S0-CBJ-522

SCANDINAVIAN MYTHOLOGY

GARLAND FOLKLORE BIBLIOGRAPHIES
(General Editor: Alan Dundes)
(VOL. 13)

GARLAND REFERENCE LIBRARY
OF THE HUMANITIES
(VOL. 394)

Garland Folklore Bibliographies

Alan Dundes, *General Editor*
University of California, Berkeley

1. *South American Indian Narrative: Theoretical and Analytical Approaches: An Annotated Bibliography*
   by Susan Niles
2. *American and Canadian Immigrant and Ethnic Folklore: An Annotated Bibliography*
   by Robert A. Georges and Stephen Stern
3. *International Proverb Scholarship: An Annotated Bibliography*
   by Wolfgang Mieder
4. *Christmas: An Annotated Bibliography*
   by Sue Samuelson
5. *Folklore and Literature in the United States: An Annotated Bibliography of Studies of Folklore in American Literature*
   by Steven Swann Jones
6. *Oral-Formulaic Theory and Research: An Introduction and Annotated Bibliography*
   by John Miles Foley
7. *Italian Folklore: An Annotated Bibliography*
   by Alessandro Falassi
8. *Fable Scholarship: An Annotated Bibliography*
   by Pack Carnes
9. *Modern Greek Folklore: An Annotated Bibliography*
   by Julia E. Miller
10. *Jewish Folklore: An Annotated Bibliography*
    by Eli Yassif
11. *Folklore and Literature of the British Isles: An Annotated Bibliography*
    by Florence E. Baer
12. *Tale Type- and Motif-Indexes: An Annotated Bibliography*
    by David S. Azzolina
13. *Scandinavian Mythology: An Annotated Bibliography*
    by John Lindow

SCANDINAVIAN MYTHOLOGY

An Annotated Bibliography

John Lindow

GARLAND PUBLISHING, INC • NEW YORK AND LONDON
1988

Lindow, John
Scandinavian mythology

(Garland folklore bibliographies ; v. 13)
Includes index.
1. Mythology, Norse—Bibliography. I. Title.
II. Series.
Z7836.L58 1988 [BL860] 016.293'13 87-29280
ISBN 0-8240-9173-6

Cover design by Valerie Mergentime

Printed on acid-free, 250-year-life paper
Manufactured in the United States of America

Contents

Editor's Preface

The Garland Folklore Bibliographies are intended to provide ready access to the folklore scholarship of a particular country or area or to the scholarship devoted to a specific folklore genre or theme. The annotations are designed to be informative and evaluative so that prospective readers may have some idea of the nature and worth of the bibliographical items listed. No bibliography is ever complete, and all are doomed to become obsolete almost immediately upon publication as new monographs and articles appear. Still, there is no substitute for a comprehensive, intelligently annotated bibliography for anyone desiring to discover what has been written on a topic under investigation.

It may strike the uninitiated as somewhat odd to compile a separate bibliography of the scholarship devoted to Scandinavian mythology. Why wouldn't such a work fit more appropriately as simply part of a larger bibliography of Scandinavian folklore scholarship or myth scholarship? The answer is that there has been such an enormous wealth of writing over the past two centuries that has explored the texts of Scandinavian mythology in infinite detail that the inclusion of such materials in a bibliography, say, of Scandinavian folklore, would occupy a disproportionate segment of that bibliography. With respect to the genre of myth, only the scholarship concerned with classical (Greek and Roman) and possibly Indic mythology can compare with the quantity and quality of Scandinavian myth studies.

The intellectual history of folkloristics owes a great deal to folklorists from Finland, Germany, Scandinavia, and elsewhere in Europe. Many of the leading folklorists were involved to some extent in the exegesis of Scandinavian mythology as part of their overall research interest in folklore in general. A list of these folklorists constitutes a virtual who's who in the history of folkloristics: S. Bugge, R. Th. Christiansen, G. Dumézil, J. Grimm, N. F. S. Grundtvig, A. Heusler, U. Holmberg, A. H. Krappe, K. Krohn, A. Kuhn, F. von der Leyen, N. Lid, W. Mannhardt, E. Meletinskij, A. Olrik, W. E. Peuckert, A. B. Rooth, D. Strömbäck, C. W. von Sydow, and J. de Vries among others. This is why the results of Scandinavian mythological scholarship are of interest to folklorists everywhere whether or not they possess any expertise in the Scandinavian myth corpus.

The task of surveying the mass of material available was an extraordinarily difficult one, requiring a knowledge of all the Scandinavian languages plus French, German, Italian, etc. Fortunately, John Lindow, Professor of Scandinavian at the University of California, Berkeley, not only possessed the requisite polyglot linguistic skills, but he is himself a scholar in the field of Scandinavian mythology and philology. He regularly offers courses in Scandinavian folklore and Scandinavian mythology on the Berkeley campus.

Born in Washington, D.C., John Lindow earned his A. B. in Scandinavian (magna cum laude) in 1968 from Harvard, where he remained for his graduate work, receiving the doctorate in Germanic Languages and Literatures in 1972. Among his books are *Comitatus, Individual and Honor: Studies in North Germanic Institutional Voca-*

bulary (Berkeley, 1976) and *Swedish Legends and Folktales* (Berkeley, 1978). He is also co-editor of *Old Norse Icelandic Literature: A Critical Guide* (Ithaca, 1985) and of *Structure and Meaning in Old Norse Literature: New Approaches to Textual Analysis and Literary Criticism* (Odense, 1986). Professor Lindow has served as Chairman of the Scandinavian Department and as Director of the Language Laboratory at Berkeley.

Folklorists and students of Scandinavian and German culture alike are surely indebted to Professor John Lindow for his carefully considered survey of the major landmarks and critical issues in *Scandinavian Mythology: An Annotated Bibliography.*

Alan Dundes, General Editor
University of California, Berkeley

Acknowledgments

Throughout this project I have enjoyed the generous support of the Committee on Research at the University of California, Berkeley. This support has provided me with bibliographic and editorial support, carried out promptly, thoroughly, and cheerfully by, at various times, Susan Shively, Pamela Ow, and Tim Tangherlini. I used, of course, many of the library facilities at my university, not least the Interlibrary Loan Service, and in acknowledging that support I would like to make particular mention of the aid I received at the Northern Regional Library Facility.

The Bibliography itself was entered and formated on central campus computing facilities provided by Campus Computing Funds made available through the College of Letters and Science. Computer professionals who gave more than generously of their time include Bill Tuthill, Jacqueline Craig, and especially Greg Shenault.

Alan Dundes has earned my thanks not only by including this volume in the series of Folklore Bibliographies, but also for his counsel during the ever-growing time period that the project consumed. During this same period, Julia Johnson, Pam Chergotis, Gary Kuris, and their colleagues at Garland Publishing displayed considerable patience, for which I am grateful.

Introduction

Scandinavian mythology comprises a body of texts, recorded mostly in the thirteenth century in Iceland and dealing with Scandinavian pagan gods. Some of the texts are in the fixed form of skaldic poetry and may therefore be presumed to derive from before the conversion to Christianity (999 or 1000 A.D.); some are in the less fixed eddic form and suggest radically different provenances, from before and after the conversion and from inside and outside Iceland; one, Snorri Sturluson's *Edda* (ca. 1220), is the work of a learned medieval Christian and the subject of an ongoing debate about its reliability as a source on Scandinavian paganism; a few others are in thirteenth-century and later prose forms and the subject of similar debates.

It follows that the study of Scandinavian mythology (as opposed to Scandinavian pagan religion) is essentially a matter of source and text criticism. Most works treating the circumstances of composition, dating, and interpretation of texts in the mythological corpus contribute to the study of Scandinavian mythology, and they have formed the initial basis of this Bibliography. Even works dealing with more directly mythological problems, such as the essence of a given god, the meaning of a given myth, or the use of a given motif, fall into this category, as the arguments they offer must of necessity draw primarily from the texts of the mythological corpus. As the texts are the written reflection of a possibly more extensive oral tradition, the study of Scandinavian mythology belongs to folklore, and prominent folklorists, such as Kaarle Krohn, Axel Olrik, and Jan de Vries, have contributed to it.

Just as older folklore studies tended to focus on origins and proto-forms, so the older study of Scandinavian mythology used the thirteenth-century recordings primarily as evidence for the study of Scandinavian or even Germanic paganism. Although I have argued that the study of Scandinavian mythology is not the study of the history of religion ("Mythology and Mythography," entry 1483 below), I cannot in this Bibliography reverse nearly two centuries of scholarship, and so I include many works whose emphasis is on religion rather than the mythological corpus. I have omitted all but the most important works that preceded the onset of scientific study, which I take to have begun roughly with the brothers Grimm; and works after 1982 or so may not yet have come to my attention.

It is important to stress that the coverage makes no attempt to be exhaustive; my goal has been to offer easy access to the more important parts of the vast amount of scholarship on the subject, most of it in languages other than English. Consultation of works cited in this Bibliography will lead the curious reader to much additional scholarship. I have, too, included many items of a bibliographical nature, so as to aid the curious reader's bibliographic searches, and I have also included many handbooks, not just in the area of Scandinavian mythology, but also in the closely related field of Germanic religion.

The annotations are intended primarily to be descriptive, and I have allowed direct value judgments only when they seemed to be beyond doubt. The length of the individual annotations offers a clue to my view of the relative importance of the various works cited, with the provision that the subject of the Bibliography is mythology;

annotations in a bibliography of Scandinavian paganism or the history of Germanic religion would certainly arrange themselves differently.

I finally chose a single index, instead of several indices, each covering a specific category (e.g., placenames, authors cited, texts), out of a belief that most users would find a single index easier and faster to use. In indexing, I have tried to be overly rather than too little inclusive, and I have permitted redundancy not only in some of the main entries but also in the relationship between main and sub-entries. Here again my major goal was speed of use, with a strong secondary goal of trying to remove my own personal biases and judgments from the user's primary tool for using the volume. In keeping with my view of the importance of extant texts, I have indexed extensively on their titles and have used individual strophes or chapters as subfields where appropriate. Beyond that, I have indexed on such important motifs as the gods themselves (e.g., Odin, Thor), other significant actors or moments in the mythology (e.g., animals, weapons), categories of interpretation (e.g., archaeology, etymology, iconography), and spheres of reception (e.g., Britain, British tradition). I have, of course, indexed references to modern scholars in the annotations.

There is, therefore, no direct entry to individual myths except insofar as they are found in single texts. Thus, for example, to find scholarship on Thor's fishing expedition for the midgard serpent, one searches either the subfield "Midgard serpent" under "Thor" or "Thor" under "Midgard serpent." This form of indexing seems to me to give a fairer picture of the entire broad reach of the scholarship.

My choice of a single alphabetical listing of works by author, with a detailed index, was the result of my own dissatisfaction with bibliographies arranged systematically. Such bibliographies are useful for indicating the way scholars divide their fields, but all such division is finally arbitrary, and it imposes preconceived notions on the material. These notions may be of no interest to the casual user of a bibliography and may even lead him or her astray. A single alphabetical listing is also more useful for the experienced user, who may seek only a quick reference, and if each author's works are arranged chronologically, as here, the reader finds a view of an individual scholar's contributions and scholarly development, which may be some compensation for the lack of the seeming order of a systematic listing.

For those who would have preferred such a listing, and to indicate the scope of scholarship covered in this Bibliography and the way I believe it could be arranged systematically, I offer the following survey of the major research areas of Scandinavian mythology.

I. Content

Higher mythology. This older term is useful to refer to works about the various gods (Odin, Týr, Thor, Njord, Freyr, Loki, Heimdall, Baldr, etc.) and goddesses (Frigg, Freyja, Eir, the Norns, etc.); their groupings (*æsir*, *vanir*); accoutrements (animals, weapons, the mead of poetry, plants and trees, natural phenomena like wind and thunder, etc.); their adversaries the giants (including Hel, the midgard serpent, Surtr, Hræsvelgr, etc.); and of course their doings—the myths. These include such well-known stories as the creation myth, the golden age, the war between the *æsir* and *vanir*, Odin's acquisition of the mead of poetry, runes, and other information; the building of Asgard, Týr's dealings with Fenrir; Thor's dealings with Hrungnir, Geirrøðr, the dwarf Alvíss, and Útgarða-Loki; Freyr's wooing of Gerðr; Íðunn and her apples; Baldr's death; and Ragnarǫk.

Lower mythology. Opposed to the so-called higher mythology is the body of belief and narratives dealing with beings neither divine nor human. For Scandinavian mythology these include primarily the dwarfs, elves, *landvættir*, and *dísir*; berserks too might fit this category. Magic (when not practiced by Odin or one of the other gods) also belongs to the lower mythology.

Other Germanic mythology (and religion). Important cognate mythological figures, objects, and motifs include Nerthus (as described by Tacitus); the Old Saxon Irmin and Irminsûl; the Old High German *Muspilli*; the Alciis and other divine twins; and so forth.

II. Method

Methodology. The Index contains many entries of works with a methodological emphasis or making methodological comments. The history of research in Scandinavian mythology was for a time identical with that of Germanic religion, as the mythology formed a major source for nineteenth-century reconstructions of Germanic paganism. The twentieth century has seen both a turn away from this view of the relationship between the mythology and Germanic religion and a modern return to it. This is not the place to undertake a description of the evolution of the field; readers are referred to the entries in the Index under "Research survey." Hans Seipp, *Entwicklungszüge der germanischen Religionswissenschaft*" (1968), is perhaps the most ambitious of these; my paper on "Mythology and Mythography" surveys the last decades. Methodologies worthy of separate mention in this context include the following.

Nature mythology. The association of certain aspects of various gods with phenomena of nature was a standard feature of early interpretations of Scandinavian mythology in the nineteenth century and still continues to find favor among a few of those who write on the mythology. Thus Thor is, represents, or derives from thunder; Odin has a similar relationship with wind, Njord with the sea, and so forth. Although the importance of phenomena of nature in early and medieval Scandinavia was surely great, this method seems to ignore other important aspects of the gods and is no longer in favor.

Comparative mythology. Even the early nature mythologists relied on comparison, which went on to become perhaps the most powerful tool of researchers in the field of Germanic religion. We may distinguish two sorts of comparison: that which sought genetic relationships and that which sought paths of diffusion. The first has naturally been the province of those familiar with the parent Indo-European tradition. After an interlude in the early part of this century when the method was not popular, it was revived by Georges Dumézil, who added two ingredients to the recipe: structuralism and relevance to social structure.

The second sort of comparison, that which seeks paths of diffusion, was the reigning mode for much of this century. The following traditions have been linked with Scandinavian mythology or Germanic religion: Greek and Roman; Finnish and Finno-Ugric, including Lapp; Irish and Welsh; Near Eastern, including Babylonian, Hittite, Sumerian, and Semitic; Indic, including Vedic and Iranian. The prevailing view has assigned origins to somewhere in the Near East, with Germanic/Scandinavian borrowing from the original source and lending to Finno-Ugric. This view is parallel to other cultural prejudices.

Linguistics and philology. Implicit to the methods thus far mentioned is the importance of historical linguistics and philology. A great deal of the research on Scandinavian mythology is informed by these disciplines, with three primary areas of application. The first is etymology: the essence of a god determined by the original meaning of his name or of epithets applied to him. The second is the study of names, particularly placenames. Etymology is a primary tool of this study, which has been particularly popular in Scandinavia. It frequently enables judgment concerning the distribution and relative chronology of the worship of a specific god. The third is the analysis of vocabulary, for example of the holy or of priesthood and temples.

Runology. The interpretation of runic inscriptions is important to Scandinavian mythology for two reasons. The first is internal to the mythology: runes are the discovery and the property of Odin and one of his tools of wisdom, and therefore their real use may illuminate the god. The second is the association in the mind of many scholars between runes and magic—an important part of the lower mythology. For these reasons I have felt it justified to include many runological works in this Bibliography.

Archaeology. Archaeology has long been a sibling of Germanic philology and has frequently been applied to the study of Germanic religion. The application to Scandinavian mythology has been less direct, as archaeological artifacts by their nature cannot directly inform narratives, but the frequent mingling of the study of religion and mythology has led to many contributions to the latter using an archaeological basis.

Iconography. Related to archaeology, iconography focuses on the interpretation of specific scenes or motifs found on archaeological artifacts. Since many of these scenes or motifs can be related to narratives, iconography is of fundamental concern to those interested in Scandinavian mythology. The greater part of the material is found on rock carvings, although bracteates have recently attracted much attention. Despite the great gap in time between the Bronze Age, when most of the rock carvings were done, and the Middle Ages, when Scandinavian mythology took its final form, scholarship on the Bronze Age rock carvings is of interest to those engaged in the study of Scandinavian mythology, and I have therefore included representative work from this field.

III. History

I use the term broadly, more or less with the sense "wie es eigentlich gewesen." This sort of history, when it tries to make sense of Scandinavian mythology and its background in paganism, attempts reconstruction of the social circumstances of two periods: 1) when the religion presumably standing behind the mythology was practiced; 2) when the mythology was actually recorded.

For the first period, we may distinguish *worship* from *social circumstances.* The emphasis of scholarship on worship has been on cult and ritual: cult of the individual gods, of animals, ancestors, and the like; and rituals of fertility, funeral practice and the dead, magic, and so forth. I have admitted many items dealing exclusively with these matters, since omitting them would have given a false picture of the scholarship. Relevant social circumstances have to do with the nature of social structure in its religious manifestations (e.g., sacral kingship—still an open question in Germanic studies—or tripartition) and even less palpable matters, such as worldview or the role of fate. The latter, for example, has been a rather popular subject, despite the necessity to rely on texts recorded centuries after the conversion. Fate is particularly relevant to Norse mythology, as the gods themselves seem subject to it.

A historical approach directed to the circumstances of the recording of the texts must of necessity begin with the conversion. This topic has attracted much attention and many various approaches, and I have included here a number of representative items. Most of these deal with the conversion in Iceland, since Iceland is the home of the literary recordings of the mythology. Others deal with the conversion of other Germanic peoples, however, because these conversions form an important background to the reconstruction of Germanic religion, itself an important foundation of Scandinavian mythology. The conversion of Iceland set the stage for early Icelandic Christianity, which greatly influenced Scandinavian mythology. With the exception of a few runic inscriptions, all of the texts comprising Scandinavian mythology were written down by Christians, and it is plain that their religion affected their view of the texts. Snorri Sturluson is now well known as a euhemerist, and his older contemporary Saxo Grammaticus went even farther in his euhemerism. Even more fundamental questions concern the amount of Christian influence on texts perhaps composed by pagans—even if they only came to be recorded by Christians centuries later—and on the religion that such pagans may have practiced. No firm answers to these questions have held the field, and the amount and nature of Christian influence on Scandinavian mythology is still debated with profit. That is as it should be for materials that at bottom are products of the recording and interpretation of once-pagan material by Christians.

In preparing a work of this nature, i.e., one intended for an audience unfamiliar with the foreign languages in which the relevant materials are found, one faces the all too familiar problems of name forms, of transliteration, and of alphabetization. Here are the solutions I have chosen.

1) *Name forms*: The more familiar gods bear the usual English forms of their names, e.g., Odin and Thor instead of Óðinn and Þórr, but Baldr, not Balder or Baldur. Less familiar figures bear the usual Old Norse-Icelandic form, in the nominative singular (e.g., Óðr). Citation of names from other traditions generally follows these principles. The cross references in the Index should reduce any inconvenience that the principles and their inherent inconsistencies cause.

2) *Transliteration*: Forms from Germanic languages are not transliterated, with the exception of the more familiar gods' names, as described above. In transliterating Russian, I have followed the Library of Congress system but have kept scholars' names in the forms they use when writing in English, e.g., Steblin-Kamenskij, Gurevich.

3) *Alphabetization*: The following system is used. Accute accents, grave accents, circumflex, and macron are ignored, but other diacritics are significant; digraphs are treated as two separate letters; and *ð* and *þ* are treated as in Icelandic.

á	>	a
à	>	a
â	>	a
ā	>	a
å	>	aa
æ	>	ae
ä	>	ae
ð	>	d
ø	>	oe
ö	>	oe
ǫ	>	oe
œ	>	oe
ü	>	ue
þ	>	at end of alphabet

Scandinavian Mythology

A

1. Ågren, Yngve. "Virrighetens apoteos." *Edda*, 1961, pp. 13-18.

Centering his discussion on the inconsistencies of *Gylfaginning*, Ågren wittily if unconvincingly argues that Snorri attempted a deliberately misleading parody of ancient myth.

2. Åkerblom, Axel. "Bidrag till diskussionen om str. 77 i Havamal: Reson och alliteration." *Arkiv för nordisk filologi*, 34 (1918), 171-73.

Comments on E. A. Kock's discussion of *Hávamál*, str. 77 ("Domen över död man" (1917)).

3. Åkerblom, Axel. "Bidrag till eddatolkningen." *Arkiv för nordisk filologi*, 36 (1920), 47-54.

Comments on Freyr's wedding gifts (*Skírnismál* and *Snorra edda*; *Hymiskviða*, str. 31; *Lokasenna*, str. 16; *Alvíssmál*, str. 16.

4. Åkerblom, Axel. "Om Vǫluspǫ́s komposition och syfte." *Arkiv för nordisk filologi*, 36 (1920), 54-62.

The outer and inner form of *Vǫluspá*. The author believes that *Vǫluspá* was once a *drápa* of some 125 stanzas, whose origin is wholly to be sought in paganism.

5. Åkerlund, Walter. *Studier över Ynglingatal.* Skrifter utgivna av vetenskapssocieteten i Lund, 23. Lund: C. W. K. Gleerup, 1939. 274 pp.

A primarily philological study of *Ynglingatal.*

6. Aakjær, Svend. "Danske stednavne fra hedenold." *Dansk udsyn*, 1927, pp. 123-25.

Danish pagan placenames.

7. Aakjær, Svend. "Hoveri, Hovgaard og Hov." *Danske folkemål*, 3 (1929), 25-34.

   Placenames with the element *Hov-*.

8. Aakjær, Svend. "Hilla, Hleiðra og Skialf." In *Studier tilegnede Verner Dahlerup paa femoghalvfjerdsaarsdagen den 31. Oktober 1934.* 52-62. Århus: Universitets forlag, 1934. Vol. was also issued as *Danske folkemaal*, vol. 8, suppl., and as *Sprog og kultur*, vol. 3, suppl.

   Sacral interpretation of placenames, associating them with ritual, particularly *seiðr*.

9. Aakjær, Svend. "Odins Vi i Salling." *Skivebogen*, 1943, pp. 33-42.

   Sacral and theophoric placenames in a Danish parish. Odin and Thor receive specific mention.

10. Aars, Jacob. "Lærer vore forfædres mytologi evige straffe?" *Tidskrift for philologi og pædagogik*, 1 (1860), 326-44.

    Denies that Norse mythology prescribed eternal punishment.

11. Abercrombie, Ralph. "Cloud-Land in Folk-Lore and in Science." *Folk-Lore Journal*, 6 (1888), 94-115.

    "I have no doubt that the old Norse idea of Thor's chariot being drawn by goats had its origin in this phase of cloud building" [cumulus clouds] (p. 101); "one-eyed Thor" [!] also explained as derived from cloud formations (p. 110).

12. Abrahamsson, David. "Solkult i nordisk bebyggelse." *Ymer*, 44 (1924), 239-59.

    Departing from the observation that the western side of Swedish churches tended to be left unsettled, Abrahamsson extrapolates pagan Germanic and older sun worship, the focus of which was the setting sun.

13. Achterberg, Eberhard. "Germanische Religion im Streit der Gegenwart." In *Reaktion oder deutscher Fortschritt in der Geschichtswissenschaft*, ed. Bernhard Kummer, 31-56. Reden und Aufsätze zum nordischen Gedanken, 32. Leipzig: A. Klein, 1935.

    A nationalistic attack on scholars who in the author's opinion fail to do justice to the Germanic "soul."

14. Achterbergranovs, Herbert. *Interpretatio Christiana: Verkleidete Glaubensgestalten der Germanen auf deutschem Boden.* Form und Geist, 19. Leipzig: H. Eichblatt, 1930. xvi, 176 pp. Diss. Greifswald.

    An attempt to reconstruct Germanic paganism from early Christian sources.

15. Aðalsteinsson, Jón Hnefill. *Kristnitakan á Íslandi*. Reykjavik: Almenna bókafélagið, 1971. 181 pp.

Preliminary version, for a popular Icelandic audience, of the author's work on the conversion of Iceland, later published as *Under the Cloak* (1978).

16. Aðalsteinsson, Jón Hnefill. *Under the Cloak: The Acceptance of Christianity with Particular Reference to the Religious Attitudes Prevailing at the Time*. Studia Ethnologica Upsaliensia, 4. Stockholm: Almqvist & Wiksell, 1978. 151 pp.

In this Uppsala dissertation, the author examines the ethnographic background of the conversion of Iceland to Christianity. After a survey of important factors and attitudes, he investigates the traditions about the formal conversion at the alþingi in 999 or 1000 A.D., according to which the pagan Þorgeirr retired under a cloak to deliberate the Icelanders' religious future. The author presents the evidence anchoring this act in ritual.

17. Adamus, Marian. *Tajemnice sag i run*. Wrocław: Zakład naradowy imiena Ossolińskich. Wydawnictwo, 1970. 375 pp.

"The secrets of the sagas and runes." Includes discussion of mythology and the Indo-European basis of early Scandinavian religion. Summary in *Bibliographie zur Symbolik, Ikonographie und Mythologie*, 6 (1973), 13-14.

18. Adinsky, E. *Tuisko oder Tuisto? Ein Beitrag zur deutschen Götterkunde*. Königsberg i. Pr.: C. Th. Nürmberger, 1903. 54 pp.

Unlearned speculation.

19. Ægidius, Jens Peter. *Vølvens spådom på dansk: En litteraer- og åndshistorisk undersøgelse*. Studier fra sprog- og oldtidsforskning, 294. Copenhagen: G. E. C. Gad, 1978. 136 pp.

On the many Danish translations of *Vǫluspá*.

20. [Afzelius, A. A.]. "Völu spá med öfversättning från isländskan." *Iduna*, 3 (1812), 3-72. 2nd. and 3rd. eds. in 1816 and 1824.

Early Swedish translation of *Vǫluspá*, with introduction and notes.

21. Agrell, Sigurd. "Der Ursprung der Runenschrift und die Magie." *Arkiv för nordisk filologi*, 43 (1927), 97-109.

Summarizes in German some of the theories of his *Runornas talmystik* (1927).

22. Agrell, Sigurd. *Runornas talmystik och dess antika förebild*. Skrifter utgivna av vetenskaps-societeten i Lund, 6. Lund: C. W. K. Gleerup, 1927. viii, 216 pp.

Agrell argues that Germanic mercenaries encountered inscriptions in the context of Mithraism and fashioned the runic system in imitation: the names of the runes have magic properties and their arrangement numerological implications. By moving the "f" rune to the end of the futhark (rune-row), Agrell can begin with "u," which he interprets as the aurochs of Mithraic mystery. "þ," the second rune, is *þurs* "giant," "a," the third rune, is *ans* "god," and so forth. Thus the number 2 is associated with giants and brings evil, and 3 is associated with the gods and brings good. In this fashion Agrell builds up an entire mythological system.

Runologists have not accepted this system, nor the theory on which it is based.

23. Agrell, Sigurd. *Zur Frage nach dem Ursprung der Runennamen*. Skrifter utgivna av vetenskaps-societeten i Lund, 10. Lund: C. W. K. Gleerup, 1928. 70 pp. English summary pp. 69-70.

German version of the second chapter of Agrell's *Runornas talmystik och dess antika förebild* (1927), addressing some of the criticisms addressed toward it by reviewers.

24. Agrell, Sigurd. "Rökstenens chiffergåtor och andra runologiska problem." *Kungliga humanistiska vetenskapssamfundet i Lund, årsberättelse*, 1929-30, pp. 25-144.

The section on the Rök stone gives prominence to Odin and Odin ritual.

25. Agrell, Sigurd. "Solbanans stjärnbilder i Eddadiktningens mytvärld." *Vetenskapssocietetens i Lund årsbok*, 1929, pp. 5-23.

Attempts to demonstrate that the dwellings of the gods in *Grímnismál* reflect late antique astrological notions.

26. Agrell, Sigurd. "Die spätantike Alphabetmystik und die Runenreihe." *Kungliga humanistiska vetenskapssamfundet i Lund, årsberättelse*, 1931-32, pp. 155-210.

More runic number magic.

27. Agrell, Sigurd. *Senantik mysteriereligion och nordisk runmagi: En inledning i den nutida runologiens grundproblem*. Stockholm: A. Bonnier, 1931. 277 pp.

The "basic problems of contemporary runology" were partly of the author's making and involved supposed numerological magic derived from oriental magic cults. Agrell summarizes here the views he put forth on these matters in earlier works.

28. Agrell, Sigurd. *Lapptrummor och runmagi: Tvenne kapitel ur trolldomsväsendets historia.* Lund: C. W. K. Gleerup, 1934. 172 pp.

Lapp shaman drums and supposed runic number magic.

29. Agrell, Sigurd. "Die pergamenische Zauberscheibe und das Tarockspiel." *Kungliga humanistiska vetenskapssamfundet i Lund, årsberättelse,* 1935-36, pp. 61-190.

Includes discussion of the mythological significance of various names of runes.

30. Agrell, Sigurd. "Lönnskrift på magiska runstenar." In *Bidrag till nordisk filologi tillägnade Emil Olson.* 302-15. Lund: C. W. K. Gleerup, 1936.

By shifting runes according to his pleasure, Agrell finds an invocation to Thor on the Stentoften runestone.

31. Agrell, Sigurd. "Die Herkunft der Runenschrift." *Kungliga humanistiska vetensskapssamfundet i Lund, årsberättelse,* 1937-38, pp. 65-117.

Ancient Italic magic writing as it bears on the question of the origin of runes. Comments on *Lokasenna* 24 and *Hávamál* 139.

32. Aho, Gary L. "*Niðarstigningarsaga*: An Old Norse Version of Christ's Harrowing of Hell." *Scandinavian Studies,* 41 (1969), 150-59.

Seeks to interpret Christ's fishing up of Leviathan in light of the myth of Thor and the midgard serpent.

33. Ahrendts, Jürgen. *Bibliographie zur alteuropäischen Religionsgeschichte,* vol. II: *1965-69: Eine interdiziplinäre Auswahl von Literatur zu den Rand- und Nachfolgekulturen der Antike in Europa unter besonderer Berücksichtigung der nichtchristlichen Religionen.* Arbeiten zur Frühmittelalterforschung, 5. Berlin and New York: Walter de Gruyter, 1974. 592 pp.

This vast bibliography differs from its predecessor, *Bibliographie zur alteuropäischen Religionsgeschichte 1954-1964* (Buchholz 1967), only in a few details of organization and in its even greater scope (7628 entries). Like its predecessor, it covers works from many disciplines relevant to non-Christian religions from the Iron Age through the Middle Ages.

34. Albertsson, Kristján. "Hverfanda hvel." *Skírnir,* 151 (1977), 57-58.

The words of the title are found in *Hávamál,* str. 84. Kristján Albertsson reads them as a kenning for "moon," as in *Alvíssmál,* str. 14.

35. Algermissen, Konrad. *Germanentum und Christentum: Ein Beitrag zur Geschichte der deutschen Frömmigkeit.* Hannover: J. Giesel, 1935. xiv, 440 pp. First of six editions; 6th ed., also 1935, was expanded to xv, 504 pp.

Early Germanic Christianity.

36. Allen, J. Romilly. "Prehistoric Art in the North." *Saga-Book of the Viking Society,* 1 (1892-96), 54-73.

Uninterpretive survey, distinguished by the following remark: "Many attempts have been made to explain the meaning of these symbols, the favourite theory being that they have to do with sun-worship. When an archaeologist is in doubt he always falls back on the sun-god" (p. 71).

37. Allen, Richard F. *Fire and Iron: Critical Approaches to Njáls saga.* [Pittsburgh]: University of Pittsburgh Press, 1971. xvi, 254 pp.

Although Allen's study does not bear directly on Norse mythology, pp. 132-34 contain a suggestive discussion of *Njáls saga* as displaced myth, possibly relevant to the context of the recording of mythology during the thirteenth century in Iceland.

38. Allén, Sture. "Baldrs draumar 14 och Guðrúnarkviða II, 9—två samhöriga eddaställen." *Arkiv för nordisk filologi,* 76 (1961), 74-95.

A proposed textual collocation, based on interpreting *menn* as "the dead."

39. Allen, W. E. D. *The Poet and the Spae-Wife: An Attempt to Reconstruct Al-Ghazal's Embassy to the Vikings.* Dublin: A. Figgis, 1960. 102 pp. Also issued as *Saga-Book of the Viking Society* 15 (1957-61), part 3.

Al-Ghazal's embassy occurred ca. 845, according to Allen among vikings in Ireland. He identifies one of the principals as Ota and discusses on pp. 47 ff. her "sybilline functions," relating her specifically to the *vanir.*

40. Alm, Jens M. "Møtet mellom Asatru og Kristendom på Dynna." *Årbok for Hadeland,* 1968, pp. 7-11.

On the burial mounds and runestone at Dynna (Norway).

41. Alme, H. A., and L. G. B. Flock. *Grundtræk af Asalæren og Völuspaa med fortolkning.* Oslo: O. Norli, 1917. 121 pp.

Theosophic reading of Norse mythology, primarily based on *Vǫluspá.*

42. Almgren, Bertil. "Hällristningar och bronsåldersdräkt." *Tor,* 6 (1960), 19-50. Summary in German, pp. 46-47.

Identifies certain images on the rock carvings as items of clothing and associates them with gifts of the gods, perhaps in the context of a ritual of the dead.

43. Almgren, Bertil. "Den osynliga gudomen." In *Proxima Thule: Sverige och Europa under forntid och medeltid: Hyllningsskrift til H. M. Konungen den 11 november 1962 utgiven av Svenska arkeologiska samfundet*. 53-71. Stockholm: P. A. Norstedt, 1962.

Almgren's premise is that cult directed at invisible gods characterized both the worship of Nerthus described by Tacitus and the religion of the Bronze Age rock carvings. Thus the wagon, ship, or footprint represented the deity, perhaps as the result of a tabu against portraying the deity itself. Symbols such as shield, spear, and ax may be connected with the gods of the mythology.

44. Almgren, Oscar. "Symboliska miniatyryxor från den yngre järnåldern." *Fornvännen*, 4 (1909), 39-42. Summary in German, p. 324.

"Thor's hammers" from the younger Iron Age in Sweden.

45. Almgren, Oscar. *Hällristningar och kultbruk: Bidrag till belysning av de nordiska bronsåldersristningarnas innebörd*. Kunglinga vitterhets historie och antikvitets akademien, handlingar, 35. Stockholm: Wahlström & Widstrand, 1926-27. 337 pp.

Swedish original of Almgren's important work on the Bronze Age rock carvings and their possible religious import.

46. Almgren, Oscar. "Die nordischen Felsenzeichnungen der Bronzezeit als religionsgeschichtliche Urkunden." In *Actes du Ve congrès international d'histoire des religions à Lund, 27-29 août 1929*. 224-31. Lund: C. W. K. Gleerup, 1930.

Lecture and discussion from an international congress on the history of religion. Almgren discusses his work on the religious significance of the rock carvings in light of international study of the history of religion.

47. Almgren, Oscar. "Bernhard Salin: Fornforskaren med konstnärshågen." *Fornvännen*, 28 (1933), 1-46.

Pp. 34-36 of this necrology treat Salin's view of the history of Scandinavian religion. This is of interest particularly because although Salin published little on the subject, he had developed strong views on it, which Almgren is able to reconstruct.

48. Almgren, Oscar. *Nordische Felszeichnungen als religiöse Urkunden*. Frankfurt a. M.: M. Diesterweg, 1934. xvi, 378 pp. German version of *Hällristningar och kultbruk* (1926-27), translated by Sigrid Vrancken.

Still the standard work on the Scandinavian rock carvings and their relationship with religion and cult. Almgren seeks to anchor the rock carvings in Bronze Age fertility cult deriving ultimately from oriental sources. He also makes some attempts to associate various figures in the carvings with the gods of the extant mythology (e.g., ithyphallic figures with Freyr, hammers with Thor).

49. Almqvist, Bo. "Um ákvæðaskáld." *Skírnir*, 135 (1961), 72-98.

On the word magic of certain powerful skalds.

50. Almqvist, Bo. *Norrön niddiktning: Traditionshistoriska studier i versmagi,* vol. 1, *Nid mot furstar.* Nordiska texter och undersökningar, 21. Stockholm: Almqvist & Wiksell, 1965. 260 pp.

The first part of Almqvist's study of Norse *níð* poetry. The first chapter treats generally the concept of *níð* and is mostly etymological and semasiological. The remaining chapters treat important passages in which *níð* occurs.

The long-term aim of these "studies," and the reason they are included in this bibliography, is the role of magic in *níð*, which in turn impinges on myth and religion.

51. Almqvist, Bo. *Norrön niddiktning,* vol. 2:1-2: *Nid mot missionärer; Senmedeltida nidtraditioner.* Nordiska texter och undersökningar, 23. Stockholm: Almqvist & Wiksell, 1974. 201 pp.

The second and concluding volume of the author's study of *níð* treats the textual traditions of four episodes. Two involve missionary activity and two are from the late Middle Ages.

52. Altheim, Franz, and Erika Trautmann (-Nehring). "Neue Felsbilder aus der Val Camonica: Die Sonne in Kult und Mythos." *Wörter und Sachen*, 19 (1938), 12-45.

On the basis of similarities between the north Italic rock carvings described here and rock carvings from Scandinavia, the authors postulate an Indo-European background.

53. Altheim, Franz, and Erika Trautmann (-Nehring). *Vom Ursprung der Runen.* Deutsches Ahnerbe, Reihe B: Fachwissenschaftliche Untersuchungen; Arbeiten zur Germanenkunde. Frankfurt a. M.: V. Klostermann, 1939. 93 pp.

Includes a section on "the spear-bearing god."

54. Altheim, Franz, and Erika Trautmann-Nehring. *Kimbern und Runen: Untersuchungen zur Ursprungsfrage der Runen.* Germanien, Beiheft 1. Berlin: Ahnenerbe-Stiftung Verlag, 1942. 65 pp.

A continuation of the authors' *Vom Ursprung der Runen* (1939), including a section on runic oracles.

55. Althin, Carl-Axel. "'Älvornas kvarnar' och 'fruktbarhetsgudens fotspår'." *Folkkultur*, 5 (1945), 5-23.

"Elf-kvarns" (cup-shaped hollows) and marks in rocks resembling footprints (of a fertility god?) as possible indications of ancient religion in Scandinavia.

56. Althin, Carl-Axel. *Studien zu den bronzezeitlichen Felszeichnungen von Skåne.* Lund: C. W. K. Gleerup, Copenhagen: E. Munksgaard, 1945. Vol. 1, 250 pp., Vol. 2 unpaginated (85 plates).

The basic premise of these studies of southern Swedish rock carvings is that the carvings grew up in a Nordic milieu of magic and ritual.

57. Ambrosiani, Sune. *Odinskultens härkomst.* Stockholm: J. Cederquist, 1907. 44 pp. Summary in German.

After calling into question the written sources for Odin's connection with Byzantium, Ambrosiani examines such evidence as bracteates and concludes that a cult of the emperor came to Scandinavia during the *Völkerwanderungszeit.*

58. Amira, Karl von. *Die germanischen Todesstrafen: Untersuchungen zur Rechts- und Religionsgeschichte.* Abhandlungen der bayerischen Akademie der Wissenschaften, phil.-hist. Kl, 31:3. Munich: Bayerische Akademie der Wissenschaften, 1922. vi, 415 pp.

This fundamental study of capital punishment in older Germanic cultures builds on a thorough presentation of the literary sources. The author enforces a strict division of Germanic penal systems into profane and sacral areas, the latter encompassing those acts that violate social codes, call forth public penalties, and label the perpetrator a *níðingr.* Within the realm of execution these acts are discussed throughout this work, and chapters 9-10 (pp. 198-235) deal explicitly with the sacral character of public execution.

The appendix (pp. 236-415) catalogs artistic representations of the material discussed. Much of this would be of value for an iconographic study of Norse mythology, but unfortunately no plates or figures are included.

59. Amira, Karl von. *Germanisches Recht*, vol. 1: *Rechtsdenkmäler,* vol. 2: *Rechtsaltertümer.* Grundriss der germanischen Philologie, 5:1-2. Berlin: W. de Gruyter, 1960-67.

The latest revision of the standard handbook of ancient Germanic law. It is of interest because of the author's conviction that law and religion are ultimately one.

60. Ampère, Jean Jacques. "Ancienne poésie scandinave." *Revue des deux mondes,* 2e. ser., 3 (1833), 420-33.

Remarks on *Vǫluspá*, *Hávamál*, and *Rígsþula.*

61. Amtoft, S. K. "Stednavne som begyggelses- og religionshistorisk kildestof: En kritisk-historisk oversigt." *Årbøger for nordisk oldkyndighed og historie*, 1941, pp. 177-312, xx-xxxii.

A useful research survey, with critical remarks and suggestions. Section C deals exclusively with theophoric placenames.

62. Amtoft, S. K. *Nordiske gudeskikkelser i bebyggesleshistorisk belysning: Studier over forholdet mellem oldtidsreligion og stednavnetyper.* Copenhagen: E. Munksgaard, 1948. 334 pp.

Applying placename evidence to Norse mythology, Amtoft seeks temporal and geographical indication of settlement history, with primary emphasis on Denmark. Some of his more interesting theories include the following. Ullr was originally worshipped throughout Denmark, whence his cult spread to Norway and Sweden; in megalithic Jutland Ullr had replaced Týr. The *vanir* were originally fertility deities, but Njord probably came to Funen in male form. There his cult coexisted for a time with that of Odin; there the marriage of both gods to Skaði (*Ynglinga saga*, ch. 8) took place. With anthropomorphization, the distinction between the earthly *vanir* and the heavenly *æsir* diminished and was finally eliminated. Baldr and Loki derived from an ethical view of the fire god, Ullr. Odin's cult grew in significance as it spread outward from Funen and was associated with that of other gods, and when Denmark was politically unified, Odin replaced Ullr as the head god.

From this it will be apparent that a central premise of the study is that a stronger centralization of religious activity for each new god who appeared characterized ancient Germanic religion; thus, Amtoft's results would largely be unacceptable to those, like Dumézil or de Vries, who feel that most or all of the gods of Norse mythology as it is recorded coexisted even in pre-Germanic times. Certainly few would accept his view of the origin of Loki and Baldr.

63. Andersen, Harry. "Viborg." *Sprog og kultur*, 4 (1935), 97-99.

Against R. Knudsen, "*Vi* og *Vis* i stednavne" (1934).

64. Andersen, Harry. "Smaa kritiske strejftog." *Arkiv för nordisk filologi*, 52 (1936), 66-75.

Opposes the etymology proposed by W. Krogmann, "Die 'Edda'" (1934).

65. Andersen, Harry. *Runestenenes forbandelsesformularer: Et tolkningsbidrag.* Studier fra sprog- og oldtidsforskning, 221. Copenhagen: Branner & Korch, 1953. 31 pp.

On the etymology and meaning of two terms found in runic curses: *rita/rata*, which Andersen reads as "one to be cast out or destroyed," and *siþi* "practicer of *seiðr*."

66. Andersen, Lise Præstgaard. *Skjoldmøer: En kvindemyte.* Copenhagen: Gyldendal, 1982.

A study, presented in semi-popular form and a rather personal perspective, of the literary archetype of the strong woman in Scandinavian tradition and its possible social background. The central figure is the valkyrie, whom the author treats in eddic poetry, Saxo, and legendary sagas and romances, and her literary descendants in family sagas and ballads.

67. Anderson, Rasmus Björn. *Norse Mythology: Or, the Religion of our Forefathers, Containing All the Myths of the Eddas, Systematized and Interpreted.* Chicago: S. C. Griggs, London: Trübner, 1875. 473 pp. 2nd ed. 1891. Rpt. (of 2nd ed.) Boston: Longwood Press, 1977.

First full-length handbook in English.

68. Anderson, William. "Åsgård: Eddans paradis och andra kultplatser i sydsvenska bygder." *Blekinge hembygdsförbunds årsbok*, 1931, pp. 138-85.

Sacral placenames in southern Sweden, related by the author to Mithraism.

69. Anderson, William. "Das altnordische Paradies." *Mannus*, 24 (1932), 19-32.

Anderson uses mountains and other elevated places to argue that Mithraism existed in Scandinavia long before Christianity arrived (and that Mithraism survived the conversion to Christianity, as a secret religion).

70. Andersson, Theodore M. "The Displacement of the Heroic Ideal in the Family Sagas." *Speculum*, 45 (1970), 575-93.

Includes discussion of the ethics of *Hávamál.*

71. Andersson, Theodore M. "The Conversion of Norway According to Oddr Snorrason and Snorri Sturluson." *Mediaeval Scandinavia*, 10 (1977), 83-91.

Snorri's narrative principles in adapting Oddr Snorrason's *Óláfs saga Tryggvasonar* and other sources for his account of the conversion in his own *Óláfs saga Tryggvasonar* included rationalization of Óláfr's itinerary and causal linking and consolidation of events. Snorri's account is thus by some standards ahistorical, but it is historical for Snorri's era insofar as it adheres to a theory that could be reconciled with the sources and was internally consistent.

72. Andersson, Thorsten. "Eigennamen als erstes Glied nordischer Ortnamen: Stamm- und Genitivkomposition." *Namn och bygd*, 67 (1979), 123-46.

Includes a section (pp. 126-31) on gods' names as first components of placenames, arguing that gods' names appear regularly in the genitive, never in the uninflected stem form.

73. Andree, Julius. *Die Externsteine: Eine germanische Kultstätte,* 2nd enlarged ed. Munster i. W.: F. Coppenrath, 1937. 67 pp.

Report of excavations of the Externsteine, arguing the holy status of the area in Germanic times.

74. Andrews, A. LeRoy. "Helge Haddingjaskati and His Place in the Old Norse Hero-Legend." *Scandinavian Studies,* 2 (1914-15), 63-78.

"Of divine brother-pair with women's coiffure or attended by priest with such coiffure ... there is no trace in these two *Haddingjar* whatever" (p. 72).

75. Andrews, A. LeRoy. "The Criteria for Dating the Eddic Poems." *Publications of the Modern Language Association,* 42 (1927), 1044-54.

The most important criteria are provided by comparison with skaldic poetry, runic inscriptions, and foreign materials in the poems.

76. Andrews, A. LeRoy. "Old Norse Notes: 7. Some Observations on Mímir." *Modern Language Notes,* 43 (1928), 166-71.

The head of Mímir may have possessed wisdom because it was actually a skull and thus a drinking vessel; as such it could designate the fountain of wisdom from which Odin drank.

77. Anholm, M. "Den bundne jætte i Kavkasus." *Danske studier,* 1 (1904), 141-51.

Anholm ends his survey of Caucasian legends of the bound giant by setting forth a few points of similarity with Loki and Ragnarǫk in Norse mythology.

78. Anjou, Sten. "Uppsalatemplets gudabeläten avbildade på bonaden från Skog." *Fornvännen,* 30 (1935), 257-64. Summary in German, p. 264.

Identifies the three figures on the Skog (Sweden) tapestry as Thor, Odin, and Freyr and compares them with Adam of Bremen's description of the idols in the pagan temple at Uppsala.

79. Anon., ed. *Snorri: átta alda minning.* Reykjavik: Sögufélagið, 1979.

A collection of essays on the author of the prose *Edda,* honoring the 800th anniversary of his birth. Of interest is the extensive collection of photographs of paintings, sketches, drawings, and sculptures of Snorri interwoven in the text, and further Helgi Þorláksson's essay, "Hvernig var Snorri í sjón?" ("What did Snorri look like?"). Directly relevant to Norse mythology and therefore receiving a separate entry in this bibliography is Óskar Halldórsson, "Snorri og Edda" (pp. 89-111).

80. Anon. "Reports of the Proceedings at the Meetings of the Club." *Saga-Book of the Viking Society*, 1 (1892-96), 5-41, 120-57, 244-84.

At the early meetings of the Viking Club (later Viking Society for Northern Research), many papers were delivered on topics dealing with Scandinavian mythology, and not all were later published. These "Reports" contain summaries and occasional publication information, and they give an interesting impression of the importance of Scandinavian mythology in late nineteenth-century Britain.

81. Aranovsky, Olga R. "On the Interpretation of the 'Knowledge by Suffering' in Aeschylus, 'Agamemnon' (176-183)." *Journal of Indo-European Studies*, 6 (1978), 243-62.

Uses *Hávamál* 138-39 as comparative evidence (pp. 248-50) and adduces an extended comparison between Odin and Apollo (pp. 251-53).

82. Arent, A. Margaret. "The Heroic Pattern: Old Germanic Helmets, *Beowulf*, and *Grettis saga*." In *Old Norse Literature and Mythology: A Symposium*, ed. Edgar C. Polomé, 130-99. Austin and London: Published for the Department of Germanic Languages, University of Texas at Austin, by the University of Texas Press, 1969.

Arent's long article departs from the premise, implicit in the work of such scholars as Höfler and F. R. Schröder, that the original context of Germanic heroic legend was mythic-religious (but cf. von See, *Germanische Heldensage* (1971)); a sacral view of the world, embodied in cult, expressed itself in plastic and literary art. Arent's study has three parts. The first investigates the archteypal character of figural representations on ancient Germanic helmets and bracteates from Torslsunda, Vendel, Valsgärde (Sweden), Gutenstein, Obrigheim, and Pliezhausen (southern Germany), and Sutton Hoo (England), delineating thematic cycles of initiation rites for the warrior and his responsibility and fate. The second part considers *Beowulf*, focusing on the pattern of the hero's life and on history as archetype, and the third seeks these features in *Grettis saga* and then contrasts the two texts, concluding that *Beowulf* revitalized ancient archetypes, whereas *Grettis saga* employed them as stereotypes. There is much to consider in this essay, even if the mapping of figural to literary materials strikes the skeptic as exaggerated.

83. Arfert, Paul. *Odin als Gott des Geistes*. Jahresbericht der Oberrealschule zu Halberstadt. Halberstadt: H. Meyer, 1904. 32 pp.

The "inner form" of Odin as a god of the Germanic spirit.

84. Arlt, Gustave Otto. "Two Old Norse Interpretations." *Scandinavian Studies*, 11 (1930-31), 173-79.

One of the interpretations associates the placename *Frekasteinn* of the Helgi poems with ritual slaying of animals.

85. Armini, Harry. "Ett par svenska ortnamn belysta av Tacitus och Iordanes." *Arkiv för nordisk filologi*, 63 (1948), 73-88.

Interprets the placename *Åsaka* as "god's drive": some attestations of the name are located roughly equal distances apart, in an area of Västergötland which may be taken as a cult center, thus suggesting the ritual migration of Nerthus in Tacitus, *Germania*, ch. 40.

86. Arntz, Helmut. *Handbuch der Runenkunde,* 2nd ed. Sammlung kurzer Grammatiken germanischer Dialekte, B, 3. Halle a .d. S.: M. Niemeyer, 1944. First edition 1935.

Handbook of runology, based on the assumption that the runes were anchored in Germanic religion and therefore functioned as a kind of cult writing system.

87. Arntz, Helmut. "Runen und Runennamen." *Anglia*, 67-68 (1944), 172-250.

Departing primarily from English sources, Arntz analyzes the names of the runes as reflections of Germanic religion. These turn, according to him, on fertility: the *vanir* and the sun.

88. Arren, J. "Om Ragnarok." *Dania*, 10 (1903), 112-25.

Commentary to A. Olrik, "Om Ragnarok" (1902); calls for a complete study of Ragnarǫk following the principles of comparative mythology.

89. Arrhenius, Birgit. "Det flammande smycket." *Fornvännen*, 57 (1962), 79-101. Summary in German.

A discussion of late Iron Age clasps ornamented with red color of garnet or carbunculus and worn by women. The author suggests possible association with worship of Freyja and with one of her attributes, the *Brísinga men.*

90. Arrhenius, Birgit. "Zum symbolischen Sinn des Almadin im früheren Mittelalter." *Frühmittelalterliche Studien*, 3 (1969), 47-59.

Includes remarks on the iconographic background of Thor's disguise as Freyja (*Þrymskviða* 12-19) and specifically on the *Brísinga men.* Following a suggestion from Dietrich Hofmann, Arrhenius reads *brísinga* as genitive plural, referring to the individual strands of the necklace.

91. Arrhenius, Birgit. "Tür der Toten: Sach- und Wortzeugnis zu einer frühmittelalterlichen Gräbersitte in Schweden." *Frühmittelalterliche Studien*, 4 (1970), 384-94.

On a grave at Helgö (Sweden) with an apparent gate or opening. Discussion of similar finds and of the possible religious and ritual background, including remarks on *Grógaldr* and the Gotland picture stones.

92. Arwidsson, Greta. "Demonmask och gudabild i germansk folkvandringstid." *Tor*, 9 (1963), 163-87. Summary in German, pp. 184-85.

Archaeological discussion of demonic masks and representations of gods during the period of Germanic migrations. Arwidsson is inclined to see southern influence on the Germanic peoples in these instances.

93. Ashdown, Margaret. "The Attitude of the Anglo-Saxons to Their Scandinavian Invaders." *Saga-Book of the Viking Society*, 10 (1919-27), 75-99.

Includes remarks on paganism, pp. 93 ff.

94. Askeberg, Fritz. *Norden och kontinenten i gammal tid: Studier i nordgermansk kulturhistoria*. Uppsala: Almqvist & Wiksell, 1944. vi, 201 pp.

Askeberg's Uppsala dissertation aims primarily at an assessment of contact between Scandinavia and the rest of Europe before and during the Viking Age. It includes a historical introduction (pp. 1-37), a chapter assigning the origins of runes to the Goths along the Vistula river (pp. 38-94), a chapter denying most usually proposed literary relationships between ancient Scandinavia and the West, i.e., Germany and Ireland (pp. 95-113), and a concluding chapter on the etymology and semantics of the terms *víkingr* and *víking*. Little of the book is directly devoted to Norse mythology, although there are occasionally relevant remarks: e.g., the suggestion that all traditions of Nerthus and Ing were North Germanic (but cf. Hans Kuhn, *Anzeiger für deutsches Altertum*, 59 (1949), 17). However, the volume is valuable for its broader analysis of cultural relationships during the pagan period in Scandinavia.

95. Auld, Richard L. "The Psychological and Mythic Unity of the God Óðinn." *Numen*, 23 (1976), 145-60.

Applies the psychological theories of Erich Neumann to Odin and Norse mythology and concludes that Odin occupies both poles in Neumann's various oppositions (male-female, matriarchal-patriarchal, unconscious-conscious, and so forth) and also frequently mediates them.

B

96. Bachlechner, Joseph. "Eine Göttin Zisa." *Zeitschrift für deutsches Altertum*, 8 (1851), 587-88.

Eliminates a hypothetical German goddess Zisa, in favor of the god Ziu/Týr.

97. Bachlechner, Joseph. "Vuldor-Ullr." *Zeitschrift für deutsches Altertum*, 8 (1851), 201-08.

Proposes a fantastic emendation to *Beowulf* and associates it with Ullr.

98. Bæksted, Anders. "Begravede runestene." *Årbøger for nordisk oldkyndighed og historie*, 1951, pp. 63-95. Summary in English.

Urges caution in assigning magic or ritual status to buried rune stones.

99. Bæksted, Anders. *Guder og helter i Norden*. Politikens håndbøger, 306. Copenhagen: Politiken, 1974. 356 pp. Fourth impression, ed. Stephen Kehler.

A survey of Norse myth and legend for a Danish audience.

100. Bæksted, Anders. *Nordiske guder og helte*. Copenhagen: Politikens forlag, 1984. 341 pp.

Lightly revised edition (by Jens Peter Schiødt) of the author's *Guder og helte i Norden* (1974).

101. Baesecke, Georg. "Die Herkunft der Runen." *Germanisch-Romanisch Monatsschrift*, 22 (1934), 413-17.

Puts the origin of runes in Germany, and connects the runes with magic and the cult of Odin.

102. Baesecke, Georg. "Muspilli II." *Zeitschrift für deutsches Altertum*, 82 (1948-50), 199-239.

Discusses a number of myths and mythological passages: Thor's battle with Hrungnir, *Vǫluspá* and Old English poetry, Snorri's mythography, and formulas of creation and destruction in Germanic.

103. Baetke, Walter. *Art und Glaube der Germanen.* Hamburg: Hanseatische Verlagsanstalt, 1934. 79 pp.

The religion of the Germanic peoples as the essence of their nature. Baetke stresses the relationship between man and god as exercised in cult, which for Baetke is of a public, political nature.

104. Baetke, Walter. *Arteigene germanische Religion und Christentum,* 2nd ed. Der Weg der Kirche, 4. Berlin: W. de Gruyter, 1936. 40 pp. 1st ed. 1933.

Germanic religion and Christianity.

105. Baetke, Walter. "Das objektive Moment in der germanischen Religion." *Zeitschrift für Theologie und Kirche,* 17 (1936), 353-76. Reprint in Baetke, *Vom Geist und Erbe Thules* (1944), pp. 16ff., and in Baetke, *Kleine Schriften* (1973), pp. 44-55.

Baetke prefers Hegel's objective theory of religion to Schleiermacher's subjective theory, and he brings this preference to bear in the analysis of Germanic religion. "The objective moment in Germanic religion lies not in its myth—the religious conceptions—nor in cult—as an expression and realization of piety—, but rather in *nomos* ['usage, convention']. Recognition of moral and social order as a holy law was the true content of Germanic religion."

106. Baetke, Walter. *Religion und Politik in der Germanenbekehrung.* Leipzig: Dörffling & Franke, 1937. 46 pp. Rpt. in Baetke, *Kleine Schriften* (1973), pp. 351-69, under the title "Religion und Politik beim Übergang der germanischen Stämme zum Christentum."

Baetke argues against separating "outer" and "inner" factors (i.e., political and religious factors) in analysis of the conversion of the Germanic peoples to Christianity, for in his opinion politics and religion were inseparable; religion as opposed to religiosity was primarily a social institution. He surveys the conversion of the various Germanic peoples, for the most part stressing outer, political factors. To the conversion of Iceland he devotes most space. He concludes that the pagan lawspeaker Þorgeirr followed primarily religious motives in his decision that Iceland should adopt the new faith: had the country not done so, peace would have been lost, and peace was, in Baetke's view, not a political but a religious matter, closely bound to cult and the social and moral order. This conversion, he argues, is in a sense paradigmatic for the others; whatever the outer circumstances, the inner process will have been something like that of Iceland. The good of the people—for Baetke a religious concept—determined the conversions.

107. Baetke, Walter. *Die Religion der Germanen in Quellenzeugnissen,* 2nd ed. Frankfurt a. M.: M. Diesterweg, 1938. xvi, 185 pp. Original 1937.

A collection of primary sources of Germanic religion in German translation.

108. Baetke, Walter. "Altgermanische Gottesverehrung und Frömmigkeit." *Zeitschrift für Deutschkunde*, 53 (1939), 100-05.

Brief essay on the outer and inner forms of Germanic religion, sounding some of Baetke's major themes, such as the relationship between Germanic public religion and law. Baetke notes that the eddic poems are not direct manifestations of religion.

109. Baetke, Walter. "Die Götterlehre der Edda und ihre Deutungen." *Velhagen und Klasings Monatshefte*, 53 (1939), 73-77. Rpt. in Baetke, *Vom Geist und Erbe Thules* (1944), pp. 140-54, and in Baetke, *Kleine Schriften* (1953), pp. 195-205.

Baetke argues that all attempts to elucidate eddic religion, or to use eddic poems as sources for Germanic religion, are doomed to failure. He surveys such attempts: the nature-mythological school, from Franz Josef Mone (1822) through Uhland; the approach linking eddic poems to cult practices (e.g., Baldr's death as fertility ritual); and attempts to isolate world view in the eddic poems—here, according to Baetke, each interpreter reaches different results. The problem is that the eddic poems are pure myth, and myth is not religion. Religion requires interaction between gods and men, a feature strikingly lacking in eddic poems. Baetke concludes by suggesting that we turn the tables: instead of using eddic myth to elucidate Germanic religion, we should use Germanic religion to explain relevant aspects of eddic myth—and the rest we should regard as literary production.

110. Baetke, Walter. *Das Heilige im Germanischen*. Tübingen: Mohr, 1942. viii, 226 pp.

Baetke's study of the concept of the holy remains fundamental to the study of Germanic religion. It consists primarily of etymological and semantic studies of the terms **wi haz* and **hailagaz* and their etyma. The first denoted the numinous or divine, the second the prosperity associated with the numen.

111. Baetke, Walter. "Der Begriff der Unheiligkeit im altnordischen Recht." *Beiträge zur Geschichte der deutschen Sprache und Literatur*, 66 (1942), 1-54. Rpt. in Baetke, *Kleine Schriften* (1973), pp. 90-128.

In a study parallel to his *Das Heilige im Germanischen* (1942), Baetke considers here the term *óheilagr* (lit. "un-holy") in Old Norse law. It is not, he finds, precisely identical to such semantically related terms as *sekr*, *ógildr*, and *útlagr*, all of which also relate to outlawry and may be applied in similar situations. A man who is *óheilagr* is not merely outside the protection of the law. That would deny him the fellowship (and therefore the aid and lack of enmity) of society and individuals within and through cult. The *óheilagr* man, rather, has lost this relationship with regard to the man or men whose legal rights he has violated and whose duty it is to seek redress, frequently vengeance. Here again Baetke stresses the social, public nature of Germanic religion and its concrete manifestation in cult.

112. Baetke, Walter. "Der Begriff des Heiligen im Germanischen." *Forschungen und Fortschritte,* 20 (1944), 3-5. Rpt. in Baetke, *Vom Geist und Erbe Thules* (1944), pp. 33-38, and in Baetke, *Kleine Schriften* (1973), pp. 83-89.

This short paper offers little more than a summary of the author's *Das Heilige im Germanischen* (1942) and "Der Begriff der Unheiligkeit im altnordischen Recht" (1942). It is organized around an attack on the notion that Germanic religion possessed a phenomenon similar to the Polynesian *mana.*

113. Baetke, Walter. "*Guð* in den altnordischen Eidesformeln." *Beiträge zur Geschichte der deutschen Sprache und Literatur,* 70 (1948), 351-71. Rpt. in Baetke, *Kleine Schriften* (1973), pp. 129-42.

The word *guð/goð* "god(s)" was originally neuter in gender; with the advent of Christianity it gradually became masculine. Certain medieval Swedish and Danish legal texts employ a neuter plural, however, and the neuter has also left traces in the medieval language of Norway and Iceland. Baetke postulates a progression from neuter plural to neuter singular (as early as during the pagan period) to masculine singular, but he does not regard use of the neuter plural in medieval Swedish legal oaths as evidence of the survival of paganism there into the thirteenth century. The original collective-abstract sense of the word made it easily applicable to the new Christian god without any sense of contradiction.

114. Baetke, Walter. *Die Götterlehre der Snorra-Edda.* Berichte über die Verhandlungen der sächsischen Akademie der Wissenschaften zu Leipzig, phil.-hist. Kl., 97:3. Berlin: Akademie-Verlag, 1950. 68 pp.

This monograph is fundamental to modern understanding of *Snorra edda.*

The first pages constitute a refutation of Hans Kuhn's bold suggestion that Snorri's version of syncretism included some form of lingering belief in the pagan gods ("Das nordgermanische Heidentum in den ersten christlichen Jahrhunderten" (1942)). Rather, argues Baetke, Snorri should be seen as a product of the Christian thirteenth century, and in this his scholarly attitude toward Norse mythology should be sought. The basic view is to be found in Romans 1:18-23: heathens once knew God, who is visible for all to see, but they turned from him and worshipped instead idols or nature. Thus men could become pagan gods, and subsequently demons could imitate them and do Satan's work. Such euhemeristic notions were clearly present in Iceland well before Snorri wrote. Snorri's *æsir* are men (men of Asia), and the tales he has them tell are their religious beliefs, tempered by Snorri's euhemerism. Thus the delusion of Gylfi concerns not the content of the myths—for the men of Asia believe them—but rather the great hall in which the encounter takes place and which later vanishes. This is necessary because Gylfi must speak with men using fictitious names in a fictitious milieu. Gylfi's later retelling of the myths explains how they survived through time, and the vexing question of how the *æsir* who tell the stories can have the same names as the "gods" they tell about is answered by Snorri's statement (ch. 43) that the men of Asia later assumed the names of their ancient gods.

Snorri's conception of the religious beliefs of the Asia men is clearly set out, according to Baetke, in the Prologue to *Snorra edda.* This posits a kind of natural religion, consistent with current medieval thought. As Snorri harmonized this with the myths as he knew them, he advanced Odin to the premier role, that of Allfather (*alfǫðr*), for the putative natural religion would have been monotheistic, with a pagan reflection of God. Snorri's intention, then, was not to Christianize Odin, but rather to clarify the religious conception of natural religion. By making Odin the Allfather he achieved this goal, and by making Allfather the father of the other gods, he created a compromise between the polytheism of Germanic mythology and the monotheism of medieval "natural religion."

115. Baetke, Walter. *Christliches Lehngut in der Sagareligion; Das Svoldr Problem: Zwei Beiträge zur Sagakritik*. Berichte über die Verhandlungen der sächischen Akademie der Wissenschaften zu Leipzig, phil.-hist. Kl., 98:6. Berlin: Akademie-Verlag, 1951. 135 pp.

The first of these two essays deals with "Christian borrowings in the religion of the sagas" (pp. 7-55; reprinted in Baetke, *Kleine Schriften* (1973), pp. 319-50). Topics treated include blessings, prayer and sacrifice, cult and magic, guilt and punishment, Christian themes, and fate and happiness. Baetke concludes that the saga authors knew virtually nothing about genuine pagan practices and often intended their accounts as Christian exempla.

116. Baetke, Walter. "Zur Christianisierung der Germanen." *Historische Zeitschrift*, 171 (1951), 112-18. Rpt. in Baetke, *Kleine Schriften* (1973), 370-74.

Baetke's review of K. D. Schmidt, *Germanischer Glaube und Christentum* (Göttingen, 1948), a study of the conversion to Christianity. It is interesting for the following remark, of methodological importance: "It is still the same, since Vilmar's interpretation of the Heliand, with the supposed points of contact in Germanic thought and belief: misjudging their true character, one takes the Christian works of the Germanic Middle Ages or Christian reports about the Germanic peoples as primary sources of heathen religiosity and infers from the Christian features, which one (naturally) finds there, by projecting them back into Germanic, a tendency of Germanic toward Christianity, one might call it a pre-stabilized harmony between the two" (*Kleine Schriften*, p. 374).

117. Baetke, Walter. "Zur Religion der Skalden." In *Atti dell'viii congresso internazionale di storia delle religioni (Roma 17-23 Aprile 1955)*. 361-64. Florence: G. C. Sansoni—Editore, 1956.

Summary of an address at the eighth international conference on the history of religions: public religion as revealed in skaldic poetry.

118. Baetke, Walter. "Fragen der altgermanischen Religionsgeschichte: Zur zweiten, völlig neubearbeiteten Auflage der 'Altgermanischen Religionsgeschichte' von Jan de Vries." *Deutsche Literaturzeitung*, 78 (1957), cols. 1062-69. Rpt. in Baetke, *Kleine Schriften* (1973), pp. 37-43.

Baetke criticizes the second (and still current) edition of the standard handbook on Germanic religion for the following reasons: 1) It depends too strongly on the theories of Dumézil, on comparative data from ancient and more recent societies, including folklore, and attempts to reconstruct Germanic religion; according to Baetke, only the religion of specific tribes may be reconstructed with any degree of certainty; 2) in the religion de Vries reconstructs, magic and mystery play too great a role, the public and institutional aspects of cult too little; 3) de Vries exaggerates the importance of the Christian mission in the conversion. Those familiar with the writings of Baetke will recognize these biases.

119. Baetke, Walter. "Die germanische Religion." In *Die Religion in Geschichte und Gegenwart*, 3rd ed. Vol. 2, cols. 1432-40. Tübingen: J. C. B. Mohr (Paul Siebeck), 1958. Rpt. in Baetke, *Kleine Schriften* (1973), pp. 28-36.

A survey of Germanic religion, written for a handbook on religions. Baetke discusses briefly Germanic religion and the state, law, and warfare, also public and private cult. He treats myth only obliquely, in a short concluding section on gods.

120. Baetke, Walter. *Die Aufnahme des Christentums durch die Germanen,* 2nd. ed. Libelli, 48. Darmstadt: Habelt, 1962.

A readable and useful survey of the conversion to Christianity among the various Germanic peoples, including the Scandinavians; here the emphasis is on Iceland.

121. Baetke, Walter. *Yngvi und die Ynglingar: Eine quellenkritische Untersuchung über das nordische 'Sakralkönigtum'.* Sitzungsberichte der sächsischen Akademie der Wissenschaften zu Leipzig, phil.-hist. Kl., 109:3. Berlin: Akademie-Verlag, 1964. 181 pp. Partial reprint (pp. 1-68 and 171-80) in Baetke, *Kleine Schriften* (1973), pp. 143-94.

The aim of this monograph is to examine the widely accepted notion of the Germanic sacral kingship through careful analysis of the sources. Part 1 deals with the supposed divine powers of the king and his sacral personage, part 2 with his supposed descent from the gods. Baetke's thesis is, to say the least, bold, for he argues that the sources show no sign of a sacral kingship.

122. Baetke, Walter. *Kleine Schriften: Geschichte, Recht und Religion in germanischem Schrifttum.* Eds. Kurt Rudolph, and Ernst Walter. Weimar: Böhlau, 1973. 387 pp.

This collection of Baetke's shorter writings includes the following works entered in this bibliography: "Die germanische Religion" (1958); "Fragen der altgermanischen Religionsgeschichte" (1957); "Das objektive Moment in der germanischen Religion" (1936); "Der Begriff der Heiligkeit im Germanischen" (1944; orig. title "Der Begriff des Heiligen im Germanischen"); "Der Begriff der Unheiligket im altnordischen Recht" (1942); "*Guð* in den altnordischen Eidesformeln" (1948); "Die Götterlehre der Edda und ihre Deutungen" (1939); *Die Götterlehre der Snorra-Edda* (1950); "Religion und Politik beim Übergang der germanischen Stämme zum Christentum" (1937; orig. title "Religion und Politik in der Germanenbekehrung"); "Zur Christianisierung der Germanen" (1951). The volume also includes excerpts from the following longer works relevant to myth and entered in this Bibliography: *Das Heilige im Germanischen* (1951); *Yngvi und die Ynglingar* (1964); "Christliches Lehngut in der Sagareligion" (1951).

123. Bailey, Richard N. *Viking Age Sculpture in Northern England.* Collins Archaeology. London: Collins, 1980. 288 pp.

Valuable especially for chapter 6, "Gods, Heroes and Christians" (pp. 101-42). Northern England stone carvings contain evidence of pagan-Christian syncretism, which Bailey examines carefully. The Gosforth monuments, in particular, seem to detail myths of Thor and of Ragnarǫk.

124. Baird, Joseph L. "Unferth the þyle." *Medium Ævum*, 39 (1970), 1-12.

Advances the hypothesis that the Old English *þyle* may have been associated with Odin.

125. Bandle, Oskar. "Strukturprobleme in der Njáls saga." In *Festschrift für Siegfried Gutenbrunner: Zum 65. Geburtstag am 26. Mai 1971 überreicht von Freunden und Kollegen*, eds. Oskar Bandle, Heinz Klingenberg, and Friedrich Maurer, 1-26. Heidelberg: C. Winter, 1972.

This structural analysis of *Njáls saga* is relevant to Scandinavian mythology for the author's insistence that the saga and its genre reflect pagan norms.

126. Bandle, Oskar, Heinz Klingenberg, and Friedrich Maurer, eds. *Festschrift für Siegfried Gutenbrunner: Zum 65. Geburtstag am 26. Mai 1971 überreicht von seinen Freunden und Kollegen.* Heidelberg: C. Winter, 1972. vii, 216 pp.

This festschrift includes the following essays relevant to Scandinavian mythology and treated separately in this bibliography: Oskar Bandle, "Strukturprobleme in der Njáls saga" (pp. 1-26); Karl Hauck, "Zur Ikonologie der Goldbrakteaten, IV" (pp. 47-70); Otto Höfler, "'Sakraltheorie' und 'Profantheorie' in der Altertumskunde" (pp. 71-116); Heinz Klingenberg, "Hávamál: Bedeutungs- und Gestaltenwandel eines Motivs" (pp. 117-44). Pp. 203-16 contain a bibliography of Gutenbrunner's writings.

127. Bang, A. Chr. *Völuspaa og de Sibyllinske orakler.* Christiania videnskabsselskabets forhandlinger, 1879, nr. 9. Oslo: J. Dybwad, in commission, 1879. 23 pp.

As the first published version of the theories developed (apparently independently?) by S. Bugge and Bang, concerning Judeo-Christian and classical influences on Old Norse literature and mythology, as transmitted via Britain, this pamphlet was quite important during the latter decades of the nineteenth and early decades of the twentieth century. The specific parallel argued here, as the title indicates, is between *Vǫluspá* and the Sibylline oracle, especially as a means of transmitting Christianity to pagans.

128. Bang, A. Chr. *Vǫluspá und die Sibyllinschen Orakel.* Vienna: Gerold's Sohn, 1880. 43 pp. Translated by Jos. Cal. Poestion.

Translation of Bang's 1879 original, somewhat enlarged by the translator.

129. Barakat, Robert A. "Odin: Old Man of *The Pardoner's Tale.*" *Southern Folklore Quarterly*, 28 (1964), 210-15.

Odin as the model of the old man in Chaucer's "The Pardoner's Tale" in *Canterbury Tales.* Refuted by P. Schmidt, "Reexamination of Chaucer's Old Man of The Pardoner's Tale" (1966), and supported by R. L. Harris, "Odin's Old Age" (1969).

Barði Guðmundsson, *see* Guðmundsson, Barði.

130. Bartsch, Karl. "Über Muspilli." *Germania*, 3 (1858), 7-21.

Germanic conceptions of the end of the world, including Ragnarǫk.

131. Baur, Grace van Sweringen. "The Disguise Motif in the Germanic Hero-Sagas." *Scandinavian Studies*, 4 (1917), 220-39.

Brief mention of Odin in the disguise of a wanderer and some indication of the broader context of this motif.

132. Bauschatz, Paul C. "Urth's Well." *Journal of Indo-European Studies*, 3 (1975), 53-86.

A discussion of fate and the experience of time in ancient Germanic culture, recovered from the symbol of Urðr's well and relevant eddic texts. The argument is expressed more fully in Bauschatz, *The Well and the Tree* (1982).

133. Bauschatz, Paul C. *The Well and the Tree: World and Time in Early Germanic Culture.* Amherst: University of Massachusetts Press, 1982. xxiii, 256 pp.

Expanded presentation of the arguments expressed in Bauschatz, "Urth's Well" (1975), on the nature and relationship of fate and time in ancient Germanic culture. Areas investigated are mythology ("Urth's Well," pp. 1-29), burial and other ritual (pp. 31-84), *Beowulf* (pp. 85-116), "Action, Space, and Time" (pp. 117-54), and language (pp. 155-87. The central hypothesis is that the basic temporal division marked past from non-past, and the discussion investigates how past and non-past influence one another.

134. Bax, Marcel, and Tineke Padmos. "Two Types of Verbal Dueling in Old Icelandic: The Interactional Structure of the *senna* and the *mannjafnaðr* in *Hárbarðsljóð.*" *Scandinavian Studies*, 55 (1983), 149-74.

Contra Clover, "*Hárbarðsljóð* as Generic Farce" (1979), the authors attempt to establish a different set of generic rules for the flyting, distinguishing between *senna* and *mannjafnaðr.* The methodology employs theories of pragmatics and conversational analysis from recent linguistic theory.

135. Beck, Heinrich. *Einige vendelzeitliche Bilddenkmäler und die literarische Überlieferung.* Sitzungsberichte der bayerischen Akademie der Wissenschaften, phil.-hist. Kl., 1964, 6. Munich: Verlag der bayerischen Akademie der Wissenschaften; C. H. Beck, in commission, 1964. 50 pp.

The Vendel helmet plates illuminated by literary sources (eddic and skaldic). Beck disassociates the images from mythology and associates them with heroic tradition.

136. Beck, Heinrich. *Das Ebersignum im Germanischen: Ein Beitrag zur germanischen Tier-Symbolik.* Quellen und Forschungen zur Sprach- und Kulturgeschichte der germanischen Völker, neue Folge, 16. Berlin: W. de Gruyter, 1965. x, 207 pp.

Monographic treatment of the boar as religious symbol in ancient Germanic cultures, building on both literary and archaeological evidence read against the broader background of Germanic animal symbolism. The author distinguishes between association of the boar with battle and warfare on the one hand and with chthonic forces of fertility on the other. Separate treatment is also given to the role of words for boar (especially *jǫfurr*) and other animals in royal naming, to the boar as devil and to the boar hunt in medieval romance, and to Norse *heitstrenging.* The frequent Celtic parallels are fully discussed.

137. Beck, Heinrich. "Die Stanzen von Torslunda und die literarische Überlieferung." *Frühmittelalterliche Studien*, 2 (1968), 237-50.

The four plates discovered in 1870 at Torslunda, Öland (Sweden), are cast bronze dies with anthropomorphic and theriomorphic motifs. Beck surveys the Germanic literary traditions relating to them and finds (as others have) that plate D (man with horned helmet and man in wolfskin) relates to Odin and the *úlfheðnar*; the helmeted man even appears one-eyed. In his discussion of plates A and B (men fighting beasts) Beck stresses the heroic pattern but does not stress Thor.

The primary value of the article will lie in the area of iconographic analysis.

138. Beck, Heinrich. "Waffentanz und Waffenspiel." In *Festschrift für Otto Höfler zum 65. Geburtstag*, eds. Helmut Birkhan and Otto Gschwantler, 1-16. Vienna: Notring, 1968.

Essentially a semantic study of Germanic **laikaz*, whose etyma usually mean "play." An equation between "battle" and "play" is basic; thus use of, e.g., Old Norse *leikr* for "battle" is not metaphoric but absolute. Pictorial representations of dancing warriors, often with gods or valkyries, strengthen this identification, which ultimately may derive from cult.

139. Beck, Heinrich. "Germanische Menschenopfer in der literarischen Überlieferung." In *Vorgeschichtliche Heiligtümer und Opferplätze in Mittel- und Nordeuropa: Bericht über ein Symposium in Reinhausen bei Göttingen vom 14.-16. Oktober 1968*, ed. Herbert Jankuhn, 240-58. Abhandlungen der Akademie der Wissenschaften in Göttingen, phil.-hist. Kl., 3. Folge, 74. Göttingen: Vandenhoeck & Ruprecht, 1970.

Considers the Germanic literary evidence for human sacrifice in five social areas: cult groups, assembly communities, cult communities, warrior bands, and households.

140. Beck, Heinrich. "Der kunstfertige Schmied—ein ikonographisches und narratives Thema des frühen Mittelalters." In *Medieval Iconography and Narrative: A Symposium*, eds. Flemming G. Andersson, Esther Nyholm, Marianne Powell, and Flemming Talbo Stubbkjær, 15-37. Odense: Odense University Press, 1980.

The effect of ancient iconographic models on pictorial and narrative traditions relating to Wayland the smith.

141. Beck, Heinrich, Herbert Jankuhn, Kurt Ranke, and Reinhard Wenskus, eds. *Reallexikon der germanischen Altertumskunde, ed. Johannes Hoops,* 2nd ed. Berlin and New York: W. de Gruyter, 1973—in progress. Vols. 1—in progress.

The second edition of Johannes Hoops's famous *Reallexikon* is completely new and expanded considerably from the original. The entries, by leading scholars, nearly all German, contain extensive notes and references. The relevant articles on gods and aspects of cult are particularly useful for their coverings of relevant archaeological data, but mythic materials also receive treatment.

142. Beck, Inge. *Studien zur Erscheinungsform des heidnischen Opfers nach altnordischen Quellen.* 1965. Diss. Munich.

Beck chose the word *Erscheinungsform* "form of appearance" for her study of pagan sacrifice in Norse sources to indicate that those sources are nonsacral and in most cases temporally removed from paganism. The work is primarily terminological and surveys place, time, person, and act. The final pages (178-83) of the exposition proper explore the nature of the *blót*. A bibliography is included.

143. Becker, C. J. "Zur Frage der eisenzeitlichen Moorgefässe in Dänemark." In *Vorgeschichtliche Heiligtümer und Opferplätze in Mittel- und Nordeuropa: Bericht über ein Symposium in Reinhausen bei Göttingen vom 14.-16. Oktober 1968*, ed. Herbert Jankuhn, 119-66. Abhandlungen der Akademie der Wissenschaften in Göttingen, phil.-hist. Kl., 3. Folge, 74. Göttingen: Vandenhoeck & Ruprecht, 1970.

Survey of evidence for possible fertility cult in Iron Age Denmark.

144. Beckman, Nathan. "Några namnstudier i terrängen." *Namn och bygd*, 9 (1921), 9-26.

Includes a section on *Odens källa* "Odin's spring."

145. Beckman, Nathan. "Några orter på den gamla dansk-svenska gränsen." *Namn och bygd*, 10 (1922), 5-12.

Includes remarks on *Gnipahellir* (*Vǫluspá* 44, 49, 58).

146. Beckman, Nathan. "Ignavi et imbelles et corpore infames." *Arkiv för nordisk filologi*, 52 (1936), 78-81.

Brief note on *ergi*.

147. Behagel, Otto. "*Wodini hailag*." *Indogermanische Forschungen*, 54 (1936), 213.

Comment on W. Krogmann, "Wodini hailag" (1936).

148. Behn, Friedrich. "Die nordischen Felsbilder." *Archiv für Religionswissenschaft*, 34 (1937), 1-13.

Calls into question a number of details of then current scholarship on Scandinavian rock carvings. Behn argues a continuous development from the Stone Age onward, questions the symbolic value of the images, and argues essentially the existence of a cult of the sun outside the context of the rock carvings. The religious background, he argues, shifted from hunting magic to agricultural ritual.

149. Bellows, Henry Adams. *The Poetic Edda, with Introduction and Notes*. New York: American-Scandinavian Foundation, 1923. xxviii, 583 pp. Numerous reprintings.

English translation of the Poetic Edda, with general introduction and head-notes and explanatory notes to the individual poems.

150. Berendsohn, Walter. "Zauberunterweisung in der Edda." *Arkiv för nordisk filologi*, 50 (1934), 250-59.

Hávamál 138-64 and *Sigrdrífumál* 5-19 as examples of instruction in magic techniques.

151. Bergeron, Tor, Magnus Fries, Carl-Axel Moberg, and Folke Ström. "'Fimbulvinter.'" *Fornvännen*, 51 (1956), 1-18.

Four short essays on Fimbulvetr: an introduction, by Moberg (pp. 1-2); the perspective of the history of religion, by Ström (pp. 3-5); the perspective of the history of vegetation, by Fries (pp. 5-10); the perspective of the history of meteorology, by Bergeron (pp. 10-18).

Ström's essay is of direct relevance to Norse mythology and is entered separately in the bibliography.

152. Bergh, L. Ph. C. van den. *Proeve van een kritisch woordenboek der nederlandsche mythologie*. Utrecht: L. E. Bosch & Zoon, 1846. xxxvi, 392 pp.

Dictionary of Netherlandic mythology. The author understands "Netherlandic" broadly and comments on evidence primarily from Germany and Scandinavia. Major inspirations appear to be Mone and Grimm. There are brief entries on the Norse gods under the German forms of their names (Thunor, Wodan), and long entries on such topics as temples and magic.

153. Bergmann, Frédéric Guillaume. *La fascination de Gulfi (Gylfa ginning),* 2nd ed. Strassburg & Paris: Treuttel & Würtz, Paris & Geneva: J. Cherbuliez, Leipzig: F. A. Brockhaus, 1871. 371 pp.

Translation of *Gylfaginning,* with Introduction (pp. 1-76) and Commentary (pp. 139-343). This, the second edition, adds additional notes (pp. 344-51), and there is a fairly extensive index.

154. Bergmann, Frédéric Guillaume. *Le message de Skirnir et les dits de Grimnir (Skirnisför-Grimnismâl, poëmes tirés de l'Edda de Sæmund, publiés avec des notes philologiques, une traduction et un commentaire perpétuel).* Leipzig: F. A. Brockhaus, 1871. x, 326 pp.

Text, translation, and commentary to *Skírnismál* and *Grímnismál.*

155. Bergmann, Frédéric Guillaume. *Des Hehren Sprüche (Hâva mâl) und altnordische Sprüche, Priameln und Rûnenlehren: Ethische und magische Gedichte aus der Sæmunds-Edda kritisch hergestellt, übersetzt und erklärt.* Strassburg: K. J. Trübner, 1877. 267 pp.

Translation and commentary to *Hávamál.*

156. Bergsland, Knut. "Hárbarðsljóð sett fra øst." *Maal og minne,* 1967, pp. 8-40.

Seen from the east, according to Bergsland (who is not a Scandinavianist), *Hárbarðsljóð* is a kind of roman-à-clef describing Haraldr Greycloak's journey to Bjarmaland. Although this conclusion has hardly generated enthusiasm, the central part of the article (pp. 19-29) may be of interest for its remarks on kinship systems in ancient Scandinavia and in the mythology.

Cf. Gösta Holm, "Hárbarðsljóð och Lappland" (1969).

157. Bergwitz, Joh. K. "Gårdnavn i det gamle Gauldøla-fylke." *Gauldalsminne,* 1 (1926), 11-16.

Includes discussion of theophoric placenames (Týr and Odin) and others reflecting ritual activity (*horg, hov*).

158. Berneker, E. "Weihen." In *Untersuchungen und Quellen zur germanischen und romanischen Philologie: Johan von Kelle dargebracht von seinen Kollegen und Schülern,* vol. 1, eds. Carl von Kraus and August Sauer, 1-6. Prager deutsche Studien, 8. Prague: C. Bellmann, 1908.

Argues that the word family of German *weihen* "to consecrate," which includes Norse *vé* "holy place," originally meant "to hang" and has to do with ritual hanging of the deity.

159. Bessason, Haraldur. "Mythological Overlays." In *Sjötíu ritgerðir helgaðar Jakobi Benediktssyni*, vol. 1, eds. Einar G. Pétursson and Jónas Kristjánsson, 273-92. Stofnun Árna Magnússonar á Íslandi, rit 12. Reykjavik: Stofnun Árna Magnússonar á Íslandi, 1977.

"It is the purpose of this article to give a few examples . . . of parallels between the Eddas and the Sagas in the use of literary technique and imagery" (p. 275). After a few examples from early sections of *Heimskringla*, including the unlikely supposition that Harald Fairhair's wooing of Gyða resonates to Freyr's wooing of Gerðr, the bulk of the article treats family sagas, primarily *Egils saga.* Here is a typical quotation: "Just as Óðinn, through his tests of prowess and endurance, finally becomes worthy of the mead [of poetry], so the poet Egill enters the spiritual realm of Ásgarðr, when he proceeds to immortalize his own sons in Sonatorrek, the only poem in which he states explicitly that his poetic talent is a gift from Óðinn" (p. 287).

160. Betz, Werner. "Sose gelimida sin." *Rheinische Viertelsblätter*, 21 (1956), 11-13.

On the last line of the second Merseburg charm.

161. Betz, Werner. "Die altgermanische Religion." In *Deutsche Philologie im Aufriss*, vol. 3, ed. Wolfgang Stammler, 2467-556. Berlin: E. Schmidt, 1957.

A thorough and excellent survey of Germanic religion, with copious bibliographic references.

162. Beyer, Paul Gerhardt. *Die Edda.* Breslau: F. Hirt, 1934. 223 pp.

Translation (sometimes paraphrase) of the Poetic Edda.

163. Beyschlag, Siegfried. "Die Betörung Gylfis." *Zeitschrift für deutsches Altertum*, 85 (1954), 163-81.

Following Walter Baetke's seminal work (1950) on Snorri's mythology, Beyschlag traces Gylfi through his interview with the *æsir* in *Gylfaginning*, seeking the specific details of the deception of Gylfi. Beyschlag regards the Prologue of Snorri's *Edda* as a statement of the kind of natural philosophy the pagan Gylfi would accept. The deception practiced by the *æsir* is to represent their mythology in these same natural philosophical terms, so that Gylfi will accept it and further it, as he does upon his return to his own people. When in ch. 43 of *Gylfaginning* the *æsir* assume the names of the "gods" they have been describing, they elevate themselves to deities of the religion Gylfi has begun to promulgate. Thus Snorri's aim in *Gylfaginning*, according to Beyschlag, was to trace and clarify the origin of Nordic pagan religion, and further to pinpoint the very moment when the "heroes" of ancient Asgard transformed themselves into gods.

164. Beyschlag, Siegfried. "Snorri Sturluson: Heidnisches Erbe und christliches Mittelalter im Geschichtsdenken Altislands." *Saeculum*, 7 (1956), 310-20.

The text of a lecture held in Erlangen in 1955. Using Snorri as a central figure, Beyschlag reviewed the still current view of the mix of pagan inheritance and medieval Christianity in thirteenth-century Iceland. The key was euhemerism: the ancient myths, and the eddic verse and skaldic kennings dependent on them, told of the deeds of former great men and hence were exempted from the Church's usual view that pagan gods (as, e.g., in *Gylfaginning*) were really visions called forth by Satan.

165. Beyschlag, Siegfried. "Zur Gestalt der Hávamál: Zu einer Studie Klaus von Sees." *Zeitschrift für deutsches Altertum*, 103 (1974), 1-19.

Beyschlag criticizes von See's monograph on *Die Gestalt der Hávamál* (1972). Besides taking up details, Beyschlag argues that von See has not demonstrated that all of the first 80 stanzas are to be understood as spoken by Odin. This article is useful not only as part of the debate on *Hávamál*, but also as a summary of von See's monograph and its relationship to earlier works on *Hávamál*.

See also von See, "Probleme der germanischen Spruchdichtung" (1975).

166. Bianchi, Ugo. *Il dualismo religioso: Saggio storico ed etnologico.* Rome: "L'Erma" di Brettschneider, 1958. 215 pp.

This study of dualism contains an appendix on Loki (pp. 194-97) relating the Norse god to Bianchi's theories about the trickster figure.

167. Bickel, Ernst. "Die Glaubwürdigkeit des Tacitus und seine Nachrichten über den Nerthuskult und den Germanennamen." *Bonner Jahrbücher*, 139 (1934), 1-20.

Expanded text of a lecture; consideration of the importance of topoi in the descriptions offered by Tacitus of the cult of Nerthus and therefore of the veracity of the account. Cf. H. Naumann, "Die Glaubwürdigkeit des Tacitus" (1934), a lecture which followed this one by a few months.

168. Biezais, Haralds. "Die vermeintlichen germanischen Zwillingsgötter." *Temenos*, 5 (1969), 22-36.

By eliminating the Baltic evidence, Biezais dismisses the so-called twin gods from the Germanic pantheon.

169. Bilfinger, Gustav. *Untersuchungen über die Zeitrechnung der alten Germanen*, vol. 1: *Das altnordische Jahr.* Stuttgart: C. Liebich, 1899. 99 pp.

Calendrical practices in ancient Scandinavia.

170. Bilfinger, Gustav. *Untersuchungen über die Zeitrechnung der alten Germanen*, vol. 2: *Das germanische Julfest.* Stuttgart: C. Liebich, 1901. 132 pp.

Pre-Christian yule ritual.

Billeskov Hjort, Vilhelm, *see* Hjort, Vilhelm Billeskov.

171. Bing, Just. "Der Götterwagen." *Mannus*, 6 (1914), 261-82.

Sacral wagons on Bronze Age rock carvings, in archaeology and in narrative.

172. Bing, Just. "Germanische Religion der älteren Bronzezeit." *Mannus*, 6 (1914), 149-80.

An attempt to interpret early Germanic religion on the basis of the Scandinavian Bronze Age rock carvings. Bing sees links both with Indo-European religion and with later religious and mythological materials and often succumbs to speculative associations.

173. Bing, Just. "Das Kivikdenkmal." *Mannus*, 7 (1915), 61-77.

An attempt at an overall interpretation of the carvings on the stone slabs from the Bronze Age grave at Kivik, Sweden. Bing argues that the scenes represent a cult act, perhaps to be associated with the burial.

174. Bing, Just. "Götterzeichen." *Mannus*, 7 (1915), 263-80.

Symbols of gods in rock carvings. Bing is inclined to find symbols of the gods of Norse mythology (ax, spear, horse, ram, etc.).

175. Bing, Just. "Ull: En mytologisk undersøkelse." *Maal og minne*, 1916, pp. 107-24.

Finds that Ullr and Odin once filled the same slot in the mythology; before then, Ullr was some kind of Dioscurian god, in connection with Freyr and Skaði.

176. Bing, Just. "Der Kultwagen von Strettweg und seine Gestalten." *Mannus*, 10 (1918), 159-78.

Interpretation of the wagon from Strettweg (early Iron Age) as a cult object and elucidation of the carvings of harts on it.

177. Bing, Just. "Rock Carvings of the Norse Bronze Age." *Saga-Book of the Viking Society*, 9 (1920-25), 275-300.

Here one finds in English much of Bing's reasoning and interpretation of the Bronze Age rock carvings, including the rather speculative connections with Norse mythology.

178. Bing, Just. "Die Götter der südskandinavischen Felsenzeichnungen." *Mannus*, 14 (1922), 259-74.

Interpretation, largely on the basis of Norse mythology, of Bronze Age rock carvings from southern Scandinavia.

179. Bing, Just. "Skibsgruppene paa helleristningene fra Berga-Tune og fra Aspeberget: En parallel." *Fornvännen*, 17 (1922), 206-13. Summary in German, p. 282.

Fertility cult in the rock carvings. Bing identifies a possible reflection of Freyr. In discussing the relative chronology of the rock carvings, he suggests that younger carvings rely more heavily on the gods and that this reliance parallels a move from cult to myth.

180. Bing, Just. *Fra trolldom til gudetro: Studier over nordiske helleristninger fra bronsealderen*. Oslo: A. W. Brøgger, 1937.

An attempt at full analysis of the religious background of the Bronze Age rock carvings. Bing offers individual analyses, much comparative material, and a proposed historical development: first gods in animal form, then animals and anthropomorphic gods portrayed separately, then a wagon cult.

The cult of the sun plays a large role in Bing's reasoning.

181. Birkeli, Emil. *Høgsætet: Det gamle ondvege i religionshistorisk belysning*. Stavanger: Dreyers grafiske anstalt, 1932. [5], 134, [1] pp.

A study of the "high-seat" and *ǫndvegi* "seat of honor" (the author distinguishes them) and the alleged religious background of the latter in ancestor worship.

182. Birkeli, Emil. *Fedrekult i Norge: Et forsøk på en systematisk-deskriptiv fremstilling*. Skrifter utgitt av det norske videnskaps-akademi i Oslo, II. hist.-filos. kl., 1938, 5. Oslo: J. Dybwad, in commission, 1938. 220 pp.

On father-cult in Norway. Although many older sources are cited and analyzed (e.g., *Snorra edda*, eddic poetry), there is no systematic discussion of mythology. Most of the source material is from more recent times and the phenomena treated belong more to "lower" than to "higher" mythology.

183. Birkeli, Emil. *Huskult og hinsidighetstro: Nye studier over fedrekult i Norge*. Skrifter utgitt av det norske videnskaps-akademie i Oslo, II. hist.-filos. kl., 1943, no. 1. Oslo: J. Dybwad, in commission, 1944. 252 pp.

A continuation of the author's *Fedrekult i Norge* (1938), on ancestor worship and attitudes toward and rites for dealing with the dead. As in *Fedrekult*, this volume is rich in detail from ancient and recent times.

184. Birkhan, Helmut. "Sîn gebaine si ûf ain irminsûl begrouben: Zur Symbolik einer Romsage." In *Volkskundliche Beiträge*, eds. Helmut Fielhauer and Ingrid Kretschmer, 9-20. Veröffentlichungen des Instituts für Volkskunde der Universität Wien, 1. Vienna: Schendl, 1966.

Symbolic use of the word *irminsûl*.

185. Birkhan, Helmut, and Otto Gschwantler, eds. *Festschrift für Otto Höfler zum 65. Geburtstag.* Vienna: Notring, 1968. xv, 523 pp. 2 vols., consecutively paginated.

Contains the following papers relevant to Scandinavian mythology and entered separately in this Bibliography: Heinrich Beck, "Waffentanz und Waffenspiel" (pp. 1-16); Helmut Fielhauer, "Das Motiv der kämpfenden Böcke" (pp. 69-106); Otto Gschwantler, "Christus, Thor und die Midgardschlange" (pp. 145-68); Maria Hornung, "Der Fastnachtlauf der 'Rollatn Lotter': Ein Relikt germanischen Brauchtums in der Osttiroler Sprachinsel Pladen in Oberkarnien" (pp. 265-72); Edith Marold, "Die Königstochter im Erdhügel" (pp. 351-61); Gunter Müller, "Altnordisch Vífill—Ein Weihename" (pp. 363-71); Kurt Schier, "Freys und Frodis Bestattung" (pp. 389-409); Ferdinand Sokolicek, "Der Hinkende im brauchtümlichen Spiel" (pp. 423-32); Gerlinde Tuppa, "Bemerkungen zu den Tierträumen der Edda" (pp. 433-43); and Herwig Wolfram, "Methodische Fragen zur Kritik am 'sakralen' Königtum" (pp. 473-90). A bibliography of Höfler's writings up to 1967, compiled by Gschwantler, completes the work (pp. 519-23).

Bjarni Einarsson, *see* Einarsson, Bjarni.

Bjarni Guðnason, *see* Guðnason, Bjarni.

186. Birkhan, Helmut. "Niederrheinisch-Friesisches in Schottland und das Alter des germanischen *a*-Umlautes von *u*." In *Antiquitates Indogermanicae: Studien zur indogermanischen Altertumskunde und zur Sprach- und Kulturgeschichte der indogermanischen Völker: Gedenkschrift für Hermann Güntert zur 25. Wiederkehr seines Todestages am 23. April 1973*, eds. Manfred Mayrhofer, Wolfgang Meid, Bernfried Schlerath, and Rüdiger Schmitt, 427-41. Innsbrucker Beiträge zur Sprachwissenschaft, 12. Innsbruck: Institut für Sprachwissenschaft der Universität Innsbruck, 1974.

Includes remarks on the transportation of the second-century Germanic mother cult of the *Mopates*.

187. Björkman, Erik. "Skjalf och Skilfing." *Namn och bygd*, 7 (1919), 163-81.

Includes remarks on *Válaskjálf* and *Hliðskjálf.*

188. Bjørn, Anathon. "Kvernstene i gravhauger." *Maal og minne*, 1927, pp. 38-43.

Reports and explores the possibility of a magico-religious interpretation of cases of mill-stones in ancient graves.

189. Bjørn, Anathon. "Et dyrehode av bronse fra Gotland." *Fornvännen*, 28 (1933), 332-40. Summary in German.

Discusses a bronze animal's head, apparently that of an elk. The author argues that the figure is wholly Nordic and relates it to cult. Ultimately, he feels, it derives from the Hallstadt culture.

Björn M. Ólsen, *see* Ólsen, Björn M.

190. Björnsson, Guðmundur. "Um jarðarfarir, bálfarir og trúna á annað líf (Alþýðufyrirlestur í Reykjavík 15. desember 1912)." *Skírnir*, 87 (1913), 97-122.

The text of an address on cremation, burial, and belief in life after death.

191. Blaas, C. M. "Sif und das Frauenhaar." *Germania*, 23 (1878), 155-58.

Sif's hair and folklore about the plant *Frauenhaar* (adiantum).

192. Blaney, Benjamin. "The Berserk Suitor: The Literary Application of a Stereotyped Theme." *Scandinavian Studies*, 54 (1982), 279-94.

The stereotyped theme involves a berserk's challenge for a woman's hand and his subsequent defeat by a hero. Blaney analyzes variations in the literary application of this theme, treating particularly the legendary *Þorsteins saga Víkingarsonar* and three family sagas: *Egils saga*, *Gísla saga*, and *Grettis saga*. The result is a rather interesting discussion of the use of a motif from mythology in later literature.

193. Blind, Karl. "The Ethic Ideas of the Edda." *Dublin University Magazine*, n.s., 1 (1878), 392-98, 520-36.

Based largely on *Hávamál*. Blind treats "rules" of hospitality, friendship, virtue, fidelity, the limits of understanding, and so forth.

194. Blind, Karl. "Discovery of Odinic Songs in Shetland." *The Nineteenth Century*, 5 (1879), 1091-113.

Alleged folklore parallels to *Hávamál*.

195. Blind, Karl. "Shetland Folklore and the Old Faith of the Scandinavians and Teutons." *Saga-Book of the Viking Society*, 1 (1892-96), 163-81. Shorter version published in the *New Review*, December, 1894.

Alleged survivals of Germanic religion/Scandinavian mythology in recent folklore of Shetland.

196. Blind, Karl. "The Boar's Head Dinner at Oxford, and a Teutonic Sun-God." *Saga-Book of the Viking Society*, 1 (1892-96), 90-105.

The "Teutonic Sun-God" is Freyr.

197. Blind, Karl. "A Pre-Historic Sun Chariot in Denmark." *Saga-Book of the Viking Society*, 3 (1901-03), 381-94.

Associates the Trundholm chariot with beliefs about Odin.

"The greater part of this lecture appeared in *The Westminster Review* of November last..." (p. 381).

198. Blinkenberg, Chr. *Tordenvåbenet i kultus og folketro: En komparativ-arkaeologisk undersøgelse.* Studier fra sprog- og oldtidsforskning, 79. Copenhagen: Tillge's boghandel, 1909. 108 pp.

The "thunder weapon" in cult and folk belief; relevant to Thor.

An English translation was issued as *The Thunderweapon in Religion and Folklore: A Study in Comparative Archaeology*, Cambridge Archaeological and Ethnological Studies (Cambridge: At the University Press, 1911, xii, 122 pp.).

199. Blinkenberg, Chr. "Tordenvåbenet i danske oldtidsfund." In *Festskrift til H. F. Feilberg fra nordiske sprog- og folkemindeforskere på 80 års dagen den 6. august 1911.* 58-71. Svenska landsmål, 1911; Maal og minne, 1911; Danske studier, 1911. Stockholm: Norstedt, Copenhagen: Gyldendal, Oslo (Kristiania): Bymaals-laget, 1911.

"The attempts to trace Thor and his hammer back to prehistoric times find, therefore, no support in ancient Danish artifacts and finds" (p. 69). Conceptions regarding Thor derive, according to the author, from oriental peoples and did not reach Denmark during the Stone or Bronze Ages.

200. Blom, Dorothea. *Tyding av Harbardljod, et Edda-kvede.* Stavanger: Dreyers grafiske anstalt, 1936. 34 pp. Summary in English, pp. 29-34.

Nature-mythological interpretation of and commentary to *Hárbarðsljóð*, with no learned apparatus. The English summary is something special, as this passage will show: "Methinks, names as hlenniman and hrossatjov strongly pleads for Tor as Loke, as the moongod with the spirals or snakes of the moonbinding" (p. 33).

201. Blom, Dorothea. *Tyding efter en grunntanke av Grimnismål, et Edda-kvede.* Stavanger: Dreyers grafiske anstalt, 1937. 17 pp.

A nature-mythological interpretation of and commentary to *Grímnismál*, with no learned apparatus.

202. Blom, Dorothea. *Tåke-hvirvlingen som nøklen eller lykelen til 'Edda''s og hedenskapets verdenanskuelse.* Stavanger: Dreyers grafiske anstalt, 1939. 46 pp.

Blom finds that the whirling of mist is the key principle of Scandinavian paganism and argues her modern nature-mythological point engagingly without scholarly underpinnings.

203. Blum, Ida. *Die Schutzgeister in der altnordischen Literatur.* Zabern: Buchdruckerei A. Fuchs, 1912. x, 45 pp. Diss. Strassburg

Study of the appearance of protective spirits (*fylgjur, dísir,* and *hamingjur*, and related phenomena) in eddic poetry, family sagas and mythical-heroic sagas.

204. Boberg, Inger M. "Baldr og misteltenen." *Årbøger for nordisk oldkyndighed og historie*, 1943, pp. 103-06.

Contra Hvidtfeldt, "*Mistilteinn* og Balders død," (1941). The sword with which Baldr is killed in Danish tradition (Saxo) was not original to the story.

205. Boberg, Inger M. "Sagnet om Harald hildetands fødsel." In *Festskrift til museumsforstander H. P. Hansen, Herning på 70-årsdagen den 2. oktober 1949*, eds. Peter Skautrup and Axel Steensberg, 208-12. Copenhagen: Rosenkilde og Bagger, 1949.

On Saxo's account of the birth of Harald wartooth (*Gesta Danorum*, Book 7) and parallel texts in Norse. Boberg puts the episode in the context of international tale-types and notes that Odin is here as elsewhere in medieval and later folk belief a replacement for Satan.

206. Boberg, Inger M. *Motif-Index of Early Icelandic Literature.* Bibliotheca Arnamagnæana, 27. Copenhagen: Munksgaard, 1966. 268 pp.

Following the format of Stith Thompson's *Motif Index of Folk Literature*, this volume opens with a section on "Mythological Motifs" (pp. 21-37) and contains in following sections a great many other motifs from the mythology. *Snorra edda* and the eddic poems are covered very thoroughly, and there are references to Saxo Grammaticus and the mythical-heroic sagas (*fornaldarsögur*). Some of the entries contain brief bibliographic information.

207. Bø, Olav. "*Hólmganga* and *einvígi*: Scandinavian Forms of the Duel." *Mediaeval Scandinavia*, 2 (1969), 132-48.

In reaching the conclusion that the *hólmganga* was a late west Scandinavian, viking form of the pan-Scandinavian *einvígi* "duel," Bø argues that the *locus classicus, Kormáks saga* ch. 10, "contains nothing to support belief in a fertility cult" (p. 135).

208. Boehmer, Heinrich. "Das germanische Christentum." *Theologische Studien und Kritiken*, 86 (1913), 165-280.

Early Christianity among the Germanic peoples; emphasis on the political mission. Boehmer found the pagan mythology quite unimportant in this context but saw many other Germanic aspects in early Germanic Christianity.

209. Boer, R[ichard] C[onstant]. "Die Béowulfsage." *Arkiv för nordisk filologi*, 19 (1902), 19-88.

Pp. 19-44 contain a useful critical survey of nineteenth-century mythic analyses of *Beowulf*, many of which restore the story to nature mythology or to thinly disguised retellings from Norse mythology. Boer's position, argued particularly in the second half of the article, is that *Beowulf* derives rather from heroic legend.

210. Boer, R[ichard] C[onstant]. "Kritik der Vǫluspá." *Zeitschrift für deutsche Philologie*, 36 (1904), 289-370.

An attempt at a full textual prehistory and history of *Vǫluspá*. Boer sees an original poem, reworked by a second pagan poet with Christian leanings. Four more redactions intervene before the extant recordings. Boer sets all of this in Iceland.

211. Boer, R[ichard] C[onstant]. "Beiträge zur Eddakritik, II: Hyndluljóð." *Arkiv för nordisk filologi*, 22 (1905), 217-56.

Analysis of four hypothetical layers of tradition in *Hyndluljóð*, including *Vǫluspá in skamma.*

212. Boer, R[ichard] C[onstant]. "Beiträge zur Eddakritik, I: Über Grímnismál." *Arkiv för nordisk filologi*, 22 (1906), 133-74.

Analysis of the original portions, expansions, and interpolations in *Grímnismál.*

213. Boer, R[ichard] C[onstant]. "Gylfes mellemværende med aserne." In *Festskrift tillägnad Hugo Pipping på hans sextioårsdag den 5 november 1924.* 17-24. Skrifter utg. av Svenska litteratursällskapet i Finland, 175. Helsinki: Mercators tryckeri, 1924.

Boer postulates the following textual history. The original *Snorra edda* (i.e., *Gylfaginning*) had Gefjon draw part of Skåne (southern Sweden, where Gylfi lived) west out to the sea. There lived the *æsir*, and there Gylfi visited them. The journey of the *æsir* from Asia belonged originally to *Ynglinga saga*. In composing *Ynglinga saga* Snorri worked in the Gefjon material chronologically and had Gefjon draw Sjælland from land near Lake Mälar. A later interpolater added the Prologue to *Snorra edda*, with its tale of the *æsir*'s journey from Asia, and revised the Gefjon material in accordance with *Ynglinga saga.*

214. Boer, R[ichard] C[onstant]. "Studier over Snorra edda." *Årbøger for nordisk oldkyndighed og historie*, 1924, pp. 145-272.

A detailed study of the style and content of *Snorra edda*, arguing that Codex Regius and Codex Trajectinus are closest to the archetype (which, however, was not Snorri's original). Continued in his "Studien über die Snorra Edda" (1926-27).

215. Boer, R[ichard] C[onstant]. "Studien über die Snorra Edda: Die Geschichte der Tradition bis auf den Archetypus." *Acta Philologica Scandinavica*, 1 (1926-27), 54-150.

A continuation of his "Studier over Snorra edda" (1924), focusing on the development of the text from Snorri's original to the archetype.

216. Börtzler, Friedr. "Edda und Muspilli vom Manichäismus beeinflusst?" *Niederdeutsche Zeitschrift für Volkskunde*, 13 (1935), 179-85.

A response to W.-E. Peuckert, "Germanische Eschatologien" (1935), dismissing the influence of Near Eastern tradition on Germanic eschatology.

217. Börtzler, Friedr. "Ymir: Ein Beitrag zu den eddischen Weltschöpfungsvorstellungen." *Archiv für Religionswissenschaft*, 33 (1936), 230-45.

Börtzler assails the common opinion that the Scandinavian conceptions of creation, and in particular the giant Ymir, derive from Iranian traditions and ultimately may have to do with the personae of fertility ritual (see especially F. R. Schröder, "Germanische Schöpfungsmythen," 1931). Ymir is represented differently in *Vǫluspá* and *Vafþrúðnismál*, and Snorri tried to reconcile the differences in his *Edda*. Börtzler draws attention to the cosmogony of Lactantius Firmianus, in which the central opposition of moisture and heat generates life, and where many other details reminiscent of Snorri's account are to be found. Lactantius, Börtzler suggests, may have given Snorri the organizing principle for the rearrangement and reconciliation of native traditions, especially regarding Ymir. This suggestion has found little favor, but the article is useful in pointing out drawbacks and alternatives to the longstanding hypothesis of Iranian influence.

218. Bogaers, J. E., and M. Gysseling. "Nehalennia, Gimbio en Ganuenta." *Naamkunde*, 4 (1972), 231-40. Summary in German. Also published in *Oudheidkundige medelingen uit het Rijksmusueum van oudheden te Leiden*, n. r. 52 (1971), 86-92.

Actually two notes: "Gimio Ganuentae consistens" (pp. 231-35, by Bogaers), and "Ganuenta" (pp. 236-39, by Gysseling). Interpretation of a Nehalennia inscription: Gimio, a donor to Nehalennia, remained in Ganuenta, a Belgian placename.

219. Bogaers, J. E., and M. Gysseling. "Over de naam van de godin Nehalennia." *Naamkunde*, 4 (1972), 221-30. Summary in German. Also published in *Oudheidkundige medelingen uit het Rijksmusueum van oudheden te Leiden*, N. R. 52 (1971), 79-85.

Actually two notes: "De kwestie van de spelling" (pp. 221-26, by Bogaers), and "Etymologie" (pp. 226-29, by Gysseling). The name of the goddess Nehalennia means "the (female) leader."

220. Bonfante, G. "Microcosmo e macrocosmo nel mito indoeuropeo." *Die Sprache*, 5 (Festschrift für Wilhelm Havers) (1959), 1-9.

Bonfante discusses the correlation between microcosmos and macrocosmos which he finds in Indo-European myth. He focuses on Norse cosmology and creation, as expressed in *Vǫluspá*, *Grímnismál*, and *Vafþrúðnismál*.

221. Bonsack, Edwin. "Wieland and Þórvarðr." *Mediaeval Scandinavia*, 1 (1968), 57-81.

On *Grímnismál* 33: the four deer represent apostles of Christ. *Dvalinn* would be an anagram for Wieland, according to Bonsack author of *Hêliand*, *Dáinn* for *Andi*, the holy spirit, *Dúneyrr* for *óreyndr*, the author of *Grímnismál*, and *Duraþrór for Þórvarðr*, the translator of *Vǫlundarkviða*. Additional speculation concerns *Hávamál* 143, in which Bonsack believes that Odin becomes the Christian god, and *Þrymskviða*, which Bonsack believes was greatly influenced by *Hêliand*.

222. Bonser, Wilfrid. "Magical Practices against Elves." *Folk-Lore*, 37 (1926), 350-63.

Attempts to link many references to elves, including those of Norse mythology.

223. Bonus, Arthur. *Zur Germanisierung des Christentums*. Zur religiösen Krisis, 1. Jena: E. Diederichs, 1911. 206 pp.

Germanic aspects of early Christianity among Germanic peoples.

224. Boor, Helmut de. "Der Zwerg in Skandinavian." In *Festschrift Eugen Mogk zum 70. Geburtstag 19. Juli 1924*. 15-29. Halle a. d. S.: M. Niemeyer, 1924.

Using both a chronological and a geographic perspective, de Boor investigates the use of the term "dwarf" and its relationship to folk belief. He concludes that dwarfs left genuine folk belief at an early date in Scandinavia and even by Old Norse times belonged primarily to the world of Märchen. Dwarfs in the eddas and other Norse texts he describes either as German imports or characters from Märchen elevated in a literary environment. His comparison with elves, whom he takes for genuine beings of folk belief and religion, enriches the article, as does the broad perspective (ancient myth to modern legend and folk belief).

225. Boor, Helmut de. "Eine griechische Romanstelle und ein nordischer Opferbrauch." In *Festskrift tillägnad Hugo Pipping på hans sextioårsdag den 5 november 1924*. 25-37. Skrifter utg. av Svenska litteratursällskapet i Finland, 175. Helsinki: Mercators tryckeri, 1924.

The Greek text in question is Xenophon, *Ephesian Histories*, book 2, ch. 13. It describes a sacrifice to Ares of men or animals, with a combination of hanging and penetration with a spear. De Boor brings it into connection with Odinic sacrifice and thinks it may be a trustworthy piece of ancient ethnography.

226. Boor, Helmut de. "Die religiöse Sprache der Vǫluspá und verwandter Denkmäler." In *Deutsche Islandforschung 1930,* vol. 1, *Kultur*, ed. Walther Heinrich Vogt, 68-142. Veröffentlichungen der schleswig-Holsteinischen Universitätsgesellschaft, 28:1. Breslau: F. Hirt, 1930.

A long, rich discussion of the vocabulary of *Vǫluspá* and other eddic poems. De Boor cites many parallels from the usage of skalds from the middle tenth century associated with the jarls of Hlaðir (near Trondheim, Norway), especially the pagan Hákon Sigurðarson; in these circles resistance to the conversion was great. It thus seems likely that *Vǫluspá* may have some association—perhaps direct—with this skaldic circle.

227. Boor, Helmut de. "Dichtung." In *Germanische Altertumskunde*, ed. Hermann Schneider, 306-430. Munich: Beck, 1939.

A historical survey of the older Germanic literatures for a comprehensive handbook of ancient Germanic culture. The author treats mythological verse and goes into particular detail regarding the relationship of mythic to heroic literature.

228. Bork, Ferdinand. "Germanische Götterdreiheiten." *Mannus*, 15 (1923), 1-19.

In part a rearrangement of the findings of J. Bing, "Germanische Religion der älteren Bronzezeit" (1914), this article makes clear from the start its true purpose: the location of lunar mythology in Germanic culture. Thus, besides the rock carvings, eddic mythological materials also receive treatment. The triads of the title are most palpable in the various magic objects of the gods, which Bork groups into threes. In each he finds a dark and light component, evidence for him of lunar mythology.

229. Bork, Ferdinand. *Die Geschichte des Weltbildes*. Ex Oriente Lux, 3:2/5. Leipzig: E. Pfeiffer, 1930. 149, [1] pp.

Cosmos and worldview from a universalist perspective, with much discussion of Scandinavian mythology. Bork regards the twelve *æsir* of Snorri's learned prehistory as zodiacal gods with a consequent association with ancient Babylon. Bork associates Ragnarǫk with Asian conceptions of the end of the world—particularly Ceylonese. These conclusions have not been accepted.

230. Bornhausen, Karl. "Die nordische Religionsvorstellung vom Sonnengott und ihr Gestaltwandel: Erweiterter Vortrag beim 6. internat. Kongress für Religionsgeschichte im Brüssel, Sept. 1935." *Archiv für Religionswissenschaft*, 33 (1936), 15-20.

Two thousand years of Nordic sun worship, extrapolated primarily from physical artifacts.

231. Bosch, H. Wirth Roeper. "Die Entstehung der Heerkönigsreligionen der eurasischen Völkerwanderungszeit und das Ende des kultischen Matriarchates." In *Atti dell'viii congresso internazionale di storia delle religioni (Roma 17-23 Aprile 1955)*. 373-75. Florence: G. C. Sansoni—Editore, 1956.

Summary of an address at the eighth international conference on the history of religions: ties in the matrones and Germanic seeresses with Eurasian religions.

232. Boudriot, Wilhelm. *Die altgermanische Religion in der amtlichen kirchlichen Literatur des Abenlandes vom 5. bis 11. Jahrhundert.* Bonn: Röhrscheid, 1964. viii, 79 pp. Unaltered reprint of the 1928 original, in Untersuchungen zur allgemeinen Religionsgeschichte, 2.

Exhaustive analysis of references to pagan Germanic religion in official and other religious literature from the Migration period to the eleventh century in Germany.

233. Bouman, Ari C. "Een dreital etymologieen: *aibr, eolete, garsecg.*" *Neophilologus,* 35 (1951), 238-41.

Associates Gothic *aibr* with phallic cult, as suggested by *Vǫlsa þáttr.* For a refutation, see E. A. Ebbinghaus, "Gothic *aibr*" (1963).

234. Boyer, Régis. "Le culte dans la religion nordique ancienne." *Inter-nord,* 13-14 (1974), 223-43.

Survey of evidence, primarily literary, of cult in ancient Scandinavian religion.

235. Boyer, Régis. "Paganism and Literature: The So-called 'Pagan Survivals' in the samtíðarsögur." *Gripla,* 1 (1975), 135-67.

Boyer investigates the religious attitudes of the so-called *samtíðarsögur* or "contemporary sagas" and finds no real evidence for a pagan renaissance of the thirteenth century.

236. Boyer, Régis. *Les sagas islandaises.* Bibliothèque historique. Paris: Payot, 1978. 230 pp.

Chapter 7 treats sagas and ancient Scandinavian religion.

237. Boyer, Régis. "La sagesse de Hávamál." In *Sagesse et religion: [Actes du] Colloque de Strasbourg, octobre 1976.* 211-32. Travaux du centre d'études supérieures specialisé d'histoire des religions du Strasbourg. Paris: Presses universitaires de France, 1979.

On the ethics of *Hávamál.*

238. Boyer, Régis. "Les Valkyries et leurs noms." In *Mythe et personification: Actes du colloque du Grand Palais (Paris), 7-8 mai 1977,* ed. Jacqueline Duchemin, 39-54. Paris: Société d'Édition "Les Belles Lettres," 1980.

A study of the names of the valkyries, starting from etymologies and aiming to place them in various religious categories.

239. Boyer, Régis. *Yggdrasill: La Religion des anciens Scandinaves.* Bibliothèque historique. Paris: Payot, 1981. 249 pp.

Boyer's synthetic treatment of Old Scandinavian religions follows two lines: the diachronic and the relatively fixed. The diachronic line fills most of the book, which, following discussion of sources and methodology (chapters 1-3), treats in successive chapters prehistory, the Bronze Age, the Iron Age, and the Viking Age. The fixed or "vertical" line, as the author terms it, consists of three aspects of nature which Boyer believes were fundamental in Old Scandinavian religion and society. These are the sun (sometimes realized as fire), liquid, and earth. Gods came to be aligned with these principles: Baldr, Týr, and Thor with the sun, Odin with liquid, the *vanir* with the earth. Only the Viking Age, however, saw a full panoply of gods aligned with the elements, along with a concomitant alignment of other forces: law and war with the solar principle; wisdom, poetry and magic with liquid; and fertility with the earth.

Although Boyer expressly argues that the difference between his scheme and that of Dumézil consists in the elimination of social structures from the model, it will be apparent that Boyer's tripartite grid could be closely mapped to Dumézil's. Some readers, too, will question the apparent tendency toward nature mythology.

The last chapters attempt synthesis: mythic history and cosmos, and the mythic icon Yggdrasill and fate.

240. Boyer, Régis. "On the Composition of *Vǫluspá*." In *Edda: A Collection of Essays*, eds. Robert J. Glendenning and Haraldur Bessason, 117-33. The University of Manitoba Icelandic Studies, 4. N. p.: University of Manitoba Press, 1983.

A reading of the Codex Regius text of *Vǫluspá*, which Boyer regards as the best of the three versions and capable of supporting a unified interpretation. He finds a symetric, carefully planned structure (diagram p. 131), composed of thirty stanzas ascending through the categories "Valfǫðr," "Disorder," "Construction," "Active/Causes," to "Fate"—the central theme of the poem—, then descending through the categories "Passive/Consequences," "Destruction," "Order," "Níðhǫggr."

241. Boyer, Régis, and Évaline Lot-Falck. *Les Religions de l'Europe du nord.* Le trésor spirituel de l'humanité. Paris: Fayard-Denoel, 1974. 753 pp.

French translations of texts pertaining to Norse mythology, principally from the two eddas. The volume contains an introductory essay by Boyer on the notion of the sacred among the Old Scandinavian peoples.

242. Branky, Franz. "Wetter- und Regenliedchen: Kinderüberlieferungen aus Niederösterreich." *Zeitschrift für deutsche Philologie*, 5 (1874), 155-59.

Includes mention of alleged survivals of Odin and Thor in recent Austrian folklore.

243. Branky, Franz. "Hans: Volksüberlieferungen aus Nieder-Österreich." *Zeitschrift für deutsche Philologie*, 8 (1877), 73-101.

P. 81 draws attention to parallels between *Hymiskviða* and Stupid Hans in Austrian folklore.

244. Branston, Brian. *Gods of the North.* New York: Vanguard Press, n. d. x, 318 pp.

This ambitious handbook begins with a lengthy historical introduction which traces links of language and culture and even discusses the meters of eddic poems. There is, however, little additional evidence of the author's expertise, despite the detail of his presentation. He contents himself largely with retelling stories, and what interpretation he ventures tends toward abandoned ideas of the nineteenth century. One even reads, in the conclusion, unblushing nature mythology: "the true Odin was originally the wind, Thor was *thunder*, Lóðurr-Ríger-Heimdallr was *beneficent fire*, Loki was destructive fire and so was Surtr" (p. 300). One seeks in vain references to recent scholarship—even in English—and the Rev. G. W. Cox and Viktor Rydberg are among the few cited as authorities on mythology (p. 309).

245. Brate, Erik. "Disen." *Zeitschrift für deutsche Wortforschung*, 13 (1911-12), 143-52.

Associates *ides* and *dísir* etymologically and interprets them as "those who return" (fem.), in light of a cult of the dead and perhaps also mother worship. Brate also comments on the etymology of Iðunn: ever-young.

246. Brate, Erik. "Höknatten." In *Festskrift til H. F. Feilberg fra nordiske sprog- og folkemindeforskere på 80 års dagen den 6. august 1911.* 404-20. Svenska landsmål, 1911; Maal og minne, 1911; Danske studier, 1911. Stockholm: Norstedt, Copenhagen: Gyldendal, Oslo (Kristiania): Bymaals-laget, 1911.

Includes remarks on pagan midwinter festivals. See *Maal og minne* 1913, pp. 42-43, for a comment on this article by Edvard Bull.

247. Brate, Erik. "Thor(s)hugle." *Arkiv för nordisk filologi*, 29 (1913), 103-09. Additional remarks on p. 386.

Philological discussion of the Swedish placename, located near Uppsala, of the title. Brate reads the name as "Thor's mound" and associates it with the worship of Thor.

248. Brate, Erik. "Wrindawi." *Arkiv för nordisk filologi*, 29 (1913), 109-19.

Brate understands the Swedish placename, near Norrköping, of the title as "Vrindr's holy place." He equates this Vrindr with Rindr of the mythology and with Saxo's Rinda and interprets her as one of the *vanir*, ultimately a representation of the earth mother.

249. Brate, Erik. "Voluspa." *Arkiv för nordisk filologi*, 30 (1914), 43-61.

Address delivered at a meeting of philologists and historians in Sweden in 1912. Because he believes it to be a *drápa*, Brate puts *Vǫluspá* no earlier than 980; but he assigns the apparent Christian elements in the poem to fourth-century Gothic influence and takes the poet for a pagan. Thus, he concludes, Hákon jarl's efforts on behalf of paganism appear to offer a likely climate for the origin of *Vǫluspá*.

250. Brate, Erik. "M. Olsen, Hedenske kultminder i norske stedsnavne I (Videnskapsselskapets skrifter II. Hist.-filos. klasse 1914, no. 4). Kristiania 1915." *Arkiv för nordisk filologi*, 34 (1918), 91-102.

Exceptionally detailed review.

251. Brate, Erik. "Andra Merseburg-besvärjelsen." *Arkiv för nordisk filologi*, 35 (1919), 287-96.

Tabu names of fertility gods.

252. Braune, Wilhelm. "Vingolf." *Beiträge zur Geschichte der deutschen Sprache und Literatur*, 14 (1889), 369-76.

Reads the word as *vín-golf* "beer-hall" and regards it as a synonym for Valhalla.

253. Braune, Wilhelm. "*Irmindeot* und *Irmingot*." *Beiträge zur Geschichte der deutschen Sprache und Literatur*, 21 (1896), 1-7.

Linguistic discussion of two Old High German terms, leading to a negative appraisal of the possibility of pagan poems being recorded among the Franks.

254. Braune, Wilhelm. "Muspilli." *Beiträge zur Geschichte der deutschen Sprache und Literatur*, 40 (1915), 425-45.

On the Old High German word *muspilli* (Old Norse *Muspell*): it derives from a proto-Germanic word meaning "world-fire." A demon, Muspellr, emerged as a personification of this world-fire but was replaced by Surtr. Surtr dwelled in Muspellr's world and may have been regarded as his son.

255. Braune, Wilhelm. "Nachtrag zu Muspilli (Beitr. 40, 425)." *Beiträge zur Geschichte der deutschen Sprache und Literatur*, 41 (1916), 192.

Linguistic addendum to Braune, "Muspilli" (1915).

256. Bray, Olive. *The Elder or Poetic Edda, Commonly Known as Saemund's Edda, I: The Mythological Poems*. Viking Club Translation Series, 2. London: Viking Club, 1908. lxxx, 327 pp. Illustrated by W. G. Collingwood.

Translation with introduction and notes.

257. Brechter, Suso. "Zur Bekehrungsgeschichte der Angelsachsen." In *La conversione al cristianesimo nell'Europa dell'alto medioevo: 14-19 aprile 1966*. 191-215. Settimane di studio del centro italiano di studi sull'alto medioevo. Spoleto: Presso la sede del centro, 1967.

A contribution to an international conference on the conversion of European peoples to Christianity; treats the Anglo-Saxons.

258. Brednich, Rolf Wilh. *Volkserzählungen und Volksglaube von den Schicksalsfrauen*. FF Communications, 193. Helsinki: Suomalainen tiedeakatemia, 1964. 244 pp.

A monograph on prophetic female beings or those who determine fate, with thorough temporal and geographic coverage. The chapter on the Germanic representatives of the category and their survival in recent folk belief (pp. 205-20) puts the norns and *vǫlur* in an interesting perspective.

259. Breitag, Byrge. "Snorre Sturluson og æsene." *Arkiv för nordisk filologi*, 79 (1964), 117-53.

Breitag contributes to the discussion on Snorri and his view of the *æsir*, earlier treated by such scholars as Kuhn, "Das nordgermanische Heidentum in den ersten christlichen Jahrhunderten" (1942), Laugesen, "Snorres opfattelse af Aserne"(1942), Baetke, *Die Götterlehre der Snorra-Edda* (1950), and Beyschlag, "Die Betörung Gylfis" (1954), and by Holtsmark, *Studier i Snorres mytologi*, in the same year (1964). In a short opening section, he argues that the Prologue and ch. 43 of *Gylfaginning* are Snorri's work (contra Laugesen). The rest of the essay deals with Snorri's attitude toward his material and attempts to derive a plausible view of the development of the theology of *Gylfaginning*. The argument may be summarized thus: long ago, the founding leader of the *æsir*, Thor, was elevated via euhemerism to the position of the *alfǫðr*, the focus of monotheistic natural religion; this is forthcoming from the Prologue and genealogies. His descendants, the *æsir*, wished to be worshipped as gods. Therefore, they represented themselves as gods to Gylfi. To do so, they pretended to have acted together with Thor. Odin, calling himself Hár in *Gylfaginning*, usurped the position of *alfǫðr*.

The argument is clever but brittle. Snorri's view of the eddic poems, in which Thor and other *æsir* act together, remains unclear, for according to the hypothesis the interaction of Thor and other gods was a pose of the *æsir* when they were deluding Gylfi. Are we thus to imagine that (perhaps in Snorri's view) these *æsir* composed the eddic poems—after Gylfi's visit?

260. Bremer, Otto. "Der germanische Himmelsgott." *Indogermanische Forschungen*, 3 (1894), 301-02.

Separates Tīwaz/Týr etymologically from Zeus and argues that although the name makes him a deity, it cannot support the notion that he once was a sky god.

261. Brennecke, Detlef. "Gab es eine *Skrýmiskviða?*" *Arkiv för nordisk filologi*, 96 (1981), 1-8.

Brennecke finds an unusual amount of alliteration in Snorri's account of Thor's dealings with the giant Skrýmir (part of the story of Thor's journey to Útgarða-Loki). This alliteration, he argues, tends to fall on words important to the narrative; the alliterative pairs have analogs in eddic and skaldic tradition; and Brennecke finds it possible to reconstruct long lines in *ljóðaháttr.* He concludes that Snorri's source was a lost poem, wholly or partly in *ljóðaháttr*, which may also have been employed by the poets of *Hárbarðsljóð* and *Lokasenna.*

262. Briem, Ólafur. *Heiðinn siður á Íslandi.* Reykjavik: Bókaútgáfa Menningarsjóðs, 1945. 190 pp.

Briem writes lucidly about many aspects of paganism in Iceland: the gods, spirits of the land, the dead, temple and sacrifice, and the decline of heathendom. He complements the literary sources with such evidence as placenames, which he analyzes in some detail. No other work is so directly aimed at Icelandic conditions, and the coverage of religious practice is valuable and useful.

263. Briem, Ólafur. "Trúin á mátt eldsins." In *Afmæliskveðja til Próf. Dr. Phil. Alexanders Jóhannessonar háskólarektors 15. Júlí 1953 frá samstarfsmönnum og nemendum*, eds. Árni Böðvarsson, Halldór Halldórsson, and Jakob Benediktsson, 164-69. [Reykjavik]: Helgafell, 1953.

On the belief in the power of fire, in Nordic mythology and later.

264. Briem, Ólafur. *Vanir og æsir.* Studia Islandica, 21. Reykjavik: Heimspekadeild Háskóla Íslands og Bókaútgáfa Menningarsjóðs, 1963. 80 pp. Summary in English.

In treating the two major groups of gods, the *æsir* and *vanir*, this brief monograph attempts nothing less than a historical reading of the mythology and the cults on which the author believes it was based. The opening chapter surveys the Norse literary evidence about the war between the *æsir* and *vanir*, and subsequent chapters treat worship of the *æsir* among the "South Germans" (i.e., West Germanic peoples); Nerthus and Njord, Freyr, Freyja, and Dís (the *dísir*); sacral kingship; the origin of the *vanir* gods; the *æsir* among the North Germanic peoples; and a conclusion. Briem's central hypothesis is that among the Germanic peoples, the cult of the *vanir* has always been more northerly than that of the *æsir.* Tacitus locates Nerthus among the Ingvaeones (in Denmark?) and seems to describe worship of the *æsir* (Mercurius, Mars, Hercules) in Germany (where worship of the *vanir* has not been traced). Later, the institution of sacral kingship, which Briem associates with the cult of the *vanir* particularly through Freyr, was centered at Uppsala, among the Svíar, while worship of Odin was typical of the Danes and Götar (cf. the Odin name Gautr). "It therefore looks as if the cult of the Æsir gradually moved northward from Germany and took root most firmly in Southern Scandinavia. It seems inevitable that the two cults must at some time have come into conflict. Although at the end of the Viking Age the conflict is at an end, it must still have been a living memory when the Eddic poems were composed. Here, therefore, is the likeliest place to seek the germ of the story of the war and the subsequent alliance between the Æsir and the Vanir" (p. 80).

Briem leaves unexplained why this conflict, which in his scheme must have been primarily centered in the more agricultural eastern sections of Scandinavia, where sacral kingship was practiced, should turn up as a fundamental aspect of the mythology recorded in West Scandinavia (Iceland).

265. Briem, Ólafur. *Norræn goðafræði*, 3rd ed. Reykjavik: Skálholt, 1968. 134 pp.

This is a handbook of Norse mythology intended for popular and school use in Iceland. Briem surveys the beings of the mythology, worship of the gods, creation and destruction, and gods and men. There are few references and much retelling of stories. The last quarter of the book offers excerpts from *Snorra edda*.

266. Brix, Hans. *Studier i nordisk runemagi*. Copenhagen: Gyldendal, 1928. 126 pp.

Magic in many runic inscriptions, including Rök.

267. Brix, Hans. "Nye studier i nordisk runemagi." *Årbøger for nordisk oldkyndighed og historie*, ser. 3, 19 (1929), 1-188.

Supposed numerological rune magic.

268. Brix, Hans. "Det indre, magiske system paa Rök-stenen." *Acta Philologica Scandinavica*, 6 (1931-32), 67-74.

More supposed runic magic.

269. Brix, Hans. "Til store Rygbjerg-stenen." *Danske studier*, 28 (1931), 83-84.

More supposed rune magic.

270. Brix, Hans. *Analyser og problemer: Studier i ældre nordisk literatur, 7:1*. Copenhagen: Gyldendal, 1955. 207 pp.

Numerology, particularly in *Vǫluspá*.

271. Bruun, Daniel, and Finnur Jónsson. "Om hove og hovudgravninger på Island." *Årbøger for nordisk oldkyndighed og historie*, 1909, pp. 245-316.

A report on excavations in Iceland which the authors interpret as evidence of pagan temples.

272. Buchholz, Peter. *Bibliographie zur alteuropäischen Religionsgeschichte 1954-1964: Literatur zu den antiken Rand- und Nachfolgekulturen im aussermediterranen Europa unter besonderer Berücksichtigung der nichtchristlichen Religionen*. Arbeiten zur Frühmittelalterforschung, 2. Berlin: W. de Gruyter, 1967. 299 pp.

Originally intended to complement the list of references in de Vries, *Altgermanische Religionsgeschichte*, 2nd ed. (1956-57), this bibliography grew to larger proportions—more than 5000 entries—as a result of the questions current during the mid-1960s concerning limitations of the concept "Germanic." Thus Buchholz offers a tool for research on "old European" religious history, i.e., the non-Christian religions of ancient Europe outside the Mediterranean area, from the Iron Age through the early Middle Ages. The bibliography is systematically organized into an introductory major section with headings of bibliography, reference works, philology, history, heroic legend and kingship, and religious relationships among Indo-European peoples; a section on theory of religious history; a section on Europe, with chronological headings, and sections divided geographically among areas of Europe. As in any systematically organized bibliography, the indices are limited—a brief index rerum is followed only by an author index—and making use of the bibliography takes practice. There are no annotations.

273. Buchholz, Peter. "Perspectives for Historical Research in Germanic Religion." *History of Religions*, 8 (1968-69), 111-38.

In his opening "General Remarks" (pp. 111-15), Buchholz discusses three questions. Were there Teutons (i.e., one Germanic people)? Buchholz doubts it, for there is "no possibility of giving a universally accepted definition of 'Teutons'" (p. 113). Was there a Germanic religion? Yes, if we understand "Germanic" as relating to the *Germani* of the lower Rhine or more broadly in the *Nordwestblock* (the area of Germanic and Celtic admixture). Did this religion have a history? "Strictly speaking, a history of Germanic religion cannot be given. However, we can arrange what we know of Germanic religion in a historical sequence" (p. 114). Buchholz does so in the remainder of the essay. His discussion of the extant sources in historical sequence surveys the pre-Roman Iron Age, the Roman Iron Age, and the Middle Ages; under the latter rubric he treats both monuments and written sources with a division between South Germanic and Scandinavian. In every case he doubts the existence of a common Germanic religion, although he does admit "striking coincidences" (p. 129).

According to Buchholz, the perspectives for historical research in Germanic religion are thus bleak if we insist on the common notion of Germanic. They brighten, however, if we abandon this notion and apply to the vast range of material the methods of the many disciplines whose relevance he claims in his "Conclusion" (pp. 136-38). These include philology, prehistory, classical archaeology, ethnology and folklore (*Volkskunde*), history, and history of art.

This article may be read as a useful adjunct to the study of Scandinavian mythology proper.

274. Buchholz, Peter. "Shamanism—the Testimony of Old Icelandic Literary Tradition." *Mediaeval Scandinavia*, 4 (1971), 7-20.

"A shortened version of two chapters from *Schaministische Züge in der altisländischen Überlieferung*" (Diss. Münster, 1968). Defines shamanism, following the works of Dominik Schröder and Karl J. Narr, then surveys Old Norse texts according to the categories of "the shaman in ecstasy" and "the role of the shaman in society."

275. Buchholz, Peter. "Im Himmel wie auf Erden: Gedanken zu Heiligtum und Kultprovinz in der Frügeschichtlichen Religion Skandinaviens." *Acta Germanica*, 7 (1972), 1-17.

Programmatic essay arguing the value of the evidence for cult and religion in grouping the early Germanic and Scandinavian peoples. Cults specifically discussed include those of the *vanir* and Odin.

276. Buchholz, Peter. "The Religious Geography of Pagan Scandinavia." *Mediaeval Scandinavia*, 5 (1972), 89-91.

Prospects and procedures for research in Scandinavian religious geography.

277. Buchholz, Peter. "Forschungsprobleme germanischer Religionsgeschichte." *Christiana Albertina—Forschungsberichte und Halbjahresschrift der Universität Kiel*, N. F., 2 (1975), 19-29.

This essay may be regarded as an update of the author's "Perspectives for Historical Research in Germanic Religion" (1968-69), and it reiterates some of the concerns addressed there. Two examples receive special attention: the documentation of Germanic religion during the Roman period, and the god Odin; both are approached from pictorial and textual evidence.

278. Buchholz, Peter. *Vorzeitkunde: Mündliches Erzählen und Überliefern im mittelalterlichen Skandinavien nach dem Zeugnis von Fornaldarsaga und eddischer Dichtung*. Skandinavistische Studien, 13. Neumünster: Karl Wachholtz, 1980. 204 pp.

A study of the oral background of the *fornaldarsögur*, in their world and medieval Scandinavian context. The final chapter, "Wahrheit und Wunder: Die Auffassung der Quellen von der Tradition" (pp. 112-21), is important for study of the mythology and other pagan material, and the entire book is relevant for the transmission of such cultural traditions. The many references and rich bibliography increase the value of the work.

279. Bülow, Werner von. *Märchendeutungen durch Runen: Die Geheimsprache der deutschen Märchen: Ein Beitrag zur Entwicklungsgeschichte der deutschen Religion*. Hellerau bei Dresden: Hakenkreuz, 1925. 107 pp.

Fantastic association of myth, runes, and Märchen.

280. Bugge, Alexander. "Vestfold og Ynglingeætten." *[Norsk] Historisk tidsskrift*, 4. række, 5 (1909), 433-54.

In the afterword to this article on Vestfold and tne Ynglingar (pp. 447-54), Bugge treats *Rígsþula*. He assigns the poem to the British Isles of the tenth century and argues that the *Konr ungr* it mentions is likely to be Guðrøðr veiðikonungr of Dublin.

281. Bugge, Alexander. "Costumes, Jewels, and Furniture in Viking Times." *Saga-Book of the Viking Society*, 7 (1910-11), 141-76.

Toward the end of the article (pp. 172 ff.), Bugge treats wine and drinking vessels in various eddic poems (*Lokasenna, Skírnismál, Rígsþula*) as examples of Western influence.

282. Bugge, Alexander. "Celtic Tribes in Jutland?: A Celtic Divinity Among the Scandinavian Gods?" *Saga-Book of the Viking Society*, 9 (1914-18), 355-71.

Explains the cult of Nerthus, and hence the *vanir*, as the result of the presence of Celtic tribes in Jutland.

283. Bugge, Sophus. "Efterslæt til min udgave af Sæmundar Edda." *Årbøger for nordisk oldkyndighed og historie*, 1869, pp. 243-76.

Notes to, inter alia, *Vǫluspá, Vafþrúðnismál, Grímnismál, Hárbarðsljóð, Hymiskviða, Lokasenna.*

284. Bugge, Sophus. *Studier over de nordiske gude- og heltesagns oprindelse,* I. række. Oslo: A. Cammermeyer, 1881-89. 572 pp.

Norwegian original of Bugge's important *Studien über die Entstehung der nordischen Götter- und Heldensagen* (1889).

285. Bugge, Sophus. "Nogle bemærkninger om sibyllinerne og Völuspá." *Nordisk tidskrift för vetenskap, konst och industri*, 4 (1881), 163-72.

Comments on V. Rydberg, "Sibyllerna och Völuspå" (1881).

286. Bugge, Sophus. "Bemærkninger til norrøne digte, I: Hyndluljóð." *Arkiv för nordisk filologi*, 1 (1883), 249-65.

Textual notes and commentary.

287. Bugge, Sophus. "Bemærkninger til norrøne digte, II: Rígsþula." *Arkiv för nordisk filologi*, 1 (1883), 305-13.

Textual notes and commentary.

288. Bugge, Sophus. "Blandede sproghistoriske bidrag." *Arkiv för nordisk filologi*, 2 (1885), 207-53.

Includes remarks on *Vǫluspá*, str. 14.

289. Bugge, Sophus. "Der Gott Bragi in den norrönen Gedichten." *Beiträge zur Geschichte der deutschen Sprache und Literatur*, 13 (1888), 187-201.

Response to E. Mogk, "Bragi als Gott und Dichter" (1887). Bugge derives the god from the noun *bragr* "poetry" and disputes the dating of Bragi the poet's verse to as early as the tenth century.

290. Bugge, Sophus. "Iduns æbler: Et bidrag til de nordiske mythers historie." *Arkiv för nordisk filologi*, 5 (1889), 1-45.

A survey of Norse stories involving apples, departing from and focusing on Ið unn's apples and the apples Skírnir offers Gerðr. Bugge offers numerous parallels from Ireland and Greek mythology and concludes that the Norse conceptions are borrowings.

291. Bugge, Sophus. *Studien über die Entstehung der nordischen Götter- und Heldensagen*. Munich: C. Kaiser, 1889. 590 pp. Translated by Oscar Brenner.

It was in this translation, authorized and checked by the author, that Bugge's famous thesis of pervasive Christian influence on Norse mythology became known to the scholarly world. Halldór Hermannsson's *Bibliography of the Eddas* (1920) lists more reviews and articles concerned with this than with any other work he cites, and all nearly all serious scholars were forced to take a stand on it.

The work itself falls into two large sections, the first on Baldr's death and the second on Odin and the world tree.

292. Bugge, Sophus. *Bidrag til den ældste skjaldedigtnings historie*. Oslo: H. Aschehoug, 1894. 184 pp.

To defend his theory of the importance of Western influence on Norse culture, Bugge investigates Bragi Boddason and *Ynglingatal* and moves the date for each up to a point consistent with his theory. The section on Bragi, in particular, has much to say of Norse mythology, and it includes the argument that the shield Bragi was describing must itself have been influenced by British traditions.

293. Bugge, Sophus. "Mindre bidrag til nordisk mythologi og sagnhistorie." *Årbøger for nordisk oldkyndighed og historie*, 1895, pp. 123-38.

On the monster called Finngálkn in the Icelandic Physiologus; not directly relevant to Norse mythology, despite the title.

294. Bugge, Sophus. "Germanische Etymologien." *Beiträge zur Geschichte der deutschen Sprache und Literatur*, 21 (1896), 421-28.

Discusses, on p. 422, the etymology of the Odin name Herjann: it is parallel to Greek *koíranos* < **kóryanos*.

295. Bugge, Sophus. "En olddansk runeoptegnelse i England." *Årbøger for nordisk oldkyndighed og historie*, 1899, pp. 263-72.

The runic text in Cotton Caligula A 15 and its relations to *Þrymskviða*.

296. Bugge, Sophus. "Nordiske runeindskrifter og billeder paa mindesmærker paa øen Man." *Årbøger for nordisk oldkyndighed og historie*, 1899, pp. 229-62.

Manx runic inscriptions and rock carvings; the final pages of the article summarize Bugge's views on the development of Scandinavian myth and religion and the role of the British Isles in that development.

297. Bugge, Sophus. "Mythiske sagn om Halvdan Svarte og Harald Haarfagre." *Arkiv för nordisk filologi*, 16 (1900), 1-37.

Traces the legends connected with Halvdan the black and Harald Fairhair to a tale of Odin's visit to Geirrøðr and associated traditions (*Grímnismál*).

298. Bugge, Sophus. "Nogle steder i Eddadigtene." *Arkiv för nordisk filologi*, 19 (1902), 1-18.

Includes textual notes to *Alvíssmál*, str. 3 and 11.

299. Bugge, Sophus, and Moltke Moe. *Torsvisen i sin norske form, udgivet med en afhandling om dens oprindelse og forhold til de andre nordiske former*. Oslo: Centraltryckeriet, 1897. 124 pp.

Edition of and commentary to the Norwegian form of the ballad of Thor's reclaiming of his hammer. *Þrymskviða* is treated on pp. 82-87.

300. Buisson, Ludwig. *Der Bildstein Ardre VIII auf Gotland: Göttermythen, Heldensagen und Jenseitsglauben der Germanen im 8. Jahrhundert n. Chr.* Abhandlungen der Adademie der Wissenschaften in Göttingen, phil.-hist. Kl., 3. Folge, 102. Göttingen: Vandenhoeck & Ruprecht, 1976. 136 pp.

As this monograph's title indicates, the Gotlandic picture stone Ardre VIII, from the second half of the eighth century, contains scenes from myth, heroic legend, and belief in the other world. Buisson offers new interpretations of two of these scenes and reinterprets several others.

From the point of view of mythology, Buisson's major contribution is identification of one of the scenes with Snorri's account of the gods fishing for Loki in *Snorra edda* (*Gylfaginning* ch. 36). Loki had invented the fishing net and changed himself into a salmon; these elements are visible on the stone. After his capture Loki was bound in punishment for his role in the death of Baldr.

Buisson also reinterprets two other scenes from the mythology: Thor's battle with a many-headed giant is now the engendering of Þruðgelmir (*Vafþrúð nismál*), and the scene with an ox and large human form is not Thor obtaining bait to fish for the midgard serpent but a representation of the beginning of the Þjazi myth.

301. Bull, Edvard. "Levninger av en hedensk høitid i kristen tid." *Maal og minne*, 1913, pp. 42-43.

An allegedly pagan holiday attached to the Icelandic bishop Guðmundr the Good.

302. Bull, Edvard. "Musen som Lokes arvtager?" *Maal og minne*, 1913, pp. 46-47.

Addendum to R. Iversen's note with the same title, pointing out additional attestations.

303. Bull, Edvard. "Det hedenske kultcentrum i søndre Gudbrandsdalen." *Maal og minne*, 1917, pp. 156-62.

The topography of a hypothetical cult center at Hundorp in the lower Gudbrandsdal, Norway. The cult center is established for Bull by the story of the conversion of Dala-Guðbrandr in the sagas of St. Olaf; Bull regards this account as derived from a local legend.

304. Burson, Ann. "Swan Maidens and Smiths: A Structural Study of *Völundarkviða*." *Scandinavian Studies*, 55 (1983), 1-19.

Following Lévi-Strauss, the author argues the essential unity of the poem on the basis of its mediation of deep opposition between nature and culture, here realized as captive and captor.

305. Busch, Werner. "Deutung der 'smyl' [Grímnismál (Edda I. Text, ed. Neckel, S. 54ff.) Z. 13: Farðu nú þar er smyl hafi þik)!]." *Zeitschrift für deutsche Philologie*, 55 (1930), 337-48.

Locates three supposed parallels between the word *smyl* and Hel: both appear to have to do with death, with devouring corpses, and with travel over water. Busch concludes that *smyl* may be a name for Hel or may represent an aspect of Hel.

306. Buschan, Georg. *Altgermanische Überlieferungen in Kult und Brauchtum der Deutschen*. Munich: J. F. Lehmann, 1936. 257 pp.

Remnants of ancient Germanic culture, including pagan religion, in German folk culture.

307. Butt, Wolfgang. "Zur Herkunft der Vǫluspá." *Beiträge zur Geschichte der deutschen Sprache und Literatur*, 91 (1969), 82-103.

Basing his argument on English parallels (Wulfstan's homilies and the poem

"The Judgement Day II"), Butt assigns the origin of *Vǫluspá* to the Danelaw during the early eleventh century.

308. Buttgereit, H. "Die Schicksalsauffassung der Germanen." *Zeitschrift für deutsche Bildung*, 15 (1939), 197-206.

Germanic conceptions of fate, from a nationalistic viewpoint.

C

309. Cahen, Maurice. *Études sur le vocabulaire religieux du vieux-scandinave: La libation.* Société de linguistique de Paris, Collection linguistique, 9. Paris: É. Champion, 1921. 325 pp.

A study, based on vocabulary, of ritual activity associated with drinking. Such activity is traced from paganism through the demise of pagan ritual to survival in later behavior, in some cases as far as the Reformation.

310. Cahen, Maurice. *Le mot "dieu" en vieux-scandinave.* Société de linguistique de Paris, Collection linguistique, 10. Paris: É. Champion, 1921. 81 pp.

The historical semantics of *guð* in pagan and Christian contexts.

311. Cahen, Maurice. "L'Adjectif 'divin' en germanique." In *Mélanges offertes à M. Charles Andler pars ses amis et ses élèves.* 79-107. Publications de la faculté des lettres de l'université de Strasbourg, 21. Strasbourg: Librairie Istra, 1924.

On the development of expressions for "holy" in Germanic languages from the pagan to Christian periods.

312. Cahen, Maurice. "L'étude du paganisme scandinave au XXme. siècle." *Revue de l'histoire des religions*, 92 (1925), 33-107.

Research survey.

313. Calissendorff, Karin. "Helgö." *Namn och bygd*, 52 (1964), 105-52. Summary in English, pp. 178-79.

The author seeks the meaning of *helg-* (cf. Old Norse *heilagr* "holy") in place-names and concludes that it had the meaning "giving sacral sanctuary," as at large religious or judicial gatherings. A more general meaning is "protected for a public purpose," which usually seems to refer to commercial centers.

314. Campbell, Joseph. *The Masks of God: Occidental Mythology.* New York: Viking, 1964. x, 564 pp.

What Campbell has to say about Germanic religion and Scandinavian mythology is to be found here in the third volume of his *Masks of God.* Pp. 473-90 ("The Weird of the Gods") treat the subject briefly, relying on translations of

Tacitus and the *Eddas*. A few words on *Beowulf* are also found on pp. 111-23 of Campbell's *The Masks of God: Creative Mythology* (New York: Viking, xviii, 730 pp.).

315. Capelle, Torsten. "Zum Runenring von Pietroassa." *Frühmittelalterliche Studien*, 2 (1968), 228-32.

The author attempts to place in a sacral context the famous rune-inscribed gold ring discovered in Pietroassa. Reference is to mythology and (primarily) to archaeological evidence.

316. Capelle, Torsten. "Ringopfer." In *Vorgeschichtliche Heiligtümer und Opferplätze in Mittel- und Nordeuropa: Bericht über ein Symposium in Reinhausen bei Göttingen vom 14.-16. Oktober 1968*, ed. Herbert Jankuhn, 214-18. Abhandlungen der Akademie der Wissenschaften in Göttingen, phil.-hist. Kl., 3. Folge, 74. Göttingen: Vandenhoeck & Ruprecht, 1970.

Comments on J. Driehaus, "Urgeschichtliche Opferfunde aus dem Mittel- und Niederrhein" (1970), H. Geisslinger, "Soziale Schichtungen in den Opferdepots der Völkerwanderungszeit" (1970), and B. Stjernquist, "Germanische Quellenopfer" (1970).

317. Capelle, Torsten. *Die Wikinger*. Urban-Taschenbücher, 140. Stuttgart: W. Kohlhammer, 1971. 139 pp.

Survey of the Viking Age, with chapters on paganism and the conversion. Unusual emphasis on contemporary iconography.

318. Capelle, Torsten. *Kunst und Kunsthandwerk im bronzezeitlichen Nordeuropa*. Neumünster: K. Wachholtz, 1974. 104 pp.

Includes discussion of the rock carvings and of magic.

319. Carlsson, Lizzie. "*Helvete* som ortnamn under medeltiden." *Namn och bygd*, 21 (1933), 138-47.

Swedish placenames in *Helvete-* "Hell" are situated north of the parish, on the road to Hel according to pagan orientation.

320. Carlsson, Lizzie. "De medeltida Helvetesnamnen än en gång." *Namn och bygd*, 22 (1934), 136-40.

A placename in *Helvete-* south of the parish center; it does not, according to the author, weaken the hypothesis advanced in her "De medeltida Helvetesnamnen" (1933).

321. Carlyle, Thomas. *On Heroes, Hero-Worship and the Heroic in History: Six Lectures, Reported with Emendations and Additions.* London: J. Fraser, 1841. 393 pp. First British edition with emendations and additions. An American edition was also issued in 1841 (New York: D. Appleton, 283 pp.), and there are numerous other editions.

The first of these lectures (delivered in May of 1840) treats "The Hero as Divinity: Odin; Paganism: Scandinavian Mythology." In it, Carlyle advances his own form of euhemerism: the prehistoric man Odin—a "Hero"—brought his view of nature and time to bear on his countrymen. The essence of the mythology, Carlyle states, in keeping with the thought of his era, is recognition of the divinity of nature.

322. Carpi, Anna Maria. "La conversione dei germani al christianesimo: nota sulla *Snorra Edda.*" *Annali della Facoltà di Lettere e Filosofia della Università di Macerata,* 5/6 (1972-73), 553-65.

Remarks on the evidence of *Snorra edda* regarding the conversion to Christianity; focus on Snorri's attitudes, especially toward the *æsir.*

323. Cassidy, Vincent H. deP. "The Location of Ginnunga-gap." In *Scandinavian Studies: Essays Presented to Dr. Henry Goddard Leach on the Occasion of His Eighty-Fifth Birthday,* eds. Carl F. Bayerschmidt and Erik J. Friis, 21-26. Seattle: Published for the American-Scandinavian Foundation by the University of Washington Press, 1965.

According to the author (not a Scandinavianist), vikings and later sailors may have regarded Ginnungagap as "a glorified strait of Gibraltar far to the west through which the waters of the outer ocean flowed in and out of a mediterranean Atlantic" (p. 36).

324. Cawley, F. Stanton. "*Loki* und *TeKþR*, ein bisher unbekannter indogermanischer Gott." *Beiträge zur Geschichte der deutschen Sprache und Literatur,* 63 (1939), 457-64.

Presentation for a German audience of the central hypothesis of Cawley's "The Figure of Loki in Germanic Mythology" (1939).

325. Cawley, F. Stanton. "The Figure of Loki in Germanic Mythology." *Harvard Theological Review,* 32 (1939), 309-26.

After a useful review of previous scholarship, Cawley posits a proto-Indo-European semi-divine culture hero **TeKþR* "he who forms or creates" and proceeds to the notion of a Germanic proto-thief **Þehsturaz,* who would be identical with Lóðurr-Loki.

326. Cederschiöld, Gustaf. *Fresta duger: Jämte andra uppsatser.* Stockholm: Norstedt, 1914. 257 pp.

Includes an essay on "Kung Orre" accepting the conclusion of Magnus Olsen, "Om Kong Orre" (1912), that the expression derives from a winter demon.

327. Cederschiöld, Louise. "Ett jämtländskt sjöfynd." *Fornvännen*, 58 (1963), 44-46.

Report on a fragment of a ring found in a lake in Jämtland, Sweden, and possibly associated with sacrifice to a fertility goddess.

328. Cederschiöld, Wilhelm. "Läkeråden i Hávamál 137." *Arkiv för nordisk filologi*, 26 (1910), 294-300.

Textual note to *Hávamál*, str. 137

329. Celander, Hilding. "Lokes mytiska ursprung." *Språkvetenskapliga sällskapets i Uppsala förhandlingar 1906-09, Uppsala universitets årsskrift*, 1910, pp. 18-140.

On the mythic origin of Loki. Proceeding on the basis partly of possible etymological similarity with the verb *locka* "tempt," Celander attempts to derive Loki from some sort of chthonic being, perhaps associated with fire or spinning, and ultimately as demon of death with Odin. His accompanying Thor would be a later accretion to the tradition.

330. Celander, Hilding. "Loke-problemet: Ett genmäle och en efterskrift." *Danske studier*, 11 (1914), 65-93.

Response ("genmäle") to A. Olrik's review of the author's study (1906-09) of Loki ("Efterslæt til Loke-myterne, II," 1912); Olrik, the journal's editor, had the last word, as the "efterskrift" is his, not Celander's.

331. Celander, Hilding. "Fella blótspán: Fornnordiska orakelformler, belysta genom nynordiska folkminnen." *Göteborgs högskolas årsskrift*, 36:3 (1930), 50-62.

The evidence of recent folk traditions brought to bear on Norse oracles. The author interprets the expression *fella blótspán* as "let fall the sacrificial bowl."

332. Celander, Hilding. "Oskoreien och besläktade föreställningar i äldre och nyare nordisk tradition." *Saga och sed*, 1943, pp. 71-175.

Celander's narrower aim in this paper is to determine the extent to which other parts of Scandinavia offer parallels to the southwest Norwegian phenomenon of the *oskorei* or wild hunt. His survey, with many citations of modern and older recordings, takes him first through west Scandinavian traditions (Norway and Iceland, with discussion of older Icelandic texts on pp. 100-113), then to east Scandinavia, for which he devotes a separate section to Odin's hunt (pp. 157-64). There follows a discussion of the age of the legend and its relation to the history of religion. Although he stresses the importance of perceptual experience in the origin of the conception, in its subsequent development Celander postulates the influence of Norse mythology.

333. Celander, Hilding. "Barfotaspringningen och vårdagsjämningstiden." *Folkminnen och folktankar*, 31 (1944), 12-26, 49-74, 85-138.

The significance for magic and fertility of ritual barefoot jumping on the vernal equinox.

334. Celander, Hilding. "Fröja och frukttträden." *Arkiv för nordisk filologi*, 59 (1944), 97-110. Also in *Festskrift till Jöran Sahlgren 8/4 1944* (Lund, C. W. K. Gleerup, 1944), pp. 417-30.

Freyja and fruit trees; emphasis on folklore.

335. Celander, Hilding. *Förkristen jul enligt norröna källor*. Göteborgs universitets årsskrift 61, 3. Stockholm: Almqvist & Wiksell, 1955. 91 pp. Summary in German.

The evidence of Old Norse sources for pre-Christian yule ritual.

336. Chadwick, H. Munro. *The Cult of Othin: An Essay in the Ancient Religion of the North*. London: C. J. Clay and Sons, 1899. 82 pp.

Still useful survey of the subject, arguing the relatively great age of the cult of Odin and importance of sacrifice in it.

337. Chadwick, H. Munro. "The Ancient Teutonic Priesthood." *Folk-Lore*, 11 (1900), 268-300.

Text of an address read May 16, 1900, before the Folk-Lore Society (London). Chadwick studies priesthood among the West and North Germanic peoples and compares the systems. His own summary of the two systems is "(1) that the priest of the ancient Germans was not a person endowed with secret knowledge but a tribal official; (2) that in the North priestly duties were always combined with temporal power" (p. 286). He finds the German system a derivation of the Northern one.

338. Chadwick, H. Munro. "The Oak and the Thunder-God." *Journal of the Anthropological Institute of Great Britain and Ireland*, 30 (1900), 22-44.

Thor's association with the oak tree.

339. Chadwick, H. Munro, and Nora K. Chadwick. *The Growth of Literature*, vol. 1: *The Ancient Literatures of Europe*. Cambridge: The University Press, 1932. xx, 672 pp.

In "Poetry and Saga Relating to Deities" (pp. 241-68), the authors consider, among other matters, Scandinavian mythology in light of their typology of poetic form.

340. Chadwick, Nora K. "Norse Ghosts." *Folk-Lore*, 57 (1946), 50-65, 106-27.

Survey of ghosts and ghost tradition in Old Norse literature, with little citation of the mythology; the cult of Freyr is mentioned on pp. 125-27. The remarks in the second part of the article on death chants are suggestive.

341. Chadwick, Nora K. "Þorgerðr Hölgabrúðr and the *trolla þing*: A Note on Sources." In *The Early Cultures of North-West Europe (H. M. Chadwick Memorial Studies)*, eds. Sir Cyril Fox and Bruce Dickins, 395-417. Cambridge: University Press, 1950.

Þorgerðr is probably best known as the supernatural ally of Hákon jarl against his foes the Jómsvíkingar, although she appears elsewhere and apparently underwent a kind of literary development before the traditions of the battle at Hjǫrungavágr came to be recorded. Chadwick argues that Þorgerðr represents a supernatural strand of traditions whose worldly strand concerns Þóra, Hákon's wife, and sets her in the context of supernatural fosterage, fertility cult—particularly of Freyr—, guardian spirits such as the *dísir* and *fylgjur*, and even royal suttee.

342. Chadwick, Nora K. "Literary Tradition in the Old Norse and Celtic World." *Saga-Book of the Viking Society*, 14 (1953-57), 164-99.

Compares the Irish Mongán and Mannanán with Heimdallr in *Rígsþula.*

343. Chadwick, Nora K. "Pictish and Celtic Marriage in Early Literary Tradition." *Scottish Gaelic Studies*, 8 (1958), 56-115.

Relevant to *Rígsþula.*

344. Chadwick, Nora K. "The Russian Giant Svyatogor and the Norse Útgartha-Loki." *Folklore*, 75 (1964), 243-59.

Parallels in Russian *byliny* to the story of Thor's visit to Útgarða-Loki and, more distantly, to Thor's visit to Geirrøðr, both in Snorri and Icelandic tradition and in Saxo. "The evidence on the whole, therefore seems to suggest that the stories relating to Svyatogor are derived from a myth which was once well known and widespread over the whole of northern Russia, where it was current at least as early as the twelfth century, and perhaps much earlier. From this region it was carried to Iceland and Denmark, where it was preserved in a coherent form, owing to the fact that it was written down at an early date by two excellent scholars" (p. 259).

345. Chaney, William A. *The Cult of Kingship in Anglo-Saxon England: The Transition from Paganism to Christianity*. Manchester: Manchester University Press, 1970. x, 276 pp.

Chaney offers "an exposition of the nature and elements of . . . sacral kingship among the Anglo-Saxons" (p. 3). Chapter 1, "The Woden-Sprung King: Germanic Sacral Kingship and Divine Descent," attempts a survey relevant to Scandinavia. The author mentions several Scandinavian texts and is in general familiar with the English and German scholarship on this controversial and once popular research topic, but he does not use secondary literature in the Scandinavian languages. The other chapters treat the royal priesthood, the sacrificial king, cult objects, the conversion of England, law, and economics of the ruler-cult.

Chantepie de la Saussaye, P. D., *see* Sassaye, P. D. Chantepie de la.

346. Charpentier, Jarl. "Zu den Namen des Schweines." *Namn och bygd*, 24 (1936), 6-33.

On Indo-European words for "pig" and "boar" and their religious significance, with remarks on Freyr and Freyja (p. 15f.).

347. Chesnutt, Michael. "An Unsolved Problem in Old Norse-Icelandic Literary History." *Mediaeval Scandinavia*, 1 (1968), 122-34.

The unsolved problem is the degree of Celtic influence, which Chesnutt believes to have been ample. Among his hypotheses is the existence of a "cross-cultural" (i.e., Celtic-Norse) poem, in Orkney and perhaps other western colonies, which may have provided Snorri for his account of the everlasting fight, the Hjaðningavíg, in *Skáldskaparmál*.

348. Christensen, Aksel E. "The Jelling Monuments." *Mediaeval Scandinavia*, 8 (1975), 7-20.

Includes discussion of the "Christianization" of the pagan Jelling site, and the original nature of the stone itself—pagan or Christian?

349. Christiansen, Reidar Th. "Litt om torsdagen i nordisk folketro." In *Festskrift til H. F. Feilberg fra nordiske sprog- og folkemindeforskere på 80 års dagen den 6. august 1911.* 183-91. Svenska landsmål, 1911; Maal og minne, 1911; Danske studier, 1911. Stockholm: Norstedt, Copenhagen: Gyldendal, Oslo (Kristiania): Bymaals-laget, 1911.

Customs and beliefs associated with Thursday. The author derives the special features of the day from its association with Thor.

350. Christiansen, Reidar Th. "Finsk sagnverden og dens sammenhæng med den nordiske." *Maal og minne*, 1913, pp. 91-106.

Review of work relating Finnish tradition to Scandinavian—much of it is in the area of Scandinavian mythology, by such scholars as J. and K. Krohn, Mansikka, and Olrik. Pp. 100-03 discuss work associating the *Kalevala* with myths of Baldr and Hǫðr.

351. Christiansen, Reidar Th. "Musen som Lokes arvtager?" *Maal og minne*, 1913, pp. 47.

Comment on R. Iversen's note with the same title, substituting the household spirit for Loki.

352. Christiansen, Reidar Th. *Die finnischen und nordischen Varianten des zweiten Merseburgerspruches: Eine vergleichende Studie.* FF Communications, 18. Hamina: Suomalainen tiedeakatemiän kustantama, 1914. vi, 218 pp.

A folkloristic study of the northern cognates of the second Merseburg charm. The deities of the Merseburg charm are in most cases replaced with Christian conceptions, but in a few cases names of the old Scandinavian gods appear (pp.53-56), probably as late literary additions rather than as genuine pagan survivals.

353. Ciklamini, Marlene. "Óðinn and the Giants." *Neophilologus*, 46 (1962), 145-58.

After a careful survey of Odin's dealings with giants, from creation to Ragnarǫk, Ciklamini concludes that Odin's relationship to the giants is ambiguous: "Though he divests them ruthlessly of their power and prized possessions, he entrusts some with important functions of the universe and accepts others as members of his pantheon. Once his reign is established, Óðinn assumes a fatalistic attitude towards the deposed race. He passively accepts the inevitability of *ragnarök* and the collapse of his rule" (p. 157).

354. Ciklamini, Marlene. "The Chronological Conception in Norse Mythology." *Neophilologus*, 47 (1963), 138-51.

"Most [mythic] adventures . . . take place in a chronological void. Even when myths can be placed in groups, the groups themselves form no chronological unity" (p. 150).

355. Ciklamini, Marlene. "Journeys to the Giant-Kingdom." *Scandinavian Studies*, 40 (1968), 95-110.

On journeys to the land of the giants in *Þorsteins þáttr bœjarmagns* and Saxo's *Gesta Danorum*, book 4; not directly relevant to Norse mythology.

356. Ciklamini, Marlene. "The Problem of Starkaðr." *Scandinavian Studies*, 43 (1971), 169-88.

Focuses on Saxo's version of Starkaðr's life (*Gesta Danorum*, books 6-8) and emphasizes the elimination of myth and the supernatural.

357. Ciklamini, Marlene. "*Ynglinga saga*: Its Function and Its Appeal." *Mediaeval Scandinavia*, 8 (1975), 86-99.

"For Snorri history was rooted in the mythical past and despite momentous political and religious changes the historical era was still subject to the forces which had shaped events of prehistoric times" (p. 98). He saw a periodicity of human affairs, a vitality to life, and these he expressed in *Ynglinga saga*.

358. Ciklamini, Marlene. *Snorri Sturluson*. Twayne's World Authors Series, 493. Boston: Twayne, 1978. 188 pp.

A brief biography of Snorri Sturluson and survey of his literary works, including his *Edda*. Bibliography on pp. 179-84.

359. Classen, Walter. *Die Germanen und das Christentum*. Das Werden des deutschen Volkes, 4. Hamburg: Hanseatische Verlagsanstalt, 1920. 184 pp.

Popular history, centered on the conversion.

360. Clausen, H. V. "Studier over Danmarks oldtidsbebyggelse." *Årbøger for nordisk oldkyndighed og historie*, 1916, pp. 1-226.

Pp. 187-226 deal with theophoric placenames and settlement patterns. The cults of Njord and Ullr receive attention.

361. Clemen, Carl. "Der Ursprung des Karnevals." *Archiv für Religionswissenschaft*, 17 (1914), 139-58.

Pp. 149-54 interpret the ritual of Nerthus, as described by Tacitus in his *Germania*, as a kind of contagious magic, possibly associated with the origin of Carneval.

362. Clemen, Carl. *Fontes historiae religionis germanicae*. Fontes Historiae Religionum ex Auctoribus Graecis et Latinos Collectos, 3. Berlin: W. de Gruyter, 1928. 112 pp.

A collection of passages dealing with Germanic religion within the works of classical authors.

363. Clemen, Carl. "Südöstliche Einflüsse auf die nordische Religion." *Zeitschrift für deutsche Philologie*, 55 (1930), 148-60.

The 1920s saw several works arguing extensive influence on Norse mythology from the Near East (e.g., works by Hempel, Neckel, Reitzenstein, and Schröder). Clemen argues against such evidence. He concludes specifically that Manichaeism exerted no influence whatever and that the hypothetical Hellenistic layer had been exaggerated.

364. Clemen, Carl. "Südöstliche Einflüsse auf die nordische Religion?" In *Actes du Ve congrès international d'histoire des religions à Lund, 27-29 août 1929*. 233-36. Lund: C. W. K. Gleerup, 1930.

Lecture and discussion from an international congress on the history of religion. Fuller version published in *Zeitschrift für deutsche Philologie*.

365. Clemen, Carl. *Urgeschichtliche Religion: Die Religion der Stein-, Bronze- und Eisenzeit,* vol. 1. Untersuchungen zur allgemeinen Religionsgeschichte, 4. Bonn: L. Röhrscheid, 1932. 140 pp.

The section on the Bronze Age (pp. 106-28) focuses on the Scandinavian rock carvings, and Scandinavian religion enters into the discussion elsewhere as well.

366. Clemen, Carl. *Urgeschichtliche Religion: Die Religion der Stein-, Bronze- und Eisenzeit,* vol. 2. Untersuchungen zur allgemeinen Religionsgeschichte, 5. Bonn: L. Röhrscheid, 1933. 52 pp.

112 plates illustrating vol. 1 of the work. Many portray the Scandinavian rock carvings.

367. Clemen, Carl. "Die Bedeutung anderer Religionen für die altnordische Religionsgeschichte." *Archiv für Religionswissenschaft*, 34 (1937), 13-18.

Argues against the influence of other religions on Scandinavian religion, especially Near Eastern religions.

368. Clemen, Carl. "Die nordeuropäischen Felszeichnungen und der Glaube der Germanen." *Zeitschrift für deutsche Philologie*, 62 (1937), [347]-58.

Skeptical appraisal of the possibility of reconstructing ancient Germanic religion on the basis of the rock carvings, particularly if they are taken as indications of the borrowing of foreign conceptions. Criticism of Almgren (1934) and other interpretations of Scandinavian rock carvings. Clemen finds no firm evidence of oriental expansion of a fertility cult to the north.

369. Clemen, Carl. "Mithrasmysterien und germanische Religion." *Archiv für Religionswissenschaft*, 34 (1937), 217-25.

Denies both the influence of Germanic religion on Mithraism and of Mithraism on Germanic religion.

370. Clemen, Carl. "Altersklassen bei den Germanen." *Archiv für Religionswissenschaft*, 35 (1938), 60-65.

Discussion and criticism of L. Weiser Aall, *Altgermanische Jünglingsweihen und Männerbünde* (1927).

371. Closs, Alois. "Neue Problemstellungen in der germanischen Religionsgeschichte." *Anthropos*, 29 (1934), 477-96.

Applies comparative ethnographic evidence to Germanic religion.

372. Closs, Alois. "Das Heidentum der Altgermanen." *Die Kirche in der Zeitwende*, 1935, pp. 120-74.

The historical evolution of Germanic paganism from its Indo-European roots, with ethnological parallels.

373. Closs, Alois. "Die Religion des Semnonenstammes." *Wiener Beiträge zur Kulturgeschichte und Linguistik*, 4 (1936), 549-673.

On the religion of the Semnones, an ancient Germanic people. Closs employs a broad ethnological perspective. The final pages discuss Wodan-Odin as a Germanic reflection of Eurasian shamanism. For methodological objections, see G. Trathnigg, "Glaube und Kult der Semnonen" (1937).

374. Closs, Alois. "Das Heilige und die Frage nach einem germanischen Totemismus." In *Festschrift Walter Baetke dargebracht zu seinem 80. Geburtstage am 28. März 1964*, ed. Kurt Rudolf et al., 79-84. Weimar: H. Böhlau, 1966.

Concludes that there is no compelling evidence for the presence of totemism in early Germanic religion, although a pre-totemic animalism is possible.

375. Closs, Alois. "Der Schamanismus bei den Indoeuropäern." In *Studien zur Sprachwissenschaft und Kulturkunde: Gedenkschrift für Wilhelm Brandenstein (1898-1967)*, ed. Manfred Mayrhofer, 289-302. Innsbrucker Beiträge zur Kulturwissenschaft, 14. Innsbruck: Gesellschaft zur Pflege der Geisteswissenschaften, 1968.

Consideration of the evidence of shamanism in Indo-European. There are passing references to Germanic, and a section devoted just to Germanic is found on p. 298.

376. Clover, Carol J. "*Hárbarðsljóð* as Generic Farce." *Scandinavian Studies*, 51 (1979), 124-45.

In this primarily literary study, Clover concludes that the genre of the flyting is the "shaping abstraction" of *Hárbarðsljóð*, against which the performance of the two interlocutors was understood by a contemporary audience. This reading leaves the mythic roles of Odin and Thor relatively intact, but it stresses that the poem is more than a comic portrayal of Thor in the context of a confrontation between mythic representatives of landowners and military aristocrats.

377. Clover, Carol J. "The Germanic Context of the Unferth Episode." *Speculum*, 55 (1980), 444-68.

Useful for the context of *Lokasenna*.

Clunies Ross, Margaret, *see* Ross, Margaret Clunies.

378. Cohen, Sidney L. *Viking Fortresses of the Trelleborg Type*. Copenhagen: Rosenkilde & Bagger, 1965. 104 pp.

"Trelleborg was most probably a sanctuary for part of its life-span. I have shown that Trelleborg is comparable to temples in Russia, whose plans were affected by religious traditions. By illustrating the connection between the number pattern of four and the worship of the god Thor, I conclude that Trelleborg's plan is associated with the same traditions. The entire layout of Trelleborg. . . is probably based upon religious considerations, rather than on military discipline" (p. 73).

379. Collinder, Björn. "Eddica." *Nordisk tidsskrift for filologi*, 4. række, 10 (1921-22), 15-47.

Philological notes on various passages from the Poetic Edda, including *Hávamál* 1, 17, 22-23, 70, and 74, *Skírnismál* 40, *Hárbarðsljóð* 50, and the prose in *Lokasenna*.

380. Collinder, Björn. "Ett nytt uppslag i den fornnordiska religionen." *Nordisk tidskrift*, 2 (1926), 220-30.

Discusses thories of Hugo Pipping.

381. Collinder, Björn. "The Name *Germani*." *Arkiv för nordisk filologi*, 59 (1944), 19-39. Also in *Festskrift till Jöran Sahlgren 8/4 1944* (Lund: C. W. K. Gleerup, 1944) pp. 339-59.

In arguing that *Germani* is the plural of Latin *germanus* "genuine," Collinder postulates sacral confederations of Germanic peoples.

382. Collinder, Björn. *Den poetiska Eddan: I översättning*. [Stockholm]: Forum, 1957. 267 pp. Reissued several times.

Swedish translation of the Poetic Edda, with introduction and notes to the individual poems.

383. Collinder, Björn. *Snorres Edda: Översättning och inledning*. [Stockholm]: Forum, 1958. 192 pp.

Translation of the Prologue, *Gylfaginning*, and *Skáldskaparmál* of *Snorra edda*, with introduction (pp. 1-31), brief commentary (pp. 157-67), index to personal names (pp. 168-87), and glossary (pp. 188-92).

384. Collinder, Björn. "Till frågan om de äldsta Eddakvädenes ålder." *Arkiv för nordisk filologi*, 80 (1965), 61-63.

Brief notes questioning points raised in various works by Birger Nerman arguing that certain eddic poems antedate the Viking Age.

385. Collinder, Björn, and Hallfrid Christiansen. "Det norrøne ord *lúðr*." *Maal og minne*, 1952, pp. 101-106.

Contra A. Holtsmark, "Det norrøne ordet lúðr" (1946), Christiansen uses modern dialect evidence as well as text interpretation to argue that *lúðr* in *Vafþrúðnismál* 35 could mean "cradle" and not only "coffin."

386. Collingwood, W. G. "Thor's Stone, or Fair Maiden Hall." *Saga-Book of the Viking Society*, 2 (1897-1900), 141-43.

A rock popularly called "Thor's stone"; Collingwood shows that there is no connection with the god.

387. Collingwood, W. G. "Some Illustrations of the Archaeology of the Viking Age in England." *Saga-Book of the Viking Society*, 5 (1906-07), 111-41.

Mythic motifs treated particularly on pp. 130-39. Collingwood concludes: "Seen in their right place these Viking monuments should be a great help to the history of the time and its thought. We have the transition from paganism to Christianity displayed, and also the process of fusion by which old folklore was developed into the strange decadent mythology of the Edda. . ." (p. 141).

388. Collitz, Hermann. "Wodan, Hermes und Pushan." In *Festskrift tillägnad Hugo Pipping på hans sextioårsdag den 5 november 1924*. 574-87. Skrifter utg. av Svenska litteratursällskapet i Finland, 175. Helsinki: Mercators tryckeri, 1924.

An attempt at Indo-European comparative mythology: Odin, Hermes, and the Indic Pūshan as three bases for the reconstruction of an Indo-European god rather like the extant Hermes.

389. Conant, Jonathan B. "Runic *alu*—A New Conjecture." *Journal of English and Germanic Philology*, 72 (1973), 467-73.

Reads runic *alu* in some cases as **allu* (neuter plural) "all" and proposes that it is prophylactic, perhaps as *ǫll goð, ǫll bǫnd*, or *ǫll regin* "all the gods."

390. Cour, Vilh. La. "Hejmdals navne." *Danske studier*, 20 (1923), 61-68.

Departing from the observation that all of Heimdallr's names are grammatical compounds, La Cour analyzes them etymologically and finds a common thread in the notion of the rays of the sun.

391. Cour, Vilh. La. "Lejrestudier: Navnet." *Danske studier*, 21 (1924), 13-22.

On Lejre, Denmark, an ancient cult place. La Cour reads the name as a common noun referring to some sort of movable cult object, perhaps used as a kind of altar.

392. Cour, Vilh. La. "Solens personifikation i vor broncealder." *Danske studier*, 21 (1924), 121-34.

Argues that certain Bronze Age rock carvings portray a personified sun.

393. Cox, George W. *The Mythology of the Aryan Nations*. London: Longmans, Green, 1870. 2 vols. Vol. 1: xx, 460 pp.; vol. 2: xv, 397 pp. Rpt. Port Washington, N.Y.: Kennikat, 1969.

Indo-European mythology and legend, based largely on Greek, Sanskrit, and Norse materials. Vol. 1, book 2, chapter 1 treats Scandinavian mythology directly under the rubric "The Ethereal Heavens."

394. Craigie, W. A. "The Oldest Icelandic Folk-Lore." *Folk-Lore*, 4 (1893), 219-32.

Translations from *Landnámabók*, including passages dealing with religious beliefs, pagan sacrifice, magic, and the *landvættir*.

395. Craigie, W. A. *The Religion of Ancient Scandinavia*. London: A. Constable, 1906. xi, 72 pp. Rpt. Freeport, N.Y.: Books for Libraries Press, 1969.

Brief handbook, stressing written sources.

396. Cramer-Peeters, Elisabeth. "Frija—Isis—Nehalennia." *Amsterdamer Beiträge zur älteren Germanistik*, 3 (1972), 15-24.

Interpretation of the inscription and iconography of the Domsburg altar. The three female figures portrayed are, according to the author, Frija/Frigg, Isis, and Nehalennia.

397. Cramer-Peeters, Elisabeth. "Zur Deutung des Names der Göttin Nehalennia." *Amsterdamer Beiträge zur älteren Germanistik*, 3 (1972), 1-14.

Reads the name of the goddess Nehalennia as "beloved of fog" and associates her with Frija/Frigg. She is a goddess of fertility and death.

398. Cramp, Rosemary. "The Viking Image." In *The Vikings*, ed. R. T. Farrell, 8-19. London and Chichester: Phillimore, 1982.

On ". . . the representations of the visible Viking Man as he saw himself" (p. 8); includes passing remarks on mythic iconography (Odin and valkyries).

399. Creuzer, Georg Friedrich. *Symbolik und Mythologie der alten Völker: Fortgesetzt von Dr. Franz Josef Mone*, vol. 5-6: *Geschichte des Heidentums im nördlichen Europa*. Leipzig and Darmstadt: C. W. Leske, 1822-23. Vol. 5: xxiv, 480 pp.; vol. 6: xvi, 607 pp.; rpt. in series Volkskundliche Quellen: Neudrucke europäischer Texte und Untersuchungen, ed. Hermann Bausinger et al., 5: Sitte (Hildesheim: Olms, 1973).

Mone's continuation of Creuzer's work was an important early source of knowledge of Scandinavian and Germanic mythology. Scandinavian mythology is treated in vol. 5, the mythology of the Germans (Saxons, Franks, and Goths) in vol. 6.

400. Crossley-Holland, Kevin. *The Faber Book of Northern Legends*. London: Faber & Faber, 1977. 236 pp.

Anthology of retellings and condensations by various authors. The myths (hardly recognizable) make up about half the book.

401. Crossley-Holland, Kevin. *The Norse Myths: Introduced and Retold*. London: A. Deutsch, 1980. xlvi, 276 pp.

"I have decided . . . to retell the myths in new versions, and hope that they are both representative of the originals and full-blooded in their own right. I have omitted nothing of any consequence . . ., but I have not hesitated to develop hints, to flesh out dramatic situations, and add snatches of dialogue."

D

402. Dahlerup, Verner. "Et par af myterne i Oehlenschlägers Nordens guder." In *Festskrift til Finnur Jónsson 29. maj 1928*. 299-303. Copenhagen: Levin & Munksgaard, 1928.

Oehlenschläger rendered *breiðar steinar* (*Þrymskviða* 16, 19) as "round stones"; Dahlerup thinks this is correct and has nothing to do with giving Thor a woman's physical appearance.

403. Dalberg, Vibeke, and John Kousgård Sørensen. *Stednavneforskning*, vol. 2: *Udnyttelsesmuligheder*. Copenhagen: Akademisk forlag, 1979. 222 pp.

Chapter 6 of this survey of the uses of placenames and placename research treats the history of religion. The authors offer a useful review of the literature and of the possible references to gods and cults in Nordic placenames, and they make clear the difficulties in interpretation. This is doubtless the most up-to-date survey of theophoric placename research.

The book also includes a short section on the evidence of placenames regarding divisions according to religious activity, based on the word for "parish" and on parish names.

404. Damico, Helen. "*Sörlaþáttr* and the Hama Episode in *Beowulf*." *Scandinavian Studies*, 55 (1983), 222-35.

Loki's theft of the *Brísinga men* from Freyja (*Sǫrla þáttr*) as a mythological analog to the Hama episode in *Beowulf* (lines 1197-1201).

405. Danielli, Mary. "Initiation Ceremonial from Norse Literature." *Folk-Lore*, 56 (1945), 229-45. Readers' comments on p. 47 and p. 151.

Although it makes no direct reference to myth, the ritual pattern suggested in this paper might be applied to Thor's giant slaying, and the suggestion of such patterns in saga literature (*Víga-Glúms saga*, *Grettis saga*, *Hrólfs saga kraka*) and in *Beowulf* may be helpful in dealing with the thirteenth-century context in which Norse mythology was recorded. In the pattern, a young man leaves home, is ignored or taunted when he arrives in a new land, but is accepted into the family when he has undertaken and won a battle with a monster. He is greeted as the equal of the head of the household and is feasted; this occurs ordinarily in winter and may ultimately have to do with conceptions of the annual reinvigoration of the earth.

406. Danielli, Mary. "Initiation Ceremonial in Norse Literature." *Folk-Lore*, 57 (1946), 151.

Response to L. W. Kingsland, "Initiation Ceremonial from Norse Literature" (1946).

407. Danielli, Mary. "The State Concept of Imerina, Compared with the Theories Found in Certain Scandinavian and Chinese Texts." *Folk-Lore*, 61 (1950), 186-202.

An unusual comparison of Madagascar, China, and the "Scandinavian system" postulated by the author in her work on "Initiation Ceremonial from Norse literature" (1945).

408. Dannwolff, Hermann. *Geschichte der germanischen Mythenforschung*. 1927. Diss. Tübingen.

Research summary.

409. Davidson, H. R. Ellis. *The Road to Hel: A Study of the Conception of the Dead in Old Norse Literature*. Cambridge: University Press, 1943. viii, 208 pp.

Lengthy study, combining archaeological, literary, and comparative materials, and focusing on death, the dead, and their world in Old Norse literature.

410. Davidson, H. R. Ellis. "Gods and Heroes in Stone." In *The Early Cultures of North-West Europe (H. M. Chadwick Memorial Studies)*, eds. Sir Cyril Fox and Bruce Dickins, 121-39. Cambridge: University Press, 1950.

Useful survey of "non-Christian subject-matter" (p. 138) in the stone carvings of the British Isles.

411. Davidson, H. R. Ellis. "The Hill of the Dragon: Anglo-Saxon Burial Mounds in Literature and Archaeology." *Folk-Lore*, 61 (1950), 169-85.

Text of an address read before the Folk-Lore Society on October 19, 1949. The author draws also on Scandinavian materials and discusses Níðhǫggr and *Vǫluspá* on p. 181. The article includes a "Note on the Resemblances between Anglo-Saxon Burial Mounds and Those of the Steppe," by G. N. Naundres (pp. 184-85), and is illustrated.

412. Davidson, H. R. Ellis. "Weland the Smith." *Folklore*, 69 (1958), 145-59.

"Behind the figure of Weland the Smith it seems possible then to discern a race of supernatural beings thought of in general as giants (but related also to dwarves and elves), who are both male and female, who live in families, who are skilled at the making of weapons and at stone-building, and whose dwellings may be reached by a descent into the earth or under the water" (p. 156).

413. Davidson, H. R. Ellis. "The Sword at the Wedding." *Folklore*, 71 (1960), 1-18. Rpt. in Davidson, *Patterns of Folklore* (Ipswich: D. S. Brewer, Totowa, N. J.: Rowman & Littlefield, 1978), pp. 95-112.

The sword as a symbol "of the continuity of the family" (p. 1), with adumbration of Scandinavian myth.

414. Davidson, H. R. Ellis. "Folklore and Man's Past." *Folklore*, 74 (1963), 527-44.

Cites, *inter alia*, folklore of Odin as a guide to ancient beliefs and cult of the god.

415. Davidson, H. R. Ellis. *Gods and Myths of Northern Europe*. Baltimore: Penguin, 1964. 251 pp.

A popular handbook, stressing the archaeological evidence.

416. Davidson, H. R. Ellis. "Thor's Hammer." *Folklore*, 76 (1965), 1-15. Rpt. in her *Patterns of Folklore* (Ipswitch: D. S. Brewer; Totowa, N. J.: Rowman & Littlefield, 1978), pp. 113-27.

On the hammer as symbol: mythological thunder weapon and prophylaxis for men in artistic representations.

417. Davidson, H. R. Ellis. *Pagan Scandinavia*. Ancient Peoples and Places, 58. London: Thames & Hudson, 1967. 214 pp.

Survey of pagan Scandinavian religion using archaeological artifacts as the primary sources. The coverage spans the entire record, from rock carvings through Viking religion.

418. Davidson, H. R. Ellis. "Germanic Religion." In *Historia Religionum*, vol. 1, eds. C. Jouco Bleeker and Geo Widengren, 611-28. Leiden: E. J. Brill, 1969.

Brief survey of Germanic religion in a collective volume that imposed a common structure on all the essays. Davidson's essay is therefore best read in the context of the other essays.

419. Davidson, H. R. Ellis. "The Chariot of the Sun." *Folklore*, 80 (1969), 174-80.

On the symbol "of the turning and travelling wheel of fire" (p. 174), including the Trundholm chariot and other Nordic artifacts.

420. Davidson, H. R. Ellis. *Scandinavian Mythology*. London: Hamlyn, 1969. 141 pp.

What distinguish this volume from other handbooks, including Davidson's *Gods and Myths of Northern Europe* (1964) are the numerous illustrations, many of them in color. They take precedence over the relatively brief text and help to give an impression of the nature and form (and beauty) of the archaeological artifacts used in the study of Scandinavian mythology.

421. Davidson, H. R. Ellis. "The Smith and the Goddess: Two Figures on the Franks Casket from Auzon." *Frühmittelalterliche Studien*, 3 (1969), 216-26.

A discussion of the smith and the goddess as dominant figures in the scenes on the Franks or Auzon casket representing themes of Germanic myth. "I believe that the main inspiration behind this particular tradition of pictorial art in pre-Christian times was the cult of the god of death and battle, the Anglo-Saxon Woden and the Scandinavian Odin, and that both smith and goddess are closely linked with this" (p. 216). The story of the smith Wayland, who violates a princess for vengeance, may be associated with myths of Odin's wanderings, especially the acquisition of the poetic mead (*Hávamál*) and the wooing of Rindr (Saxo). The goddesses on the casket may be understood as valkyries. A figure on the casket of a warrior with helmet and mail may represent an Odin worshipper.

422. Davidson, H. R. Ellis. *The Battle God of the Vikings: The First G. N. Garmonsway Memorial Lecture Delivered 29 October 1971 in the University of York.* University of York Medieval Monograph Series, 1. York: University of York, Centre for Medieval Studies, 1972. [ii,] 33 pp.

Archaeologically oriented lecture, illustrated, on the cult of Odin as god of battle.

423. Davidson, H. R. Ellis. "Scandinavian Cosmology." In *Ancient Cosmologies*, eds. Carmen Blacker and Michael Loewe, 172-97. London: Allen & Unwin, 1975.

The first half of the essay focuses on the World Tree. The remainder treats mythological beings, creation, and destruction.

This essay is also reportedly available in German, in *Die Kosmologien der alten Kulturvölker* (Düsseldorf: Diederichs, 1975).

424. Davidson, H. R. Ellis. *Wit and Eloquence in the Courts of Saxo's Early Kings.* Ed. Karsten Friis-Jensen. Copenhagen: Museum Tusculanum Press, 1981.

The title refers to verbal, versified exchanges which the author believes were popular in medieval Scandinavia, particularly Norway. "The number of Edda poems and legendary sagas which show the gods themselves, as well as lesser supernatural figures such as giants and dwarfs and troll-women, taking part in such contests suggests that this type of game, rather than more elaborate mythological dramas, such as Bertha Phillpotts claimed, lay behind the dialog poems of the Poetic Edda" (p. 43). Saxo will have dignified these exchanges in placing them in Danish courtly settings.

425. Davidson, H. R. Ellis. "Insults and Riddles in the *Edda* Poems." In *Edda: A Collection of Essays*, eds. Robert J. Glendenning and Haraldur Bessason, 25-46. The University of Manitoba Icelandic Studies, 4. N. p.: University of Manitoba Press, 1983.

A survey of exchanges of insults and of riddles in the Poetic Edda, seen against similar episodes in the *Gesta Danorum* of Saxo Grammaticus and in more modern customs and lore, e.g., mumming and Irish wakes. "There may have been certain forms of intellectual activity which flourished particularly in Norway and Denmark, and which are in keeping with the activities of gods and heroes as represented in the *Edda*. . . . it must be recognized that there is much in the *Edda* in keeping with traditions which are found in Saxo against a secular background, and which were evidently familiar in his own time" (p. 44).

426. Davidson, H. R. Ellis, and Peter Fischer. *Saxo Grammaticus, the History of the Danes: Books I-IX.* Vol. 1: *English text*, transl. Peter Fischer, 229 pp. Vol. 2: *Commentary*, xiv, 209 pp. Towota, N.J.: Rowman & Littlefield, Cambridge: D. S. Brewer, 1979-80.

Vol. 1 contains an English translation of the first nine books of Saxo's *Gesta Danorum*; these contain the mythic and heroic material for which Saxo is such an important source. Although there are occasional textual remarks in vol. 1, most of Davidson's commentary is in vol. 2. This detailed running commentary is preceded by remarks on Saxo's life and work and followed by a useful bibliography and indices. This important work is a welcome addition to the study of Scandinavian mythology, even for those who can cope with Saxo's baroque Latin.

427. Delbono, Francesco. "La letteratura catechetica di lingua tedesca (Il problema della lingua nell'evangelizzazione)." In *La conversione al cristianesimo nell'Europa dell'alto medioevo: 14-19 aprile 1966.* 697-741. Settimane di studio del centro italiano di studi sull'alto medioevo. Spoleto: Presso la sede del centro, 1967.

A contribution to the international symposium on the conversion of various European peoples to Christianity; discussion of religious literature in Germany in light of the question of continuity from paganism to Christianity.

428. Denecke, Ludwig. *Ritterdichter und Heidengötter (1150-1220).* Form und Geist, Arbeiten zur germanischen Philologie, 13. Leipzig: H. Eichblatt, 1930. xvi, 190 pp.

The reception of pagan gods in medieval German literature; little direct reference to Norse mythology.

429. Derolez, R. L. M. *De godsdienst der Germanen.* Roermond en Maaseik: J. J. Romen, 1959. Available in French as *Les dieux et la religion des Germains* (Paris: Payot, 1962, 268 pp.) and in German as *Götter und Mythen der Germanen* (Einsiedeln: Benziger, 1963, 334 pp.).

A popular handbook emphasizing the personae of the gods and the myths in which they figure. As the author is a prominent runologist, special attention is devoted to runic inscriptions.

430. Derolez, R. L. M. "Les germains." In *Les celtes et les germains*. 61-137. Religions du monde. Paris: Bloud & Gay, 1965.

Popular survey of Scandinavian religion, from the Bronze Age up to the end of paganism, with emphasis on the gods of the mythology. The other essay in the volume, by André Varagnac, treats the religion of the Celts.

431. Detter, Ferdinand. "Nahanarvali." *Zeitschrift für deutsches Altertum*, 31 (1887), 207-08.

Includes etymological interpretation of Naglfar: "ship of the dead."

432. Detter, Ferdinand. "Der Finnenkönig Gusi." *Zeitschrift für deutsches Altertum*, 32 (1888), 449-54.

Associates Gúsi in *Ketils saga hængs* with Ullr and ultimately with myths of attempted usurping of Odin's power.

433. Detter, Ferdinand. "Der Mythus von Hölgi, Þorgerðr und Irpa." *Zeitschrift für deutsches Altertum*, 32 (1888), 394-402.

Associates the complex with the cult of Jumali/Jómali.

434. Detter, Ferdinand. "Der Baldermythus." *Beiträge zur Geschichte der deutschen Sprache und Literatur*, 19 (1894), 495-516.

After a summary of the relevant sources, including *Beowulf* and Saxo, *Gesta Danorum*, Detter attempts a reconstruction of the original Baldr myth. He finds that Odin was the original slayer of Baldr (who he thinks may be equivalent to Freyr), and that by killing Baldr, Odin played the devil and assumed the guilt of all the *æsir*. All the motifs of the myth find parallels in Scandinavian heroic legend and indeed in biblical tradition as well.

435. Detter, Ferdinand. "Der Siegfriedmythus." *Beiträge zur Geschichte der deutschen Sprache und Literatur*, 18 (1894), 194-202.

Includes discussion of the myth of Njord and Skaði as the possible background to heroic legend.

436. Detter, Ferdinand. "Hárr." *Beiträge zur Geschichte der deutschen Sprache und Literatur*, 18 (1894), 202-03.

The etymology of the Odin name *Hárr*: "one-eyed."

437. Detter, Ferdinand. "Zur Ynglingasaga." *Beiträge zur Geschichte der deutschen Sprache und Literatur*, 18 (1894), 72-105.

Critical discussion of *Ynglinga saga* and its sources and analogs. Three of the article's five sections are directly relevant to Norse mythology in their discussion of mythic patterns: 1) Njord, Skaði, and the Nibelungen (pp. 72-82); 2) the Baldr myth and King Hygelac (*Beowulf*) (pp. 82-88); 3) Freyr, Beli, and Fjǫlnir (pp. 88-90). Detter's basic principle is to explain myths as inventions intended to clarify poetic expressions.

438. Detter, Ferdinand. "Mûspilli." *Beiträge zur Geschichte der deutschen Sprache und Literatur*, 21 (1896), 107-10.

The etymology of Old High German *muspilli* (and Old Norse *Muspell*): < Old Saxon **mûð-spilli* "oral declaration," i.e., prophecy, with the sense of the end of the world.

439. Detter, Ferdinand. "Erwiderung." *Arkiv för nordisk filologi*, 13 (1897), 207-08.

The reviewer's reaction to an author's reprise, i.e., Eiríkr Magnússon, "Yggdrasill" (1897).

440. Detter, Ferdinand. *Die Völuspa herausgegeben und erklärt*. Sitzungsberichte der kaiserlichen Akademie der Wissenschaften, phil.-hist. Kl., 140:5. Vienna: C. Gerold's Sohn, 1899. 56 pp.

Edition of and commentary to *Vǫluspá*.

441. Detter, Ferdinand, and R. Heinzel. "Hœnir und der Vanenkrieg." *Beiträge zur Geschichte der deutschen Sprache und Literatur*, 18 (1894), 542-60.

A reflection of the war between the *æsir* and the *vanir* in Saxo, *Gesta Danorum*, book 6, in the adventures of King Fridlevus. Saxo's Hiarne must be equivalent to Hœnir, whose name, according to Detter and Heinzel, means "the singer" and probably ultimately denotes Odin. The mythic core of the *æsir-vanir* war, they believe, is an opposition between the agricultural and shipfaring *vanir* and the aristocratic *æsir*, realized as an opposition between Freyr and Odin.

442. Dibelius, Otto. *Die Germanisierung des Christentums: Eine Tragödie. His* Christus und die Deutschen, 1. Berlin: Kranz-Verlag, 1934. 61 pp.

The "Germanicization" of Christianity among the Goths. As the last words of the title indicate, the essay is programmatic.

443. Dickins, Bruce. "English Names and Old English Heathenism." *Essays and Studies by Members of the English Association*, 19 (1933), 148-60.

Theophoric placenames in England.

444. Dickins, Bruce. "Þrymskviða 81-83." *Leeds Studies in English and Kindred Languages*, 4 (1935), 79-80.

On the line *vit scolom aca tvau* in *Þrymskviða*, str. 20. Dickins favors retention of the neuter plural *tvau*, which he believes that Loki uses "to accentuate Thor's humiliation" (p. 80).

445. Dieck, Alfred. "Selbsttötung bei den Germanen." *Archiv für Religionswissenschaft*, 36 (1939), 391-96.

Attempts to remove Germanic suicide from the realm of cult.

446. Dietrich, Franz. "Zu Havamal." *Zeitschrift für deutsches Altertum*, 3 (1843), 385-432.

Early study of *Hávamál*, taking the form of a commentary. Dietrich recognizes the following divisions: rules of hospitality and travel; friendship; the good things of life; time; untrustworthy matters; love; the seduction of Gunnlǫð; the *Loddfáfnismál* (an interpolation).

447. Dietrich, Franz. "Alter der Völuspâ." *Zeitschrift für deutsches Altertum*, 7 (1849), 304-18.

Dates *Vǫluspá* to the eighth century.

448. Dietrich, Franz. "Drei altheidnische Segensformeln: Nebst einigen jüngeren, auf Runendenkmälern und in Hss. aufgefundenen." *Zeitschrift für deutsches Altertum*, 13 (1867), 193-217.

The first charm discussed is the runic invocation to Thor in Cotton Caligula A 15, fol., 122.

449. Dillmann, François-Xavier. *Culture et civilisation vikings: Une bibliographie de langue française*. Publications du centre de recherches sur les pays du nord et du nord-ouest de l'université de Caen. Caen: Centre de recherches sur les pays du Nord et du Nord-Ouest de l'Université de Caen, 1975. 48 pp.

Bibliography of works in French on Viking civilization; pp. 32-33 cover the Christian mission and early Christianity.

450. Döhrung, A. "Kastors und Balders Tod." *Archiv für Religionswissenschaft*, 5 (1902), 38-63, 97-104.

Draws a series of parallels between the deaths of Castor and Baldr (especially as told by Saxo) and concludes that the underlying mythic core is a myth of the sunset.

451. Döhrung, A. *Etymologische Beiträge zur griechischen und deutschen Mythologie.* Programm des königlichen Friedrichs-Kollegiums, 6. Königsberg: Hartung, 1907. 30 pp.

Etymological notes on solar mythology in Greek and German (Scandinavian) tradition. Focus is more on Greek than Germanic.

452. Dölvers, Horst. "Text, Gliederung und Deutung der Vǫluspá." *Zeitschrift für deutsches Altertum*, 98 (1969), 241-64.

"Stylistically separated sections may be observed in *Vǫluspá*, the analysis of which reveals a hitherto overlooked contrastive division within the poem" (p. 241). The poem has, according to Dölvers, an "open" form of composition, in which the parts are connected somewhat randomly, as if in memory—established by the ficticious narrative situation. Dölvers analyzes five gross constituent elements: magic wisdom, creation and order, the *dvergjatal*, the arrival of the three (str. 17), and Gullveig.

453. Doht, Renate. *Der Rauschtrank im germanischen Mythos.* Wiener Arbeiten zur germanischen Altertumskunde und Philologie, 3. Vienna: K. M. Halosar, 1974. xi, 379 pp.

This monograph subjects to detailed source criticism the various Germanic narratives about and references to intoxicating drink in its mythic context (primarily Scandinavian). Doht's approach is Dumézilian insofar as the monograph attempts to relate intoxicating drink to all three of the major functions (sovereignty, force, fertility) and thereby indicate the fundamental nature of the subject.

454. Dolfini, Georgio. *Snorri Sturluson: Edda.* Biblioteca Adelphi, 61. Milan: Adelphi Edizione, 1975. 184 pp.

A translation into Italian of *Gylfaginning* and *Skáldskaparmál*, with introduction (pp. 9-44).

455. Domaszewski, Alfred von. "Die Iuppitersäule in Mainz." *Archiv für Religionswissenschaft*, 9 (1906), 303-11.

Report on the find of the "Jupiter column" in Mainz, putting it into a Gallo-Roman religious context.

456. Dorph, Christian. *Grundriss der nordischen Mythologie: Zum Gebrauch beim Studium der germanischen Götterlehre.* Neuwied: Heuser, 1882. 59 pp. Translated by Eugen Liebich.

German translation of Dorph's Danish sketch of the mythology.

457. Dorph, Christian. *Omrids af den nordiske mythologi: Til skolebrug*, 9th ed. Copenhagen: E. L. Thaarup, 1883. 40 pp.

Brief sketch of the mythology, for use in Danish schools.

458. Driehaus, Jürgen. "Urgeschichtliche Opferfunde aus dem Mittel- und Niederrhein." In *Vorgeschichtliche Heiligtümer und Opferplätze in Mittel- und Nordeuropa: Bericht über ein Symposium in Reinhausen bei Göttingen vom 14.-16. Oktober 1968*, ed. Herbert Jankuhn, 40-54. Abhandlungen der Akademie der Wissenschaften in Göttingen, phil.-hist. Kl., 3. Folge, 74. Göttingen: Vandenhoeck & Ruprecht, 1970.

The archaeology of prehistoric cult in the Rhineland. For discussion see T. Capelle, "Ringopfer" (1970).

459. Drobin, Ulf. "Myth and Epical Motifs in the Loki-Research." *Temenos*, 3 (1968), 19-39.

About half this article is a useful methodological discussion of the problem of myth and scholarly treatments of Loki. The rest analyzes Loki's epic role: "In a series of incidents Loki causes something that he is compelled to restore, the consequences of which *could* be important mythical events. . . . Loki is the originator of fateful events, of the chaos-monsters as well as of the most useful treasures of the gods" (p. 37). He is one of those figures who "make possible the chains of intrigues, which are necessary to express the religious ideas and concepts in an epical form" (p. 37).

460. Dronke, Ursula. "Art and Tradition in *Skírnismál*." In *English and Medieval Studies Presented to J. R. R. Tolkien on the Occasion of his Seventieth Birthday*, eds. Norman Davis and C. L. Wrenn, 250-68. London: Allen & Unwin, 1962.

An appreciative essay on *Skírnismál*, stressing the unity of the poem and the artistry of the poet. Dronke finds that ". . . there once existed a coherent pattern of ideas, rooted in universal and ancient belief, from which a poem such as *Skírnismál* might have sprung" (pp. 259-60). This pattern involved elements of sun and fertility, of the *hieros gamos*.

461. Dronke, Ursula. "Beowulf and Ragnarǫk." *Saga-Book of the Viking Society*, 17 (1968), 302-325.

Dronke's aim in this extremely perceptive article is to explore the possibility that the *Beowulf* poet euhemerized versions of ancient Germanic myth similar to the myths recorded in Scandinavia. In so doing she revives an interpretation put forth by Tolkien in his famous essay "*Beowulf*: the Monsters and the Critics" (1936), that the gods who fell at Ragnarǫk parallel the hero Beowulf, who dies defending his kingdom from a dragon. Dronke argues for the age and essential unity of the Ragnarǫk conception within Norse and lucidly demonstrates its role in the mythology (pp. 307-13); these pages, anchored both in philological scholarship and in recent theories of myth, have independent value. She rejects Hermann Schneider's finding in his paper "Muspilli" (1936) that there is nothing in the German poem *Muspilli* but the name and concludes that Germanic traditions other than Norse may have told of a god and his enemy who killed each other at the end of the world. Beowulf, then, can have been a euhemerization of this god.

Two other mythic moments seem to be present in *Beowulf*: the Baldr story (in the Herebeald-Hæðcyn episode), which relates to eschatology, and the *Brísinga men*, which perhaps belonged to the context of an ancient mythic battle between a good and an evil god (Heimdallr and Loki). Taken together, these three parallels support the possibility that the *Beowulf* poet knew myths—or a mythology—not significantly different from those recorded in Scandinavia and that he drew upon them in fashioning his epic.

462. Dronke, Ursula. "*Völuspá* and Satiric Tradition." *Annali: Sezione germanica: Studi nederlandesi, studi nordici*, 22 (1979), 57-86.

Reconstruction of the lost source of *Vǫluspá* 25-26, a "lay of Svaðilfari," the master-builder's horse. Dronke also proposes this as the source of Snorri's remarks on the master-builder, against J. Harris, "The Master-Builder Story in Snorri's *Edda* and Two Sagas" (1976), who argued that Snorri had adapted an international folktale and some Icelandic redactions of it in his interpretation of the appropriate stanzas in *Vǫluspá.*

463. Dronke, Ursula. "Sem jarlar forðum: The Influence of Rígsþula on Two Saga-Episodes." In *Speculum Norroenum: Norse Studies in Memory of Gabriel Turville-Petre*, eds. Ursula Dronke, Guðrún P. Helgadóttir, Gerd Wolfgang Weber, and Hans Bekker-Nielsen, 56-72. N.p.: Odense University Press, 1981.

The two episodes are *Víga-Glúms saga*, ch. 26, and parallel incidents in *Bjarnar saga Hítdœlakappa*, ch. 21, and *Eyrbyggja saga*, ch. 40. In the first a verse of Glúmr makes apparent allusion to *Rígsþula*'s Jarl, who won lands by force, and the verse thus points up Glúmr's aristocratic leanings, against the general Odinic background of Glúmr's character. In the second episodes a hero recognizes an illegitimate son in a verse which echoes both Rígr's emergence from the bush to acknowledge his son Jarl and the snake's eyes of Jarl.

464. Dronke, Ursula, and Peter Dronke. "The Prologue of the Prose *Edda*: Explorations of a Latin Background." In *Sjötíu ritgerðir helgaðar Jakobi Benediktssyni*, vol. 1, eds. Einar G. Pétursson and Jónas Kristjánsson, 153-76. Stofnun Árna Magnússonar á Íslandi, rit 12. Reykjavik: Stofnun Árna Magnússonar á Íslandi, 1977.

Asks "Why should such a master of the art of realistic historical narrative as Snorri value so highly, and return so often to, the fictions about the heathen gods?" Suggests that "Snorri was convinced that the heathen traditions had a positive intellectual value for a Christian Norseman, and that he could have found confirmation for his conviction in certain Christian writings." These writings are primarily the twelfth-century Latin humanists, such as William of Conches, Thierry of Chartres, Hugh of Saint-Victor, or Alan of Lille, whom Snorri may have read or heard discussed by "scholars who had studied in France or through teachers who had undergone this platonizing influence." The argument centers on the role of the "argument by design" and attitude toward earthly wisdom displayed in the Prologue to Snorri's *Edda*.

465. Düwel, Klaus. "Germanische Opfer und Opferriten im Spiegel altgermanischer Kultworte." In *Vorgeschichtliche Heiligtümer und Opferplätze in Mittel- und Nordeuropa: Bericht über ein Symposium in Reinhausen bei Göttingen vom 14.-16. Oktober 1968*, ed. Herbert Jankuhn, 219-39. Abhandlungen der Akademie der Wissenschaften in Göttingen, phil.-hist. Kl., 3. Folge, 74. Göttingen: Vandenhoeck & Ruprecht, 1970.

The vocabulary of sacrifice in Germanic languages.

466. Düwel, Klaus, Günter Müller, and Karl Hauck. "Zur Ikonologie der Goldbrakteaten, IX: Die philologische und ikonographische Auswertung von fünf Inschriftenprägungen." *Frühmittelalterliche Studien*, 9 (1975), 143-85.

Actually a group of shorter essays joining philological and iconographic analysis of five bracteates. Müller's contribution, "Individualname oder Sakralname?" (pp. 159-65), raises the possibility that names on the bracteates refer to Odin or Baldr, or aspects relating to them, and Hauck then evaluates the implications of such a possibility in light of the iconography.

467. Dumézil, Georges. *Le festin d'immortalité, étude de mythologie comparée indo-européenne.* Annales du musée Guimet, bibliothèque d'études, 34. Paris: Geuthner, 1924. xix, 318 pp.

Includes discussion of the Norse mead of poetry.

468. Dumézil, Georges. *Mythes et dieux des germains: Essai d'interprétation comparative.* Mythes et religions, 1. Paris: PUF, 1939. xvi, 157 pp.

Dumézil's first programmatic analysis of an Indo-European mythology into the tripartite division of functions of sovereignty, force, and fertility. Revised version published 1959 as *Les dieux des germains.*

469. Dumézil, Georges. *Mitra-Varuna: Essai sur deux réprésentations indo-européennes de la souveraineté.* Bibliothèque de l'école des hautes études, sciences réligieuses, 46. Paris: PUF, 1940. xii, 150 pp.

Dumézil develops the division of the first function (sovereignty) into magico-religious and legal-contractual elements. Extensive discussion of Odin and Týr.

470. Dumézil, Georges. *Jupiter, Mars, Quirinus: Essai sur la conception indo-européenne de la société et sur les origines de Rome.* Collection la montagne Sainte-Geneviève, 1. Paris: Gallimard, 1941. 264 pp.

With remarks on the war between the *æsir* and *vanir.*

471. Dumézil, Georges. *Tarpeia: Essais de philologie comparative indo-européenne. His* Les mythes romains, 3. Paris: Gallimard, 1947. 294 pp.

With remarks on the treasures of the gods and on the war between the *æsir* and *vanir.*

472. Dumézil, Georges. *Loki.* Les dieux et les hommes, 1. Paris: G. -P. Maisonneuve, 1948. 203 pp.

A monograph on Loki, noteworthy for its rebuttal of Eugen Mogk's aspersions on Snorri's credibility. A major focus of the book is comparison of Loki with traditions about Syrdon, a trickster figure of Ossetic lore. Dumézil does not argue common derivation from Indo-European tradition; rather he discusses the probable similarities of situation which might cause similarity of attributes of the two figures.

Revised German translation in 1959.

473. Dumézil, Georges. "Deux petits dieux scandinaves: Byggvir et Beyla." *La nouvelle clio*, 3 (1952), 1-31.

A primarily philological study of the minor figures Byggvir and Beyla, Freyr's servants in *Lokasenna.* They are the barley and the bee, each of whom is instrumental in furnishing man with intoxicating drink. English translation in Dumézil, *Gods of the Ancient Northmen* (1973), pp. 90-117.

474. Dumézil, Georges. "La 'gestatio' de Frotho III et le folclore du Frodebjerg." *Études germaniques*, 7 (1952), 156-60.

A folklore parallel to the death and funeral of Frotho III in Saxo's *Gesta Danorum.*

475. Dumézil, Georges. *La saga de Hadingus (Saxo Grammaticus I, V-VIII), du mythe au roman.* Bibliothèque de l'école des hautes études, sciences religieuses, 66. Paris: PUF, 1953. 174 pp.

First version of Dumézil's study of the displacement of myth in Saxo's account of Hadingus. Revised version published in 1970.

476. Dumézil, Georges. "Njörðr, Nerthus et le folclore scandinave des génies de la mer." *Revue de l'histoire des religions*, 147 (1955), 210-26.

Folklore parallels to Nerthus/Njord.

477. Dumézil, Georges. *Aspects de la fonction guerrière chez les indo-européens.* Bibliothèque de l'école des hautes études, sciences religieuses, 68. Paris: PUF, 1956. 111 pp.

The first version of Dumézil's comprehensive study of the second (warrior) function. Includes discussion of the hero Starkaðr. Revised version issued in 1969.

478. Dumézil, Georges. "L'étude comparée des religions des peuples indo-européens." *Beiträge zur Geschichte der deutschen Sprache und Literatur* (Tübingen), 78 (1956), 173-80.

A response to Karl Helm, "Mythologie auf alten und neuen Wegen" (1955).

479. Dumézil, Georges. "La Rígsþula et la structure sociale indo-européenne." *Revue de l'histoire des religions*, 154 (1958), 1-9.

Reads *Rígsþula* as a mythic account of the origin of the three socio-mythic functions: Karl is the third function, Jarl the second function, and *kon ungr* the first. The thralls fall, like the Indic untouchables, beneath the system.

480. Dumézil, Georges. *Les dieux des germains: essai sur la formation de la religion scandinave.* Mythes et religions, 38. Paris: PUF, 1959. 128 pp.

A revised version of his *Mythes et dieux des germains* (1939), this is Dumézil's fullest treatment of Norse mythology as a whole. The first chapter treats the war of the *æsir* and *vanir* and their subsequent truce as a mythic integration of the functions of sovereignty and force with fertility. The second chapter treats the division of the first function (sovereignty) into magico-religious and legal-contractual aspects; the roles are filled by Odin and Týr. The third chapter analyzes the role of Baldr's death in Norse eschatology, and the fourth chapter compares Thor's aspects of fertility with those of the *vanir* Njord, Freyr, and Freyja. In each chapter but the fourth an Indic parallel is of importance in arguing Indo-European origins for Norse mythic conceptions.

It is probably significant that Dumézil dropped the word "myth" from the title of this revision of a study twenty years old. At least in the Norse area Dumézil's modus operandi ordinarily involves a focus on specific deities and their individual roles rather than on entire myths.

This volume is available in English, with selected additional writings of Dumézil, in his *Gods of the Ancient Northmen* (1973).

481. Dumézil, Georges. *Loki.* Darmstadt: Wissenschaftliche Buchgesellschaft, 1959. Translated by Inge Köck.

A revised German translation of Dumézil's monograph on Loki, with a preface by Otto Höfler.

482. Dumézil, Georges. "Notes sur le bestiaire cosmique de l'Edda et du Rg Veda." In *Mélanges de linguistique et de philologie, Fernand Mossé, In Memoriam.* 104-12. Paris: Librairie Marcel Didier, 1959.

Vedic parallels to Yggdrasill, Læráðr, Hvergelmir, Níðhǫggr, and similar conceptions. English translation in Dumézil, *Gods of the Ancient Northmen* (1973), pp. 141-50.

483. Dumézil, Georges. "Remarques comparatives sur le dieu scandinave Heimdallr." *Études celtiques*, 8 (1959), 263-83.

A parallel in Celtic folklore to the nine mothers of Heimdallr, indicating that they are waves of the sea. English translation in Dumézil, *Gods of the Ancient Northmen* (1973), pp. 126-40.

484. Dumézil, Georges. "Høtherus et Balderus." *Beiträge zur Geschichte der deutschen Sprache und Literatur* (Tübingen), 83 (1961), 259-70.

Remarks on Saxo's version of the Baldr story.

485. Dumézil, Georges. *De nordiska gudarna: En undersökning av den skandinaviska religionen.* Aldusbok, 50. Stockholm: Aldus/Bonniers, 1962. 122 pp. Translated by Åke Ohlmarks.

Swedish translation of *Les Dieux des Germains* (1959), with a preface by Geo Widengren.

486. Dumézil, Georges. "Le dieu scandinave Víðarr." *Revue de l'histoire des religions*, 168 (1965), 1-13.

Comparative remarks on Víðarr.

487. Dumézil, Georges. *Heur et malheur du guerrier: Aspects mythiques de la fonction guèrriere chez les indo-européens.* Paris: PUF, 1969. 148 pp.

Revised version of Dumézil's study of the warrior function among the Indo-Europeans (1956). Includes detailed discussion of books 6-8 of Saxo's *Gesta Danorum*, treating Starcatherus (Starkaðr). According to the analysis, this hero's three evil deeds follow Dumézil's tripartite structure: he kills a monarch (first function), flees in battle (second function), and kills a defenseless king in the bath (third function (?)). English translation in Dumézil, *The Destiny of the Warrior* (1970).

488. Dumézil, Georges. *Du mythe au roman: La saga de Hadingus (Saxo Grammaticus, I, V-VIII) et autres essais.* Paris: PUF, 1970. 208 pp.

Revised version of Dumézil's study of Hadingus (1953). Dumézil argues that Hadingus, a figure in book 1 of Saxo's *Gesta Danorum*, represents a transposition of the god Njord: he marries twice and is associated with the sea. In his lifetime he passes through the three functions, ending as an Odin hero. Here according to Dumézil we may perceive another parallel with Njord, who progressed from the *vanir* to the *æsir*.

489. Dumézil, Georges. *The Destiny of the Warrior.* Chicago and London: University of Chicago Press, 1970. xv, 168 pp. Translated by Alf Hiltebeitel.

English translation of *Heur et malheur du guerrier* (1969).

490. Dumézil, Georges. *Mythe et épopée,* vol. 2: *Types épiques indo-Européens: Un héros, un sorcier, un roi.* [Paris]: Gallimard, 1971.

Includes remarks on Starkaðr.

491. Dumézil, Georges. *From Myth to Fiction: The Myth of Hadingus.* Chicago: University of Chicago Press, 1973. Translated by Derek Coltman.

English translation of Dumézil's study of Hadingus (1970).

492. Dumézil, Georges. *Gods of the Ancient Northmen.* Publications of the UCLA Center for the Study of Comparative Folklore and Mythology, 3. Berkeley and Los Angeles: University of California Press, 1973. xlvi, 157 pp.

This volume contains English translations of Dumézil's *Dieux des germains* (1959) and four articles: "Two Minor Scandinavian Gods: Byggvir and Beyla" (1952), pp. 89-117; "The *Rígsþula* and Indo-European Social Structure" (1958), pp.118-25; "Comparative Remarks on the Scandinavian God Heimdallr" (1959), pp.126-40; "Notes on the Cosmic Bestiary of the *Edda* and the *Rig Veda*" (1959), pp. 141-50. A two-part Introduction by C. Scott Littleton (pp. ix-xviii) and Udo Strutynski (pp. xix-xliii) discusses the scholarly context of Dumézil's work.

493. Dumézil, Georges. "'Le Borgne' and 'le Manchot': The State of the Problem." In *Myth in Indo-European Antiquity,* eds. Gerald James Larson, C. Scott Littleton, and Jaan Puhvel, 17-28. Berkeley and Los Angeles: University of California Press, 1974.

The comparative Indo-European context of Odin and Týr.

494. Durmayer, Johan. *Reste altgermanischen Heidentums in unseren Tagen.* Nürnberg: F. Korn, 1883. 68 pp.

Survivals of Norse mythology in nineteenth-century German lore.

495. Dyroff, Adolf. "Zur griechischen und germanischen Kosmogonie." *Archiv für Religionswissenschaft,* 31 (1934), 105-23.

By comparing *Vǫluspá* with similar cosmogonic passages in ancient Greek tradition, Dyroff tries to show that the conceptions of *Vǫluspá* are pre-Christian.

496. Dyroff, Karl. "Eine Frage zu Völuspá 5, 1-4 (*Sól varp sunnan* usw.)." *Zeitschrift für deutsche Philologie,* 40 (1908), 430-32.

Textual note to *Vǫluspá,* str. 5. Dyroff understands *himins iodyr* as the zodiac.

E

497. Ebbinghaus, Ernst A. "Gothic *aibr.*" *Journal of English and Germanic Philology*, 62 (1963), 718-21.

Against A. C. Bouman, "Een dreital etymologieen: *aibr, eolete, garsecg*" (1951), who had interpreted the Gothic term in light of alleged Germanic phallic cult, as suggested by *Vǫlsa þáttr.* In a footnote Ebbinghaus has this to say: "Both Germanic and Indo-European are linguistic terms and should not be used otherwise. The 'IE religion' of which some contemporary scholars seem to know so much was invented in the earlier part of the nineteenth century A.D. Neither daring etymologies, nor the rehashing of Adalbert Kuhn's comparison of myths can make it any older" (p. 719, fn. 11).

498. Ebel, Else, ed. *Jacob Grimms Deutsche Altertumskunde.* Göttingen: Vandenhoeck & Ruprecht, 1974. 187 pp.

Jacob Grimm's lectures reprinted. The third major section is on mythology.

499. Ebel, Uwe. "Studien zur Rezeption der 'Edda' in der Neuzeit." *Literaturwissenschaftliches Jahrbuch*, n. s., 14 (1973), 123-82.

Useful analysis of two aspects of the reception of the Poetic Edda: the importance of Resen's edition and Herder's translation techniques.

500. Ebenbauer, Alfred. "Ursprungsglaube, Herrschergott und Menschenopfer: Beobachtungen zum Semnonkult (Germania c. 39)." In *Antiquitates Indogermanicae: Studien zur indogermanischen Altertumskunde und zur Sprach- und Kulturgeschichte der indogermanischen Völker: Gedenkschrift für Hermann Güntert zur 25. Wiederkehr seines Todestages am 23. April 1973*, eds. Manfred Mayrhofer, Wolfgang Meid, Bernfried Schlerath, and Rüdiger Schmitt, 233-49. Innsbrucker Beiträge zur Sprachwissenschaft, 12. Innsbruck: Institut für Sprachwissenschaft der Universität Innsbruck, 1974.

The sacrifice in the grove of the Semnones combined aspects of fertility—by echoing the dismemberment of the proto-being—and of the political security of the ruling clan. Ebenbauer's conclusion has more general implications: "It therefore seems as though the functions of fertility and of sovereignty fall together in cosmogonic rituals of regeneration. In this regard should not perhaps the argument over the æsir or vanir character of Baldr be superfluous?" (p. 249).

501. Eckhardt, Karl August. *Irdische Unsterblichkeit: Germanischer Glaube an die Wiederverkörperung in der Sippe.* Studien zur Rechts- und Religionsgeschichte, 1. Weimar: H. Böhlau, 1937. viii, 130 pp.

Argues a Germanic belief in reincarnation within the family, most often in the form of grandfather-grandson, and attempts an Indo-European derivation of the phenomenon.

502. Eckhardt, Karl August. *Studien zu Rechts- und Religionsgeschichte.* Weimar: Hermann Böhlau, 1939. 150 pp.

Consists of two works: "Ingwi und die Ingweonen," first published in *Zeitschrift der Savigny-Stiftung für Rechtsgeschichte,* Germ. Abt., 59, here with two appendices, and later published separately in a second edition (1940); and "Irdische Unsterblichkeit."

503. Eckhardt, Karl August. *Der Wanenkrieg.* Germanenstudien, 3. Bonn: L. Röhrscheid, 1940. 109 pp.

A broad interpretation of the war between the *æsir* and *vanir* and the development of Germanic myth and religion. Eckhardt argues a historical development still visible in the extant Norse mythology: Týr and Njord and an entire older generation replaced by conceptions of Odin. Perhaps the most curious part of the argument is postulation of a family of beings (including Týr) descending from Hymir. The author also attempts correlation with the history of peoples, the *vanir* representing an older layer of population overrun by the Indo-European *æsir.*

504. Eckhardt, Karl August. *Ingwi und die Ingweonen in der Überlieferung des Nordens,* 2nd ed. Germanenstudien, 1. Weimar: L. Röhrscheid, 1940. i, 98 pp. 1st. ed. issued 1939 as part of the author's *Studien zu Rechts- und Religionsgeschichte.*

On Ingwi/Yngvi and the Germanic people known as the Ingvaeones, with remarks on religion. Njord, the god of the proto-Ingvaeones, was later replaced (in name) by Ingwi/Yngvi.

505. Edsman, Carl-Martin. "Återspeglar Vǫluspá 2:5-8 ett schamanistiskt ritual eller en keltisk åldersvers?" *Arkiv för nordisk filologi,* 63 (1948), 1-54.

The author asks whether the disputed lines in *Vǫluspá* 2:5-8 on the nine worlds recalled by the sibyl reflect a shamanistic ritual or Celtic verse and concludes that it does neither, although neither theory is without merit. The article is valuable for its survey of earlier work, i.e., that of Palmér, Pipping, Schröder, Höckert, and Ranke.

506. Edzardi, A. "Kleine Beiträge zur Geschichte und Erklärung der Eddalieder, III, 10: Zur Lokasenna." *Germania,* 23 (1878), 418-21.

Textual note, especially to str. 28-29.

507. Edzardi, A. "Kleine Beiträge zur Geschichte und Erklärung der Eddalieder, III, 11: Zur Hýmiskviða." *Germania*, 23 (1878), 421-40.

An attempt to eliminate the extraneous from the original *Hymiskviða*, which Edzardi takes to be the quest for the kettle.

508. Edzardi, A. "Fensalir und Vegtamskviða 12, 5 ff." *Germania*, 27 (1882), 330-39.

On the riddles posed in *Baldrs draumar*, str. 12, and *Vafþrúðnismál*, str. 54, and intended as refutation of S. Bugge's reading of the stanzas. Edzardi postulates a nature myth in connection with Baldr's death and sees it in *Baldrs draumar* 12: Frigg (who lives at *Fensalir*—"bog or pond halls," according to Edzardi), weeps tears of gold that draw Baldr back.

509. Edzardi, A. "Über die Heimat der Eddalieder." *Beiträge zur Geschichte der deutschen Sprache und Literatur*, 8 (1882), 349-70.

Critical discussion of Guðbrandur Vigfússon's "Prologomena" to *Sturlunga saga*. Most of the analysis focuses on heroic poetry, but it is applicable to the mythological verse, and the last pages concern *Rígsþula*.

510. Eeden, W. van. "Een opmerking over de 'Edda'." *Neophilologus*, 31 (1947), 16-18.

Questions whether Snorri was the author of the *Bragarœður*.

511. Eggers, Hans Jürgen. *Die magischen Gegenstände der altisländischen Prosaliteratur*. Form und Geist; Arbeiten zur germanischen Philologie, 27. Leipzig: H. Eichblatt, 1932.

Magic objects in family sagas, *fornaldarsögur*, and lying sagas. Useful in providing context to the thirteenth-century and later reception of the mythology.

512. Eggers, Hans Jürgen. "Altgermanische Seelenvorstellungen im Lichte der Heliand." *Niederdeutsche Jahrbücher*, 80 (1957), 1-24.

The evidence of the Old Saxon *Hêliand* for early Germanic conceptions of the soul.

513. Ehrismann, Gustav. "Religionsgeschichtliche Beiträge zum germanischen Frühchristentum." *Beiträge zur Geschichte der deutschen Sprache und Literatur*, 35 (1909), 209-39.

The interaction between paganism and early Germanic Christianity, including an explanation for the relative ease of the conversion: Christianity offered a more reassuring picture of life after death.

514. Eike, Christine N. F. "Oskoreia og ekstasriter." *Norveg*, 23 (1980), 227-309.

Departing from the theories of Höfler and others, Eike studies Norwegian traditions of the Oskorei/wild hunt in the context of ecstasy. She concludes that ecstatic rites (related to the cult of Odin) form the core of Oskorei legends.

515. Eikeland, I. Berner. "Vettekult i Sirdal." *Frå bygd og by i Rogaland*, 1962, pp. 37-53.

Placename evidence for worship of spirits in Sirdal (Rogaland, Norway).

516. Eikeland, I. Berner. "Vettekult: Hellige tre og lunder." *Frå bygd og by i Rogaland*, 1963, pp. 62-74.

Cult activity at such natural features as trees and groves.

517. Einarsdóttir, Ólafia. "Árið 1000." *Skírnir*, 141 (1967), 128-38.

Translation of a chapter of the author's *Studier i kronologisk metode i tidlig islandsk historieskrivning* (1964), placing the conversion of Iceland in the year 999 A. D.

518. Einarsson, Bjarni. "'Að ósi skal á stemma.'" *Andvari*, 1961, pp. 47-50.

The title repeats Thor's words when he casts a stone at the giantess flooding the river Thor must cross on his visit to Geirrøðr, according to *Snorra edda*, and they are reflected in Snorri's *Óláfs saga helga*. Bjarni Einarsson offers here a few remarks on the possible background in real life of the formula.

519. Einarsson, Bjarni. "The Last Hour of Hallfreðr vandræðaskáld as Described in *Hallfreðarsaga*." In *Proceedings of the Eighth Viking Congress Århus 24-31 August 1977*, eds. Hans Bekker-Nielsen, Peter Foote, and Olaf Olsen, 217-21. Mediaeval Scandinavia Supplements, 2. Viborg, Denmark: Odense University Press, 1981.

The version in *Óláfs saga Tryggvasonar hin mesta* omits a *fylgja* found in the version in *Möðruvallabók* and includes a highly Christian verse. The author argues that the "bigoted compiler" of the *Óláfs saga* version may have made these changes to "get rid of a partly heathen episode and at the same time express a real Christian death-bed remorse and fright for the fate of his soul after death" (p. 220).

520. Einarsson, Stefán. "Notes on Gísla saga." *Acta Philologica Scandinavica*, 9 (1934-35), 85-96.

Pp. 85-91 on the technicalities of cutting the *jarðarmen*, the piece of turf under which men passed as part of a bloodbrother ritual (*Gísla saga*, ch. 6).

521. Einarsson, Stefán. "The Freydís-Incident in Eiríks saga rauða, Ch. 11." *Acta Philologica Scandinavica*, 13 (1938-39), 246-56.

Associates the incident with "ancient magical behaviour" (p. 256), with distant reference to berserks.

522. Einarsson, Stefán. "Eddu-smælki." *Skírnir*, 122 (1948), 142-45.

Argues that the word *hórdómr* "adultery" in the description of Ragnarǫk in *Vǫluspá* 41 reflects Norwegian as opposed to Icelandic churchly use. For a response see Einar Ól Sveinsson, "Lítil athugasemd," directly following in the same number of the journal.

523. Einarsson, Stefán. "Alternate Recitals by Twos in Wídsíþ (?), Sturlunga and Kalevala." *Arv*, 7 (1951), 59-83.

Postulates an ancient Lappish-Finnish ritual as the basis of a dream sequence in *Sturlunga saga.*

524. Einarsson, Stefán. "Horse Dance in the Sturlunga saga." *Saga och sed*, 1960, pp. 114-17. Rpt. in *Folkloristica: Festskrift till Dag Strömbäck 13 Augusti 1960* (Uppsala: Almqvist & Wiksell, 1960), pp. 290-93.

Relevant to Norse mythology as an early instance of "Cult Remnants in Early Icelandic Dances" (1948), which Dag Strömbäck had traced to ancient mumming and ultimately to fertility ritual.

525. Einarsson, Stefán. "Some Parallels in Norse and Indian Mythology." In *Scandinavian Studies: Essays Presented to Dr. Henry Goddard Leach on the Occasion of His Eighty-Fifth Birthday*, eds. Carl F. Bayerschmidt and Erik J. Friis, 21-26. Seattle: Published for the American-Scandinavian Foundation by the University of Washington Press, 1965.

The author suggests several speculative equivalences centering on motifs associated with the mead of poetry. The Icelandic folktale cow Búkolla is said to parallel Indic milkgiving cows in the hands of monsters, and Tvashtri, possessor of soma, is equated with Þjazzi [sic], who kidnapped Iðunn and her apples.

526. Einarsson, Stefán. "'Askr Yggdrasils', 'Gullnar töflur' (Völuspá)." In *Studies in Language and Literature in Honor of Margaret Schlauch*, eds. M. Brahmer, S. Helsztyński, and J. Kryżanowski, 111-15. Warsaw: PWN, 1966.

In this brief article the author points out parallels between aspects of Norse mythology and ancient Near Eastern myth and religion. A tree of life reminiscent of Yggdrasill is found in Babylonian tradition (*Gilgamesh*) and Sumerian, and Babylonian Tables of Destiny are arguably parallel to the *gullnar tǫflur* "gold gaming pieces" of *Vǫluspá* 61.

Eiríkr Magnússon, *see* Magnússon, Eiríkr.

527. Eitrem, S. "Lina laukar." In *Festskrift tilegnet førstebibliothekar A. Kjær av venner 26. september 1924.* 85-94. Oslo: Cammermeyer, J. Dybwad, Grøndahl & Søn, 1924.

The expression occurs on the runic inscription on the scraper found at Fløksand (Norway); Eitrem attempts to set it in the context of fertility cult.

528. Eitrem, S. "Köning Aun in Upsala und Kronos." In *Festskrift til Hjalmar Falk 30. desember 1927 fra elever, venner og kolleger.* 245-61. Oslo: H. Aschehoug (W. Nygaard), 1927.

The Greek Kronos (in myth and ritual) and King Aun of *Ynglinga saga* and *Ynglingatal*, set in Frazerian context. Both the Greek and Norse complexes involve periodicity of rule and sacrifice of sons. Eitrem cites an Irish parallel (pp. 258-59) and the presence of several Märchen motifs (pp. 259-61).

529. Ejder, Bertil. "Eddadikten Vafþrúðnismál." *Vetenskapssocietetens i Lund årsbok*, 1960, pp. 3-20.

Takes up a number of details in *Vafþrúðnismál*: the element of the *mannjafnaðr; the word lúðr*; the name *Gagnraðr*; and the unity of the poem, including the manuscript evidence that can be brought to bear.

530. Ejerfeldt, Lennart. "Helighet, 'karisma' och kungadöme i forngermansk religion." *Kungl. humanistiska Vetenskaps-samfundet i Uppsala, Årsbok*, 1969-70, pp. 112-75.

Inclines to the opinion that what may appear to be sacral kingship in the written sources is in fact the medieval Christian notion of the divine grace of kings.

531. Ekdahl, Sven, ed. *Kirche und Gesellschaft im Ostseeraum und im Norden vor der Mitte des 13. Jahrhunderts.* Visby: Museum Gotlands fornsal, 1969. 257 pp.

An international symposium on church and society in the Baltic and Scandinavia before the mid-thirteenth century; many of the essays treat problems of paganism, syncretism, or the conversion to Christianity, and are hence entered in this bibliography. They include Mårten Stenberger, "Christliche Einflüsse im archäologischen Material der Wikingerzeit in Schweden" (pp. 9-20); Gustaf Trotzig, "Gegensätze zwischen Heidentum und Christentum im archäologishen Material des 11. Jahrhunderts auf Gotland" (pp. 21-30); Ella Kivikoski "Christliche Einflüsse in dem archäologischen Material der Wikingerzeit und der Kreuzzugszeit Finnlands" (pp. 31-41); Olaf Olsen, "Die alte Gesellschaft und die neue Kirche" (pp. 43-54); Sven Ulrik Palme, "Die Kirche in der Gesellschaft der Landschaftsgesetze" (pp. 55-63); Percy Ernst Schramm, "Nordeuropa im Licht der Staatssymbolik" (pp. 99-112).

532. Ekenvall, Verner. "Två heiti i Snorres Edda." *Arkiv för nordisk filologi*, 58 (1944), 36-39. Also in *Festskrift till Jöran Sahlgren 8/4 1944* (Lund: C. W. K. Gleerup, 1944), pp. 36-39.

The *heiti eyþveri* "ox" may originally have meant "island-drill" and thus referred to Gefjon's plowing of Sjælland.

533. Ekholm, Gunnar. "De skandinaviska hällristningarna och deras betydelse." *Ymer*, 36 (1916), 275-308.

Important older article. Scandinavian rock carvings and the cult of the dead: oriental and Egyptian parallels.

534. Ekholm, Gunnar. "Hällristningsproblemet: Ett genmäle." *Fornvännen*, 17 (1922), 213-29. Summary in German, p. 283.

Response to B. Schnittger, "En hällristning vid Berga-Tuna i Södermanland" (1922), defending among other things Ekholm's theory that the rock carvings reflect a cult of the dead.

535. Ekholm, Gunnar. "Om hällristningarnas kronologi och betydelse: Slutord till antikvarien Schnittger." *Fornvännen*, 17 (1922), 239-59. German summary, pp. 284-85.

Response to B. Schnittger, "Hällristningarnas kronologi och betydelse" (1922).

536. Ekholm, Gunnar. "Gödåker: En förberedande studie." *Namn och bygd*, 13 (1925), 75-103.

Included in the author's argumentation is the supposition that Gödåker (Sweden) was an ancient cult center, a predecessor to Gamla Uppsala. The discussion includes remarks on the cults of Nerthus and Frigg.

537. Ekholm, Gunnar. "Brudvælte." *Namn och bygd*, 24 (1936), 192-96.

The association with Nerthus cult of placenames in *Brud-*, as supported by archaeological finds of horns allegedly used in such ritual.

538. Ekholm, Gunnar. "Hällristningsproblem." *Tor*, 12 (1967-68), 7-11. Summary in German.

Draws attention to two works of B. Almgren: "Hällristningar och bronsålderdräkt" (1960), and "Den osynlige gudomen" (1962).

539. Ekwall, Eilert. "Grim's Ditch." In *Studier Germanica tillägnade Ernst Albin Kock den 6 december 1934*. 41-44. Lund: C. Blom, 1934.

Reads the placename of the title as containing the Odin name *Grímr* and gathers other possible Grímr placenames in England.

540. Ekwall, Eilert. "Some Notes on English Place-Names Containing Names of Heathen Deities." *Englische Studien*, 70 (1935-36), 55-59.

Theophoric placenames in England.

541. Eldjárn, Kristján. *Kuml og haugfé: Úr heiðnum sið á Íslandi.* Akureyri: Norðri, 1956. 460 pp.

Exhaustive catalog and description of pagan grave sites and burial customs in Iceland.

542. Eldjárn, Kristján. "Fornþjóð og minjar." In *Saga Íslands*, ed. Sigurður Líndal, 99-152. Reykjavík: Hið íslenzka bókmenntafélag—Sögufélag, 1974.

A survey of the ancient populace and archaeological monuments of Iceland, for a volume of general essays on the country's history. This contribution is useful mainly as a brief survey of Icelandic archaeology, but it also contains a sober appraisal of the witness of archaeology with regard to ancient religious belief (pp. 110-12).

543. Eldjárn, Kristján. "The Bronze Image from Eyarland." In *Speculum Norroenum: Norse Studies in Memory of Gabriel Turville-Petre*, eds. Ursula Dronke, Guðrún P. Helgadóttir, Gerd Wolfgang Weber, and Hans Bekker-Nielsen, 73-84. N. p.: Odense University Press, 1981.

The small bronze image from Eyarland (Iceland), portraying a bearded man seated on a chair holding a cross-shaped object, has since its discovery early in the nineteenth century been identified with greater or lesser certainty as a representation of the god Thor. Eldjárn's purpose here is to call this identification into question: the object held by the figure differs significantly from the amulets known as Thor's hammers; the figure may date from after the conversion of Iceland to Christianity; and despite its similarity to the Rällinge image commonly identified as Freyr, it resembles even more closely a whalebone image from Baldursheimur (Iceland). This image has no obvious religious significance, but the grave in which it was found contained gaming pieces. Eldjárn wonders, tentatively, whether the Baldursheimur and Eyarland images might not then have been the die (*hnefi*) for the game *hnefitafl*.

544. Elgqvist, Eric. "Studier i södra Smålands bebyggelseshistorie: Anmärkningar till en karta över Värends järnåldersbebyggelse." *Hyltén-Cavallius föreningen, årsbok*, 1931, pp. 1-233.

Includes a section on thing places and cult places.

545. Elgqvist, Eric. "Brudhammare och hammarsäng." *Folkminnen och folktankar*, 21 (1934), 1-19.

Associates the blessing of the bride with Thor's hammer (in the end of *Þrymskviða*) with folk customs.

546. Elgqvist, Eric. *Skälv och skilfingar: Vad nordiska ortnamn vittna om svenska expansionssträvanden omkring mitten av första årtusendet e. kr.* Lund: Olins antikvariat, 1944. 161 pp.

The name of the Skilfingar, Sweden's ancient royal family, is reflected in the placename *Skälv* (older *skialf*). Elgqvist argues that *skialf* placenames are characteristically located at strategically important places and that the term itself means "watch tower." By tracing the names he attempts to follow the expansion of the Svea imperium.

Chapter 6 (pp. 57-64) treats the mythic name *Hliðskjálf* (Odin's high seat), explaining it as "portal tower."

547. Elgqvist, Eric. *Ullvi och Götevi: Studier rörande Götalandskapens införlivande med Sveaväldet.* Lund: Olins antikvariat, 1947. 158 pp.

As the subtitle indicates, the main focus of this monograph is the process of the incorporation of Götaland with or into the kingdom of the Svear as that kingdom expanded to the south. Placenames form the materials of the study, and the first four of the seven chapters treat theophoric placenames. The author concludes that placenames compounded with the name of the god Ullr show close association with and apparent importance to the Svea kingdom; they occupy central positions, near administrative and commercial centers or paths of transportation, and the Eriksgatan appears to have passed near twelve sanctuaries to Ullr. In Götaland theophoric placenames in *-Göta-* are evidence, to the author, of the participants in a phallic cult related to Odin (cf. the Odin names *Gautr* and *Gauti*). This cult was practiced later than the eastern Swedish cult of Ullr and Njord but coexisted with it for a time, and the distribution of the names referring to it is associated with the boundary between Svear and Götar.

548. Elgqvist, Eric. *Studier rörande Njordkultens spridning bland de nordiska folken.* Lund: Olins antikvariat, 1952. 181 pp. Summary in English.

An extremely thorough study of the cult of Nerthus and the hypothetical relationship of that cult to various Germanic peoples. The evidence is largely from placenames, but runological and archaeological data are also adduced. Elgqvist localizes the cult originally to southern Jutland and finds evidence of it in southern and western Norway and in central Sweden, frequently in areas where districts meet (i.e., peripheral to the areas of oldest settlement). This distribution suggests that the cult was spread by a people emigrating from southern Jutland, and Elgqvist nominates the Heruli, the eastern portion of whose territory was conquered by the Danes in the third century A. D., an event presumably causing emigration.

549. Elgqvist, Eric. *Ullvi och Ullinshov: Studier rörande Ullkultens uppkomst och utbredning.* Lund: Olins antikvariat, 1955. 179, [1] pp.

Ullr as a god originally associated with springs and worshipped by the Svear. Certain of his characteristics enabled Ullr to be associated with other deities: Freyr, Skaði, Hǫrn, Njord, and the *dísir.* The cult was spread from the Mäler region to southeast Norway, where the placename *Ullinhov* indicates a later form of the cult. The spreading of the cult may have occurred in connection with the expansion of the Svear in the sixth century.

550. Elgqvist, Eric. "Guden Höner." *Arkiv för nordisk filologi*, 72 (1957), 155-72.

Elgqvist argues that Hœnir is to be understood as a god in the form of a crane, with many of the crane's attributes. He may, Elgqvist thinks, have been associated with the vernal equinox and rites pertaining to it.

551. Elgqvist, Eric. "Vad svioniska ortnamn vittnar om grundandet av det danska väldet." *Arkiv för nordisk filologi*, 74 (1959), 161-217.

In the course of asserting, on the basis of placename evidence, that a tribe from Swedish Svealand was instrumental in the foundation of a Danish empire in Sjælland, Elgqvist discusses the distribution of the cults of the various gods. The Danish placename Torsager parallels the Swedish Torsåker and indicates that Thor was a fertility god in Sjælland as well as in Sweden; and a few other placenames suggest that Freyr, who was popular in Sweden, Norway, and Iceland, may also have been worshipped in Denmark.

552. Ellekilde, Hans. "Om Sighvat skjalds alfeblotsstrofer og Alfhildssagnet i Hervararsaga." *Acta Philologica Scandinavica*, 8 (1933-34), 182-92.

A response to J. de Vries, "Über Sigvats Álfablót-Strophen" (1932-33), defending the notion that the ritual behind Sigvatr's description was that of female worship, similar to the *dísablót* and cult of Vǫlsi, and defending also the source value of *Hervarar saga*.

553. Elliger, Walter. *Gottes- und Schicksalsglauben im frühdeutschen Christentum.* Kieler Universitätsreden, Neue Folge, 6. Hamburg: Hanseatische Verlagsanstalt, 1935. 21 pp.

Concepts of god and fate in early Germanic Christianity.

554. Elmevik, Lennart. "Fsv. *lytir (*Lytir): Ett etymologiskt och religionshistoriskt bidrag." *Namn och bygd*, 54 (1966), 47-61.

This contribution is primarily etymological, but it suggests too that Old Swedish may have had a noun **lytir* "diviner of lots" or the name **Lytir*, "the god with lots," who decides men's fates; this would be Freyr.

555. Elmevik, Lennart. "Fisl. einherjar 'krigare i Valhall' och några andra fornnord. sammansättningar med -ein." *Saga och sed*, 1982, pp. 75-84.

The etymology of *einherjar*: "peerless warriors."

556. Engelstad, Eivind S. *Østnorske ristninger og malinger av den arktiske gruppe.* Instituttet for sammenlignende kulturforskninger, ser. B, 26. Oslo: H. Aschehoug, Cambridge, Mass.: Harvard University Press, 1934. 144, [2] pp. With summary in German.

East Norwegian rock carvings.

557. Engfield, Roy. "Der Selbstmord in der germanischen Zeit." *Seminar*, 8 (1972), 1-14.

Suicide among the Germanic peoples, explained in part by reference to religion and ritual.

558. Envall, Petrus. *Falun och Falköping: Strängnäs: Forntida handels- och kultplatser.* Ortnamn och kulturhistoria, 3. Stockholm: Almqvist & Wiksell, 1962. 55 pp.

Besides the argument that Strängnäs, an episcopal see in Sweden, may have been an ancient cult site, Envall's little book is worth noting for its insistence that the most mundane explanation for a placename is not always the most convincing.

559. Envall, Petrus. *Gudastolpen: Rod och råd: En studie i fornnordisk språk- och religionshistoria.* Stockholm: Almqvist & Wiksell, 1969. 289 pp.

The author finds references to fertility gods and fertility ritual throughout Nordic placenames. Nordic placename scholars find the book unworthy of serious discussion (e.g., Thorsten Andersson in *Namn och bygd* 57 (1969), 184).

560. Erben, J. "Der Schluss des zweiten Merseburger Zauberspruchs." In *Festschrift Walter Baetke dargebracht zu seinem 80. Geburtstag am 28. März 1964*, ed. Kurt Rudolf et al., 118-21. Weimar: Böhlau, 1966.

On the ending of the second Merseburg charm.

561. Eriksson, Manne. "Ortnamnet Ål." *Namn och bygd*, 24 (1936), 139-50.

Another example of the reaction against overly zealous interpretation of placenames as theophoric. Names with *ål-* as first component reflect not a cult word (cf. runic *alu*) but rather a terrain word.

562. Eriksson, Manne. "Tallen på torpet." *Svenska landsmål och svenskt folkliv*, 81 (1958), 83-105. Summary in French.

Primarily on the etymology and meaning of Old Norse *þorp*, but with discussion of *Hávamál*, str. 50.

563. Eriksson, Manne, and Delmar Olof Zetterholm. "En amulett från Sigtuna: Ett tolkningsförsök." *Fornvännen*, 28 (1933), 129-56. Summary in German.

Attempts to read a runic amulet discovered in 1931 in Sigtuna, Sweden, as an invocation to Thor, a charm to be used against illness. It opens, according to this interpretation, "May Thor wound you, lord of giants," and also refers to the adversary as a wolf.

Cf. also I. Lindquist, *Religiösa runtexter, 1: Sigtuna-galdern* (1932), and H. Pipping, *Sigtuna amuletten* (1933).

564. Estrich, Robert M. "The Throne of Hrothgar—*Beowulf*, ll. 168-169." *Journal of English and Germanic Philology*, 43 (1944), 384-89.

Argues that the monster Grendel leaves Hrothgar's throne unmolested because, "as a symbol of semi-divine royalty, it was sacrosanct. . . . The pagan beliefs here briefly touched by the poem had their origin in the basic concepts of Germanic kingship and were strong enough to retain some value after the Conversion" (pp. 384-85).

565. Ettlinger, Ellen. "The Mythological Relief of the Oseberg Wagon Found in Southern Norway." *Folklore*, 87 (1976), 81-88.

Adaptation of the legend of Herakles on the Oseberg wagon.

566. Ettmüller, Ludwig. *Vaulu-spá: Das älteste Denkmal germanisch-nordischer Sprache, nebst einigen Gedanken über Nordens Wissen und Glauben und nordische Dichtkunst.* Leipzig: Weidmann, 1830. lv, 168 pp.

Edition of and commentary to *Vǫluspá.*

567. Ettmüller, Ludwig. "Beiträge zur Kritik der Eddalieder." *Germania*, 14 (1869), 305-23.

Textual notes to *Lokasenna*, *Grógaldr*, and *Fjǫlsvinnsmál.*

568. Evans, David A. H. "King Agni: Myth, History or Legend." In *Speculum Norroenum: Norse Studies in Memory of Gabriel Turville-Petre*, eds. Ursula Dronke, Guðrún P. Helgadóttir, Gerd Wolfgang Weber, and Hans Bekker-Nielsen, 89-105. N.p.: Odense University Press, 1981.

The Agni of *Ynglingatal*, adapted into Snorri's *Ynglinga saga* in *Heimskringla*, belonged neither to history nor myth; he was a figure of legend, as was his wife Skjálf, even before Þjóðólfr composed *Ynglingatal.*

569. Evans, David. "Dodona, Dodola, and Daedala." In *Myth in Indo-European Antiquity*, eds. Gerald James Larson, C. Scott Littleton, and Jaan Puhvel, 99-

130. Berkeley and Los Angeles: University of California Press, 1974.

Primarily a study of the oracle of Zeus at Dodona, seeking comparison in other Indo-European thunder gods, including Thor.

F

570. Falck-Kjällquist, Birgit. "Namnet *Ullerö*." *Namn och bygd*, 71 (1983), 152-56. Summary in English.

The name *Ullerö* (Värmland, Sweden) has ordinarily been associated with the god Ullr. Falck-Kjällquist proposes a different solution, analyzing the first component as the genitive of a river name **Ull* or **Ulla* "the bubbling or boiling river."

571. Falk, Hjalmar. "Oldnorske ordforklaringer." *Arkiv för nordisk filologi*, 5 (1889), 111-24.

Analysis of words occurring, inter alia, in *Hávamál* 145, *Hárbarðsljóð* 50, and *Lokasenna* 16.

572. Falk, Hjalmar. "Martianus Capella og den nordiske mythologi." *Årbøger for nordisk oldkyndighed og historie*, 1891, pp. 266-300.

Relates eddic mythology to *De Nuptiis Philologiae et Mercurii* of Martianus Capella: the creation of humans; the shield of the sun; Óðr-Adonis; Loptr; the rivers of *Grímnismál*; conceptions of the moon; demons; Yggdrasill's animals and astrology; Lyfjaberg.

573. Falk, Hjalmar. "Hávamál strofe 74." *Maal og minne*, 1922, pp. 173-75.

Textual note.

574. Falk, Hjalmar. "Mytologiens gudesønner." In *Festskrift tilegnet førstebibliothekar A. Kjær av venner 26. september 1924*. 1-8. Oslo: Cammermeyer, J. Dybwad, Grøndahl & Søn, 1924.

The father-son relationships in Norse mythology.

575. Falk, Hjalmar. *Odinsheite*. Skrifter utg. av det norske videnskaps-akademi i Oslo, II. hist.-filos. kl., 1924:10. Oslo (Kristiania): J. Dybwad, 1924. 46 pp.

A study of the *heiti* (poetic synonyms and nicknames) for Odin.

576. Falk, Hjalmar. "De nordiske hovedguders utviklingshistorie." *Arkiv för nordisk filologi*, 43 (1926), 34-44.

On the history of the development of the principal gods. *Nerthus* means "strength" and is to be associated with Celtic **nerto*, Irish *nert* "strength." The association of Fjǫrgyn with the Baltic Perkunas is not justified.

577. Falk, Hjalmar. "'Sjelen' i hedentroen." *Maal og minne*, 1926, pp. 169-74.

An attempt to apply Frazer's concept of the soul to Old Scandinavian conceptions, as exemplified primarily in vocabulary. Includes also discussion of fate and of burial customs.

578. Falk, Hjalmar. "Ordstudier I." *Arkiv för nordisk filologi*, 44 (1928), 315-24.

Includes discussion of *Jǫlfuðr*, an Odin name associating the god with bears.

579. Falk, Hjalmar. "Tre Edda-ord." *Norsk tidsskrift for sprogvidenskap*, 1 (1928), 5-9.

Etymologies of *hýnótt* (*Skírnismál* 42) and *mǫsmar* (*Rígsþula* 38).

580. Falk, Hjalmar. "Nogen Edda-studier." In *Studier tillägnade Axel Kock, tidskriftens redaktör, 1888-1925*. 223-31. Arkiv för nordisk filologi, 40, supplement. Lund: C. W. K. Gleerup, 1929. Also issued separately, under title *Studier tillägnade Axel Kock*.

Philological notes to *Hávamál* 6 and 120, *Rígsþula* 2, 14, 16, and *Hárbarðsljóð* 50.

581. Faraday, Lucy Winifred. *The Edda*, I: *The Divine Mythology of the North*. Popular Studies in Mythology, Romance & Folklore, 12. London: D. Nutt, 1902. 51 pp.

Popular sketch.

582. Faraday, Lucy Winifred. "Custom and Belief in the Icelandic Sagas." *Folk-Lore*, 17 (1906), 387-426.

Excerpted material, primarily from family sagas and kings' sagas, grouped under the following rubrics: the gods; hero-worship and underworld deities; burial customs and hero-cults; tomb treasures; divination; feasts and sacrifice.

583. Faulkes, Anthony. "Edda." *Gripla*, 2 (1977), 32-39.

Faulkes offers a new etymology of the title *Edda*: a neologism from Latin *edo*, here with the sense "I compose poetry."

584. Faulkes, Anthony, ed. *Edda Islandorum: Völuspá. Hávamál: P. H. Resen's Editions of 1665.* Reykjavik: Stofnun Árna Magnússonar, 1977. 104 pp. Additional unfoliated material.

Contains facsimiles of the first editions of Snorri's *Edda* and of *Vǫluspá* and *Hávamál*, the first two eddic poems to be published. All were edited by Peder Hansen Resen (1625-1688) and were published in Copenhagen in 1665. Faulkes's "Introduction" (pp. 9-104) clarifies the complex textual history of the manuscripts Resen used, many of them the work of other Danish and Icelandic humanists. Thus the volume is useful in illuminating the rediscovery of Norse mythology by the humanists.

585. Faulkes, Anthony. "The Genealogies and Regnal Lists in a Manuscript in Resen's Library." In *Sjötíu ritgerðir helgaðar Jakobi Benediktssyni 20. júlí 1977*, eds. Einar G. Pétursson and Jónas Kristjánsson, 177-90. Stofnun Árna Magnússonar á Íslandi, rit 12. Reykjavik: Stofnun Árna Magnússonar, 1977.

The manuscript AM 1 e beta fol. contains on leaves 85v-91r a compilation of genealogical and regnal lists copied from a mid-thirteenth-century vellum destroyed in the Copenhagen fire of 1728. A similar compilation seems to have formed part of the basis of the Prologue to *Snorra edda*. Snorri may have had no greater knowledge of Anglo-Saxon genealogy than was available in such lists, but the use of such a list in parts of *Heimskringla* and in the Prologue to *Snorra edda* "provides further support for the view that the prologue is also by Snorri Sturluson" (p. 187).

586. Faulkes, Anthony. "Descent from the Gods." *Mediaeval Scandinavia*, 11 (1979-80), 92-125.

A thorough discussion of learned Icelandic genealogies tracing descent from the gods and the important factors behind them, namely euhemerism and the Trojan material. Detailed discussion of textual relationships, with special discussion of the Prologue to *Snorra edda.*

587. Faulkes, Anthony, ed. *Edda Magnúsar Ólafssonar (Laufás Edda).* Reykjavik: Stofnun Árna Magnússonar, 1979.

An edition of the so-called "*Laufás edda*," an arrangement of Snorri's *Edda* carried out by the clergyman Magnús Ólafsson (ca. 1573-1636) during the end of the first decade of the seventeenth century. Magnús collected all the narratives from *Gylfaginning* and *Skáldskaparmál* into a section of *apologi* or *dæmisögur* and followed this with a section in which the kennings and heiti are arranged into groups according to their referents, in alphabetical order. His work (which was extremely popular in Iceland—it survives in more than 100 manuscripts) presents a view of later reception of Snorri's *Edda.*

Faulkes's "Introduction" (pp. 13-186) is a monograph on the sources and textual history of Magnús's *Edda.*

588. Faulkes, Anthony. "Pagan Sympathy: Attitudes to Heathendom in the Prologue to *Snorra edda.*" In *Edda: A Collection of Essays*, eds. Robert J. Glendenning and Haraldur Bessason, 283-314. The University of Manitoba Icelandic Studies, 4. N. p.: University of Manitoba Press, 1983.

Analogs from classical writers and medieval Christendom to various passages in the Prologue to *Snorra edda.* The Prologue takes an essentially historical view of Nordic paganism and is consistent with *Gylfaginning* when the author's sources and aims are considered.

589. Feilberg, H. F. *Jul*, vol. 1: *Allesjælestiden, hedensk, kristen julefest.* Copenhagen: Rosenkilde & Bagger, 1962. 363 pp. Rpt. of the 1904 original.

The first two sections, on the cults of the dead and Yule in ancient Scandinavia, are relevant to the study of Norse mythology.

590. Feist, Sigmund. "Zur Deutung der deutschen Runenspangen." *Zeitschrift für deutsche Philologie*, 47 (1916-18), 1-10.

Attempts to bring the runic brooches found on German soil into a greater context of late paganism, especially through the alleged magic use of the runes and the formulaic language of the inscriptions.

591. Feist, Sigmund. "Runen und Zauberwesen im germanischen Altertum." *Arkiv för nordisk filologi*, 35 (1919), 243-87.

Survey article arguing the magic use of runes, concentrating on the elder futhark.

592. Feist, Sigmund. "Die Runeninschrift der grösseren Nordendorfer Spange." *Zeitschrift für deutsche Philologie*, 49 (1921-23), 1-10.

Interpretation of the runic inscription on the Nordendorf brooch as a pagan invocation.

593. Feist, Sigmund. "Die religionsgeschichtliche Bedeutung der ältesten Runeninschriften." *Journal of English and Germanic Philology*, 21 (1922), 601-11.

Attempts to demonstrate borrowings of Near Eastern religious materials in elder futhark runic inscriptions containing "I" formulas: e.g., "I so-and-so carved the runes." The materials cited come from various Near Eastern traditions and have to do with the power of names.

594. Feist, Sigmund. "Neuere Germanenforschung." *Acta Philologica Scandinavica*, 1 (1926-27), 156-69.

Includes an explanation of the discrepancy between the accounts of Germanic gods by Caesar and Tacitus: Tacitus had a source consistent with later Germanic cult, whereas Caesar describes the gods of the "Germanic Celts" (p. 166).

595. Fell, Christine. "From Odin to Christ." In *The Viking World*, ed. James Graham-Campbell, 172-93. London: F. Lincoln, New Haven: Ticknor & Fields, 1980.

Brief survey in a lavishly illustrated popular volume.

596. Fell, Christine. "Gods and Heroes of the Northern World." In *The Northern World: The History and Heritage of Northern Europe, AD 400-1100*, ed. David M. Wilson, 15-46. New York: Harry N. Abrams, London: Thames & Hudson, 1980.

Brief survey in a lavishly illustrated popular volume.

597. Fett, Eva Nissen. "Kultminne i fornfund." In *Religionhistorie*, ed. Nils Lid, 5-27. Nordisk kultur, 26. Stockholm: A Bonnier, Oslo: H. Aschehoug, Copenhagen: J. H. Schultz, 1942.

A survey of cult remains in ancient archaeological evidence, treating sacrifice, graves, iconography, amulets, and cult places. Coverage begins with the Stone Age and extends through the end of paganism (younger Iron Age).

598. Fidjestøl, Bjarne. "Ein idrett utan lyte." In *Fra skald til modernist: Dikterens roll gjennom tidene*, ed. Andreas Skartveit, 9-23. Perspektivbøkene, 26. Oslo: Dreyer, 1967.

Argues the importance of pagan magic in early skaldic poetry.

599. Fielhauer, Helmut. "Das Motiv der kämpfenden Böcke." In *Festschrift für Otto Höfler zum 65. Geburtstag*, eds. Helmut Birkhan and Otto Gschwantler, 69-106. Vienna: Notring, 1968.

The fighting rams investigated here are found in southern German and east Alpine folk narrative and art, but the discussion ranges widely and even embraces Yggdrasill and Heiðrún (p. 98f.). The parallels adduced by the author might be useful in further study of these phenomena in Norse mythology.

600. Finger, Heinz. *Untersuchungen zum 'Muspilli.'* Göppinger Arbeiten zur Germanistik, 244. Göppingen: Kümmerle Verlag, 1977. 235 pp.

Finger's results, if accepted, would reduce the value of the parallel between the Old High German poem *Muspilli* and Ragnarǫk in Scandinavian tradition. Finger argues patristic influence on much of *Muspilli* and rejects the notion that the encounter between Elias and the antichrist is a duel without legal connotations.

601. Finnbogason, Guðmundur. "Um Þórsdrápu: Nokkrar athugasemdir." *Skírnir*, 98 (1924), 172-81.

Textual notes to *Þórsdrápa*.

602. Finnbogason, Guðmundur. "Simul." *Skírnir*, 102 (1928), 222.

On a name for Freyja in Egill's *lausavísa* 17: *Simul* "the fainter" as a reference to a shamanistic trance.

603. Finnbogason, Guðmundur. "Nokkrar athugasemdir við Hávamál." *Skírnir*, 103 (1929), 103-08.

Textual remarks to *Hávamál* 2, 31, and 53, and discussion of the use of the expressions *geð* and *lof ok líknstafir*.

604. Finnbogason, Guðmundur. *Íslendingar: Nokkur drög að þjóðarlýsingu.* Reykjavik: Menningarsjóður, 1933. 386 pp.

Historically oriented description of the Icelandic people, with chapters on the philosophy of life and religion (pagan and Christian) and on the supernatural.

Finnbogi Guðmundsson, *see* Guðmundsson, Finnbogi.

Finnur Jónsson, *see* Jónsson, Finnur.

Finnur Magnússon, *see* Magnússon, Finnur.

605. Fischer, Rudolf W. "Gullveigs Wandlung: Versuch einer läutender Deutung des Kultes in Hars Halle." *Antaios*, 4 (1963), 581-96.

In *Vǫluspá* 21 the seeress recalls the first war in the world, when the *æsir* studded Gullveig with spears and burned her three times in Hár's hall; three times she arose reborn, and she lives yet. Fischer sees this passage as the reflection of ancient ritual used in the purification of gold.

606. Fiske, Christabel F. "The British Isles in Norse Saga." *Scandinavian Studies*, 2 (1914-15), 196-214.

"Possibly the British Isles appear most interestingly in Norse saga as a source of Christian influence" (p. 206). Fiske supports this statement with a discussion of the meeting of paganism and the conversion in Old Icelandic literature, especially the kings' sagas.

607. Flade, Gottfried. "Zur Germanen-Mission." *Zeitschrift für Kirchengeschichte*, 54 (1935), 301-22.

On the supposed predisposition of the Germanic peoples to convert to Christianity, based on inadequacies in their own pagan religion.

608. Fleck, Jere. "Drei Vorschläge zu *Baldrs draumar*." *Arkiv för nordisk filologi*, 84 (1969), 19-37.

Textual notes to *Baldrs draumar* 12 and 13.

609. Fleck, Jere. "*Konr–Óttarr–Geirroðr*: A Knowledge Criterion for Succession to the Germanic Sacred Kingship." *Scandinavian Studies*, 42 (1970), 39-49.

"In summary, according to my interpretation the *Rígsþula*, *Hyndluljóð* and *Grímnismál* offer us three variants of the same functional narrative. A godly figure accepts the individual consecration of a royal younger or youngest son. He then provides his human protégé with that numinous knowledge necessary to decide the succession in the latter's favor despite the principle of primogeniture" (p. 46).

610. Fleck, Jere. "Óðinn's Self-Sacrifice–A New Interpretation, I: The Ritual Inversion." *Scandinavian Studies*, 43 (1971), 119-42.

On *Hávamál* 135. "I have presented evidence that in his self-sacrifice in Hávamál Óðinn hung in inverted position. I have accepted the well-known theory that this self-sacrifice represented an initiation, but have drawn attention to the 'lifting up' of the runes as a symbolization of Óðinn's acquisition of numinous knowledge. Furthermore, I have presented material supporting the formula that the acquisition of such knowledge within the framework of an initiation may lead to the throne–in the case of a god, obviously a 'ritual kingship'" (p. 142).

Continued in "Óðinn's Self-Sacrifice–A New Interpretation, II: The Ritual Landscape" (1971).

611. Fleck, Jere. "Óðinn's Self-Sacrifice–A New Interpretation, II: The Ritual Landscape." *Scandinavian Studies*, 43 (1971), 385-413.

Continuation of "Óðinn's Self-Sacrifice–A New Interpretation, I: The Ritual Inversion" (1971).

The tree; the cosmos; the fountain or lake; Mímr and Kvasir; the horn; sexual symbolism of Odin's self-sacrifice. "From his spear-wound, the stigma of his ritual slaughter, his blood drips down into the spring below, paralleling the cosmic seed which drips down *Yggdrasill* into the same brunnr. Óðinn's sperm is not only the source of his own ritual rebirth, but remains preserved in the spring in two separate functions: as the 'poet's mead' and as *Valfǫðs veð*, the cosmic father's 'pledge' of fertility to rejuvenate the universe after each cyclical *ragnarǫk*" (p. 411).

612. Fleck, Jere. "The 'Knowledge-Criterion' in the *Grímnismál*: The Case Against Shamanism." *Arkiv för nordisk filologi*, 86 (1971), 49-65.

This is, in effect, two papers. The first (pp. 49-58) argues that according to a strict ethnographic definition (i.e., that of Vajda, "Zur phraseologischen Stellung des Schamanismus") there was no shamanism in Germanic. The second (pp. 58-65) argues that *Grímnismál* implies a ritual of accession to sacral kingship.

The first is useful for its brief review of scholarly concepts of shamanism.

613. Flodström, Isidor. "Växtnamnet baldersbrå." *Arkiv för nordisk filologi*, 48 (1932), 174-202, 265-84.

In part a response to J. Palmér, "Baldersbrå" (1918), this paper covers the distribution of the name, the botanical background, and linguistic aspects of both components, generally accepting that the first component has to do with the god Baldr.

614. Flom, George T. "A Group of Words from *Hávamál I* in the Light of Modern Norwegian and Icelandic Dialects." *Scandinavian Studies*, 1 (1911-14), 251-73.

Textual notes to the first section of *Hávamál* (str. 1-80). Words and expressions treated are *illr* (str. 9, 51); *illa* (str. 22); *óminnes hegri* (str. 13); *hæþenn, glisser, glame* (str. 31); *snóper, solgen* (str. 33); *snaper* (str. 62); *dælsk* (str. 57). Flom concludes that this section of *Hávamál* was composed during the ninth century. "The real home of the *Hávamál I* remains . . . that [region] bounded by West Telemarken and Hardanger on the east and north–then to the coast on the west and south" (p. 272).

615. Flom, George T. "South Scandinavian Rock-Tracings: A Survey of the Material and a Brief Account of Like Sculpturings in England and Scotland." *Scandinavian Studies*, 7 (1921), 1-29.

Includes an interesting survey of early discoveries, published reproductions, and interpretations.

616. Flom, George T. "Old Norse *fránn* 'Gleaming'; Orkedal Dial. *fræna*, 'To Rain': A Study in Semantics." *Journal of English and Germanic Philology*, 25 (1926), 299-329.

Of interest for its remarks on the meaning and usage of *fránn* when applied (as it often is) to dragons, including the midgard serpent and the dragon of *Vǫluspá* 66.

617. Flom, George T. "The Drama of Norse Mythology." *Scandinavian Studies*, 15 (1938-39), 135-57.

Text of a lecture: the "drama" is understood as an ethicized struggle between helpful (gods) and harmful (giants) natural forces. Act I is creation and the golden age, Act II the giants' challenge to the rule of the gods, Act III Baldr's death. This is the climax of Flom's drama; although he alludes to the aftermath of Ragnarǫk, he does not seem to include it in the script.

618. Foerste, William. "Die germanischen Stammesnamen auf -varii." *Frühmittelalterliche Studien*, 3 (1969), 60-70.

Foerste argues that *-varii*, the second component of many Germanic names of peoples and groups, made reference to the political and corporate structure of such groups, which were probably joined by a common leader, system of defense, or cult. He mentions Schwabian worshippers of Ziu (the Old High German cognate of Týr) (p. 69f.).

619. Förstemann, E. "Noch etwas über Idisi." *Germania*, 5 (1843), 219-21.

Commentary to the first Merseburg charm.

620. Fontaine, Jacques. "Conversion et culture chez les wisigoths d'Espagne." In *La conversione al cristianesimo nell'Europa dell'alto medioevo: 14-19 aprile 1966.* 87-147. Settimane di studio del centro italiano di studi sull'alto medioevo. Spoleto: Presso la sede del centro, 1967.

A contribution to an international symposium on the conversion of European peoples; treats the Visigoths.

621. Fontenrose, Joseph. *Python: A Study of Delphic Myth and its Origins.* Berkeley and Los Angeles: University of California Press, 1959. xx, 617 pp. Rpt. 1980 with new "Foreword" and "Addenda et Corrigenda."

A now classic study of the "myth of combat" (between a god and a monster). Fontenrose summarizes the Norse material, i.e., the creation myth, in an appendix entitled "The Combat in Germanic Myth and Legend" (pp. 521-44). The summary draws out the similarities to the themes Fontenrose has enumerated throughout the book; some of these themes, and the extent to which the Norse creation myth shares them, may be found in tables 9-10 (pp. 359-61).

622. Fontenrose, Joseph. "The Building of the City Walls: Troy and Asgard." *Journal of American Folklore*, 96 (1983), 53-63.

The Trojan parallel, long recognized, to Snorri's tale of the building of the walls of Asgard is in books 7 and 21 of the *Iliad* and elsewhere: Poseidon (in some sources Apollo) built the walls of Troy for Laomedon, who refused to make payment for the work. Fontenrose finds eleven common "significant themes," which taken together make up a kind of tale type. According to Fontenrose, no other variants of the tale are so closely related as these two. He sees common origin, perhaps in early Indo-European walled settlements.

623. Foote, Peter G. "Observations on 'Syncretism' in Early Icelandic Christianity." *Árbók vísindafélags Íslendinga*, 1974, pp. 69-86. Rpt. with postscript in Foote, *Árvandilstá: Norse Studies* (N.p.: Odense University Press, 1984), pp. 84-100.

Argues against the presence of pagan-Christian syncretism in several literary passages, all of which Foote interprets in purely Christian terms.

624. Foote, Peter G. "Secular Attitudes in Early Iceland." *Mediaeval Scandinavia*, 7 (1974), 31-44. Rpt. in Foote, *Aurvandilstá*, Viking Collection, 2 (N.p.: Odense University Press, 1984), pp. 31-46.

Evidence primarily from contemporary sagas on secular attitudes in twelfth- and thirteenth-century Iceland.

625. Foote, Peter G. "[On the Conversion of the Icelanders]." *Arv*, 35 (1979), 155-59. Rpt. in Foote, *Árvandilstá: Norse Studies* (N.p.: Odense University Press, 1984), pp. 54-64.

Detailed review of Jón Hnefill Aðalsteinsson, *Under the Cloak* (1978). The title cited above is found only in the reprint; the original is headed as an ordinary review.

626. Frank, Roberta. "Snorri and the Mead of Poetry." In *Speculum Norroenum: Norse Studies in Memory of Gabriel Turville-Petre*, eds. Ursula Dronke, Guðrún P. Helgadóttir, Gerd Wolfgang Weber, and Hans Bekker-Nielsen, 155-70. N.p.: Odense University Press, 1981.

Frank investigates Snorri's story of the acquisition of the mead of poetry and concludes that he may present a version based not on pagan myth but on later attempts to understand certain kennings associated with the story. These attempts may have been made by twelfth-century mythographers, or perhaps even by Snorri himself.

627. Franquinet, G. D. *Noordsche litteratuer: Verhandeling over de Volö-spâ, met mythologische en taelkundige noten voorafgegaen van eene inleiding over de Edda van Soemund den wyzen*. Antwerp: J. E. Buschmann, 1846. 130 pp.

Edition of and commentary to *Vǫluspá*.

628. Franz, Leonhard. "Die Geschichten vom Monde in der Snorra-Edda." *Mitteilungen der Islandfreunde*, 10 (1922-23), 45-48.

On the presumed importance of the moon in Germanic religion and folk belief, departing from Snorri's brief remarks in *Gylfaginning*.

629. Franz, Leonhard. "Zur altnordischen Religionsgeschichte." *Mannus*, 19 (1927), 135-48.

Attempts to align Swedish history of the third to the sixth centuries with the history of religion. Franz distinguishes the religious "systems" of worship of *æsir* and *vanir*. He associates the *vanir* with Svealand and the *æsir*, in the form of Odin, with Götaland. The accommodation of the two systems accompanied the conquering of the Götar by the Svear.

630. Franzén, Anne-Marie. "Odens öga." *Fornvännen*, 53 (1958), 195-98.

On the tapestry from Skog, Sweden, which allegedly portrays Odin, Thor, and Freyr. The author reports nine small holes in the area where the one-eyed figure's other eye should be and interprets this as evidence that the figure once had two eyes and therefore probably does not represent Odin.

631. Franzén, Gösta. "Harstena." *Namn och bygd*, 67 (1979), 65-69. Summary in English.

Franzén points out that the placename element *-harg* (cf. Norse *hǫrgr*) may mean "cairn" or "boundary-mark" and concludes that these meanings must be considered in interpretations of *-harg* placenames. Thus some names previously interpreted as theophoric may need reconsideration.

632. Fredsjö, Åke, Sverker Janson, and Carl-Axel Moberg. *Hällristningar i Sverige*, 2nd. ed. När-var-hur-serien. Stockholm: Forum, 1969. 139 pp. 1st ed. 1956.

Popular introduction to the Swedish rock carvings, with some discussion of their possible religious import.

633. Freij, Henry. "'Balkåtrumman'–i solkultens tjänst?" *Fornvännen*, 72 (1977), 129-35. Summary in English.

A Bronze Age artifact interpreted as a burning mirror used in worship of the sun.

634. Friberg, Sven. *Studier över ortnamnen i Kållands härad*. Nomina Germanica, 5. Uppsala: Appelbeg, 1938. xiv, 144 pp.

With a section on faith, customs, and cult.

635. Friedrichs, Gustav. *Grundlage, Entstehung und genaue Einzeldeutung der bekanntesten germanischen Märchen, Mythen und Sagen*. Leipzig: W. Heims, 1909. xv, 495 pp.

Nature-mythological readings of Norse mythology and German narrative folklore, with an attempt to derive the latter in part from the former.

636. Friedrichs, Gustav. *Deutung und Erklärung der germanischen Märchen und Mythen*. Quellen und Forschungen zur Erd- und Kulturkunde, 12. Leipzig: W. Heims, 1934. 88 pp.

Argues a nature-mythological interpretation of myth, and Märchen as the derivative of myth. Much overlap, some word for word, with the following entry.

637. Friedrichs, Gustav. *Die Grundlagen des germanischen Götterglaubens*. Quellen und Forschungen zur Erd- und Kulturkunde, 13. Leipzig: W. Heims, 1934. 127 pp.

Argues a nature-mythological interpretation of Germanic myth. Much overlap, some word for word, with the preceding entry.

638. Friesen, Otto von. "Om några fornvestnordiska vers." *Arkiv för nordisk filologi*, 18 (1902), 62-75.

Includes a textual note on *Hávamál*, str. 1 (pp. 72-75).

639. Friesen, Otto von. "Tors fiske på en uppländsk runsten." In *Festschrift Eugen Mogk zum 70. Geburtstag 19. Juli 1924*. 474-83. Halle a. d. S.: M. Niemeyer, 1924.

Despite the title, most of this paper is a standard runological description of the Altuna stone (Uppland, Sweden). The last pages offer analysis of the pictorial representation of Thor's fishing expedition to the midgard serpent. The absence of Hymir in the picture von Friesen ascribes to lack of room (the corresponding absence in *Hymiskviða* to a "defective text" (p. 482)). The impetus to include such description on a runestone is said (implausibly) to derive from similar decorative practices on shields or indoors.

640. Friesen, Otto von. "Till Sigvats Bergsøglisvísur strof 6." In *Festskrift til Finnur Jónsson 29. maj 1928*. 258-62. Copenhagen: Levin & Munksgaard, 1928.

Includes discussion of the etymology of the name *Heimdallr*: the first component may have been an adjective, **heimr* "shining."

641. Friesen, Otto von. "Har det nordiska kungadömet sakralt ursprung? En ordhistorisk utredning." *Saga och sed*, 1932-34, pp. 15-34.

The etymology of *konungr* "king." The author derives the first component from *kvena/kona* "woman" and explains the term as "the fertility goddess's mate," an indication of sacral kingship.

642. Frings, Th. "Langbärte und Wollbärte." *Beiträge zur Geschichte der deutschen Sprache und Literatur*, 65 (1942), 153-54.

An Irish parallel to the story of the "long-beards" as the origin of the Langobards (Odin and Frigg, in West Germanic guise, figure in the Langobard story).

643. Fritzner, Johan. "Þing eðr þjóðarmál (Hávamál 114)." *Arkiv för nordisk filologi*, 1 (1883), 22-32.

Textual note to *Hávamál*, str. 114.

644. Fromm, Hans. "Lemminkäinen und Baldr." In *Märchen, Mythos, Dichtung: Festschrift zum 90. Geburtstage Friedrich von der Leyens am 19. August 1963*, eds. Hugo Kuhn and Kurt Schier, 287-302. Munich: C. H. Beck, 1963.

Examines the parallels between the Lemminkäinen material in the *Kalevala* and the myth of Baldr's death. Concludes that both derive from initiation ritual.

645. Fry, Donald K. *Norse Sagas Translated into English: A Bibliography*. New York: AMS Press, 1980. xx, 139 pp.

Includes translations of *Snorra edda*.

646. Fuchs, Theodor. "Ueber die Bedeutung des Rîgs-Mâl." *Mitteilungen der anthropologischen Gesellschaft in Wien*, 9 (1880), 142-54.

Argues that *Rígsþula* does not present three successive cultural layers; rather, it represents the three classes of ancient German(ic) society, as a glance at older German laws will show. Thus, *Rígsþula* explains the origin of the class system.

647. Funke, Ulrich. *Enthalten die deutschen Märchen Reste der germanischen Götterlehre?* Düren-Rhld: Danielewski, 1932. 85 pp. Diss. Bonn.

Useful only as a survey of older research on the question of the retention of Germanic mythology in modern German folktales.

G

648. Gaerte, Wilhelm. "Das Schuhsohlen-, Rad- und Kreuzsymbol auf den schwedischen Felszeichnungen." *Mannus*, 15 (1923), 271-85.

Offers a non-religious interpretation of some common symbols on the rock carvings: footprints, wheels, and crosses have to do with legal rituals of taking possession of territory.

649. Gaerte, Wilhelm. *Altgermanisches Brauchtum auf nordischen Steinbildern.* Leipzig: C. Kabitzsch, 1935. 147 pp.

Customs and lore on the rock carvings.

650. Garmonsway, G. N. "Old Norse *jarðarmen.*" In *The Early Cultures of North-West Europe (H. M. Chadwick Memorial Studies)*, eds. Sir Cyril Fox and Bruce Dickens, 419-25. Cambridge: University Press, 1950.

Primarily on the passage in *Njáls saga*, ch. 119, in which Skarpheðinn accuses Skapti Þóroddsson of going under a *jarðarmen* "strip of earth; earth-necklace." Garmonsway suggests that the ritual behind the accusation may have been intended to propitiate Freyr.

651. Gaster, M. "The Letter of Toledo." *Folk-Lore*, 13 (1902), 115-34.

Issued in 1184, the letter predicted the end of the world two years later. Gaster traces the tradition through various forms, including *Vǫluspá* and *Muspilli.*

652. Gebhardt, August. "Miscellen." *Beiträge zur Geschichte der deutschen Sprache und Literatur*, 24 (1899), 406-13.

Pp. 412-13 offer a textual note on *Vǫluspá*, str. 5.

653. Gehl, Walther. *Der germanische Schicksalsglaube.* Berlin: Junker und Dünnhaupt, 1939. 265 pp.

The classic treatment of Germanic concepts of fate, departing from etymology and semantics. Although Gehl seeks to separate fate from religion, it impinges on mythology in the persons of the norns and other collective beings associated with fate, and the terms for them also collectively refer to the gods (*bǫnd, regin, hapt*). Only Odin, however, has according to Gehl a direct connection with fate, and that only during late paganism.

A planned second volume on the Indo-European and proto-Germanic background never appeared.

654. Gehl, Walther. "Das Problem des germanischen Tempels." *Zeitschrift für deutsches Altertum*, 78 (1941), 37-49.

Building on Å. Ohlmarks, "Isländska hov och gudahus" (1936), and F. Oelmann, "Zum Problem des gallischen Tempels" (1933), Gehl argues that the roughly square temple type was associated with the cult of the *vanir* and in West Scandinavian was called *hǫrgr*; the oblong type was associated with the *æsir*, and *hof* could refer to either type. The roughly square shape of stave churches accords with the hypothetical temple type of the *vanir*. In Norway and Iceland the two temple types may have influenced one another.

655. Gehrts, Heino. *Das Märchen und das Opfer: Untersuchungen zum europäischen Brüdermärchen*. Bonn: Bouvier, 1967. 309 pp.

Proposes a ritual background for the tale type of the two brothers, having to do with worship of the Dioscurii in Männerbünde. Although not directly aimed at Norse mythology, this study provides useful background.

656. Gehrts, Heino. "Die Gullveig-Mythe der Vǫluspá." *Zeitschrift für deutsche Philologie*, 88 (1969), 312-78.

This lengthy article attempts to anchor in cult *Vǫluspá* 21-26. The triple burning of Gullveig would represent a ritual sacrifice and the ensuing battles ritual combat.

657. [Geijer, Erik Gustav]. "Wegtams quida: Öfwersättning." *Iduna*, 1 (1811), 60-69. 2nd ed. 1816, 3rd ed. 1824

Swedish translation of *Baldrs draumar*, with introduction.

658. [Geijer, Erik Gustav]. "Betraktelse i afseende på de nordiska mythernas anwändande i skön konst." *Iduna*, 7 (1817), 86-132.

The famous Swedish romantic's views on the use of Norse mythology in literature and art.

659. Geisslinger, Helmut. "Soziale Schichtungen in den Opferdepots der Völkerwanderungszeit." In *Vorgeschichtliche Heiligtümer und Opferplätze in Mittel- und Nordeuropa: Bericht über ein Symposium in Reinhausen bei Göttingen vom 14.- 16. Oktober 1968*, ed. Herbert Jankuhn, 198-213. Abhandlungen der Akademie der Wissenschaften in Göttingen, phil.-hist. Kl., 3. Folge, 74. Göttingen: Vandenhoeck & Ruprecht, 1970.

Distinguishes two social layers, with individual offerings characterizing women and collective offerings characterizing men. For discussion see T. Capelle, "Ringopfer" (1970).

660. Gelbe, Theodor. "Zu Simrocks Mythologie." *Germania*, 30 (1885), 382-83.

Brief addendum to K. Simrock, *Handbuch der deutschen Mythologie mit Einschluss der Nordischen* (1869).

661. Gellerstedt, Nils. "Hednatemplet i Gamla Uppsala." *Fornvännen*, 45 (1950), 193-219. Summary in German.

Survey of previous attempts at reconstruction of the pagan temple at Uppsala, followed by the author's own attempt. Illustrated with plans, elevations, sections, sketches, and a photo.

662. Gellerstedt, Nils. "Uppsala och Arkona." *Fornvännen*, 47 (1952), 21-57. Summary in German, pp. 56-57.

Comparison of the reconstructed pagan temple at Arkona, Rügen, with the Uppsala temple, and consideration of the possibilities for similar reconstruction.

663. Gelling, Margaret. "Place-Names and Anglo-Saxon Paganism." *University of Birmingham Historical Journal*, 8 (1962), 7-25.

Alternative explanations for supposed theophoric placenames in England.

664. Gelling, Margaret. "Further Thoughts on Pagan Place-Names." In *Otium et Negotium: Studies in Onomatology and Library Science Presented to Olof von Feilitzen*, ed. Folke Sandgren, 109-28. Acta Bibliothecae Regiæ Stockholmiensis, 16. Stockholm: Norstedt, 1973.

Additional alternative explanations of supposed theophoric placenames in England. Pp. 120-27 contain a catalog of most of the names (after F. Stenton, "The Historical Bearing of Place-Name Studies" (1941)), with relevant evidence and interpretation.

665. Gelling, Peter, and Hilda Ellis Davidson. *The Chariot of the Sun, and Other Rites and Symbols of the Northern Bronze Age*. London: J. M. Dent, New York: Praeger, 1969. ix, 200 pp.

An attempt to reconstruct the religious background of the southern Scandinavian rock carvings of the Bronze Age, by Gelling, followed by a chapter by Davidson tracing the conceptions into Norse mythology. Gelling finds that sun worship was a basic trait of Bronze Age religion in Scandinavia and isolates a sword-god (perhaps Freyr) and a spear-god (perhaps Odin). Davidson argues a great deal of continuity over several millennia in Scandinavian religious history.

666. Genzmer, Felix. "Das Eddische Preislied." *Beiträge zur Geschichte der deutschen Sprache und Literatur*, 44 (1920), 146-68.

On *Haraldskvæði, Eiríksmál, Hákonarmál*, and *Darraðarljóð*. Pp. 165-68 discuss their inclination toward mythological material.

667. Genzmer, Felix. "Der Spottvers des Hjalti Skeggjason." *Arkiv för nordisk filologi*, 44 (1928), 311-14.

Textual note. Genzmer reads the verse as support for the conversion.

668. Genzmer, Felix. "Die Gefjonstrophe." *Beiträge zur Geschichte der deutschen Sprache und Literatur*, 56 (1932), 414-36.

Interpretation of *Ragnarsdrápa* 13.

669. Genzmer, Felix. "Die ersten Gesätze der Thorsdrapa." In *Studia Germanica tillägnade Ernst Albin Kock den 6 december 1934*. 59-73. Lund: C. Blom, 1934.

Textual notes to the first strophe of *Þórsdrápa*.

670. Genzmer, Felix. "Ein germanisches Gedicht aus der Hallstattzeit." *Germanisch-Romanisch Monatsschrift*, 24 (1936), 14-21.

Based on the account of creation in Tacitus, *Germania*, ch. 2, Genzmer postulates and attempts to recreate a proto-Germanic song of creation.

671. Genzmer, Felix. *Edda: Götter- und Heldendichtung*. Jena: E. Diederichs, 1937. 461 pp. Monumentalausgabe.

German translation of the Poetic Edda.

672. Genzmer, Felix. *Germanische Schöpfungssagen*. Deutsche Reihe, 149. Jena: E. Diederichs, 1944. 64 pp.

In this little volume intended primarily for a popular audience, Genzmer gathered and discussed the "Germanic legends of creation," by which he meant Tacitus, the Norse sources, the creation episode of the *Guta saga*, and the *Wessobrunner Gebet*. In general he regarded the Germanic material as the heir to Indo-European tradition.

673. Genzmer, Felix. "Die Götter des zweiten Merseburger Zauberspruchs." *Arkiv för nordisk filologi*, 63 (1948), 55-72.

In the second Merseburg charm, Fol (Phol) is the male counterpart to Folla, who in turn is equivalent to the Norse Fulla; cf. Freyr and Freyja.

674. Genzmer, Felix. "Das Alter einiger Eddalieder." *Zeitschrift für deutsche Philologie*, 71 (1951-52), 134-51.

On dating the eddic poems. Focus is on the younger heroic poems, but Genzmer discusses many mythic poems as well. Among his conclusions are the early dating of the gnomic section of *Hávamál* and the dating of *Vǫluspá* to before ca. 1050.

675. Genzmer, Felix. "Die Geheimrunen der Egilssaga." *Arkiv för nordisk filologi*, 67 (1952), 39-47.

One example of a magic use of runes, with its mythological context.

676. Genzmer, Felix, ed. *Edda,* vol. 2: Götterdichtung und Spruchdichtung. Düsseldorf and Cologne: M. Niemeyer, 1962. 204 pp.

A German translation of eddic mythological verse, with introductions and commentary by Andreas Heusler, brought up to 1941 by Felix Genzmer. This reprint contains a postscript by Hans Kuhn.

677. Gering, Hugo. "Der zweite Merseburger Spruch." *Zeitschrift für deutsche Philologie*, 26 (1894), 145-49.

Criticism of F. Kauffmann, "Der zweite Merseburger Zauberspruch" (1891).

678. Gering, Hugo. "Noch einmal der zweite Merseburger Spruch." *Zeitschrift für deutsche Philologie*, 26 (1894), 462-67.

Response to F. Kauffmann's immediately preceding article with the same title.

679. Gering, Hugo. "Zur Lieder-Edda." *Zeitschrift für deutsche Philologie*, 26 (1894), 25-30.

Textual notes to the Poetic Edda.

680. Gering, Hugo. "Zur Lieder-Edda, II." *Zeitschrift für deutsche Philologie*, 29 (1897), 49-63.

Textual notes: *Alvíssmál*, str. 5 and *Hávamál*, str. 106.

681. Gering, Hugo. "Zu Hǫvamǫl Str. 100." *Zeitschrift für deutsche Philologie*, 34 (1902), 133-34.

Textual note, correcting the interpretation of K. Gjellerup.

682. Gering, Hugo. *Vollständiges Wörterbuch zu den Liedern der Edda*. Die Lieder der Edda, ed. B. Sijmons and H. Gering, vol. 2; Germanistische Handbibliothek, 7:4-5. Halle a. d. S.: Buchhandlung des Waisenhauses, 1903. xiii, 1404 pp.

This glossary to eddic poetry contains an index of names. Under the names of the various gods, one finds a list of their actions in the eddic poems indexed to poem and stanza.

683. Gering, Hugo. "Zur Lieder-Edda, III." *Zeitschrift für deutsche Philologie*, 43 (1911), 132-40.

Textual notes to, inter alia, *Vǫluspá* 17, *Skírnismál* 17, 18, 23, 30, and 39; *Lokasenna* 34 and 39; *Þrymskviða* 4 and 27.

684. Gering, Hugo. "Grottasǫngr (Eine Probe aus dem Eddakommentar)." In *Festschrift Eugen Mogk zum 70. Geburtstag 19. Juli 1924*. 30-53. Halle a. d. S.: M. Niemeyer, 1924.

Contains a detailed, primarily philologically oriented commentary to the eddic poem *Grottasǫngr* and its accompanying prose.

685. Gerschel, Lucien. "Sur un schème trifonctionnel dans une famille de légendes germaniques." *Revue de l'histoire des religions*, 150 (1956), 55-92.

Gerschel attempts to identify Dumézil's tripartite scheme in recent German and Swiss legends.

686. Gerschel, Lucien. "Un épisode trifonctionnel dans la saga de Hrolfr Kraki." In *Hommages à Georges Dumézil*. 104-16. Collection Latomus, 45. Brussels: Latomus: Revue d'études latines, 1960.

Marshalls evidence in support of a Dumézilian triad in *Hrólfs saga kraka*: the hero Bǫðvarr bjarki is a second function (warrior) figure, and his brothers Þórir (who becomes a king) and Elgfróði (who aspires to riches) represent the first and third functions, respectively.

687. Gerstein, Mary R. "Germanic Warg: The Outlaw as Werwolf." In *Myth in Indo-European Antiquity*, eds. Gerald James Larson, C. Scott Littleton, and Jaan Puhvel, 131-56. Berkeley and Los Angeles: University of California Press, 1974.

Following extensive discussion of terminology, Gerstein concludes: "the Gmc. *warg* is ultimately the human representative of the *Roggenwolf*, the dread and mysterious disease wolf, the supernatural demonic wolf who is the negative aspect of the wolf-god who protects the fertility of the community, allows the grain to grow, and punishes criminals" (p. 156).

688. Giffen, A. E. van. "Totenritus bei den Nordmannen oder Wikingern an der Wolga im zehnten Jahrhundert." *Numen*, 10 (1963), 228-35.

Context and summary of Ibn Fadlan's description of a Rus funeral.

689. Gimbutas, Marija. "The Lithuanian God Velnias." In *Myth in Indo-European Antiquity*, eds. Gerald James Larson, C. Scott Littleton, and Jaan Puhvel, 87-92. Berkeley and Los Angeles: University of California Press, 1974.

Comparison with Odin and Varuna.

690. Girvan, Ritchie. *Beowulf and the Seventh Century: Language and Content.* Methuen's Old English Library [C. Studies, 1]. London: Methuen, 1935. viii, 86 pp.

With remarks on ship burials and the necessity of preventing a return of the corpse; some relevance to Baldr's funeral.

691. Gíslason, Konráð. "Om navnet Ýmir." *Det kongelige danske videnskabernes selskabs skrifter*, 5. ser., hist.-phil. kl., 4 (1874), 433-55.

Establishes the proper forms of Hymir, the giant involved in Thor's battle with the midgard serpent, and Ýmir [sic], the proto-giant. The latter derives from a root meaning "plenty, multitude."

692. Gíslason, Konráð. "Œgir og Ægir." *Årbøger for nordisk oldkyndighed og historie*, 1876, pp. 312-30.

Establishes the name of the giant or god of the sea as Ægir, not Œgir.

693. Gíslason, Konráð. "En bemærking om edda som navn paa et skrift." *Årbøger for nordisk oldkyndighed og historie*, 1884, pp. 143-56.

Derives the title *Edda* from *óðr* "poetry."

694. Gjessing, Gutorm. "Hesten i førhistorisk kunst og kultus." *Viking*, 7 (1943), 5-143.

The horse in prehistoric art and cult. The perspective is historical, with chapters on the Bronze and Stone Ages (pp. 5-22), the gold bracteates (pp. 23-42), the Migration period (pp. 42-57), and the burial rituals of the Merovingian and Viking periods (pp. 57-64), followed by detailed discussion of Viking Age traditions: the development of Sleipnir (pp. 92-105), the Oseberg burial (pp. 105-22), and a concluding discussion on "the unbroken line" (pp. 125-33). Gods receiving particular mention are Freyr and Odin.

695. Gjessing, Helge. "Et gammelt kultsted i Sandeid: Frugtbarhetsgudeparrets dyrkelse i Ryfylke og paa Jæderen." *Maal og minne*, 1915, pp. 65-79.

The discussion centers around the "holy white stones" described by Th. Petersen, *Nogle bemerkninger om de saakaldte 'hellige, hvide stene'* (1905; and cf. Petersen, "Zwei neugefundene Kultobjekte aus der älteren Eisenzeit" (1924)) and assigned by Petersen to the cult of Njord. Gjessing demurs, and using partly iconographic evidence, he argues that the stones are to be seen in light of the myth retained in *Skírnismál* (as interpreted by Magnus Olsen), a divine marriage of a sacral couple.

696. Glendinning, Robert J. "The Archetypal Structure of Hymisqviða." *Folklore*, 91 (1980), 92-110.

Argues a structural unity of *Hymiskviða*, on narrative and (Jungian) archetypal levels. Although Glendinning finds some similarity in this unity with typological methods of biblical exegis, he is inclined to seek archetypes at the heart of it.

697. Glob, P. V. "Kultbåde fra Danmarks bronzealder." *Kuml*, 1961, pp. 9-18. Summary in English.

Cult ships in the rock carvings.

698. Glob, P. V. *Danske oldtidsminder.* Copenhagen: Gyldendal, 1967. 275 pp.

Popular introduction to Danish archaeology, including a chapter on rock carvings and other religious manifestations of the Bronze Age.

699. Glob, P. V. *Helleristninger i Danmark.* Jysk arkæologisk selskabs skrifter, 7. Copenhagen: Gyldendal, 1969. 333 pp.

A survey of Danish Bronze Age rock carvings, many of which seem to have had religious significance. Glob attempts a historical survey of various symbols and is able to enforce a distinction between grave custom and ritual associated exclusively with the living.

700. Goedheer, A. J. *Irish and Norse Traditions about the Battle of Clontarf.* Haarlem: H. D. Tjeenk Willink & Zoon, 1938. xiii, 124 pp.

The author's discussion of *Darraðarljóð* includes some general treatment of norns and valkyries.

701. Goegginger, Wolf H. "Hermann Güntert als Religionsforscher." *Numen*, 14 (1967), 150-58.

Life and works on the history of religion of H. Güntert.

702. Goegginger, Wolf H. "Das Werden des indoeuropäischen Gottesbegriffes." In *Antiquitates Indogermanicae: Studien zur indogermanischen Altertumskunde und zur Sprach- und Kulturgeschichte der indogermanischen Völker: Gedenkschrift für Hermann Güntert zur 25. Wiederkehr seines Todestages am 23. April 1973*, eds. Manfred Mayrhofer, Wolfgang Meid, Bernfried Schlerath, and Rüdiger Schmitt, 165-73. Innsbrucker Beiträge zur Sprachwissenschaft, 12. Innsbruck: Institut für Sprachwissenschaft der Universität Innsbruck, 1974.

Includes discussion of differentiation of functions and attributes among Odin, Thor, and Freyr. Also remarks on O. Almgren, *Nordische Felszeichnungen als religiöse Urkunden* (1934).

703. Göransson, Johan. *De yfverborna atlingars eller sviogöthars ok nordmänners patriarkaliska lära, eller sådan hon var före Odhin II:s tid; af Sämund hin frode på Island, efter gamla runoböcker år Chr. 1090 afskrefven; men nu efter trenne kongl. antiqvitets archivet tillhöriga göthiska handksrifter med svensk öfversättning utgifven.* Stockholm: J. Merckell, 1750. 24 pp.

Early Swedish edition and translation of *Vǫluspá*, with interpretive notes.

704. Götlind, Johan. "Valhall och ättestupa i västgötsk tradition." In *Folkminnesstudier tillägnade Hilding Celander den 17 Juli 1926*, eds. David Arill, Elof Lindälv, Sverker Ek, and Waldemar Liungman, 69-84. Folkloristiska studier och samlingar, 2. Gothenburg: Elander, 1926.

Argues an ancient and genuine association between conceptions of Valhalla and those of the *ättestupa* in Västergötland, Sweden (*ättestupa* "cliff over which aged family members throw themselves").

705. Goette, Rudolf. "Die Schwertrune und der Schwertgott." *Am Urds-Brunnen*, 5 (1887-88), 177-82.

Týr the sun-god and the t-rune his sword and a ray of sunshine.

706. Goette, Rudolf. "Erwiderung auf die Abhandlung des Herrn Sz. 'Der germanische Kriegsgott Tyr' in Nr. 1-5 des laufenden Jahrgangs dieser Zeitschrift." *Am Urds-Brunnen*, 6 (1888-89), 99-100.

Response to an article by G. von Szcepański criticizing the author's "Die Schwertrune und der Schwertgott" (1887-88).

707. Goette, Rudolf. "Nochmals die Forschungen des Herrn von Sz." *Am Urds-Brunnen*, 6 (1888-89), 158-59.

Response to G. von Szcepański, "Die Frage- und Ausrufungszeichen des Herrn R. Goette" (1888-89).

708. Golther, Wolfgang. "Studien zur germanischen Sagengeschichte, I: Der Valkyrjenmythus." *Abhandlungen der philos.-philol. Cl. der königlichen bayerischen Akademie der Wissenschaften*, 18 (1888), 401-38.

Presents the myths of the valkyries as Scandinavian creations of the ninth and tenth centuries.

709. Golther, Wolfgang. *Handbuch der germanischen Mythologie*. Leipzig: S. Hirzel, 1895. xi, 668 pp.

Important nineteenth-century handbook, accepting extensive Christian influence on the mythology. Following a succinct research history, Golther offers major sections on the lower mythology, the gods, creation and cosmos, and forms of worship.

710. Golther, Wolfgang. *Religion und Mythus der Germanen*. Leipzig: Deutsche Zukunft, 1909. iv, 115 pp.

Popular handbook.

711. Gould, Chester N. "*Hávamál*, Stanza 75." *Modern Philology*, 24 (1926-27), 385-88.

Proposed emendation: *af ǫldrom* for *aflauðrom*.

712. Gould, Chester N. "They Who Await the Second Death: A Study in the Icelandic Romantic Sagas." *Scandinavian Studies*, 9 (1926-27), 167-201.

Although not directly relevant to Scandinavian mythology, this essay treats parallel material in the *fornaldarsögur*: the corpse, figures with attributes of living corpses, and dwarfs.

713. Gould, Chester N. "Which Are the Norns Who Take Children from Mothers?" *Modern Language Notes*, 42 (1927), 218-21.

Translates *Fáfnismál* 12: "Which are the norns / who move in haste / and take mothers from children?"

714. Gould, Chester N. "Dwarf-Names in Old Icelandic." *Publications of the Modern Language Association*, 44 (1929), 949-67.

A list of some 190 dwarfs in Norse sources, divided into the following major categories: 1) behavior; 2) battle; 3) appearance (lustre); 4) association with death; 5) wisdom; 6) association with nature; 7) craftsmanship and tools; 8) association with the supernatural. The names are said to derive from attributes or activities of persons newly dead and buried.

For a criticism of Gould's procedure—registering variant names separately and ignoring context—see the "Nachwort" by Dietrich Hofmann to Lotte Motz, "New Thoughts on Dwarf-Names in Old Icelandic" (1973), pp. 116-17. Motz, pp. 112-15, offers a corrected list.

715. Gould, Chester N. "Blótnaut." In *Studies in Honor of Hermann Collitz, Professor of Germanic Philology, Emeritus, in the Johns Hopkins University, Baltimore, Maryland: Presented by a Group of his Pupils and Friends on the Occasion of his Seventy-Fifth Birthday, February 4, 1930.* 141-54. Baltimore: The Johns Hopkins Press, 1930.

On cattle worship among the ancient Scandinavians. After cataloging the evidence, Gould concludes that it is genuine and that "cattle-worship, and in the light of the accounts we have collected here, bull-worship mainly, was the chief animal-cult known in Icelandic tradition and practice."

716. Gould, Chester N. "Gematria." *Modern Language Notes*, 45 (1930), 465-68.

Negative judgement of S. Agrell's theories of numerological magic in runic inscriptions.

717. Gräter, F. D. "Thrym, oder die Wiederlangung des Hammers." *Bragur*, 1 (1791), 306-24.

Introduction, Norse text, Danish translation, and notes to *Þrymskviða.*

718. Gräter, F. D. "Das berühmte Grimnis-Maal oder Die Fabel von Grimnir aus der ältern Edda zum ersten Mal ins Teutsche übersetzt." *Idunna und Hermode*, 1814, pp. 57-59, 117-18, 159-61, 205-07.

First German translation of *Grímnismál*, with occasional commentary in footnotes.

719. Gräter, F. D. "Freya, die Göttin teustcher Liebe und Freue: Ein mythologischer Versuch." *Idunna und Hermode*, 1814, pp. 2-3, 6-7, 37-38.

Early study of Freyja, relying on the Eddas.

720. Gräter, F. D. "Blumenlese zur Geschichte des teutschen Heidenthums." *Idunna und Hermode*, 1816, pp. 69-70, 77-78.

Texts relevant to pagan customs in Germany.

721. Gräter, F. D. "Proben von den Zusätzen zu der neuen Ausgabe der Nordischen Blumen: 1., Der Wurdarborn, oder der Brunnen der Vergangenheit." *Idunna und Hermode*, 1816, pp. 85-87.

Remarks on the well of Urðr.

722. Gräter, F. D. "Proben von den Zusätzen zu der neuen Ausgabe der Nordischen Blumen: 2., Die Schicksalsgöttin Urd, und das Zauberlied Urdarlokur." *Idunna und Hermode*, 1816, pp. 93-96.

Comparative remarks on Urðr.

723. Graf, Heinz Joachim. "Zur Frage der Felsbildluren." *Mannus*, 32 (1940), 408-10.

The horns apparently portrayed on some rock carvings are here interpreted as accompaniments to cult.

724. Grahn, Heinz A. "Völuspá: Versuch einer Deutung." *Wirkendes Wort*, 17 (1967), 289-301.

Attempt at a comprehensive, unified interpretation of *Vǫluspá*. Focus on the poet's understanding of time.

725. Grambo, Ronald. "De tre legende møyer i norske trollformler: En motivhistorisk undersøkelse." *Maal og minne*, 1974, pp. 72-89. Summary in English.

Historically oriented analysis of the motif of three healing maidens who appear in Norwegian magic formulas. The obvious association with the Germanic *matres/matrones* and norns, and the spinning of fate, receives treatment on pp. 77-79. "The conception of the maidens as manifested in our charms must certainly be influenced by old Germanic birth goddesses and goddesses of fatality" (p. 87).

726. Grape, Anders, Gottfrid Kallstenius, and Olof Thorell, eds. *Snorre Sturlassons Edda: Uppsala-handskriften DG 11,* vol. 2. Uppsala: Almqvist & Wiksell International, 1977.

An edition of one of the major manuscripts of Snorri's *Edda*. Contains the transcribed text of DG 11 4to and an extensive palaeographic commentary, both the work of all three editors. The introduction and complete word index were done by Thorell. The volume was issued as part of the 500-year anniversary of the University of Uppsala.

727. Gras, Elizabeth J. "Hávamál." *Neophilologus*, 15 (1930), 131-35.

The construction of the poem.

728. Gras, Elizabeth J. "Lok-Loki." *Neophilologus*, 15 (1930), 219-20.

On an Icelandic scribal error which seems to suggest that *Loki* means "fire."

729. Gras, Elizabeth J. *De noordse Loki-mythen in hun onderling verband.* Neederlandsche bijdragen op het gebied van germaansche philologie en linguistiek, 2. Haarlem: H. D. Tjeenk Willink & Zoon, 1931. 130 pp.

The results of this Utrecht dissertation may be summarized thus. Loki is identical with Lóðurr and was originally a cobold or elf; through his association with Odin he joined the fellowship of the gods, later becoming the companion of Thor. Christianity, however, altered his position. His battle with Heimdallr could be viewed ethically, and he was drawn into the Baldr story to replace Hǫðr. A migratory legend of the bound giant, applied to him as part of the story of his punishment, associated him with the giants. It caused him to join them at Ragnarǫk and to be viewed as the father of the midgard serpent, Fenrir, and Hel.

Perhaps because it is written in Dutch, this attempt to order chronologically Loki's principal characteristics has not been cited as frequently as some other studies of Loki. It must be admitted, however, that the work is speculative, in that the entire hypothetical development is to have taken place before any of the texts were composed, let alone written down.

730. Gras, Elizabeth J. "Mistilteinn." *Neophilologus*, 17 (1932), 293-98.

Finds the mistletoe in the Baldr myth to be original. The sword in Saxo's version is a Nordic replacement.

731. Green, W. C. "East Anglia." *Saga-Book of the Viking Society*, 2 (1897-1900), 262-64.

Cites a folklore parallel in East Anglia to one of the riddles of Gestumblindi in *Heiðreks saga.*

732. Green, W. C. "Fylgja and Fetches." *Saga-Book of the Viking Society*, 3 (1901-03), 207-09.

Scottish, classical, and Old Norse fetches.

733. Greene, Jesse Laurence. "Indo-European Social Tripartism in Book I of the Cædmonian Paraphrase." *Journal of Indo-European Studies*, 6 (1978), 263-78.

"Book I of the Cædmonian Paraphrase (Bodleian MS. Junius 11) provides a clearer insight into the nature and structure of Anglo-Saxon culture and religion than any other single document" (p. 263). Dumézilian tripartition, often based on analysis of vocabulary, with frequent reference to Norse mythology.

734. Greenway, John L. *The Golden Horns: Mythic Imagination and the Nordic Past.* Athens: University of Georgia Press, 1977. 226 pp.

An examination of the "myth" of Nordic origins as a symbolic paradigm for recognizing forms, as manifested in texts from throughout northern Europe, from the Middle Ages to modern times. Includes treatment of *Vǫluspá* (ch. 2, pp. 24-41) and the displacement of the myths of *Vǫluspá* into the family sagas (ch. 3, pp. 42-59).

735. Grienberger, Theodor von. "Germanische Götternamen auf rheinischen Inschriften." *Zeitschrift für deutsches Altertum*, 35 (1891), 388-401.

First of two parts. Interpretation of the following divine names on inscriptions from the Rhineland: Mars halamardus; Dea sandraudiga; Mercurius leudisio; Dea vagdavercustis; Hercules Saxanus.

736. Grienberger, Theodor von. "Germanische Götternamen auf rheinischen Inschriften." *Zeitschrift für deutsches Altertum*, 36 (1892), 308-15.

Second of two parts. Names treated are Dea hariasa; Vihansa; and Dea vagdavercustis.

737. Grienberger, Theodor von. "Dea Garmangabis." *Zeitschrift für deutsches Altertum*, 38 (1894), 189-95.

The etymology and meaning of the name of one of the matrones.

738. Grienberger, Theodor von. "Die Merseburger Zaubersprüche." *Zeitschrift für deutsche Philologie*, 27 (1895), 433-62.

Linguistic analysis and interpretation of the Merseburg charms. In the second charm, Grienberger sees Phol as a German god, perhaps the equivalent of Baldr.

739. Grienberger, Theodor von. "Zu den Merseburger Zaubersprüchen." *Zeitschrift für deutsche Philologie*, 31 (1899), 139.

Addendum to the author's article "Die Merseburger Zaubersprüche" (1895); etymological note to the name *Phol.*

740. Grienberger, Theodor von. "Múspell." *Indogermanische Forschungen*, 16 (1904), 40-63.

Argues that the term is common Germanic and originally meant "mass death" or "mass destruction."

741. Grienberger, Theodor von. "Althochdeutsche Texterklärungen." *Beiträge zur Geschichte der deutschen Sprache und Literatur*, 45 (1921), 212-38.

Pp. 231-34 discuss the Merseburg charms, including the divine name *Phol.*

742. Grimm, Jacob. "Altfriesische Kosmogonie." *Zeitschrift für deutsches Altertum*, 1 (1841), 1-2.

Syncretism in a Frisian cosmogonic passage.

743. Grimm, Jacob. "Schon mehr über Phol." *Zeitschrift für deutsches Altertum*, 2 (1842), 252-57.

Discussion of the German divine name *Phol*, including placename evidence.

744. Grimm, Jacob. "Zu den Merseburger Gedichten." *Zeitschrift für deutsches Altertum*, 2 (1842), 188-90.

On the number of goddesses in the second Merseburg charm.

745. Grimm, Jacob. "Der heilige Hammer." *Zeitschrift für deutsches Altertum*, 5 (1845), 72-74.

An English and German custom possibly associated with Donar/Thor.

746. Grimm, Jacob. "Wodan und Frea bei den Winilen." *Zeitschrift für deutsches Altertum*, 5 (1845), 1-2.

Paul the Deacon on Wodan and Frea/Frigg.

747. Grimm, Jacob. *Abhandlungen zur Mythologie und Sittenkunde. His* Kleinere Schriften, 2. Berlin: F. Dümmler, 1865. 462 pp.

Collection of Grimm's shorter works on mythology. Important for the subject of this bibliography are: "Über zwei entdeckte Gedichte aus der Zeit des deutschen Heidenthums," pp. 1-29 (originally published in 1842; describes and reads the Merseburg charms); "Deutsche Grenzalthümer," pp. 30-74 (originally published in 1843; includes discussion of Donar/Thor and Wuotan/Odin as boundary figures); "Über Schenken und Geben, pp. 173-210 (originally published in 1848; wide-ranging philological essay on the verbs for giving in European languages, ancient and modern; includes reference to Norse mythological themes, such as the drink at the beginning of a contest of wisdom); "Über das Verbrennen der Leichen," pp. 211-313 (originally published in 1849; cremation in ancient Europe, as attested in literary sources, with ample discussion of Norse mythology); "Über den Liebesgott," pp. 314-32 (originally published in 1851; reconstructs a god of love or desire in Indo-European; in Norse sources, both Freyr and Odin are involved); "Über die Namen des Donners," pp. 402-38 (originally published in 1853; words for thunder in Finnish and Indo-European languages; much discussion of Thor).

748. Grimm, Jacob. *Teutonic Mythology*. New York: Dover, 1966. 4 vols. Translated by James Steven Stallybrass.

A translation of the fourth edition of *Deutsche Mythologie* (first ed. 1835), the first systematic study of the myth and religion of the Germanic peoples and the foundation of the discipline. Still useful for its vast collection of data.

749. Grimm, Wilhelm. "Die mythische Bedeutung des Wolfes." *Zeitschrift für deutsches Altertum*, 12 (1860-65), 203-28.

The (unfortunate) mythic image of the wolf in Germanic and German culture. Most of the materials cited come from the German Middle Ages. Karl Müllenhoff adds a brief footnote to the article under the title "Wolf und Wölfin" on p. 252 of the same number of the journal.

750. Grimstad, Kaaren. "The Revenge of Vǫlundr." In *Edda: A Collection of Essays*, eds. Robert J. Glendenning and Haraldur Bessason, 187-209. The University of Manitoba Icelandic Studies, 4. N. p.: University of Manitoba Press, 1983.

Reads *Vǫlundarkviða* on two levels: ". . . the tale of an elf, who wreaks vengeance on the mortal who has stolen his property, imprisoned and crippled him. The poem's dramatic structure is that of the folk legend. . . . On a second level, we have entertained the hypothesis of a substructure in the poem depicting a double initiation rite. On the one hand the king's sons are initiated by Vǫlundr through ritual death to a new level of manhood, perhaps as warriors, and, on the other hand, Vǫlundr himself suffers mutilation through which he increases his power and ascends to a higher realm. . ." (p. 204).

751. Grønbech, Vilhelm. *Lykkemand og niding*. Vor folkeætt i oldtiden, 1. Copenhagen: V. Pio, 1909. 220 pp.

First volume of Grønbech's major study of the inner culture of the Germanic peoples. In this instance, Grønbech probes the essential concepts of peace, honor, and happiness (Danish *lykke*, which Grønbech equates essentially with the force of life). He concludes that all were possible for the ancient Germanic individual only insofar as the individual was part of a kin group.

752. Grønbech, Vilhelm. *Midgård og menneskelivet*. Vor folkeætt i oldtiden, 2. Copenhagen: V. Pio, 1912. 271 pp.

Second volume of Grønbech's major study of the inner culture of the Germanic peoples. Here Grønbech studies the physical and spiritual world of the ancient Germanic peoples and takes up life and death and their interaction with the kin system.

753. Grønbech, Vilhelm. *Hellighed og helligdom*. Vor folkeætt i oldtiden, 3. Copenhagen: V. Pio, 1912. 208 pp.

Third volume of Grønbech's major study of the inner culture of the Germanic peoples. This one, according to its title, studies cult and cult place, but Grønbech takes an extremely broad view of the subject. He allows it to include many forms of interpersonal relationships outside the kin group: special weapons, naming and inheritance, the exchange of gifts, mercantile activity, sharing food, and cult. The underlying notion is the creation of a substitute for the kin group.

754. Grønbech, Vilhelm. *Menneskelivet og guderne.* Vor folkeætt i oldtiden, 4. Copenhagen: V. Pio, 1912. 133 pp.

Fourth volume of Grønbech's major study of the inner culture of the Germanic peoples. As the culmination of the work, Grønbech takes up the relationship between the Germanic peoples and their gods. The focus is not on mythology but on cult: festival, prayer, sacrifice, oaths.

755. Grønbech, Vilhelm. *The Culture of the Teutons.* London: Oxford University Press, Copenhagen: Jespersen og Piøs forlag, 1932. 3 vols. Translated by W. Worster.

Enlarged translation of *Vor folkeæt i oldtiden* (1909-12).

756. Grønbech, Vilhelm. *Kultur und Religion der Germanen.* Hamburg: Hanseatische Verlagsanstalt, 1942. 2 vols. Vol. 1, 343 pp; vol. 2, 337 pp. 1st ed. 1937.

German translation by Ellen Hoffmeyer, edited with a brief introduction by Otto Höfler. The translation follows the Danish original, sometimes using the enlarged English edition.

Höfler's laudatory introduction will serve as a brief summary of the major parts of Grønbech's argument.

757. Gröndal, Benedict. "Um Sæmundar-Eddu og norræna goðafræði, skoðanir Bugges og Rydbergs." *Tímarit hins íslenzka bókmenntafélags*, 13 (1892), 82-169.

Critical survey of the views of S. Bugge and V. Rydberg.

758. Grønvik, Ottar, and Per Hovda. "Über norwegische Gebirgsnamen." *Namn och bygd*, 47 (1959), 149-70.

The mountain *Vesaldo* (Stavanger, Norway), means "the mountain of the holy ones (the dead)."

759. Grønvik, Ottar. *Runene på Tunesteinen: Alfabet, språkform, budskap.* Oslo: Universitetsforlaget, 1981. 263 pp.

Argues the association of ritual and legal activity in Norse funerals, particularly as evidenced by the Tune runestone.

760. Groth, P. "Sjá hǫlf hýnótt." In *Festskrift til Finnur Jónsson 29. maj 1928.* 240-43. Copenhagen: Levin & Munksgaard, 1928.

On the etymology of *hýnótt* (*Skírnismál* 42) and its use in the phrase *sjá hǫlf hýnótt*, which Groth understands as ironic: "this night when the wedding is only half completed."

761. Grottanelli, Christiano. "Un passo del libro dei Giudici alla luce della comparazione storico-religiosa: Il guidice Ehud e il valore della mano sinistra." In *Atti del 1. convegno italiano sul vicino oriente antico (Roma, 22-24 aprile 1976).* 35-45. Orientis Antiqui Collectio, 13. Rome: Centro per le antichità e la storia dell'arte dei vicino oriente, 1978.

Drawing on the myth of Týr as one of three major examples, Grottanelli analyzes the symbolic value of the left hand: in a right-left binary scheme, it is powerful but impure.

762. Gruber, Loren C. "The Rites of Passage: *Hávamál*, Stanzas 1-5." *Scandinavian Studies*, 49 (1977), 330-39.

Gruber offers a "mythic" reading of the openings stanzas of *Hávamál* in the spirit of Joseph Campbell and Mircea Eliade: the guest crossing thresholds echoes archetypes of birth (the child entering the world; the soul entering the body) and death (arrival in Valhalla). Gruber finds additional examples of the theme of crossing thresholds to acquire knowledge in *Hávamál* 92 and 106 (reference to Odin's gaining of knowledge in giantland) and 134-35 (guests equated with "shrivelled bags" from which clear words issue).

This article represents one of the few attempts to apply archetypal criticism to Norse materials.

Grüner Nielsen, H., *see* Nielsen, H. Grüner.

763. Grundtvig, N. F. S. *Nordens mythologi eller sindbilled-sprog, historisk-poetisk udviklet og oplyst,* 3rd ed. Copenhagen: J. H. Schuboth, 1870. xx, 586 pp. 1st ed. 1808. Rpt. (of this 3rd ed.) 1983.

Grundtvig's interpretation of the mythology is important in the history of ideas in nineteenth-century Denmark. In effect, he used the mythology as a springboard for a philosophical commentary.

764. Grundtvig, N. F. S. *Nordens mythologie: Fotografisk optryk af 3. udgave fra 1870.* Copenhagen: Samlerens forlag, 1983. 15, xx, 586 pp.

Rpt. of Grundtvig's *Nordens mythologi eller sindbilled-sprog, historisk-poetisk udviklet og oplyst* (1870), with foreword (pp. 6-15 of the new front matter) by Poul Engberg.

765. Gruppe, Otto. *Die griechischen Culte und Mythen in ihren Beziehungen zu den orientalischen Religionen,* vol. 1: *Einleitung* [All that appeared]. Leipzig: B. G. Teubner, 1887. xviii, 706 pp.

In passing, argues also for a Near Eastern background for Germanic myth and religion.

766. Gsänger, Hans. *Die Externsteine,* 2nd ed. Mysterienstätten der Menschheit. Freiburg: Die Kommenden, 1968. 241 pp.

Proposes a series of chronological cult layers for the *Externsteine*, of which one is a "Wodan-layer" (ca. 1500-530 B.C.) and one a "Germanic layer" (ca. 2-772 A.D.).

767. Gschwantler, Otto. "Christus, Thor und die Midgardschlange." In *Festschrift für Otto Höfler zum 65. Geburtstag*, eds. Helmut Birkhan and Otto Gschwantler, 145-68. Vienna: Notring, 1968.

The author attempts to demonstrate that early Christianity deliberately seized on the similarity between the legend of Christ and Leviathan and the myth of Thor and the midgard serpent, in order to make use of the myth as Christian allegory. Besides narrative traditions, the Gosforth and Kirk Andreas crosses receive analysis as examples of the importance of the old myth in the new context.

768. Guðmundsson, Barði. *The Origin of the Icelanders (Uppruni Íslendinga).* Lincoln: University of Nebraska Press, 1967. x, 173 pp. Translated by Lee M. Hollander. Icelandic original 1959.

Argues that Iceland was settled not by Norwegian nobles but rather by an East Scandinavian upper-class group ultimately of Herulean origin. This people differed from the West Scandinavians in several important ways, including the prominence of the cult of Freyr.

769. Guðmundsson, Finnbogi. "Hvernig lýsir Snorri Sturluson orðfæri manna?" In *Á góðu dægri: Afmæliskveðja til Sigurðar Nordals 14. sept. 1951 frá yngstu nemendum hans.* 58-75. [Reykjavik]: Helgafell, [1951?].

On Snorri Sturluson's literary portrayals of men of few words, compared with Snorri's own apparent taciturnity. Many examples from *Snorra edda.*

770. Guðmundsson, Valtýr. *Island i fristatstiden.* Folkelæsning, 338. Copenhagen: G. E. C. Gad, in commission, 1924. 186 pp.

Popular account of Iceland during the saga period, with discussion of religious attitudes and cult (chapter 1) and the conversion and early Christianity (chapter 5).

Guðmundur Björnsson, *see* Björnsson, Guðmundur.

Guðmundur Finnbogason, *see* Finnbogason, Guðmundur.

771. Guðnason, Bjarni. "Þankar um siðfræði Íslendingasagna." *Skírnir*, 139 (1965), 65-82.

Explores the difficulties of explaining family saga ethics as either pagan or Christian, with comparison of ethics in *Hávamál* and family sagas.

772. Güntert, Hermann. *Über altisländische Berserker-geschichten*. Beilage zum Jahresbericht des Heidelberger Gymnasiums 1912. Heidelberg: J. Hörning, 1912. 33 pp.

Early study of narratives concerning berserks.

773. Güntert, Hermann. *Von der Sprache der Götter und Geister: Bedeutungsgeschichtliche Untersuchungen zur homerischen und eddischen Göttersprache*. Halle a. d. S.: M. Niemeyer, 1921. viii, 183 pp.

The first part of this study of "the language of the gods and spirits" deals generally with word-superstition, word magic, and such related topics as glossolalia. Güntert then examines two examples of the language of gods among Indo-Europeans: in Homer and related later Greek poets (pp. 89-130) and in the eddic *Alvíssmál* (pp. 130-60). The later section is of interest to students of Norse mythology in part for its analysis of detail, in part for its attempts to distinguish archaic material from metaphorical; Güntert finds more of the latter than the former.

774. Güntert, Hermann. *Der arische Weltkönig und Heiland: Bedeutungsgeschichtliche Untersuchungen zur indo-iranischen Religionsgeschichte und Altertumskunde*. Halle a. d. S.: M. Niemeyer, 1923. x, 439 pp. Rpt. Hildesheim: Gerstenberg, 1977.

This justly famous treatment of Indic religion touches frequently on Germanic and is particularly useful for its remarks on proto-beings and the myths of creation (pp. 315-94).

775. Güntert, Hermann. *Altgermanischer Glaube nach Wesen und Grundlage*. Kultur und Sprache, 10. Heidelberg: C. Winter, 1937. 141 pp.

Idiosyncratic survey of ancient Germanic belief, stressing the opposition between the cultures of aboriginal megalithic agriculture and Indo-European peoples.

776. Günther, Hans F. K. *The Religious Attitudes of the Indo-Europeans*. London: Clair Press, 1967. 127 pp. Translation, by Vivian Bird in collaboration with Roger Pearson, of the author's *Frömmigkeit nordischer Artung*, 6th ed., Bebenburg: Pähl, 1963.

The opening chapter puts Germanic religion in its Indo-European context, stressing Odin as a latecomer; thereafter mention of Germanic religion and Norse mythology recurs at frequent intervals. The work offers an interesting alternative to the theories of Dumézil and his followers.

777. Guerber, H. A. *Myths of Northern Lands: Narrated with Special Reference to Literature and Art.* New York, Cincinnati, Chicago: American Book Co., 1895. 319 pp. Rpt. Detroit: Singing Tree Press, 1970.

Handbook, arranged by gods and inclining toward nature mythology. The last chapter compares Greek and Norse mythology (pp. 274-92).

778. Guggisberg, Kurt. *Germanisches Christentum im Frühmittelalter.* Bern: H. Lang, 1935. 30 pp.

Inaugural lecture, treating early Germanic Christianity.

779. Guichard, René. *De la mythologie scandinave: Des Eddas, des sagas, des drapas, des runas: Suite à l'essai sur l'histoire du peuple burgonde.* Paris: A. & J. Picard, 1971. 76 pp.

Brief dictionary of Scandinavian mythology and related subjects, followed by a previously published essay on the history of the Burgundians.

780. Gunnarsson, Gunnar. *Nordischer Schicksalsgedanke, eine Rede.* Munich: A. Langen, G. Müller, 1936. 18 pp. Translated by Helmut de Boor.

Nordic belief in fate, from an essentially racist point of view.

781. Gurevich, A. Ya. "Space and Time in the *Weltmodell* of the Old Scandinavian Peoples." *Mediaeval Scandinavia,* 2 (1969), 42-53.

On space: the cosmos is parallel to the farmstead, with an enclosed, cultivated center and a surrounding outer area. The conception of the cosmos was primarily horizontal, not vertical as in Christianity.

On time: the perception of time involved not duration but some specific content, frequently anthropomorphous—thus, e.g., *ǫld* meant "age" and "men." Time was generally cyclic, referenced to the mythic beginning, and chronology was basically only reckoned in terms of genealogy—Gurevich calls this phenomenon "kinship time." Further, time was as tangible as the real world. It was ordered by the gods at creation.

"Thus the mythological vision of the universe was characterized by the qualitative heterogeneity of both time and space. Some points of time, as well as some places, were sacral and specially protected by divine forces. Such were the periods of festivities and of the established peace, and the sanctuaries, burial grounds, public assembly places, farmsteads dedicated to the gods. Space was perceived symbolically. This was the way the ancient Scandinavians viewed the whole world, as may be seen from their poetry and arts" (p. 53).

782. Gurevich, A. Ya. "Saga and History: The Historical Conception of Snorri Sturluson." *Mediaeval Scandinavia,* 4 (1971), 42-53.

"To find the 'general tenor' concealed in *Heimskringla* means to evaluate it as a historical source, and in particular as a monument formed under the impress of a developing historical outlook in a society which thought mainly in categories of myth" (p. 43). Gurevich offers analysis, mainly centering on *Ynglinga saga*, of luck and fate as fundamental concepts in Snorri's view of history.

783. Gurevich, A. Ya. *Istoriya i saga*. Moscow: Nauka, 1972. 198 pp.

A study of *Heimskringla* as a historical source, with several sections pertinent to the interpretation of Scandinavian myth and religion: dreams and visions (pp. 42-51), myth and legend (pp. 74-81), and the paganism of Christians or the Christianity of pagans (pp. 166-75).

784. Gurevich, A. Ya. "On the Nature of the Comic in the Elder Edda: A Comment on an Article by Professor Höfler." *Mediaeval Scandinavia*, 9 (1976), 127-37.

Occasioned by Otto Höfler's "Götterkomik: Zur Selbstrelativierung des Mythos" (1971), Gurevich's perceptive comment focuses on *Lokasenna* and Loki but is addressed to all the "burlesque" in the Poetic Edda. Gurevich finds the comic "an integral part of the sacral" (p. 132), a part which demonstrates the freedom of the gods from tabus and other constraints on men and hence reaffirms the sanctity of the deities.

785. Gurevich, A. Ya. "Om det heroiskas natur i germanfolkens poesi (företrädesvis i 'Den ældre Eddan')." *Scandia*, 44 (1978), 99-228. Translated by Marianne Sahlen. Summary in English.

Finds a ritual layer behind the "most archaic" and puzzling motifs in Germanic heroic poetry.

786. Gurevich, A. Ya. *'Edda' i saga*. Moscow: Izdatel'stvo "Nauka", 1979. 192 pp.

The opening chapter (pp. 7-24) of this handbook of edda and saga conains introductory remarks on the mythic and ritual background of the Poetic Edda, and a later chapter (pp. 71-90) treats its "comic nature."

787. Gurevich, A. Ya. "'Pryad o Torsteyne moroz-po-kozhe': Zagrobniy mir i islandskiy yumor." *Skandinaviskii sbornik*, 24 (1979), 125-32. Summary in Swedish.

On the influence of the mixture of pagan and Christian elements in the formation of *Þorsteins þáttr skelks.*

788. Gurevich, A. Ya. *Das Weltbild des mittelalterlichen Menschen,* 3rd ed. Munich: C. H. Beck, 1986. 423 pp. Translated by Gabriele Lossack with Hubert Mohr. Russian orig. 1972; 1st German ed. Dresden: VEB Verlag der Kunst, 1978.

Although direct references to Norse mythology are only sporadic in this work, it is important in putting the Norse material in the context of medieval European world view. The focus of the work is on space and time.

789. Gustavson, Herbert. "Gotlands ortnamn." *Ortnamnssällskapets i Uppsala årsskrift*, 3 (1938), 1-58.

With discussion of theophoric and cult placenames on Gotland.

790. Gutenbrunner, Siegfried. "Beiträge zur Deutung einiger Runendenkmäler." *Acta Philologica Scandinavica*, 11 (1936-37), 162-73.

The Frøihov (Norway) bronze figurine may contain a reference to the long-haired priest of the *dioscurii*; the Kragehul shaft may be dedicated to Ómi, an ancient Odin name; the word *leþro* on the Staarup diadem may mean "the leather one," perhaps a reference to Nerthus.

791. Gutenbrunner, Siegfried. *Die germanischen Götternamen der antiken Inschriften.* Rheinische Beiträge und Hülfsbücher zur germanischen Philologie und Volkskunde, 24. Halle a. d. S.: M. Niemeyer, 1936. xii, 260 pp.

Monographic treatment of the names of Germanic gods on ancient inscriptions.

792. Gutenbrunner, Siegfried. "Zur Gutasaga." *Zeitschrift für deutsches Altertum*, 73 (1936), 159-63.

On the mythic and religious background of *Guta saga.*

793. Gutenbrunner, Siegfried. "Der Kult des Weltherrschers bei den Semnonen und ein altnorwegischer Rechtsbrauch." *Acta Philologica Scandinavica*, 14 (1939-40), 102-08.

Gutenbrunner compares the prescriptions on fallen worshippers of the *regnator omnium deus* among the Semnones (Tacitus, *Germania*, ch. 39) with the legal expression *veltask ór* "to fall out of" attested in various descriptions of ancient Naumudal, Norway. He finds that an involuntary act among the Semnones may have become the voluntary act of the Norwegians and centers the complex on ancestor worship. The fall of Geirrøðr on his sword (*Grímnismál* 53 and prose frame) may also be relevant.

794. Gutenbrunner, Siegfried. "Die Inschrift von Eggjum und die Geschichte von Kjalar." *Beiträge zur Geschichte der deutschen Sprache und Literatur*, 64 (1940), 229-37.

Interpretation of the apparent Odin name *Kjalarr* (*Grímnismál* 49) and similar evidence, in light of the Eggjum runic inscription.

795. Gutenbrunner, Siegfried. "Eddica." *Zeitschrift für deutsches Altertum*, 77 (1940), 12-15.

Includes textual remarks on *Hymiskviða* 2.

796. Gutenbrunner, Siegfried. "*Fanesii* und *Fenrir.*" *Zeitschrift für deutsches Altertum*, 77 (1940), 25-26.

Brief note associating the *Fanesii* in Pliny with Fenrir.

797. Gutenbrunner, Siegfried. "Der Büchertitel Edda." *Beiträge zur Geschichte der deutschen Sprache und Literatur*, 66 (1942), 276-77.

The author draws attention to other shortened titles, e.g., *Njála* or *Skalda*, and speculates whether Snorri's account might have been called **Eddumál* or **Eddusaga.*

798. Gutenbrunner, Siegfried. "Über die Träger des Himmelgewölbes im germanischen Mythos." *Archiv für Religionswissenschaft*, 37 (1942), 270-72.

Alamannic evidence to support the mythic authenticity of Snorri's statement that four dwarfs hold up the sky.

799. Gutenbrunner, Siegfried. "Der zweite Merseburger Spruch im Lichte nordischer Überlieferungen." *Zeitschrift für deutsches Altertum*, 80 (1943-44), 1-5.

Proposed emendation to the second Merseburg charm, making possible close association with Baldr myth.

800. Gutenbrunner, Siegfried. *Schleswig-Holsteins älteste Literatur von der Kombernzeit bis zur Gudrundichtung.* Kiel: W. G. Mühlau, 1949. 103 pp.

Includes discussion of *Vǫluspá.*

801. Gutenbrunner, Siegfried. "Über zwei germanische Heiligtümer bei Plinius und bei Ptolemaios." *Zeitschrift für deutsches Altertum*, 83 (1951-52), 157-62.

Using a passage in Pliny's *Natural History* and two placenames in Ptolemy's *Geography*, Gutenbrunner constructs sacred groves in oak forests and associates them with Odin.

802. Gutenbrunner, Siegfried. "Heldenleben und Heldendichtung: Eine Nachlese zu Otto Höflers Rökbuch." *Zeitschrift für deutsche Philologie*, 73 (1954), 365-406.

First of two parts probing the findings of O. Höfler, *Germanisches Sakralkönigtum* (1952). Gutenbrunner approves.

803. Gutenbrunner, Siegfried. "Heldenleben und Heldendichtung: Eine Nachlese zu Otto Höflers Rökbuch." *Zeitschrift für deutsche Philologie*, 74 (1955), 113-26.

Second of two parts probing the findings of O. Höfler, *Germanisches Sakralkönigtum* (1952). Gutenbrunner approves.

804. Gutenbrunner, Siegfried. "Über die Zwerge in der Völuspá." *Arkiv för nordisk filologi*, 70 (1955), 61-75.

On the list of dwarf names in *Vǫluspá*, str. 10-16. The ritual text to an *álfablót* may stand behind the names in str. 11-12.

805. Gutenbrunner, Siegfried. "Balders Wiederkehr: Südostgermanisches in der Völuspá?" *Germanisch-Romanisch Monatsschrift*, 37 (1956), 67-72.

Explores the possibility that the Baldr myth may have originated as a Gothic loan.

806. Gutenbrunner, Siegfried. "Eddastudien II: Skuld helt skildi, / en Skǫgul ǫnnor." *Arkiv för nordisk filologi*, 71 (1956), 14-24.

The subtitle is a line from *Vǫluspá*, str. 30, which Gutenbrunner sets alongside str. 20. He constructs an elaborate set of parallels between the norns Verðandi and Skuld and the valkyries Skǫgul and Skuld, in light of various other Germanic figures and their hypothetical associations with cult.

807. Gutenbrunner, Siegfried. "Vorindogermanisches bei den rheinischen Germanen?" *Zeitschrift für deutsches Altertum*, 88 (1957-58), 241-49.

Speculation regarding pre-Indo-European strata in the Rhineland, in large part from a religious perspective. A proto-Herjann, associated with horses, will have been the chief god of the Istaevones and may have taken over traits and cult of earlier deities.

808. Gutenbrunner, Siegfried. "Eddastudien III: Über *ek* und *hon* in der *Völospa*." *Arkiv för nordisk filologi*, 72 (1957), 7-12.

On the variation between first and third person to refer to the seeress in *Vǫluspá*. Gutenbrunner sees two sides to the poem, represented by the two pronouns. "I" stands for the kernel of knowledge and power of personality of the seeress, "she" for the seeress's immanence (*Bestimmtsein*) and relation to Odin. These in turn, Gutenbrunner feels, may ultimately have to do with two traditions in which the poem was used: one of performance and one of learned wisdom.

809. Gutenbrunner, Siegfried. "Über Ausstrahlungen deutscher Lyrik in die Edda." *Zeitschrift für deutsche Philologie*, 77 (1958), 245-59.

Proposes influence of German lyric on, inter alia, the gnomic section of *Hávamál*.

810. Gutenbrunner, Siegfried. "Vortragsregeln für die Vǫluspá." *Zeitschrift für deutsche Philologie*, 77 (1958), 1-25.

Gutenbrunner attempts to elicit rules for the dramatic recitation of *Vǫluspá*.

811. Gutenbrunner, Siegfried. "Sprachliche Toreutik der Skalden." In *Die Wissenschaft von deutscher Sprache und Dichtung: Methoden, Probleme, Aufgaben [Festschrift für Friedrich Maurer zum 65. Geburtstag am 5. Januar 1963]*, ed. Siegfried Gutenbrunner et al., 284-304. Stuttgart: E. Klett, 1963.

With remarks on Egill Skallagrímsson's religious attitude as reflected in *Sonatorrek* (pp. 292-93).

812. Gutenbrunner, Siegfried. "Ritennamen—Kultnamen—Mythennamen der Götter." In *Namenforschung: Festschrift für Adolf Bach zum 75. Geburtstag am 31. Januar 1965*, eds. Rudolf Schützeichel and Matthias Zender, 17-31. Heidelberg: C. Winter, 1965.

Distinguishes three levels of significance in religion: ritual, cult, and myth, and attempts to apply this distinction to the second Merseburg charm. Gutenbrunner's findings include: the name *Phol* derives from *Fol*, a ritual name related to *full* and thus to ritual libation; *Sinhtgunt* "she who restrains the journey to the thing" and *Sunna* "she who acknowledges legitimate dealings" are valkyrie-like figures; Baldr is the cult name of a young noble worthy of royal dignities because of his birth but hindered by his early death from carrying out a warlike deed—earlier it was a ritual name.

813. Gutenbrunner, Siegfried. "Ostern: Neue Materialien zum Synkretismus der Merowingerzeit." In *Festschrift Walter Baetke dargebracht zu seinem 80. Geburtstage am 28. März 1964*, ed. Kurt Rudolf et al., 122-29. Weimar: H. Böhlau, 1966.

In arguing that Old High German *ôstarun* (German *Ostern*, English *Easter*) is an early Germanic translation of *pascha* "Savior's redemptive death on the cross," Gutenbrunner discusses the root *ausa-* as part of a complex having to do with ritual and myth of the god sacrificed on the tree (Odin and Baldr).

H

814. Hachmann, Rolf. *The Germanic Peoples.* Archaeologia Mundi. Geneva: Nagel, 1971. 208 pp. Translated by James Hogarth.

Handbook of Germanic archaeology, with much discussion of cult and religion.

The German original was issued simultaneously in the same series as *Die Germanen* (Geneva: Nagel, 203 pp.).

815. Hachmeister, Carl Ernst. *Nordische Mythologie nach den Quellen bearbeitet und systematisch zusammengestellt: Ein Handbuch.* Hannover: Hahn'sche Hofbuchhandl., 1832. xi, 316 pp.

Early handbook.

816. Hægstad, Marius. "Um namnet Oskoreidi." *Maal og minne,* 1912, pp. 80-85.

Derives the Norwegian term *Oskoreidi* "Wild Hunt" from older *ásgoðreið* "those who accompany the *æsir* gods."

817. Hagberg, Ulf Erik. "Skedemosse—en första presentation." *Fornvännen,* 56 (1961), 237-55. Summary in German.

On excavations on the island of Öland, Sweden, with important information on sacrifice and sacrificial customs.

818. Hagberg, Ulf Erik. "Blotare i Skedemosse." *Tor,* 9 (1963), 144-62. Summary in German, pp. 158-61.

Archaeological report on an apparent sacrificial site on Öland, Sweden.

819. Hagberg, Ulf Erik. "Järnålderns offerfynd ur svenskt perspektiv." *Tor,* 10 (1964), 222-36. Summary in German, pp. 233-35.

Archaeological treatment of apparent sacrificial rites. The focus is on Skedemosse, Öland, Sweden.

820. Hagberg, Ulf Erik. "Religionsgeschichtliche Aspekte des Moorfundes vom Skedemosse auf Öland." In *Vorgeschichtliche Heiligtümer und Opferplätze in Mittel- und Nordeuropa: Bericht über ein Symposium in Reinhausen bei Göttingen vom 14.-16. Oktober 1968*, ed. Herbert Jankuhn, 167-71. Abhandlungen der Akademie der Wissenschaften in Göttingen, phil.-hist. Kl., 3. Folge, 74. Göttingen: Vandenhoeck & Ruprecht, 1970.

Archaeological interpretation of a single cult area, according to the author an important one.

821. Hagen, Friedrich Heinrich von der. *Lieder der älteren oder Sämundischen Edda*. Berlin: Bei Haude und Spener, 1812. xii, cxviii, 98 pp.

Early edition and study of eddic poetry.

822. Hagen, Friedrich Heinrich von der. *Irmin; seine Säule, seine Strasse und sein Wagen: Einladung zu Vorlesungen über altdeutsche und altnordische Götterlehre*. Breslau: J. Max, 1817. iv, 68 pp.

Early study of Irmin.

823. Hagen, Friedrich Heinrich von der. *Die Nibelungen, ihre Bedeutung für die Gegenwart und für immer*. Breslau: Max, 1819. 224 pp.

Early study linking heroic poetry and religion.

824. Hagen, Friedrich Heinrich von der. "Die deutschen Wochentagegötter." *Germania*, 1 (1836), 18-38, 344-77.

Solar, lunar, and astral myth and customs associated with the names of the weekdays. P. 377 promises a conclusion to follow.

825. Hagen, Friedrich Heinrich von der. "Heidnischer Aberglaube aus dem Gewissensspiegel des Predigers Martin von Amberg." *Germania*, 2 (1837), 63-65.

Presents a brief German text on superstition.

826. Hagen, Friedrich Heinrich von der. "Urkunden des deutschen Heidenthums zur Zeit des Heiligen Bonifacius." *Germania*, 2 (1837), 59-63.

Three eighth-century German documents relating to paganism.

827. Hagen, S. N. "Om navnet Fenrisulfr." *Maal og minne*, 1910, pp. 57-59.

Suggests an etymology for the Fenris wolf: **fen-hrís-ulfr* "fen-bush-wolf, i.e., wolf lying in the swamp." This would be associated with the description of Behemoth in the Book of Job.

828. Hagen, S. N. "On the Origin of the Name *Kvasir*." *Arkiv för nordisk filologi*, 28 (1912), 127-39.

Any journal article bearing a disclaimer from the editor (p. 127, fn. 1) must raise suspicion. Here one's suspicions will be justified, for Hagen's attempt to show that the main features of Snorri's account of the origin of Kvasir "are based upon Latin stories concerning Orion" (p. 129) relies on an improbable Latin misreading and leads to the postulation of the borrowing of a story which in fact shares little with the Kvasir myth.

829. Hagman, Nore. "Kring några motiv i Håvamål." *Arkiv för nordisk filologi*, 72 (1957), 13-24.

Parallels between *Hávamál* and Ecclesiastes of the Old Testament.

830. Hahn, E. E. *Heiligtümer der German: Ausradiert, Rekonstruiert: Eine Dreiheit germanischer Naturheiligtümer und ein Opferplatz im süddeutschen Raum.* Gerabronn: Hohenloher, 1970. 48 pp.

A triplet of natural cult places: rock, spring, tree; general treatment of early south Germanic cult activity.

831. Hahne, Hans. *Totenehre im alten Norden.* Jena: E. Diederichs, 1929. vii, 144 pp. With 77 drawings by Kurt Richter.

Cult of the dead.

832. Hald, Kristian. "The Cult of Odin in Danish Place-names." In *Early English and Norse Studies Presented to Hugh Smith in Honour of his Sixtieth Birthday*, eds. Arthur Brown and Peter Foote, 99-109. London: Methuen, 1963.

As Danish placenames in *-vi* are always compounded with the name of Odin, Hald concludes that "a single god, Odin, played a completely dominant role in the public cult" (p. 107). As the official, higher religion of the Danes, the cult of the single god, Odin, may have eased the transition to Christianity.

Halldór Hermansson, *see* Hermansson, Halldór.

833. Hale, Christopher S. "The River Names in *Grímnismál* 27-29." In *Edda: A Collection of Essays*, eds. Robert J. Glendenning and Haraldur Bessason, 165-86. The University of Manitoba Icelandic Studies, 4. N. p.: University of Manitoba Press, 1983.

A survey, primarily linguistic, of the names in question. All could once have referred to real rivers, mostly in Norway and the rest of Scandinavia. They may have been found in doggerels used to recall boundaries (*deildevers*) and been combined therefrom in an interpolation into *Grímnismál.*

834. Hallberg, Peter. "Världsträdet och världsbranden: Ett motiv i Völuspá." *Arkiv för nordisk filologi*, 67 (1952), 145-55.

Interpretation of *Vǫluspá*, str. 57: *aldnari* refers to the world tree, not fire, and the line in question means "fire rages at the world tree, the high flame plays against heaven itself." To support the interpretation, Hallberg discusses the other occurrences of the world tree in the poem and assigns the tree a dominant role, carefully and esthetically planned and carried out by the poet.

835. Hallberg, Peter. "Om Þrymskviða." *Arkiv för nordisk filologi*, 69 (1954), 51-77.

Argues that Snorri composed Þrymskviða. Cf. G. Lindblad, "Snorre Sturlasson och eddadiktningen" (1978).

836. Hallberg, Peter. "Elements of Imagery in the *Edda*." In *Edda: A Collection of Essays*, eds. Robert J. Glendenning and Haraldur Bessason, 47-85. The University of Manitoba Icelandic Studies, 4. N. p.: University of Manitoba Press, 1983.

Includes discussion of the mythological poems. More generally, concludes Hallberg: "Mythology and human life intermingle. Not only do gods and valkyries appear from time to time among men, giving them advice and directing the course of events, in the kennings men are also seen as gods, women as goddesses or valkyries. The supernatural creatures of myth have their counterparts in the social life of men" (p. 83).

837. Halldórsson, Óskar. "Snorri og Edda." In *Snorri: Átta alda minning*. 89-111. Reykjavik: Sögufélagið, 1979.

A survey of the background and contents of Snorri's *Edda* for a popular Icelandic volume honoring the 800th anniversary of Snorri's birth.

838. Halleux, Pierre. "Hrafnkel's Character Reinterpreted." *Scandinavian Studies*, 38 (1966), 36-44.

In part on Hrafnkell's attitude toward the god Freyr.

839. Hallström, Gustaf. *Monumental Art of Northern Europe from the Stone Age*, vol. 1: *The Norwegian Localities*. Stockholm: Thule, 1938. 544 pp.

Stone Age rock carvings from Norway.

840. Halsall, Maureen. *The Old English Rune Poem: A Critical Edition*. McMaster Old English Studies and Texts, 2. Toronto: University of Toronto Press, 1981. x, 197 pp.

Contains general introductory material on runes (pp. 3-20) emphasizing alleged magical use.

841. Hamel, A. G. van. "Vǫluspá 27-29." *Arkiv för nordisk filologi*, 41 (1925), 293-305.

Attempts to clarify the expression *veð Valfǫðrs* "pledge of Valfǫðr" on the basis of folk beliefs; argues that *Mímr* is the original form, not *Mímir*.

842. Hamel, A. G. van. "Gods, Skalds and Magic." *Saga-Book of the Viking Society*, 11 (1928-36), 129-52.

Loosely organized paper, with many good points, ranging from Germanic religion to recent Icelandic folklore. The central elements include the need of gods and men to get into contact with secret powers outside of and within themselves and thus "to rule an often ill-favoured and hostile world. . ." (p. 152). Magic is the means; gods are the mediators who bring it to men; skalds control it with their craft.

843. Hamel, A. G. van. "The Conception of Fate in Early Teutonic and Celtic Religion." *Saga-Book of the Viking Society*, 11 (1928-36), 202-14.

Stresses the importance of death as the focus of Germanic fatalism; even the gods die, at Ragnarǫk. Each man and god, however, has the freedom to pursue his own course.

844. Hamel, A. G. van. "The Prose-Frame of Lokasenna." *Neophilologus*, 14 (1929), 204-14.

The redactor of *Lokasenna*, according to van Hamel, added the prose frame to reconcile conflicting versions of myths of Loki, in particular as concerns the origin of the net used to capture Loki and the circumstances of his entering and re-entering the hall. Originally the gods met to determine the punishment of Loki; later their meeting was identified with an ordinary banquet.

845. Hamel, A. G. van. "De samenhang der *Vǫluspá*." *Neophilologus*, 16 (1931), 196-205.

Reading of *Vǫluspá*, stressing its inner unity.

846. Hamel, A. G. van. "Óðinn Hanging on the Tree." *Acta Philologica Scandinavica*, 7 (1932-33), 260-88.

On *Hávamál*, str. 138-42. After a review of previous interpretations, van Hamel undertakes to explain the myth on its own terms, without recourse to Christian influence. He draws a parallel with *Grímnismál*: in each text Odin endures suffering in order to call up his divine magic power (*ásmegin*). "Óðinn is not the absolute master of his own divine power. He is like a mortal in this that the supernatural force within him is of a magical character and must be actualized by means of magic. Once it has been animated, no magic can resist it. In the rune-myth he desires to become the lord of the runes, and attains this on the ninth day after a period of fasting and torturing himself against their magic power. In Grímnismál we find the fasting and the fire-test, intended as a torture by Geirrøðr, but in the deeper sense an expedient to raise the god's *ásmegin*. Geirrøðr is annihilated just as the runes must yield. There is the identical result in the two cases" (p. 286).

847. Hamel, A. G. van. "Gambanteinn." *Neophilologus*, 17 (1932), 136-43 and 234-39.

Discussion of the term *gambanteinn* (*Skírnismál* 32; *Hávamál* 90) and other words in *gamban-*. The root is said to be related to *afl* "wealth," implying a development from wealth to power to supernatural power.

848. Hamel, A. G. van. "The Game of the Gods." *Arkiv för nordisk filologi*, 50 (1934), 218-42.

Interprets *Vǫluspá*: the game played by the gods during the golden age (str. 8) ruled the world, independently of their will. The end of the game resulted in *Ragnarǫk*, and thereafter the survivors find the game board (str. 61) and initiate a new golden age. Cites a Welsh parallel, which, however, Reidar Th. Christiansen rejected in his *Studies in Irish and Scandinavian Folktales* (Copenhagen: Rosenkilde and Bagger, for Coimisiún Béaloideasa Éireann, 1959), pp. 218-19.

849. Hamel, A. G. van. "The Mastering of the Mead." In *Studia Germanica tillägnade Ernst Albin Kock den 6 december 1934*. 76-85. Lund: C. Blom, 1934.

Derives Snorri's account of the acquisition of the mead of poetry from two variants supposedly concatenated and adapted by Snorri: in the first Odin obtained the mead from Baugi, in the second from Suttungr's daughter. In each, Odin escaped by drilling his way out of the mountain. The source of the first was "popular tradition," of the second *Hávamál* 104-10. Snorri prefaced his account by adapting a legend of the devil (Odin's tricking Baugi's workers to kill each other). Speculative.

850. Hamel, A. G. van. "De islandse gang tegen de zon." *Neophilologus*, 20 (1935), 212-23.

On the ritual, attested in medieval Icelandic literature and later, or riding against the path of the sun (*andsœlis*). Van Hamel puts the ritual in the context of the oldest Germanic sun worship and of conceptions suggested by eddic poetry.

851. Hammarstedt, N. E. "Kvarlevor av en Frös-ritual i en svensk bröllopslek." In *Festskrift til H. F. Feilberg fra nordiske sprog- og folkemindeforskere på 80 års dagen den 6. august 1911*. 489-517. Svenska landsmål, 1911; Maal og minne, 1911; Danske studier, 1911. Stockholm: Norstedt, Copenhagen: Gyldendal, Oslo (Kristiania): Bymaals-laget, 1911.

Alleged traces of fertility ritual, centered on Freyr, in a Swedish bridal custom.

852. Hammarstedt, N. E. "Olsmessa och Torsblot." *Fataburen*, 1915, pp. 32-40, 89-91.

Finnish and Swedish harvest ceremonies around the feast of St. Olaf associated with hypothetical older worship of Thor. Hammarstedt suggests that the older pagan ceremonies may have been assimilated by Christianity.

Pp. 89-91 comprise a supplement.

853. Hammarstedt, N. E. "Elias, Åskguden: Ännu ett tillägg till 'Olsmessa och Torsblot.'" *Fataburen*, 1916, pp. 21-29.

Supplement to the author's "Olsmessa och Torsblot" (1915), spreading a wider net over traditions of harvest ceremonies.

854. Hammerbacher, H. W. *Irminsul und Lebensbaum*. Heusenstamm: Orion-Heimreiter, 1973. 223 pp.

In its appeal to a German spirit, this tracing of the image of the Irminsûl/tree of life in German history is something of a throwback to earlier German scholarship.

855. Hammerich, Frederik. *Nordens ældste digt, oplyst og oversat*. Copenhagen: Gyldendal (F. Hegel), 1876. 138 pp.

Lengthy discussion of *Vǫluspá*, followed by text and Danish translation.

856. Hammerich, L. L. "Ein Reiterstück (Tacitus, *Germania* c. 6)." In *Fragen und Forschungen im Bereich und Umkreis der germanischen Philologie: Festgabe für Theodor Frings zum 70. Geburtstag, 23 Juli 1956*, eds. Elisabeth Karg-Gasterstädt and Johannes Erben, 283-97. Deutsche Akademie der Wissenschaften zu Berlin; Veröffentlichungen des Instituts für deutsche Sprache und Literatur, 8. Berlin: Akademie-Verlag, 1956.

An alleged ritual in Tacitus: a rider follows the path of the sun to encircle something for a magic purpose.

857. Hammerich, Martin Johannes. *Om Ragnaroksmythen og dens betydning i den oldnordiske religion*. Copenhagen: J. D. Quist, 1836. xii, 167, [4] pp. Diss. Copenhagen. Also issued as vol. 1 of Hammerich's *Smaaskrifter om cultur og underviisning*.

Early study of Ragnarǫk.

858. Hanna, Helen I. "Siegfried-Arminius." *Journal of English and Germanic Philology*, 19 (1920), 439-85.

Contains a useful research summary of earlier work linking the historical Arminius with the legendary Siegfried, through a mythologizing process.

859. Hannaas, Torleiv. "Til Hávamál." In *Festskrift til Finnur Jónsson 29. maj 1928.* 229-39. Copenhagen: Levin & Munksgaard, 1928.

Notes to stanzas 2, 19, 22, 31, 49, 68, 82, 86, 90.

860. Hannesson, Jóhann S. *Bibliography of the Eddas: A Supplement to Bibliography of the Eddas (Islandica XIII), by Halldór Hermansson.* Islandica, 37. Ithaca: Cornell University Press, 1955. xiii, 113 pp.

Important bibliography of works up to around 1955 dealing with the Poetic Edda and *Snorra edda.* Same coverage and systematic arrangement as that of Halldór Hermansson, *Bibliography of the Eddas* (1920).

861. Hansen, Finn. "Benbrud og bane i blåt." *Scripta Islandica,* 30 (1979), 13-24.

Hansen investigates the well-known impulse of characters in the family sagas to dress in blue/black (*blár*), frequently a blue cape, when violence or death is imminent. He sees this against a mythic background: the goddess Hel was blue/black, and Odin frequently wore such a cape. Understanding the symbolic function of such matters assumes that the saga audience made a connection between mythology and the saga text. Hansen excerpts occurrences of the formula *blá(r)* + article of clothing in ten sagas and argues the connotative and symbolic use of the formula against its mythic background.

862. Hansen, Martin A. *Orm og tyr.* Copenhagen: Wivel, 1952. 381 pp. With illustrations by Sten Havsteen-Mikkelsen. Many subsequent printings and editions.

The famous Danish novelist's attempt at a presentation of older Nordic worldview and religion, from prehistory through the early Middle Ages, is more a work of art than of scholarship. It argues a continuity among the "folk" from paganism to Christianity. Norse mythology appears throughout but is the particular focus of the last chapter of book 1; Ragnarǫk is stressed.

863. Hansen, Søren. "Trællen i Rigsthula: Lange hæle." *Danske studier,* 9 (1912), 112-15.

Textual note to *Rígsþula,* str. 8, *langir hælir,* in an old-fashioned physical anthropological vein.

864. Hansen, Søren. "Rigstula." *Nordisk tidskrift för vetenskap, konst och industri,* n. s., 7 (1931), 89-101.

Interpretation and appreciation of *Rígsþula,* based on the notion that it stems from the time of Harald Fairhair.

Haraldur Bessason, *see* Bessason, Haraldur.

865. Harder, Anna. *Der germanische Ächter*. Bonner Beiträge zur deutschen Philologie, 5. Wurzburg-Aumühle: K. Triltsch, 1938. v, 98 pp.

The final chapter of this monograph on the Germanic outlaw relates the phenomenon to mythology: Odin, Loki, Ragnarǫk.

866. Harder, Hermann. "Zur Herkunft von ahd. *thuris*, ags. *þyrs*, aisl. *þurs*." *Archiv für das Studium der neueren Sprachen und Literaturen*, 175 (1939), 90.

The etymology of *þurs* "giant": "large, swollen."

867. Harris, Joseph. "Cursing with the Thistle: 'Skírnismál' 31, 6-8, and OE Metrical Charm 9, 16-17." *Neuphilologische Mitteilungen*, 76 (1975), 26-33.

Comparison of Skírnir's curse of Gerðr in *Skírnismál* 31:6-8 with Old English metrical charm 9:16-17 permits postulation of a possible common Germanic curse in which the victim is likened to a brittle thistle of late autumn, about to burst with seed and die. As a metaphor, the thistle links the four paradigmatic spheres Harris locates: social life, mental life, private life, and physical life. At this level, argues Harris, magic and rhetoric are indistinguishable.

868. Harris, Joseph. "The Masterbuilder Tale in Snorri's *Edda* and Two Sagas." *Arkiv för nordisk filologi*, 91 (1976), 66-101.

In the spirit of modern Snorri criticism, Harris attempts an explanation of the story of the building of Asgard in *Gylfaginning*. He locates a new analog in two family sagas, *Eyrbyggja saga* and *Heiðarvíga saga*, and postulates an oral local legend at Berserkjahraun, in turn based on an international migratory legend. Snorri adapted the local legend in light of *Vǫluspá* 25-26 and an account of the building of Troy in *Trójumanna saga*. There was, accordingly, no pagan myth of the building of Asgard; for this loss, our compensation is increased understanding of Snorri's literary procedures.

869. Harris, Joseph. "The *senna*: From Description to Literary Theory." *Michigan Germanic Studies*, 5 (1979), 65-74.

Relevant to *Lokasenna*.

870. Harris, Richard L. "Odin's Old Age: A Study of the Old Man in *The Pardoner's Tale*." *Southern Folklore Quarterly*, 33 (1969), 24-38.

Revives the notion of Odin as a model for the old man in "The Pardoner's Tale" (cf. R. A. Barakat, "Odin: Old Man of *The Pardoner's Tale*" (1964) and P. Schmidt, "Reexamination of Chaucer's Old Man of The Pardoner's Tale" (1966)).

871. Hartmann, Elisabeth. *Die Trollvorstellungen in den Sagen und Märchen der skandinavischen Völker*. Tübinger germanistische Arbeiten, 23 (Studien zur nordischen Philologie, 4). Stuttgart and Berlin: W. Kohlhammer, 1936. xxiv, 222 pp.

Conceptions of trolls and other supernatural beings in Scandinavian folk belief and recent Märchen, including some historical perspective.

872. Hartmann, Elisabeth. "Der Ahnenberg: Eine altnordische Jenseitsvorstellung." *Archiv für Religionswissenschaft*, 34 (1937), 201-17.

Folkloristically oriented study of the notion of the mountain wherein dead ancestors dwell, a motif attested in Norse literature and, according to Hartmann, of importance in ancient Scandinavian worldview. Aspects of the complex probably had to do with Odin cult and conceptions of Valhalla.

873. Hartner, Willy. *Die Goldhörner von Gallehus: Die Inschriften, die ikonographischen und literarischen Beziehungen, das Entstehungsdatum*. Wiesbaden: F. Steiner, 1969. x, 115 pp. Summary in English.

Hartner offers a noteworthy attempt to place the (lost) gold horns of Gallehus (Denmark) in astrological, religious and mythological, numerological, and historical context. He believes the horns were made and decorated in Gallehus during the fifth century A.D., as a response to an eclipse and the implicit association with Ragnarǫk. Hartner recognizes many Norse gods and mythological figures (e.g., Týr, Odin, Thor, Garmr, Loki, and Njord) in the decoration on the horns, and he treats the relevant mythological passages in connection with them.

874. Hasenfratz, Hans-Peter. *Die Toten Lebenden: Eine religionsphänomenologische Studie zum sozialen Tod in archaischen Gesellschaften: Zugleich ein kritischer Beitrag zur sogennanten Strafopfertheorie*. Zeitschrift für Religions- und Geistesgeschichte, Beiheft 24. Leiden: E. J. Brill, 1982. xii, 167 pp.

The "living dead" studied here, mostly on the basis of Germanic materials, are those put by society outside its laws: outlaws. The last word of the second title refers to the theory—refuted here—that capital punishment is a form of sacrifice. The study is generally relevant to the context of Scandinavian mythology because it illuminates the sacral worldview, particularly as regards the cosmos and its inhabitants.

875. Hauck, Karl. "Geblütsheiligkeit." In *Liber Floridus: Mittelalterliche Studien Paul Lehmann zum 65. Geburtstag am 13. Juli 1949 gewidmet von Freunden, Kollegen und Schülern*, eds. Bernhard Bischoff and Suso Brechter, 187-240. St. Ottilien: EOS Verlag der Erzabtei, 1950.

"Sainthood by affinity" among early Germanic Christian kings may be related to an earlier sacral kingship. This article is noteworthey as one of the early contributions to the problem of pagan-Christian continuity, which has been of concern particularly to German scholars during the last decades.

876. Hauck, Karl. "Herrschaftszeichen eines wodanistischen Königtums." In *Festgabe Anton Ernstberger: Dargebracht zum 60. Geburtstag am 22. Nov. 1954*, ed. Heinz Löwe, 9-65. Jahrbücher für fränkische Landesforschung, 14. Kallmünz-Oberpfalz: Lassleben, 1954.

Symbols of the sovereignty of an Odinic kinghsip within the Sutton Hoo find.

877. Hauck, Karl. "Lebensnormen und Kultmythen in germanischen Stammes- und Herrschergenealogien." *Saeculum*, 6 (1955), 186-223.

An attempt to rehabilitate mythic royal genealogies among the Germanic peoples as valid historical sources relevant to the organization of the state and the Christian mission. So long as these genealogies are based on oral traditions, reflect a rational worldview, and present recognizable mythological types, the author believes they are useful. Rulers will have traced their ancestry to pagan gods even during and after the conversion to Christianity. Among the peoples studied are the Semnones (*Germania*), Anglo-Saxons, Merovingians, Langobards, Ynglingar, and Saxons. Origin myths also receive special attention.

878. Hauck, Karl. "Brieflicher Hinweis auf eine kleine ostnordische Bilder-Edda." In *Sonderband [*of Beiträge zur Geschichte der deutschen Sprache und Literatur (Halle)] *Elisabeth Karg-Gasterstädt zum 75. Geburtstag gewidmet*, eds. Gertraud Müller and Rudolf Grosse, 47-67. Halle: M. Niemeyer, 1961. Rpt. in K. Hauck, ed., *Zur germanisch-deutschen Heldensage: Sechzehn Aufsätze zum neuen Forschungsstand*, Wege der Forschung, 14 (Darmstadt: Wissenschaftliche Buchgesellschaft, 1965), pp. 427-49.

The author presumably intended the term *Bilder-Edda* "Pictorial edda" as a direct parallel to *Lieder-Edda* "Poetic edda." The East Norse Pictoral edda is to be found represented on such artifacts as the Överhogdal (Sweden) tapestry and on the Gotland picture stones. Hauck interprets the Överhogdal panels as a pictorial memorial encomium to Theodoric of Verona and generally regards Theodoric as a sacral hero; the last pages of the essay are important for the modern case for the relationship between Germanic myth and legend.

The perhaps puzzling adjective *brieflich* in the title refers to the essay's conceit as a letter to the recipient of the Festschrift.

879. Hauck, Karl. "Carmina antiqua: Abstammungsglaube und Stammesbewusstsein." In *Land und Volk, Herrschaft und Staat in der Geschichte und Geschichtsforschung Bayerns: Karl Alexander von Müller zum 80. Geburtstag*. 1-33. Zeitschrift für bayerische Landesgeschichte, 27. Munich: C. H. Beck, 1964.

Departing from the account of creation in Tacitus, *Germania*, ch. 2, Hauck investigates the probable relationship between creation myth and ethnicity within the elite among ancient Germanic peoples.

880. Hauck, Karl. "Von einer spätantiken Randkultur zum karolingischen Europa: Hermann Hempel zum 19. Sept. 1966 gewidmet." *Frühmittelalterliche Studien*, 1 (1967), 3-93.

Hauck focuses on the growth of the Frankish imperium and its transition from peripheral culture to Carolingian Europe. He regards the conversion to Christianity as pivotal and investigates its political and missionary aspects in detail.

881. Hauck, Karl. "Vom Kaiser- zum Götter-Amulett: Die Bildformeln der Inschriften-Brakteaten." *Frühmittelalterliche Studien*, 3 (1969), 27-46.

An expanded version of Appendix G to Hauck's *Goldbrakteaten aus Sievern* (1970), on the typology and relative chronology of the gold bracteates with inscriptions. Hauck remarks on the iconography of the wind-god on horseback (Odin) and its relationship to the second Merseburg charm and worship of Odin and Baldr, and he finds arguments for centering this cult around Odense, on the island of Funen, Denmark.

882. Hauck, Karl. *Goldbrakteaten aus Sievern: Spätantike Amulett-Bilder der 'Dania Saxonica' und die Sachsen-'Origo' bei Widukind von Corvey.* Münstersche Mittelalter-Schriften, 1. Munich: W. Fink, 1970. 488 pp. With contributions by K. Düwl, H. Tiefenbach, and H. Vierck.

Hauck interprets gold bracteates from Sievern (Wesermünde, Germany) as remnants of traditions about Saxon settlement. The bracteates frequently portray a figure whom Hauck understands to be a "wind-god" (Odin), and the most important aspect of this wind-god seems to be curing the leg of a horse, thus making the bracteates iconographic parallels to the second Merseburg charm.

There are twelve appendices, including contributions by K. Düwel, H. Tiefenbach, and H. Vierck.

883. Hauck, Karl. "Völkerwanderungszeitliche Bilddarstellungen des zweiten Merseburger Spruchs als Zugang zu Heiligtum und Opfer." In *Vorgeschichtliche Heiligtümer und Opferplätze in Mittel- und Nordeuropa: Bericht über ein Symposium in Reinhausen bei Göttingen vom 14.-16. Oktober 1968*, ed. Herbert Jankuhn, 297-319. Abhandlungen der Akademie der Wissenschaften in Göttingen, phil.-hist. Kl., 3. Folge, 74. Göttingen: Vandenhoeck & Ruprecht, 1970.

The evidence of the bracteates applied to questions of cult and sacrifice.

884. Hauck, Karl. "Bilddenkmäler: Zur Religion." In *Reallexikon der germanischen Altertumskunde,* 2nd ed., vol. 2, ed. Kurt Ranke et al., cols. 577-91. Berlin and New York: W. de Gruyter, 1972.

A survey of pictorial representations of Germanic religion, with extensive bibliography.

885. Hauck, Karl. "Zur Ikonologie der Goldbrakteaten, I: Neue Windgott-Amulette." In *Festschrift für Hermann Heimpel zum 70. Geburtstag am 19. September 1971*, vol. 3. 627-60. Veröffentlichungen des Max-Planck-Instituts für Geschichte, 36:3. Göttingen: Vandenhoeck & Ruprecht, 1972.

Focuses on the "god-horse formula" on the so-called C-bracteates.

886. Hauck, Karl. "Zur Ikonologie der Goldbrakteaten, IV: Metamorphosen Odins nach dem Wissen von Snorri und von Amuletten der Völkerwanderungszeit." In *Festschrift für Siegfried Gutenbrunner: Zum 65. Geburtstag am 26. Mai 1971 überreicht von seinen Freunden und Kollegen*, eds. Oskar Bandle, Heinz Klingenberg, and F. Maurer, 47-70. Heidelberg: C. Winter, 1972.

Hauck identifies the god Odin in artistic representations of birds and snakes in metamorphosis on bracteates from the Migration period.

887. Hauck, Karl. "Zur Ikonologie der Guldbrakteaten, XI: Methoden der Brakteaten-Deutung." *Mitteilungen der Berliner Gesellschaft für Anthropologie, Ethnologie und Urgeschichte*, 1974-76, pp. 156-75.

The text of an address, delivered in 1974, on the methodology devised by Hauck and his Münster colleagues for the interpretation of the gold bracteates. The three-god and wind-god types are discussed.

888. Hauck, Karl. "Zur Ikonologie der Goldbrakteaten, V: Ein neues Drei-Götter-Amulett." In *Geschichte in der Gesellschaft: Festschrift für Karl Bosl zum 65. Geburtstag, 11.XI.1973*, eds. Friedrich Prinz, Franz-Josef Schmale, and Ferdinand Seibt, 92-159. Stuttgart: A. Hiersemann, 1974.

The discovery of a bracteate in Funen with three figures on it leads Hauck to a consideration of the entire group of "three-god" amulets. He interprets the three as Odin, Baldr, and Loki and argues that here Loki has a special place: he procures Baldr's sword and presides at Baldr's sacrifice. More generally, the bracteates permit analysis of variants and indicate different cult centers during the Migration period.

889. Hauck, Karl. "Zur Ikonologie der Goldbrakteaten, X: Formen der Aneignung spätantiker ikonographischer Konventionen im paganen Norden." In *Simboli e simbologia nell'alto medioevo*. 81-106. Settimane di studio del centro italiano di studi sull'alto medioevo, 23. Spoleto: Presso la sede del centro, 1976.

Adaptation of classical iconography: Odin as Jonas and the midgard serpent as Leviathan. The text was delivered at a symposium, and pp. 107-21 contain discussion.

890. Hauck, Karl. "Zur Ikonologie der Goldbrakteaten, XII: Die Ikonographie der C-Brakteaten." *Archäologisches Korrespondenzblatt*, 6 (1976), 235-42.

The iconography of Odin as a healing god.

891. Hauck, Karl. "Schlüsselstücke zur Entzifferung der Ikonographie der D-Brakteaten." In *Studien zur Sachsenforschung*, ed. Hans-Jürgen Hässler, 161-96. Hildesheim: Lax, 1977.

Adaptation of classical iconography: the midgard serpent as Leviathan.

892. Hauck, Karl. *Wielands Hort: Die sozialgeschichtliche Stellung des Schmiedes in frühen Bildprogrammen nach und vor dem Religionswechsel.* Kungliga vitterhets historie och antikvitets akademien, Antikvariskt arkiv, 64. Stockholm: Almqvist & Wiksell, 1977. 31 pp.

Hauck juxtaposes literary and archaeological-iconographic evidence about the figure of the smith in ancient Germanic culture. He finds a striking continuity of pagan themes, in pictorial art and arguably therefore in oral tradition, of both Wayland the smith and a group of three valkyries. He analyzes the traditions particularly on the Gotland picture stone Ardre VIII and the Franks (Auzon) casket; on the latter a remarkable syncretism of Mediterranean and Germanic motifs obtains.

893. Hauck, Karl. "Zur Ikonologie der Goldbrakteaten, XIV: Die Spannung zwischen Zauber- und Erfahrungsmedizin, erhellt an Rezepten aus zwei Jahrtausenden." *Frühmittelalterliche Studien*, 11 (1977), 414-510.

This far-ranging monograph finds elements of the divine healer or healing god on the gold bracteates of the Germanic Migration period and specifically correlates some of them with worship of Odin (pp. 479-83). Virtually the entire piece is helpful toward an understanding of the social, religious, and iconographic context of the role of the gods in medicine.

894. Hauck, Karl. "Zur Ikonologie der Goldbrakteaten, XV: Die Artzfunktion des seegermanischen Götterkönigs, erhellt mit der Rolle der Vögel auf den goldenen Amulettbildern." In *Festschrift für Helmut Beumann zum 65. Geburtstag*, eds. Kurt-Ulrich Jäschke and Reinhard Wenskus, 98-116. Sigmaringen: Thorbecke, 1977.

The iconography of a hypothetical Nordic healing-god, associated with birds and other animal helpers.

895. Hauck, Karl. "Bildforschung als historische Sachforschung: Zur vorchristlichen Ikonographie der figuralen Helmprogramme aus der Vendelzeit." In *Geschichtsschreibung und geistiges Leben im Mittelalter: Festschrift für Heinz Löwe zum 65. Geburtstag*, eds. Karl Hauck and Hubert Mordek, 27-70. Cologne: Böhlau, 1978.

Programmatic essay on iconographic research, with many specific examples cited from the helmet Valsgärde 7; these include Odin and the Dioscurii.

896. Hauck, Karl. "Gott als Arzt." In *Text und Bild: Aspekte des Zusammenwirkens zweier Künste im Mittelalter und früher Neuzeit*, eds. Christel Meier and Uwe Ruberg, 19-62. Wiesbaden: L. Reichert, 1980.

The concept of the "healing god" on the bracteates, from three religious traditions: the Asclepius cult, early Christianity, and Norse adaptations. In the latter case, older Germanic religious conceptions afforded an important basis.

897. Hauer, Jakob Wilhelm. *Deutsche Gottschau: Grundzüge eines deutschen Glaubens,* 4th ed. Stuttgart: K. Gutbrod, 1935. 288 pp. 1st ed. 1934.

Essentially racist remarks on German belief.

898. Hauge, Hans-Egil. "Traditioner kring tandfällningen." *Arv,* 16 (1960), 144-54. English summary, pp. 153-54.

Recent Nordic traditions of what one does with a child's lost tooth are of interest because in seventeen (of the 205) Swedish recordings one throws the tooth into the fire and says: "Loke, Loke, give me a bone-tooth instead of a gold tooth." Older scholars saw a sacrifice to Loki as a fire-demon; Hauge inclines rather to the notion that the tooth is to be kept out of the hands of the supernatural beings. *Loke* would be an insignificant epic variation.

899. Haugen, Einar. "The Mythical Structure of the Ancient Scandinavians: Some Thoughts on Reading Dumézil." In *To Honor Roman Jakobson: Essays on the Occasion of his Seventieth Birthday.* 855-68. The Hague: Mouton, 1967.

Depending heavily on the theories of Lévi-Strauss, Haugen maps the tripartite scheme of Dumézil's functions onto a series of oppositions with mediators. Thus among the *æsir* Odin and Thor are in opposition, with Heimdallr the mediator (on not fully convincing evidence); *æsir* oppose *vanir,* with Kvasir the mediator; gods oppose giants, with Loki the mediator; these supernatural beings oppose men, with divine heroes (e.g., Starkaðr) as mediators; these men oppose animals, with dragons or berserks as mediators; and these living creatures oppose the dead, with the world tree Yggdrasill as mediator.

For criticism see U. Strutynski, "History and Structure in Germanic Mythology: Some Thoughts on Einar Haugen's Critique of Dumézil" (1974).

900. Haugen, Einar. "The *Edda* as Ritual: Odin and his Masks." In *Edda: A Collection of Essays,* eds. Robert J. Glendenning and Haraldur Bessason, 3-24. The University of Manitoba Icelandic Studies, 4. N. p.: University of Manitoba Press, 1983.

"The question I wish to raise is simply this: how great is the step between the ritual occasions when the gods were worshipped and when they were offered sacrifices of animals and even men, and the occasions when the Eddic poems were recited?" (p. 4). Not far, according to the author. He concentrates primarily on Odin and the poems in which Odin figures: *Grímnismál, Vafþrúðnismál, Hávamál, Baldrs draumar,* also *Vǫluspá, Sigrdrífumál*; emphasis is on the possibility of abstracting "a conception of the religious beliefs and practices of the Germanic tribes. I am convinced that the texts as we have them are very close to the cultic rituals which were enacted among them as among most other archaic peoples" (p. 21).

901. Hauser, Otto. *Die Edda: Übertragen und erläutert.* Weimar: A. Dunckler, 1926. 432 pp.

Translation with commentary of the Poetic Edda.

902. Hazelius, Artur Immanuel. *Inledning till Hávamál eller Odens sång.* Uppsala: C. A. Leffler, 1860. 39 pp. Diss. Uppsala.

Discussion of the transmission, translation, metrics, and contents of *Hávamál.*

903. Heanley, Robert M. "Lincolnshire Superstitions." *Folk-Lore*, 9 (1898), 186-87.

Alleged survivals of Odin and Loki.

904. Heanley, Robert M. "The Vikings: Traces of Their Folklore in Marshland." *Saga-Book of the Viking Society*, 3 (1901-03), 35-62.

Many references to supposed survivals of Norse mythology in Lincolnshire.

905. Hearn, Lafcadio. "The Havamal: Old Northern Ethics of Life." In Hearn, *Interpretations of Literature,* vol. 2, pp. 200-19. New York: Dodd, Mead, 1915. Ed. John Erskine. Reprinted in several other editions of Hearn's works.

Introductory essay on the ethics of *Hávamál*, for a Japanese audience.

906. Heiermeier, Annie. *Der Runenstein von Eggjum: Ein Beitrag zu seiner Deutung.* Halle a. d. S.: M. Niemeyer, 1934. 100 pp.

Against interpretation of the Eggjum runestone as magic.

907. Heinertz, N. Otto. "Drottning und käring (mit einem Nachtrag über das Wort *konungr*): Ein Beitrag zur germanischen Kulturgeschichte." *Acta Philologica Scandinavica*, 10 (1935-36), 145-62.

Analyzes the Swedish terms *drottning* "queen" and *käring* "old woman" as "offspring of the king" and "offspring of the man" respectively and relates these to the role of women in fertility cult. An appendix (pp. 158-62) treats von Friesen's discussion of *konungr* in "Har det nordiska kungadömet sakralt ursprung?" (1932-34).

908. Heinrichs, Heinrich Matthias. "Lokis Streitreden." *Island: Deutsch-Isländisches Jahrbuch*, 6 (1968-69), 41-65.

Translation of *Lokasenna*, with introductory remarks and interspersed commentary. Heinrichs distinguishes Loki's trickster functions from a less visible cosmogonic and eschatological function, and he sees no impediment to assigning the poem to the pagan period.

909. Heinrichs, Heinrich Matthias. "Satirisch-parodistische Züge in der Þrymskviða." In *Festschrift für Hans Eggers zum 65. Geburtstag*, ed. Herbert Backes, 501-10. Beiträge zur Geschichte der deutschen Sprache und Literatur (Tübingen), 94, Supplement. Tübingen: M. Niemeyer, 1972.

By pointing out the contrast between the solemn language of *Þrymskviða* (appropriate in other poems) and the actual contexts in which it is employed, Heinrichs seeks out the satiric-parodic elements of the poem.

910. Heinze, R. L. "Über die Anwendung der nordischen Mythologie auf Germanien." *Idunna und Hermode*, 1812, pp. 113-16.

Early consideration of the application of Scandinavian mythology to Germany.

911. Hektor, Enno. "Der nordische Mythus vom Dichtertrank." *Am Urdhs-Brunnen*, 2 (1884), 61-78.

Nature mythology: rain as the mead of poetry.

912. Helgason, Jón. "Bæn Glúms Þorkelssonar." In *Festskrift til Finnur Jónsson 29. maj 1928*. 377-84. Copenhagen: Levin & Munksgaard, 1928.

A prayer in *galdr*-form.

913. Helgason, Jón. "Två isländska textställen." In *Scandinavica et Finno-Ugrica: Studier tillägnade Björn Collinder den 22 Juli 1954*. 75-77. Stockholm: Almqvist & Wiksell, 1954. Summary in French, p. 77

Textual note to *Skírnismál* 36: postulates the nominae agentis **ergir* "a staff that makes one *argr*" and **œðir* "a staff that makes one *óðr*."

Helgi Hálfdanarson, *see* Hálfdanarson, Helgi.

Helgi Pjetursson, *see* Pjetursson, Helgi.

914. Hellberg, Lars. "Himmelsända: Ett sörmländsk ortnamn och ett Edda-ord." *Ortnamnssällskapets i Uppsala årsskrift*, 1950, pp. 55-60.

Postulates an appellative *himmelsända* "world's horizon," which he finds mythologically represented in the locations of Hræsvelgr (*Vafþrúðnismál* 37) and Hymir (*Hymiskviða* 5).

915. Hellquist, Elof. "Om Fornjótr." *Arkiv för nordisk filologi*, 19 (1902), 134-40.

Hellquist regards the Fornjótr story as a philosophizing parallel to the more brutal origin myth of Ymir. He reads the name as *Forn-jótr* "proto-man" and equates it with Mannus as described by Tacitus.

916. Hellquist, Elof. "Om naturmytiska element i Hymiskviða." *Arkiv för nordisk filologi*, 18 (1902), 353-68.

On the basis of a study of the "nature-mythological" elements of *Hymiskviða*, Hellquist derives the major moment of the poem, Thor's obtaining of the kettle, from "a primeval myth of autumn, in which the sky-god Týr and the thunder-god Thor appear in opposition to the demon of the cloudy sky, Hymir, in whose power has fallen a goddess of light, 'Týr's mother'" (p. 368).

917. Hellquist, Elof. "Ett par mytologiska bidrag." *Arkiv för nordisk filologi*, 21 (1905), 132-40.

Two brief mythological notes. "Om jättenamnet Þjaze" (pp. 132-38) suggests that *Þjazi* was a hypocoristic name for the storm-demon Allvaldi/Ölvaldi. "Ett östnordiskt jätte- eller jättinnenamn" (pp. 138-40) analyzes a Swedish placename as containing the giant name Harðgreip.

918. Hellquist, Elof. "Richard M. Meyer, Altgermanische Religionsgeschichte." *Arkiv för nordisk filologi*, 29 (1913), 193-205.

Exceptionally detailed review of Meyer's 1910 handbook.

919. Hellquist, Elof. "Svenska ortnamn (Guden Höner)." *Namn och bygd*, 4 (1916), 127-54.

Associates the name of the god Hœnir with etyma of *hani* "rooster."

920. Hellquist, Elof. "Jöran Sahlgren." In *Handlingar rörande tillsättandet av det efter professorn Hellquist lediga professorsämbetet i nordiska språk vid universitetet i Lund*. 92-109. Lund: Lunds universitet, 1928-29.

Includes criticism of Sahlgren's theories on *Skírnismál*.

921. Helm, Karl. "Die germanische Weltschöpfungssage und die Alvíssmaál." *Beiträge zur Geschichte der deutschen Sprache und Literatur*, 32 (1907), 99-112.

A detailed and convincing refutation of Gudmund Schütte's postulation of textual relationship between the old German and Norse creation stories, as based on the notion that *Alvíssmál* glosses the creation story and marks specially the non-Norse words of the tale. See Schütte, "Die Schöpfungssagen in Deutschland und im Norden" (1905).

922. Helm, Karl. "Hluðana." *Beiträge zur Geschichte der deutschen Sprache und Literatur*, 37 (1911), 337-38.

Restores the name of the goddess Hluðana to the stone at Monterberg bei Calcar.

923. Helm, Karl. *Altgermanische Religionsgeschichte,* vol. 1. Germanische Bibliothek, 1. Abteilung, 5. Reihe, 2; Religionswissenschaftliche Bibliothek, 5. Heidelberg: C. Winter, 1913. x, 411 pp.

What distinguishes Helm's handbook on Germanic religion from those of his predecessors is his de-emphasis of mythology and corresponding focus on the "historical record" (broadly speaking) and also the division of the book by chronological criteria. After a lengthy introduction, the rest of the book is in two sections: prehistory, and pre-Roman and Roman times. The chapters within these divisions, furthermore, are not devoted to individual gods. The first section treats such matters as additional chronological presentations, and the second divides common Germanic phenomena from those limited to individual tribes and branches.

924. Helm, Karl. "Isis Sueborum?" *Beiträge zur Geschichte der deutschen Sprache und Literatur,* 43 (1918), 527-34.

Support for deleting *Sueborum* from the phrase concerning a goddess (Isis) in *Germania,* ch. 9.

925. Helm, Karl. "Lollus?" *Beiträge zur Geschichte der deutschen Sprache und Literatur,* 43 (1918), 158-63.

Strikes from the record a certain Lollus, said to be a Germanic god in a now lost passage of Caesar.

926. Helm, Karl. "Waluburg, die Wahrsagerin." *Beiträge zur Geschichte der deutschen Sprache und Literatur,* 43 (1918), 337-41.

On the formation of the name *Waluburg,* the (nick-)name of a seeress of the Semnones.

927. Helm, Karl. "Spaltung, Schichtung und Mischung im germanischen Heidentum." In *Vom Werden des deutschen Geistes: Festgabe Gustav Ehrismann zum 8. Oktober 1925 dargebracht von Freunden und Schülern,* eds. Paul Merker and Wolfgang Stammler, 1-20. Berlin and Leipzig: W. de Gruyter, 1925.

A classic statement of the "historicist" position.

928. Helm, Karl. "Die Entwicklung der germanischen Religion; ihr Nachleben in und neben dem Christentum." In *Germanische Wiederstehung: Ein Werk über die germanischen Grundlagen unserer Gesittung,* ed. Hermann Nollau, 292-422. Heidelberg: C. Winter, 1926.

Survey of Germanic religion, in a volume of essays on various aspects of Germanic culture and ethics.

929. Helm, Karl. "Die Zahl der Einherjar." *Arkiv för nordisk filologi*, 42 (1926), 314-19.

On the number of the *einherjar* according to *Grímnismál*, str. 23: 540 doors, each with 800 warriors. Helm criticizes F. R. Schröder's hypothesis, advanced in *Germanentum und Hellenismus* (1924), that the product of the two numbers—432,000, a holy number in the Middle East—should be regarded as a Hellenistic loan. The significant numbers are 540 and 800, and the correspondence between their product and holy numbers elsewhere may be just coincidence.

930. Helm, Karl. "Germanisches und aussergermanisches Heidentum." *Mitteilungen des Universitätsbundes (Marburg)*, 26 (1929), 29-33.

Contacts between Germanic religion and other religions: Roman, Celtic, Finnish.

931. Helm, Karl. *Altgermanische Religionsgeschichte*, vol. 2: *Die nachrömische Zeit*, part 1: *Die Ostgermanen*. Germanische Bibliothek, 1. Abteilung, 5. Reihe, 2; Religionswissenschaftliche Bibliothek, 5. Heidelberg: C. Winter, 1937. 76 pp.

Continuation of the author's history of Germanic religion (1913; 1953). In the second volume, Helm moves on to the post-Roman period, and in this first part he takes up the East Germanic peoples. The relative paucity of the data restricts the work considerably, but Helm gives fair treatment to conceptions of the soul and cult of the dead; demons; magic and property; the gods; the historical position of the East Germanic peoples within Germanic paganism; and the conversion to Christianity.

932. Helm, Karl. "Zu den gotländischen Bildsteinen." *Beiträge zur Geschichte der deutschen Sprache und Literatur*, 62 (1938), 357-61.

Notes on the interpretation of the Gotland picture stones, including a suggestion that Týr and Fenrir appear on the Alskog Tjängvide stone.

933. Helm, Karl. "Über einige grundsätzliche Fragen der germanischen Bekehrungsgeschichte." *Nachrichten der Giessener Hochschulgesellschaft*, 13 (1939), 61-78.

Some fundamental problems of the history of the conversion, treated here in the context of the discussion in Germany during the period when the author was writing. Helm stresses the lengthy duration of the conversions of the various Germanic peoples and the possibilities for syncretism.

934. Helm, Karl. "Weltwerden und Weltvergehen in altgermanischer Sage, Dichtung und Religion." *Hessische Blätter für Volkskunde*, 38 (1940), 1-35.

Karl Helm's aim is to trace certain aspects of Norse cosmogony from prehistory to their use in the written sources. He is disposed to find nature legends as the original stage of many Norse cosmogonic conceptions. To these simple etiological legends were later added the gods, and only then could the legends be involved with religion. Thus, for example, the cow Auðumla is merely an occurrence of the common motif of life originating from some object, paralleled by Líf and Lífþrasir, who seem to originate in wood. The formation of the cosmos from Ymir's body Helm dismisses as a loan, seeing the original legend in the rising of the earth out of the sea, for *Vǫluspá* 59 has this occur after Ragnarǫk for the second time.

Helm finds the legends of Ragnarǫk more complex, with much foreign material. Here he seeks primarily an ancient Germanic core, illuminated by comparison with conceptions of the world's end from throughout the world. Finally he analyzes the uses to which these building blocks were put in Norse literature. Only *Vǫluspá*, he finds, elevated them to a kind of pagan theology; the gods must submit to their fate, occasioned by their own transgressions; but in combatting it they introduce an ethical dimension.

This paper relies heavily on Olrik's study of Ragnarǫk and Nordal's of *Vǫluspá*. The most original notion is the unverifiable progression from etiological legend to narrative of the gods to theology.

935. Helm, Karl. "Balder in Deutschland?" *Beiträge zur Geschichte der deutschen Sprache und Literatur*, 67 (1944), 216-27.

Baldr in Germany? Not according to Karl Helm, who claims there is no compelling evidence for the worship of Baldr anywhere on the Continent.

936. Helm, Karl. *Wodan: Ausbreitung und Wanderung seines Kultes*. Giessener Beiträge zur deutschen Philologie, 85. Giessen: W. Schmidt, 1946. 71 pp.

A classic monograph on the historical and geographical distribution of the cult of Wodan/Odin, addressing the question whether the god was common to all the Germanic peoples as the highest god or whether his influence expanded outward from a given area. Helm opts for the latter view, arguing that the Wodan cult first grew up along the lower Rhine and during the first centuries A. D. gradually spread throughout the Germanic area.

937. Helm, Karl. "Ver sacrum bei den Germanen?" *Beiträge zur Geschichte der deutschen Sprache und Literatur*, 69 (1947), 285-300.

Traces the ritual of the *Ver sacrum* among migration legends of the Germanic peoples.

938. Helm, Karl. "Erfundene Götter." In *Studien zur deutschen Philologie des Mittelalters: Festschrift zum 80. Geburtstag von Friedrich Panzer*, ed. Richard Kienast, 1-11. Heidelberg: C. Winter, 1950.

The "invented gods" discussed here include the German Balder (second Merseburg charm), Frô, and Ingun. Cf. Helm's earlier response to the question: "Baldr in Deutschland?" (1944).

939. Helm, Karl. *Altgermanische Religionsgeschichte,* vol. 2: *Die nachrömische Zeit,* part 2: *Die Westgermanen.* Germanische Bibliothek, 5. Reihe. Heidelberg: C. Winter, 1953. 292 pp.

The final part of the author's history of Germanic religion (1913; 1937). A third part of vol. 2, treating the North Germanic peoples, was once projected but never appeared. In this part Helm treats the pagan religion of the West Germanic peoples: Franks, Alemans, Bavarians, Thuringians, Saxons, Friesians, Langobards, Anglo-Saxons. Topics treated are cult of the dead and conception of the soul; mythic fauna and demons; magic and prophecy; cult; deities; belief in fate; cosmogony. In an interesting Afterword (p. 289), Helm reminisces on the work, whose progress unfolded over half a century.

940. Helm, Karl. "Mythologie auf alten und neuen Wegen." *Beiträge zur Geschichte der deutschen Sprache und Literatur* (Tübingen), 77 (1955), 333-65.

A survey of various lines of scholarship within Germanic religion. Notable for its critical but still sympathetic introduction of the theories of Georges Dumézil. Dumézil's reply, and Helm's response, appeared in the same journal a year later.

941. Helm, Karl. "Zu vorstehendem Aufsatz von G. Dumézil." *Beiträge zur Geschichte der deutschen Sprache und Literatur* (Tübingen), 78 (1956), 181.

Response to G. Dumézil, "L'étude compareé des religions des peuples indo-européens" (1956), which in turn was a response to Helm, "Mythologie auf alten und neuen Wegen" (1955).

942. Helten, W. van. "Über *Marti Thincso, Alaesiagis Bede et Fimmilene* (?), *Tuihanti,* (langob.) *thingx,* (got.) *þeihs* und (mnl.) *dinxen-, dijssendach* etc., (mnd.) *dingsedagh* etc." *Beiträge zur Geschichte der deutschen Sprache und Literatur,* 27 (1902), 137-53.

The many words of the title, and the focus of this article, relate to inscriptions on Borovicium votive altars. Mars Thincsus is often taken to be Týr in an association with *þing* meetings; van Helten thinks it likely, however, that *thincsus* may mean something like "warrior," and he interprets the female figures who accompany the god, Alaesigis Bede and Fimmilene, in martial ways.

943. Hempel, Heinrich. "Hellenistisch-orientalisches Lehngut in der germanischen Religion." *Germanisch-Romanisch Monatsschrift,* 16 (1928), 185-202. Revised version in Hempel, *Kleine Schriften* (1966), 35-49.

This essay derives from an address delivered in 1926, when scholars like Schröder and Neckel had made the influence of a syncretic Hellenistic-Oriental culture seem likely on Germanic religion. Although Hempel sees the Goths as an important link in the dissemination of this influence, he regards it as likely that there were contacts during the millennia before the birth of Christ.

Aspects attributed to Hellenistic-Oriental influence in this survey include the magic force of numerals, various aspects of cosmology (e.g., Valhalla), and eschatology (Ragnarǫk and the Baldr story). Many others have discussed these parallels; Hempel's contribution may be the insistence that as they turn up in Scandinavian sources, they help to establish the existence of a Germanic religion, as opposed to the notion of religions of various Germanic peoples.

944. Hempel, Heinrich. "Der Ursprung der Runenschrift." *Germanisch-Romanisch Monatsschrift*, 23 (1935), 401-26.

The origin of runic writing, with emphasis on the alleged religious background.

945. Hempel, Heinrich. "Matronenkult und germanische Mütterglaube." *Germanisch-Romanisch Monatsschrift*, 27 (1939), 245-70. Revised version in Hempel, *Kleine Schriften* (1966), 13-37.

The *matres* or *matronae* are known from numerous inscriptions from the Roman period, mostly from Germania inferior, the area west of the lower Rhine. They are female deities who tend to come in threes. Hempel argues that they are Germanic, not Celtic, and surveys sources from the conversion period, from modern lore, and from Scandinavian mythology. The discussion of the latter centers on the norns, valkyries, *dísir*, *fylgjur*, and *hamingjur*. The origin of the cult of the *matronae*, which these Norse figures dimly reflect, Hempel sets in a special cult of dead female members of the family who involve themselves with the family's affairs–particularly at childbirth–and by virtue of dwelling underground are also involved with the fertility of crops.

946. Hempel, Heinrich. "Altgermanische Götterlieder." *Zeitschrift für deutsche Bildung*, 17 (1941), 273-86. Revised version in Hempel, *Kleine Schriften* (1966), 50-63.

The contents of *Vafþrúðnismál* and *Grímnismál* are "among the most ancient and valuable religious-historical material Scandinavia has to offer" (p. 52), but the frames were invented by poets. The Thor poems have approached heroic poetry: Thor is a divine hero, treated with light irony. The poets saw Loki as Thor's heroic opposite and also set Thor once against Odin (*Hárbarðsljóð*). As a group these narrative poems (*Vafþrúðnismál*, *Grímnismál*, *Þrymskviða*, *Hymiskviða*, *Skírnismál*) are of very limited value in the history of religion. *Vǫluspá* and Odin's self-sacrifice in *Hávamál* appear to be of more use. In general, the gods are treated differently; only Odin is taken seriously. "The mythological poems of the Edda grew in the soil of prevailing belief in Odin as prepared by the warlike court culture of the Viking Age. They are elitist poetry, created for an audience of princes and warriors" (p. 52). Snorri's account of Thor's battle with Hrungnir may retain some of the old reverence for that god and his cosmic role. The mythological poems are thus of greater interest for cultural history than religious history.

947. Hempel, Heinrich. *Kleine Schriften zur Vollendung seines 80. Lebensjahres am 27. August 1965*. Ed. Heinrich Mattias Heinrichs. Heidelberg: C. Winter, 1966. 447 pp.

The contents include the following articles relevant to mythology and separately treated in this bibliography: "Matronenkult und germanischer Mütterglaube" (1939), "Hellenistisch-orientalisches Lehngut in der germanischen

Religion" (1928), "Altgermanische Götterlieder" (1941). The volume closes with a bibliography of Hempel's writings (pp. 442-46).

948. Herford, C. H. *Norse Myth in English Poetry*. Manchester: Manchester University Press, New York: Longmans, Green, 1919. 31 pp.

The reception of Scandinavian mythology in English literature.

Hermann Pálsson, *see* Pálsson, Hermann.

949. Hermansson, Halldór. *Bibliography of the Eddas*. Islandica, 13. Ithaca: Cornell University Library, 1920. x, 95 pp. Rpt. New York, 1966.

Important bibliography of works up to around 1920 dealing with the Poetic Edda and *Snorra edda*. Includes editions, translations, and individual works, arranged systematically.

950. Hermansson, Halldór. *Sæmund Sigfússon and the Oddaverjar*. Islandica, 22. Ithaca: Cornell University Press, 1932. 52 pp.

On the background of the environment where Snorri Sturluson was raised.

951. Herrmann, Paul. *Nordische Mythologie in gemeinverständlicher Darstellung*. Leipzig: W. Engelmann, 1903. xii, 634 pp.

Handbook of Scandinavian mythology.

952. Herrmann, Paul. *Deutsche Mythologie in gemeinverständlicher Darstellung*, 2nd. ed. Leipzig: W. Engelmann, 1906. 445 pp. 1st ed. 1898.

Handbook of German and Germanic mythology.

953. Herrmann, Paul. *Erläuterungen zu den ersten neun Büchern der dänischen Geschichte des Saxo Grammaticus*, part 2: *Kommentar*. Leipzig: W. Engelmann, 1922. xxiv, 668 pp.

Commentary to the first nine books of Saxo's *Gesta Danorum*, focusing largely on questions of sources. Herrmann has much to say about the Baldr story: he sees no Danish version in Saxo, only the reflection of Icelandic sources.

954. Herrmann, Paul. *Das altgermanische Priesterwesen*. Deutsche Volkheit, [64]. Jena: E. Diederichs, 1929. 79 pp.

Pagan priests in Germanic culture. After an opening discussion presenting the Germanic peoples as combining aristocratic and democratic tendencies, Herrmann offers large sections on priesthood and sanctuaries. Under the first he treats priests, seeresses, prophecy, and magic; under the second holy places, temples, idols, and the ambience of the temple.

955. Herrmanowski, Paul. *Die deutsche Götterlehre und ihre Verwertung in Kunst und Dichtung*. Berlin: Nicolai, 1891. Two vols. Vol. 1, 284 pp.; vol. 2, 278 pp.

Vol. 1 (*Deutsche Götterlehre*) is a handbook of Norse/Germanic mythology intended to inspire German artists to use the mythology in their work. Vol. 2 (*Germanische Götter und Helden in Kunst und Dichtung*) focuses on already existing artistic and literary use of the mythology.

956. Herte, Adolf. *Die Begegnung des Germanentums mit dem Christentum; ein erweiteter Vortrag*. Paderborn: Verlag der Bonifacius-Druckerei, 1935. 86 pp.

Early Germanic Christianity.

957. Hertlein, Friedrich. *Die Juppitergigantensäulen*. Stuttgart: E. Schweizerbart, 1910. vi, 168 pp.

The "Jupiter-columns" of the Rhineland, interpreted as sacral objects of early Germanic religion.

958. Herwegen, Ildefons. *Antike, Germanentum und Christentum: Drei Vorlesungen*. Bücherei der Salzburger Hochschulwochen, 1. Salzburg: A. Pustet, 1932. 80 pp.

Germanic religion and early Germanic Christianity.

959. Heskestad, Peter. "Med tavl på tunet." *Frå bygd og by i Rogaland*, 14 (1967), 114-16.

Brief remarks on some ancient Norwegian gaming pieces in the context of *Vǫluspá* 61 and *Rígsþula*.

960. Hesselman, Bengt. "Ivar Lindquist." In *Handlingar rörande tillsättandet av det efter professorn Hellquist lediga professorsämbetet i nordiska språk vid universitetet i Lund*. 132-43. Lund: Lunds universitet, 1929.

With discussion of Lindquist's *Galdrar* (1923).

961. Heusler, Andreas. *Vǫlo spǫ́: Die Weissagung der Seherin: Aus dem Altnordischen übersetzt und erläutert*. Berlin: G. Reimer, 1887. 59 pp.

Translation of and commentary to *Vǫluspá*.

962. Heusler, Andreas. "Heimat und Alter der eddischen Gedichte: Das isländische Sondergut." *Archiv für das Studium der neueren Sprachen und Literaturen*, 116 (1906), 249-81.

On the Icelandic component of eddic poetry. Most of the mythological poems reflect common Germanic inheritance, but the *þulur* and *Alvíssmál* are later Icelandic productions, and *Rígsþula* is the "most Icelandic" eddic poem, probably dating from the time of Snorri. *Baldrs draumar*, *Vafþrúðnismál*, and *Grímnismál* are difficult cases.

963. Heusler, Andreas. *Die gelehrte Urgeschichte im altisländischen Schrifttum.* Abhandlungen der königlichen preussischen Akademie der Wissenschaften, phil.-hist. Kl, 1908, 3. Berlin: Verlag der königlichen preussischen Akademie der Wissenschaften, G. Reimer in commission, 1908. 102 pp. Rpt. in Heusler, *Kleine Schriften*, vol. 2 (Berlin: W. de Gruyter, 1969), pp. 80-161.

Still a standard work on the "learned prehistory," Heusler's monograph sureveys medieval learned prehistory, its Icelandic manifestations, the origins of those manifestations, and Snorri's and Saxo's euhemerism. Among the more famous of Heusler's arguments is the assigning of the Prologue of *Snorra edda* to a hand other and later than Snorri's.

964. Heusler, Andreas. "Geschichtliches und Mythisches in der germanischen Heldensage." *Sitzungsberichte der Königlichen preussischen Akademie der Wissenschaften,* 1909, no. 37, 1909, pp. 920-45.

Argues against the idea, then being debated by German philologists, that heroic legend was the result of a blending of history and myth.

965. Heusler, Andreas. "Sprichwörter in den eddischen Sittengedichten." *Zeitschrift für Volkskunde*, 25 (1915), 42-57.

Proverbs in *Hávamál* and other eddic poetry.

966. Heusler, Andreas. "Die zwei altnordischen Sittengedichte der Havamal nach ihre Strophenfolge." *Sitzungsberichte der preussischen Akademie der Wissenschaften*, 1917, pp. 105-35.

Reconstruction of two original ethical poems embedded in the extant *Hávamál.*

967. Heusler, Andreas. "Preface." In *Codex Regius of the Elder Edda; MS. No. 2365 4to in the Old Royal Collection in the Royal Library of Copenhagen.* 7-35. Corpus Codicum Islandicorum Medii Ævi, 10. Copenhagen: Levin & Munksgaard, 1937.

Introduction to a facsimile edition of Codex Regius of the Poetic Edda, with description of the manuscript and discussion of the recording of eddic poetry.

968. Heusler, Andreas, and Wilhelm Ranisch, eds. *Eddica Minora: Dichtung eddischer Art aus den Fornaldarsögur and anderen Prosawerken.* Darmstadt: Wissenschaftliche Buchgesellschaft, 1974. cx, 160 pp.

A photomechanical reprint of the 1903 edition, which gave the name "Eddica minora" to eddic poetry in *fornaldarsögur* and other prose texts. This verse contains frequent references to the pagan gods and represents a late primary source for the study of Norse mythology.

The volume contains an extensive introduction to the texts which, although somewhat dated, remains useful.

969. Higgens, T. W. E. "A Survival of Odin-Worship in Kent." *Folk-Lore*, 7 (1896), 298-99.

Hanging dead animals in trees.

970. Hildebrand, Hans Olof Hildebrand. *Svenska folket under hednatiden*, 2nd ed. Stockholm: J. Seligmann, 1872. xi, 242 pp. 1st ed. 1866.

The first great work on Swedish prehistory; includes a chapter on pagan religion.

971. Hildebrand, Karl. *Die Lieder der älteren Edda (Sæmundar Edda)*. Bibliothek der ältesten deutschen Litteratur-Denkmäler, 7. Paderborn: F. Schöningh, 1876. xiv, 323 pp. Completed after Hildebrand's death by Theodor Möbius.

Edition of the Poetic Edda, with brief commentary.

972. Hill, Thomas D. "The Confession of Beowulf and the Structure of Volsunga Saga." In *The Vikings*, ed. R. T. Farrell, 165-79. London and Chichester: Phillimore, 1982.

Argues that the Vǫlsung legend interweaves two great themes: the excess of the hero and the violation of kinship. Hill relates the latter theme to Ragnarǫk.

973. Hirschfeld, Max. *Untersuchungen zur Lokasenna*. Acta Germanica, 1:1. Berlin: Mayer & Müller, 1889. 85 pp.

Introduction, text, translation, and commentary to *Lokasenna*. The interpretation is nature-mythological.

974. His, Rudolf. *Der Totenglaube in der Geschichte des germanischen Strafrechts: Rede bei der Übernahme des Rektorates am 15. Oktober 1928*. Schriften der Gesellschaft zur Förderung der Westfälischen Wilhelms-Universität zu Münster, 9. Münster in Westfalen: Aschendorffsche Verlagsbuchhandlung, 1929. 24 pp.

Beliefs concerning the dead in the penal codes of Germanic law.

975. Hjärne, Erland. "Svethiud: En kommentar till Snorres skildring av Sverige." *Namn och bygd*, 40 (1952), 91-183.

The conclusion reached in the first section (pp. 91-116) of this detailed study may be of interest in the study of Norse mythology: Snorri is said to have used an old source, and perhaps a younger intermediate source, in his description of Sweden in *Ynglinga saga*. Part of the argument turns on Odin's establishment of cult.

976. Hjelmqvist, Theodor. "Havamal: Ett föredrag." *Läsning för folket*, 1895, pp. 161-77, 241-57.

Text of a popular lecture on *Hávamál*, focusing on the picture of Odin and speculating on the character of the ancient Nordic peoples.

977. Hjort, Vilhelm Billeskov. *Eddasangene forklarede som bidrag til verdensaandens historie*. Horsens: A. C. Andersen, 1863. 239 pp.

Eddic poetry as the product of a last age of Scandinavian paganism.

978. Höckert, Robert. "Vǫlsupá och vanakriget." In *Festskrift tillägnad Vitalis Norström på 60-årsdagen den 29 janaari 1916*. 293-309. Gothenburg: Wettergren & Kerber, 1916.

Extends the part of *Vǫluspá* dealing with the war between the *æsir* and *vanir* through str. 29 and reads the war as the central focus of the poem. Indeed, Höckert inclines to the opinion that *Vǫluspá* originated in Sweden in connection with religious struggles between the cult of the *vanir* and the cult of Odin.

979. Höckert, Robert. *Vǫluspá och Vanakulten*, vol. 1. Uppsala: Almqvist & Wiksell, 1926. 113 pp.

Develops further some of the ideas presented in the author's "Vǫluspá och Vanakriget" (1916), seeking traces of the cult of the *vanir* in *Vǫluspá*. The procedure is close reading: "spurious" strophes are distinguished syntactically from genuine ones. Many words and expressions receive close scrutiny, including Gullveig, Heiðrún, and Mímir. *Hávamál* 104-10 are also discussed.

980. Höckert, Robert. *Vǫluspá och Vanakulten*, vol. 2. Uppsala: Almqvist & Wiksell, 1930. 163 pp.

Essentially a response to E. Wessén's review in *Arkiv för nordisk filologi*, 43 (1927) of vol. 1 of Höckert's study.

981. Hoefer, Albert. "Zur Mythologie und Sittenkunde aus Pommern." *Germania*, 1 (1856), 101-10.

Pagan remnants in Pomerania, including Odin and the Wild Hunt.

982. Höfler, Otto. *Kultische Geheimbünde der Germanen*, vol. 1 [all that appeared]. Frankfurt a. M.: M. Diesterweg, 1934. xiv, 357 pp.

A now classic work on the role of cult—particularly Odin cult—in Germanic *Männerbünde*, focusing on the Wild Hunt. An excursus (pp. 163-268) deals with Old Norse tradition.

983. Höfler, Otto. "Der germanische Totenkult und und die Sagen vom Wilden Heer." *Oberdeutsche Zeitschrift für Volkskunde*, 10 (1936), 33-49.

Presentation of Höfler's position on the religious background of the cult of the dead, focused on Odin, and its reflection in modern legends of the Wild Hunt. The article takes the form of a discussion and rebuttal of F. von der Leyen's review of Höfler's *Kultische Geheimbünde der Germanen* (1934), in *Anzeiger für deutsches Altertum*, 54 (1935), 153-65.

984. Höfler, Otto. "Über germanische Verwandlungskulte." *Zeitschrift für deutsches Altertum*, 73 (1936), 109-15.

Defense of the author's *Kultische Geheimbünde der Germanen* (1934) against criticism advanced by F. von der Leyen (review in *Anzeiger für deutsches Altertum*, 54 [1935], 153-65) and B. Kummer, "Kultische Geheimbünde der Germanen?" (1935).

985. Höfler, Otto. "Die Trelleborg auf Seeland und der Runenstein von Rök." *Anzeiger der Österreichischen Akademie der Wissenschaften, phil.-hist. Kl.*, 85 (1948), 9-37.

Höfler connects the mathematically precise count of four groups of five "kings" of the Rök inscription with the ground plan of the military encampment at Trelleborg, with its division into precise quarter-units. The word *ualkaR* on the inscription suggests to the author a group of warriors with a bird totem, involved with the cult of Odin.

986. Höfler, Otto. "Balders Bestattung und die nordischen Felszeichnungen." *Anzeiger der Österreichischen Akademie der Wissenschaften, phil.-hist. Kl.*, 88 (1951), 343-72.

In this speculative essay, Höfler seeks to interpret Snorri's account of Baldr's funeral on the basis of the ancient rock carvings of Bohuslän (Sweden) and Østfold (Norway), and the cult milieu they seem to imply. Höfler imagines that similar motifs were carved on the decorative panels at Óláfr Peacock's hall at Hjarðarholt (Iceland), ca. 980, which Úlfr Uggason described in his poem *Húsdrápa*, one of Snorri's major sources, and that Snorri misunderstood these carvings. Thus the funeral ship being launched and later set afire will have been, according to this interpretation, a ship wagon pulled about the countryside and later set afire; Hyrrokkin will have been the one who pulled it, and Litr a cult dancer leaping high (Snorri will randomly have assigned them these names); the giants at the funeral will have been masked cult participants; Snorri called the ship *Hringhorni* because it will have had a sun-ring on its prow; he had the gods kill Hyrrokkin's horse because the pictorial stone will have showed a ritual slaying of animals; and he had the gods ride to the funeral because the pictorial source showed numerous small carts around the cult ship wagon.

Against the 1500-year chronological gap separating the rock carvings from the wood carvings at Hjarðarholt Höfler argues continuity of cult and perhaps also of iconography in now lost wood carvings.

The argument is clever but will strike some as close to circular: Höfler uses ancient rock carvings and Snorri's alleged misunderstandings to reconstruct the carvings at Hjarðarholt, but he does not subject *Húsdrápa*, commonly regarded as a direct description of these carvings, to close scrutiny. The reconstruction then serves as evidence of cult continuity.

987. Höfler, Otto. *Germanisches Sakralkönigtum*, vol. 1: *Der Runenstein von Rök und die germanische Individualweihe.* Tübingen: M. Niemeyer, 1952. xix, 412 pp.

This book centers on the interpretation of the Rök stone and the relationship of an individual warrior to his leaders and gods—particularly Odin. According to Höfler, the carver of the Rök stone addressed his message to his younger son, informing him that he was born to avenge his fallen brother and through his mother's sacrifice made holy to Theodoric of Verona—an Odinic sacral king. The son is to take vengeance on twenty viking sea kings in Sjælland. The book is full of detail, nearly all of it relevant to the study of Norse mythology, cult, and sacral kingship.

988. Höfler, Otto. "Das Opfer im Semnonenhain und die Edda." In *Edda, Skalden, Saga: Festschrift zum 70. Geburtstag von Felix Genzmer*, ed. Hermann Schneider, 1-67. Heidelberg: C. Winter, 1952.

A study of the the human sacrifice undertaken by the Semnones in a sacred forest (according to Tacitus, *Germania*, ch. 39), illuminated by parallels in the Poetic Edda.

989. Höfler, Otto. "Der Sakralcharakter des germanischen Königtums." In *Atti dell'viii congresso internazionale di storia delle religioni (Roma 17-23 Aprile 1955)*. 359-61. Florence: G. C. Sansoni—Editore, 1956.

Summary of an address at the eighth international conference on the history of religions: types of sacral kingship among the Germanic peoples.

990. Höfler, Otto. *Siegfried, Arminius und die Symbolik: Mit einem historischen Anhang über die Varusschlacht.* Heidelberg: C. Winter, 1961. 190 pp.

A reprinting of Höfler's essay with the same title, originally published (1960) in the Schröder Festschrift. This edition contains a second essay, localizing the victory of Arminius over Varus on the Knetterheide.

The main essay suggests that the figure of Siegfried derived from the historical figure Arminius and with subtle argumentation seeks to develop many of the motifs in the extant medieval legends from symbolism, cult, and myth.

991. Höfler, Otto. "Der Rökstein und die Sage." *Arkiv för nordisk filologi*, 78 (1963), 1-121.

Contra E. Wessén, *Runstenen vid Röks kyrka* (1958), and L. Jacobsen, "Rökstudier" (1961). Höfler argues a single interpretation of both major parts of the inscription. The stone is a consecrated object that presents Theodoric in mythic form.

992. Höfler, Otto. "Zum Streit um den Rökstein." *Arkiv för nordisk filologi*, 81 (1966), 229-54.

Part of the debate with Wessén on the Rök inscription.

993. Höfler, Otto. "Götterkomik: Zur Selbstrelativierung des Mythos." *Zeitschrift für deutsches Altertum*, 100 (1971), 371-89.

Comparing ancient Greek, Indic, and eddic traditions, Höfler argues that comedy among the gods (as, for example, in *Lokasenna*) is possible only when gods are represented in some concrete form. This form is different from their divine substance, and comedy underscores the difference.

994. Höfler, Otto. "Spervogel—Herger—*Harugwari." In *Mediævalia litteraria: Festschrift für Helmut de Boor zum 80. Geburtstag*, eds. Ursula Hennig and Herbert Kolb, 211-27. Munich: C. H. Beck, 1971.

Höfler investigates the relationship between the name Spervogel "sparrow" (under whose name the earliest traces of German gnomic poetry are gathered) and Hergêre, the name of the elder of the two persons said to bear the name Spervogel. Höfler derives Hergêre from **harug-wari* "the sacred functionary (*wari*) of the cult place (*harug-*)" and seeks Germanic evidence of the recitation of gnomic verse at a cult place; here he relies on *Hávamál* 164 and 111. The connection with "sparrow" will strike some as very subtle: *Hávamál* mentions the seat of the *þulr*, whom Höfler takes for the reciter of gnomic verse in the cult. The verb describing his action, *þylja*, is in some contexts similar to *gala* "to chant magic," which Ivar Lindquist has equated with the sound of a bird (*Galdrar* I, 1923, pp. 3 ff.). Thus Hergêre, the cult reciter, might also be called "sparrow."

995. Höfler, Otto. "Brakteaten als Geschichtsquelle: Zu Karl Haucks 'Goldbrakteaten aus Sievern.'" *Zeitschrift für deutsches Altertum*, 101 (1972), 161-86.

A review article of a volume by Karl Hauck and others (1970) on the representations on gold bracteates from Saxony (fourth-sixth centuries A. D.) and their relationship to the origin of the Saxons. ". . . Hauck's interpretations of the bracteates have achieved a surprisingly rich supply of mythic and cultural-historical data which open for us, around three quarters of a millennium before Snorri and the edda-codex, an unexpectedly lively view of important beliefs of the world of this era" (pp. 182-83). Höfler sees on the bracteates reflections of a cult of transformation, centered on Odin. Baldr was already known in this cult; Týr receives only minor mention, and Thor and the female deities are unknown. Höfler's most startling suggestion is that the Scandinavian bracteates found in the area of the Elbe and Saale rivers indicate that the Merseburg charms, one of which mentions the goddess Fulla, may be of Nordic origin.

996. Höfler, Otto. "'Sakraltheorie' und 'Profantheorie' in der Altertumskunde." In *Festschrift für Siegfried Gutenbrunner zum 65 Geburtstag am 26. Mai überreicht von seinen Freunden und Kollegen*, eds. Oskar Bandle, Heinz Klingenberg, and Friedrich Maurer, 71-116. Heidelberg: C. Winter, 1972.

Höfler attacks the procedure he ascribes to such Germanists as Heusler and von See of wrenching phenomena like art or law out of their sacred context: a belief in holy values associated with the community of cult. Von See offered a response: *Kontinuitätstheorie und Sakraltheorie in der Germanenforschhung* (1972).

997. Höfler, Otto. *Verwandlungskulte, Volkssagen und Mythen*. Sitzungsberichte der Österreichischen Akademie der Wissenschaften, phil.-hist. Kl., 279:2. Vienna: Verlag der Österreichischen Akademie der Wissenschaften, 1973. 290 pp.

Höfler's aim here is primarily methodological: to support the use of modern lore in the analysis of myth and cult. The volume includes extensive criticism of the work of Friedrich Ranke and others who had differed sharply with Heusler on the value of such data. As with much of Höfler's work, emphasis is on the Wild Hunt and myths of Odin, which Höfler views as two sides of a cult of transformation.

998. Höfler, Otto. "Zwei Grundkräfte im Wodankult." In *Antiquitates Indogermanicae: Studien zur indogermanischen Altertumskunde und zur Sprach- und Kulturgeschichte der indogermanischen Völker: Gedenkschrift für Hermann Güntert zur 25. Wiederkehr seines Todestages am 23. April 1973*, eds. Manfred Mayrhofer, Wolfgang Meid, Bernfried Schlerath, and Rüdiger Schmitt, 133-44. Innsbrucker Beiträge zur Sprachwissenschaft, 12. Innsbruck: Institut für Sprachwissenschaft der Universität Innsbruck, 1974.

Two impulses united in the cult and mythology of Odin and, more generally, in Germanic culture: the ecstatic and the mathematic-rational. The second finds expression in skaldic poetry, runic numerology, and strict military and social organization (e.g., Trelleborg or military formations).

999. Höfler, Otto. "Der Rökstein und Theodorich." *Arkiv för nordisk filologi*, 90 (1975), 93-110.

A part of the debate with Wessén on the Rök inscription.

1000. Höfler, Otto. *Über somatische, psychische und kulturelle Homologie*. Sitzungsberichte der Österreichischen Akademie der Wissenschaften, phil.-hist. Kl., 366. Vienna: Verlag der Österreichischen Akademie der Wissenschaften, 1980. 55 pp.

A summary of the author's critical theories and methodology, applicable to his work on cult, myth, religion, and literature.

Høgsbro Østergaard, K., *see* Østergaard, K. Høgsbro.

1001. Høst, Gerd. *Våre eldste norske runeinnskrifter*. Oslo: Aschehoug, 1976. 132 pp.

The corpus of elder futhark inscriptions in Norway, arranged geographically. The presentation and interpretation draw heavily on the view of runes as essentially magic and closely linked to religion.

1002. Hoffory, Julius. "Über zwei Strophen der Vǫluspá." *Sitzungsberichte der königlich preussischen Akademie der Wissenschaften zu Berlin*, 1885, pp. 551-58.

Analysis of *Vǫluspá*, str. 5-6. Hoffory finds that they are interpolations from a lost poem on the original ordering of the world, which he assigns to Norway.

1003. Hoffory, Julius. *Eddastudien*, vol. 1. Berlin: G. Reimer, 1889. 173 pp.

Textual note to *Vǫluspá* (pp. 71-85); study of the Germanic sky god (pp. 143-73).

1004. Hofmann, C. "Zum Mythus von Baldurs Tod." *Germania*, 2 (1857), 48.

A Judaic parallel to the myth of Baldr's death.

1005. Hofmann, Erich. *Die heiligen Könige bei den Angelsachsen und den skandinavischen Völkern*. Quellen und Forschungen zur Geschichte Schleswig-Holsteins, 69. Neumünster: K. Wachholtz, 1975. 238 pp.

The "holy kings" were the sainted kings of early Christian Scandinavia, e.g., St. Olaf, St. Knut, St. Erik. The author seeks the immediate roots of the beatification of kings both in such practices among other Germanic peoples, especially the Anglo-Saxons, and in the putative sacral kingship of Nordic and Germanic paganism. Much of this is relevant to Scandinavian mythology, particularly to Odin.

1006. Hofsten, Nils von. *Eddadikternas djur och växter*. Skrifter utgivna av kungliga Gustav Adolfs akademien, 30. Uppsala: Lundequistska bokhandeln, in distribution, 1957. 111 pp. English summary, pp. 107-11.

The author, a professional biologist, lists and examines the forty or so different animals and twenty-five or so plants in the Poetic Edda, dividing his treatment among older mythological poems, younger mythological poems, and heroic poems. Insofar as the flora and fauna enter into the mythology (e.g., ash tree or wolf), the discussion provides useful background.

1007. Holder, Alfred. *Die ältere Edda, übers. und erklärt: Vorlesungen von Adolf Holtzmann*. Leipzig: B. G. Teubner, 1875. viii, 603 pp.

Early edition with translation and notes.

1008. Hollander, Lee M. "Notes on the *Nornagests þáttr*." *Scandinavian Studies*, 3 (1916), 105-11.

". . . I am not claiming Gest to be Odin himself, but that the author of the þáttr, in casting about for attributes to give the figure of the wanderer some fullness, simply borrowed the stereotype features of the ancient godhead" (p. 108).

1009. Hollander, Lee M. "Eddic Notes." *Scandinavian Studies*, 7 (1921), 113-21.

Brief textual note touching on the tree imagery of *Hávamál* 49 and on the presence of beer in Ægir's hall according to *Hymiskviða* 1.

1010. Hollander, Lee M. "Hávamál strofe 81." *Maal og minne*, 1922, pp. 175-77.

Textual note.

1011. Hollander, Lee M. "Recent Studies in the Helgi Poems." *Scandinavian Studies*, 8 (1924-25), 108-25.

Pp. 119-25 describe critically B. Phillpotts, *The Elder Edda and Ancient Scandinavian Drama* (1920).

1012. Hollander, Lee M. "Were the Mythological Poems of the Edda Composed in the Pre-Christian Era?" *Journal of English and Germanic Philology*, 26 (1927), 96-105.

Hollander offers an intelligent account, with more than merely historical interest, of the difficulties of dating the mythological eddic poems. He stresses the possibility that the conversion to Christianity may not represent a terminus ante quem; poets could imitate older forms, tolerance toward the pagan material seems to have been the rule, and there is no firm linguistic or other evidence that the poems must antedate the conversion.

1013. Hollander, Lee M. "Is the Lay of Eric a Fragment?" *Acta Philologica Scandinavica*, 7 (1932-33), 249-57.

On the text of *Eiríksmál*. Accepting that *Hákonarmál* imitates *Eiríksmál*, Hollander concludes that *Eiríksmál* is probably complete in its retained form.

1014. Hollander, Lee M. "Two Eddic Cruxes." *Germanic Review*, 7 (1932), 280-87.

Includes remarks on *Hávamál* 111.

1015. Hollander, Lee M. "Observations on Bernhard Kummer's *Midgards Untergang*." *Journal of English and Germanic Philology*, 33 (1934), 255-69.

A rather sympathetic rebuttal of some of the theses aired in Kummer's book (1927).

1016. Hollander, Lee M. "Comments on Lokasenna 5, 3; and Skírnismǫl 27, 3." *Scandinavian Studies*, 19 (1947), 298-305.

Proposed emendations, of no particular mythological import.

1017. Hollander, Lee M. "The Old Norse God Óðr." *Journal of English and Germanic Philology*, 49 (1950), 304-08.

Hollander disputes the association of Óðr with Odin and with Adonis/Baldr. He argues instead that Snorri's story about Óðr (*Gylfaginning* ch. 22) is a reworking of the popular story of Psyche and Cupid, made famous by Apuleius: Psyche discovers the real nature of her lover, who leaves her, and she searches disconsolately for him. This causes a (rather awkward) reversal: in Greek myth "the soul" searches for Cupid, in Norse Freyja/Venus tries to find Óðr "the soul."

Cf. de Vries, "Über das Verhältnis von Óðr und Óðinn" (1954).

1018. Hollander, Lee M. *A Bibliography of Skaldic Studies*. Copenhagen: E. Munksgaard, 1958. 117 pp.

Useful for poems on preChristian topics, such as Eilífr's *Þórsdrápa*.

1019. Hollander, Lee M. *The Poetic Edda*, 2nd. rev. ed. Austin: University of Texas, 1962. xxix, 343 pp. 1st ed. Austin: University of Texas Press, 1922, xxxi, 396 pp.

An English translation, with competent introduction, headnotes to the individual poems, and footnotes. The deliberately archaic translation is not always easy to read.

1020. Hollander, Lee M. "For Whom Were the Eddic Poems Composed?" *Journal of English and Germanic Philology*, 62 (1963), 136-42.

On the audience of eddic poetry. Among other matters, Hollander suggests that the wisdom poetry–*Grímnismál, Vafþrúðnismál, Alvíssmál, Baldrs draumar, Hyndluljóð, Grógaldr,* and *Fjǫlsvinnsmál, Reginsmál, Fáfnismál,* and *Sigrdrífumál*–"all appear to have a more or less pleasing framework invented for presenting mythologic, runic, gnomic, and in the case of *Hyndluljóð*, genealogic, lore, effected in charcteristic medieval fashion by means of dialogue. . . . [W]e may well imagine gifted pupils sitting at the feet of recognized skalds and with their prodigious memories committing 'lays' like the above as well as the *þulur* composed precisely for the purpose indicated. Insofar, then, we would seem to know the audience for which they were composed" (pp. 136-37).

1021. Hollander, Lee M. "Recent Works and Views on the Poetic Edda." *Scandinavian Studies*, 35 (1963), 101-09.

Research survey.

1022. Hollander, Lee M. "*Skírnismál* 29,4, *Grípisspá* 40,1-4, *Fáfnismál* 38,3, *Sigrdrífumál* 16,3, Hamþismál 7,3." *Arkiv för nordisk filologi*, 82 (1967), 243-49.

The note on *Skírnismál* occupies pp. 243-44. It proposes a reordering of stanzas in the curse section.

1023. Hollowell, Ida Masters. "*Scop* and *woðbora* in OE Poetry." *Journal of English and Germanic Philology*, 77 (1978), 317-29.

Criticism of E. Werlich, *Der Westgermanische Skop* (1964): Old English *scop* and *woðbora* are not synonyms. The *woðbora* was something like a seer or druid, and "A link with Wodenesque ecstasy is as conceivable for the OE *woð bora* as for the Celtic *vates*" (p. 327), "[b]ut the figure may have had at one time some of the attributes of Woden besides wisdom and poetic inspiration" (p. 328).

1024. Holm, Gösta. "Hárbarðsljóð och Lappland." *Maal og minne*, 1969, pp. 93-103.

Opposes the geographic localization of the events in *Hárbarðsljóð* to Lapland, as proposed by Knut Bergsland, "Hárbarðsljóð sett fra øst" (1967).

1025. Holmberg, Maj-Lis. "Om Finland och övriga finnländer i den isländska fornlitteraturen." *Arkiv för nordisk filologi*, 91 (1976), 166-91.

This survey of Finland and other Finno-Ugric lands and peoples in medieval Icelandic literature is relevant to Norse mythology because of the importance of Finns and Lapps in magic. *Ynglinga saga*, quite naturally, merits a good deal of discussion.

1026. Holmberg, Uno (Harva). "Valhall och världsträdet." *Finsk tidskrift för vitterhet, vetenskap, konst och politik*, 48 (1917), 349-77.

Using analogs from folk belief, mostly Finno-Ugric, Holmberg argues that Valhalla and the world tree are native old Scandinavian conceptions. Valhalla was atop the tree. Icelandic conceptions of Eikþyrnir derive from observation of the constellation Ursa Major.

1027. Holmberg, Uno (Harva). *Der Baum des Lebens*. Suomalaisen tiedeakatemian toimituksia; Annales Academiæ Scientiarum Fennicæ, B 16:3. Helsinki: Suomalaisen tiedeakatemia, 1922-23. 157 pp.

This "Rundgang durch den Sagenschatz der verschiedenen Völker" (p. 68) makes it clear that most of the conceptions connected with the world tree in Old Norse have parallels elsewhere.

1028. Holmberg, Uno (Harva). "De finska fornsångernas Sampo." *Saga och sed*, 1943, pp. 16-55.

Concludes that tales of the *sampo* derive ultimately from Nordic culture, perhaps the theft by Finns of a Freyr-idol or talisman from a sacred site in Sweden or Gotland.

1029. Holmgren, Gustaf. "Taga och vräka konung." *Fornvännen*, 32 (1937), 19-26. Summary in German.

The title refers to a passage from *Västgötalagen*, the medieval law of

Västergötland, Sweden, which expresses the people's right to take and to depose a king. Holmgren argues that the passage makes reference to ceremonies which he interprets as rituals of initiation and separation.

1030. Holmqvist, Wilhelm. "Hednisk kult på Helgö." In *Septentrionalia et Orientalia: Studia Bernhardo Karlgren A.D. III non. oct. anno mcmlix dedicata*. 203-12. Kungliga vitterhets historie och antikvitets akademiens handlingar, 91. Stockholm: Kungliga vitterhets historie och antikvitets akademien, 1959.

Archaeological evidence for pagan cult at Helgö: millstones, stone globes, and representational art.

1031. Holthausen, Ferdinand. "Etymologien." *Indogermanische Forschungen*, 20 (1906-07), 316-32.

P. 317 correlates the second component of Heimdallr and the first of Dellingr with roots meaning "bloom, blossom."

1032. Holthausen, Ferdinand. "Wortdeutungen." *Indogermanische Forschungen*, 48 (1930), 254-67.

P. 267 associates Old English *geneorð* "satisfied" with Nerthus/Njord and *neorxna-wang*.

1033. Holthausen, Ferdinand. "Zu den Eddaliedern." *Zeitschrift für deutsches Altertum*, 80 (1944), 155-56.

Philological notes on *Vǫluspá* 2, *Hávamál* 70, 75, 139 and 151, *Hárbarðsljóð* 41, and *Vǫlundarkviða* 5.

1034. Holtsmark, Anne. "Vitazgjafi." *Maal og minne*, 1933, pp. 111-33.

On the literary placename *Vitazgjafi*: Holtsmark tries to prove that it referred to Freyr as fertility god.

1035. Holtsmark, Anne. "Vefr Darraðar." *Maal og minne*, 1939, pp. 74-96.

Philological treatment of the *Darraðarljóð*, with remarks on the weaving valkyries who play the role of norns.

1036. Holtsmark, Anne. "Tillegg til 'Vefr Darraðar'." *Maal og minne*, 1940, pp. 7-8.

Addendum to the author's "Vefr Darraðar" (1939).

1037. Holtsmark, Anne. "Kong Atles eder." *Maal og minne*, 1941, pp. 1-10.

Pp. 8-9 treat oaths sworn on the ring of Ullr and Odin's *baugeiðr* (*Hávamál* 110).

1038. Holtsmark, Anne. "Gevjons plog." *Maal og minne*, 1944, pp. 169-79.

On Bragi's Gefjon stanza. The word *djúprǫðull* means "deep-wheel." It refers to the wheel-plow, which is not attested archaeologically in Iceland, and the reference thus assures the reliability of Icelandic tradition in this instance.

1039. Holtsmark, Anne. "*Bil* og *Hjuke*." *Maal og minne*, 1945, pp. 139-54.

An analysis of Snorri's remarks (cf. *Gylfaginning*, ch. 6) on the children of the moon. Snorri's source was probably in verse, which Holtsmark ingeniously reconstructs. She discusses the etymology and meaning of the names: Bil is the waning moon, Hjúki the waxing moon. The one stunts growth, the other promotes it. The verse was a learned riddle, and neither Bil nor Hjúki was a moon deity. From the etymology of her name, Bil may have been associated with the notion of an inexplicable loss of will, which can have drawn her into the riddle. She may have been one of the *dísir*.

1040. Holtsmark, Anne. "Det norrøne ordet *lúðr*." *Maal og minne*, 1946, pp. 49-65.

The word *lúðr* is best known from *Vafþrúðnismál* 35, which states that Bergelmir was placed on one; since the first half of the verse mentions his birth, it has been assumed that the word refers to a bed or cradle. Apparently following *Vafþrúðnismál*, Snorri has Bergelmir climb on a *lúðr* to escape from the flood of gore rushing from Ymir's slaughter. The word is also attested in *Grógaldr* 11 and in a kenning of the skald Ormr Steinþórsson. After a thorough etymological and semantic study, Holtsmark argues that the gloss "bed" is impossible; the primary meanings are "coffin, chest; millbank; case sheath." Thus *Vafþrúðnismál* 35b probably refers to the death and funeral of Bergelmir, and Snorri misunderstood the context of the verse.

1041. Holtsmark, Anne. "Ísarnkol." *Maal og minne*, 1947, pp. 119-23.

The word *ísarnkol* is found in *Grímnismál* and interpreted by Snorri as bellows to cool the horses pulling the chariot of the sun. Holtsmark shows that the word must rather refer to bellows used to keep the sun burning brightly, and she understands Snorri's interpretation as learned speculation.

1042. Holtsmark, Anne. "Myten om *Idun* og *Tjatse* i Tjodolvs *Haustlǫng*." *Arkiv för nordisk filologi*, 64 (1949), 1-73.

Holtsmark investigates the skaldic poem *Haustlǫng* by Þjoðolfr of Hvin, which contains the story of the kidnapping of Iðunn by Þjazi; as a secondary concern she discusses the pictures upon which the poem is said to be based. Her bold attempt to derive poem and picture from ritual drama of the religious festivals of the year has not gained favor, but the philological discussion of the poem remains important.

For a review in English see Odd Nordland in *Humaniora Norvegica* 1 (1950) [1954], 99-102.

1043. Holtsmark, Anne. "Sarþuara—*Sárþvara*." *Arkiv för nordisk filologi*, 66 (1951), 216-20.

On the Canterbury runic curse with consequent discussion of Thor in a magic formula.

1044. Holtsmark, Anne. "Skáro á skíði: Til tolkningen av Voluspå str 20." *Maal og minne*, 1952, pp. 81-89.

Vǫluspá 20 states that the norns cut marks on a stick (*skáro á skíði*). Holtsmark argues that these marks were not runes and offers an ethnographic survey of the uses of cutting marks on sticks for various kinds of reckoning. She concludes that the norns may have reckoned the length of people's lives with their marks on the stick.

Review in English by Ludwig Holm-Olsen in *Humaniora Norvegica* 2 (1950-52) [1958], 200-01.

1045. Holtsmark, Anne. "Til Hávamál str. 52." *Maal og minne*, 1959, pp. 1.

Textual note.

1046. Holtsmark, Anne. "Fód báis—banaþúfa—heillaþúfa." *Lochlann*, 2 (Norsk tidsskrift for sprogvidenskap, suppl. 6) (1962), 122-27.

Old Norse *banaþúfa* is a loan translation of Old Irish *fód báis* and has undergone further semantic development: 1) the place of one's death, determined by fate; 2) stumbling as an omen of death; 3) a sod to which one leans or falls in the moment of death. "The thought that fate intervenes and gets people to stumble has been amalgamated with the notion of the Irish *fód báis*; *banaþúfa* is the sod one stumbles against and which is the cause of one's death" (p. 126).

1047. Holtsmark, Anne. "Loki: en omstridt skikkelse i nordisk mytologi." *Maal og minne*, 1962, pp. 81-89.

Research survey, treating de Vries, *The Problem of Loki* (1933); Dumézil, *Loki* (1948); Ström, *Loki* (1956); and Rooth, *Loki in Scandinavian Mythology* (1961).

1048. Holtsmark, Anne. "Den uløselige gåten." *Maal og minne*, 1964, pp. 101-05.

The unanswerable riddle: what did Odin say to Baldr on the funeral pyre? It occurs in *Vafþrúðnismál* 54 and in the *Heiðreksgátur* of *Hervarar saga*; and *Baldrs draumar* 12 (*Hveriar ro þær meyiar*?) and even the unasked riddle one would expect at the end of *Gylfaginning* are parallels. Holtsmark warns against trying to find the answer to the riddle; the situation is poetic, and the point is that only Odin can know the answer.

1049. Holtsmark, Anne. *Studier i Snorres mytologi.* Skrifter utg. av det norske videnskaps-akademi i Oslo, II. Hist. -filos. kl., N.s., 4. Oslo: Universitetsforlaget, 1964. 86 pp.

Probably the most important of the most recent works on Snorri's mythology. Holtsmark's studies take the form of several short chapters of a few thousand words each on the following subjects: the vocabulary of the Prologue and *Gylfaginning*, Snorri's euhemerism, irony, the "credo," cosmos, *Alfheimr* and the heavens, Hliðskjálf, the "golden age," Hvergelmir, Bifrǫst, Asgard and Troy, the creation of humans, Loki and the devil, Gefjon, Baldr and Forseti, etymologies and origins, and an epilog. Holtsmark's aim is to distinguish between Snorri the author and his sources (p. 5). She uses basically philological methodology and concentrates for the most part on vocabulary, suggesting parallels in such Christian texts as the *Elucidarius*, which was well known during the age and in his circles when Snorri was alive.

1050. Holtsmark, Anne. "Et gammelnorsk ordsprog." *Norveg*, 13 (1968), 106-12. Summary in English, p. 112.

Comments on a proverb in *Hárbarðsljóð*, str. 22.

1051. Holtsmark, Anne. "Iðavǫllr." In *Festschrift für Konstantin Reichardt*, ed. Christian Gellinek, 98-102. Bern and Munich: Francke, 1969.

Explores the idea that the name *Íðavǫllr* (she uses a long initial *Í*) from *Vǫluspá*, str. 7, may have been an invention of the poet, who might have understood the term as "plain of the pursuits [of the gods]."

1052. Holtsmark, Anne. *Norrøn mytologi: Tru og mytar i vikingtida.* Oslo: Det norske samlaget, 1970. 192 pp. Also issued in a *bokmål* version.

Handbook of Scandinavian mythology.

1053. Holtsmark, Anne. *Forelesninger over Voluspá: Høsten 1949.* Oslo: Universitetsforlaget, 1971. iii, 88 pp. Re-issue of the 1949 mimeographed ed.

Useful series of lectures on *Vǫluspá*, comprising a commentary on the major problems of the poem.

1054. Holtsmark, Anne, and Jón Helgason, eds. *Edda [Snorra Sturlusonar]: Gylfaginning og prosafortellingene av Skaldskaparmal.* Copenhagen: Munksgaard, Olso: Dreyer, Stockholm: Svenska Bokförlaget (Norstedt), 1965. 107 pp.

A normalized edition of the narrative sections of *Snorra edda* with brief introduction and variant apparatus.

1055. Holtzmann, A. "Wôdan." *Zeitschrift für deutsche Mythologie und Sittenkunde*, 3 (1855), 393-94.

Draws attention to a passage in the life of the martyr Apollinaris describing worship of Wodan/Odin.

1056. Hornung, Maria. "Der Fastnachlauf der 'Rollatn Lotter': Ein Relikt germanischen Brauchtums in der Osttiroler Sprachinsel Pladen in Oberkarnien." In *Festschrift für Otto Höfler zum 65. Geburtstag*, eds. Helmut Birkhan and Otto Gschwantler, 265-71. Vienna: Notring, 1968.

A supposed relic of berserk cult in the use of ritual masks in the East Tyrol.

1057. Horowitz, Sylvia Huntley. "The Ravens in *Beowulf*." *Journal of English and Germanic Philology*, 80 (1981), 502-11.

Draws Odin's ravens into the discussion.

1058. Hovda, Per. "Eldre norske inndelingsnamn." *Namn och bygd*, 66 (1978), 63-78. With discussion.

This treatment of older Norwegian names for administrative divisions touches on the relationship between parish, church, and older pagan cult. Although the parish boundaries may be presumed to derive from communities of cult, and although it is often assumed that churches were regularly erected on the sites of pagan cults, in the cases studied here the placenames indicating such cult are far from the sites of the old churches.

1059. Hovstad, Johan. *Heim, hov og kyrkje: Studiar i norrøn etikk*. Oslo: Det norske samlaget, 1948. 295 pp.

Analysis of ethics in ancient Scandinavia. The last two of the three major sections deal with religion and ethics and the conversion to Christianity, and there is a separate chapter on Ragnarǫk (pp. 155-62).

1060. Huisman, J. A. "Geysteren en Wanssum: Twee germaanse cultusplaatsen?" *Neerlands volksleven*, 24 (1974), 105-20.

Ancient holy wells.

1061. Huisman, J. A. "Christianity and Germanic Religion." In *Official and Popular Religion: Analysis of a Theme for Religious Studies*, eds. Pieter Hendrik Vrijhof and Jacques Waardenburg, 55-70. Religion and Society, 19. The Hague: Mouton, 1979.

Brisk survey of the meeting between Germanic (popular) religion and Christianity as an official religion. Huisman starts with the Bronze Age and continues through modern times, with the result that despite its emphasis on the conversion period, the survey sometimes seems superficial.

1062. Hume, Kathryn. "The Function of the *Hrefn Blaca: Beowulf* 1801." *Modern Philology*, 67 (1969-70), 60-63.

Odin's ravens as a good omen.

1063. Hummelstedt, Eskil. "Norr. vilmógom Hávamál 134." *Studier i nordisk filologi*, 39; *Skrifter utg. av svenska literatursällskapet i Finland*, 323 (1949), 25-27.

Textual note to *Hávamál* 134; *vilmógom* is dat. pl. of a term meaning "animal's intestines" and refers to a kind of rope from which Odin is suspended when being hung (indoors, according to the author) on the world tree.

1064. Hungerland, Heinz. "Über Spuren altgermanischen Götterdienstes in und um Osnabrück." *Mitteilungen des Vereins für Geschichte und Landeskunde von Osnabrück*, 46 (1924), 151-375.

Recent folk traditions from around Osnabrück, Germany, associated by the author with Germanic religion and Norse mythology.

1065. Hunke, Waltraud. "'Sie schufen das Schicksal'." *Germanien, Monatshefte für Germanenkunde*, 14 (1942), 409-14.

Brief note on worship of the norns and folk belief.

1066. Hunke, Waltraud. "Odins Geburt." In *Edda, Skalden, Saga: Festschrift zum 70. Geburtstag von Felix Genzmer*, ed. Hermann Schneider, 68-71. Heidelberg: C. Winter, 1952.

This suggestive essay investigates the possible implications of *Hávamál* 141 that Odin was born while hanging on the tree, (*þá nam ec frævaz*). The name of his mother, Bestla, < **Bastilo n*, "is probably best understood as the bark, which protects the life with the tree by encircling it," and thus Bestla is "the maternal tree out of which Odin was born" (p. 69). There is no contradiction with theories regarding this as an initiation sequence, for initiations require a rebirth. It would be tempting to regard Odin's nine nights on the tree as equivalent to the nine months of human gestation, but *Sólarljóð* 51 has wisdom gained in nine days in a holy place. Perhaps Odin entered this myth when the one who taught him the nine *fimbulljóð* was secondarily made into Bolþorn's son (p. 70). Hunke concludes by noting the homonym of *áss* "god" meaning "beam, post" and the carving of idols from wood; the conception of Odin's birth advanced here may be relevant.

1067. Huth, Otto. "Der Durchzug des wilden Heeres." *Archiv für Religionswissenschaft*, 32 (1935), 193-210.

Draws attention to one aspect of legends of the Wild Hunt—rushing through a house— and, finding in it ancient Rome and modern Germany, assigns it to Germanic and Indo-European cult.

1068. Huth, Otto. "Die Kulttore der Indogermanen." *Archiv für Religionswissenschaft*, 34 (1937), 371-77.

Addendum to the author's "Der Durchzug des wilden Heeres" (1935), presenting examples from various Indo-European traditions so as to support the proto-Indo-European nature of the phenomenon.

1069. Huth, Otto. "Der Feuerkult der Germanen: Hat der lateinische Vestakult eine germanische Entsprechung?" *Archiv für Religionswissenschaft*, 36 (1939), 108-34.

Indo-European background and folklore survivals of alleged Germanic fire cult. In Norse tradition, the seeresses are supposed to have been some kind of Vestal princesses, with Menglǫð and Brynhild their literary reflections.

1070. Hveberg, Harald. "Ullanhaug—Jåtten: Barlinden i Ulls kultus." *Maal og minne*, 1937, pp. 49-67.

Reminiscence of the cult of Ullr in Jæren, Norway, in placenames containing the god's name and in others referring to the yew tree.

1071. Hveberg, Harald. *Of Gods and Giants: Norse Mythology*. Oslo: J. G. Tanum, 1961. 72 pp. Translated by Pat Shaw Iversen.

Popular retellings.

1072. Hvidtfeldt, Arild. "Mistilteinn og Balders død." *Årbøger for nordisk oldkyndighed og historie*, 1941, pp. 169-75. Summary in French, appendix p. ixx.

Saxo's was the older version of Baldr's death. In this version, Baldr was killed by a sword called Mistilteinn "mistletoe," which name it bore because of a runic formula on it. The Icelandic versions, and particularly Snorri's, are explained by a misunderstanding of the sword name.

1073. Hvidtfeldt, Arild. "Nordisk mytologi og moderne videnskab." *Danske studier*, 38 (1941), 154-56.

Dismissal, on methodological grounds, of H. Kyrre, *Liv og sjæl i myte, menneskentanke og kunst* (1941).

1074. Hyde, James. "The Under-Thought of the 'Elder Edda'." *Transactions of the Royal Society of Literature*, 2nd ser., 30 (1910), 97-134.

Reads Norse mythology, primarily *Vǫluspá*, as an allegory of the development of the human mind.

I

1075. Institut für Ur- und Frühgeschichte der Humboldt-Universität zu Berlin (K. H. Otto, dir.). *Bibliographie zur archäologischen Germanenforschung: Deutschsprachige Literatur 1941-1955*. Berlin: VEB Deutscher Verlag der Wissenschaften, 1966. 221 pp.

German-language archaeological scholarship on Germanic culture is the subject of this bibliography. It is of value because it covers the war years, when journals were unable to continue their regular bibliographic coverage. The indices, divided by periods, contain main headings for cult and religion with numerous sub-headings.

1076. Iversen, Ragnvald. "Musen som Lokes arvtager?" *Maal og minne*, 1912, pp. 116.

The mouse as the recipient of teeth in a fire ceremony in Trøndelag and therefore theoretically as a Loki figure.

J

1077. Jacobsen, Lis. *Eggjum-stenen: Forsøg paa en filologisk tolkning.* Copenhagen: Levin & Munksgaard, 1931. 111 pp.

A reading of the Eggjum runestone, accepting the reference to a blood sacrifice in the second line and rejecting any notion of number magic.

A six-page addendum mentions that scuttling a boat may have been part of the burial rites referred to on the stone.

1078. Jacobsen, Lis. *Forbandelsesformularer i nordiske runeindskrifter.* Kungliga vitterhets, historie, och antikvitetsakademiens handlingar, 39:4. Stockholm: Wahlström & Widstrand, in distribution, 1935. 81 pp. Summary in English.

The Stentoften and Björketorp stones and other runic inscriptions cursing those who break the sanctity of the grave. Assigns invocations to Thor to late paganism, as reactions to Christianity.

1079. Jacobsen, Lis. "Rökstudier." *Arkiv för nordisk filologi*, 76 (1961), 1-50.

Investigation of the Rök runic inscription, departing from the premise that the second part of the inscription represents a sample of texts anchored in pagan piety.

1080. Jacoby, Michael. "Die Übernahme orientalisch-mittelmeerischer Zodiac-Systeme in die Germania." *Amsterdamer Beiträge zur älteren Germanistik*, 18 (1982), 63-77. Summary in English.

Includes speculation on an Arabic background to Ginnungagap and the Elivágar.

1081. Jaekel, Hugo. "Die Alaisiagen Bede und Fimmilene." *Zeitschrift für deutsche Philologie*, 22 (1890), 257-77.

Reading of the inscriptions on the Borovicium altars.

1082. Jaekel, Hugo. "Ertha Hludana." *Zeitschrift für deutsche Philologie*, 23 (1891), 129-45.

On the goddess Hludana. Jaekel sees her as *Airtha Hlo þunja Fairgunja*, a representation of earth and the chief goddess of the Frisians, married to Tius/Týr.

1083. Jaekel, Hugo. "Die Hauptgöttin der Istavaeen." *Zeitschrift für deutsche Philologie*, 24 (1892), 289-311.

On the principal goddess of the peoples around the Rhineland, based to a certain extent on epigraphic evidence. Names treated include *Nehalennia, Aiwa,* and *Tamfana.*

1084. Jahn, Ulrich. *Die deutschen Opfergebräuche bei Ackerbau und Viehzucht: Ein Beitrag zur deutschen Mythologie und Alterthumskunde.* Germanistische Abhandlungen, 3. Breslau: W. Koebner, 1884. viii, 350 pp.

Modern German agricultural customs and folklore as reflections of ancient sacrifice, sometimes assigned by Jahn to specific gods of Norse mythology.

1085. Jakobsen, Alfred. "Til strofe 2:5-6 i Vǫluspá." *Maal og minne*, 1963, pp. 79-93. Rpt. in his *Studier i norrøn filologi* (1979), 11-25.

Textual note with proposed emendation to *Vǫluspá* 2:6: *nío híbili* "nine households."

1086. Jakobsen, Alfred. "Strofe 33 i Grímnismál." *Arkiv för nordisk filologi*, 80 (1965), 87-94. Rpt. in his *Studier i norrøn filologi* (1979), 27-34.

Textual comment. Jakobsen argues that *hæfingar* (*Grímnismál* 33) means "high branch-tops," and that the stanza may be interpolated.

1087. Jakobsen, Alfred. "Et problem i Helgakviða Hundingsbana I." *Maal og minne*, 1966, pp. 1-10. Rpt. in his *Studier i norrøn filologi* (1979), 49-58.

A mythic echo in *Helgakviða Hundingsbana I*, str. 3: *þá er borgir braut í Brálundi* "when strongholds were burst." Jakobsen finds the parallel in *Vǫluspá*, str. 21-24, and the myth of the first battle of peoples.

1088. Jakobsen, Alfred. "Et par Eddastrofer revurdert." *Arkiv för nordisk filologi*, 90 (1975), 41-48. Rpt. in his *Studier i norrøn filologi* (1979), 35-42.

Proposes a reading of *Hárbarðsljóð* 44-45.

1089. Jakobsen, Alfred. "Bera tilt með tveim: Til tolkningen av Lokasenna 38." *Maal og minne*, 1979, pp. 34-39. Rpt. in his *Studier i norrøn filologi* (1979), 43-48.

The words in the main title occur in *Lokasenna* 38 and are addressed to Týr. They are usually understood as "[You never know how] to make peace among two [men]." Jakobsen thinks such a reading stands behind Snorri's statement that Týr is not a peacemaker. He prefers, however, a literal reading relating directly to the rest of the strophe: "[You never know how] to carry with two [hands]."

If Jakobsen's hypotheses are correct, there is no evidence that Týr was an inciter of men.

1090. Jakobsen, Alfred. *Studier i norrøn filologi.* N. p.: Tapir, 1979. 200 pp.

Five of the articles reprinted here are relevant to Norse mythology and are entered separately in this bibliography: "Til strofe 2:5-6 i Vǫluspá" (1963), pp. 11-25; "Strofe 33 i Grímnismál" (1965), pp. 27-34; "Et par Edda-strofer revurdert" (1975), pp. 35-42; "Bera tilt með tveim" (1979), pp. 43-48; "Et problem i Helgakviða Hundingsbana I" (1966), pp. 49-58.

1091. Jankuhn, Herbert. "Das Missionsfeld Ansgars." *Frühmittelalterliche Studien*, 1 (1967), 213-21.

Archaeological finds (paticularly grave customs) suggest that in his missionary activity, Ansgar will have found most receptive the merchants of Schleswig, Ripen, and Birka.

1092. Jankuhn, Herbert, ed. *Vorgeschichtliche Heiligtümer und Opferplätze in Mittel- und Nordeuropa: Bericht über ein Symposium in Reinhausen bei Göttingen in der Zeit vom 14. bis 16. Oktober 1968.* Göttingen: Vandenhoeck & Ruprecht, 1970. 319 pp.

Proceedings of a symposium on cult and sacrificial sites. The following papers are entered separately in this bibliography: J. Driehaus, "Urgeschichtliche Opferfunde aus dem Mittel- und Niederrhein" (pp. 40-54); B. Stjernquist, "Germanische Quellenopfer" (pp. 78-99); G. Kunwald, "Der Moorfund im Rappendam, Seeland, Dänemark" (pp. 100-18); C. J. Becker, "Zur Frage der eisenzeitlichen Moorgefässe in Dänemark" (pp. 119-66); U. E. Hagberg, "Religionsgeschichtliche Aspekte des Moorfundes vom Skedemosse auf Öland" (pp. 167-71); M. Ørsnes, "Der Moorfund von Ejsbøl bei Hadersleben und die Deutungsprobleme der grossen nordgermanischen Waffenopferfunde" (pp. 172-87); K. Raddatz, "Religionsgeschichtliche Probleme des Thorsberger Moorfundes" (pp. 188-97); H. Geisslinger, "Soziale Schichtungen in den Opferdepots der Völkerwanderungszeit" (pp. 198-213); T. Capelle, "Ringopfer" (pp. 214-18); K. Düwel, "Germanische Opfer und Opferriten im Spiegel altgermanischer Kultworte" (pp. 219-39); H. Beck, "Germanische Menschenopfer in der literarischen Überlieferung" (pp. 240-58); O. Olsen, "Vorchristliche Heiligtümer in Nordeuropa" (pp. 259-78); H. Leuner, "Über die historische Rolle magischer Pflanzen und ihrer Wirkstoffe" (pp. 279-96); K. Hauck, "Völkerwanderungszeitliche Bilddarstellungen des zweiten Merseburger Spruchs als Zugang zu Heiligtum und Opfer" (pp. 297-319).

1093. Janssen, Hans Lüitjen. "Die Toten in Brauchtum und Glauben der germanischen Vorzeit." *Mitteilungen der anthropologischen Gesellschaft in Wien*, 72 (1942), 1-242.

Beliefs and customs concerning the dead in ancient Germanic culture.

1094. Jansson, Sven B. F. "Snorre." *Scripta Islandica*, 4 (1953), 31-38.

Appreciation of Snorri Sturluson and his literary works.

1095. Jansson, Valter. "Niflheim." *Språkvetenskapliga sällskapets i Uppsala förhandlingar, 1934-36; Uppsala universitets årsskrift*, 10 (1936), 75-102.

The etymology and usage of *nifl(-)*. *Niflhel* (perhaps "the deep Hel") and *Hel* are roughly synonymous terms for the realm of the dead.

1096. Janzén, Assar. "Religion und Ortsnamen." *Deutsch-schwedisches Jahrbuch*, 1939, pp. 41-44.

Placenames and East Scandinavian myth especially relating to Ullr.

1097. Jensen, Knud B. "Til Gefjon-spørgsmaalet." *Danske studier*, 16 (1919), 92-94.

Notes on the discussion of the placenames *Gjæw* and *Gieffnskouff* in A. Olrik, "En oldtidshelligdom" (1911).

1098. Jerrold, Clare. "The Balder Myth and Some English Poets." *Saga-Book of the Viking Society*, 3 (1901-03), 94-116.

Pp. 115-16 treat then current speculations on Hel and the world of the dead.

1099. Jessen, E. "Über die Eddalieder." *Zeitschrift für deutsche Philologie*, 3 (1871), 1-84.

Important early study of the eddic poems. Jessen assigns the poems to Norway in the tenth century and suggests that they may have been literary products based on older materials. Although many of the details of this view are now untenable, the theory as a whole is remarkably modern.

1100. Jessen, E. "Etymologiserende notitser, IX." *Nordisk tidsskrift for filologi*, 4. række, 5 (1916-17), 113-24.

With a suggestion on the etymology of *Heimdallr* (p. 116).

1101. Jørgensen, Ove Bruun. "Myter og ristninger." *Kuml*, 1976, pp. 99-128. Summary in English.

Interpretation of Scandinavian rock carvings as Ugaritic myth.

Jóhann S. Hanneson, *see* Hanneson, Jóhann S.

1102. Johannesson, A. "Zu Snorris Skaldskaparmal." *Zeitschrift für deutsche Philologie*, 59 (1934-35), 126-36.

Primarily on the circumstances of composition of *Snorra edda*, with emphasis on Snorri's knowledge of mythological and poetic traditions. Pp. 128-33 offer examples of the breadth of Snorri's mythological sources.

1103. Johannesson, Kurt. *Saxo Grammaticus: Komposition och världsbild i Gesta Danorum*. Lychnos-bibliotek, 31. Stockholm: Almqvist & Wiksell, 1978. 348 pp.

A reinterpretation of the structure of Saxo's *Gesta Danorurm*. It is divided into four sections of four books each; each section illustrates one of the cardinal virtues, and each book contrasts its virtue with some vice or another virtue. Further, the work illustrates the development of arts and science in Denmark, and Saxo was a twelfth-century Platonist.

Since these theories deal more with organization than with content, they leave the mythic material in Saxo more or less intact.

1104. Jóhannesson, Jón. *A History of the Old Icelandic Commonwealth: Íslendinga saga*. University of Manitoba Icelandic Studies, 2. Manitoba: University of Manitoba Press, 1974. xi, 407 pp. Translated by Haraldur Bessason. Icelandic original: *Saga Íslands*: vol. 1, *Þjóðveldisöld* (1956), vol. 2, *Fyrirlestrar og ritgerðir um tímabilið 1262-1550* (1968).

Besides its value as general historical orientation, this volume contains a useful chapter on the conversion and early Icelandic Christianity (pp. 118-221).

1105. Johansen, Øystein. "Forhistorien, religionsforskningens grense?" *Viking*, 43 (1980), 96-106. Summary in English, pp. 105-06.

Although it deals with prehistoric religion in Norway, this article is of interest for its methodological remarks on archaeology and religion.

1106. Johansons, Andrejs. "Kultverbände und Verwandlungskulte." *Arv*, 29-30 (1973-74), 149-57.

Summary of Otto Höfler, *Verwandlungskulte, Volkssagen und Mythen* (1973), with additional supporting evidence of werewolfism in Latvia.

1107. Johansson, Karl Ferdinand. *Über die altindische Göttin Dhisána und Verwandtes: Beiträge zum Fruchtbarkeitskultus in Indien*. Skrifter utgivna af kungliga humanistiska vetenskapssamfundet i Uppsala, 20:1. Uppsala: Akademiska bokhandeln, 1917. 170 pp.

Includes references to and analysis of fertility cult in Scandinavia, e.g., phallus cult, the divine pair, and the *vanir*.

1108. Johansson, Karl Ferdinand. "Germ. Alcis (germ. Dioskurer)." *Arkiv för nordisk filologi*, 35 (1919), 1-22.

The Germanic Alciis as the representatives of Indo-European *dioscurii*: twin gods, in horse form, who provide help. Johansson's main contribution is etymological. He reads *Alciis* as a hypocoristic nominative plural of a base form **alhi-ehwa-* "the two dioscurii."

1109. Johns, Ellen. "The Change in Status of Women in Iceland from Pagan to Christian Times." In *Traditions in Contact and Change: Selected Proceedings of the XIVth Congress of the International Association for the History of Religions*, eds. Peter Slater and Donald Wiebe, 377-82. Waterloo, Ontario: Canadian Corporation for Studies in Religion/Wilfred Laurier University Press, 1983.

Women as the focus of cult and "lower mythology."

1110. Johnston, Alfred W. "Ragna-rök and Orkney." *Scottish Historical Review*, 9 (1911-12), 148-58.

Finds that poetic traditions about Ragnarǫk were extant and collected in the Orkneys.

Jón Helgason, *see* Helgason, Jón.

Jón Hnefill Aðalsteinsson, *see* Aðalsteinsson, Jón Hnefill.

Jón Jóhannesson, *see* Jóhannesson, Jón.

Jón Jónsson, *see* Jónsson, Jón.

Jón Steffensen, *see* Steffensen, Jón.

1111. Jones, Gwyn. "Mabinogi and Edda." *Saga-Book of the Viking Society*, 1946-53, pp. 23-47.

Norse-Welsh parallels, including the deaths of Baldr and Branwen.

1112. Jones, Gwyn. *A History of the Vikings*, rev. ed. Oxford and New York: Oxford University Press, 1984. xviii, 504 pp. 1st ed. 1968.

Besides many passing references, contains a brief discussion of religion, worldview, and mythology, in the context of a more general discussion of "The Scandinavian Community: Culture and Image" (pp. 315-55).

1113. Jónsson, Finnur. "Hárbarþsljóð: En undersøgelse." *Årbøger for nordisk oldkyndighed og historie*, 1886, pp. 139-79.

Reconstructed text of *Hárbarðsljóð*; little mythological interpretation.

1114. Jónsson, Finnur. "Vingolf." *Arkiv för nordisk filologi*, 6 (1890), 280-84.

Contra W. Braune, "Vingolf" (1889). Finnur Jónsson argues that the word and concept are extremely old.

1115. Jónsson, Finnur. "Mytiske forestillinger i de ældste skjaldekvad." *Arkiv för nordisk filologi*, 9 (1893), 1-22.

In this useful article Finnur Jónsson shows how widespread the conceptions of Norse mythology were among the earliest skalds.

1116. Jónsson, Finnur. "Hvar eru Eddukvæðin til orðin?" *Tímarit hins íslenzka bókmenntafélags*, 16 (1895), 1-41.

Response to Björn M. Ólsen's article (1894) with the same title.

1117. Jónsson, Finnur. "De ældste skjalde og deres kvad." *Årbøger for nordisk oldkyndighed og historie*, 1895, pp. 271-359.

The essential aim of this long article, as the author states in the opening pages, is to demonstrate the inconsistencies of Bugge's mythological and skaldic theories, thus disproving both.

1118. Jónsson, Finnur. "Tilnavne i den islandske oldlitteratur." *Årbøger for nordisk oldkyndighed og historie*, 1897, pp. 161-381.

See p. 300 for a brief list of mythological nicknames in Old Icelandic literature.

1119. Jónsson, Finnur. "Edda Snorra Sturlusonar: Dens oprindelige form og sammensætning." *Årbøger for nordisk oldkyndighed og historie*, 1898, pp. 283-357.

Argues that Codex Regius (GkS 2367 4to) most closely represents the original text of Snorri's *Edda.*

1120. Jónsson, Finnur. "Odin og Tor i Norge og Island og på Island i det 9. og 10. årh." *Arkiv för nordisk filologi*, 17 (1901), 219-47.

A survey, using primarily skaldic sources, of knowledge of Odin and Thor during the early Viking Age.

1121. Jónsson, Finnur. "Völuspá." *Skírnir*, 81 (1907), 326-41.

A running commentary to *Vǫluspá*, stressing interpretation of the content. Finnur Jónsson regarded the poem as the composition of a pagan poet who may have been the first to combine the various traditions he found into a kind of mythic history, based on the unending opposition between giants and gods.

1122. Jónsson, Finnur, and Daniel Bruun. "Finds and Excavations of Heathen Temples in Iceland." *Saga-Book of the Viking Society*, 7 (1910-11), 25-37.

Abridged English translation of Bruun and Finnur Jónsson, "Om hove og hovudgravninger på Island" (1909).

1123. Jónsson, Finnur. *Völu-spá, Völvens spådom*. Studier fra sprog- og oldtidforskning, 84. Copenhagen: Tillge, 1911. 52 pp.

An essay on *Vǫluspá*, assigning it to Norway toward the end of the first half of the tenth century. Pp. 42-52 comprise a commentary to the poem's individual stanzas.

1124. Jónsson, Finnur. *Goðafræði Norðmanna og Íslendinga efter heimildum*. Reykjavik: Hið íslenska bókmenntafélag/Prentsmiðjan Gutenberg, 1913. 158 pp.

Icelandic handbook of Scandinavian mythology.

1125. Jónsson, Finnur. "Rígsþula." *Arkiv för nordisk filologi*, 33 (1916-17), 157-71.

Reactions to treatments of the poem by K. Lehmann (1904) and A. Heusler. Finnur Jónsson argues for an early date and Norwegian provenance.

1126. Jónsson, Finnur. "Gudenavne—dyrenavne." *Arkiv för nordisk filologi*, 35 (1919), 309-14.

Brief catalog of the gods in animal form, based mostly on their secondary names. Finnur Jónsson concludes that virtually all household animals are indicated and that Odin plays the largest role.

1127. Jónsson, Finnur. "Eddatolkning: Nogle modbemærkninger." *Arkiv för nordisk filologi*, 37 (1921), 313-27. Rpt. in Finnur Jónsson, *Seks afhandlinger om Eddadigtene* (1933), pp. 170-85.

Defense of the author's readings of eddic poetry, including some from *Vǫluspá* and *Hávamál*, against some interpretations proposed by E. A. Kock, "Bidrag till eddatolkning" (1919 and 1921).

1128. Jónsson, Finnur. *Norsk-islandske kultur- og sprogforhold i 9. og 10. årh.* Det kgl. danske videnskabs selskab, historiske-filologiske meddelser, 3:2. Copenhagen: A. F. Høst, in commission, 1921. 330 pp.

Chapter IV of Part A of this discussion of Norse-Icelandic cultural relations during the ninth and tenth centuries treats mythology and legends (pp. 80-117). It summarizes and discusses the views of Sophus Bugge, Axel Olrik, C. W. von Sydow, and Heinrich Zimmer. In each case Finnur Jónsson argues, ad operam et ad hominem, that these scholars exaggerated the contacts between Norse and Celtic traditions.

1129. Jónsson, Finnur, ed. *Edda Snorra Sturlusonar: Codex Wormianus AM 242, fol.* Copenhagen and Oslo (Kristiania): Gyldendalske Boghandel—Nordisk Forlag (for Kommissionen for det Arnamagnæanske legat), 1924.

An edition of one of the major manuscripts of Snorri's *Edda.*

1130. Jónsson, Finnur. *Hávamál.* Copenhagen: G. E. C. Gad, 1924. 170 pp.

An edition of the poem, with commentary and translation.

1131. Jónsson, Finnur. "Eddadigtenes samling." *Arkiv för nordisk filologi*, 42 (1926), 215-33. Rpt. in Finnur Jónsson, *Seks afhandlinger om Eddadigtene* (1933), pp. 1-20.

On the collection of the eddic poems. On the basis of "loans" (parallels) between eddic and datable skaldic verse and verse in *fornaldarsögur*, Finnur Jónsson believes that there must have been one or more written collections of eddic poems by 1200 at the latest. Systematic reworking followed, according to a "saga principle" (arranging texts to create a saga-like chronology) and a "summary principle" (placing texts summarizing large bodies of material, e.g., *Vǫluspá*, before other texts dealing in greater detail with the same material).

1132. Jónsson, Finnur, ed. *Snorri Sturluson: Edda,* 2nd ed. Copenhagen: G. E. C. Gad, 1926.

An edition of Snorri's *Edda*, based primarily on Codex Regius (GkS 2367 4to). Superseded by Finnur Jónsson's 1931 edition.

1133. Jónsson, Finnur. "Samlingen af Eddadigte i Codex Regius." In *Studier tillägnade Axel Kock, tidskriftens redaktör, 1888-1925.* 1-13. Arkiv för nordisk filologi, 40, supplement. Lund: C. W. K. Gleerup, 1929. Also issued separately, under title *Studier tillägnade Axel Kock.*

Further considerations on the problem of the collection of Codex Regius, reaching the same conclusion as in the author's "Eddadigternes samling" (1926).

1134. Jónsson, Finnur. "Brage skjald." *Acta Philologica Scandinavica*, 5 (1930-31), 237-86.

Includes textual notes to *Ragnarsdrápa*: Thor and the midgard serpent (pp. 239-50), the Gefjon myth (pp. 250-54), and the Hjaðningavíg (p. 268).

1135. Jónsson, Finnur. "Rúnafræði í ágrip." *Ársrit hins íslenzka fræðafélags*, 1930, pp. 1-62.

Popular summary of runology, with short section on magic particularly relevant to Iceland.

1136. Jónsson, Finnur, ed. *Edda Snorra Sturlusonar udgivet efter håndskrifterne.* Copenhagen: Gyldendalske Boghandel–Nordisk Forlag (for Kommissionen for det Arnamagnæanske legat), 1931.

The standard edition of Snorri's *Edda*, with variant readings from the various manuscripts and a useful index of names in the text. Finnur Jónsson's "Indledning" (pp. i-lix) surveys the manuscript tradition.

1137. Jónsson, Finnur. *Lexicon Poeticum Antiquae Linguae Septentrionalis: Ordbog over det norsk-islandske skjaldesprog oprindelig forfattet af Sveinbjörn Egilsson*, 2nd. ed. Copenhagen: S. L. Møller, 1931. xvi, 667 pp. 1st ed. 1913-16. Rpt. 1966.

Finnur Jónsson's adaptation of Sveinbjörn Egilsson's 1860 dictionary of Old Norse-Icelandic poetic language is useful for the study of mythology insofar as it includes the names of the gods as head-words and under them catalogs the various occurrences of those names.

1138. Jónsson, Finnur. *De gamle Eddadigte udgivne og tolkede.* Copenhagen: G. E. C. Gad, 1932. xv, 371 pp.

An edition of the Poetic Edda, with introduction, commentary, and indices.

1139. Jónsson, Finnur. "Þulur." *Acta Philologica Scandinavica*, 8 (1933-34), 262-72.

Includes and puts into context sections on mythological river names (pp. 263-64) and on mythological names for the earth (pp. 269-70), namely *fjǫrgyn*, *hlǫð yn*, and *sif.*

1140. Jónsson, Finnur. *Seks afhandlinger om Eddadigtene.* Copenhagen: G. E. C. Gad, 1933. 185 pp.

Reprint of six of Finnur Jónsson's essays on eddic poetry. Three are separately entered in this bibliography: "Eddadigtenes samling" (1926), pp. 1-20; "Samlingen af Eddadigte i Codex Regius (1929), pp. 21-32; "Eddatolkning: Nogle modbemærkninger" (1921), pp. 170-85, printed here without the subtitle.

1141. Jónsson, Finnur. "Þulur: Søkonge- og jættenavneremserne." *Acta Philologica Scandinavica*, 9 (1934-35), 289-308.

Pp. 292-308 treat *þulur* with the names of giants.

1142. Jónsson, Finnur. "Til belysing af Snorri Sturlusons behandling af hans kilder." *Arkiv för nordisk filologi*, 50 (1934), 181-96.

Snorri's use of his sources in *Ynglinga saga*, with occasional comparison to *Snorra edda.*

1143. Jónsson, Finnur. "Til belysning af Snorri Sturlusons behandling af hans kilder." *Arkiv för nordisk filologi*, 50 (1934), 181-96.

On Snorri's treatment of his sources in both *Snorra edda* and *Ynglinga saga.* Finnur Jónsson finds that Snorri has not always acted consistently.

Pp. 183-84 assail E. Mogk's surmise of a mythological school surrounding Snorri.

1144. Jónsson, Jón. "Liserus.—Beów." *Arkiv för nordisk filologi*, 15 (1899), 255-61.

The first half of the article (pp. 255-58) seeks to show that Saxo's Liserus is identical to Lýsir; that Lýsir in turn is identical to Heimdallr; and that Lýtir is a name for Heimdallr.

1145. Jónsson, Jón. "Haddingssaga Saxa." *Arkiv för nordisk filologi*, 22 (1905), 256-71.

On the sources and literary relations of Saxo's story of Hadingus.

1146. Jónsson, Þorleifr, ed. *Edda Snorra Sturlusonar.* Copenhagen: Gyldendal, 1875. xxiv, 326 pp.

Edition of *Snorra edda.*

1147. Jordan, Wilhelm. *Die Edda.* Frankfurt a. M.: W. Jordan, 1889. iv, 534 pp.

German translation of the Poetic Edda.

1148. Jordans, Wilhelm. *Der germanische Volksglaube von den Toten und Dämonen im Berg und ihrer Beschswichtigung.* Bonner Studien zur englischen Philologie, 17. Bonn: P. Hanstein, 1933. 71 pp.

Beliefs about the dead and demons in mountains.

1149. Joseph, Brian D. "The Old English Hengest as an Indo-European Twin Hero." *Mankind Quarterly*, 24 (1983-84), 105-15.

Hengest and Horsa as Dioscuric figures.

1150. Joseph, Herbert S. "Völsa þáttr: A Literary Remnant of a Phallic Cult." *Folklore*, 83 (1972), 245-52.

Concludes that the verses in the *þáttr* "give indications that they have come from a tradition of folk humor rather than from any specific religious source" (p. 252); however, "this þáttr is certainly amongst those rare literary works which in some way or other hearkens [sic] back to the common repository of Indo-European folk myth. . ." (p. 252).

1151. Jostes, Franz. "Idis." *Indogermanische Forschungen*, 2 (1893), 197-98.

The etymology of *idis*: a compound meaning "water woman," in which the second component is identical with Old Norse *dís*.

1152. Jostes, Franz. *Sonnenwende: Forschungen zur germanischen Religions- und Sagengeschichte,* vol. 1: *Die Religion der Keltogermanen.* Münster: Aschendorff, 1926. 238 pp.

First of a two-part work arguing the ultimate Egyptian/astrological origin of Germanic religion and seeking its remains even in recent lore. This volume focuses particularly on the supposed Celtic intermediary.

1153. Jostes, Franz. *Sonnenwende: Forschungen zur germanischen Religions- und Sagengeschichte,* vol. 2: *Germanische Wanderungssagen, die Religion der heidnischen Merowinger, der Mythus in Kult und Legende.* Münster: Aschendorff, 1930. 691 pp.

Second of a two-part work arguing the ultimate Egyptian/astrological origin of Germanic religion and seeking its remains even in recent lore. This volume focuses more on the later survivals.

1154. Jung, Erich. "Irmensul und Rolandsäule: Ein Beitrag zur Rechtsarchäologie." *Mannus*, 17 (1925), 1-34.

Connects the Irminsûl and other ancient columns in Germany with the god Ziu/Týr, especially in his role as god of law.

1155. Jung, Erich. "Altgeweihte Stätten: Archäologische Beiträge zur deutschen Rechtsgeschichte und Glaubensgeschichte." In *Festgabe für den 70jährigen Gustaf Kossinna von Freunden und Schülern.* 333-49. Mannus, 6, Ergänzungsband. Leipzig: C. Kabitzsch, 1928.

Touches on possible remnants of belief in Wodan/Odin and Ziu/Týr in parts of Germany.

1156. Jung, Erich. "Götter, Heilige und Unholde: Archäologische Beiträge zur deutschen Glaubens- und Rechtsgeschichte." *Mannus*, 20 (1928), 118-61.

Remnants of paganism and syncretism in German archaeological finds and early art.

1157. Jung, Erich. *Germanische Götter und Helden in christlicher Zeit: Urkunden und Betrachtungen zur deutschen Glaubensgeschichte, Rechtsgeschichte, Kunstgeschichte und allgemeinen Geistesgeschichte,* 2nd ed. Munich: J. F. Lehmann, 1939. 393 pp. 1st ed. (1922) bore the subtitle *Beiträge zur Entwicklungsgeschichte der deutschen Geistesform.*

Pagan remnants in medieval art and archaeology.

1158. Jungandreas, Wolfgang. "Die germanische Runenreihe und ihre Bedeutung." *Zeitschrift für deutsche Philologie*, 60 (1935), 105-21.

After reconstructing the proto-Germanic names for the runes of the elder futhark, Jungandreas groups them, in part after the grouping proposed by F. von der Leyen, "Die germanische Runenreihe und ihre Bedeutung" (1930), and proceeds to draw various conclusions. He assigns the origin of the rune-row to southern Germany, roughly during the first century A. D., and comments on the implications of the proposed pairing of the rune names. The cosmos was divided into three parts: sky, earth, and sea. The major gods were **teiwos* (> Týr) and **ingwos* (> Ing, Yngvi); the *æsir* (sing. **ansos*) did not at that time have the status of gods, as they were paired with the giants.

1159. Jungandreas, Wolfgang. "Zur Runenreihe." *Zeitschrift für deutsche Philologie*, 61 (1936), 227-32.

Additional note to the author's "Die germanische Runenreihe und ihre Bedeutung" (1935), defending the basic findings.

1160. Jungner, Hugo. "Om Kung Orre: Några funderingar." *Maal og minne*, 1914, pp. 123-46.

Against Magnus Olsen, "Kung Orre" (1912), who had argued that King Orre was a winter demon. Jungner associates the name with the Swedish King Eric of Pomerania.

1161. Jungner, Hugo. "Uppsala- och Vendel-konungarnas mytiska ättefäder." *Fornvännen*, 1919, pp. 79-102.

Archaeological evidence suggests that the cult of Freyr was practiced at Uppsala, that of Odin at Vendel: the Uppsala mounds contain rich finds but no weapons, in contrast to the weapons in graves at Ulltuna and Vendel; and the ornamentation on the Vendel and Valsgärde helmets seems to point to Odin. The cult of Odin, according to the author, was probably an import from Götaland, in that warriors from there may have been part of the army that overran the Yngling lands in the mid-seventh century or so.

1162. Jungner, Hugo. *Gudinnan Frigg och Als härad: En studie i Västergötlands religions-, språk-, och bebyggelsehistorie.* Uppsala: Wretmans boktryckeri, 1922. viii, 416 pp. 4 maps. Diss. Uppsala.

Als härad, a district in Västergötland, Sweden, bears striking onomastic similarity to an area some 30-40 kilometers to the northwest. Jungner thinks Als härad was settled from that area around 100 B. C. and devotes much of this dissertation to the consequences of such a premise. The placenames involved are largely theophoric and indicative of the worship of Frigg (e.g., *Friggeråker* "Frigg's field").

The central chapters (4-6) discuss Frigg's cult in detail, arguing that it was associated with a strong cultural influence from the Near East, including particularly an agrarian cult. According to the author, then, Frigg was originally identical to Freyja and one of the *vanir.* She was the sister of a male god (*Friggi), whose name and some of whose attributes may be a loan from the cult of Priapus. The goddess herself, however, would go back to the Bronze Age in Scandinavia.

1163. Jungner, Hugo. "Om Friggproblemet: Några kritiska anmärkningar." *Namn och bygd,* 12 (1924), 1-36.

A response to criticism of the author's *Gudinnan Frigg och Als härad* (1922).

1164. Jungner, Hugo. "Den gotländska runbildstenen från Sanda: Om Valhallstro och hednisk begravningsritual." *Fornvännen,* 25 (1930), 65-82. Summary in German.

Interprets the carving on the top portion of the Sanda, Gotland, runic picture stone. After cremating their kinsman, three relatives walk away. Each carries an object associated with one of the major gods: spear (Odin); hammer (Thor); and spade (Freyr). The inset portion above may show the reception of the dead man in Valhalla; Odin and Frigg are seated there, and a stork may be the messenger who transported the dead man to Valhǫll.

1165. Jungner, Hugo. "Högstena-galdern: En västgötsk runbesvärjelse mot gengångare." *Fornvännen,* 31 (1936), 278-304. Summary in German.

A runic charm against revenants.

1166. Jungner, Hugo. "När kristendom och fornsvensk gudatro möttes." *Religion och kultur,* 9 (1938), 70-75.

Runic evidence for the meeting of paganism and Christianity in Sweden: the Sparlösa and Oklunda inscriptions.

1167. Jungner, Hugo. "Sparlösastenen: Västergötlands Rök—ett hövdingamonument från folkvandringstiden." *Fornvännen,* 1938, pp. 193-229.

The runes on the Sparlösa stone may have been consecrated by a priest or guardian of the sanctuary (*vé-vǫrðr*).

K

1168. Kabell, Aage. *Balder und die Mistel.* FF Communications, 196. Helsinki: Suomalainen tiedeakatemia, 1965. 21 pp.

The mistletoe said to have killed Baldr is in its cultural context an unlikely weapon, according to Kabell, for mistletoe ordinarily confers health and good fortune. Kabell argues that Snorri misunderstood the poetic expression *viðar teinungr*, originally a metaphor for Hǫðr. As in the Herebeald episode in *Beowulf*, an inexperienced youth accidentally kills his brother.

1169. Kabell, Aage. "Nordendorf A." *Beiträge zur Geschichte der deutschen Sprache und Literatur* (Tübingen), 92 (1970), 1-16.

Interpretation of the runic inscription "A" on the Nordendorf brooch. Kabell reads the triad as Wodan/Odin, Vingþórr, and "flame-drier" (logaþore).

1170. Kabell, Aage. "Harja." *Zeitschrift für deutsches Altertum*, 102 (1973), 1-15.

Suggests that etymological syncretism created a single root (*har*) combining such notions as "hairy," "powerful," "one-eyed," "involved with battle," and so forth, which was instrumental in the development of the mythological conception of Odin.

1171. Kabell, Aage. "Baugi und der Ringeid." *Arkiv för nordisk filologi*, 90 (1975), 30-40.

Despite the title, this article has little to do directly with Baugi (brother of Suttungr in Snorri's version of the acquisition of the mead of poetry). According to Kabell, Snorri misunderstood the word *baugeiðr* "ring-oath" in *Hávamál* 10 and created Baugi from it. Indeed, Kabell argues, the "ring-oath" is a late Icelandic antiquarian production with no basis in paganism; most of the article presents evidence for this hypothesis.

1172. Kabell, Aage. "Der Fischfang Þórs." *Arkiv för nordisk filologi*, 91 (1976), 123-29.

Derives the account of Thor's fishing expedition for the midgard serpent from Christian and particularly Judaic allegory. The Judaic influence (Behemoth, Hiob, Leviathan) will have reached Scandinavia as a result of the expansion of

Jewish culture in Spain, the Carolingian empire, and England from the eighth century onward, and the Nordic version of the myth was created among the skalds.

1173. Kabell, Aage. *Skalden und Schamanen.* FF Communications, 227. Helsinki: Suomalainen tiedeakatemia, 1980. 44 pp.

Explores the possibility that the old mythological skaldic poems, i.e., *Ragnarsdrápa*, *Haustlǫng*, and *Húsdrápa*, are texts that were recited accompanied by Lapp shaman drums. On these drums were mythological scenes to which the skalds alluded.

1174. Kahl, Hans-Dietrich. "Europäische Wortschatzbewegungen im Bereich der Verfassungsgeschichte: Ein Versuch am Beispiel germanischer und slawischer Herrschernamen. Mit Anhang: Zum Ursprung von germ. König." *Zeitschrift der Savigny-Stiftung für Rechtsgeschichte*, 77, Germanistische Abteilung (1960), 154-240.

The appendix, on the Germanic word for "king" (pp. 198-240), makes extensive use of *Rígsþula* and throws interesting light on the institutional background of the poem.

1175. Kahle, Bernhard. "Das Christentum in der altwestnordischen Dichtung." *Arkiv för nordisk filologi*, 17 (1901), 1-40, 97-160.

Well-known discussion of the treatment of Christianity and Christian themes in Old Norse verse. Pp. 5-20 deal directly with pagan elements, and much of the rest of the work seeks to put Christianity in the context of relatively new converts with an essentially pagan poetic diction.

1176. Kahle, Bernhard. "Altwestnordische Namenstudien." *Indogermanische Forschungen*, 14 (1903), 133-224.

Includes explanation of many mythological names, some of which are the following: Andhrímnir, Árvakr, Auðumla, Boðn, Dáinn, Draupnir, Dvalinn, Eldhrímnir, Fenrir, Fjalarr, Garmr, Gjallarbrú, Gjallarhorn, Grímr, Hræsvelgr, Hrungnir, Huginn, Jǫrmungandr, Mjǫllnir, Muninn, Naglfar, Níðhǫggr, Ratatǫskr, Skíðblaðnir, Sleipnir, Yggdrasill.

1177. Kahle, Bernhard. "Der gefesselte Riese." *Archiv für Religionswissenschaft*, 8 (1905), 314-16.

Note to M. Anholm, "Den bundne jætte i Kavkasus" (1904).

1178. Kahle, Bernhard. "Der Ragnarökmythus." *Archiv für Religionswissenschaft*, 8 (1905), 431-55.

First of two parts: critical evaluation of A. Olrik, "Om Ragnarok" (1902).

1179. Kahle, Bernhard. "Der Ragnarökmythus." *Archiv für Religionswissenschaft*, 9 (1906), 61-72.

Second of two parts: critical evaluation of A. Olrik, "Om Ragnarok" (1902).

1180. Kahle, Bernhard. "Zum Nerthuskult." *Archiv für Religionswissenschaft*, 14 (1911), 310-13.

On the Nerthus cult as described by Tacitus: Kahle sees it as a *hieros gamos* followed by lustration of the goddess and leaves unexplained the drowning of the slaves.

1181. Kalinke, Marianne. "*Ynglinga saga*, Chapter 21: A Case of Once Too Often." *Scandinavian Studies*, 50 (1978), 72-75.

On Snorri's stylistic revision of an episode in *Ynglingatal*, his source.

1182. Kallas, Oskar Ph. "Scandinavian Elements in Estonian Folklore." *Saga-Book of the Viking Society*, 10 (1919-27), 100-12.

Pp. 108 ff. rehearse some of Kaarle Krohn's hypotheses about the parallels to Norse mythology in Finnish and Estonian culture.

1183. Karlowicz, Jan. "Germanische Elemente im slavischen Mythus und Brauch." *Archiv für Religionswissenschaft*, 3 (1900), 184-93.

Germanic (mostly German) loans in the "lower mythology" of Slavic peoples.

1184. Karlsson, Stefán. "Íviðjur." *Gripla*, 3 (1979), 227-28.

The reading of *Vǫluspá*, str. 6: *íviðjur.*

1185. Karlsson, Stefán. "Þorp." *Gripla*, 3 (1979), 115-23. Summary in English, p. 123.

Karlsson proposes emending *á* to *án* in *Hávamál* 50:1-2 and understands *þorp* there as "group of trees." The emendation permits this reading: "That pine withers which stands without [the protection of] a group of trees.

1186. Karsten, T. E. "Einige Zeugnisse zur altnordischen Götterverehrung in Finland." In *Festgabe für Vilhelm Thomsen,* part 1. 307-16. Finnisch-Ugrische Forschungen, 12. Leipzig: O. Harrassowitz, 1912.

Treats the cults of Thor and of Freyr in Finland, stressing the role of Finno-Swedish culture in the transmission from Scandinavian to Finnish.

1187. Karsten, T. E. "Tīwaz." *Namn och bygd*, 2 (1914), 195-204.

Primarily concerned with survival of the god's name **Tīwaz* (> Týr) in Finno-Swedish and Swedish onomastic and popular traditions. Also attacks the etymology proposed by Adolf Noreen ("Tiveden och tibast," 1911), linking the placename Tiveden not with Týr but with the plant *Daphne mezereum*.

1188. Karsten, T. E. *Germanisch-finnische Lehnwortstudien: Ein Beitrag zu der ältesten Sprach- und Kulturgeschichte der Germanen*. Acta Societatis Scientiarum Fennicae, 45:2. Helsinki: Druckerei der finnischen Literaturgesellschaft, 1915. iv, 280 pp.

Well-known monograph on Germanic loanwords in Finnish and their implications. The first section deals with cult and treats most of the major gods, fertility cult, and cult of the dead. The second section, too, on the Germanic consonant shift, offers mythological notes in passing.

1189. Karsten, T. E. "Fenno-Skandinavisches." *Acta Philologica Scandinavica*, 5 (1930-31), 193-210.

Pp. 200-10 treat Aarnio, the Finnish fire-demon, and his relationship to Germanic peoples. As opposed to Hjalmar Lindroth, "Härnevi" (1913), Karsten holds that Aarnio has nothing to do with the placename *Härnevi*, although the name has Germanic cognates and the concept may have been influenced by Germanic gold depots of the Migration period.

1190. Karsten, T. E. "Die Inschrift des Goldrings von Pietroassa." In *Beiträge zur Runenkunde und nordischen Sprachwissenschaft: Gustav Neckel zum 60. Geburtstag*. 78-82. Leipzig: O. Harrassowitz, 1938.

Interpretation of the Pietroassa runic ring, leading to discussion of the terminology of the sacred (*helga, heilagr*).

1191. Kaspers, Wilhelm. "Germanische Götternamen." *Zeitschrift für deutsches Altertum*, 83 (1951-52), 79-91.

A series of shorter studies on the names of the Germanic gods: Donar/Thor in Roman inscriptions; Ambiomarcus (possible connection with Wodan/Odin); Duisburg-Marxloh-Dinxlaken (theophoric placenames).

1192. Kaspers, Wilhelm. "Ein neuer Matronenname." *Beiträge zur Geschichte der deutschen Sprache und Literatur* (Halle), 78 (1956), 470-79.

A new Matrona, possibly Germanic: Hurstvaheni(s), which Kaspers reads as "goddess of the forest or bush."

1193. Kaspers, Wilhelm. "Der Name der Dea Hurstrga." *Beiträge zur Geschichte der deutschen Sprache und Literatur* (Halle), 80 (1958), 422-23.

Additional evidence for the author's postulation, in "Ein neuer

Matronenname" (1956), of a Matrona-name Hurstvaheni(s), which Kaspers reads as "goddess of the forest or bush."

1194. Kauffmann, Friedrich. "Der zweite Merseburger Zauberspruch." *Beiträge zur Geschichte der deutschen Sprache und Literatur*, 15 (1891), 207-10.

"Probably Vol and Friia are originally only hypostases of various attributes of one and the same divine woman, the wife of the highest god" (p. 210).

1195. Kauffmann, Friedrich. "Mythologische Zeugnisse aus römischen Inschriften." *Beiträge zur Geschichte der deutschen Sprache und Literatur*, 15 (1891), 553-62.

The first of a series of articles on Roman inscriptions; deals with a Hercules Magusanus, who has obvious affinities with Thor.

1196. Kauffmann, Friedrich. "Mythologische Zeugnisse aus römischen Inschriften." *Beiträge zur Geschichte der deutschen Sprache und Literatur*, 16 (1892), 200-34.

The second of a series of articles on Roman inscriptions. Pp. 200-10 (part 2 of the series) treat Mars Thincsus and the Alciis, and pp. 210-34 discuss a deity called Dea Nehalennia, a goddess perhaps reminiscent of the *vanir*.

1197. Kauffmann, Friedrich. "Vingolf." *Zeitschrift für deutsches Altertum*, 36 (1892), 32-41.

"*Vingolf* is the 'hall of lovers,' where the shield-maiden makes the deathless hero happy, where, in Scandinavian terminology, valkyries and einherjar in free love enjoy the most blessed passions" (p. 37).

1198. Kauffmann, Friedrich. "Mythologische Zeugnisse aus römischen Inschriften." *Beiträge zur Geschichte der deutschen Sprache und Literatur*, 18 (1894), 134-94.

The third of a series of articles on Roman inscriptions, comprising the fourth and fifth parts of the series. "Dea Hluđana" (pp. 134-57) discusses a figure, perhaps identical to Hlóđyn, who inhabits the woods. "Deus Requalivahanus" (pp. 157-94) presents a figure Kauffmann interprets as "the god who lives in darkness" and associates with the Baldr myth.

1199. Kauffmann, Friedrich. "Noch einmal der zweite Merseburger Spruch." *Zeitschrift für deutsche Philologie*, 26 (1894), 454-62.

Response to H. Gering, "Der zweite Merseburger Spruch" (1894).

1200. Kauffmann, Friedrich. "Mythologische Zeugnisse aus römischen Inschriften." *Beiträge zur Geschichte der deutschen Sprache und Literatur*, 19 (1895), 526-34.

The sixth part in a series of articles on Roman inscriptions, this bears the subtitle "Dea Garmangabis." Kauffmann interprets the name as "goddess of wealth" and associates her with Nerthus.

1201. Kauffmann, Friedrich. *Deutsche Mythologie*, 2nd ed. Sammlung Göschen, 15. Stuttgart: G. J. Göschen, 1896. 119 pp. 1st ed. 1890.

Handbook of German mythology.

1202. Kauffmann, Friedrich. "Ein gotischer Göttername?" *Zeitschrift für deutsche Philologie*, 31 (1899), 138.

Dismisses a hypothetical Gothic god, Hore.

1203. Kauffmann, Friedrich. "Muspilli." *Zeitschrift für deutsche Philologie*, 33 (1901), 5-7.

The meaning of *muspilli*: "destruction of the earth."

1204. Kauffmann, Friedrich. *Balder: Mythus und Sage, nach ihren dichterischen und religiösen Elementen untersucht.* Texte und Untersuchungen zur altgermanischen Religionsgeschichte, Untersuchungen, 1. Strassburg: K. J. Trübner, 1902. ix, 308 pp.

Monograph on Baldr, seeking to derive the myth from a heroicized royal sacrifice.

1205. Kauffmann, Friedrich. *Northern Mythology*. London: J. M. Dent, 1903. xii, 106 pp. Translated by M. Steele Smith. Rpt. Philadelphia: R. West, 1977.

Translation of the author's *Deutsche Mythologie* (orig. 1890).

1206. Kauffmann, Friedrich. "Altgermanische Religion." *Archiv für Religionswissenschaft*, 8 (1905), 114-28.

Research survey.

1207. Kauffmann, Friedrich. "Mercurius Cimbrianus." *Zeitschrift für deutsche Philologie*, 38 (1906), 289-97.

The epigraphic evidence for a German Mercury, god of merchants and, according to Kauffmann, identical with Wodan/Odin.

1208. Kauffmann, Friedrich. "Altgermanische Religion." *Archiv für Religionswissenschaft*, 11 (1907-08), 105-26.

Research survey.

1209. Kauffmann, Friedrich. "Altgermanische Religion." *Archiv für Religionswissenschaft*, 20 (1920-21), 205-29.

Research survey.

1210. Kauffmann, Friedrich. "Über den Schicksalsglauben der Germanen." *Zeitschrift für deutsche Philologie*, 50 (1923-26), 361-408.

A study, drawing on vocabulary and textual examples, of the varieties of belief in fate among Germanic peoples. Kauffmann investigates the bonds of fate, powers of fate, and various manifestations of fate. The latter section relates to mythological beings (matrones, norns, gods, etc); Kauffmann concludes that originally power over fate resided not with the gods but with giants. Only during late paganism were such powers associated with the gods.

1211. Kauffmann, Friedrich. "Altgermanische Religion." *Archiv für Religionswissenschaft*, 27 (1929), 334-45.

Research survey.

1212. Kauffmann, Friedrich. "Altgermanische Religion." *Archiv für Religionswissenschaft*, 31 (1934), 124-36.

Research survey.

1213. Kaufmann, Alex. "Zur Thrymsquidha." *Zeitschrift für deutsche Mythologie und Sittenkunde*, 3 (1855), 107-09.

An alleged folktale analog to *Þrymskviða*.

1214. Keller, Gustav. *Tanz und Gesang bei den alten Germanen*. Bern: Stämpfli, 1927. 87 pp.

In arguing (against Heusler) the primacy of song and dance among the ancient Germanic peoples, Keller discusses ritual warrior dances and other examples of dance in cult, and he connects mythological eddic poetry with these.

1215. Ker, W. P. "Notes on Orendel and Other Stories." *Folk-Lore*, 8 (1897), 289-307.

Touches on the possibility that the name *Orendel* is equivalent to Aurvandill and concludes with a consideration of solar mythology and *Grógaldr*, *Fjǫlsvinnsmál*, and related texts.

1216. Ker, W. P. *Epic and Romance: Essays on Medieval Literature* [2nd ed]. London: Macmillan, 1908. xxiv, 398 pp. 1st ed. 1897; rpt. New York: Dover Publications, 1957.

Ker's classic study of medieval epic and romance is useful for placing Norse mythological traditions in their literary context. See especially the chapters on "Romantic Mythology" (pp. 35-49), "The Teutonic Epic" (pp. 65-122), and "The Style of the Poems" (pp. 133-43).

1217. Kermode, P. M. C. "Saga Illustrations of Early Manks Monuments." *Saga-Book of the Viking Society*, 1 (1892-96), 350-69.

Scandinavian myth and legend on Manx stones, with illustrations.

1218. Kermode, P. M. C. *Traces of the Norse Mythology in the Isle of Man*. London: Bemrose, 1904. 30 pp.

Text of an address; illustrated. Kermode interprets pictorial motifs from Manx crosses as instances of Norse mythology.

1219. Kermode, P. M. C. *Manx Crosses: Or, the Inscribed and Sculptured Monuments of the Isle of Man from About the End of the Fifth to the Beginning of the Thirteenth Century*. London: Bemrose, 1907. xxii, 221 pp.

Identifies Norse mythological scenes on a number of crosses.

1220. Keyser, R. *Nordmændenes videnskabelighed og literatur i middelalderen*. Oslo: P. L Malling, 1866. viii, 588 pp. Vol. 1 of Keyser's *Efterladte Skrifter*, ed. O. Rygh.

These posthumous lectures of R. Keyser offer nothing less than a handbook of Old Norse literature, with emphasis on the poetic materials, especially *Snorra edda* and eddic poetry.

1221. Kienle, Mathilde von. "Der Schicksalsbegriff im Altdeutschen." *Wörter und Sachen*, 15 (1933), 81-111.

Semantic study of Old High German vocabulary of the concept of fate. Relevant to the norns and to such Norse terms as *mjǫtuðr* and *regin*.

1222. Kienle, Richard von. "Das Auftreten keltischer und germanischer Gottheiten zwischen Oberrhein und Limes." *Archiv für Religionswissenschaft*, 35 (1938), 252-87.

Islands of possible Germanic cult within areas of Celtic settlement in the Rhineland.

1223. Kienle, Richard von. *Germanische Gemeinschaftsformen*. Deutsches Ahnerbe, B: Fachwissenschaftliche Untersuchungen, Arbeiten zur Germanenkunde, 4. Stuttgart: W. Kohlhammer, 1939. ix, 325 pp.

On Germanic social forms; accepts the presence of *Männerbünde* but disassociates them from the sacral.

1224. Kiil, Vilhelm. "Er de nordiske Solberg minner om soldyrkelse?" *Maal og minne*, 1936, pp. 126-75.

Using placename evidence, Kiil argues that sun worship was associated from the Bronze Age onward in Scandinavia—particularly Norway—with high, isolated mountain areas. Such worship was allegedly deeply rooted in Scandinavia also in later periods and manifested itself in such placenames as *Solberg* "sun-mountain," where people gathered on important days for cult activity directed toward the sun.

1225. Kiil, Vilhelm. "Eilífr Goðrúnarson's Þórsdrápa." *Arkiv för nordisk filologi*, 71 (1956), 89-167.

Detailed edition and extended commentary to the poem, one of the most important skaldic mythological texts.

1226. Kiil, Vilhelm. "Ladejarlenes ennidúkr og fjordens díar." *Maal og minne*, 1958, pp. 98-106.

In interpreting a kenning in Einarr skálaglamm's *Vellekla*, Kiil proposes that the word *díar* in Kormakr's *Sigurðardrápa* refers specifically to functionaries in the Trondheim area who looked after sacrifice. Kiil goes on to examine Snorri's use of the word *díar* in *Ynglinga saga* for the twelve divine priests established by Odin, and he concludes that Kormakr's poem may have influenced Snorri there and in *Skáldskaparmál*. In any case, argues Kiil, the word is unlikely to be an Irish loan.

1227. Kiil, Vilhelm. "De to *vísur* Torvald veile og Ulv Uggason imellom." *Maal og minne*, 1959, pp. 2-19.

Interpretation of the skaldic exchange between Þorvaldr veili and Ulfr Uggason in connection with the conversion of Iceland.

1228. Kiil, Vilhelm. "Tjodolvs *Haustlǫng*." *Arkiv för nordisk filologi*, 74 (1959), 1-104.

An extensive commentary to Þjóðolfr's poem. The first four pages contain criticism of A. Holtsmark, "Myten om *Idun* og *Tjatse* i Tjodolvs *Haustlǫng*" (1949).

1229. Kiil, Vilhelm. "Fra andvegissúla til omnkall: Grunndrag i Torskulten." *Norveg*, 7 (1960), 183-246. Illustrated. Summary in English.

Connects the worship of Thor with pillars and interprets some of the myths of

Thor in this context. The whetstone in Thor's head reflects nails driven ritually into the pillar, and the alternation of an image of Thor and a terrifying mask atop pillars may have to do with his visit to Geirrøðr and general opposition to the giants.

See the criticism of A. Ropeid, "Vilhelm Kiil og Tors-kulten" (1963).

1230. Kiil, Vilhelm. "*Hliðskjálf* og *seiðhjallr*." *Arkiv för nordisk filologi*, 75 (1960), 84-112.

Interprets Hliðskjalf, Odin's high seat according to Snorri, as originally a common noun identical with *seiðhjallr*, the term denoting the platform on which a seeress carried out her magic acts. Among the more interesting suggestions is the notion that scenes from the Bayeaux tapestry may show the platform, and that placenames in *-skjalf* have much to say about ancient cult activity.

1231. Kiil, Vilhelm. "Hyndluljóð's skautgjarn jǫtunn." *Maal og minne*, 1962, pp. 97.

Kiil reads *skautgjarn jǫtunn* (*Hyndluljóð* 30) as "the giant greedy for the sail's sheet," support for Kiil's notion that Þjazi, to whom the epithet pertains, was a wind demon probably to be equated with Hræsvelgr.

1232. Kiil, Vilhelm. "The Norse Prophetess and the Ritually Induced Prostitution." *Norveg*, 9 (1962), 159-74.

States that "partly ritually induced prostitution was practiced by the professional sibyls, *vǫlur*. This statement, perhaps astonishing to the reader, we will confirm from various Old Norse literary sources" (p. 160). These sources are primarily poetic and difficult to interpret. Kiil adds: "we may presume that the earthly counterpart of *Vingolf*, the hǫrgr, which is known to be the domain of the priestess and a sanctuary especially for the gods of fertility, has also included sexual intercourse in its rituals" (p. 171).

1233. Kiil, Vilhelm. "Gevjonmyten og Ragnarsdråpa." *Maal og minne*, 1965, pp. 63-70.

Following his arguments about "The Norse Prophetess and the Ritual Prostitution" (1961), Kiil interprets the first part of the first helming of *Ragnarsdrápa* as follows: "Gefjon, happy, drew wages of arousal from Gylfi's homestead" (the second clause he interprets in the normal way). The interpretation is based on postulation of a direct object, *djúprǫðul æðla*, literally "gold of arousals."

1234. Kilger, P. Laurenz. "Bekehrungsmotive in der Germanenmission." *Zeitschrift für Missionswissenschaft*, 27 (1937), 1-19.

Motivation for the conversion of the Germanic peoples to Christianity: the Christian God was more powerful than pagan gods and the pagan notion of fate. Kilger sees the conversion as partly a political matter, as chieftains led the way.

1235. Kingsland, L. W. "Initiation Ceremony from Norse Literature." *Folk-Lore*, 57 (1946), 47.

Brief comment on M. Danielli, "Initiation Ceremony from Norse Literature" (1945).

1236. Kirby, W. F. "The Voluspá, the Sibyl's Lay in the Edda of Sæmund." *Saga-Book of the Viking Society*, 8 (1912-13), 44-52.

Essentially a summary of the poem, arguing against Christian influence but admitting some Celtic influence.

1237. Kivikoski, Ella. "Christliche Einflüsse in dem archäologischen Material der Wikingerzeit und der Kreuzzugszeit Finnlands." In *Kirche und Gesellschaft im Ostseeraum und im Norden vor der Mitte des 13. Jahrhunderts*. 31-41. Acta Visbyensia, 3; Visby-symposiet för historiska vetenskaper 1967. Visby: Museum Gotlands Fornsal, 1969.

A paper delivered at an international conference on church and society in Viking Scandinavia and the Baltic; treats possible Christian influence on pagan grave materials in Finland.

1238. Kjær, A. "Nogle stedsnavne." *Maal og minne*, 1914, pp. 204-23.

Includes a section on the Norwegian fjord names **Fjǫlna, Fjǫlnir*, arguing that these are not associated with the mythological name Fjǫlnir.

1239. Kjærum, Poul. "Tempelhus fra stenalder." *Kuml*, 1955, pp. 7-34. Summary in English.

Archaeological description of a neolithic temple in eastern Jutland.

1240. Kjellberg, Carl M. "Thorshugle." *Namn och bygd*, 1 (1913), 126-32.

On the specific location of a placename, Thorshugle, in Uppsala (Sweden), which the author takes as definite indication of the worship of Thor.

1241. Kjerulf, E. *Völuspá fornritanna og ýmiskonar athuganir*. Reykjavik: Ísafoldarprentsmiðja h. f., 1945. 229 pp.

Edition, with notes and commentary, of *Vǫluspá*. The apparatus ranges far in attempting to show that *Vǫluspá* and other Old Icelandic texts, or sections of texts, would, if written with runes, tend toward a total number of characters divisible by eight. It is difficult to take seriously such argumentation.

1242. Klare, Hans-Joachim. "Die Toten in der altnordischen Literatur." *Acta Philologica Scandinavica*, 8 (1933-34), 1-56.

A systematic study of the dead in Old Norse literature. The survey purports to be complete, and the essential finding is that all the Norse dead were "living corpses." They were three-dimensional beings of flesh and blood, possessing many of the usual characteristics of the living, but their appearance was that of corpses. They were quite similar to human magicians in their interactions with the ordinary human community.

Pp. 15-17 treat *Hávamál* 157 and Odin's association with the dead.

1243. Klein, Ernst. "Der Ritus des Tötens bei den nordischen Völkern." *Archiv für Religionswissenschaft*, 28 (1930), 166-82.

On animal and human sacrifice in Scandinavia. The article has as much a theoretical as a practical cast, but some of the materials chosen, such as *níð*, are relevant to Norse mythology.

1244. Klein, Ernst. "Der Ritus des Tötens bei den nordischen Völkern." In *Actes du Ve congrès international d'histoire des religions à Lund, 27-29 août 1929*. 205-08. Lund: C. W. K. Gleerup, 1930.

Lecture and discussion from an international congress on the history of religion. A longer version of this lecture appeared under the same title in *Archiv für Religionswissenschaft*.

1245. Klingenberg, Heinz. "Alvíssmál: Das Lied vom überweisen Zwerg." *Germanisch-Romanisch Monatsschrift*, 48 (1967), 113-42.

Klingenberg finds considerable order and design in *Alvíssmál*. Thor's questions fall in six linked categories, plus one which implies a missing category. In the eleventh question, that category is night, and the missing category is the sun, which destroys Alvíss. In using thirteen categories, argues Klingenberg, Thor calls on magic, and Klingenberg subdivides the responses too into groups of thirteen. The final category, beer, relates to such contests of wisdom, and apparently Alvíss lost track of his identity during the exchange.

1246. Klingenberg, Heinz. "Hávamál: Bedeutungs- und Gestaltenwandel eines Motivs." In *Festschrift für Siegfried Gubenbrunner: Zum 65. Geburtstag am 26. Mai 1971 überreicht von seinen Freunden und Kollegen*, eds. Oskar Bandle, Heinz Klingenberg, and F. Maurer, 117-44. Heidelberg: C. Winter, 1972.

Klingenberg analyzes the structure of the *Ljóðatal*, the list of charms acquired by Odin in *Hávamál* and listed in stanzas 146-63. He divides the eighteen charms into two groups of nine, in which the first half involve reduction and the second half increase. Klingenberg associates this grouping and procession with the phases of the moon and postulates a connection with the immediately preceding stanzas 138-45, which detail Odin's famous self- sacrifice; there too a progression of reduction and increase may be observed, in the circumstances of the gods.

1247. Klingenberg, Heinz. *Runenschrift, Schriftdenken, Runeninschriften*. Germanische Bibliothek, 3. Reihe, Untersuchungen und Einzeldarstellungen. Heidelberg: C. Winter, 1973. 415 pp.

Klingenberg argues that older runic inscriptions repeatedly show multiples of 13 in a great many ways (few of them convincing). Since the name of the thirteenth rune in the elder futhark is "yew tree," Klingenberg speculates that use of that rune and the hypothetical multiples of 13 symbolize the world tree of myth. The relevance to Scandinavian mythology and Germanic religion of this attempt to demonstrate the presence of precise numerological speculation in the Gallehus horn and other older runic inscriptions lies in the implied correlation of such rational thinking and calculation with the irrational, with myth and cult. See Otto Höfler's review in *Anzeiger für deutsches Altertum*, 136 (1975), 49-61, especially p. 61.

1248. Klingenberg, Heinz. *Edda—Sammlung und Dichtung*. Beiträge zur nordischen Philologie, 3. Basel and Stuttgart: Kohlhammer, 1974. 186 pp.

Despite its turgid prose and repetitions, this monograph is of unusual interest. Klingenberg investigates the hypothetical role of the compiler of Codex Regius of the Poetic Edda, and draws the following conclusions: 1) the section containing heroic poems deliberately recapitulates the mythological section; *Helgakviða Hundingsbana I* as a synopsis of what is to follow parallels *Vǫluspá*, and *Hamð ismál* presents a heroic parallel to Ragnarǫk; 2) the redactor of Codex Regius composed *Helgakviða Hundingsbana I*; 3) further concern with the curve of mythic structure, leading to a heroic Ragnarǫk, manifests itself in a "second language" with many intimations of the end of the world; 4) the concern with myth and the end of the world derives from the thirteenth-century context of the redaction of Codex Regius.

1249. Klingenberg, Heinz. "Die Drei-Götter-Fibel von Nordendorf bei Augsburg: Zum Typus der mythologischen, exemplarisch-aktuellen Runeninschrift." *Zeitschrift für deutsches Altertum*, 105 (1976), 167-88.

Analyzing the runic inscription on brooch I from Nordendorf, Klingenberg proposes a typology of three-god inscriptions.

1250. Klingenberg, Heinz. "Types of Eddic Mythological Poetry." In *Edda: A Collection of Essays*, eds. Robert J. Glendenning and Haraldur Bessason, 134-64. The University of Manitoba Icelandic Studies, 4. N. p.: University of Manitoba Press, 1983.

Klingenberg distinguishes two types of eddic mythological poetry: a continuous narrative type and a more common enumerative type. He discusses in detail two examples of each type: *Þrymskviða* and *Hymiskviða* (continuous narrative) and *Lokasenna* and *Grímnismál* (enumerative). These discussions are informative as regards the texts themselves and include some interesting suggestions: *Hymiskviða* shows traces of a thirteenth-century neomythographer; *Lokasenna* represents the trial of Loki for the murder of Baldr; in *Grímnismál* Odin shows Geirrøðr a vision of what he would have had as an Odin hero and then denies it to him.

1251. Kluge, Friedrich. "Ôstarûn." *Zeitschrift für deutsche Wortforschung*, 2 (1902), 42-43.

Goddess of the new year?

1252. Kluge, Friedrich. "Tuisco deus et filius Mannus Germ. 2." *Zeitschrift für deutsche Wortforschung*, 2 (1902), 43-45.

Proposes the following genealogy: Ti wos, Ti wisko, Mannus, Manniskones (men).

1253. Knudsen, Gunnar. "Hjemligt hedenskab." *Danske studier*, 16 (1919), 186-88.

Review of G. Schütte, *Hjemligt hedenskab i almenfattelig fremstilling* (1919).

1254. Knudsen, Gunnar. "Balder." *Danske studier*, 17 (1920), 184-85.

Review of G. Neckel, *Die Überlieferungen vom Gotte Balder* (1920).

1255. Knudsen, Gunnar. "Norrøne gude- og heltesagn." *Danske studier*, 19 (1922), 187-88.

Review of P. A. Munch, *Norrøne gude- og heltesagn* (1922).

1256. Knudsen, Gunnar. "Baldersbrønde." In *Festskrift til Finnur Jónsson 29. maj 1928*. 463-73. Copenhagen: Levin & Munksgaard, 1928.

The placename *Baldersbrønde* has nothing to do with the god Baldr, although the second component may refer to a sacred spring.

1257. Knudsen, Gunnar. "Runemagi." *Danske studier*, 28 (1931), 88-89.

Review of S. Agrell, *Senantik mysteriereligion och nordisk runmagi* (1931).

1258. Knudsen, Gunnar. "Brudevælte." *Danske studier*, 32 (1935), 161-67.

Contra G. Ekholm, "Brudevælte" (1936): the name makes no reference to cult.

1259. Knudsen, Gunnar. "Religionshistorie." *Danske studier*, 33 (1936), 188.

Review of J. de Vries, *Altgermanische Religionsgeschichte* (1st ed., 1935).

1260. Knudsen, Gunnar. "Navnestudier." *Danske studier*, 35 (1938), 49-63.

Review article on placename studies; pp. 56-61 discuss the differing methodological premises employed by J. de Vries, H. Ellekilde, and Aug. F. Schmidt.

1261. Knudsen, Gunnar. "Pseudotheofore stednavne." *Namn och bygd*, 27 (1939), 105-115.

The author introduces the term "pseudotheophoric" for placenames wrongly assigned to the sphere of cult. Examples are from Denmark and relate, among others, to the goddess Hǫrn.

1262. Knudsen, Gunnar. "Kultminne i stadnamn: Danmark." In *Religionshistorie*, ed. Nils Lid, 28-40. Nordisk kultur, 26. Stockholm: A. Bonnier, Oslo: H. Aschehoug, Copenhagen: J. H. Schultz, 1942.

A critical survey of references to cult in Danish placenames, including discussion of earlier work and ample references.

1263. Knudsen, Regnar. "*Visby*: Bemerkninger om navnet og stedet." *Gotländskt arkiv*, 5 (1933), 26-36.

Against derivation of the placename *Visby* from *vi-* "sanctuary."

1264. Knudsen, Regnar. "*Vi* og *Vis* i stednavne." In *Studier tilegnede Verner Dahlerup paa femoghalvfjerdsaarsdagen den 31. oktober 1934*. 196-204. Århus: Universitets forlag, 1934. Also issued as *Danske folkemaal*, vol. 8, suppl., and *Sprog og kultur*, vol. 3, suppl.

False theophoric placenames.

1265. Koch-Olsen, Ib. *Danmarks kulturhistorie—tiden indtil 1600.* Copenhagen: Grafisk forlag, 1968. 560 pp.

Illustrated cultural history of Denmark. The chapters on the period 400-1200 A.D. offer a popular account of myth and religion.

1266. Kock, Axel. "Om Ynglingar såsom namn på en svensk konungaätt." *[Svensk] Historisk tidskrift*, 15 (1895), 157-70.

On the Swedish royal line, the Ynglingar. Kock sees a progression from an *Inguna árfreyr* (Yngvi-Freyr) "lord of the Ingvaeonic peoples," which indicates cult in eastern Denmark. This cult was brought to Sweden, where later kings considered themselves descendants of Yngvi-Freyr.

1267. Kock, Axel. "Die Göttin Nerthus und der Gott Niorþr." *Zeitschrift für deutsche Philologie*, 28 (1896), 289-94.

Linguistic evidence for the pairs Nerthus-Njǫrðr and Freyr-Freyja: with the weakening of the feminine u-stem nouns and their syncretism with masculines, it became possible to call the masculine companion of Nerthus by the same name as the goddess; adding *freyr* "lord" and *freyja* "lady" was thus necessary to distinguish the two. Later, when the feminine u-stem nouns were lost and the terms *Freyr* and *Freyja* were used alone, only Njord remained of the "original" pair.

1268. Kock, Axel. "Etymologisch-mythologische Untersuchungen." *Indogermanische Forschungen*, 10 (1899), 90-111.

Proposes several etymologies with mythological interpretation.

Loki's name means "fire." His secondary name Loptr means "lightning." His brother's name, Byleiptr, means "storm lightning," and Helblindi is the darkness between flashes of lightning. Nál and Laufey are associated with the origin of fire in trees struck by lightning, and Sigyn has to do with rain clouds.

Fornjótr was originally "the ancient storm."

Other names treated more briefly are Gleipnir, Són and Boðn, Mjǫllnir, and Vingþórr.

1269. Kock, Axel. "Bidrag till nordisk ordforskning." *Arkiv för nordisk filologi*, 20 (1903), 44-56.

Pp. 44-47 propose an etymology for Old Norse-Icelandic *dísarsalr*: < **di s-aiR-salR* "cult hall of the *dísir*.

1270. Kock, Axel. "Ordforskning i den äldre Eddan." *Arkiv för nordisk filologi*, 27 (1911), 107-40.

Includes etymological discussion of Bergelmir and Óskopnir, and also of several common nouns from mythological poetry.

1271. Kock, Axel. "Besvärjelse-formler i forndanska runinskrifter." *Arkiv för nordisk filologi*, 38 (1922), 1-21.

Primarily philological notes on curses in Old Danish runic inscriptions.

1272. Kock, Ernst A. "Domen över död man." *Arkiv för nordisk filologi*, 33 (1917), 175-78.

Discussion of *Hávamál*, str. 77.

1273. Kock, Ernst A. "Bidrag till eddatolkningen." *Arkiv för nordisk filologi*, 35 (1919), 22-29.

Commentary to *Vǫluspá*, str. 23, 34; *Lokasenna*, str. 28; *Hávamál*, str. 2, 57, 76, 95.

1274. Kock, Ernst A. "Bidrag till eddatolkningen (Jfr Arkiv 35, 22-29)." *Arkiv för nordisk filologi*, 37 (1921), 105-35.

The second of Kock's "bidrag" includes commentary on, inter alia, *Hymiskviða*, str. 31; *Alvíssmál*, str. 4, 16; *Hávamál*, str. 7, 54, 70, 77, 155.

1275. Kock, Ernst A. "Bidrag till eddatolkningen (Jfr Arkiv 35, 22-29, 37, 105-135)." *Arkiv för nordisk filologi*, 38 (1922), 269-94.

The third of Kock's "bidrag" includes commentary on, inter alia, *Vǫluspá*, str. 31, 41, 55; *Baldrs draumar*, str. 14, *Hymiskviða*, str. 10, 39; *Grímnismál*, str. 29; *Hávamál*, str. 6, 36-37, 63, 99; several verses in *Rígsþula*; *Skírnismál* 22. Pp. 292-94 contain indices of passages, words, and subjects treated in the three articles.

1276. Kögel, Rudolf. "Idis und Walküre." *Beiträge zur Geschichte der deutschen Sprache und Literatur*, 16 (1892), 502-08.

Etymologies concerned with female figures in religion and myth.

1277. Kögel, Rudolf. "Germanische Etymologien." *Indogermanische Forschungen*, 4 (1894), 312-20.

Pp. 312-14 treat the etymology of the first component of the name Heimdallr: "gleaming."

1278. Köhler, Reinhold. "Zum zweiten Merseburger Zauberspruch." *Germania*, 8 (1863), 62-63.

Scottish parallels.

1279. Kölbing, E. "Zu Œgisdrekka." *Germania*, 21 (1876), 27-28.

Notes to *Lokasenna*, str. 19 and 24.

1280. Kohl, R. "Die Augsburger Cisa—eine germanische Göttin?" *Archiv für Religionswissenschaft*, 33 (1936), 21-40.

Careful consideration of the evidence for and against a hypothetical German goddess Cisa. The article is of some methodological interest, as it uses such unusual sources as art history and the humanistic tradition.

1281. Kohlschmidt, Werner. "Zur religionsgeschichtlichen Stellung des Muspilli." *Zeitschrift für deutsches Altertum*, 64 (1927), 294-98.

Explores the possibility that the figure of Elias in *Muspilli* may exhibit traits of the Germanic thunder god.

1282. Koht, Halvdan. "Sjælevandring og opkaldelse." *Maal og minne*, 1915, pp. 64.

Comment on G. Storm, "Vore forfædres tro paa sjælevandring og deres opkaldelsessystem" (1892).

1283. Koht, Halvdan. "Sild og–bukker?" *Maal og minne*, 1917, pp. 163-64.

Restores oats for goats, as suggested by O. Nordgaard, "Tors frokost" (1917), for Thor's breakfast in *Hárbarðsljóð*.

1284. Kolb, Herbert. "Vora demo muspille: Versuch einer Interpretation." *Zeitschrift für deutsche Philologie*, 83 (1964), 2-33.

On the German poem *Muspilli*, arguing its literary unity and unique standing. Of interest to the study of Scandinavian mythology is Kolb's interpretation of the term *muspilli* as "last judgment."

1285. Kolsrud, Oluf. "Dísaþing." *Maal og minne*, 1912, pp. 114.

Attestation of *dísaþing* in a Norwegian placename.

1286. Kolsrud, Oluf. "To hittil ukjendte hov i Løten." *Maal og minne*, 1914, pp. 95-100.

Placenames indicating cult activity in Hedmark, Norway.

1287. Konow, Sten. "Njord og Kāli : En parallel en antydning." In *Festskrift tilegnet førstebibliothekar A. Kjær av venner 26. september 1924*. 53-60. Oslo: Cammermeyer, J. Dybwad, Grøndahl & Søn, 1924.

Comparison of Njord and Kāli as fertility figures.

1288. Konrad, Karl. *Die Edda des Snorri Sturluson*. Thüringen: Urquell-Verlag, 1926. 187 pp.

German translation of *Snorra edda*, with introduction and commentary.

Konráð Gíslason, *see* Gíslason, Konráð.

1289. Kopperstad, Knut. "Det pers. pron. 'Hann' som subjekt for 'upersonlege' verber." *Maal og minne*, 1920, pp. 94-100.

Includes the suggestion that Njord may be the underlying subject of the expression *hann rignir* "it is raining."

For a rebuttal see M. Olsen, "Er 'han' i upersonlege uttrykk Njord?" (1920).

1290. Korsun, A. I. *Starshaya Edda: Drevneskandskie pesni o bogach i geroyach*. Leningrad and Moscow: Nauka, 1963. 259 pp.

A Russian translation of the eddic poems. Of some interest for the introduction and commentary, both by M. I. Steblin-Kamenskij.

1291. Kossinna, Gustaf. "Zum Haaropfer (oben S. 64 ff.)." *Mannus*, 16 (1924), 112.

Brief note to G. Wilke, "Ein altgermanisches Haaropfer" (1924).

1292. Kossinna, Gustaf. "Germanischer Götterdienst in der Vorgeschichte (Kurzer Auszug)." *Mannus*, 7, Ergänzungsband (1929), 38-40. Also printed in *Forschungen und Fortschritte*, 4 (1928), 307-08; there the title lacks the words "Kurzer Auszug."

Summary of a lecture on Germanic cult and archaeology. The emphasis is on the rock carvings.

Kousgård Sørensen, John, *see* Sørensen, John Kousgård.

1293. Kragerud, Alv. "De mytologiske spørsmål i Fåvnesmål." *Arkiv för nordisk filologi*, 96 (1981), 9-48.

Fáfnismál contains a mythological question-answer sequence in which the dying Fáfnir answers Sigurd's questions: which norns deliver mothers, and on what island will Surtr meet the gods? Kragerud sets this sequence in its direct context, in the context of the entire poem, and in the context of other eddic wisdom poetry. He offers intelligent remarks on the genealogy of the norns and the traditions of Ragnarǫk and more generally on wisdom poetry. Poems treated include *Reginsmál* (str. 3-4), *Alvíssmál*, *Baldrs draumar*, *Vafþrúðnismál*, the verse in *Sǫgubrot*, ch. 3, *Fjǫlsvinnsmál*, and *Grímnismál*. Kragerud tends toward interpretation associating the poems with oracle and particularly necromancy. The dead (*Baldrs draumar*) or dying (*Fáfnismál*) being is forced to answer questions, and the answers are of a mantic nature and function almost as ideograms.

1294. Krahe, Hans. "Altgermanische Kleinigkeiten." *Indogermanische Forschungen*, 66 (1960), 35-43.

Pp. 39-43 discuss the name *Veleda*, which was borne by a seeress, and they take up generally the formation of the names of Germanic seeresses. *Veleda* is likely to be a Celtic loan.

1295. Kraig, Bruce. "Symbolism in Burial Orientations among Early Indo-Europeans." *Journal of Indo-European Studies*, 6 (1978), 149-72.

With remarks on early Indo-European worldview, symbolic classification, and ritual, relevant to Norse mythology.

1296. Krappe, Alexander Haggerty. "The Legend of Walther and Hildegund." *Journal of English and Germanic Philology*, 22 (1923), 75-88.

Includes in its attempt at a stemma the accounts of Hildr and Heðin in Norse tradition (the eternal battle of the Hjaðningar).

1297. Krappe, Alexander Haggerty. "The Myth of Balder: A Study in Comparative Mythology." *Folk-Lore*, 34 (1923), 184-215.

By comparison with Greek myths, Krappe seeks to support the following conclusion: Baldr was "an Indo-European Dioscuric vegetation demon and culture hero, originally probably a tree-spirit, but not connected with the oak. He was developed by both Hellenes and Teutons into a divinity of light. Both as a Dioscure and a culture hero he was the centre of a ritual and of an elaborate myth, relating his love for a woman and his premature death at the hands of his twin brother and rival" (p. 215).

1298. Krappe, Alexander Haggerty. "La légende de Gunnar Half (Olafs saga Tryggvasonar, Chap. 173)." *Acta Philologica Scandinavica*, 3 (1928-29), 226-33.

Krappe analyzes the tale of Gunnarr helmingr, who impersonated Freyr in a ritual procession through Sweden, reaping rich gifts and making the priestess pregnant. On the basis of Roman and Hellenic analogs and their interpretation, Krappe argues that the story lacks a direct historical basis but reflects actual ritual in which a man played the role of Freyr during sacred processional.

1299. Krappe, Alexander Haggerty. *Études de mythologie et de folklore germaniques.* Paris: E. Leroux, 1928. viii, 192 pp.

Something more than half of this book deals with mythology; from 115ff. Krappe considers folklore, later Icelandic literature, and German medieval material. The mythological section treats various topics, including Týr (originally a wolf), Odin (the Gunnlǫð episode derives from vegetation ritual), Thor (relations with fertility), and the folktale figure Frau Holle (originally a Germanic goddess). Few of these findings have proved lasting.

1300. Krappe, Alexander Haggerty. "Les dieux jumeaux dans la religion germanique." *Acta Philologica Scandinavica*, 6 (1931-32), 1-25.

Departing from *Germania*, ch. 43, Krappe puts the Germanic divine twins in their religious context. The exposition is wide-ranging, with evidence cited from Baltic, Greek, and even Zulu culture. The twins are associated with trees, with fertility, with animals, and with the sky god.

1301. Krappe, Alexander Haggerty. "Anses." *Beiträge zur Geschichte der deutschen Sprache und Literatur*, 56 (1932), 1-10.

Derives the *anses/æsir* from a pair of divine twins.

1302. Krappe, Alexander Haggerty. "Odin entre les feux (Grímnismál)." *Acta Philologica Scandinavica*, 8 (1933-34), 136-45.

On the situation in *Grímnismál*. Without knowing it, the poet will have employed for his frame an account of an ancient ritual act reflected among the Celts as the fires of Beltane, replacing the sacrificial victim with the god Odin. The origin of a corresponding myth would, according to Krappe, derive from the opposition between the new cult of the *æsir* and the old cult of the *vanir*, which would see in Odin an evil sorcerer. The myth also, in its extant form, has moral effect.

1303. Krappe, Alexander Haggerty. "Alces." *Beiträge zur Geschichte der deutschen Sprache und Literatur*, 57 (1933), 226-30.

Identifies the *alces* (Tacitus, *Germania*, book 43) as divine twins of Germanic religion.

1304. Krappe, Alexander Haggerty. "Riesen und Göttinnen." *Zeitschrift für deutsches Altertum*, 70 (1933), 206-08.

Derives the motif of the giants' lust for goddesses from classical tradition.

1305. Krappe, Alexander Haggerty. "Alexandrinische Nachklänge in der älteren Skaldendichtung." *Zeitschrift für deutsches Altertum*, 71 (1934), 181-86.

Possible Greek influence on *Eiríksmál* and *Hákonarmál.*

1306. Krappe, Alexander Haggerty. "Appolon emintheús and the Teutonic Mysing." *Archiv für Religionswissenschaft*, 33 (1936), 40-56.

Mysing is, according to the prose of *Grottasǫngr*, the destroyer of the kingdom of Fróði. Krappe equates the term with Greek *emintheús* "mouse-god" and associates the complex with accounts of the plague. Further, he suggests that the Scandinavian story is borrowed from Greek and Near Eastern sources.

1307. Krappe, Alexander Haggerty. "Die Blendwerke der Æsir." *Zeitschrift für deutsche Philologie*, 62 (1937), 113-24.

Treats three "deludings" in Norse tradition involving the *æsir*: that of Gylfi (*Gylfaginning*), that of Hrolf kraki by Hrani (Odin) (*Hrólfs saga kraka*), and that of Thor in the Útgarða-Loki episode of *Snorra edda*. After a broad review of ancient, classical, medieval, and folklore analogs, Krappe concludes that the Norse "delusions" derive from Irish models.

1308. Krappe, Alexander Haggerty. "Aegean Culture Currents in the Baltic." *Scandinavian Studies*, 16 (1940-41), 165-84.

On *Ynglinga saga*, ch. 14-15, the Anglo-Saxon *Rune Poem*, and *Grottasǫngr*. Krappe associates them with Greek (Aegean) tradition, with Thracian intermediaries.

1309. Krappe, Alexander Haggerty. "The Snake Tower." *Scandinavian Studies*, 16 (1940), 22-33.

Comparative discussion of Gunnarr in the snake pit, leading to consideration of the bound Loki. This aspect of Loki's career will have reached Scandinavia, according to the author, during the Viking Age, via England, ultimately from Near Eastern sources.

1310. Krappe, Alexander Haggerty. *The Science of Folklore.* New York: Barnes & Noble, 1962. xxi, 344 pp. Issued originally as *The Science of Folk-lore* (New York: L. MacVeigh; The Dial Press, 1930); rpt. W. W. Norton, 1964.

In this handbook on folklore, the chapters on "Custom and Religion" and "Folk-lore, Myth and Religion" contain material taken from Norse mythology.

1311. Krappe, Edith Smith. "The *Casina* of Plautus and the *Þrymskviða.*" *Scandinavian Studies*, 6 (1920), 198-201.

"The plot of the disguised bride does not occur in Western European literature in any form which does not go back to Plautus or to the *Þrymskviða*, the *Casina* and the Eddic song being the only independent plots of this nature. We can, then, be fairly certain that the *Þrymskviða* is not of old Scandinavian origin, but was introduced and incorporated to the Thor legends during the Viking period by reason of Scandinavian contact with Western Europe, i.e., probably Ireland" (p. 201).

1312. Kratz, Henry. "Was Vamoþ Still Alive? The Rök-Stone as an Initiation Memorial." *Mediaeval Scandinavia*, 11 (1978-79), 9-29.

The central premise of this attempt at a unified interpretation of the Rök inscription is that Væmoþ is dead only in a symbolic way, as the initiand in a ritual of initiation into a secret, warrior society. Vilin, then, would be his father only in the sense that he was Væmoþ's mentor.

Ample citation of earlier work.

1313. Krause, H. "Nachträge und Berichtigungen." *Zeitschrift für deutsche Mythologie und Sittenkunde*, 3 (1855), 116-22.

Treats, inter alia, Donar/Thor, Sif, and Hel.

1314. Krause, Wolfgang. "Vingþórr." *Zeitschrift für deutsches Altertum*, 64 (1927), 269-76.

On several of Thor's names in *Ving/Vé* and similar. *Ving-* is derived from the root of *vé* and *vígja* and is akin to *Véorr*; the names mean "consecrating Thor." *Wigiþonar* on the Nordendorf brooch I is probably also related. Other names discussed are *Vingiþórr, Véuðr*, and *Vingnir.*

1315. Krause, Wolfgang. "Runica II." *Nachrichten von der Gesellschaft der Wissenschaften zu Göttingen, phil.-hist. Kl.*, 1929, pp. 35-56.

Includes a section on the Gimsø stone, which Krause reads as a prophecy: Thor will rise again.

1316. Krause, Wolfgang. "Beiträge zur Runenforschung." *Schriften der Königsberger Gelehrten Gesellschaft, geisteswissenschaftliche Kl.*, 9:2 (1932), [1]-29.

The first section treats the Kylver stone in light of rune-magic.

1317. Krause, Wolfgang. "Beiträge zur Runenforschung: Zweites Heft." *Schriften der Königsberger Gelehrten Gesellschaft, geisteswissenschaftliche Kl.*, 11:1 (1934), 1-17.

On runic *laukaR* and the leek as a magic spell.

1318. Krause, Wolfgang. "Húsdrápa 9." In *Studia Germanica tillägnade Ernst Albin Kock den 6 december 1934*. 116-20. Lund: C. Blom, 1934.

Identifies a kenning for warrior in which various Odin myths are employed: victory bush of the slurp of the holy sacrifice.

1319. Krause, Wolfgang. *Was man in Runen ritzte*. Schriften der Königsberger Gelehrten Gesellschaft, geisteswissenschaftliche Kl., 12: 2. Halle a. d. S.: M. Niemeyer, 1935. viii, 53 pp. 2nd ed. 1943.

Sections relating to magic, burial, and fertility.

1320. Krause, Wolfgang. "Die Runen als Begriffszeichen." In *Beiträge zur Runenkunde und nordischen Sprachwissenschaft: Gustav Neckel zum 60. Geburtstag*. 35-53. Leipzig: O. Harrassowitz, 1938.

With remarks on the importance of the rune names referring to gods: **ansuz*, which Krause understands as Odin, and **tīwaz* "Týr."

1321. Krause, Wolfgang. "Ing." *Nachrichten der Akademie der Wissenschaften in Göttingen, phil.-hist. Kl., no. 10*, 1944, pp. 229-54.

A discussion primarily of the linguistic and runological aspects of the figure Ing. The name derives from **Ingwaz*, the eponymous founder of the Inguiones (according to Krause the correct form for the tribe called Ingvaeones by Tacitus). The word originally meant "man, male," as is appropriate for the son of Mannus (Tacitus, *Germania*, ch. 2). Personal names in Ing- probably derive from the people, not from the god, and Yngvi-Freyr should be understood as "the lord of the Inguiones." Krause also comments on the forms Ingunar- and Yngvin.

According to Krause, Ing was a fertility god who acted through the sun.

1322. Krause, Wolfgang. "Untersuchungen zu den Runennamen, I: Die Lauch-Rune." *Nachrichten der Akademie der Wissenschaften in Göttingen, phil.-hist. Kl.*, 1946-47, pp. 60-63.

Krause argues that the original name of the l-rune was not *laguR* but *laukaR*, which derives from the realm of pagan magic; *laguR* was probably a Christian replacement.

1323. Krause, Wolfgang. "Untersuchungen zu den Runennamen, II: Runennamen und Götterwelt." *Nachrichten der Akademie in Göttingen, phil.-hist. Kl.*, 1948, pp. 93-108.

This article argues a close connection between the names of the runes and the world of cult and religion. The names of the twenty-four runes fall into the following eight categories: 1) gods and demons; 2) animals; 3) plants; 4) celestial bodies and weather; 5) negative powers; 6) reference to cult; 7) uncertain references (joy, delight); 8) non-cultic (the first and last runes of the futhark). By far the most important category is 1), with seventeen of the twenty-four names; names here with direct mythological import include **þurisaz* (> *þurs* 'giant'), **ansuz* (> *áss* 'god'), **so wilo* (> *sól* 'sun'), **teiwaz* (> Týr), **mannaz* (cf. Mannus in *Germania*, book 2), **ingwaz* (cf. Ing and Yngvi). According to Krause, the few names in the other categories made reference to cult, too.

Thus the animals were worshipped as gods (this is not explained clearly), **raido* may denote a chariot used in cult, and so forth.

1324. Krause, Wolfgang. "Erta, ein anglischer Gott." *Die Sprache*, 5 (*Festschrift für Wilhelm Havers*) (1959), 46-54.

Identifes on the Franks (Auzon) casket a god's name Erta as a secondary form of the English Woden.

1325. Krause, Wolfgang. "Gullveig und Pandora." *Skandinavistik*, 5 (1975), 1-6.

Gullveig compared to Pandora.

1326. Kretschmer, Paul. "Das älteste germanische Sprachdenkmal." *Zeitschrift für deutsches Altertum*, 66 (1929), 1-14.

On the inscription on the helmet from Negau. Kretschmer discusses the linguistic implications of reading *teiwa* as cognate to Týr.

1327. Kristensen, Anne K. G. *Tacitus' germanische Gefolgschaft*. Det kongelige danske videnskabernes selskab, hist.-filos. meddelelser, 50:5. Copenhagen: Munksgaard, in commission, 1983. 93 pp.

A study of the Germanic *comitatus* as presented by Tacitus, drawing heavily on the notion of the *Männerbund* as proposed by Weiser-Aall and Höfler.

1328. Kristensen, Marius. "Bidrag til tolkning af danske stednavne." *Namn och bygd*, 8 (1920), 115-25.

Jersdal (near Haderslev, Denmark) originally meant "the goddess Eir's cult place" (pp. 119-20).

1329. Kristensen, Marius. "Skjaldenes mytologi." *Acta Philologica Scandinavica*, 5 (1930-31), 67-92.

On the mythology of the skalds.

1330. Kristensen, Marius. *Gamle navne: Spredte iagttagelser og overvejelser*. Studier fra sprog- og oldtidsforskning, 177. Copenhagen: P. Branner, 1938. 72 pp.

Includes discussions of placenames with the name of the god Thor.

Kristján Albertsson, *see* Albertsson, Kristján.

Kristján Eldjárn, *see* Eldjárn, Kristján.

1331. Kroes, H. W. J. "Die Balderüberlieferung und der 2. Merseburger Zauberspruch." *Neophilologus*, 35 (1951), 201-13.

Kroes argues (with Neckel and against de Vries) that the Baldr myth derives from the Near East and originally did not belong to the heroic sphere, although certain elements in time became more "Germanic." The second Merseburg charm is evidence that the myth was known in Germany; *Phol* is to be read as *Vol* and refers to Baldr.

1332. Kroes, H. W. J. "So se gelimida si n." *Germanisch-Romanisch Monatsschrift*, 34 (1953), 152-53.

On the etymology of *gelimida* in the last verse of the second Merseburg charm: "limed" or bound together.

1333. Kroes, H. W. J. "Die Sage vom Nibelungenhort und ihr mythischer Hintergrund." In *Fragen und Forschungen im Bereich und Umkreis der germanischen Philologie: Festgabe für Theodor Frings zum 70. Geburtstag, 23 Juli 1956*, eds. Elisabeth Karg-Gasterstädt and Johannes Erben, 323-37. Deutsche Akademie der Wissenschaften zu Berlin; Veröffentlichungen des Instituts für deutsche Sprache und Literatur, 8. Berlin: Akademie Verlag, 1956.

Argues a mythic basis for the legend of the treasure of the Nibelungen. This basis is primarily that of conceptions of fertility.

1334. Kroes, H. W. J. "Muspilli." *Germanisch-Romanisch Monatsschrift*, 38 (1957), 393-94.

The etymology of *muspilli*: "destruction by mouth," a reference to the swallowing of the sun.

1335. Kroesen, Riti. "Thor and the Giant's Bride." *Amsterdamer Beiträge zur älteren Germanistik*, 17 (1982), 59-67.

On Thor and females: "his deeds fit the general pattern of the saviour-god who protects the vital forces of the world from destruction, although in some stories this pattern is given a negative twist" (p. 67).

1336. Krogmann, Willy. "Mûdspelli." *Germanisch-Romanisch Monatsschrift*, 17 (1929), 231-38.

The etymology of the term. See Krogmann, *Mudspelli auf Island* (1933).

1337. Krogmann, Willy. "Hœ́nir." *Acta Philologica Scandinavica*, 6 (1931-32), 311-27.

The etymology of Hœnir: < **huhnijaz* "the gleaming one." As the root is old, so, according to Krogmann, must the god be. The term *aurkonungr*, however, is a relatively recent formation.

1338. Krogmann, Willy. "Mûdspelli." *Wörter und Sachen*, 14 (1932), 68-85.

The etymology of the term. See Krogmann, *Muspelli auf Island* (1933).

1339. Krogmann, Willy. "Jul." *Zeitschrift für vergleichende Sprachforschung*, 60 (1933), 114-29.

The etymology and meaning of *yule* and related terms: it is a verbal abstract meaning "sacrifice." The original verb meant "to speak solemnly" and the semantic association was in the importance of ritual language in cult.

1340. Krogmann, Willy. *Mudspelli auf Island: Eine religionsgeschichtliche Untersuchung*. Wismar: Hinstorff, 1933. 74 pp.

Krogmann expands on two of his earlier essays on the etymology and use of the term *mudspelli* in *Hêliand*; these appeared in *Germanisch-Romanisch Monatsschrift*, 17 (1929), 231-38, and *Wörter und Sachen* 14 (1932), 68-85. In them he had argued that the term means "he who destroys with his mouth," i.e., Christ, and refers to the Last Judgment. Here he again takes up that etymology and interpretation and applies it to traditions relating to the Icelandic term *múspell(r)* or *muspell(r)*, whose principal attestation is in *Vǫluspá*. He tries to demonstrate that these traditions are wholly Christian or of Christian origin (example: since Christ will come with fire to the Last Judgment, *muspell* was associated with the fire demon Surtr).

The monograph was not well received upon publication. Linguists doubted the etymology, and other reviewers pointed out the failure to consider important secondary works, e.g., Nordal's *Völuspá* (1923).

1341. Krogmann, Willy. "Die 'Edda.'" *Arkiv för nordisk filologi*, 50 (1934), 243-49.

On the title *Edda*: the underlying form is **o þiðo n* "poetics," for a poet was *óðr* "possessed."

1342. Krogmann, Willy. "Christus in der Edda." *Westermanns Monatshefte*, 157 (1935), 436-40.

Popular treatment of the term *muspell* in Eddic poetry.

1343. Krogmann, Willy. "Hera duoder." *Beiträge zur Geschichte der deutschen Sprache und Literatur*, 59 (1935), 102-43.

The words in question are from the first Merseburg charm. Krogmann denies them, and the preceding *idisi*, any mythic import.

1344. Krogmann, Willy. "Wodini hailag." *Indogermanische Forschungen*, 54 (1936), 42-44.

Reading of the runic inscription on the Kehrlich brooch. Krogmann reads the words *Wodini hailag* as "made holy by Odin."

For criticism see O. Behagel "*Wodini hailag*" (1922)

1345. Krogmann, Willy. "Loki." *Acta Philologica Scandinavica*, 12 (1937-38), 59-70.

Loki as the *logaþore* of the runic Nordendorf brooch I. His original identity, clarified by an Old English gloss, had nothing to do with fire or fertility; the etymology shows him to be "the cunning, evil one."

1346. Krogmann, Willy. "Era duoder." *Zeitschrift für deutsches Altertum*, 83 (1951-52), 122-25.

Dismisses the goddess Eir from the first Merseburg charm but admits female helpers.

1347. Krogmann, Willy. "Phol im Merseburger Pferdesegen." *Zeitschrift für deutsche Philologie*, 71 (1951-52), 152-62.

Removes the god Phol from the second Merseburg charm.

1348. Krogmann, Willy. "As. mu ðspelli und die Esra-Apokalypse." *Zeitschrift für deutsche Wortforschung*, 20 ([1964?]), 98-114.

Includes comments on Icelandic conceptions of Muspell.

1349. Krohn, Kaarle. "Sampsa Pellervoinen < Njordr, Freyr?" *Finnisch-Ugrische Forschungen*, 4 (1904), 231-48.

Argues that the Finnish traditions of Sämpsä Pellervoinen derive from fertility cult similar to that of Nerthus, later equivalent to Njord and Freyr.

1350. Krohn, Kaarle. "Lemminkäinens Tod < Christi > Balders Tod." *Finnisch-Ugrische Forschungen*, 5 (1905), 83-138.

The Christ story as the basis for the traditions both of Lemminkäinen's death and Baldr's death; thus no direct relationship will have obtained between Nordic and Finnish traditions in this case.

1351. Krohn, Kaarle. "Lappische Beiträge zur germanischen Mythologie." *Finnisch-Ugrische Forschungen*, 6 (1906), 155-80.

On Lapp religion and Germanic mythology. For Krohn, Lapp religion offers a kind of control: material common to the two was borrowed by the Lapps at an early date and establishes the authenticity and age of that material in Germanic religion.

1352. Krohn, Kaarle. "Germanische Elemente in der finnischen Volksdichtung." *Zeitschrift für deutsches Altertum*, 51 (1909), 13-22.

The first of the Germanic elements in Finnish tradition taken up have to do with pre-Christian religion: cult of the dead, Freyr, and Thor.

1353. Krohn, Kaarle. "Tyrs högra hand, Freys svärd." In *Festskrift til H. F. Feilberg fra nordiske sprog- og folkemindeforskere på 80 års dagen den 6. august 1911.* 541-47. Svenska landsmål, 1911; Maal og minne, 1911; Danske studier, 1911. Stockholm: Norstedt, Copenhagen: Gyldendal, Oslo (Kristiania): Bymaalslaget, 1911.

Argues Christian models. For the myth of Týr's hand: God stretched out and sacrificed his right hand to bind evil. For Freyr's loss of his sword: David's loss of his sword after having Uriah killed and marrying Bathsheba.

1354. Krohn, Kaarle. "Das Schiff Naglfar." In *Festgabe für Vilhelm Thomsen,* part 1. 154-55. Finnisch-Ugrische Forschungen, 12. Leipzig: O. Harrassowitz, 1912.

Finnish folk beliefs about the devil's use of fingernails to make a ship; one recording associates the ship with the end of the world. Krohn explains the parallel to Naglfar by deriving both the Finnish folk belief and the eddic mythic motif from medieval Christian popular conceptions.

1355. Krohn, Kaarle. *Skandinavisk mytologi (Olaus Petri föreläsningar).* Helsinki: H. Schildt, 1922. 228 pp.

Here is the great Finnish folklorist's statement on Norse mythology. It grew out of lectures delivered at Uppsala on Norse mythology from the perspective of

Finnish folk traditions, and Finnish scholarly traditions have shaped the result. Just as the "Finnish method" focuses not on an artifact itself but rather on the diffusion of its archetype, so Krohn regards no god or myth as of native Scandinavian origin; everything came from somewhere else. There was, indeed, no mythology until after the period of Germanic migrations.

This theory is of course untenable as a whole, but the book is more than a scholarly curiosity, for Krohn's remarks on individual points, extracted from the overall theory, remain provocative and worth consulting.

1356. Krohn, Kaarle. "Die Bedeutung der finnischen Mythologie für die Skandinavische." In *Actes du Ve congrès international d'histoire des religions à Lund, 27-29 août 1929.* 198-200. Lund: C. W. K. Gleerup, 1930.

Lecture and discussion from an international congress on the history of religion. Finnish tradition as a relic area for loans from Scandinavian mythology.

A slightly longer version of this paper was published in *Studi e materiali di storia delle religioni*, 6 (1930), 1-8.

1357. Kroll, Adolf. *Die Edda: Erläutert.* Kleine "Germanen-Bücherei," 5. Berlin-Steglitz: Kraft & Schönheit, 1919. 28 pp.

Philosophical interpretation of the mythology.

1358. Kühnhold, Christa. "Zwei Miszellen zur altisländischen Dichtung." *Zeitschrift für deutsches Altertum*, 107 (1978), 179-83.

The first of these notes treats: "Die Lebenswerte der Hávamál strophe 68" (pp. 179-81). According to Kühnhold, these life values are three in number, not four as Heusler stated in *Die zwei Sittengedichte der Hávamál nach ihrer Strophenfolge* (1917), pp. 119-20. They are fire, sun, and health without blemish.

1359. Kuhn, Adalbert. "Über die Bedeutung des Namens Ziu." *Zeitschrift für deutsches Altertum*, 2 (1842), 231-35.

On the etymology of Ziu/Týr, illuminated by means of the Indo-European cognates, and showing the god as the gleaming sky-father.

1360. Kuhn, Adalbert. "Ueber den Namen Ostara." *Germania*, 6 (1844), 244-50.

Ostara as a Germanic goddess of the sun, symbolic of the victory of spring over winter.

1361. Kuhn, Adalbert. "Zur deutschen Mythologie." *Zeitschrift für deutsches Altertum*, 4 (1844), 385-91.

Survivals in northern German lore, mostly of the "lower mythology."

1362. Kuhn, Adalbert. "Wodan." *Zeitschrift für deutsches Altertum*, 5 (1845), 472-94.

Survivals of Wodan/Odin in northern German lore.

1363. Kuhn, Adalbert. "Zur deutschen Mythologie." *Zeitschrift für deutsches Altertum*, 5 (1845), 373-81.

Survivals in northern German lore, mostly of the "lower mythology."

1364. Kuhn, Adalbert. "Zur Mythologie." *Zeitschrift für deutsches Altertum*, 6 (1848), 117-34.

Legends of Odin reconstructed from Indic and Germanic materials.

1365. Kuhn, Adalbert. "Der Schuss des wilden Jägers auf den Sonnenhirsch: Ein Beitrag zur vergleichenden Mythologie der Indogermanen." *Zeitschrift für deutsche Philologie*, 1 (1869), 89-119.

Reconstructs the following nature-myth: the storm-god (Odin in Scandinavia), probably with the help of an evening-goddess, pursues and wounds the sun-god, who has taken the form of a stag.

P. 119 contains the interesting methodological note that recent folklore may give a truer picture of ancient mythology than do the Eddas.

1366. Kuhn, Adalbert. "Über Entwicklungsstufen der Mythenbildung." *Abhandlungen der preussischen Akademie der Wissenschaften zu Berlin, phil.-hist. Kl.*, 58 (1873), 123-51.

Theoretical and practical discussion of the stages of the formation of myth, with remarks on the derivation of the Germanic gods. Kuhn leans toward phenomena of nature as an ultimate explanation, particularly storm clouds.

1367. Kuhn, Adalbert. *Die Herabkunft des Feuers und des Göttertranks: Beitrag zur vergleichenden Mythologie der Indogermanen.* Gütersloh: C. Bertelsmann, 1886. iv, 240 pp. 2nd ed, issued as Kuhn's *Mythologische Studien*, ed. Ernst Kuhn; 1st ed. 1859.

Important early study of fire and the drink of the gods, from a comparative Indo-European perspective.

1368. Kuhn, Hans. "König und Volk in der germanischen Bekehrungsgeschichte." *Zeitschrift für deutsches Altertum*, 77 (1940), 1-11. Rpt. in Kuhn, *Kleine Schriften*, vol. 2 (1971), pp. 277-86.

A contribution to a contemporary debate on the role of kings and more generally politics in the conversions of the Germanic peoples. Kuhn argues against a strong role for kings and politics and stresses the importance of the cult community.

1369. Kuhn, Hans. "Das nordgermanische Heidentum in den ersten christlichen Jahrhunderten." *Zeitschrift für deutsches Altertum*, 79 (1942), 132-66. Rpt. in Kuhn, *Kleine Schriften*, vol. 2 (1971), pp. 296-326.

In this important and controversial paper, Kuhn argued that the break with paganism implied by the conversion to Christianity has been exaggerated by scholars. This break had been extrapolated from the literary sources, primarily on the basis of pagan kennings, which scholars argued increased during waning paganism, virtually vanished with the conversion, and were restored with the "renaissance" of the mid-twelfth century. The work most associated with this view is Jan de Vries, "De skaldenkenningen met mythologischen inhoud" (1934), which Kuhn criticizes energetically. He concludes that pagan kennings continued in use and that there was no abrupt change in the use of kennings ca. 1150. During the first centuries of Christianity in Scandinavia, particularly in Iceland, syncretism prevailed, and according to Kuhn, even Snorri may have been affected by this syncretism.

De Vries responded with "Kenningen und Christentum" (1956-57).

1370. Kuhn, Hans. "Und hvera lundi." *Namn och bygd*, 33 (1945), 171-95.

The title is from *Vǫluspá* 35:2, in which some observers saw a reference to Iceland's hot springs and hence an opportunity to assign Icelandic provenance to the poem. Kuhn demurs, arguing that the word *hverr* came to mean "hot spring" only after *Vǫluspá* was composed. The evidence is largely from Icelandic placenames.

1371. Kuhn, Hans. "Es gibt kein *balder* 'Herr.'" In *Erbe der Vergangenheit: Germanistische Beiträge, Festgabe für Karl Helm zum 80. Geburtstage 19. Mai 1951.* 37-45. Tübingen: M. Niemeyer, 1951. Rpt. in Kuhn, *Kleine Schriften*, vol. 2 (1971), pp. 332-38.

Kuhn rebuts the common notion that the Old English noun *bealdor* and its Germanic cognates mean "lord." This is important because understanding his name as "lord" has long been used to link Baldr with the dying gods of Near Eastern tradition, whose names frequently mean "lord."

Old English *bealdor* may be grouped with a series of nouns which in kenning-like expressions mean "lord." These include *ealdor* "hedge," *helm* "helmet, covering, protection," *hleo* "protection, lee," and *ord* "point of a weapon." Thus Kuhn concludes that *bealdor* should have a similar meaning. He tentatively proposes "guardian" but notes that the word had long been out of active use when the poetic sources were composed or recorded.

1372. Kuhn, Hans. "Die norwegischen Spuren in der Liederedda." *Acta Philologica Scandinavica*, 22 (1954), 65-80. Rpt. in Kuhn, *Kleine Schriften*, vol. 1 (1969), pp. 205-18.

Contra Seip, "Har nordmenn skrevet opp Eddadiktningen?" (1951). Kuhn argues that most if not all of the supposed Norwegianisms Seip had isolated in the Poetic Edda are in fact to be postulated for Icelandic scribal practice as well, so close were the West Norwegian and Icelandic writing traditions.

1373. Kuhn, Hans. "Gaut." In *Festschrift für Jost Trier zu seinem 60. Geburtstag am 15. Dezember 1954*, eds. Benno von Wiese and Karl Heinz Borck, 417-33. Meisenheim/Glan: A. Hain, 1954. Rpt. in Kuhn, *Kleine Schriften*, vol. 2 (1971), pp. 364-77.

Kuhn proposes that *gautr* means: "the one chosen or made holy for sacrifice." Thus Odin is, e.g., *alda* or *aldinn gautr*, and he bears the name Gautr. Etymologically *gautr* < **gautaz* and is related to **geutan* "to pour," i.e., "to sacrifice."

1374. Kuhn, Hans. "Das Fortleben des germanischen Heidentums nach der Christianisierung." In *La conversione al cristianesimo nell'Europa dell'alto medioevo: 14-19 aprile 1966*. 743-57. Settimane di studio del centro italiano di studi sull'alto medioevo. Spoleto: Presso la sede del centro, 1967.

A contribution to a symposium on the conversion to Christianity among the European peoples. Kuhn summarizes the somewhat radical position he took in his "Das nordgermanische Heidentum in den ersten christlichen Jahrhunderten" (1942), arguing that the early Church acknowledged the existence of other gods, so long as its God was highest. Also treated are the nature of paganism and early Christianity and the limits of a definition of religion within this discussion.

1375. Kuhn, Hans. "Die Religion der nordischen Völker in der Wikingerzeit." In *I normanni e la loro espansione in Europa nell'alto medioevo: 19-24 aprile 1968*. 117-29. Settimane di studio del centro italiano di studi sull'alto medioevo, 16. Spoleto: Presso la sede del centro, 1968. Discussion on pp. 161-63.

A contribution to a colloquium on the Normans in Europe. Kuhn begins with a polemic against current trends in research in Germanic religion, especially the tendency toward scholarly reconstruction. The foundation of myth in cult is not an important question, according to Kuhn, but these are: the relative importance of the individual elements of the religion, the role of religion in people's lives and their attitude toward it. Kuhn surveys the all-important period when Scandinavian paganism was under Christian influence, particularly from northern England; this tenth-century syncretism paved the way for the conversion. Concrete examples include the elevation of Odin and the changing concepts of Valhalla and the abode of the dead.

Textual analysis centers on skaldic poetry; *Hávamál*, *Vǫluspá*, and *Eiríksmál* also receive mention.

1376. Kuhn, Hans. "Kämpen und Berserker." *Frühmittelalterliche Studien*, 2 (1968), 218-27. Rpt. in Kuhn, *Kleine Schriften*, vol. 2 (1971), pp. 521-31.

Includes etymological and semantic remarks on the term *berserkr*, which Kuhn understands as "bare-shirted," and discussion of relevant passages in Norse literature. In general Kuhn inclines toward the notion of Roman influence on these Norse conceptions.

1377. Kuhn, Hans. "Das älteste Christentum Islands." *Zeitschrift für deutsches Altertum*, 100 (1971), 4-40. Rpt. in Kuhn, *Kleine Schriften*, vol. 4 (1978), pp. 167-200.

Discussion of the first centuries of Christianity in Iceland, stressing what is unique in Icelandic Christianity and in the Icelandic situation.

1378. Kuhn, Hans. *Das alte Island.* Dusseldorf: E. Diederichs, 1971. 287 pp.

Contains summary chapters on paganism and Christianity and on ethics.

1379. Kuhn, Hans. "Rund um die Vǫluspá." In *Mediaevalia Litteraria: Festschrift für Helmut de Boor zum 80. Geburtstag*, eds. Ursula Hennig and Herbert Kolb, 1-14. Munich: C. H. Beck, 1971. Rpt. in Kuhn, *Kleine Schriften*, vol. 4 (1978), pp. 135-47.

The starting point for this essay is de Boer's complex study of the religious vocabulary of *Vǫluspá*, "Die religiöse Sprache der Vǫluspá und verwandter Denkmäler" (1930). Kuhn reviews several of de Boor's findings, primarily concerning new theophoric kenning types seemingly originating around 950 in the circle of the Hlaðir jarls, and other questions of religious vocabulary. Of greatest interest is Kuhn's suggestion (p. 4) of the possibility "that de Boer explained something as a special possession of the circle of the Trondheim jarls, which belonged legally to all the skalds composing in Norway."

1380. Kuhn, Hans. "Die gotische Mission: Gedanken zur germanischen Bekehrungsgeschichte." *Saeculum*, 27 (1976), 50-65. Rpt. in Kuhn, *Kleine Schriften*, vol. 4 (1978), pp. 201-22.

The conversion of the Goths as something of a special case among the various Germanic conversions; most of these, Kuhn argues, should be viewed as accessions to the power of the Roman imperium.

1381. Kuhn, Hans. "Philologisches zur altgermanischen Religionsgeschichte." In Kuhn, *Kleine Schriften: Aufsätze und Rezensionen aus den Gebieten der germanischen und nordischen Sprach-, Literatur- und Kulturgeschichte*, vol. 4: *Aufsätze aus den Jahren 1968-1976*. 223-321. Berlin and New York: W. de Gruyter, 1978.

Sixteen short essays on philological problems relating to Germanic religion. According to the preface (pp. 223-25), some of the essays were written as early as the 1930s, and others are recent; three (on the *æsir*, elves, and Anglo-Saxon mission) are reprinted from the new edition of the *Reallexikon der germanischen Altertumskunde*. Those not printed before are as follows: "Ingvaeones, Erminones and Istaevones" (pp. 225-31); "Germanic priesthood" (pp. 231-42), a terminological review stressing the difficulty of reconstructing a Germanic priesthood; "Germanic sacral kingship" (pp. 242-47), skeptical survey of the evidence; "The spear of death: Odin as god of death" (pp. 247-58); "'God' in Old Norse" (pp. 258-65); "The *vanir*" (pp. 269-77); "Freyr's game" (pp. 277-79), reads the kenning as a reference to cult; "Gná and Sýr: Foreign names in the Germanic myths" (pp. 280-89), finds evidence of southern influence; "Jǫrmunr and the lists of names in *Snorra edda*" (pp. 289-94), distinguishes three levels of Odin names; "Asgard, midgard and utgard" (pp. 295-302), questions the age of the division of the world implied by the terms; "The giants' weapons" (pp. 302-09); "Belief" (pp. 309-17), review of terminology, with remarks on the conversion to Christianity; "Ansgar" (pp. 320-21), an appreciation.

1382. Kuhn, Hans. "Des Schenken in unserem Altertum." *Zeitschrift für deutsches Altertum*, 109 (1980), 181-92.

In the course of this discussion of gift-giving in Germanic society Kuhn mentions several sections of *Hávamál* (str. 1-80) and the *tannfé* which Freyr received from the other gods (*Grímnismál* 5).

1383. Kukovszky, Stefan. "Vǫluspá 5, 1-4." *Zeitschrift für deutsches Altertum*, 75 (1938), 119-20.

Interprets *sól varp sunnan* as a reference to the midday sun in winter.

1384. Kummer, Bernhard. "Kultische Geheimbünde der Germanen?" *Reden und Aufsätze zum nordischen Gedanke*, 32 (1935), 57-77.

Criticism of Otto Höfler's monograph with the same title—except for the question mark (1934). For a rebuttal see Höfler, "Über germanische Verwandlungskulte" (1936).

1385. Kummer, Bernhard. *Midgards Untergang: Germanischer Kult und Glaube in den letzten heidnischen Jahrhunderten,* 4th ed. Leipzig: A. Klein, 1938. 352 pp. 1st ed. 1927.

A highly idiosyncratic reading of late Germanic paganism, based to a large extent on the sagas and the author's notion of the Germanic mind.

1386. Kummer, Bernhard. *Brünhild und Ragnarök: Die Gestaltung der isländischen Brünhilddichtung aus dem Erlebnis des Glaubenswechsels.* Lübeck: H. Dittmer, 1950. 60 pp.

A reading of the Brynhild legends in light of religion, experience, and myth, especially the associations between conceptions of Ragnarǫk and the conversion.

1387. Kummer, Bernhard. "Sverre und Magnus: Ein Lebensbeispiel zur Frage nach Ursprung und Fortwirkung demokratischen und sakralen Königtums in Skandinavien." In *Atti dell'viii congresso internazionale di storia delle religioni (Roma 17-23 Aprile 1955).* 368-71. Florence: G. C. Sansoni—Editore, 1956.

Summary of an address at the eighth international conference on the history of religions: using *Sverris saga* as an example, Kummer stresses the importance of considering the medieval point of view in seeking models of sacral and democratic kingship.

1388. Kummer, Bernhard. *Die Lieder des Codex Regius (Edda) und verwandte Denkmäler,* vol. 1: *Mythische Dichtung,* part 1: *Die Schau der Seherin (Vǫluspá): Text, Übersetzung, Erläuterungen, Exkurse und religionsgeschichtliche Ergänzungen.* Bremen: Verlag der Forschungsfragen unserer Zeit, 1961. 140 pp.

An edition of *Vǫluspá*, with translation and extensive commentary, especially on religious and mythic topics. Not considered trustworthy.

1389. Kunwald, Georg. "Der Moorfund im Rappendam, Seeland, Dänemark." In *Vorgeschichtliche Heiligtümer und Opferplätze in Mittel- und Nordeuropa: Bericht über ein Symposium in Reinhausen bei Göttingen vom 14.-16. Oktober 1968*, ed. Herbert Jankuhn, 100-18. Abhandlungen der Akademie der Wissenschaften in Göttingen, phil.-hist. Kl., 3. Folge, 74. Göttingen: Vandenhoeck & Ruprecht, 1970.

Archaeological evidence for a possible Nerthus cult.

1390. Kunze, Friedrich. "Der Birkenbesen, ein Symbol des Donar: Eine mythologische Untersuchung." *Internationales Archiv für Ethnographie*, 13 (1900), 81-162.

The birch broom as a symbol of Donar/Thor, the thunderer.

1391. Kvillerud, Reinert. "Några anmärkningar till Þrymskviða." *Arkiv för nordisk filologi*, 80 (1965), 64-86.

After a sketch of recent work on *Þrymskviða*, inclining toward P. Hallberg's nomination of Snorri Sturluson as the author of the poem (1954), Kvillerud considers parallelism and repetition. He then turns to the interpretation of specific passages, including str. 12, 15, 16, 19, 20, and 32.

1392. Kyrre, Hans. *Liv og sjæl i myte, menneksetanke og kunst*. Copenhagen: J. Gjellerup, 1941. 176 pp.

Norse mythology and modern biology as parallel thought processes.

1393. Kyrre, Hans. "Myte og menneksetanke: Nogle bemærkninger til Arild Hvidtfeldt's anmeldelse." *Danske studier*, 39 (1942), 77-80.

Response to A. Hvidtfeldt, "Nordisk mytologi og moderne videnskab" (1941).

L

La Cour, Vilh., *see* Cour, Vilh. La.

1394. Lacy, Alan F. "What Kind of Demon did Gothic *skohsl* Imply?" *Acta Philologica Scandinavica*, 32 (1978-79), 117-20.

The Gothic Bible renders Greek *daímōn* and *daimónion* with *skohsl*, which Lacy derives from Germanic **skeg-* + *ilo-* "that which causes to shake." This "originally meant the inhabitant of the grave who returned and terrorized the living" (p. 119). If so, belief in such spirits may be older than the references to *draugar* in Norse tradition and probably is common Germanic.

1395. Läffler, L. Fr. "Lytir, en hittils förbisedd fornsvensk gud." *Arkiv för nordisk filologi*, 26 (1910), 96.

Suggests accepting as true the account in *Þáttr Hauks Hábrókar* of the worship of a god Lytir at Uppsala.

1396. Läffler, L. Fr. "Det evigt grönskande trädet vid Uppsala hednatämpel." In *Festskrift til H. F. Feilberg fra nordiske sprog- og folkemindeforskere på 80 års dagen den 6. august 1911.* 617-96. Svenska landsmål, 1911; Maal og minne, 1911; Danske studier, 1911. Stockholm: Norstedt, Copenhagen: Gyldendal, Oslo (Kristiania): Bymaals-laget, 1911.

A detailed study of Adam of Bremen's account of the evergreen tree at the pagan temple in Uppsala. Läffler concludes that the four scholiae are essentially correct in their descriptions of the building of the temple and the rites associated with it. The original conception of the evergreen tree, in both Norway and Sweden, was of an ash tree; the myth took new form and was spread from Sweden to Norway.

1397. Läffler, L. Fr. "Det evigt grönskande trädet vid Uppsala hednatämpel: Tillägg till Festskrift til H. F. Feilberg." *Maal og minne*, 1913, pp. 49-52.

Supplement to the author's study of the evergreen tree by the pagan temple in Uppsala (1911), organized in the form of short notes to individual pages.

1398. Läffler, L. Fr. "Det evigt grönskande trädet i den fornnordiska mytologien och det fno. ordet *barr*, fisl. *barr*." *Arkiv för nordisk filologi*, 30 (1914), 112-23.

Response to criticism by H. Lindroth (in *Arkiv för nordisk filologi* 29, p. 274, fn. 3 [!]) of Läffler's article "Det evigt grönskande trädet vid Uppsala hednatempel" (1911).

1399. Läffler, L. Fr. "Hávamál 53:1-3." *Arkiv för nordisk filologi*, 32 (1916), 316-21.

Response to a reading proposed by B. M. Ólsen in his "Til Eddakvadene, II: Til Havamal" (1915).

1400. Läffler, L. Fr. "Till Hávamáls strof 155." *Arkiv för nordisk filologi*, 32 (1916), 83-113.

Response to B. M. Ólsen, "Hávamál v. 155 (Bugge)" (1915-16).

1401. Läffler, L. Fr. "Till Alvíssmál str. 12:6 och 16:6." *Arkiv för nordisk filologi*, 37 (1921), 328-29.

Proposed emendations of *Alvíssmál*, str. 12 and 16.

1402. Landmark, Knut. "När författades Valans spådom?" *Cassiopeia, årsbok*, 1940, pp. 92-97.

On the dating of *Vǫluspá*.

1403. Lange, Wolfgang. "Altnordisch Ómi." *Beiträge zur Geschichte der deutschen Sprache und Literatur*, 75 (1953), 421-30.

On the Odin name Ómi, attested inter alia in *Grímnismál*, str. 49. Lange finds that the name is old. He explores associating it with the word *uma* in the runic inscription on the Kragehul spear shaft. This association, if correct, would demonstrate an early cult of Odin.

1404. Lange, Wolfgang. "Zahlen und Zahlenkompositionen in der Edda." *Beiträge zur Geschichte der deutschen Sprache und Literatur (Halle)*, 77 (1955), 306-48.

The use of numerals in the Poetic Edda.

1405. Lange, Wolfgang. "Über religiöse Wurzeln des Epischen." In *Indogermanica: Festschrift für Wolfgang Krause zum 65. Geburtstag am 18. September 1960 von Fachgenossen und Freunden dargebracht.* 80-93. Heidelberg: C. Winter, 1960.

Lange's purpose is to refute the notion of Johan Huizinga, *Homo ludens* (1938; English translation 1950), that play is central to poetry. Following Von der Leeuw's *Phänomenologie der Religion* (2nd ed. 1956), Lange finds roots of narrative in religious feeling and act. In reciting Thor's giant-slaying, Vetrliði

Sumarliðason brought the past into the present (p. 86); his oral recitation paralleled the representation of cult. Using Germanic examples, Lange finds a religious aspect to heroic poetry, even in the Christian Middle Ages, and he concludes that *homo faber*, who was also *homo religiosus*, stood at the origin of poetry. *Homo ludens* came only later.

1406. Lange, Wolfgang. *Texte zur germanischen Bekehrungsgeschichte.* Tübingen: M. Niemeyer, 1962. xiv, 258 pp.

A collection of texts representative of the conversion of the Germanic peoples (including Scandinavians) to Christianity.

1407. Lange, Wolfgang. *Die Germania des Tacitus: Erläutert von Rudolf Much,* 3rd ed. Heidelberg: C. Winter, 1967. 581 pp.

For Germanic philologists, archaeologists, and cultural historians, this is the standard edition of the *Germania* of Tacitus. The extensive commentary, originally by Rudolf Much, is here brought up to date by Wolfgang Lange and Herbert Jankuhn.

1408. Langenfelt, Gösta. "Gallehus-problemet." *Fornvännen*, 41 (1946), 290-93.

Interprets *holtijaR* on the Gallehus horn as "belonging to a holy grave." For a contrary opinion see E. Moltke, "Hvad var Lægæst, guldhornets mester, magiker, præst eller guldsmed" (1947).

1409. Langenhove, George van. *Linguistische Studien, 2: Essai de linguistique indo-européenne.* Rijksuniversiteit te Gent, werken uitgegeven door de faculteit van de weisbegeerte en letteren, 87. Antwerp: De Sikkel, The Hague: M. Nijhoff, 1939. xvii, 151 pp.

Many of the terms treated in this etymological treatise are from the mythology: *vanir*, Lóðurr, Hœnir, Hrungnir.

1410. Larsen, Alf. "Nyt om Njord." *Danske studier*, 4 (1907), 144-45.

Review of M. Olsen, *Det gamle norske ønavn Njarðarlǫg* (1905).

1411. Larsen, Knud A. "Solvogn og solkult." *Kuml*, 1955, pp. 46-64.

Sun worship as an Indo-European cult. In this cult, horses and dawn play an important role.

1412. Larsen, Martin. *Den ældre Edda og Eddica minora,* vol. 1. Copenhagen: E. Munksgaard, 1943. 263 pp.

Danish translation of mythological eddic poetry, with an introduction and commentary.

1413. Larsen, Thøger. "Verdens oprindelse i de nordiske sagn." *Atlantis*, 2 (1924), 218-31, 408-11.

Attempts to associate Bacchus with Ymir and Suttungr.

1414. Larsen, Thøger. "Yggdrasils dyr." *Atlantis*, 2 (1924), 176-86.

Attempts to associate the animals of Yggdrasill with the constellations.

1415. Larsen, Thøger. *Forklaringer og noter til edda-myterne.* Lemvig: H. Bech, 1926-27. 123 pp.

Commentary to Danish translations of mythological eddic poems and *Snorra edda.*

1416. Lárusson, Magnús Már. "Um Niðurstigningarsögu." *Skírnir*, 129 (1955), 159-68.

Draws attention to Old Norse glosses of Leviathan as *miðgarðsormr* "midgard serpent" in *Niðarstigningarsaga* and discusses briefly the significance of the equation.

1417. Lárusson, Magnús Már. "Frændsemis- og sifjaspell." *Skírnir*, 140 (1966), 128-42.

On incest in ancient Icelandic culture, particularly law: possible pagan background and relation to *Vǫluspá*'s *Brœðr munu berjask / ok at bǫnum verðask* (str. 45).

1418. Lárusson, Ólafur. "Vísa Þorvalds veila." In *Festskrift til Finnur Jónsson 29. maj 1928.* 263-73. Copenhagen: Levin & Munksgaard, 1928.

According to the author, Þorvaldr's verse, directed at the missionary Þangbrandr, threatens Þangbrandr with the supposed Germanic sacral death penalty of being pushed over a cliff.

1419. Lárusson, Ólafur. "Kultminne i stadnamn, 4: Island." In *Religionshistorie*, ed. Nils Lid, 74-79. Nordisk kultur, 26. Stockholm: A. Bonnier, Oslo: H. Aschehoug, Copenhagen: J. H. Schultz, 1942.

A survey of references to cult in Icelandic placenames: *Hof-* and *Goð-* are common first components, and Thor is the most frequently encountered god.

1420. László, Gyula. *Steppenvölker und Germanen: Kunst der Völkerwanderungszeit.* Vienna and Munich: A. Schroll, 1970. 152 pp.

Includes a chapter on mythology (pp. 102-48), putting several Germanic myths in the context of related material from such peoples as the Huns, Avars, and Slavs.

1421. Laugesen, Anker Teilgård. "Snorres opfattelse af Aserne." *Arkiv för nordisk filologi*, 56 (1942), 301-15.

Takes up the problem of the apparently differing views of the *æsir* in Snorri's *Ynglinga saga*, *Gylfaginning*, and the Prologue to *Snorra edda* and ch. 43 of *Gylfaginning*. *Ynglinga saga* is based on *Lokasenna* and *Hávamál*, with *Vǫluspá* in the background. The frame of *Gylfaginning* is firmly based on *Vafþrúðnismál*. For example, the two kinds of *æsir* in *Gylfaginning* (those with whom Gangleri talks and those of whose exploits he hears) recall Odin in *Vafþrúðnismál* telling of his own deeds; Gylfi's entry into Hárr's hall mirrors Odin's into Vafþrúðnir's. Snorri chose Gylfi so as to create a source for oral traditions, a Norseman who was contemporaneous with the Asiamen. Laugesen dismisses most of the Prologue and ch. 43 as interpolations.

1422. Laugesen, Anker Teilgård. *Syv-ni-tolv: Nogle iagttagelser over typiske tal i litteraturen*. Studier fra sprog- og oldtidforskning, 237. Copenhagen: G. E. C. Gad, 1959. 56 pp.

The use of numerals in older literature, including the Poetic Edda.

1423. Laur, Wolfgang. "Die germanischen Frauennamen auf *-gard/-gerðr* und ihr Ursprung aus dem Bereich des Kultischen." *Beiträge zur Geschichte der deutschen Sprache und Literatur*, 73 (1951), 321-46.

Drawing on the myth of *Skírnismál*, Laur sets women's names in *-gerðr* (German *-gard*) in the context of cult. Since many such names have the name of an important god as first component, Laur believes that the names in *-gerðr* once referred to priestesses of those gods.

1424. Laur, Wolfgang. "Die Heldensage vom Finnsburgkampf." *Zeitschrift für deutsches Altertum*, 85 (1954-55), 107-36.

Laur finds the earliest traces of the Finnsburg legend in (reconstructed) Masterbuilder traditions, which he thinks gave rise to *Alvíssmál* and the Norse Masterbuilder legend on one hand and to the continental Scandinavian Finn legends on the other. The latter developed ultimately into the Finnsburg legend.

Pp. 133-34 contain theoretical remarks on the relationship between myth and heroic legend.

1425. Laur, Wolfgang. "Theophore Ortsnamen und Kultstätten." In *Studien zur europäischen Vor- und Frühgeschichte*, eds. Martin Claus, Werner Haarnagel, and Klaus Raddatz, 359-68. Neumünster: K. Wachholtz, 1968.

Investigates the degree of overlap between archaeologically defined cult places and theophoric placenames and finds such overlap to be infrequent.

1426. Lavrsen, Jytte. "Om votivfund fra bronzealderens slutning." *Kuml*, 1958, pp. 63-71. Summary in English.

Weapons and ornaments as votive finds associated with Bronze Age deities.

1427. Lawrence, William Witherle. *Beowulf and Epic Tradition.* Cambridge, Mass.: Harvard University Press, 1930. xiv, 349 pp.

The chapter on "Scyld and Breca" (pp. 129-60) treats the supernatural in *Beowulf,* seen against Norse mythological sources. Fertility myth and ritual form the basic of the discussion, which also summarizes some older work (e.g., Müllenhoff).

1428. Laxness, Halldór. "Forneskjutaut." *Skírnir,* 147 (1973), 5-31.

Religious attitudes in Iceland during and around the conversion, as reflected in later literature, especially such family sagas as *Eyrbyggja saga.*

1429. Legis, Gustav Thormond (pseud. for Anton Thormond Glückselig). *Handbuch der altdeutschen und nordischen Götterlehre,* 2nd ed. Leipzig: F. Volckmar, 1833. viii, 191 pp. 1st ed. 1831.

Early handbook of the mythology.

1430. Lehmann, Edvard. "Tvekønnede frugtbarhedsguder i Norden." *Maal og minne,* 1919, pp. 1-4.

Uses apparently hermaphroditic figures on rock carvings to argue that Nerthus/Njord and Skaði may reflect self-impregnating fertility deities.

1431. Lehmann, Karl. "Grabhügel und Königshügel in nordischer Heidenzeit." *Zeitschrift für deutsche Philologie,* 42 (1910), 1-15.

Survey of Norse literary evidence concerning grave mounds. Lehmann reasons that grave mounds were cult sites and that the mounds on which kings sat, according to the literary evidence, were grave mounds and places of assembly.

1432. Lehmann, Karl. "Grabhügel und Königshügel in nordischer Heidenzeit." *Zeitschrift für deutsche Philologie,* 44 (1912), 78-79.

Addendum to Lehmann's article of 1910 with the same title, primarily commenting on A. Olrik, "At sidde paa høj" (1909).

1433. Lehmann, Winfred P. "*Lín* and *laukr* in the Edda." *Germanic Review,* 30 (1955), 163-71.

The words *lín* "flax, linen" and *laukr* "leek" occur in many eddic poems, including *Vǫluspá, Þrymskviða, Vǫlundarkviða,* and *Rígsþula.* Lehmann stresses that interpretation must bear in mind the role of these words and/or the objects they represent as fertility symbols.

1434. Lehmann, Winfred P. "On Reflections of Germanic Legal Terminology and Situations in the *Edda*." In *Old Norse Literature and Mythology*, ed. Edgar C. Polomé, 227-43. Austin and London: Published for the Department of Germanic Languages of the University of Texas, Austin, by the University of Texas Press, 1969.

Among the passages discussed are *Hárbarðsljóð* 48, 11-12, 40-43; and *Hávamál* 49. The readings proposed do not change the mythological functions of the gods involved.

1435. Leithe, H. "Zu Völuspá 50 6/7." *Zeitschrift für deutsche Philologie*, 66 (1941), 9-10.

A putative trace of Christian eschatology in *Vǫluspá* 50: carrion attracts the eagle (Matthew 24:28; Luke 17:37).

1436. Leitzmann, Albert. "Ags. *neorxna-wong*." *Beiträge zur Geschichte der deutschen Sprache und Literatur*, 32 (1907), 60-66.

The etymology of Old English *neorxnawong* "Paradise": "field of those belonging to Nerthus."

1437. Leo, H. "Etymologische Vergleichung der deutschen Götternamen mit keltischen Wortfamilien." *Zeitschrift für deutsches Altertum*, 3 (1843), 224-26.

Contrived etymological cognates in Celtic to Norse (not German, as the title promises) mythological figures.

1438. Leoni, Federico Albano. "Rúnar munt þú finna oc ráðna stafi (Su *Háv*. 142 e altri luoghi eddici)." *Studi germanici*, n. s., 10 (1972), 99-120.

Semantic study of the terms *rún* "rune" and *stafr* "stave," bearing on their collocation in *Hávamál*, str. 142. Leoni explores the possibility of synonymy.

1439. Leuner, Hanscarl. "Über die historische Rolle magischer Pflanzen und ihrer Wirkstoffe." In *Vorgeschichtliche Heiligtümer und Opferplätze in Mittel- und Nordeuropa: Bericht über ein Symposium in Reinhausen bei Göttingen vom 14.-16. Oktober 1968*, ed. Herbert Jankuhn, 279-96. Abhandlungen der Akademie der Wissenschaften in Göttingen, phil.-hist. Kl., 3. Folge, 74. Göttingen: Vandenhoeck & Ruprecht, 1970.

Hallucinogenic plants and ecstatic religion, with references to berserks and shamans.

1440. Levy, Janet E. "Religious Ritual and Social Stratification in Pre-Historic Societies: An Example from Bronze Age Denmark." *History of Religions*, 21 (1981-82), 172-88.

Analysis of hoard finds in Denmark. "In summary, I believe that the ritual hoards represent a ranked society with differential access to sumptuary goods and, by analogy, to power, authority, and, probably, wealth. The hoards further represent offerings apparently related to fertility rituals. Thus, the hoards seem to represent the intersection of religious concerns and the organizations of a social hierarchy" (p. 187).

1441. Leyen, Friedrich von der. *Das Märchen in den Göttersagen der Edda*. Berlin: G. Reimer, 1899. 83 pp.

Points out the presence of folktale motifs and structures in the extant eddic mythology. Von der Leyen assigned a late date to the folktale-like material and wished to separate it from genuine Germanic mythology.

1442. Leyen, Friedrich von der. "Der gefesselte Unhold: Eine mythologische Studie." In *Untersuchungen und Quellen zur germanischen und romanischen Philologie: Johan von Kelle dargebracht von seinen Kollegen und Schülern*, vol. 1. 7-35. Prager deutsche Studien, 8. Prague: C. Bellmann, 1908.

Comparative study of the bound monster, including Loki.

1443. Leyen, Friedrich von der. "Útgarðaloke in Irland." *Beiträge zur Geschichte der deutschen Sprache und Literatur*, 33 (1908), 382-91.

The Irish folktale of Diarmuid's acquisition of beauty as a borrowing of the Útgarða-Loki story.

1444. Leyen, Friedrich von der. "Die Entwicklung der Göttersagen in der Edda." *Germanisch-Romanisch Monatsschrift*, 1 (1909), 284-91.

"I repeat in this article in a different arrangement, much explaining, much expanding, some of the thoughts of my book *Die Götter und Göttersagen der Germanen*" (1909).

1445. Leyen, Friedrich von der. *Die Götter und Göttersagen der Germanen*. Deutsches Sagenbuch, 1. Munich: C. H. Beck, 1909. 253 pp.

The first of the four parts of the "Deutsches Sagenbuch," an attempt to present the German public with all aspects of its legend tradition. As such, the volume comprises not only a handbook of Germanic mythology, but also an introduction to von der Leyen's views on legends and legend research. The opening chapter (pp. 13-45) offers a research history, and the next (pp. 46-90) treats the origin of myth. A survey of the various gods makes up the bulk of the work.

1446. Leyen, Friedrich von der. "Die grosse Runenspange von Nordendorf." *Zeitschrift des Vereins für Volkskunde*, 25 (1915), 136-46.

The significance of this study of the Nordendorf brooch I is that here the identification of the runic *logaþore* with the Loki-name *Lóðurr* was first made.

1447. Leyen, Friedrich von der. "Die germanische Runenreihe und ihre Namen." *Zeitschrift für Volkskunde*, 40 (1930), 170-82.

The three "families" or groups of eight of the characters of the elder runic alphabet represent, according to von der Leyen, three different divine principles: the thunder god; good and evil forces of wealth and prosperity; and sky gods.

1448. Leyen, Friedrich von der. *Die Götter der Germanen*. Munich: C. H. Beck, 1938. xii, 322 pp.

Survey of Germanic religion and mythology. The extant mythology is a product of the Viking Age and tends toward the heroic and the poetic.

1449. Leyen, Friedrich von der. "Zur grösseren Nordendorfer Spange." *Beiträge zur Geschichte der deutschen Sprache und Literatur* (Tübingen), 80 (1958), 208-13.

On Logaþore, Logþer, Loki, and tricksters. The author finds the inscription on the Nordendorf brooch I the oldest Germanic magic charm and possibly the most noteworthy, from the point of view of the history of Germanic religion, of all continental runic inscriptions.

1450. Liberman, Anatoly. "Germanic *sendan* 'To Make a Sacrifice.'" *Journal of English and Germanic Philology*, 77 (1978), 473-88.

Argues that the Germanic verb **sendan* (usually glossed "to send") could also mean "to sacrifice." The evidence is primarily from *Beowulf* 600 (Grendel's killing of Hondscio) and *Atlakviða* 37:5-8. *Hávamál* 144-45 and the mock sacrifice of Víkarr in *Gautreks saga* are also adduced.

1451. Lid, Nils. "At hitta í lið: Til Hávamál 66,6." *Maal og minne*, 1925, pp. 18-24.

Textual note to *Hávamál*, str. 66.

1452. Lid, Nils. "Ullins øyra." In *Heidersskrift til Marius Hægstad*. 128-44. Oslo: O. Norli, 1925.

On modern folk customs and beliefs concerning small outgrowths on the hearts of slaughtered animals. Terms for these growths in some Scandinavian dialects begin with *ull-*, which Lid interprets as "Ullr."

1453. Lid, Nils. "Gand og tyre." In *Festskrift til Hjalmar Falk fra elever, venner og kolleger*. 331-50. Oslo: H. Aschehoug, 1927. Rpt. in Lid, *Trolldom: Nordiske studiar* (Oslo: Cammermeyer (G. E. Raabe), [1950]), pp. 37-58.

Treats the words *gand* (Norwegian) and *tyre* (Swedish dialect), both of which came to mean "magic" from original meanings "painted stick, projectile." Discussion of the implications of the semantic shift.

1454. Lid, Nils. *Joleband og vegetasjonsguddom.* Skrifter utgitt av det norske videnskaps-akademie i Oslo, II. hist.-filos. kl, 1928, 4. Oslo: J. Dybwad, in commission, 1928. 286 pp.

A study of vegetation beliefs and rites associated primarily with Christmas in Norway. The older mythology is mentioned only in passing, e.g., Freyr (pp. 147-56) and Fróði (pp. 172-74).

1455. Lid, Nils. "Altnorw. Þorri." *Norsk tidsskrift for sprogvidenskap,* 7 (1934), 163-69.

Ullr as "the wooly," a name indicating fertility.

1456. Lid, Nils. "Til varulvens historia." *Saga och sed,* 1937, pp. 3-25. Rpt. in Lid, *Trolldom: Nordiske studiar* (Oslo: Cammermeyer (G. E. Raabe), n.d. [1950]), pp. 82-108.

General treatment of werewolves and shape-changing in Nordic tradition, including berserks and *úlfheðnar.*

1457. Lid, Nils. "Gudar og gudedyrking." In *Religionshistorie,* ed. Nils Lid, 80-153. Nordisk kultur, 26. Stockholm: A. Bonnier, Oslo: H. Aschehoug, Copenhagen: J. H. Schultz, 1942.

Here Nils Lid attempts a history of Scandinavian paganism. Topics treated are: sacrifice and temple (pp. 80-91); Baldr (pp. 91-95); Freyr (pp. 95-109); Njord (pp. 109-15); Ullr (pp. 115-24); Thor (pp. 124-29); Odin (pp. 129-35); valkyries and *dísir* (pp. 135-42); cosmos (pp. 142-46). From the point of view of mythology the emphasis is not usual: Ullr, a shadowy figure, receives more attention than Odin or Thor, and Freyr more than both of these *æsir* together. The reason is, of course, that for Lid the mythology is only one of several major sources illuminating his major subject, cult.

The perspective may be said to be typical of contemporary Nordic research of that time in the subject. Philology (broadly defined) is the major tool, and it is used to seek the history through time and space of the individual gods' cults.

1458. Lid, Nils, ed. *Religionshistorie.* Stockholm: Bonniers, Oslo: Aschehoug, Copenhagen: J. H. Schultz, 1942. 163 pp.

Following a brief introduction by the editor, this volume in the important series Nordisk kultur contains the following essays, each given a separate entry in this bibliography: Eva Nissen Fett, "Kultminne i fornfund"; "Kultminne i stadnamn," "1: Danmark" by Gunnar Knudsen, "2: Sverige" by Oskar Lundberg, "3: Norge" by Magnus Olsen, "4: Island" by Ólafur Lárusson; Nils Lid, "Gudar og gudedyrking." An index is found on pp. 154-59.

Given the national divisions and different emphases of the articles—particularly the placename articles—and the consequent scattering of data, this can hardly be recommended as a general handbook, but for a philological perspective on cult it is still useful.

1459. Lid, Nils. *Light-Mother and Earth-Mother.* Studia Norvegica, 4. Oslo: H. Aschehoug, 1946. 20 pp.

The term "earth-mother" (*jordmoder* and similar forms) for "midwife" probably reflects an old stratum of belief in guardian figures like norns.

1460. Lid, Nils. "Scandinavian Heathen Cult Places." In *Atti dell'viii congresso internazionale di storia delle religioni (Roma 17-23 Aprile 1955).* 366-68. Florence: G. C. Sansoni—Editore, 1956.

Summary of an address at the eighth international conference on the history of religions: cult places, primarily elucidated through placename evidence.

1461. Lie, Haakon. "En gamal kultus." *Maal og minne,* 1939, pp. 11-13.

The placename *Jøgelkonta* (Norway) as a derivative of ancient fertility cult.

1462. Lie, Hallvard. "Sonatorrek str. 1-4." *Arkiv för nordisk filologi,* 61 (1946), 182-207.

The last pages discuss the erotic connotations of the Odin name Hroptr.

1463. Lie, Hallvard. "Skaldestil-studier." *Maal og minne,* 1952, pp. 1-92.

Includes discussion of *Hymiskviða* and *Ragnarsdrápa* (p. 33) and representations in viking art of Thor's expedition fishing for the midgard serpent (pp. 40-41).

1464. Lie, Hallvard. "Naglfar og Naglfari." *Maal og minne,* 1954, pp. 152-61.

On the meaning of *Naglfar* (*Vǫluspá,* str. 50). Following Snorri, most observers take it to be the name of a specific ship, but Lie thinks instead that it simply means "ship," through metonymy: it is literally "row of nails" (a reference to the nailing together of a ship's planks).

The article bears methodological importance for its insistence on consideration of contextual and stylistic unity in interpreting texts.

1465. Lie, Hallvard. "Þórsdrápa." *Kulturhistoriskt lexikon för nordisk medeltid,* 20 (1976), cols. 397-400.

A helpful encyclopedia article on the most important skaldic source concerning Thor's visit to the giant Geirrøðr.

1466. Liebrecht, Felix. "Ein Fuchsmythus." *Germania,* 11 (1866), 99-102.

German custom associated with Thor and given a nature-mythological explanation.

1467. Liebrecht, Felix. "Germanische Mythen und Sagen im alten Amerika." *Germania*, 16 (1871), 37-42.

Points out Central American parallels to Germanic myths.

1468. Liestøl, Aslak. "Freyfaxi." *Maal og minne*, 1945, pp. 59-66.

The horse Freyfaxi in *Hrafnkels saga* as it relates to horse-cult and Freyr-cult.

1469. Liestøl, Aslak. "Det norske runediktet." *Maal og minne*, 1948, pp. 65-71.

Suggests pagan-Christian syncretism in the Norwegian rune-poem.

1470. Liestøl, Knut. "Jøtnarne og joli." In *Festskrift til H. F. Feilberg fra nordiske sprog- og folkemindeforskere på 80 års dagen den 6. august 1911.* 192-205. Svenska landsmål, 1911; Maal og minne, 1911; Danske studier, 1911. Stockholm: Norstedt, Copenhagen: Gyldendal, Oslo (Kristiania): Bymaals-laget, 1911.

In the course of arguing late medieval origins to the association between giants and Christmas, Liestøl draws a distinction between popular beliefs, which associated giants closely with nature, and literary conceptions, like those of Norse mythology.

1471. Liestøl, Knut. *Draumkvæde: A Norwegian Visionary Poem from the Middle Ages.* Studia Norvegica, 3. Oslo: H. Aschehoug (W. Nygaard), 1946. 144 pp.

This translation and discussion of the Norwegian dream ballad includes remarks on the Gjallarbrú.

1472. Liliencron, R. von. "Das Harbardslied." *Zeitschrift für deutsches Altertum*, 10 (1855-56), 180-96.

Reading of *Hárbarðsljóð*, attempting to place the poem in the context of the cults of Thor and Odin.

1473. Lincoln, Bruce. "The Lord of the Dead." *History of Religions*, 20 (1980-81), 224-41.

Indo-European *Yemo (Old Norse Ymir) as the first sacrifice and lord of the other world. Nordic evidence relies primarily on the death and realm of Guðmundr in *Hervarar saga.*

1474. Líndal, Sigurður. "Upphaf kristni og kirkju." In *Saga Íslands: Samin að tilhlutan þjóðhátíðarnefndar 1974,* vol. 1, ed. Sigurður Líndal, 225-88. Reykjavik: Hið íslenzka bókmenntafélag—Sögufélag, 1974.

A survey of the origins of Christianity and the Church in Iceland, for a volume of general essays on the history of Iceland. The sections on early

Christianity (pp. 231-38) and the conversion (pp. 239-48) illuminate the interplay between pagan and Christian, and the entire work provides useful background on the spiritual circumstances of the culture in which Scandinavian mythology lived and was later recorded.

1475. Lindblad, Gustav. *Studier i codex regius av äldre eddan* I-III. Lundastudier i nordisk språkvetenskap, 10. Lund: C. W. K. Gleerup, 1954. xxiv, 328 pp. Summary in English.

Lindblad's study of the palaeography, orthography, and phonology of Codex Regius of the Poetic Edda leads to the following conclusions. The manuscript was written by a single scribe, ca. 1270. However, a palaeographic-orthographic boundary seems to exist between the last mythical poem (*Alvíssmál*) and the first heroic poem (*Helgakviða Hundingsbana I*), suggesting that originally the mythic and heroic poems were recorded in two separate collections. *Vǫlundarkviða* belonged with the mythic poems, not the heroic poems, as is usually asserted, and therefore AM 748 I 4to (the other major manuscript of eddic poetry) probably never contained the Helgi and Niflung lays. The two separate collections probably did not contain all the lays now in Codex Regius. Recording of eddic verse occurred before 1240, but *Vafþrúðnismál* and *Hymiskviða* were probably recorded some decades earlier. The original source(s) of Codex Regius, however, cannot antedate 1200. Norwegianisms in Codex Regius are the result of general Norwegian scribal influence.

1476. Lindblad, Gustav. "Centrala eddaproblem i 1970-talets forskningsläge." *Scripta Islandica*, 28 (1977), 3-26.

A critical survey of central problems in research on eddic poetry, stressing the author's earlier findings (1954). A collection of heroic eddic poems existed before Snorri wrote his *edda* (ca. 1222-25), but mythological poems had been collected to a much lesser extent. "Despite the Icelanders' remarkable tolerance, they will have found it distasteful to write down either verse or prose records of the old pagan worldview. Snorri, in his enthusiasm for skaldic poetry, will have been the first with such strong motivation that he felt himself compelled to set aside this earlier attitude" (p. 20).

1477. Lindblad, Gustav. "Snorre Sturlasson och eddadiktningen." *Saga och sed*, 1978, pp. 17-34.

The author evaluates the importance of Snorri Sturluson for eddic poetry and concludes that it was minimal: Snorri did not provide the impetus for recording eddic poetry, as written collections, at least of heroic poetry, were apparently undertaken before Snorri wrote his *Edda*; *Snorra edda* may, however, have influenced the collection and concatenation of mythological poetry. Snorri himself will not have had a hand in this; nor was he the author of *Þrymskviða*, contra Hallberg ("Om Þrymskviða," 1954).

1478. Lindblad, Gustav. "Poetiska eddans förhistoria och skrivskicket i Codex Regius." *Arkiv för nordisk filologi*, 95 (1980), 142-67.

In this important article Lindblad offers a detailed addition and complement to his study of Codex Regius, the major manuscript of the Poetic Edda (*Studier i codex regius av äldre eddan* (1954)). He repeats his conclusion that Codex Regius goes back to two written compilations combined for the first time in that manuscript ca. 1270. The scribe of Codex Regius was therefore the redactor of the Poetic Edda.

1479. Linde, Gunnar. "Den äldsta bebyggelsen i Kåkinds härad." *Ortnamnssällskapets i Uppsala årsskrift*, 1951, pp. 36-46.

Includes discussion of the placename *Skövde*, which some scholars have interpreted as identical to *Skadevi*, i.e., "Skaði's holy place." Linde offers instead an explanation based purely on the topology of the area.

1480. Lindén, Bror. "Hanaknä." *Namn och bygd*, 24 (1936), 114-21.

Contra Hellquist, "Svenska ortnamn (Guden Höner)," *Namn och bygd* 4 (1916), 127-54, esp. 141f. "I must however confess that in reading various religiously oriented interpretations of placenames, advanced by noted scholars, I have been unable to suppress the feeling that in many cases they have overshot the goal and unnecessarily preferred complex, abstract explanations over more real ones that indeed lie closer to hand, even if they are not always so easily discernible for modern cultural man." A long sentence (and no more elegant in Swedish), but typical of the sober reappraisal of early zealous identification of theophoric placenames.

1481. Lindow, John. "A Mythic Model in *Bandamanna saga* and its Significance." *Michigan Germanic Studies*, 3 (1977), 1-12.

Given similarities between *Bandamanna saga* and *Lokasenna*, this article explores the parallel of the character Ófeigr with Loki the trickster and with Odin.

1482. Lindow, John. "The Two Skaldic Stanzas in *Gylfaginning*: Notes on Sources and Text History." *Arkiv för nordisk filologi*, 92 (1977), 106-24.

Argues that the Gefjon stanza is interpolated in *Gylfaginning*, and that Snorri cited *Haraldskvæði* lla (on Valhalla) because of the description of jesters in str. 22-23 of that poem, thus denigrating the *æsir* with whom Gylfi meets.

1483. Lindow, John. "Mythology and Mythography." In *Old Norse-Icelandic Literature: A Critical Guide*, eds. Carol J. Clover and John Lindow, 21-67. Islandica, 45. Ithaca: Cornell University Press, 1985.

Bibliographically-oriented essay summarizing research trends in Scandinavian mythology.

1484. Lindquist, Ivar. "Till två små dikter i Hávamál." *Ver Sacrum*, 1917, pp. 126-35.

Textual notes to *Hávamál*, str. 50 and 62.

1485. Lindquist, Ivar. *Ordstudier och tolkningar i Havamal.* Studier i nordisk filologi, 9:1; Skrifter utgivna av Svenska literatursällskapet i Finland, 139. Helsinki: Svenska literatursällskapet i Finland, 1918. 17 pp.

Textual remarks on *Hávamál*, str. 1, 4, 8-9, 41, 52, 123.

1486. Lindquist, Ivar. *Galdrar: De gamla germanska trollsångernas stil undersökt i samband med en svensk runinskrift från folkvandringstiden.* Göteborgs högskolas årsskrift 1923:1. Gothenburg: Wettergren & Kerber, 1923. 193 pp.

The author investigates the style of Norse magic charms and proposes a metrical "*galdr*-form." He considers the two Merseburg charms and, in the longest section of the book (pp. 61-187), takes up in great detail the Stentoften inscription.

1487. Lindquist, Ivar. "Eddornas bild av Ull—och guldhornens." *Namn och bygd*, 14 (1926), 82-103.

Lindquist identifies Ullr in the pictures on the Gallehus horns and concludes that they verify Snorri's information on Ullr. (This argument may be somewhat circular.)

1488. Lindquist, Ivar. *Religiösa runtexter, I: Sigtuna-galdern: Runinskriften på en amulett funnen i Sigtuna 1931.* Skrifter utgivna av vetenskaps-societeten i Lund, 15. Lund: H. Ohlsson, 1932. 115 pp. Summary in English, pp. [106]-11.

Reads the newly discovered (1931) Sigtuna amulet as a magic spell against illness, but without the reference to Thor found by M. Eriksson and D. O. Zetterholm, "En amulett från Sigtuna" (1933).

Cf. part 2 of the study (Lindquist 1940) and H. Pipping, *Sigtuna-amuletten* (1933).

1489. Lindquist, Ivar. "Kritisk undersökning av sista raden i Skírnismál." In *Studia Germanica tillägnade Ernst Albin Kock den 6 december 1934.* 128-37. Lund: C. Blom, 1934.

The last line of *Skírnismál* may reflect in part a magic charm.

1490. Lindquist, Ivar. "Egendomliga *u*-stammar." In *Bidrag till nordisk filologi tillägnade Emil Olson.* 230-41. Lund: C. W. K. Gleerup, 1936.

Óðr in *Hyndluljóð* 47.

1491. Lindquist, Ivar. "Trolldomsrunorna från Sigtuna." *Fornvännen*, 31 (1936), 29-46. Summary in German.

Interpretation of the Sigtuna amulet: a magic charm against illness, but with no invocation to Thor. Cf. Manne Eriksson and D. O. Zetterholm, "En amulett från Sigtuna" (1933).

1492. Lindquist, Ivar. "Guden Heimdall enligt Snorres källor." *Vetenskaps-societeten i Lund, årsbok*, 1937, pp. 53-98.

Detailed criticism of Åke Ohlmarks, *Heimdalls Horn und Odins Auge* (1937).

1493. Lindquist, Ivar. "*Hlewagastir* och *Harigasti Teiua*: Studier i germansk epigrafik och i runologiens hjälpvetenskaper." In *Beiträge zur Runenkunde und nordischen Sprachwissenschaft: Gustav Neckel zum 60. Geburtstag*. 86-102. Leipzig: O. Harrassowitz, 1938.

With discussions of names in *Þór-*.

1494. Lindquist, Ivar. *Religiösa runtexter, II: Sparlösa-stenen. Ett svenskt runmonument från Karl den stores tid upptäckt 1937*. Skrifter utgivna av vetenskaps-societeten i Lund, 24. Lund: C. W. K. Gleerup, 1940. 213 pp. Summary in English, pp. 202-07.

Reads the Sparlösa stone as a remnant of Indo-European and Germanic religion.

1495. Lindquist, Ivar. "Kungadömet i hednatidens Sverige." *Arkiv för nordisk filologi*, 58 (1944), 221-34. Also in *Festskrift till Jöran Sahlgren 8/4 1944* (Lund: C. W. K. Gleerup, 1944), pp. 221-34.

On kingship in pagan Sweden. The king had political and sacral obligations, the latter centering on his descent from Freyr.

Opposes von Friesen's etymology of the word *konungr* "king."

1496. Lindquist, Ivar. *Die Urgestalt der Hávamál: Versuch zur Bestimmung auf synthetischem Wege*. Lundastudier i nordisk språkvetenskap, 11. Lund: C. W. K. Gleerup, 1956. 271 pp.

Lindquist seeks to reconstruct a proto-text of *Hávamál*, moving stanzas around, borrowing material from other sources, and even composing lines of his own. His analysis is of interest because of the theoretical premise: the poem is regarded as the words of Odin, thereby presupposing a ritual, presumably initiation into an Odin cult.

1497. Lindqvist, Natan. *Bjärka-Säby ortnamn*. Uppsala: Svenska kyrkans diakonistyrelses förlag, 1926. 488 pp.

Includes a warning against uncritical acceptance of theophoric elements in placenames.

1498. Lindqvist, Natan. *Stort och smått i språkets spegel*. Uppsala: Almqvist & Wiksell, 1927. 97 pp.

Includes a chapter on "placenames derived from magic acts": the component *vret/vreta-* "clearing by burning" reflects a magic act in which a furrow around an area to be burned is intended to keep the fire from spreading.

1499. Lindqvist, Sune. "Ett 'Frös-vi' i Nerike." *Fornvännen*, 5 (1910), 119-38.

Description and analysis of an excavation in Närke, Sweden, which the author interprets as a cult area sacred to Freyr.

1500. Lindqvist, Sune. "Snorres uppgifter om hednatidens gravskick och gravar." *Fornvännen*, 15 (1920), 56-105.

Understands the inconsistencies in Snorri's accounts of burial practice in *Snorra edda* and *Ynglinga saga* as the result of his trying to deal with disparate sources. Lindqvist also takes up the question of Odin's immigration to Scandinavia with the *æsir* and concludes that between composing *Snorra edda* and *Heimskringla*, Snorri came across a Swedish source previously unknown to him.

1501. Lindqvist, Sune. "Ynglingaättens gravskick." *Fornvännen*, 16 (1921), 83-194.

Departing from a description of the excavation of Ingjaldshögen, a mound in Södermanland, Sweden, Lindqvist develops a theory of house cremation funeral ritual, practiced by the early ruling Upplandic family, the Ynglingar. A lengthy section of the essay (pp. 111-67) surveys literary evidence: eddic poetry, laws, *Ynglinga saga* and *Ynglingatal*, *Beowulf*, and skaldic poetry. This section offers several remarks concerning Odin and valkyries.

1502. Lindqvist, Sune. "Hednatemplet i Uppsala." *Fornvännen*, 18 (1923), 85-118. German summary.

An attempt to evaluate the description of the pagan temple at Uppsala in Adam of Bremen's history of the archbishopric of Hamburg-Bremen. Lindqvist imagines that some of it is an eyewitness report given by someone who had seen the temple at a distance and misunderstood certain basic features of site and construction.

On p. 118 Emil Eckhoff adds a brief untitled note on the article.

1503. Lindqvist, Sune. *Svenskarna i heden tid.* Stockholm: A. Bonnier, 1935. 264 pp.

Popular treatment of ancient Sweden, stressing archaeology. Chapter 6, "Andlig odling," deals in part with religion: votive finds, rock carvings, and the Uppsala temple.

1504. Lindqvist, Sune. "Hunningestenen och Franks skrin." *Saga och sed*, 1940, pp. 55-63.

The Hunninge (Gotland) stone and Auzon (Franks) casket portray, according to the author, variants of a now lost legend of vengeance.

1505. Lindqvist, Sune. *Gotlands Bildsteine*. Stockholm: Kungliga vitterhets historie och antikvitets akademien, 1941-42. Vol. 1 (1941), 151 pp. and 183 plates (unfoliated); vol. 2 (1942), 147 pp.

The Gotland picture stones contain scenes which have been identified with Norse myth, heroic legend, and otherworld belief, and taken together they represent perhaps the most important iconographic source for the study of this material. Lindqvist's is the standard edition of the corpus. Vol. 1 offers a general introduction and survey, with sections devoted to forms, pictures, and chronology; a chapter on the scenes from the mythology appears on pp. 95-101, and the chapters on symbols (pp. 91-95) and heroic legend (pp. 101-07) are also relevant to Germanic myth and religion. Vol. 2 contains detailed descriptions of the individual stones.

1506. Lindqvist, Sune. "En detalj i Gudingsåkrarnas problem." *Gotländsk arkiv*, 17 (1945), 31-32.

Brief comment on M. Stenberger, "Gudingsåkrarna" (1943), associating sacrificial ritual with a bird cult.

1507. Lindqvist, Sune. "Valhall—Colosseum eller Uppsalatemplet?" *Tor*, [2] (1949-51), 61-103.

On an archaeological basis, and using several reconstructions, Lindqvist rejects the notion advanced by M. Olsen, "Valhall med de mange dörer" (1931-32), that the description of Valhalla in *Grímnismál* reflects the Colosseum. Instead, argues Lindqvist, it may equally represent some northern building, perhaps the pagan temple at Gamla Uppsala.

1508. Lindroth, Hjalmar. "Hymiskviða str. 38." In *Sertum philologicum Carolo Ferdinando Johansson oblatum: Festskrift tillegnad Karl Ferdinand Johansson på hans 50-årsdag den 16 september 1910*. 52-61. Gothenburg: W. Zachrisson, 1910.

Textual note: the stanza combines the description of a god's transport-animal failing with a later one of the slaughter, eating, and resurrection of an animal.

1509. Lindroth, Hjalmar. "Två uppsalienska vattendragsnamn." *Namn och bygd*, 1 (1913), 35-44.

Includes discussion of an ancient cult place, perhaps relating to the *dísir*, near a watercourse in Uppsala (Sweden).

1510. Lindroth, Hjalmar. "Yggdrasils 'barr' och eviga grönska: En replik." *Arkiv för nordisk filologi*, 30 (1914), 218-26.

Response to Läffler, "Det evigt grönskande trädet i den fornnordiska mytologien och det fno. ordet *barr*, fisl. *barr*" (1930).

1511. Lindroth, Hjalmar. "Boðn, Són och Óðrœrir." *Maal og minne*, 1915, pp. 174-77.

Of the three names Snorri assigns to the vessels used to contain the mead of poetry, only *boðn*, according to Lindroth, meant "pot." *Són* meant "reconciliation" and *Óðrœrir* referred to the mead itself. The trinity *Boðn, Són,* and *Óð rœrir* thus reveals itself as three heterogeneous entities.

1512. Lindroth, Hjalmar. "Gudanamnet Tor." *Namn och bygd*, 7 (1919), 186.

Derives the name of Thor from **þunraR* "thunderer."

1513. Lindroth, Hjalmar. "*Skee—Skövde—Skedevi.*" *Göteborgs högskolas årsskrift*, 36:3 (1930), 38-49.

Etymological remarks on placenames containing, according to the author, the name of the ancient goddess Skedja (related to Skaði).

1514. Lindroth, Hjalmar. "En hällristning och ett ortnamn: En lockande sammanställning." *Göteborgs och Bohusläns fornminnesförenings tidsskrift*, 1942, pp. 1-23.

The placename is *Hovträd*; a nearby rock carving tempts the author to connect possible cult activity there with the placename.

1515. Lindsten, Egil. "Fyndet från Alva myr." *Fornvännen*, 28 (1933), 321-31. Summary in German.

The find from the Alva (Gotland) bog, made in 1929, was of an oak chest dating from the Bronze Age. Lindsten speculates on the possible religious and superstitious (he favors the latter) background of this and other finds indicating burial in a bog. He suggests that bogs and moors were regarded as evil and thus suitable places for burial of wrongdoers or even secondary burial of revenants.

1516. Linnig, Franz. *Deutsche Mythen-Märchen: Beitrag zur Erklärung der Grimmschen Kinder- und Hausmärchen.* Paderborn: F. Schöningh, 1883. xii, 213 pp.

Alleged survivals of Germanic mythology, mostly understood as nature mythology and in German form, in ca. forty of the tales of the Brothers Grimm.

1517. Lippert, Julius. *Die Religionen der europäischen Culturvölker, der Litauer, Slaven, Germanen, Griechen und Römer in ihrem geschichtlichen Ursprunge.* Berlin: T. Hofmann, 1881. xvi, 496 pp.

Animism, drawing occasionally on Germanic materials.

1518. Lippert, Julius. *Christenthum, Volksglaube und Volksbrauch: Geschichtliche Entwicklung ihres Vorstellungsinhaltes.* Berlin: T. Hofmann, 1882. xvi, 696 pp.

The meeting of early Christianity and the cult of the soul in many European cultures, including Germanic.

1519. Lithberg, Nils. "Mutterrechtliche Züge in der altnordischen Götterwelt." In *Actes du Ve congrès international d'histoire des religions à Lund, 27-29 août 1929.* 200-05. Lund: C. W. K. Gleerup, 1930.

Lecture and discussion from an international congress on the history of religion. Lithberg finds traces of *Mutterrecht* among the ancient Germanic peoples and thinks that the figure of Nerthus-Njord may be an archaic survival.

1520. Lithberg, Nils. "Att helga torsdag." *Vetenskapssocietetens i Lund årsbok*, 1933, pp. 3-30.

On the folklore concerning Thursday as a special day. "What is Germanic and what is Roman about the hallowing of Thursday, what is mythological or astrological about the *dies Jovis*, what Jupiter the god of the week can have borrowed from Jupiter the planet—and its eastern predecessor in the star of Bel-Marduk—, what Thor with Thursday the intermediary can have borrowed from Jupiter the god or the planet; all this we must leave untouched in the absence of richer materials, both classical and modern. What we can ascertain with certainty is that the hallowing of the fifth day of the week *did not originate* on Germanic soil. The tips of its roots lead most likely down to eastern astrological theories."

1521. Littleton, C. Scott. "Is the 'Kingship in Heaven' Theme Indo-European?" In *Indo-European and Indo-Europeans: Papers Presented at the Third Indo-European Conference at the University of Pennsylvania*, eds. George M. Cardona, Henry M. Hoenigswald, and Alfred Senn, 383-404. Philadelphia: University of Pennsylvania Press, 1970.

Includes a section on "The Norse Version" (pp. 390-92), betraying no direct knowledge of the Icelandic language or literary tradition.

1522. Littleton, C. Scott. "The 'Kingship in Heaven' Theme." In *Myth and Law Among the Indo-Europeans: Studies in Indo-European Comparative Mythology*, ed. Jaan Puhvel, 83-121. Publications of the UCLA Center for the Study of Comparative Folklore and Mythology, 1. Berkeley and Los Angeles: University of California Press, 1970.

Littleton argues the existence of the following pattern in Hittite, Phoenician, Babylonian, and Norse traditions: "an existing generation of gods was preceded by two (and in some cases three) earlier generations of supernatural beings, each succeeding generation being presided over by a 'king in heaven' who has usurped (or at least assumed) the power of his predecessor. Moreover, there is generally a fourth figure, a monster of some sort, who, acting on behalf of the deposed 'king'. . . presents a challenge to the final heavenly ruler and must be overcome before the latter can assert full and perpetual authority" (p. 84). Analysis of

Norse material (pp. 106-09) focuses on the creation story as recounted by Snorri and the eddic poems. It will not convince specialists.

1523. Liungman, Waldemar. *Traditionswanderungen Euphrat-Rhein: Studien zur Geschichte der Volksbräuche.* FF Communications, 118-19. Helsinki: Suomalainen tiedeakatemia, 1937-38. 1220 pp. 2 vols. Summary in English, pp. 1124-47.

Traces the spread of customs, including many with a possible cultic background (e.g., the Wild Hunt), from a hypothetical Near Eastern origin to transplanted identity in Germanic lands.

1524. Ljungberg, Helge. *Den nordiska religionen og kristendomen: Studier över det nordiska religionsskiftet under vikingatiden.* Nordiska texter och undersökningar, 11. Stockholm: H. Geber, Copenhagen: Levin & Munksgaard, 1938. ix, 342 pp. German translation issued in 1940: *Die nordische Religion und das Christentum* (Gütersloh: C. Bertelsmann).

A full study of the meeting of paganism and Christianity in Scandinavia, emphasizing the conversion. Ljungberg studies both classical Norse sources (sagas, skaldic poetry) and East Scandinavian materials. Here the emphasis is on Sweden, and among the interesting suggestions is that the high incidence of runic inscriptions in eleventh-century Uppland is a reaction to the proximity of the pagan temple at Uppsala.

With an extensive bibliography, pp. 317-42.

1525. Ljungberg, Helge. "*Trúa*: En ordhistorisk undersökning till den nordiska religionshistorie." *Arkiv för nordisk filologi*, 62 (1947), 151-71.

A semantic and comparative study of the Norse verb *trúa* "believe (in)." Its usage changed greatly with the conversion, when it was first given a religious sense; paganism stressed the *act* of cult, not belief.

1526. Ljungberg, Helge. *Tor: Undersökningar i indoeuropeisk och nordisk religionshistoria,* vol. I: *Den nordiska åskguden och besläktade indoeuropeiska gudar: Den nordiska åskguden i bild och myt.* Uppsala universitets årsskrift, 1947:9. Uppsala: Lundequistska Bokhandeln, 1947. 251 pp. Summary in French.

Perhaps the greatest value of this detailed study of Thor against the Indo-European and Nordic background is its gathering of sources (texts, pictures, kennings, and *heiti*) and its review of previous scholarship. After two chapters questioning identification of Norse gods with the account of Germanic religion given by Tacitus, Ljungberg surveys Thor's relations to other Indo-European gods: Perkúnas, Taranis, Horagalles, Ukko (the latter two are not Indo-European but borrow characteristics of the Indo-European sky god), Indra, Hercules, and Taara. The following chapters treat the psychological and metereological basis for belief in a thunder god and the reflexes of such belief in Scandinavian myth and pictorial tradition. Here the most interpretive parts of the study occur. Thunder is divided into two aspects: a positive aspect, which is correlated with the gods, and a negative aspect correlated with the giants; thus gods and giants are essentially similar, but thus myths of Thor also stress his battles with the giants. The cult, according to the author, was associated with spring and summer in eastern Scandinavia, when violent thunderstorms tend to occur, but this association was impossible in Iceland, where thunder was rare in summer. Thus the thunder god could be viewed jocularly there (i.e., *Þrymskviða*).

Vol. 2 never appeared.

1527. Ljungberg, Helge. "The Religious Interpretation of the Scandinavian Myths." In *Proceedings of the 7th Congress for the History of Religions: Amsterdam, 4th-9th September 1950*, eds. C. J. Bleeker, G. W. J. Drewes, and K. A. H. Hidding, 152-53. Amsterdam: North-Holland Publishing Company, 1951.

Summary of a lecture delivered before an international congress on the history of religion: "It seems to me, as if it were impossible to penetrate the nature of the Scandinavian myths, without first thoroughly dealing with the descriptive material, as it is preserved in rock-carvings and descriptions found in literature, and then confronting the material with what can be said about the Scandinavian cult after research of place-names and folklore" (p. 153).

1528. Ljungberg, Helge. "Das sakrale Königtum im Norden während der Missionszeit im 10. und 11. Jahrhundert." In *Atti dell'viii congresso internazionale di storia delle religioni (Roma 17-23 Aprile 1955)*. 364-66. Florence: G. C. Sansoni—Editore, 1956.

Summary of an address at the eighth international conference on the history of religions: sacral kingship and the conversion, particularly in Sweden.

1529. Ljungberg, Helge. *Röde Orm och Vite Krist: Studier till Sveriges kristnande.* Skrifter utgivna av samfundet Pro Fide et Christianismo, 1. Stockholm: Proprius, 1980. 140 pp.

A survey of the conversion of Sweden to Christianity.

1530. Ljunggren, Karl Gustav. "Anteckningar till Skírnismál och Rígsþula." *Arkiv för nordisk filologi*, 53 (1937), 190-232.

First part of an article published in two parts. Textual notes to *Skírnismál* str. 28, 31, and 42.

1531. Ljunggren, Karl Gustav. "Anteckningar till Skírnismál och Rígsþula." *Arkiv för nordisk filologi*, 54 (1938-39), 9-44.

Second part of an article published in two parts. Textual notes to *Rígsþula*: prose frame and str. 2, 10, and 15.

1532. Ljunggren, Karl Gustav. "Några ortnamn från Halmstads härad, 5: Onsjö." *Namn och bygd*, 29 (1941), 29-32.

On Odin placenames, with remarks on local lore.

1533. Ljunggren, Karl Gustav. "Färöarnas gamla kultcentrum." *Arkiv för nordisk filologi*, 72 (1957), 1-6.

The placenames *Kirkjubøur, Velbastaður*, and *Tórshavn* as indications of a cult center, dedicated to Thor, on southern Streymøy in the Faroes.

1534. Ljunggren, Karl Gustav. "Eine Gruppe südskandinavischer Altertümer in philologischer Beleuchtung." In *Festschrift Walter Baetke dargebracht zu seinem 80. Geburtstage am 28. März 1964*, ed. Kurt Rudolf et al., 261-70. Weimar: H. Böhlau, 1966.

A reworking, with additional material, of Ljunggren, "Ales stenar: En fornminnesgrupp i filologisk belysning," *Sydsvenska ortnamnssällskapets årsskrift* 1959-60, pp. 3-18. Departing from the popular name *Ales stenar* "Ale's stones" for the *skeppsättning* (series of stones arranged in ship form) at Kåseberga (Skåne, Sweden), Ljunggren attempts to recover an otherwise unrecorded Nordic appellative **al* "holy place," cognate with Gothic *alhs* "temple" and certain West Germanic onomastic forms; and he seeks further attestations in other south Scandinavian placenames.

1535. Ljunggren, Karl Gustav. "Några sydsvenska kultnamn." *Sydsvenska ortnamnssällskapets årsskrift*, 1968, pp. 3-37. Summary in English. Posthumous.

On theophoric placenames in Halland, southern Sweden. Gods mentioned are Odin, Thor, Freyr, and Freyja. Nouns for cult places include **hof* and **al.*

1536. Lodin, S. "Till frågan om Södermanlands kristnande med särskild hänsyn till runstenarnas vittnesbörd." *Teologisk årsbok*, 1937, pp. 71-96.

The Christianization of the Swedish province Södermanland, with evidence from runic inscriptions.

1537. Lönnroth, Lars. "The Noble Heathen: A Theme in the Sagas." *Scandinavian Studies*, 41 (1969), 1-29.

A stock character in the family sagas who seems to represent the saga authors' views toward the possibilities of paganism before the conversion to Christianity.

1538. Lönnroth, Lars. *Njáls saga: A Critical Introduction*. Berkeley and Los Angeles: University of California Press, 1976. xi, 275 pp.

The section on "The Language of Tradition" (pp. 42-103) relates character types, in passing, to the mythological plane.

1539. Lönnroth, Lars. "Skirnismal och den fornisländska äktenskapsnormen." In *Opuscula Septentrionalia: Festskrift til Ole Widding 10.10.1977*, ed. Bent Chr. Jacobsen et al., 154-78. Copenhagen: C. A. Reitzel, 1977.

A structural analysis leading to a social interpretation of the myth recounted in *Skírnismál*. The myth mediates, according to Lönnroth, a socially based opposition between marriage and love—especially, as in this case, love awakened by magic—and a psychologically based opposition between responsibility and desire.

1540. Lönnroth, Lars. "The Riddles of the Rök Stone: A Structural Approach." *Arkiv för nordisk filologi*, 92 (1977), 1-57.

In the course of a structural analysis of the inscription on the Rök (Sweden) runestone, Lönnroth suggests that one of the "riddles" in the inscription is based on a myth in which a hero Vilin killed a dragon and then fostered an even greater hero—Thor (pp. 42-49). Vilin "was an aged hero who in spite of his age managed to perform better than the official leader of the gods in dealing with a threat against the *vé* ["holy place"]. His short term solution of the problem was to slay a giant, but he also had a long term solution which consisted in fathering a new and even more efficient giant-slayer" (p. 48). Elements of such a story may be seen, Lönnroth argues, in reports concerning Vili and Vé, Thor and Váli, Frigg and the earth goddess, and so forth. This and the other "riddles" of the inscription functioned as a kind of secret lore among the elite (p. 55).

1541. Lönnroth, Lars. *Den dubbla scenen: Muntlig diktning från Eddan till Abba*. Stockholm: Prisma, 1978. 432 pp.

The second of these essays on the "double scene"—the interplay between the scene of an oral performance and the scene the performer describes—deals with the origin myth of the first eight strophes of *Vǫluspá*. It describes how the performer in the role of the seeress creates an image of the creation of Midgard in the consciousness of the medieval Icelandic listeners, partly through their knowledge of the ancient cosmology, more directly through mythic reference to their everyday world. Thus the construction of Midgard finds parallels in the construction of an Icelandic chieftain's hall and further in the formation of the Icelandic state during the Viking Age, and Lönnroth understands the gods' establishment of the divisions of time as an attempt to legitimize through myth the division of the workday common on Icelandic farms during the Middle Ages. The threat to order posed by the three women in str. 8 may have gained resonance through the audience's knowledge of the feuds that eroded and finally ended the "golden age" when Iceland was first settled.

Of all the vast literature on *Vǫluspá* and Norse mythology, Lönnroth's essay is virtually alone and therefore all the more significant in its treatment of the poem not as a philological ruin but rather as the expression of a specific audience's possible reaction to it—the reaction of a known audience to a known text.

1542. Lönnroth, Lars. "Iǫrð fannz æva né upphiminn: A Formula Analysis." In *Speculum Norroenum: Norse Studies in Memory of Gabriel Turville-Petre*, eds. Ursula Dronke, Guðrún P. Helgadóttir, Gerd Wolfgang Weber, and Hans Bekker-Nielsen, 310-27. N.p.: Odense University Press, 1981.

Establishes "norms" for the use of the *jǫrð—upphiminn* "earth—heaven" formula and related motifs in early Germanic texts dealing with creation (*Vǫluspá*, *Wessobrunner Gebet*, *Andreas*, *Hêliand*, *Vafþrúðnismál*, and the Old English psalms), destruction (*Christ*, the Skarpåker runestone, *Oddrúnargrátr*, and *Þrymskviða*), and magic formulas. The core of the argument is that the formulaic complex arose during Germanic times and maintained its basic context during oral transmission, thus explaining its appearance in a variety of otherwise unrelated texts.

1543. Lönnroth, Lars. "Den oldnordiske kultur ca. 800-1200." In *Dansk Literaturhistorie, I: Fra runer til ridderdigtning o. 800-1480.* 11-112. Copenhagen: Gyldendal, 1984.

The opening section of a collectively written history of Danish literature in nine volumes, Lönnroth's contribution (the authorial attribution is on p. 9) is noteworthy for its attempt at a popular presentation of the mythology in social and cultural context (pp. 49-66).

1544. Loewe, Richard. "Der Goldring von Pietroassa." *Indogermanische Forschungen*, 26 (1909-10), 203-08.

Interpretation of the runic inscription on the Pietroassa ring: "sacred to the Jupiter of the Goths" (i.e, Donar/Thor).

1545. Loewe, Richard. "Die Inschrift des Goldrings von Pietroassa." *Zeitschrift für deutsches Altertum*, 67 (1930), 49-54.

On the interpretation proposed by R. Meissner, "Die Inschrift des Bukarester Ringes" (1929).

1546. Loewenthal, John. "Drei Götternamen." *Arkiv för nordisk filologi*, 31 (1915), 153-54.

Etymological remarks on the theophoric names Yngvi, Phol, and Loki.

1547. Loewenthal, John. "Zur germanischen Wortkunde." *Arkiv för nordisk filologi*, 32 (1916), 270-301.

Etymological remarks on the mythological names Mars Thincsus, Alciis, Embla, Askr, and Nerthus.

1548. Loewenthal, John. "Zur germanischen Wortkunde." *Arkiv för nordisk filologi*, 33 (1917), 97-131.

Etymological remarks on the mythological names Baldr, Hœnir, Fjǫrgyn, Ing, Ostarun.

1549. Loewenthal, John. "Zur germanischen Wortkunde." *Arkiv för nordisk filologi*, 35 (1919), 229-42.

The etymologies of, inter alia, *blót, þulr*, and Ægir.

1550. Loewenthal, John. "Anord. *Loki.*" *Indogermanische Forschungen*, 39 (1921), 113-14.

Etymological note associating Loki with the word *logi* "flame."

1551. Loewenthal, John. "Religionswissenschaftliche Parerga zur german. Altertumskunde." *Beiträge zur Geschichte der deutschen Sprache und Literatur*, 45 (1921), 239-65. Corrections and additions, p. 477.

Notes, primarily with a linguistic orientation, on various topics: holy animals (bear, horse, swan, spider); cult relationships (Ingvaeones, Istaevones, Frisaevones, Erminones); the vocabulary of ritual (*blóta, halshǫggva, díar, jól).*

1552. Loewenthal, John. "Germanische Culturaltertümer." *Beiträge zur Geschichte der deutschen Sprache und Literatur*, 47 (1923), 261-89.

Twelve notes primarily on matters of myth and religion. These are relevant: Hræsvelgr; Thor's stone (*Eyrbyggja saga*); Hallinskíði; Yngvi; Embla; Locke Ran; *sóa* "to sacrifice"; East Germanic **Lagringōs* and cult; Afrikaans *dadsisas* and death ritual; Old Norse *dís.*

1553. Loewenthal, John. "Cultgeschichtliche Fragen." *Beiträge zur Geschichte der deutschen Sprache und Literatur*, 49 (1924-25), 63-88.

Primarily etymological. Treats, inter alia, Gungnir, Baldr, Askr, Embla, and the term *heðinn* "pagan."

1554. Loewenthal, John. "Etymological Parerga." *Beiträge zur Geschichte der deutschen Sprache und Literatur*, 49 (1924-25), 421-23.

The first section of this short article bears the title "Zur Religionsgeschichte" (pp. 421-22) and treats the etymology of *ingi* "prince"; cf. Yngvi.

1555. Loewenthal, John. "Etymologische Miscellen." *Beiträge zur Geschichte der deutschen Sprache und Literatur*, 49 (1925), 5-20.

Includes brief discussion of the etymology of the term *áss.*

1556. Loewenthal, John. "Fricco." *Beiträge zur Geschichte der deutschen Sprache und Literatur*, 50 (1926), 287-96.

Attacking H. Jungner, *Gudinnan Frigg och Als härad*, Loewenthal derives *Fricco* from Proto-Germanic **friðkan-* "lover," and *ingi* (cf. Yngvi) from the verb **aigan* "to possess."

1557. Loewenthal, John. "Alcis." *Beiträge zur Geschichte der deutschen Sprache und Literatur*, 51 (1927), 287-89.

The etymology of *Alciis* or divine twins: from a root **algīz* "driving snow."

1558. Loewenthal, John. "Wortdeutungen." *Beiträge zur Geschichte der deutschen Sprache und Literatur*, 51 (1927), 137-39.

Proposed etymology of *Kvasir*: parallel to Low German *quasen* "to chatter."

1559. Loewenthal, John. "Etymologica." *Beiträge zur Geschichte der deutschen Sprache und Literatur*, 52 (1928), 457-59.

The etymology of *dvergr* "dwarf ": "splendid fated thing."

1560. Loewenthal, John. "Etymoligica." *Beiträge zur Geschichte der deutschen Sprache und Literatur*, 54 (1930), 156-57.

Includes an etymology of West Germanic *Garmangabis*, a matrona; the first component may be related to *Garmr*.

1561. Loewenthal, John. "Germāni ." *Beiträge zur Geschichte der deutschen Sprache und Literatur*, 54 (1930), 478.

Raises the possibility that the name of the hound *Garmr* may be related etymologically to that of the *Germani* "Germanic peoples."

1562. Loewenthal, John. "Etymologica." *Beiträge zur Geschichte der deutschen Sprache und Literatur*, 55 (1931), 317-18.

Rindr associated with Serbo-Croatian *rudina* "large grassy plain."

1563. Lohse, Eduard. *Versuch einer Typologie der Felszeichnungen von Bohuslän*. Dresden: Gittel, 1934. 36 pp. Diss. Leipzig.

A typology of the Bronze Age rock carvings from Bohuslän, Sweden, based on a detailed presentation of some 500 individual motifs.

1564. Lommel, Hermann. "Eine Beziehung zwischen Veda und Edda." *Zeitschrift für deutsches Altertum*, 73 (1936), 245-51.

A Vedic charm compared with the curse in *Skírnismál*.

1565. Loorits, Oskar. "Das Märchen vom gestohlenen Donnerinstrument bei den Esten." *Sitzungsberichte der Gelehrten Estnischen Gesellschaft*, 1930, pp. 47-121.

Derives *Þrymskviða* (and the Estonian variants of the Märchen of the stolen thunder weapon) from a Christian legend, possibly of Russian provenance.

1566. Losch, Friedrich. *Balder und der weisse Hirsch: Ein Beitrag zur deutschen Mythologie*. Stuttgart: F. Frommann, 1892. iv, 197 pp.

Focuses particularly on survivals of hypothetical ancient Baldr worship in Germany. The "white stag" connects the god with seasonal ritual.

1567. Losch, Friedrich. "Mythologische Studien im Gebiet des Baldermythus." *Archiv für Religionswissenschaft*, 3 (1900), 358-74.

Using charms and Saxo to establish his bases (Baldr is equivalent to a stag; Baldr's connection with wells is original), Losch examines the German legends of Oswalt as heroicized mythic complexes of Baldr myth. These have, he believes, to do with the struggle between light and dark.

1568. Louis-Jensen, Jonna, and Stéfan Karlsson. "En marginal i Codex regius af Den ældre Edda." *Opuscula*, 4 (1970), 80-82. Bibliotheca Arnamagnæana, 30. Copenhagen: Munksgaard.

A marginal notation in the major manuscript of eddic poetry indicates that the manuscript was called "Sæmundar edda" even before the time of Bishop Brynjólfur Sveinsson, who is usually credited with (or blamed for) the creation of this misguided name.

1569. Löwe, Heinz. "Pirmin, Willibrord und Bonifatius: Ihre Bedeutung für die Missionsgeschichte ihrer Zeit." In *La conversione al cristianesimo nell'Europa dell'alto medioevo: 14-19 aprile 1966*. 217-61. Settimane di studio del centro italiano di studi sull'alto medioevo. Spoleto: Presso la sede del centro, 1967.

A contribution to an international symposium on the conversion of the European peoples to Christianity; treats the missionary saints Pirminius, Willibrord, and Boniface.

1570. Lütolf, Alois. "Heimdall und Wilhelm Tell." *Germania*, 8 (1863), 208-16.

Argues that Heimdallr was reformulated as Wilhelm Tell in the historical consciousness of the Swiss Uri.

1571. Lukas, Franz. *Die Grundbegriffe in den Kosmogonien der alten Völker*. Leipzig: W. Friedrich, 1893. vi, 277 pp.

Includes discussion of eddic cosmogonic concepts.

1572. Lukman, Niels. "An Irish Source and Some Icelandic *fornaldarsögur*." *Mediaeval Scandinavia*, 10 (1977), 41-57.

The Irish source is a fragment from the annals; the *fornaldarsögur* include *Sǫrla þáttr* and other texts dealing with the Hjaðningavíg. The Irish source does not, however, include *Sǫrla þáttr*'s mythological frame.

1573. Lund, Harald E. "En sentralhelligdom for det gamle håløyske riket?" *Naturen*, 66 (1942), 67-77.

Discusses the archaeological evidence for central cult-place in Hålågaland, Norway.

1574. Lundahl, Ivar. "Västergötlands ortnamn: En kort översikt." *Namn och bygd*, 43 (1955), 137-44.

This survey repeats the received opinion that Götaland has fewer theophoric placenames than Svealand and that Odin is the most widely attested god in Västergötland's placenames.

1575. Lundberg, Oskar. "Ortnamnet Dejbjerg." In *Festskrift til H. F. Feilberg fra nordiske sprog- og folkemindeforskere på 80 års dagen den 6. august 1911*. 303-17. Svenska landsmål, 1911; Maal og minne, 1911; Danske studier, 1911. Stockholm: Norstedt, Copenhagen: Gyldendal, Oslo (Kristiania): Bymaals-laget, 1911.

Interprets the Danish placename *Dejbjerg* as "the place made holy for the dead."

1576. Lundberg, Oskar. "Den heliga murgrönan: Till ortnamnet Vrindavi." *Namn och bygd*, 1 (1913), 49-58.

On placenames perhaps associated with the goddess Rindr. Lundberg finds the goddess's name identical to a plant name denoting Hedera helix and Lycopodium clavatum and derives her, then, from a sacred evergreen.

1577. Lundberg, Oskar. "'Odins häst.'" *Namn och bygd*, 5 (1917), 160.

Brief notice concerning a windmill with eight blades, called "Odin's horse" by the local population and thus reminiscent of Sleipnir.

1578. Lundberg, Oskar. "Kultminne i stadnamn, 2: Sverige." In *Religionshistorie*, ed. Nils Lid, 41-58. Nordisk kultur, 26. Stockholm: A. Bonnier, Oslo: H. Aschehoug, Copenhagen: J. H. Schultz, 1942.

Critical survey of references to cult in Swedish placenames, with brief research history and remarks on methodology.

1579. Lundberg, Oskar. *Ön allgrön: Är Eddans Harbardsljod ett norskt kväde?*. Arctos Svecica, 2. Stockholm: H. Geber, 1944. 32 pp. Summary in English.

Associates the name *Algrœn* (*Hárbarðsljóð* 16) with the Norwegian placename *Algrøn* (Søndre Bergenhus) and questions therefore whether the poem might not be of Norwegian origin.

Textual remarks to str. 16-18.

1580. Lundberg, Oskar. "Holmgång och holmgångsblot." *Arv*, 2 (1946), 125-38.

This discussion of the duel (*holmgangr*) in ancient Scandinavia implies association with fertility cult: the *tjǫsnur* "pegs" marking the field of combat had phallic form.

1581. Lundberg, Oskar, and Hans Sperber. *Härnevi.* Uppsala universitets årsskrift, 1911:1, Meddelanden från nordiska seminariet, 4. Uppsala: Akademiska boktryckeriet, 1912. 49 pp.

On the Swedish placename *Härnevi*: it reflects the name of a fertility goddess whose name would be *Hǫrn* in West Scandinavian. *Hǫrn* is indeed attested as a name for Freyja.

1582. Lundgren, Magnus Fredrik. *Språkliga intyg om hednisk gudatro i Sverge.* Gothenburg: D. F. Bonnier, 1878. 86 pp.

Pioneering work on theophoric placenames in Sweden.

1583. Lundgren, Magnus Fredrik. *Spår af hednisk tro och kult i fornsvenska personnamn.* Uppsala universitetets årsskrift 1880; filosofi, språkvetenskap och historiska vetenskaper, 4. Uppsala: E. Edquist, 1880. vi, 58 pp.

Pioneering work on theophoric personal names in Sweden.

M

1584. Maack, Karl. "Die Insel der Nerthus, ein historisch-antiquarischer Versuch." *Germania*, 4 (1859), 385-414.

Localizes the Nerthus cult to Holstein and identifies the site and sacred lake. Pp. 408-13 seek to separate the cult from the Freyr cult of Sjælland.

1585. MacArthur, William. "Norse Myths Illustrated on Ancient Manx Crosses." *Notes and Queries*, Ser. 11, 5 (1912), 506.

Brief note; motifs mentioned include Odin, Valhalla, Hræsvelgr, Heimdallr, Bifrǫst, and Ragnarǫk.

1586. MacCulloch, John Arnott. *The Mythology of All Races,* vol. 2: *Eddic*. Boston: Archaeological Institute of America/M. Jones, 1930. xi, 400 pp. Rpt. New York: Cooper Square Publishers, 1964.

Handbook, in a vast and well-known series; Axel Olrik was originally to have written the volume, but death intervened.

MacCulloch keeps clear the distinction between eddic mythology (stories about gods in the Icelandic eddas and related texts) and Germanic religion. The thirty-three chapters are devoted virtually all to mythological beings: gods, animals, norns, trolls, etc.; only the chapters on euhemerism, nature, magic, the otherworld, and cosmology violate this principle, and these chapters, too, stress narrative.

The volume has a color frontispiece and forty-eight monochrome plates following the final page.

1587. MacCulloch, John Arnott. *The Celtic and Scandinavian Religions.* Hutchinson's University Library, World Religions, 10. London and New York: Hutchinson's University Library, [1948]. 180 pp.

Handbook.

1588. MacCulloch, John Arnott. "Trees in Ritual and in Myth (Scandinavian and Celtic)." In *Proceedings of the 7th Congress for the History of Religions: Amsterdam, 4th-9th September 1950*, eds. C. J. Bleeker, G. W. J. Drewes, and K. A. H. Hidding, 153-54. Amsterdam: North-Holland Publishing Company, 1951.

Summary of a lecture delivered before an international congress on the history of religion: Scandinavian and Celtic sacred groves and trees compared.

1589. Mackensen, Lutz. *Name und Mythos: Sprachliche Untersuchungen zur Religionsgeschichte und Volkskunde.* Form und Geist: Arbeiten zur germanischen Philologie, 4. Leipzig: H. Eichblatt, 1927. 54 pp.

Monograph on myth and language, focusing on legends. Portions apply to Norse mythology.

1590. Mackenzie, Donald A. *Teutonic Myth and Legend: An Introduction to the Eddas & Sagas, Beowulf, The Nibelungenlied, etc.* New York: W. H. Wise, 1934. xlvii, 469 pp.

Retellings in an archaic style.

1591. Mackenzie, Donald A. *The Migration of Symbols and Their Relations to Beliefs and Customs.* New York: AMS Press, 1970. xvi, 219 pp. First published 1926 (New York: Knopf). Additional reprint 1968 (Detroit: Gale Research Co.).

With many references to Norse mythology.

1592. Magerøy, Hallvard. "Þrymskviða." *Edda*, 58 (1958), 256-70.

Mageróy accepts the standard view of *Þrymskviða* as a late poem but rejects the suggestion of Hallberg (1954) that Snorri Sturluson composed it.

1593. Magerøy, Hallvard. *Norsk-islandske problem (Omstridde spørsmål i nordens historie, 3).* Foreningene Nordens historiske publikasjoner, 4. Oslo: Universitetsforlaget, 1965. 113 pp.

Includes a chapter on the age and home of the eddic poems.

1594. Magnússon, Eiríkr. "[*Hávamál* 2, 3]." *Proceedings of the Cambridge Philological Society*, 1884, pp. 21-31.

Textual notes to str. 2 and 3 of *Hávamál.*

1595. Magnússon, Eiríkr. "[*Hávamál*]." *Proceedings of the Cambridge Philological Society*, 1887, pp. 5-18.

Textual notes.

1596. Magnússon, Eiríkr. "'Edda.'" *Saga-Book of the Viking Society*, 1 (1892-96), 219-39.

The meaning of the title *Edda*: "the book of, or at Oddi" (p. 237).

1597. Magnússon, Eiríkr. *Odin's Horse Yggdrasill: A Paper Read before the Cambridge Philological Society, January 24, 1895.* London: Society for Promoting Christian Knowledge, New York: E. & J. B. Young, 1895. 64 pp.

Text of an address. As the title suggests, Eiríkr Magnússon regards Yggdrasill not as the name of the world tree but of Odin's horse, which he believes ultimately reflects the wind.

1598. Magnússon, Eiríkr. "The Conversion of Iceland to Christianity, A.D. 1000." *Saga-Book of the Viking Society*, 2 (1897-1900), 348-74.

Following the suggestion that worship of the *landvættir* was replacing that of the *æsir*, the author argues a political explanation of the conversion. Discussion following the oral presentation of the paper appears in the same number of the journal, pp. 255-56.

1599. Magnússon, Eiríkr. "Yggdrasill." *Arkiv för nordisk filologi*, 13 (1897), 205-07.

Response to a review by F. Detter (pp. 99-100 of the same journal) of the author's *Odin's Horse Yggdrasill* (1895).

1600. Magnússon, Eiríkr. "Vilmǫgum or vílmǫgum." *Arkiv för nordisk filologi*, 15 (1899), 319-20.

Textual note to *Hávamál*, str. 133.

1601. Magnússon, Eiríkr. "Notes on Shipbuilding and Nautical Terms of Old in the North." *Saga-Book of the Viking Society*, 4 (1904-05), 182-237.

Besides the many allusions to ships in the mythology—typical of the general interest in the subject around the turn of the century—, this article is of interest for an excursus (pp. 206-08) exploring a possible relationship between the *vanir* and the Veneti of western Gaul.

1602. Magnússon, Finnur. "Digter-drikken, en oldnordisk mythe, med tilhørende forklaring." *Athene*, 6 (1816), 242-60.

Discussion of the myth of Odin's acquisition of the mead of poetry in *Hávamál*, followed by translation, accompanied by commentary, of str. 104-10.

1603. Magnússon, Finnur. "Indledning til forelæsninger over den ældre Edda's mythiske og ethiske digte." *Athene*, 6 (1816), 101-40.

Introduction to eddic mythological poetry and *Snorra edda*; focus on the texts themselves.

1604. Magnússon, Finnur. "Indledning til forelæsninger over den ældre Edda, 2det cursus, begyndt i efteraaret 1816." *Dansk minerva*, Feb. (1817), 53-74.

Introduction to eddic mythological poetry and *Snorra edda*; focus on the early secondary literature.

1605. Magnússon, Finnur. *Eddalæren og dens oprindelse eller nöjagtig fremstilling af de gamle nordboers digtninger og meninger om verdens, gudernes, aandernes og menneskenes tilblivelse, natur og skjæbne. . . .* Copenhagen: Gyldendal, 1824-26. 4 vols.

Early comparative study of eddic mythological conceptions.

1606. Magnússon, Finnur. *Priscae Veterum Borealium Mythologiae Lexicon. . . .* Copenhagen: Gyldendal, 1828. viii, 874 pp.

Separate printing of Finnur Magnússon's early attempt at systematization in vol. 3 of the Arnamagnaean edition of the Poetic Edda issued 1787-1828.

1607. Magoun, Francis P. "Fi feldor and the Name of the Eider." *Namn och bygd*, 28 (1940), 94-114.

Includes remarks on some placenames including the name of Ægir (pp. 109-12).

1608. Major, Albany F. "Ship Burials in Scandinavian Lands and the Beliefs that Underlie Them." *Folk-Lore*, 35 (1924), 113-50.

Mostly derivative summary of the archaeological and literary (including mythic) evidence. In the final pages, Major seems to argue that aspects of Norse mythology postdate the Viking Age.

1609. Makaev, E. A. "Pesni Eddy i ustnaya traditsiya." In *Problemy sravnitel'noi filologii: Sbornik statei k 70-letio chlena-korrespondenta AN SSSR V. M. Zhirmunskogo*, ed. Akademia nauk SSSR, Otdelenie literatury i yazyka, 408-17. Leningrad and Moscow: Naukal, 1964.

Makaev elucidates oral tradition within the eddic poems, using both internal and comparative evidence.

1610. Mallet, Paul Henri. *Introduction à l'histoire de Dannemarc, où l'on traite de la religion, des loix, des mœurs et des usages des anciens danois.* Copenhagen: Berling, 1755. 256 pp.

First work to make Scandinavian myth, religion, and ancient culture widely known in Europe.

1611. Mallet, Paul Henri. *Northern Antiquities: Or, A Description of the Manners, Customs, Religion and Laws of the Ancient Danes, and Other Northern Nations; including those of our Own Saxon Ancestors; with a Translation of the Edda, Or System of Runic Mythology, and Other Pieces, from the Ancient Icelandic Tongue. . . .* London: T. Carnan, 1770. 2 vols. Translated by Bishop Percy.

Bishop Percy's translation of Mallet is the first important work in English on Scandinavian mythology. Mallet's knowledge of the mythological sources was limited to Resen's editions of *Vǫluspá* and *Hávamál* (1665).

1612. Mallet, Paul Henri. *Northern Antiquities; Or, an Historical Account of the Manners, Customs, Religion and Laws, Maritime Expeditions and Discoveries, Language and Literature of the Ancient Scandinavians.* London: H. G. Bohn, 1847. 578 pp. Translated by Bishop Percy; new ed. by I. A. Blackwell.

New and considerably enlarged edition of an important work. Blackwell added several chapters and sections, of which the most important in this context are his new translation of *Gylfaginning* and the *Bragarœður* of *Snorra edda* (pp. 397-463), which marked the first time that a text other than that of Resen was known in English; his "Critical Examination of the Leading Doctrines of the System of Scandinavian Mythology" (pp. 464-507); and an interpretative "Glossary to the Prose Edda" (pp. 540-70).

The volume also contains an abstract of *Eyrbyggja saga* by Sir Walter Scott.

1613. Malmer, Mats P. "Bronsristningar." *Kuml*, 1970, pp. 189-210. Summary in English, pp. 206-07.

"Rock engravings are a peripheral phenomenon, in Scandinavia as in Europe as a whole. In Central Sweden and South Norway, people engraved pictures of offerings and cult processions; but in Southern Scandinavia they had the economic resources to make *real* offerings and carry out *real* cult processions, either with human actors or with the aid of small bronze figurines and miniature wagons" (p. 207).

1614. Malone, Kemp. "Ne. *Leed* and nsw. *Luggude*." *Namn och bygd*, 20 (1932), 244.

The underlying form **Liuðguða* means "vegetation goddess."

1615. Malone, Kemp. "The Votaries of Nerthus." *Namn och bygd*, 22 (1934), 26-51.

The title refers to the seven tribes who, according to Tacitus (*Germania*, ch. 40-41), worship Nerthus. Malone surveys other classical references to these tribes and localizes their cult to an unidentified island near the Lim fjord (Jutland, Denmark).

1616. Malone, Kemp. "Hrungnir." *Arkiv för nordisk filologi*, 61 (1946), 284-85.

The etymology of Hrungnir: "big person, tall man."

1617. Mannhardt, Wilhelm. "Frô-Donar." *Zeitschrift für deutsche Mythologie und Sittenkunde*, 3 (1855), 86-107.

Phallic aspects of Thor's hammer, and consequent association with Freyr.

1618. Mannhardt, Wilhelm. *Germanische Mythen; Forschungen.* Berlin: F. Schneider, 1858. xxi, 759, [1] pp.

Early study of Germanic myths by the great nineteenth-century comparatist.

1619. Mannhardt, Wilhelm. "Die Einweihung des Scheiterhaufens durch den Donnerhammer." *Zeitschrift für deutsche Mythologie und Sittenkunde*, 4 (1859), 295-98.

Indic parallel to the consecration of Baldr's funeral pyre by Thor's hammer.

1620. Mannhardt, Wilhelm. "Nachträge und Berichtungen zu den 'Germanischen Mythen.'" *Zeitschrift für deutsche Mythologie und Sittenkunde*, 4 (1859), 418-49.

Additions and corrections to the author's *Germanische Mythen; Forschungen* (1858).

1621. Mannhardt, Wilhelm. *Die Götterwelt der deutschen und nordischen Völker: Eine Darstellung.* Berlin: H. Schindler, 1860. 328 pp.

First part of a never completed study of German and Nordic mythology.

1622. Mannhardt, Wilhelm. "Übereinstimmungen deutscher und antiker Volksüberlieferungen." *Zeitschrift für deutsches Altertum*, 22 (1878), 1-18.

Additional notes to the author's *Antike Wald- und Feldkulte* (1875-77), some with relevance to Norse mythology (e.g., Odin's hunt).

1623. Mannhardt, Wilhelm. *Mythologische Forschungen: Aus dem Nachlasse.* Quellen und Forschungen zur Sprach- und Culturgeschichte der germanischen Völker, 51. Strassburg: K. J. Trübner, 1884. xl, 382 pp.

Posthumous mythological studies of Mannhardt, with introductory essays by K. Müllenhoff and W. Scherer. The emphasis is on Greco-Roman materials, but Nordic topics appear occasionally.

1624. Mannhardt, Wilhelm. *Wald- und Feltkulte.* 2nd ed. by W. Heuschkel. Vol. 1: *Der Baumkultus der Germanen und ihrer Nachbarstämme: Mythologische Untersuchungen.* Berlin: Borntræger, 1904. xviii, 648 pp. 1st ed. 1875. Rpt. Darmstadt: Wissenschaftliche Buchgesellschaft, 1966.

This, the second edition of Mannhardt's famous work, differs from the first edition only in orthography and the correction of minor details. As is well known, Mannhardt proposed to elucidate religion on the basis of customs, primarily recent agricultural customs. Nevertheless, he hardly ignores the mythology. He cites *Hávamál* 50 in the second section of chapter 1 (p. 6) and devotes the next section to Askr and Embla (pp. 7-8). Yggdrasill receives treatment on pp. 54-58 and Irminsûl on pp. 303-10. Nerthus is the subject of an entire chapter (pp. 567-602), the aim of which is to present her ritual as that of a vegetation demon.

1625. Manselli, Raoul. "La conversione dei popoli germanici al cristianesimo: La discussione storiografica." In *La conversione al cristianesimo nell'Europa dell'alto medioevo: 14-19 aprile 1966*. [13]-42. Settimane di studio del centro italiano di studi sull'alto medioevo. Spoleto: Presso la sede del centro, 1967.

The inaugural address to an international symposium on the conversion of the European peoples to Christianity; surveys the historical discussion.

1626. Marchant, Francis P. "The First Christian Martyr in Russia." *Saga-Book of the Viking Society*, 6 (1908-09), 28-30.

Includes a comparison of Thor and Perkunas.

1627. Marchant, Francis P. "The Vikings and the Wends." *Saga-Book of the Viking Society*, 8 (1912-13), 108-29.

Possible worship of Odin among the Wends is discussed on pp. 124-26.

1628. Mari-Catani, Alessandro. "Dodici anni di studi eddici." *Annali; Filologia germanica*, 22 (1979), 343-86.

Bibliographic essay on eddic scholarship during the 1960s.

1629. Maringer, Johannes. *The Gods of Prehistoric Man*. London: Weidenfeld & Nicolson, 1960. xviii, 219 pp. Translated by Mary Ilford.

Translation of *Vorgeschichtliche Religion: Religionen im steinzeitlichen Europa* (Einsiedeln: Benziger, 1956, 328 pp.). Useful background, particularly for the rock carvings and other archaeological artifacts. Northern Europe is mentioned occasionally, particularly in the treatment of the neolithic period.

1630. Maringer, Johannes. "Grave and Water in Prehistoric Europe." *Journal of Indo-European Studies*, 3 (1975), 121-45.

Ancient European peoples tended to conduct burial rites near or with water, and Indo-European peoples continued the practice from the Bronze Age onward. Perhaps this provides context to accounts of Viking and Norse funeral ritual?

1631. Markey, Thomas L. "Nordic níðvísur: An Instance of Ritual Inversion?" *Mediaeval Scandinavia*, 5 (1972), 7-18.

"I conclude that Nordic *níð* is a ritual expression of status reversal, an instance of ritual inversion. At its oldest derivational level based on comparative evidence *níð* implied a curse of lack of masculinity, a lack of *argr* [which Markey derives from Indo-European **orghi-* "testicles"], and was dependent on divinities (*landvættir* or the gods) for its effect" (p. 18).

1632. Markey, Thomas L. "Germanic *li þ-/laiþ-* and Funerary Ritual." *Frühmittelalterliche Studien*, 8 (1974), 179-94.

Derives from Proto-Indo-European **le i/lei* "pour, flow" both the verb *li þan* "sail; move gradually" and the noun **li þu-* "fruit wine; strong drink" (as in Norse *líð*, a *heiti* for beer). Through reference to the myth of the mead of poetry and other sources, Markey concludes "that the custom of funerary and commemorative libations was deeply embedded in Germanic pagan tradition and that it was specifically associated with Odin" (p. 191).

1633. Markey, Thomas L. "Delabialization in Germanic." *Folia Linguistica Historica*, 1 (1980), 285-93.

Includes proposal of an etymology for Garmr, making the name cognate with *warm*, through personification of fire as howling dog.

1634. Marold, Edith. "Die Königstochter im Erdhügel." In *Festschrift für Otto Höfler zum 65. Geburtstag*, eds. Helmut Birkhan and Otto Gschwantler, 351-61. Vienna: Notring, 1968.

Aspects of the folktale of the princess in the mound are reflected in Saxo's *Gesta Danorum* and in *Ásmundar saga kappabana*. These traditions may, like the legend of Hetel and Hilde (cf. F. R. Schröder, "Die Sage von Hetel und Hilde" (1958), derive from cult.

1635. Marold, Edith. "Das Walhallbild in den Eiríksmál und den Hákonarmál." *Mediaeval Scandinavia*, 5 (1972), 19-33.

A comparison of the varying conceptions of Valhalla in *Eiríksmál* and *Hákonarmál.* That of *Eiríksmál* is more straightforward: Odin chooses and welcomes Erik into Valhalla. *Hákonarmál*, on the other hand, shows a fearsome Odin, but Hákon's reception in Valhalla is essentially positive: all the gods (*ráð ǫll ok regin*) invited him there. Marold's ingenious explanation involves assigning Danish provenance to Erik's personal relationship with Odin and Norwegian provenance—in two layers—to *Hákonarmál*'s conception. The awesome Odin of death—perhaps inspired in the poet Eyvindr by imagination of the battlefield—represents an older conception, replaced gradually among the circles of the Hlað ir jarls, among whom Eyvindr worked, by more collective conceptions such as *ráð ǫll ok regin.*

1636. Marold, Edith. "'Thor weihe diese Runen.'" *Frühmittelalterliche Studien*, 8 (1974), 195-222.

Derives the runic formula "May Thor hallow these runes" from the Christian-pagan syncretism of the conversion period.

1637. Marstrand, Vilhelm. *Astronomisk bestemmelse af tiden for Vølvens spådom og Erik blodøxes regering.* Copenhagen: Trykt til deltagerne i det den 13de februar 1926 af undervisningsminister Nina Bang i Skolemusæet afholdte møde om tilrettelæggelsen af en topografisk og kildekritisk undersøgelse af Danmarks ældste historie, 1926. 29 pp.

Uses solar eclipses to support Finnur Jónsson's dating of *Vǫluspá* to 935 A. D.

1638. Marstrander, Carl J. S. "Tor i Irland." *Maal og minne*, 1915, pp. 80-89.

Evidence for knowledge and worship of Thor in Ireland, from Irish literary sources and placenames, purporting to be complete. As in West Scandinavia, Thor seems to have been regarded as the pagan opposite of Christ and was certainly the most worshipped of the Norse gods. Marstrander also cites brief evidence for worship of Baldr and perhaps for Frigg as well.

1639. Marstrander, Carl J. S. "Om runene og runenavnenes oprindelse." *Norsk tidsskrift for sprogvidenskap*, 1 (1928), 85-188. Summary in French, pp. 180-88.

Comprehensive attempt to locate the origin of runes and the names of the runes, with emphasis on magic, religious, and ritual traditions. Marstrander derives the names of the runes from gods and demons.

1640. Marstrander, Carl J. S. "De gotiske runeminnesmerker." *Norsk tidsskrift for sprogvidenskap*, 3 (1929), 25-157. Summary in French, pp. 149-57.

Monograph arguing that most older runic inscriptions are Gothic, with discussion of several inscriptions. The reading of the Vimose brooch includes remarks on the worship of Odin and Frigg, on *gandr*, and on the valkyries.

1641. Marstrander, Carl J. S. "Tunestenen." *Norsk tidsskrift for sprogvidenskap*, 4 (1930), 294-358. Summary in English, pp. 350-58.

Finds an Odin name in the memorial formula.

1642. Marstrander, Sverre. *Østfolds jordbruksristninger: Skjeberg.* Instituttet for sammenlignende kulturforskning, serie B: skrifter, 53. Oslo: Universitetsforlaget, 1963. 481 pp. 2 vols. Summary in English, pp. 440-61.

Survey of agricultural rock carvings from eastern Norway. The discussion of human and animal figures relies heavily on a religious interpretation.

1643. Marstrander, Sverre. "Nye resultater i utforskningen av bronsealderens helleristninger (jordbrugsristningene)." *Det kongelige norske videnskabers selskab museet årbok*, 1966, pp. 103-20.

Agricultural ritual in Bronze Age rock carvings, associated with changes in social structure accompanying the introduction of fixed cultivation of the land.

1644. Marstrander, Sverre. "A Newly Discovered Rock-Carving of Bronze Age Type in Central Norway." In *Valcamonica Symposium*, ed. Emmanuel Anati, 261-68. Capo di Ponte: Centro camuno di studi preistorici, [1970]. Summaires in French and German, p. 268.

The first processional scene to be discovered among the Norwegian rock carvings.

1645. Martin, E. "Muspilli." *Zeitschrift für deutsches Altertum*, 38 (1894), 186-89.

The meaning of the first component of Old High German *muspilli*: "sod, turf."

1646. Martin, John Stanley. *Ragnarǫk: An Investigation into Old Norse Concepts of the Fate of the Gods.* Melbourne Monographs in Germanic Studies, 3. Assen: Van Gorcum, 1972. viii, 151 pp.

In investigating Ragnarǫk, Martin notes similarities to certain West Asian societies suggesting a link between myth and ritual. These lead him to propose that a "ritual of reinvigoration" may once have been associated with the traditions concerning Ragnarǫk. The epic battle between gods and giants he regards as of native origin, perhaps influenced by Irish or Christian conceptions, and the death of Baldr may have arisen from a seasonal ritual not directly connected to Ragnarǫk.

Despite its careful source criticism, this monograph offers rather speculative conclusions, insofar as it proceeds from typological similarities and seeks to reconstruct pagan ritual from medieval myth.

1647. Martin, John Stanley. "Ár vas alda: Ancient Scandinavian Creation Myths Reconsidered." In *Speculum Norroenum: Norse Studies in Memory of Gabriel Turville-Petre*, eds. Ursula Dronke, Guðrún P. Helgadóttir, Gerd Wolfgang Weber, and Hans Bekker-Nielsen, 357-69. N.p.: Odense University Press, 1981.

Distinguishes between genetic similarity, typological similarity, and manifestation of the human psyche, none of which yields complete interpretation in the study of myth. "We need to go deeper than the superficial morphology of the motifs to see them functioning in the mythopoeic situation" (p. 365). This we do by examining the nature of myth and its function in more richly documented societies. "Cosmogonic myths link all aspects of nature and human life to the divine activity at the laying of the foundation of all things" (p. 366), and this may be applied to the literary forms of the Norse sources.

1648. Masing, Uku. "Die Entstehung des Märchens vom gestohlenen Donnerinstrument (Aarne-Thompson 1148B)." *Zeitschrift für deutsches Altertum*, 81 (1944), 23-31.

Derives the myth of *Þrymskviða* and the stolen thunder weapon from Asia Minor, ultimately from northern Syria.

1649. Masser, Achim. "Zum zweiten Merseburger Zauberspruch." *Beiträge zur Geschichte der deutschen Sprache und Literatur* (Tübingen), 94 (1972), 19-25.

Makes *Phol* the subject of the accident in the second Merseburg charm and regards *balderes* as secondary.

1650. Massmann, H. F. "Der Bukarester Runenring." *Germania*, 2 (1857), 209-13.

The Pietroassa ring in a cultic context.

1651. Mastrelli, Carlo Alberto. *L'Edda: Carmini norroeni*. Classici della religione, 1. Florence: G. C. Sansoni—Editore, 1951. civ, 600 pp.

An Italian translation of the Poetic Edda, with lengthy introduction and commentary. An imposing but somewhat idiosyncratic bibliography is included (pp. 533-68).

1652. Mastrelli, Carlo Alberto. "Sul nome della gigantessa Rán." *Studi germanici*, n. s. 4, 3 (1966), 253-64.

Philological remarks on the name *Rán*, according to *Snorra edda* wife of Ægir and hence a sea figure.

1653. Matras, Christian. "Et færøsk ordsprog og en strofe i Hávamál." *Maal og minne*, 1938, pp. 151-52.

Textual note to *Hávamál*, str. 41.

1654. Matthíasson, Steingrímur. "Líkbrensla." *Skírnir*, 79 (1905), 48-55.

Short note on cremation funerals.

1655. Matthiessen, C. C. "Hǫll havll) viþ hýrogi." *Danske studier*, 55 (1960), 93.

Textual note to *Hávamál*, str. 137.

1656. Maurer, Konrad. *Die Bekehrung des norwegischen Stammes zum Christenthume, in ihrem geschichtlichen Verlaufe quellenmässig geschildert*. Munich: C. Kaiser, 1855-56. 2 vols.; vol. 1, xii, 660, vol. 2, vii, 732. Rpt. Osnabrück, 1965.

Important older treatment of the conversion in Norway. The second volume treats the religious aspects and is therefore of greater interest to the student of Scandinavian mythology. The treatment is divided into three parts: paganism, the clash between paganism and Christianity, and early Christianity.

1657. Maurer, Konrad. "Zur Urgeschichte der Godenwürde." *Zeitschrift für deutsche Philologie*, 4 (1873), 125-30.

Speculation on the prehistory of the institution of the *goði*: what in Denmark and Norway had been largely a religious office, subordinate to central administrative power, in Iceland assumed an administrative function because of the absence of such functions elsewhere.

1658. Maurer, Konrad. "Das Gottesurtheil im altnordischen Rechte." *Germania*, 19 (1874), 139-48.

Steps through the Norwegian and Icelandic evidence for divine ordeal. The extant legal provisions do not for the most part seem to be of native origin, but Maurer finds other evidence suggesting pagan divine ordeals.

1659. Maurer, Konrad. *Über die Wasserweihe des germanischen Heidenthumes.* Abhandlungen der königlichen bayerischen Akademie der Wissenschaften, I. Cl., 15:3. Munich: G. Franz, 1880. 81 pp.

On pagan "baptism" in ancient Germanic culture. Maurer sees the Scandinavian form of it as a pre-Christian loan from Britain.

1660. Mawer, Allen. "The Scandinavian Settlements in England as Reflected in English Place-Names." *Acta Philologica Scandinavica*, 7 (1932-33), 1-30.

With remarks on sacred groves (pp. 5-6).

1661. McCreesh, Bernadine. "Structural Patterns in the *Eyrbyggja Saga* and Other Sagas of the Conversion." *Mediaeval Scandinavia*, 11 (1978-79), 271-80.

Argues the existence of a structural parallel between pagan and Christian events.

1662. McCreesh, Bernadine. "How Pagan Are the Icelandic Family Sagas?" *Journal of English and Germanic Philology*, 79 (1980), 58-66.

Not very.

1663. McTurk, R. W. "Sacral Kingship in Ancient Scandinavia: A Review of Some Recent Writings." *Saga-Book of the Viking Society*, 19 (1974-77), 139-69.

Useful review essay, touching on the writings of, among others, W. Baetke, J. M. Wallace-Hadrill, F. Ström, O. von Friesen, V. Grønbech, and L. Ejerfeldt. It contains the following definition: "a sacral king is one who is marked off from his fellow men by an aura of specialness which may or may not have its origin in more or less direct associations with the supernatural" (p. 156).

1664. Meaney, A. L. "Woden in England: A Recondsideration of the Evidence." *Folklore*, 77 (1966), 105-15.

A criticism of J. S. Ryan, "Othin in England" (1963), concluding that Ryan's "most interesting ideas. . . are unfortunately incapable of proof" (p. 114). "The moral is, then, not to let oneself be carried away. There is some evidence which it is legitimate to use in an attempt to assess the importance of the heathen religion in England. Little though it is, one should confine oneself to it, and attempt, by examining it more closely, to see if it will yield anything more than what we already know. We should not try to extend it by reading heathen memories into passages of poetic description which a much more prosaic explanation would illuminate as well, if not better" (p. 115).

1665. Medioevo, Centro italiano di studi sull'alto. *La conversione al cristianesimo nell'Europa dell'alto medioevo: 14-19 aprile 1966*. Settimane di studio del centro italiano sull'alto medioevo, 14. Spoleto: Presso La Sede del Centro, 1967. 865 pp.

The proceedings of an international congress on the conversion to Christianity of the various European peoples. The relevant contributions, entered separately in this bibliography, include the following: Suso Brechter, "Zur Bekehrungsgeschichte der Angelsachsen," pp. 191-215; Francesco Delbono, "La letteratura catechetica di lingua tedesca (Il problema della lingua nell'evangelizzazione)" pp. 697-741; Jacques Fontaine, "Conversion et culture chez les wisigoths d'Espagne" pp. 87-147; Hans Kuhn, "Das Fortleben des germanischen Heidentums nach der Christianisierung" pp. 743-57; Heinz Löwe, "Pirmin, Willibrord und Bonifatius: Ihre Bedeutung für die Missionsgeschichte ihrer Zeit" pp. 217-61; Raoul Manselli, "La conversione dei popoli germanici al cristianesimo: La discussione storiografica" pp. 13-42; Lucien Musset, "La pénétration chrétienne dans l'Europe du nord et son influence sur la civilisation scandinave" pp. 263-325; Piergiuseppe Scardigli, "La conversione dei goti al cristianesimo" pp. 47-86; Marco Scovazzi, "Paganesimo e cristianesimo nelle saghe nordiche" pp. 759-84; Georges Tessier, "La conversion de Clovis et la christianisation des Francs" pp. 149-89.

1666. Meer, Gay van der, and Lars O. Lagerqvist. "Ett anglosaxiskt mynt med inristade fågelbilder." *Fornvännen*, 55 (1960), 92-99. Summary in English, p. 99.

On a coin with small figures of birds scratched into it, and, more generally, on the iconographic context of such scratchings, which the authors relate to Nordic paganism.

1667. Meid, Wolfgang. "Der germanische Personenname *Veleda*." *Indogermanische Forschungen*, 69 (1964), 256-58.

Counters Krahe, "Altgermanische Kleinigkeiten" (1960) on the name of the seeress, Veleda. It is not a Celtic loan; instead it reflects the Germanic root **wel*, which is also found in the name Ullr/Ullinn.

1668. Meier, John. *Untersuchungen zur deutschen Volkskunde und Rechtsgeschichte: Ahnengrab und Rechtsstein.* Deutsche Akademie der Wissenschaften zu Berlin: Veröffentlichungen der Kommission für Volkskunde, 1. Berlin: Akademie-Verlag, 1950. viii, 158 pp.

Folkloristic study of the intersection between ancestors' graves and legal disputes.

1669. Meisen, Karl. *Die Sagen vom Wütenden Heer und Wilden Jäger.* Volkskundliche Quellen, 1. Münster i. W.: Aschendorff, 1935. 144 pp.

Collection of texts of the Wild Hunt, with summary of previous research; relevant to Odin and Odinic cult.

1670. Meissner, Rudolf. "Die Inschrift des Bukarester Ringes." *Zeitschrift für deutsches Altertum*, 66 (1929), 54-60.

Interprets the runic inscription on the Pietroassa ring as *wi h gutanijo* "holy place of the Gutanijos"—these were "female protective spirits (*dísir*)."

1671. Meissner, Rudolf. "Die Inschrift des Bukarester Ringes: (Nachtrag)." *Zeitschrift für deutsches Altertum*, 66 (1929), 213-16.

Addition to the author's earlier paper on the Pietroassa ring.

1672. Meissner, Rudolf. "Heilig." *Zeitschrift für deutsches Altertum*, 67 (1930), 54.

The earliest usage of *heilagr* "holy."

1673. Meissner, Rudolf. "Rígr." *Beiträge zur Geschichte der deutschen Sprache und Literatur*, 57 (1933), 109-30.

Association of Heimdallr with Rígr is not original to the poem *Rígsþula*, which shows Celtic influence and derives from a milieu when the past was not too distant to be mixed with the present.

1674. Meissner, Rudolf. "Das 'Blutopfer' in der Inschrift von Eggjum." *Zeitschrift für deutsches Altertum*, 71 (1934), 189-200.

Dismisses the hypothetical burial sacrifice from the Eggjum runic inscription.

1675. Meissner, Rudolf. "Litilla sanda litilla sęva." *Zeitschrift für deutsches Altertum*, 75 (1938), 83-86.

Interpretation of *Hávamál* 53.

1676. Meissner, Rudolf. "Vǫluspá 2, 5-8." *Zeitschrift für deutsches Altertum*, 76 (1939), 218-21.

On the seeress of *Vǫluspá* and her relationship to the rest of the text.

1677. Meissner, Rudolf. "Vǫluspá 2:5-8." *Zeitschrift für deutsches Altertum*, 76 (1939), 218-21.

The words *mjǫtviđ mæran* are to be understood parenthetically, not as apposition to *níu íviđi*, and together these two expressions refer to the present and the past, the full extent of the seeress's knowledge.

1678. Meletinskij, Eleazar. "Scandinavian Mythology as a System." *The Journal of Symbolic Anthropology*, 1, 2 (1973-74), 43-58, 57-78.

An attempt at a structural model of the mythology taken as a system. The cosmic model distinguishes horizontal and vertical axes, and the pantheon makes a kind of eschatological system. In vol. 2, pp. 66-78, Meletinskij applies these findings in a section entitled "The semantics of narrative mythological plots."

1679. Meletinskij, Eleazar. "O semantike mifologicheskih syuzhetov v drevneskandinavskoy (eddicheskoy) poezii i proze." *Skandinavisky sbornik*, 18 (1973), 145-58.

An earlier version of the author's structural model.

1680. Meletinskij, Eleazar. "Drevnskandinavskaya mifologicheskaya sistema." In *Materialy vsesoyuzkogo simpoziuma po vtorichnym modeliruyshchim sistemam 1:5*, ed. Y. M. Lotman, 16-26. Tartu: Tartuskij gos., 1974.

Early version of the author's interpretation of the Norse mythological system.

1681. Meletinskij, Eleazar. "Skandinavskaya mifologiya kak sistema." *Trudy po znakovym sistemam: Uchenye zapiski Tartuskogo sosudarstvennogo universiteta*, 7 (1975), 38-51.

Russian version of "Scandinavian Mythology as a System" (1973).

1682. Meletinskij, Eleazar. "Scandinavian Mythology as a System of Oppositions." In *Patterns in Oral Literature*, eds. Heda Jason and Dimitri Segal, 252-60. World Anthropology. The Hague and Paris: Mouton, 1977.

A summary of Meletinskij's various writings on the structural models applicable to Scandinavian mythology.

1683. Menzel, Wolfgang. "Von Thors Müttern und Frauen." *Germania*, 6 (1861), 287-94.

Nature-mythological interpretation of Thor's "two mothers" (Jǫrð and Fjǫrgyn/Hloðyn) and "two wives" (Járnsaxa and Sif).

1684. Meringer, Rudolf. "Wörter und Sachen II." *Indogermanische Forschungen*, 17 (1904-05), 100-66.

Pp. 159-60 discuss the relationship and possible religious significance of the homonym pair *áss* "beam" / *áss* "god."

1685. Meringer, Rudolf. "Wörter und Sachen III." *Indogermanische Forschungen*, 18 (1905-06), 204-96.

Pp. 277-88 discuss Indo-European worship of wood blocks, including the *æsir* and Baldr.

1686. Meringer, Rudolf. "Wörter und Sachen V." *Indogermanische Forschungen*, 21 (1907), 277-314.

Pp. 296-306 discuss Indo-European worship of wood blocks, including the *æsir*, the Irminsûl, and Baldr.

1687. Meringer, Rudolf. "Indogermanische Pfahlgötzen (Alche, Dioskuren, Asen)." *Wörter und Sachen*, 9 (1926), 107-22.

Numbers the *æsir* among Indo-European "post-idols."

1688. Merkel, R. F. "Anfänge der Erforschung germanischer Religion." *Archiv für Religionswissenschaft*, 34 (1937), 18-41.

The early study of Norse mythology and Germanic religion. In Scandinavia it focused on the eddas, in Germany initially on Tacitus.

1689. Meschke, Kurt. *Schwerttanz und Schwerttanzspiel im germanischen Kulturkreis.* Leipzig and Berlin: B. G. Teubner, 1931. vii, 225 pp.

Thorough study of the sword dance in Germanic culture, including consideration of its possible role in cult.

1690. Metzger, G. "Aisl. *fiarg-*, *fiorgu* pl. Gott, Götter." *Arkiv för nordisk filologi*, 57 (1941), 112-13.

Approves the emendation of *fiorgvall* (*Lokasenna* 19) to *fiorg oll* "all the gods."

Meulengracht Sørensen, Preben, *see* Sørensen, Preben Meulengracht.

1691. Meyer, Elard Hugo. *Indogermanische Mythen,* I: *Gandharven-Kentauren.* Berlin: F. Dümmler, 1883. ii, 243 pp.

Equation of the Vedic Gandharvas and the centaurs, with occasional forays into Germanic myth and recent German lore.

1692. Meyer, Elard Hugo. *Indogermanische Mythen,* II: *Achilleis.* Berlin: F. Dümmler, 1887. viii, 710 pp.

Reconstructs an elaborate Indo-European myth of the storm and thunder god, applied to Germanic heroic legend and to the mythology in the latter part of the book.

1693. Meyer, Elard Hugo. *Völuspa: Eine Untersuchung.* Berlin: Mayer & Müller, 1889. 298 pp.

Reads *Vǫluspá* as an almost completely Christian poem, based on biblical and patristic sources, among whom Honorius of Autun is particularly important. *Vǫluspá* would thus be a late poem, and Meyer inclines toward the twelfth century for a date and to Sæmundr Sigfússon the Learned as a possible author.

For an extended review, see A. Noreen, "Ett nytt uppslag i fråga om den nordiska mytologien" (1890).

1694. Meyer, Elard Hugo. *Die eddische Kosmogonie: Ein Beitrag zur Geschichte der Kosmogonie des Altertums und des Mittelalters.* Freiburg i. Br.: J. C. B. Mohr (P. Siebeck), 1891. 118 pp.

Study of the Norse and other cosmogonic myths. Meyer concludes that the Norse conceptions, as expressed in such poems as *Vǫluspá*, *Vafþrúðnismál*, and *Grímnismál*, are the products of authors extremely well versed in Christian theology. Ultimately, however, he finds that Indo-European cosmogony derives from Babylonian conceptions.

1695. Meyer, Elard Hugo. *Germanische Mythologie.* Lehrbücher der germanischen Philologie, 1. Berlin: Mayer & Müller, 1891. xi, 354 pp.

Important nineteenth-century handbook. Meyer stresses the similarity with material from other traditions and argues the influence of these traditions on Germanic mythology.

1696. Meyer, Elard Hugo. "Hercules Saxanus." *Beiträge zur Geschichte der deutschen Sprache und Literatur,* 18 (1894), 106-33.

Argues that Hercules Saxanus is neither Germanic nor Celtic but Roman.

1697. Meyer, Elard Hugo. *Mythologie der Germanen, gemeinfasslich dargestellt.* Strassburg: K. J. Trübner, 1903. xii, 526 pp.

Survey of Germanic mythology for a popular audience.

1698. Meyer, Herbert. "Menschengestaltige Ahnenpfähle aus germanischer und indogermanischer Frühzeit." *Zeitschrift der Savigny Stiftung für Rechtsgeschichte,* Germanistische Abteilung, 58 (1938), 42-68.

The *trémenn* of the eddas and of *Ragnars saga loðbrókar,* in the context of Germanic and Indo-European ancestor worship.

1699. Meyer, Karl. "Beiträge zur deutschen Mythologie." *Germania,* 17 (1872), 197-206.

Identifies the Aesti as the Germanic tribe among whom worship of the *vanir* originated and from whom it spread.

1700. Meyer, Richard M. *Die altgermanische Poesie nach ihren formelhaften Elementen beschrieben.* Berlin: W. Hertz, 1889. xx, 549 pp.

Chapters 2 and 3 discuss the typical motifs of Old Germanic poetry and comment often on the mythology.

1701. Meyer, Richard M. "Ymi und die Weltschöpfung." *Zeitschrift für deutsches Altertum,* 37 (1893), 1-8.

Argues against the derivation from learned sources of the creation of the cosmos out of Ymir's body; the motif itself is widespread and developed, according to Meyer, polygenetically among the Germanic peoples during pagan times.

1702. Meyer, Richard M. "Der Urriese." *Zeitschrift für deutsches Altertum,* 41 (1897), 180-87.

Defense of the author's "Ymi und die Weltschöpfung" (1893), against the criticism of E. H. Meyer, review of W. Golther, *Handbuch der germanischen Mythologie* (1895), in *Literaturblatt für germanische und romanische Philologie,* 17 (1896), 217-25.

1703. Meyer, Richard M. "Über den Begriff des Wunders in der Edda." *Zeitschrift für deutsche Philologie,* 31 (1899), 315-27.

Unusual article on the concept of the marvelous in eddic poetry. Meyer surveys the actions of the various beings, with emphasis on the gods, and concludes that the wondrous tends to cluster around ecstasy, death, night, and specially marked periods of time, especially the end of the world.

1704. Meyer, Richard M. "Ikonische Mythen." *Zeitschrift für deutsche Philologie,* 38 (1906), 166-77.

By "iconic myths" Meyer means, in effect, etiological legends. Within Scandinavian mythology, Meyer assigns the following to such an origin: Skaði (originally a Finnish deity whose myths in the guise in which we know them may have explained an idol); Yggdrasill as the world tree (learned speculation); Glitnir and

Valhalla (temple decorations as a means of differentiating gods); Sif's golden hair (an idol decorated with gold).

1705. Meyer, Richard M. "Fetischismus." *Archiv für Religionswissenschaft*, 11 (1907-08), 320-38.

The sacred mountain at Þórsnes, Iceland, as an early fetish (pp. 323-24).

1706. Meyer, Richard M. "Beiträge zur altgermanischen Mythologie." *Arkiv för nordisk filologi*, 23 (1907), 245-56.

Three notes. In "Tuisto" (pp. 246-48), Meyer argues the identity of Tuisto and Ymir. In "Dea Sandraudiga" (pp. 249-50), he argues the identity of this minor figure with Fulla and Nerthus. In "Heimdall" (pp. 250-56), he argues that Heimdallr was an original god of social divisions and creative activity who was later systematized into a position at the border of the world of the gods, as Loki's opponent.

1707. Meyer, Richard M. "Mythologische Fragen." *Archiv für Religionswissenschaft*, 10 (1907), 88-103.

Second part of an article treating various mythological problems, primarily from classical tradition (the first part is in *Archiv für Religionswissenschaft*, 9 (1906), 417-28). Pp. 93-96 treat the death of Baldr.

1708. Meyer, Richard M. "Ymi-Tuisto." *Arkiv för nordisk filologi*, 25 (1909), 333.

Addendum to the author's "Beiträge zur altgermanischen Mythologie" (1907), arguing the identity of Tuisto and Ymir.

1709. Meyer, Richard M. *Altgermanische Religionsgeschichte*. Leipzig: Quelle & Meyer, 1910. xx, 645 pp.

Handbook of Germanic religion.

1710. Meyer, Richard M. "Trier und Merseburg." *Zeitschrift für deutsches Altertum*, 52 (1910), 390-96.

Takes up the question posed by Edward Schröder in F. W. E. Roth and Schröder, "Althochdeutsches aus Trier," in the same number of the journal, p. 180, whether the Germanic charms may not be reformations of Christian charms. Meyer uses the Trier and Merseburg charms to argue that the opposite may have occurred: pagan charms reinterpreted in a Christian light.

1711. Meyer, Richard M. "Snorri als Mythograph." *Arkiv för nordisk filologi*, 28 (1911), 109-21.

Explores medieval Latin descriptions of pagan mythology as possible models or sources for *Snorra edda*, primarily *Gylfaginning*. Mentioned are Servius (the

Scholiae to Vergil), Hyginus, Isidore—none of which seems a likely immediate source—and the three Vatican mythographers. Four elements are said to be shared by Snorri and Latin mythographers: 1) use of "phantoms," 2) allegory, 3) etymology, 4) overall form: verses as evidence, lists of names, attributes. The tendency toward a strict rank order and precise moral characterization of the gods would, however, remain Snorri's own. Useful as a suggestion of one aspect of the context in which Snorri wrote.

1712. Meyer, Richard M. "Schwurgötter." *Archiv für Religionswissenschaft*, 15 (1912), 435-50.

Comparative study of gods involved in the ritual of swearing oaths, proposing a development in five stages, from pledging one's mastery of an important object, such as a weapon, through the development of gods of oaths, to an all-encompassing oath. Meyer relies heavily on Germanic material, and Ullr receives frequent mention.

1713. Meyer, Richard M. "Theophore und theriophore Namen in der germanischen Mythologie." In *Actes du IVe congrès international d'histoire des religions tenu à Leide du 9e-13e septembre 1912.* 145. Leiden: E. J. Brill, 1913.

Capsule summary of a lecture delivered before an international congress on the history of religion. Personal names referring to Odin's animals may reflect Odin worship.

1714. Meyer, Rudolf. *Nordische Apokalypse.* Stuttgart: Verlag Urachhaus, 1967. 250 pp.

Argues that the "experience" of apocalypse is more important than source criticism of the texts.

1715. Mezger, Fritz. "Á aldinn mar." *Arkiv för nordisk filologi*, 50 (1934), 271-72.

The expression, found in *Hávamál* 62 and elsewhere, means "the high sea."

1716. Mezger, Fritz. "A Note on the Meaning of 'Hveim er fúss er fara,' Fǫr Skírnis 13, 2." *Scandinavian Studies*, 17 (1942), 154-55.

Textual note to *Skírnismál*, str. 13.

1717. Mezger, Fritz. "A Semantic and Stylistic Study of Eddic *brek, súsbreki*." *Journal of English and Germanic Philology*, 42 (1943), 236-39.

Textual note to *Skírnismál*, str. 29: *súsbreki* means "grief," and the line containing it is balladic.

1718. Miedema, H. T. J. "Thor en de Wikingen in Friesland: Oudfries *Thôresday 'Donderdag.'" *Naamkunde*, 4 (1972), 1-20.

The Old Frisian form for "Thursday" as a relic of Old Norse influence in Frisia, including presumably worship of Thor.

1719. Mikkola, J. J. "Zur Vanenmythe." In *Festskrift tillägnad Hugo Pipping på hans sextioårsdag den 5 november 1924.* 376-78. Skrifter utg. av Svenska litteratursällskapet i Finland, 175. Helsinki: Mercators tryckeri, 1924.

Discusses the possibility of a trace of the *vanir* in a Slavic placename in Mecklenburg (northern Germany), where some scholars have placed the "historical" war between the indigenous *vanir* and invading *æsir.*

1720. Milroy, James. "The Story of Ætternisstapi in *Gautreks saga.*" *Saga-Book of the Viking Society*, 17 (1966-69), 206-23.

Urges a cautious attitude in approaching Old Icelandic literature as a potential source for the study of myth and religion.

1721. Milroy, James. "Starkaðr: An Essay in Interpretation." *Saga-Book of the Viking Society*, 19 (1974-77), 118-38.

Skirts the "mythic" interpretations of such scholars as Dumézil and de Vries and attempts instead to interpret Starkaðr as a "*literary* myth, or to put it another way, as a set of data that underlie and give inspiration to the later literature" (p. 137). For Milroy, Starkaðr's ideals are "those of the fiercely independent freeman" (pp. 137-38).

1722. Mitchell, Stephen A. "*Fǫr Scírnis* as Mythological Model: Frið at kaupa." *Arkiv för nordisk filologi*, 98 (1983), 108-22.

Structural reading of *Skírnismál* and *Þrymskviða*, along the lines made famous by Lévi-Strauss. Mitchell sees two major oppositions at work in both poems: gods—giants and creative—anticreative. Ultimately, Mitchell believes, "the myth provides a matrix for resolving the inherent conflict between groups through a system of exchange and inter-marriage and an alternating pattern of creative and anti-creative behavior" (p. 122).

1723. Mitchell, Stephen A. "The Whetstone as Symbol of Authority in Old English and Old Norse." *Scandinavian Studies*, 57 (1985), 1-31.

Linguistic and textual evidence in support of the hypothesis set forth in the title. Besides touching on the possible relationship between the whetstone and sky gods such as *Tīwaz (> Týr), Mitchell puts into context the two mythological narratives in which whetstones appear: Odin and Baugi's nine thralls, who fight over Odin's hone, and Thor's battle with Hrungnir, who is armed with a hone. Further: "As *Tīwaz* receded into the mythological background, his attributes tended to be inherited by Óðinn and Þórr as the gods of battle and thunder; it is therefore hardly surprising to find that it is the two of them in the mythological texts who are connected with whetstones" (p. 21).

1724. Mittner, Ladislaus. *Wurd: Das Sakrale in der altgermanischen Epik.* Bibliotheca Germanica, 6. Bern: Francke, 1955. 204 pp.

A study of kennings and the grammatical forms in which concepts of fate are realized (or, according to the author, displaced). Includes discussion and passages from mythological texts, e.g., *Ynglingatal* and *Vǫluspá* (esp. pp. 82-88).

1725. Moberg, Carl-Axel. "Boskapsfålla i stället för solskiva?" *Fornvännen*, 47 (1952), 119-20.

Proposes substituting a cattle pen for the sun in the interpretation of certain Bronze Age rock carvings and thus moving that particular motif "away from the subtle speculations of history, closer to a more practical reality connected with the supernatural" (p. 120).

1726. Moberg, Carl-Axel. "Vilka hällristningar är från bronsåldern?" *Tor*, 3 (1957), 49-64. Summary in English, p. 62.

On dating the rock carvings.

1727. Moberg, Carl-Axel. "Regional och global syn på hällristningar." *Kuml*, 1970, pp. 223-32.

Review article on P. V. Glob, *Helleristninger i Danmark*, stressing general methodological considerations.

1728. Moberg, Lennart. "The Languages of *Alvíssmál*." *Saga-Book of the Viking Society*, 18 (1970-73), 299-323.

A discussion of the poetic vocabulary of *Alvíssmál.* Moberg agrees that at least three "languages" (i.e., groups of words) are to be distinguished. These are the language of men (common, prosaic words); language of gods (solemn, poetic, archaic words); and the language of giants (heavy, clumsy words). Moberg cautions, however, that the poem is the virtuoso performance of a poet with a rich vocabulary, who left "the impression that [he] did not himself take the fiction of the languages of different worlds all that seriously" (p. 323).

1729. Modéer, Ivar. "Järsyssla vid Skara." *Ortnamnssällskapets i Uppsala årsskrift*, 1947, pp. 38-46.

Includes discussion of the proximity and overlap of ancient administrative and cult divisions.

1730. Moe, Moltke. *Sophus Bugge og mytegranskningarne hans.* Norske folkeskrifter, 6. Oslo: Norigs ungdomslag og student-maallaget, 1903. 24 pp.

Survey of S. Bugge's mythological interpretations.

1731. Møhl, Ulrik. "Bjørnekløer og brandgrave: Dyreknogler fra germansk jernalder i Stilling." *Kuml*, 1977, pp. 119-29. Summary in English.

Interpretation of possible cultic background and significance of cremation grave-finds, including bear-claws, from the early Germanic Iron Age in Jutland.

1732. Möller, Hermann. "Zum Fiölsvinnsmál." *Germania*, 20 (1875), 356-60.

Textual note.

1733. Mogk, Eugen. "Ginnungagap." *Beiträge zur Geschichte der deutschen Sprache und Literatur*, 8 (1882), 153-160.

The point of Mogk's paper is to demonstrate that Ginnungagap was the realization of formless mass—chaos—from before the period of Ymir, when the cosmos was formed. The first component derives from *gína* "to gape"; the second may be the gen. sing. of *-ungi*, a noun formant; and the third is "gap." Mogk postulates a being called *Ginnungi, a personification of the unfulfilled, unrealized world space that stretches everywhere.

1734. Mogk, Eugen. "Bragi als Gott und Dichter." *Beiträge zur Geschichte der deutschen Sprache und Literatur*, 12 (1887), 383-92.

Proposes the following progression: the historical poet Bragi lived early in the ninth century and invented skaldic poetry. He therefore lived on in the legends of skalds, who by the end of the ninth century had him living among the gods. Perhaps as early as by the tenth century he had come to be regarded as a god of poetry, and at some point, to avoid confusion with the principal god of poetry, Bragi was made Odin's son.

1735. Mogk, Eugen. "Bragi." *Beiträge zur Geschichte der deutschen Sprache und Literatur*, 14 (1889), 81-90.

Response to S. Bugge, "Der Gott Bragi in den norrönen Gedichten" (1888).

1736. Mogk, Eugen. "Das angebliche Sifbild im Tempel zu Guðbrandsdalir." *Beiträge zur Geschichte der deutschen Sprache und Literatur*, 14 (1889), 90-93.

The hypothetical idol of Sif in the temple of Hákon at Hlaðir, mentioned by several nineteenth-century scholars, is here shown to derive from misunderstanding.

1737. Mogk, Eugen. "Eine Hǫvamǫlvísa in der Njála." *Beiträge zur Geschichte der deutschen Sprache und Literatur*, 14 (1889), 94.

The sentiment of *Hávamál*, str. 42, in a dialog of *Njáls saga.*

1738. Mogk, Eugen. "Menschenopfer bei den Germanen." *Abhandlungen der Königlichen Sächischen Akademie der Wissenschaften, phil.-hist. Kl.*, 27 (1909), 601-43.

On human sacrifice among the Germanic peoples, stressing the importance of careful text criticism.

1739. Mogk, Eugen. "Ein Nachwort zu den Menschenopfern bei den Germanen." *Archiv für Religionswissenschaft*, 15 (1912), 422-34.

Addendum to Mogk's "Menschenopfer bei den Germanen" (1909). Mogk takes up the remarks of Tacitus on Mercury/Odin and human sacrifice and stresses that all Germanic sacrifice has to do with protection from death; Odin was drawn into this picture as god of the dead.

1740. Mogk, Eugen. "Die heidnisch-germanische Sittenlehre im Spiegel der eddischen Dichtung." In *Von deutscher Sprache und Art*, vols. 10-11, ed. Alfred Bass, 3-9. Leipzig: Der Ritter von Hakenkreuz, 1921.

Popular treatment of ethics, building primarily on *Hávamál.*

1741. Mogk, Eugen. *Novellistische Darstellung mythologischer Stoffe Snorris und seiner Schule.* FF Communications, 51. Helsinki: Suomalainen tiedakatemia, 1923. 33 pp.

In this short monograph Mogk first advanced his skepticism regarding the value of *Snorra edda* as a source of pagan mythology and religion. Snorri and members of his "school" (for the existence of which Mogk advances no compelling argument) at Reykjaholt will have composed "mythological novellas" on the basis of older sources known to them (and generally also to us). As specific examples Mogk considers the war between the *æsir* and *vanir* and the origin of the mead of poetry.

The argument is no doubt an exaggeration, but Mogk's skepticism was instrumental in leading to modern assessment of Snorri. See, e.g., Walter Baetke, *Die Götterlehre der Snorra-Edda* (1950), or Anne Holtsmark, *Studier i Snorres mytologi* (1964). Mogk's attitude was criticized by Dumézil in a number of works, e.g., *Loki* (1948; German translation 1959).

1742. Mogk, Eugen. "Zur Bewertung des Cod. Upsaliensis der Snorra-Edda." *Beiträge zur Geschichte der deutschen Sprache und Literatur*, 49 (1924-25), 402-14.

Concludes that Codex Upsaliensis is closer to the original text of Snorri's *Edda* than are the other major manuscripts.

1743. Mogk, Eugen. "Die Überlieferungen von Thors Kampf mit dem Riesen Geirröð." In *Festskrift tillägnad Hugo Pipping på hans sextioårsdag den 5 november 1924*. 379-88. Skrifter utg. av Svenska litteratursällskapet i Finland, 175. Helsinki: Mercators tryckeri, 1924.

On the various recordings of the tale of Thor's journey to and battle with

Geirrøðr. Eilífr's *Þórsdrápa*, the earliest source, had according to Mogk itself a reworked literary version of the myth. The version in *Snorra edda* is a mythic novella, that of Saxo was affected by contemporary vision literature, and the transposed version of *Þorsteins saga bæjarmagns* is a mythic folktale.

1744. Mogk, Eugen. *Lokis Anteil an Baldrs Tode.* FF Communications, 57. Helsinki: Suomalainen tiedeakatemia, 1924. 5 pp.

As part of his skepticism about Snorri's value as a source of myth and religion, Mogk argued here that Loki originally played no role in Baldr's death. Snorri added him to the story to provide motivation.

1745. Mogk, Eugen. "Nordgermanische Götterverehrung nach den Kultquellen." In *Germanica: Eudard Sievers zum 75. Geburtstage.* 258-72. Halle: M. Niemeyer, 1925.

Primarily on Odin: the god was not strongly represented in cult in Iceland, therefore Odin poems were not composed there. The etymology of the name: "leader of the band of the dead."

1746. Mogk, Eugen. "Nordgermanische Götterverehrung nach den Kultquellen." In *Germanica: Eduard Sievers zum 75. Geburtstage 25. November 1925.* 258-72. Halle a. d. S.: M. Niemeyer, 1925.

In this useful article, Mogk gathered all the written documentation for cult worship in Norway and Iceland of the major gods: Odin, Thor, Freyr. The focus is primarily on Odin: the god was not strongly represented in cult in Iceland; therefore Odin poems were not composed there. The etymology of the name: "leader of the band of the dead."

1747. Mogk, Eugen. *Zur Gigantomachie der Vǫluspá.* FF Communications, 58. Helsinki: Suomalainen tiedeakatemia, 1925. 10 pp.

On *Vǫluspá*, str. 21-26. Mogk reads them as a battle between gods and giants (not between *æsir* and *vanir*), and he separates them from building of Asgard (Snorri's interpretation).

1748. Mogk, Eugen. *Germanische Religionsgeschichte und Mythologie,* 3rd. ed. Sammlung Göschen, 15. Berlin and Leipzig: W. de Gruyter, 1927. 140 pp.

Mogk's popular survey in the Göschen series is competent and informative. It separates myth from religion and is otherwise typical of its era in stressing supposed Near Eastern origins.

1749. Mogk, Eugen. *Zur Bewertung der Snorra-Edda als religionsgeschichtliche und mythologische Quelle des nordgermanischen Heidentums.* Berichte über die Verhandlungen der sächischen Akademie der Wissenschaften zu Leipzig, Phil.-hist. Kl., 84:2. Leipzig: S. Hirzel, 1932.

A restatement of some of Mogk's earlier work on Snorri and an analysis of

Snorri's creation story and cosmogony, repeating Mogk's contention that *Snorra edda* has no value as religious history or myth, except in cases where Snorri actually cites a poetic source.

1750. Mohr, Wolfgang. *Kenningstudien: Stilgeschichte der altgermanischen Dichtung.* Tübinger germanistische Arbeiten; Studien zur nordischen Philologie, 19. Stuttgart: W. Kohlhammer, 1933. 213 pp.

Standard general treatment of kennings.

1751. Mohr, Wolfgang. "Altgermanische Kultdichtungen." *Zeitschrift für Deutschkunde*, 54 (1940), 129-40.

Three examples of Germanic cult verse: the Old English metrical charm "For Unfruitful Land," the eddic *Sigrdrífumál*, and the eddic *Hyndluljóð*.

1752. Mohr, Wolfgang. "Mephistopheles und Loki." *Deutsche Vierteljahrsschrift für Literaturwissenschaft und Geistesgeschichte*, 18 (1940), 173-200.

Comparison of Loki and the Mephistopheles of the Faust legend, getting at a consideration of the nature of evil, irony, and fate among the Germanic peoples.

1753. Mohr, Wolfgang. "Thor im Fluss: Zur Form der altnordischen mythologischen Überlieferung." *Beiträge zur Geschichte der deutschen Sprache und Literatur*, 64 (1940), 209-229.

Deals primarily with the question of the form in which myth was transmitted, using the specific example of Thor's perils in the river Vímur while on his way to Geirrøðr (*Skáldskaparmál*, ch. 27).

1754. Mohr, Wolfgang, and Walter Haug. *Zweimal 'Muspilli.'* Untersuchungen zur deutschen Literaturgeschichte, 18. Tübingen: M. Niemeyer, 1977. 80 pp.

This volume contains two essays on the medieval German poem *Muspilli*, where a parallel to Ragnarǫk takes the form of an encounter between Elias and the Antichrist as the world ends. What is particularly relevant to Scandinavian mythology is Mohr's notion that the Old High German poem retains pagan notions.

1755. Molenaar, H. A. "Concentric Dualism as Transition between a Lineal and Cyclic Representation of Life and Death in Scandinavian Mythology." *Bijdragen tot de taal-, land- en volkenkunde*, 138 (1982), 29-53.

The theoretical framework of the article is provided by notions of kinship and social structure advanced by Lévi-Strauss. The myths analyzed most closely center on Baldr, but cosmological conceptions also receive scrutiny. Molenaar posits three spatial arrangements, of which the second is transitional: a diametric dualism between Hel and Asgard, a concentric dualism between Utgard and Asgard, and a triadic relationship among these three worlds. These correspond, according to the author, to theories of Lévi-Strauss concerning reciprocity.

1756. Moltke, Erik. "Sigurd Agrell: Runornas talmystik och dess antika förebild." *Acta Philologica Scandinavica*, 3 (1928-29), 90-96.

Critical review of Agrell's work of the same name (1927).

1757. Moltke, Erik. "Bidrag til tolkning af Gørlev-stenen." *Acta Philologica Scandinavica*, 4 (1929-30), 172-85.

With remarks on the magic powers of runes.

1758. Moltke, Erik. "Glavendrup-stenen og de nyfundne runer." *Acta Philologica Scandinavica*, 7 (1932-33), 83-96.

The final pages attempt to formulate a distinction between the terms *þulr* and *goði*.

1759. Moltke, Erik. "Professor Hans Brix's talmagi: En lille praktisk orientering." *Danske studier*, 30 (1933), 43-45.

Criticism of H. Brix, *Systematiske beregninger i danske runinskrifter* (1932).

1760. Moltke, Erik. "Runetrolddom." *Nordisk tidskrift för vetenskap, konst och industri*, 10 (1934), 427-39.

Runes and magic.

1761. Moltke, Erik. "Hvad var Lægæst, guldhornets mester, magiker, præst eller guldsmed?" *Fornvännen*, 42 (1947), 336-42.

Contra Langenfelt, "Gallehus-problemet" (1946); Moltke finds no reference to magic or cult in the inscription on the Gallehus horn.

1762. Moltke, Erik. "En grønlandsk runeindskrift fra Erik den rødes tid: Narssaq-pinden." *Grønland*, 1961, pp. 401-10.

Interpretation of a Viking Age Greenlandic rune stick. The text appears to be mythological: "On the sea, on the sea, the sea is where the *æsir* lurk. Bifrau is the name of the maid who sits on the blue [heaven?]."

1763. Moltke, Erik, and Lis Jacobsen. "Troldtal." *Tilskueren*, 45 (1928), 155-73.

Critical review of H. Brix, *Runernes magt* (1927).

1764. Montelius, Oscar. *Die Kultur Schwedens in vorchristlicher Zeit*. Berlin: G. Reimer, 1885. 198 pp. Translation, by Carl Appel, of the Swedish 2nd ed.

Archaeological treatise on prehistoric Sweden, with discussion of paganism.

1765. Montelius, Oscar. "Solgudens yxa och Tors hammare." *Svenska fornminnesföreningens tidskrift*, 10 (1900), 277-96. English version published as "The Sun-God's Axe and Thor's Hammer," *Folk-Lore*, 21 (1910), 60-78.

Through comparison, primarily with Classical and Near Eastern sources, Montelius equates the ax of sun gods with Thor's hammer. He concludes that Thor originally was both thunder god and sun god, a figure whose roots extended to prehistory and who lived on in the popular cult of St. Olaf and in modern folklore. Illustrated.

1766. Montelius, Oscar. *Kulturgeschichte Schwedens von den ältesten Zeiten bis zum elften Jahrhundert nach Christus*. Leipzig: E. A. Seemann, 1906. 336 pp.

Cultural history of ancient Sweden, based on archaeology; many comments on paganism.

1767. Morgenstierne, Georg. "Åss og (J)as (osseter)." *Maal og minne*, 1975, pp. 30-31.

Brief note on *Ynglinga saga*'s *Åsaland*, near the Don. According to Morgenstierne, Snorri identified the mythological *áss* "god" (plural *æsir*) with the ethnic name As (Ás), an Iranian people once living on the steppes near the Don and later known in the Caucasus as the Ossetes.

1768. Mortensen, Karl. *Nordisk mytologi*. Copenhagen: Nordisk forlag, 1898. [7], 164 pp. A 2nd ed. was issued under the title *Nordisk mytologi i kortfattet populær fremstilling* (Copenhagen and Oslo: Gyldendal, 1906, 164 pp.).

Popular handbook, including treatment of higher and lower mythology, cult and ritual, and heroic legend.

1769. Mortensen, Karl. *A Handbook of Norse Mythology*. New York: T. Y. Crowell, 1913. viii, 208 pp. Translated by A. Clinton Crowell.

Translation of Mortensen, *Nordisk mythologi* (1st ed. 1898), a popular handbook.

1770. Mortensen, Rasmus. "Balders offerplads." *Vejle amts aarbøger*, 1919, pp. 198-206.

Toponymic evidence for the worship of Baldr at Møgelbjerg, Denmark.

1771. Mortensson-Egnund, Ivar. *Eddakvæde: Norrøne fornsongar paa nynorsk*. Gammelnorsk bokverk, 21. Oslo: Johansen & Nielsen, 1944. 271 pp.

Nynorsk translation of the eddic poems, with notes and commentary.

1772. Moschkau, Rudolf. "Nachtrag zum germanischen Haaropfer." *Mannus*, 17 (1925), 121.

Brief comment on G. Wilke, "Ein altgermanisches Haaropfer" (1924).

1773. Mosher, Arthur D. "The Story of Baldr's Death: The Inadequacy of Myth in the Light of Christian Faith." *Scandinavian Studies*, 55 (1983), 305-15.

"In this study, we explore how the story of Baldr's death, as encountered by Snorri in the written records and in oral transmission, could have presented itself to him as a similar, yet inadequate, even twisted representation of the story central to Christian faith, namely the crucifixion of Christ" (p. 307).

1774. Motz, Lotte. "New Thoughts on Dwarf-Names in Old Icelandic." *Frühmittelalterliche Studien*, 7 (1973), 100-17. With "Nachwort" by Dietrich Hofmann.

Motz attempts to relate dwarf names to "the actors of the pageantry which moves through the wintry landscape of Europe in the observance of the ancient traditions of the Christmas and Carneval season" (p. 100). Especially important is the figure of the smith and association with Odin. Pp. 113-15 contain a list of dwarf names, indicating variant forms, context, and meaning. Hofmann's "Nachwort" comments on the need for such a list to replace that found in Chester N. Gould, "Dwarf-Names in Old Icelandic" (1929).

1775. Motz, Lotte. "Withdrawal and Return: A Ritual Pattern in the Grettis saga." *Arkiv för nordisk filologi*, 88 (1973), 91-110.

Grettis saga and other Norse texts as reflections of ancient initiation ritual. For criticism see I. Whitaker, "Some Anthropological Perspectives on *Gretla*" (1977).

1776. Motz, Lotte. "The King and the Goddess: An Interpretation of the *Svipdagsmál*." *Arkiv för nordisk filologi*, 90 (1975), 133-50.

Motz offers a novel interpretation of *Svipdagsmál*: the poem incorporates "the elements of an initiatory sequence leading to admission into the secret house of a goddess. This course of events, containing echoes of the rites of puberty initiation, parallels also that of the rites of some mystery religions in which the chosen reenact through their agony and their final union the drama of the resurrection of the god, the son or lover of the great goddess whose cult or priesthood they are about to enter" (pp. 149-50); the initiand may be regarded as a king or priest-king in the service of the goddess. Thus the poet "modernized a myth" (p. 150). The author is concerned more with pointing out parallels–some from rather distant cultures–than with tracing the course of the myth allegedly modernized.

1777. Motz, Lotte. "Snorri's Story of the Cheated Mason and its Folklore Parallels." *Maal og minne*, 1977, pp. 115-22.

Some folklore analogs to the story of the building of Asgard in *Snorra edda*.

1778. Motz, Lotte. "The Hero and his Tale: Response to Whitaker." *Arkiv för nordisk filologi*, 93 (1978), 145-48.

Response to I. Whitaker, "Some Anthropological Perspectives on *Gretla*" (1977), which was a dismissal of Motz, "Withdrawal and Return" (1973).

1779. Motz, Lotte. "Driving Out the Elves: A Euphemism and a Theme of Folklore." *Frühmittelalterliche Studien*, 13 (1979), 439-41.

As the Icelandic expression *ganga álfrek* "relieve oneself" may be understood literally as "drive off elves," Motz adduces examples from German folklore where human waste causes supernatural beings to depart. "If the tales reflect, as folktales may, actual historical events, then the family of spirits might be representative of an older social order or of an older faith" (p. 441). Further explanation is wanting.

1780. Motz, Lotte. "Sister in the Cave; the Stature and the Function of the Female Figures in the Eddas." *Arkiv för nordisk filologi*, 95 (1980), 168-82.

Although the *ásynjur* "do not exercise the talents or qualities assigned to them by Snorri" and are "ineffectual" and "treated casually," there are "female forces of great potency." These supposedly represent an "older order," whom the gods overcame through marriage.

1781. Motz, Lotte. "Aurboða-Eyrgjafa: Two Old Icelandic Names." *Mankind Quarterly*, 22 (1981-82), 93-103.

The etymological discussion is soon broadened and general conceptions of the giants are taken up.

1782. Motz, Lotte. "The Chanter at the Door." *Mankind Quarterly*, 22 (1981-82), 237-56.

Treatment of dwarfs in Scandinavian myth.

1783. Motz, Lotte. "Gerðr: A New Interpretation of the Lay of Skírnir." *Maal og minne*, 1981, pp. 121-36.

According to Motz, *Skírnismál* does not portray a sacral marriage; the name *Gerðr* has to do etymologically with "enclosure" and Freyr's penetration of her enclosure is an act with parallels in the heroic literature. Ultimately the story may be "a possible reflection of the struggle between two dynasties of gods which ends with the triumph of the *Æsir*. The superhuman battle may reflect, in its turn, a historical reality: the conquest of a land which was invaded, as Gymir's dwelling was by Skírnir, by a grim and warlike nation and its gods" (p. 133). So ends the essay, with no further clarification.

1784. Motz, Lotte. "Freyja, Anat, Ishtar and Inanna: Some Cross-Cultural Comparisons." *Mankind Quarterly*, 23 (1982-83), 195-212.

"In this paper I attempted to obtain, through a close reading of the Old Icelandic texts, a more specific picture of the northern goddess" (pp. 195-96).

1785. Motz, Lotte. "The Northern Heritage of Germanic Religion." *Mankind Quarterly*, 23 (1982-83), 365-82.

Argues an arctic context.

1786. Motz, Lotte. "Giants in Folklore and Mythology: A New Approach." *Folklore*, 93 (1982), 70-84.

Contra von Sydow, "Jättarna i mytologi och folktro" (1919), Motz argues four points: giants of the eddas and modern folklore are related (Motz uses German folklore, but Scandinavian lore would have yielded the same results); size is not their most basic quality; they originated not in speculation but in myth; the giants were the creators of the world. They represented non-sexual creativity, later displaced by the sexual creativity of the gods. Thus belief and tales about giants would, according to Motz, represent survivals of an ancient creation myth.

1787. Motz, Lotte. "Gods and Demons of the Wilderness: A Study in Norse Tradition." *Arkiv för nordisk filologi*, 99 (1984), 175-87.

"In this paper I pointed to those qualities of the Norse giants which would characterize them as spirits and godheads of the wilderness" (p. 186). "We may receive from the continuous bitter struggle of the gods against the trolls, from the trolls' station in the far North of Europe and their affinity with frost and cold, phenomena of the northern landscape, added confirmation of the origin of giants in the culture and belief of the northern lands" (p. 187).

1788. Much, Rudolf. "Germanische Matronennamen: Ein Excurs zu Saitchamims." *Zeitschrift für deutsches Altertum*, 35 (1891), 315-24.

Grammatical remarks on the form *Saitchamims*.

1789. Much, Rudolf. "Jupiter Tanarus." *Zeitschrift für deutsches Altertum*, 35 (1891), 372-74.

Thor in Anglo-Roman guise.

1790. Much, Rudolf. "Mercurius Hanno." *Zeitschrift für deutsches Altertum*, 35 (1891), 207-08. Addendum in *Anzeiger für deutsches Altertum*, 16 (1891), 184.

Grammatical interpretation of the form on a German inscription.

1791. Much, Rudolf. "Nehalennia." *Zeitschrift für deutsches Altertum*, 35 (1891), 324-28.

Etymology and discussion of the form *Nehalennia*, in part illuminated against the myths and cult of the *vanir*.

1792. Much, Rudolf. "Requalivahanus." *Zeitschrift für deutsches Altertum*, 35 (1891), 374-76.

The form *Requalivahanus* means "the dark one" and refers to a god of the underworld.

1793. Much, Rudolf. "Dea Harimella." *Zeitschrift für deutsches Altertum*, 36 (1892), 44-47.

Interprets the name of the Germanic goddess Harimella, apparently attested on the Thingsus stone, Scotland, as a goddess of battle.

1794. Much, Rudolf. "Eddica." *Zeitschrift für deutsches Altertum*, 37 (1893), 417-19.

Textual notes to *Vǫluspá*, str. 46-47, and *Rígsþula*, str. 10.

1795. Much, Rudolf. "Ulls Schiff." *Beiträge zur Geschichte der deutschen Sprache und Literatur*, 20 (1895), 35-36.

Linguistic explanation of the shield-kenning "Ullr's ship."

1796. Much, Rudolf. "Gapt." *Zeitschrift für deutsches Altertum*, 41 (1897), 95-96.

A possible Greek source for the name Gapt, which is often associated with Gautr/Odin.

1797. Much, Rudolf. "Der germanische Himmelsgott." In *Abhandlungen zur germanischen Philologie: Festgabe für R. Heinzel*. 189-278. Halle a. d. S.: M. Niemeyer, 1898.

Historical study of the Germanic sky god and derivatives, including comparison with Celtic and Slavic myth. Much finds that the wind god Odin came to replace the original sky god atop the pantheon and assumed many of that god's features and characteristics.

1798. Much, Rudolf. "Der Sagenstoff der Grimnismal." *Zeitschrift für deutsches Altertum*, 46 (1902), 309-29.

Finds that the original legendary core of *Grímnismál* involved the death of a hero by his own sword as a punishment for blasphemy. Much speculates further on a historical background in accounts of the death of the Persian king Kambyses, which might have reached and been developed by the Germanic peoples.

1799. Much, Rudolf. "Undensakre-Untersberg." *Zeitschrift für deutsches Altertum*, 47 (1903-04), 67-72.

Placename evidence of conceptions of the otherworld.

1800. Much, Rudolf. "Zur Rígsþula." In *Untersuchungen und Quellen zur germanischen und romanischen Philologie: Johan von Kelle dargebracht von seinen Kollegen und Schülern,* vol. 1. 225-39. Prager deutsche Studien, 8. Prague: C. Bellmann, 1908.

Reconstruction of str. 7 of *Rígsþula.*

1801. Much, Rudolf. "Vagdavercustis." *Zeitschrift für deutsches Altertum*, 55 (1914-17), 284-96.

Interprets the name as that of a warlike goddess.

1802. Much, Rudolf. "Harimalla-Harimella." *Zeitschrift für deutsches Altertum*, 63 (1926), 19-22.

Against E. Schröder, Much separates the placename Hermalle and the goddess Harimella.

1803. Much, Rudolf. "Waren die Germanen des Caesar und Tacitus Kelten?" *Zeitschrift für deutsches Altertum*, 65 (1928), 1-50.

In disputing the notion put forth by Siegmund Feist that the ancient Germanic tribes were actually Celtic, Much offers occasional discussion of religion and cult.

1804. Much, Rudolf. "Der nordische Widdergott." In *Deutsche Islandforschung 1930,* vol. 1: *Kultur*, ed. Walther Heinrich Vogt, 63-67. Veröffentlichungen der Schleswig-Holsteinischen Universitätsgesellschaft, 28:1. Breslau: F. Hirt, 1930.

On Heimdallr. He is principally a ram: the name *Hallinskíði* refers to butting, and *Gullintanni* to gold flashes that Much argues appear on the teeth of ruminants. Much explains Heimdallr's nine mothers as reflections of a practice of breeding a male animal successively with his female offspring, a practice he observes also in *Rígsþula.*

1805. Much, Rudolf. "Aurvandils tá." *Altschlesien*, 5 (1934), 387-88.

Speculates that *tá* may refer not to Aurvandil's toe but to the planet Venus.

1806. Much, Rudolf. "Mondmythologie und Wissenschaft." *Archiv für Religionswissenschaft*, 37 (1941-42), 231-61.

An attack on scholarly attempts to elevate the moon to an important position in various mythologies, particularly Germanic.

1807. Mudrak, Edmund. "Zur germanischen Kosmologie." In *Festgabe für Wolfgang Jungandreas zum 70. Geburtstag am 9. Dezember 1964: Beiträge zur deutschen Sprachgeschichte, Landes-, Volks- und Altertumsgeschichte*, ed. Richard Laufner, 50-65. Schriftenreihe zur Trierischen Landesgeschichte und Volkskunde, 13. Trier: Arbeitsgemeinschaft für Landesgeschichte und Volkskunde des Trierer Raumes, Sektion der Gesellschaft für nützliche Forschungen, 1964.

Using the *Wessobrunner Gebet* and *Vǫluspá* (str. 3), Mudrak seeks to demonstrate the existence in ancient Germanic cosmology of a tripartition into heaven, earth, and sea. (Note the brief criticism by Walter Röll (1966) in *Germanistik* 7:155.)

1808. Müllenhoff, Karl. "Der Mythus von Beóvulf." *Zeitschrift für deutsches Altertum*, 7 (1849), 419-41.

Beowulf as seasonal myth, associated with the *vanir* and particularly with Freyr.

1809. Müllenhoff, Karl. "Donar und Wuotan." *Zeitschrift für deutsches Altertum*, 7 (1849), 529-30.

Donar/Thor and Wuotan/Odin in German cult.

1810. Müllenhoff, Karl. "Lust und Unlust." *Zeitschrift für deutsches Altertum*, 9 (1853), 127-28.

On the interpretation of *Vǫluspá*, str. 1.

1811. Müllenhoff, Karl. "Zur deutschen Mythologie." *Zeitschrift für deutsches Altertum*, 12 (1860-65), 401-09.

Brief mythological notes on German material.

1812. Müllenhoff, Karl. "Mythologisches." *Zeitschrift für deutsches Altertum*, 13 (1867), 577-78.

Brief notes, mostly on Donar/Thor.

1813. Müllenhoff, Karl. "Mennor und Wippeon." *Zeitschrift für deutsches Altertum*, 16 (1873), 143-46.

Medieval German parallel to the origin myth of Tuisto-Mannus in Tacitus, *Germania*.

1814. Müllenhoff, Karl. "Um Ragnaröckr." *Zeitschrift für deutsches Altertum*, 16 (1873), 146-48.

On the replacement of *ragna rǫk* "fates of the gods" with *ragna røkkr* "twilight of the gods."

1815. Müllenhoff, Karl. "UUâra und uuara." *Zeitschrift für deutsches Altertum*, 16 (1873), 148-56.

Argues that the goddesses Vǫr and Vár in some redactions of *Snorra edda* were once one and the same and, in particular, that Codex Upsaliensis is the best manuscript of *Snorra edda.*

1816. Müllenhoff, Karl. "Ein gotischer Göttername?" *Zeitschrift für deutsches Altertum*, 23 (1879), 43-46.

Expresses grave doubts as to the existence of a Gothic deity named Hore.

1817. Müllenhoff, Karl. "Irmin und seine Brüder." *Zeitschrift für deutsches Altertum*, 23 (1879), 1-23.

On the formation of the tribal names Erminones, Istaevones, Ingvaeones.

1818. Müllenhoff, Karl. "Tanfana." *Zeitschrift für deutsches Altertum*, 23 (1879), 23-25.

Notes on the German goddess Tanfana, relating to *Hávamál*, str. 144-45.

1819. Müllenhoff, Karl. *Deutsche Altertumskunde,* Vol 5:1. Berlin: Weidmann, 1883. vii, 356 pp.

An important monument of nineteenth-century scholarship, this last section of Müllenhoff's *Deutsche Altertumskunde* is devoted primarily to the texts of Scandinavian mythology. Pp. 3-157 comprise a defense of *Vǫluspá* against A. Chr. Bang and S. Bugge, who sought to deny it its place in Germanic antiquity, and a text and translation of the poem. Pp. 157-356 consider the remainder of the written sources. Here Müllenhoff issued still well-known opinions on *Snorra edda* and Codex Regius of the Poetic Edda; the Uppsala codex is in his opinion closest to Snorri's original, and smaller pamphlets, according to Müllenhoff, preceded the composition of Codex Regius of the Poetic Edda.

1820. Müllenhoff, Karl. "Frija und der Halsbandmythus." *Zeitschrift für deutsches Altertum*, 30 (1886), 217-60.

Posthumous essay on Fri ja/Frigg and the myth of the necklace later associated with Freyja. Ranging widely, Müllenhoff treats the entire mythic complex associated with the "goddess of heaven," a complex he believed to have been formed before the worship of Odin grew to importance. Much of the article focuses on Heimdallr, Loki, and the Hjaðningavíg.

1821. Müllenhoff, Karl. *Deutsche Altertumskunde,* vol. 5, 2nd ed. Ed. Max Rödiger. Berlin: Weidmann, 1908. xi, 436 pp.

Reprint of the first edition, with three mythological articles appended.

1822. Müller, Friedrich Wilhelm. *Untersuchungen zur Uppsala Edda.* Dresden: M. Dittert, 1941. 150 pp. Also issued as inaug. diss., Leipzig.

A thorough study comparing the text of Codex Upsaliensis of Snorri's *Edda* with the other major maunscripts. Müller concludes that Codex Upsaliensis is probably closer to Snorri's original text than are the other major manuscripts.

1823. Müller, Günter. "Zum Namen *Wolfhetan* und seine Verwandten." *Frühmittelalterliche Studien,* 1 (1967), 200-12.

A discussion of the name *Wolfhetan* (Norse *Úlfheðinn*), leading to consideration of use of animal masks for battle and perhaps also for cult.

1824. Müller, Günter. "Altnordisch Vífill—Ein Weihename." In *Festschrift für Otto Höfler zum 65. Geburtstag,* eds. Helmut Birkhan and Otto Gschwantler, 363-72. Vienna: Notring, 1968.

The etymology of the West Norse personal name *Vífill*: "young consecrated [male]" (< **wi gilaz*); the name form Þórifill denotes a youth consecrated to Thor. In general, argues Müller, the name was applied to men with specialized functions, such as rune masters or cult priests.

1825. Müller, Günter. "Germanische Tiersymbolik und Namengebung." *Frühmittelalterliche Studien,* 2 (1968), 202-17.

In the course of a review of pertinent scholarship, the author calls for consideration of all aspects of animal symbolism in discussion of theophoric personal names among the Germanic peoples. The same animals appear in various contexts: in plastic art, as components of men's names, and as sacral objects in the mythology. Although he readily admits a connection to religion, Müller cautions against immediate acceptance of such theories as, for example, that theophoric personal names are tabu replacements of hypothetical theophoric personal names. All chronological, distributional, linguistic, and mythological factors must be considered.

Pp. 214-15 contain remarks on Germanic animal cult and animal worship.

1826. Müller, Günter. "Harald Gormssons Königsschicksal in heidnischer und christlicher Deutung." *Frühmittelalterliche Studien,* 7 (1973), 118-42.

A detailed analysis of the many sources dealing with the career of the tenth-century Danish king Haraldr Gormsson, often called "blue-tooth" or "battle-tooth" and said to have been a favorite of Odin. According to Müller's hypothesis, the actual occurrences of the tenth century were followed by two stages. The first, during the conversion period, was characterized by oral accounts of intervention of pagan gods in Haraldr's spectacular rise and fall. In the second, historicized Odin fables were compiled with other information on Haraldr's career. Thus such written sources as *Jómsvíkinga saga*, Sven Aggesen, Saxo Grammaticus, and the Danish annals permit reconstruction of a pagan sense of history.

1827. Müller, Günter. "Zur Heilkraft der Walküre: Sondersprachliches der Magie in kontinentalen und skandinavischen Zeugnissen." *Frühmittelalterliche Studien*, 10 (1976), 350-61.

Primarily on *Sigrdrífumál* 11, in which the valkyrie Sigrdrífa teaches Sigurd about *limrúnar*. The Hilde legend, myths of the *einherjar*, and *rúnatal* of *Hávamál* provide context, and the author regards *Sigrdrífumál* as a more valuable source on the history of religion than previous observers have allowed. Müller proposes the reading *límrúnar*, whose first component would be associated with *gali mida* of the second Merseburg charm. This enables him to interpret *Sinhtgunt* on the charm as a valkyrie name.

1828. Müller, Peter Erasmus. "Om autenthien af Snorres Edda, og beviset derfra kan hentes for asalærens æghed." *Det skandinaviske litteraturs selskabs skrifter*, 8 (1812), 1-97.

Early discussion of the source value of *Snorra edda*.

1829. Müller, Sophus. "Votivfund fra sten- og bronzealderen." *Årbøger for nordisk oldkyndighed og historie*, 1886, pp. 216-51.

Catalog of finds interpreted as sacral offerings.

1830. Müller, Sophus. *Nordische Altertumskunde: Nach Funden und Denkmälern aus Dänemark und Schleswig gemeinfasslich dargestellt.* Strassburg: K. J. Trübner, 1897-98. Translated by Otto Luitpold Jiriczek. Vol. 1: *Steinzeit-Bronzezeit* (1897), xi, 472 pp; vol. 2: *Eisenzeit* (1898), 324 pp.

Popular presentation of Danish archaeology, with chapters in each of the three major sections (Stone Age, Bronze Age, Iron Age) on art and religion.

1831. Müller, Sophus. *Vor oldtid: Danmarks forhistoriske archæologi almenfattelig fremstillet.* Copenhagen: Det nordiske forlag, 1897.

Danish original of the author's *Nordische Altertumskunde* (1897-98).

1832. Müller, Wilhelm. "Gefjon." *Zeitschrift für deutsches Altertum*, 1 (1841), 95-96.

Gefjon as goddess of the sea.

1833. Müller, Wilhelm. *Versuch einer mythologischen Erklärung der Nibelungensage.* Berlin: G. Reimer, 1841. vi, 148 pp.

Myth in heroic legend.

1834. Müller, Wilhelm. "Siegfried und Freyr." *Zeitschrift für deutsches Altertum*, 3 (1843), 43-53.

Argues the derivation of Siegfried legend from Freyr myth.

1835. Müller, Wilhelm. *Geschichte und System der altdeutschen Religion*. Göttingen: Vandenhoeck & Ruprecht, 1844. xvi, 424 pp.

One of the first serious attempts at a history of Germanic religion.

1836. Müller, Wilhelm. *Mythologie der deutschen Heldensage*. Heilbronn: Henninger, 1886. vii, 260 pp.

Myth in heroic legend.

1837. Müller, Wilhelm. *Zur Mythologie der griechischen und deutschen Heldensage*. Heilbronn: Henninger, 1889. iv, 177 pp.

The hypothetical mythological background of Greek and Germanic heroic legend.

1838. Mulot, Arno. *Frühdeutsches Christentum: Die Christianisierung Deutschlands im Speigel der ältesten deutschen Dichtung*. Stuttgart: J. B. Metzler, 1935. 149 pp.

Early Christianity in German literature; includes consideration of possible pre-Christian survivals.

1839. Munch, Peter Andreas. *Norse Mythology: Legends of Gods and Heroes*. Scandinavian Classics, 27. New York: The American-Scandinavian Foundation, 1963. xix, 392 pp. Revised ed. by Magnus Olsen. (Originally publ. 1927.) Translated by Sigurd Bernhard Hustvedt.

Munch's retelling of Scandinavian mythology appeared first in 1840. This translation follows the 1927 revision by Magnus Olsen but omits the appendix on Norwegian theophoric placenames and relegates many of Olsen's textual notes to a section at the end of the volume. One thus can appreciate–if that is the word–without encumbrance Munch's 1840 text. It summarizes such literary documents as the two eddas and Saxo's *Gesta Danorum* with virtually no source criticism and hence is of little value to serious study of Norse myth or religion.

1840. Munch, Peter Andreas. *Norrøne gude- og heltesagn*. N. p.: Universitetsforlag, 1967. 351 pp. Revised ed. by Anne Holtsmark.

Anne Holtsmark's is the fourth revision of Munch's famous book on Norse myth and legends (see Munch (1963) for an English translation of an earlier edition). Holtsmark added extensive source-critical and bibliographic notes, which amount to a brief introduction to Norse myth and legend. In the area of myth she has also taken care to distinguish possible cult practices from Munch's broad summaries of literary sources.

1841. Mundal, Else. *Fylgjemotiva i norrøn litteratur.* Skrifter for nordisk språk og litteratur ved universitetene i Bergen, Oslo, Trondheim og Tromsø, 5. Oslo, Bergen, Tromsø: Universitetsforlag, 1974. 150 pp.

Mundal surveys the literary traditions relating to *fylgjur*, both the animal fetches and the female guardian spirits, using both literary and folkloristic methodology. The last chapter treats the development of belief in *fylgjur* from Norse to modern times. The volume has several useful charts registering the attestations of various motifs.

1842. Murray, Alexander Stuart. *Manual of Mythology: Greek and Roman, Norse and Old German, Hindoo and Egyptian Mythology,* rev. ed. Philadelphia: D. McKay, 1895. xi, 368 pp. 1st ed. 1885.

Handbook treating many mythologies, including "Norse and Old German."

A facsimile reprint of the 1885 edition was issued in 1970 by Gale Research Co., Detroit.

1843. Murray, Margaret A. *The Divine King in England: A Study in Anthropology.* London: Faber & Faber, 1954. 279 pp.

Focuses on late and postmedieval times; not directly relevant to Norse mythology.

1844. Murray, Margaret A. "The Divine King in England." In *Atti dell'viii congresso internazionale di storia delle religioni (Roma 17-23 Aprile 1955).* 378-80. Florence: G. C. Sansoni—Editore, 1956.

Summary of an address at the eighth international conference on the history of religions: sacral kingship in England, elucidated in part with Swedish evidence.

1845. Musset, Lucien. "La pénétration chrétienne dans l'Europe du nord et son influence sur la civilisation scandinave." In *La conversione al cristianesimo nell'Europa dell'alto medioevo: 14-19 aprile 1966.* 263-325. Settimane di studio del centro italiano di studi sull'alto medioevo. Spoleto: Presso la sede del centro, 1967.

A contribution to an international symposium on the conversion of European peoples to Christianity; Musset treats the Scandinavians' conversion and its effects, and the article is therefore directly relevant to the study of Scandinavian mythology.

1846. Must, Gustav. "English *holy*, German *heilig*." *Journal of English and Germanic Philology*, 59 (1960), 184-89.

Includes speculation on the unsuitability of Germanic **hailagaz/hailaz* "complete, whole, healthy" for pagan gods as opposed to the Christian God.

N

1847. Naert, Pierre. "Grímnismál 33." *Arkiv för nordisk filologi*, 81 (1966), 117-19.

Textual note.

1848. Nagy, Gregory. "Perku´nas and Perunj." In *Antiquitates Indogermanicae: Studien zur indogermanischen Altertumskunde und zur Sprach- und Kulturgeschichte der indogermanischen Völker: Gedenkschrift für Hermann Güntert zur 25. Wiederkehr seines Todestages am 23. April 1973*, eds. Manfred Mayrhofer, Wolfgang Meid, Bernfried Schlerath, and Rüdiger Schmitt, 113-31. Innsbrucker Beiträge zur Sprachwissenschaft, 12. Innsbruck: Institut für Sprachwissenschaft der Universität Innsbruck, 1974.

Linguistic evidence that the Indo-European thunder god was involved with the creation of man from oak or stone; occasional reference to Norse myth.

1849. Naumann, Hans. "Sôse gelîmida sîn." *Zeitschrift für deutsche Philologie*, 51 (1926), 477.

Textual note on a line from the second Merseburg charm: *gelîmida* means "glued, attached."

1850. Naumann, Hans. "Die Glaubwürdigkeit des Tacitus." *Bonner Jahrbücher*, 139 (1934), 21-33.

Text of a lecture insisting on the veracity of Tacitus, *Germania*. Cf. E. Bickel, "Die Glaubwürdigkeit des Tacitus und seine Nachrichten über den Nerthuskult und den Germanennamen" (1934), a lecture which preceded this one by a few months.

1851. Naumann, Hans. *Germanische Schicksalsglaube*. Jena: E. Diederichs, 1934. 95 pp.

Standard treatment of fate in Germanic culture. The first few chapters treat the mythology directly.

1852. Naumann, Hans. *Rede zum Geburtstag des Führers: (Germanische Götterlieder)*. Bonner Akademi, Reden, 27. Bonn: Scheur, 1937. 10 pp.

Þrymskviða and *Skírnismál* as living literature in Nazi Germany.

1853. Naumann, Hans. "Der König und die Seherin." *Zeitschrift für deutsche Philologie*, 63 (1938), 347-58.

The social role and position of the seeress in ancient germanic culture, clarified by materials ranging from Roman times to medieval Icelandic.

1854. Naumann, Hans. "Zur altgermanischen Götterdichtung." In *Beiträge zur Runenkunde und nordischen Sprachwissenschaft: Gustav Neckel zum 60. Geburtstag.* 147-54. Leipzig: O. Harrassowitz, 1938.

On *Vǫlundarkviða*, *Hymiskviða*, and *Lokasenna*.

1855. Naumann, Hans. "Germanen in Glaubenswechsel." *Deutsche Vierteljahrsschrift für Literaturwissenschaft und Geistesgeschichte*, 17 (1939), 277-300.

The conversion to Christianity of the Germanic peoples.

1856. Naumann, Hans. *Altdeutsches Volkskönigstum: Reden und Aufsätze zum germanischen Überlieferungszusammenhang*. Stuttgart: J. B. Metzler, 1940. 244 pp.

Twelve essays relevant to the problem of Germanic continuity and sacral kingship.

1857. Naumann, Hans. "Neue Beiträge zum altgermanischen Dioskurenglauben." *Bonner Jahrbücher*, 150 (1950), 91-101.

A study of the *dioscurii* or divine twins in Germanic mythology. Naumann concludes that there were several pairs: Vili and Vé near the beginning of mythic time, and in the new age after Ragnarǫk, Baldr and Hǫðr, Víðarr and Váli, Móði and Magni, and perhaps the sons of Vili and Vé.

1858. Naumann, Hans-Peter. "Tell und die nordische Überlieferung: Zur Frage nach dem Archetypus vom Meisterschützen." *Schweizerisches Archiv für Volkskunde*, 71 (1975), 108-28.

In tracing the master archer into Nordic tradition, Naumann devotes several paragraphs to the Norse mythic archer Ullr (pp. 123-25). This god will not easily fit into Dumézil's tripartite scheme. However, such sources as *Gesta Danorum*, book 3, suggest the existence of older myths involving conflict between tyrannical sovereignty and some other triumphant power, realized in symbols like bow and ax. This conflict may ultimately have been rooted in the ideology of the Germanic chieftain-retainer relationship.

1859. Nebel, Gerhard. *Die Not der Götter: Welt und Mythos der Germanen*. Hamburg: Hofmann & Campe, 1957. 216 pp.

Historically conscious (see the first chapter, on "Teutonism") treatment of Germanic mythology, relying heavily on Scandinavian sources. The treatment is essentially comparative and philosophical.

1860. Neckel, Gustav. "Hundum verpa." *Arkiv för nordisk filologi*, 24 (1908), 199-200.

Textual note to *Rígsþula*, str. 35.

1861. Neckel, Gustav. "Kleine Beiträge zur germanischen Altertumskunde." *Beiträge zur Geschichte der deutschen Sprache und Literatur*, 33 (1908), 459-82.

Pp. 459-66 treat the line *skáro á skíði* (*Vǫluspá*, str. 20).

1862. Neckel, Gustav. "Zur Einfürung in die Runenforschung, II: Die Runen kulturhistorisch betrachtet." *Germanisch-Romanisch Monatsschrift*, 1 (1909), 81-95.

Includes discussion of hypothetical magic and oracular use of runes.

1863. Neckel, Gustav. *Walhall, Studien über germanischen Jenseitsglauben.* Dortmund: F. W. Ruhfus, 1913. iv, 144 pp.

A survey and analysis of conceptions of Valhalla, still useful and important. Neckel distinguishes an older layer, the fallen on the battlefield, from a younger mythological layer, the *æsir* in Odin's palace.

1864. Neckel, Gustav. "Hamalt fylkia und svínfylkja." *Arkiv för nordisk filologi*, 34 (1918), 284-349.

On the two names for military formations and their connections with the gods, particularly Odin.

1865. Neckel, Gustav. *Studien zu den germanischen Dichtungen vom Weltuntergang.* Sitzungsberichte der Heidelberger Akademie der Wissenschaften, phil.-hist. Kl, 1918, 7. Heidelberg: C. Winter, 1918. 52 pp.

Study of the traditions of Ragnarǫk. For Neckel, the oldest layer consisted of a heavenly battle of gods and fire demons, a conception which he believes can only have originated in the Caucasus and been transported via the Goths to Scandinavia.

1866. Neckel, Gustav. *Die Überlieferungen vom Gotte Balder.* Dortmund: F. W. Ruhfus, 1920. vii, 267 pp.

Although initial reviewers' enthusiasm for Neckel's wide reading and erudition was tempered with skepticism, the book proved epochal and remains fundamental to modern study of the Baldr myth—and indeed all Norse mythology—as an example of the hypothesis of Near Eastern origins. In this Neckel followed his teacher Axel Olrik, who sought to demonstrate the same hypothesis for the conceptions of Ragnarǫk (German translation 1920).

The first three chapters subject the sources to close analysis. Neckel regards Snorri as the most important source (and Codex Regius of *Snorra edda* as Snorri's text) but analyzes other sources, including Saxo. Of some historical interest is his discussion of the pictorial representations said to underlie

Húsdrápa, which he treats as an independent and valid source of the myth (and traces to Asia Minor). The pivotal fourth chapter scrutinizes the cult of Baldr and argues association with the cults of Freyr, Fróði, and Nerthus. The fifth chapter assigns the origin of this cult to fertility rituals of Tammuz and Ishtar on the one hand and Adonis, Attis, and Orpheus on the other: the dying god who annually revivifies fertility. The last chapter argues that this cult and accompanying myths reached the Goths via the Thracians. Ca. 575 some poet, perhaps a Dane, composed two Baldr poems and recited them before a southern Scandinavian court, and from these the extant traditions descend.

There are no loose ends here, but as the last supposition shows, speculation tied the ends of the theory together. Although de Vries seemed to have removed the underpinning of Neckel's major argument with his 1956 study of Baldr, scholars still consult Neckel, and Kurt Schier now argues a typological parallel with the Near Eastern dying gods ("Balder," 1981).

1867. Neckel, Gustav. "Snorri Sturlusons Edda: Vortrag bei der Hauptversammlung der Islandfreunde am 3. April 1925 in der Universität Berlin." *Mitteilungen der Islandfreunde*, 12 (1924-25), 53-57.

An appreciation of Snorri, stressing the value of the *Edda* and of his other writings.

1868. Neckel, Gustav. "Regnator omnium deus." *Neue Jahrbücher für Wissenschaft und Jugendbildung*, 2 (1926), 139-50.

On *Germania*, ch. 39, and the cult therein described. Neckel finds that the *regnator omnium deus* is Odin and offers a number of observations on the worship of Odin. The god was known in North Germanic as well as in West Germanic, and a spread from south to north seems unlikely; indeed, spread in the opposite direction is possible. Since Neckel's methodology is basically historicist, it is interesting to note that this finding contradicts the classical historicist postulation of spread from the south.

1869. Neckel, Gustav. "Die altgermanische Religion." *Zeitschrift für Deutschkunde*, 1927, pp. 465-94.

Seeks to interpret the verb *sóa* "to sacrifice" as relating to expiation through cult drink.

1870. Neckel, Gustav. "Zu den Eddaliedern." *Arkiv för nordisk filologi*, 43 (1927), 358-73.

Includes comments on *Hávamál*, str. 107.

1871. Neckel, Gustav. "Runische Schmuckformen." *Buch und Schrift*, 2 (1928), 31-38.

Against the interpretation of runes as magic.

1872. Neckel, Gustav. "Der Tylorsche Seelenbegriff und die germanischen Quellen." In *Actes du Ve congrès international d'histoire des religions à Lund, 27-29 août 1929*. 218-24. Lund: C. W. K. Gleerup, 1930.

Lecture and discussion from an international congress on the history of religion: Tylor's animism and Germanic sources.

1873. Neckel, Gustav. "Island und die Edda." *Germanisch-Romanisch Monatsschrift*, 5 (1931), 512-27.

Pp. 518-21 discuss the dating and location of the mythological eddic poems.

1874. Neckel, Gustav. "Die Bekehrung der Germanen im Lichte der Quellen." *Reden und Aufsätze*, 18 (1934), 3-34.

"The conversion in light of the sources," in light of 1930s German nationalism.

1875. Neckel, Gustav. "Walhall und Hel." *Die Sonne: Monatschrift für Rasse, Glauben und Volkstum*, 12 (1935), 132-35.

Brief note stressing the logical separation of Valhalla and Hel (one for warriors, the other for the rest of the population) and suggesting that it may be old.

1876. Neckel, Gustav. "Die Runen." *Acta Philologica Scandinavica*, 12 (1937-38), 102-15.

With remarks on the magic-symbolic value of certain runes and rune names.

1877. Negelein, Julius von. *Germanische mythologie,* 3rd ed. Leipzig: B. G. Teubner, 1919. 128 pp. 1st ed. 1906.

Handbook of Germanic mythology.

1878. Nerman, Birger. *Studier över Sveriges hedna literatur*. Uppsala: K. W. Appelberg, 1913. xiii, 213 pp. Diss. Uppsala.

Topics treated include the oldest form of the Baldr story; Swedish tales of shield maidens; and the tale of the *dioscurii.*

1879. Nerman, Birger. "Baldersagans älsta [sic] form." *Edda*, 3 (1915), 1-10.

The digression on Herebeald and Hæðcyn in *Beowulf* as the hypothetical "oldest form" of the Baldr story. According to Nerman, this oldest form actualized the euhemerization of an actual historical event, the accidental murder of brother by brother. Nerman dates the story, on text-critical and archaeological grounds, to the fifth century.

1880. Nerman, Birger. "Ynglingasagan i arkeologisk belysning." *Fornvännen*, 12 (1917), 226-61.

The thrust of Nerman's argument is that archaeological evidence emphatically supports the historicity of *Ynglinga saga*. This support extends even to the opening chapters on Odin's immigration to Scandinavia, which Nerman associates with the evidence for an invasion of Scandinavia during the third and fourth centuries A.D. by peoples from north of the Black Sea.

1881. Nerman, Birger. *The Poetic Edda in the Light of Archaeology*. The Viking Society for Northern Research, Extra Series, 4. Coventry: Curtis & Beamish, 1931. vii, 94 pp.

Surveying the archaeological background of the eddic poems, Nerman concludes that, because of the emphasis on gold and absence of silver, they must have originated before the Viking Age. Today few would accept such a generalized dating, even if the evidence were compelling.

1882. Nerman, Birger. "En kristen mission på Gotland vid tiden omkring år 800 e. kr.?" *Fornvännen*, 36 (1941), 30-40. Summary in English, pp. 39-40.

Based on grave evidence at a single site, Nerman wonders whether a Christian mission, perhaps from the Carolingian empire, may not have visited Gotland ca. 800 A.D.

1883. Nerman, Birger. "Forngutniska 'kokkamrater.'" *Fornvännen*, 36 (1941), 238-42. Summary in English, p. 242.

An attempt to verify archaeologically some of the details of the sacrificial feasts described in *Guta saga*.

1884. Nerman, Birger. "En fornsvensk fågelkult." *Fornvännen*, 37 (1942), 385-89. Summary in English, pp. 388-89.

Tries to locate an archaeological parallel on Gotland to a statement by Emperor Constantine VII Porphyrogennetos (died 959) that the *rhōs* (*rus'*—whom Nerman understands as Swedes in Russia) practiced a bird cult.

1885. Nerman, Birger. *När Sverige kristnades*. Stockholm: Skoglund, 1945. 192 pp.

Popular treatment of the Christian mission and conversion to Christianity in Sweden.

1886. Nerman, Birger. "Rígsþula 16:8 *dvergar á ǫxlom*, arkeologiskt belyst." *Arkiv för nordisk filologi*, 69 (1954), 210-13. Illustrated.

On part of Amma's clothing in *Rígsþula*, str. 16. Nerman associates the expression *dvergar á ǫxlom* with grave finds, from ca. 650-1000, of objects near women's shoulders and concludes that the dates of the grave finds set termini for the dating of the poem.

1887. Nerman, Birger. "Hur gammal är Vǫluspá?" *Arkiv för nordisk filologi*, 73 (1958), 1-4.

On archaeological grounds, Nerman dates *Vǫluspá* to the second half of the seventh century or later.

1888. Nerman, Birger. "Det heliga tretalet och Vǫluspá." *Arkiv för nordisk filologi*, 74 (1959), 264-67.

The predilection for three or multiples of three in *Vǫluspá* finds a supposed parallel in artifacts from Gotland dated by archaeologists to the seventh century. Nerman regards the parallels as significant for the dating of *Vǫluspá*. Cf. Nerman, "Hur gammal är Vǫluspá" (1958), and Rokkjær "Arkæologisk datering af poetiske tekster"(1959).

1889. Nerman, Birger. "Hjälmbärare." *Fornvännen*, 57 (1962), 233-38. Summary in English.

Late sixth-century bronze buckles from Gotland are ornamented with a helmeted man's head. Drawing attention to the Odin names *Hjálmberi* "helmet bearer" and *Síðhǫttr* "deep-hatted," Nerman speculates that the figure may represent Odin.

1890. Nerman, Birger. "Två unga eddadikter: Arkeologisk belysning av Þrymskviða och Atlamál." *Arkiv för nordisk filologi*, 78 (1963), 126-33.

Comparison with archaeologists' datings of objects apparently mentioned in the poems leads Nerman to date *Þrymskviða* and *Atlamál* to the Viking Age—a radically early dating by today's standards.

1891. Nerman, Birger. "Vǫluspá 61:3 gullnar tǫflor." *Arkiv för nordisk filologi*, 78 (1963), 122-25.

Nerman identifies as gold bracteates the gold objects which the surviving gods find in the grass after Ragnarǫk in *Vǫluspá* (str. 61 in the usual ordering).

1892. Nerman, Birger. "Bröt-Anunds död." *Arkiv för nordisk filologi*, 79 (1964), 241-42.

Argues that Snorri misunderstood his sources in describing Braut-Önundr's death in *Ynglinga saga*, ch. 35.

1893. Nerman, Birger. "Svenskar i Balticum under 'Grobintiden.'" *Saga och sed*, 1967, pp. 102-11.

Suggests that Starkaðr was an eighth-century figure, born in the East Baltic Swedish colonies.

1894. Nerman, Birger. "Rígsþulas ålder." *Arkiv för nordisk filologi*, 84 (1969), 15-18.

Archaeological dating of *Rígsþula* to the second half of the tenth century.

1895. Nerman, Birger. "Fimbultýs fornar rúnar." *Arkiv för nordisk filologi*, 85 (1970), 206-07.

The title is a line from *Vǫluspá*, str. 60. Nerman relates Fimbultýr's ancient runes to fifth- and sixth-century bracteates and reiterates his dating of the poem to ca. 650-700. See also his "Hur gammal är Völuspá?" (1958).

1896. Nerman, Birger. "De äldsta eddadikterna." *Arkiv för nordisk filologi*, 86 (1971), 19-37.

On archaeological grounds *Skírnismál* and *Vǫlundarkviða* are among the oldest eddic poems.

1897. Nesheim, Asbjørn. "Omkring harpen i Voluspå." *By og bygd*, 20 (1968), 1-10.

An attempt to join the two parts of *Vǫluspá* 42. In the first Eggþér plays a harp; in the second Fjalarr crows *í gaglviði*. Nesheim understands this as a kenning whose referent is "harp"; the crowing would be, then, the playing of the harp.

1898. Netter, Irmgard. *Germanisches Frauentum*. Die Welt der Germanen, 4. Leipzig: Quelle & Meyer, 1935. 82 pp.

Includes discussion of women in the mythological poetry (pp. 25ff.).

1899. Neuhaus, Johannes. "Halfdan Frode Hadbardernes konge, hvis rige forenes med det danske." *Nordisk tidsskrift for filologi*, 4th series, 6 (1917), 78-80.

Fróði as a historical entity.

1900. Neumann, Eduard. *Das Schicksal in der Edda*, vol. 1: *Der Schicksalsbegriff in der Edda*. Beiträge zur deutschen Philologie, 7. Giessen: W. Schmitz, 1955. 197 pp.

Neumann divides conceptions of fate in the Poetic Edda into two groups: those mirroring an impersonal fate, and those deriving from the active intervention of some personal agency. To the former, he believes, belong the *vanir*, and to the latter the *æsir*.

1901. Neumann, Eduard, and Helmut Voigt. "Germanische Mythologie." In *Wörterbuch der Mythologie*, vol. 2: *Götter und Mythen im alten Europa*, ed. Hans Wilhelm Haussig, 21-98. Stuttgart: E. Klett, 1973.

Brief dictionary of Germanic mythology, concentrating on Scandinavian sources. There are occasional references to secondary literature and—more interesting—cross references to articles in other sections of the book, dealing with other old European mythologies.

1902. Neumann, Friedrich. "Tell—Dellingr—Heimdall." *Germania*, 26 (1881), 343-48.

Wilhelm Tell as the sun that pierces the clouds, and therefore, according to the author, as a descendant of Dellingr and Heimdallr.

1903. Niedner, Felix. "Skírnis för." *Zeitschrift für deutsches Altertum*, 30 (1886), 132-50.

Regards the extant *Skírnismál* as an artistic, carefully constructed reworking, by an Odin worshipper, of an archaic myth of spring.

1904. Niedner, Felix. "Das Hárbarðsljóð." *Zeitschrift für deutsches Altertum*, 31 (1887), 217-82.

Detailed introduction, text, translation, and commentary to *Hárbarðsljóð*.

1905. Niedner, Felix. "Bemerkungen zu den Eddaliedern." *Zeitschrift für deutsches Altertum*, 36 (1892), 278-95.

Notes on the structure, composition, and contents of *Þrymskviða*, *Vǫluspá*, *Lokasenna*.

1906. Niedner, Felix. *Zur Liederedda.* Wissenschaftliche Beilage zum Jahresbericht des Friedrichs-Gymnasium zu Berlin, Ostern 1896 . . .Programm, nr. 53. Berlin: R. Gaertner, 1896. 32 pp.

Treats, inter alia, *Hávamál* and *Hárbarðsljóð*.

1907. Niedner, Felix. "Baldrs Tod." *Zeitschrift für deutsches Altertum*, 41 (1897), 305-34.

Defends the Germanic origin of the story of Baldr's death. An original form, in which Odin played a major role, was later replaced by a form in which Frigg was more important.

1908. Niedner, Felix. "Eddische Fragen." *Zeitschrift für deutsches Altertum*, 41 (1897), 33-64.

Pp. 33-44 discuss the relationship between *Vǫluspá* and Christianity.

1909. Niedner, Felix. "Die Dioskuren im Beowulf." *Zeitschrift für deutsches Altertum*, 42 (1898), 229-58.

Parallels to the Baldr story in *Beowulf*, understood in light of Dioscurian myth. Niedner concludes that the original Nordic Baldr-Váli-Hǫðr myth parallels the old morning Dioscurii.

1910. Niedner, Felix. "Der Mythus des zweiten Merseburger Spruches." *Zeitschrift für deutsches Altertum*, 43 (1899), 101-12.

The epic plot of the second Merseburg charm as a myth of morning, parallel (in Niedner's interpretation) to other occurrences of the myth of Baldr.

1911. Niedner, Felix. "Ragnarök in der Völuspa." *Zeitschrift für deutsches Altertum*, 49 (1908), 239-98. Addendum in *Anzeiger für deutsches Altertum*, 31 (1908), 208-09.

After a detailed analysis of the manuscript transmission, settling on the text in Codex Regius as the only one worthy of the "higher criticism," Niedner proceeds to Ragnarǫk itself. He stresses the genuine pagan nature of the account and unity with the rest of the poem. Despite the title's emphasis on Ragnarǫk, the article treats the entire poem.

1912. Niedner, Felix. "Þórsdrápa des Eilífr Guðrúnarson." *Mitteilungen der Islandfreunde*, 17 (1930), 59-63.

Translation of *Þórsdrápa*.

1913. Nielsen, Ax. "Guldhornene." *Danske studier*, 37 (1940), 96-119.

Interpretation of the decorations on the now lost Gallehus horns, based to a great extent on Norse mythology. The horns were, Nielsen believes, associated with the cult of Týr.

1914. Nielsen, Ax. "Guldhornskalendere: Supplement til artiklen 'Guldhornene' i DSt. 1940." *Danske studier*, 41 (1944), 139-41.

Supplementary note to the author's "Guldhornene" (1940).

1915. Nielsen, H. Grüner. "Torsvisen på Færøerne." In *Festskrift til H. F. Feilberg fra nordiske sprog- og folkemindeforskere på 80 års dagen den 6. august 1911*. 72-76. Svenska landsmål, 1911; Maal og minne, 1911; Danske studier, 1911. Stockholm: Norstedt, Copenhagen: Gyldendal, Oslo (Kristiania): Bymaalslaget, 1911.

Evidence that a ballad based on *Þrymskviða* was sung on the Faroes during the nineteenth century.

1916. Nielsen, H. Grüner, and Axel Olrik. "Efterslæt til Loke-myterne, I: Loeke, Lodder i flamsk folketro." *Danske studier*, 9 (1912), 87-90.

Note following Olrik's studies on Loki; argues the existence of a Loki figure in Flemish folklore.

1917. Nielsen, Niels Åge. *Runestudier.* Odense Studies in Scandinavian Languages, 1. Odense: Odense University Press, 1968. 125 pp.

Two essays on runic inscriptions. The first, "Sydskandinaviske runestenes værneformler" (pp. 9-52), treats prophylactic formulas on the following stones: Glavendrup, Skern 2, Tryggevælde, Glemminge, Saleby, Sønder-Vinge 2, Sparlösa, Stentoften, and Björketorp, and concludes that the strength of such formulas lay in questioning the social status of a person who violated the formula, by equating such a person with magic, particularly *seiðr.* The last section in this essay (pp. 48-52) treats *seiðr* exclusively. The second essay treats the inscription on the Eggjum stone. Nielsen finds that the main part of the text falls into two parts, a memorial poem and an invocation to Odin in the form of a question and answer. A protective formula and a warning formula comprise the rest of the inscription.

1918. Nielsen, Niels Åge. "Freyr, Ullr, and the Sparlösa Stone." *Mediaeval Scandinavia,* 2 (1969), 102-28.

Argues that the entire text of the Sparlösa runic inscription is in verse and relates to the god Ullr; no previous interpretation had found this name in the inscription. Furthermore, Nielsen argues that the inscription supports the notion that Ullr and Freyr were identical, and that the pictures on the stone relate to this god: rider, horse, and dog; ships and birds; house, cats, owl, and snakes (these indicate to Nielsen that Freyr-Ullr was associated with death).

1919. Nielsen, Niels Åge. *Runerne på Rökstenen.* Odense Studies in Scandinavian Languages, 2. Odense: Odense University Press, 1969. 68 pp.

Nielsen offers a new interpretation of the Rök runestone, dividing the inscription into three sections (this parallels his reading of the Eggjum stone) and reading the entire text as verse. The three parts are a memorial poem, an invocation to Odin, and an invocation to Thor (the "parallel section" of the Eggjum stone has a warning formula).

The Odin invocation makes reference to a (hypothetical) myth, in which Odin cursed two objects so that each of them twelve times caused its owner's death, to Theodorik as an Odin name, and perhaps ultimately to the endless battle of the Hjaðningar. The Thor invocation makes reference to the Hrungnir myth; Thor (here the son of Ingald, understood by Nielsen as an Odin name) was ninety years old when he sired Magni (here called Vilin). By defeating the greatest of giants, he laid claim to men's invocations and requests for protection.

It need hardly be said that the reading is conjectural.

1920. Nielsen, Niels Åge. "Notes on Early Runic Poetry." *Mediaeval Scandinavia,* 3 (1970), 138-41.

Includes interpretation of the Sjælland bracteate 2 as an amulet which gives protection through threefold repetition of the name of the god Týr.

1921. Nilsson, Albert. "Balders död och återkomst." In *Festskrift tillägnad Axel Herrlin den 30 mars 1935: Studier och uppsatser överräckta på sextiofemårsdagen av kolleger, lärjungar och vänner*, eds. Alf Nyman, Elof Gertz, and Herman Siegvald, 295-310. Lund: C. Blom, 1935.

Deals mostly with modern Swedish poetic treatments of Baldr's death in the context of the mythological debate. Viktor Rydberg receives special treatment. Insofar as he takes a position, Nilsson seems to incline toward Christian influence.

1922. Nilsson, Bruce E. "The Runic 'Fish-Amulet' from Öland: A Solution." *Mediaeval Scandinavia*, 9 (1976), 236-45.

This runic inscription seems to be a magic injunction to protect a fisherman; it contains the line "May Thor protect him with that hammer which came from the sea, (and which) fled from evil." As the inscription may be dated to the eleventh or early twelfth century, it should be understood as an example of syncretism.

1923. Nilsson, Martin P. "Studien zur Vorgeschichte des Weihnachtsfestes." *Archiv für Religionswissenschaft*, 19 (1916-19), 50-150.

In part 2, pp. 94-149, Nilsson carefully brings out much that is Germanic in yule ritual, and in the last pages he weighs the evidence of Norse literature.

1924. Nilsson, Martin P. "Zur Deutung der Juppitergigantensäulen." *Archiv für Religionswissenschaft*, 23 (1925), 175-84.

On the larger context of the so-called "Jupiter-columns." Nilsson does not include them in the Germanic dossier, although he does see Gallic (pre-Germanic) possibilities.

1925. Nilsson, Victor. *Loddfáfnismál: An Eddic Study*. Minneapolis: University Press of Minnesota, 1898. 47 pp.

Published dissertation, putting the Loddfáfnismál section of *Hávamál* into the context of heroic poetry. Nilsson reads Loddfáfnir as Sigurðr and the counselor as Grípir.

1926. Ninck, Martin. *Wodan und germanischer Schicksalsglaube*. Jena: E. Diederichs, 1935. 357, [1] pp. Rpt. Darmstadt: Wissenschaftliche Buchgesellschaft, 1967.

An attempt to present the German reader of the 1930s with the essence of two important aspects of the religion of their forebears, Odin and fate, with the emphasis on Odin. Ninck stresses the deep contrast in the being of Odin: god of death and god of life.

Some of the reasoning may strike the modern reader as largely intuitive and the nationalistic purpose distracting.

1927. Ninck, Martin. *Götter und Jenseitsglauben der Germanen.* Jena: E. Diederichs, 1937.

Beliefs in the otherworld among the Germanic peoples, as exemplified primarily in Norse literature. The emphasis is, as one would expect, on Odin. The author stresses the relationship between myth and literary creation.

1928. Nordal, Sigurður. "Snorri Sturluson: Brot úr mannlýsingu." *Skírnir*, 90 (1916), 225-55.

A description of Snorri's life and literary works, with emphasis on his relation to his contemporaries.

1929. Nordal, Sigurður. *Snorri Sturluson.* Reykjavik: Þ. B. Þorláksson, 1920. viii, 266 pp.

Standard account of Snorri's life and literary works.

1930. Nordal, Sigurður. *Völuspá: Gefin út með skyringum.* Árbók háskóla Íslands, 1922-23, supplement. Reykjavik: Háskóli Íslands, 1923. vi, 142 pp. 2nd printing Reykjavik: Helgafell, 1952.

Edition of *Vǫluspá* with reconstructed text and important commentary. Nordal sets the poem in Iceland toward the end of the tenth century.

1931. Nordal, Sigurður. "Átrúnaður Egils Skallagrímssonar." *Skírnir*, 98 (1924), 145-65.

On the religious faith of Egill Skallagrímsson, eponymous hero of *Egils saga Skallagrímssonar.* Nordal argues that when Egill's sons died, he experienced a crisis in his faith in Odin and expressed that crisis in his poem *Sonatorrek.*

1932. Nordal, Sigurður. "Völu-Steinn." *Iðunn*, 8 (1924), 161-78. Rpt. in Nordal, *Áfangar*, vol. 2 (Reykjavik: Helgafell, 1944), pp. 83-102; Danish translation in Nordal, *Islandske streiflys* (Bergen: Universitetsforlaget, 1965), pp. 50-65.

Icelandic original of Nordal, "The Author of *Völuspá*" (1978-81).

1933. Nordal, Sigurður. *Völuspá: Vølvens spådom.* Copenhagen: H. Aschehoug, 1927. xviii, 157 pp. Translated by Hans Albrectsen.

Danish translation of Nordal's important study of *Vǫluspá* (1923).

1934. Nordal, Sigurður. "Billings mær." In *Bidrag till nordisk filologi tillägnade Emil Olson.* 288-95. Lund: C. W. K. Gleerup, 1936.

Interpretation of *Hávamál* 96-102: the wife of Billingr thwarts Odin's advances by deflecting his magic powers onto a dog in her bed.

1935. Nordal, Sigurður. "Snorri Sturluson: Nokkurar hugleiðingar á 700. ártíð hans." *Skírnir*, 115 (1941), 5-33.

Personal reminiscence of the author's scholarly work on Snorri Sturluson, occasioned by the 700th anniversary of Snorri's death.

1936. Nordal, Sigurður. *Íslenzk menning,* vol. 1. Reykjavik: Mál og menning, 1942. 359, [1] pp. Half-title: Arfur Íslendinga.

Sigurður Nordal's classic treatment of Old Icelandic literary culture contains a chapter on paganism, with particularly sensitive remarks on the spiritual world of Egill Skallagrímsson and other heroes. Topics treated in this context include fate, heroism, and Ragnarǫk (*Vǫluspá*).

1937. Nordal, Sigurður. "Three Essays on Völuspá." *Saga-Book of the Viking Society*, 18 (1970-73), 79-135. Translated by B. S. Benedikz and J. S. McKinnell.

Translations from Nordal's *Völuspá* (1923).

1938. Nordal, Sigurður. "The Author of *Völuspá.*" *Saga-Book of the Viking Society*, 20 (1978-81), 114-30. Translated by B. S. Benedikz.

Translation of Sigurður Nordal, "Völu-Steinn" (1923-24). He identifies the author as one Völu-Steinn, a Norwegian settler in Bolungarvík, Iceland, from Hálogland. By the end of the tenth century, Nordal's date for the poem, Völu-Steinn was a grown man, and his mother had been a seeress. Völu-steinn is known to have composed two half-stanzas (outside of *Vǫluspá*) of a mythological nature.

1939. Nordal, Sigurður. *Vǫluspá.* Durham and St. Andrews Medieval Texts, 1. Durham: Department of English Language and Medieval Literature, 1978. viii, 165 pp. Translated by B. S. Benedikz and John McKinnell.

English translation of Nordal's famous study of *Vǫluspá* (1923), slightly rearranged and including a glossary.

1940. Nordal, Sigurður. *Völuspá.* Texte zur Forschung, 33. Darmstadt: Wissenschaftliche Buchgesellschaft, 1980. xxvi, 161 pp. Translated with a foreword by Ommo Wilts.

Translation of Nordal's famous study of *Vǫluspá* (1923).

1941. Nordén, Arthur. "Hällristningarnas kronologi och betydelse." *Ymer*, 37 (1917), 57-83.

Older article on the Bronze Age rock carvings. Nordén's interpretation follows the lines set forth in the same journal by G. Ekholm one year earlier ("De skandinaviska hällristningarna och deras betydelse") in setting the rock carvings in the context of magic surrounding the cult of the dead.

1942. Nordén, Arthur. *Spår av hedendom vid Norrköping.* Norrköping: A. Lundberg, 1921. 47 pp.

Traces of Norse myth and religion in recent folklore from near Norrköping, Sweden.

1943. Nordén, Arthur. *Felsbilder der Provinz Ostgotland in Auswahl,* 2nd ed. Werke der Urgermanen, Schriften zum Wiederaufbau der alten nordischen Kulturen, 2; Schriften-Reihe Kulturen der Erde, 10. Hagen i W. and Darmstadt: Folkwang, 1923. 43 pp.

Rock carvings from Östergötland, Sweden.

1944. Nordén, Arthur. "Den heliga murgrönens offerställe: Ett bidrag till frågan om vi-namnens äkthetsbevis." *Sydsvenska ortnamnsällskapets årsskrift,* 1925, pp. 40-46.

Argues that the Swedish placename Vrinnevi meant "Rind's holy place."

1945. Nordén, Arthur. "Sankt Olofsyxan: En studie över kultövningens lokala kontinuitet." *Fornvännen,* 20 (1925), 1-17. Summary in German, p. 17.

St. Olaf as the heir to the cult of Thor and to older Bronze Age cult in and around Norrköping, Sweden.

1946. Nordén, Arthur. "Baldershagen och tempelhelgden: Oklunda-inskriften, en rättsurkund från en forn-östgötsk blotlund." *Ord och bild,* 39 (1930), 255-61.

A runic inscription interpreted as a legal document: a convicted manslaughterer seeks sanctuary at a holy place.

1947. Nordén, Arthur. "Ett rättsdokument från en fornsvensk offerlund: Oklundaristningen, en nyupptäckt östgötsk rökrune-inskrift." *Fornvännen,* 26 (1931), 330-51.

A reading of the legalistic runic inscription from Oklunda, Sweden. In the last pages the author discusses the placename and suggests that this part of Östergötland was an important cult area.

1948. Nordén, Arthur. "Från Kivik till Eggjum, I: De gravmagiska bildristningarna." *Fornvännen,* 29 (1934), 35-53.

Explores the notion of continuity from Bronze Age rock carvings to later runic inscriptions in the area of grave magic. The article includes a survey of relevant grave sites.

1949. Nordén, Arthur. "Från Kivik till Eggjum, II: Runristningar med gengångarbesvärjelse." *Fornvännen*, 29 (1934), 97-117.

Prophylaxis against revenants on early runic inscriptions.

1950. Nordén, Arthur. "Från Kivik till Eggjum, III: Fågel—fisk—magien och vattnet som gengångarskydd." *Fornvännen*, 31 (1936), 241-48.

On the Eggjum runic inscription; the importance of water as a means of defense against revenants.

1951. Nordén, Arthur. "Magiska runinskrifter." *Arkiv för nordisk filologi*, 53 (1937), 147-89.

On magic in several runic inscriptions, mostly from Sweden.

1952. Nordén, Arthur. "Söderköpingsstenen: En nyfunnen runsten med magiskt syfte från 'övergångstiden.'" *Fornvännen*, 32 (1937), 129-56. Summary in German, pp. 155-56.

Description and interpretation of a runestone from Söderköping, Sweden, to which the author ascribes a magic purpose.

1953. Nordén, Arthur. "Söderköpingsstenen: En nyfunnen runsten med magiskt syfte från 'övergångstiden.'" *Fornvännen*, 32 (1937), 129-56.

Interpretation of a then newly discovered runestone as magic against desecration of the grave or possible revenants.

1954. Nordén, Arthur. "Bidrag till svensk runforskning." *Kungliga vitterhets historie och antikvitets akademiens handlingar*, 55; Antikvariska studier, 1 (1943), 143-232.

On magic and cult use of runes, emphasizing Swedish inscriptions. The first part continues Nordén's article, "Magiska runinskrifter" (1937); the second argues the existence of a formal office of guardian or defender of the pagan temple. Here the evidence comes from the Kälvesten, Sparlösa, and Rök inscriptions.

1955. Nordenstreng, Rolf. "Ett förslag till texträttelse i Hávamál." *Arkiv för nordisk filologi*, 25 (1909), 190-91.

Textual note to *Hávamál*, str. 36-37.

1956. Nordenstreng, Rolf. "Guden *Váli*." In *Festskrift tillägnad Hugo Pipping på hans sextioårsdag den 5 november 1924*. 392-94. Skrifter utg. av Svenska litteratursällskapet i Finland, 175. Helsinki: Mercators tryckeri, 1924.

Proposes an etymology from **waihala* or **waihula* "little warrior," and argues that the god, and perhaps the Baldr myth, may be old.

1957. Nordenstreng, Rolf. "Namnet Yggdrasill." In *Studier tillägnade Axel Kock, tidskriftens redaktör, 1888-1925*. 194-99. Arkiv för nordisk filologi, 40, supplement. Lund: C. W. K. Gleerup, 1929. Also issued separately, under title *Studier tillägnade Axel Kock*.

The name *Yggdrasill* means "the powerful, knotty, hanging yew."

1958. Nordgaard, O. "Tors frokost." *Maal og minne*, 1917, pp. 79-80.

Substitutes goats for oats on Thor's breakfast menu in *Hárbarðsljóð*, str. 3 (*hafra*).

Disputed by H. Koht, "Sild og—bukker?" (1917); defended by Nordgaard a year later.

1959. Nordgaard, O. "Mere om Tors frokost." *Maal og minne*, 1918, pp. 82-84.

Defense of goats, not oats, on Thor's breakfast table.

1960. Nordland, Odd. "Valhall and Helgafell: Syncretistic Traits of the Old Norse Religion." In *Syncretism: Based on Papers Read at the Symposium on Cultural Contact, Meeting of Religions, Syncretism Held at Åbo on the 8th-10th of September, 1966*, ed. Sven S. Hartman, 66-99. Scripti Instituti Donneriani Aboensis, 3. Stockholm: Almqvist & Wiksell, 1969.

The syncretism treated here is between Scandinavian and Finno-Ugric (Lapp and Finnish), and Nordland dates it back to the meeting of an indigenous population from northern Scandinavia with an invading population from the south, a meeting that occurred thousands of years ago. He traces the intermingling of the two cultures in cult reconstructed from Norwegian placenames.

1961. Nordlander, Johan. "Minnen af heden tro och kult i norrländska ortnamn." *Ymer*, 28 (1908), 113-21.

Argues the existence of theophoric placenames in Jämtland, Medelpad, and Ångermanland, Sweden. Includes a map with hypothetical cult places.

1962. Noreen, Adolf. "Ett nytt uppslag i fråga om den nordiska mytologien." *Nordisk tidskrift för vetenskap, konst och industri*, n. f. 3 (1890), 201-12.

Extended review of E. H. Meyer, *Völuspá* (1889).

1963. Noreen, Adolf. "Fornnordisk religion, mytologi och teologi: Populär föreläsning, hållen til förmån för egyptiska museet i Upsala den 9 mars 1892." *Svensk tidskrift*, 2 (1892), 172-82.

Text of a lecture on the methodological bases of research in ancient Nordic religion. Noreen operates within the confines of nature mythology, but he stresses the differing conceptions of various social classes and differing times, separating the mythology of purely pagan speculators from the theology of those influenced by Christianity.

1964. Noreen, Adolf. "Mytiska beståndsdelar i Ynglingatal." In *Uppsalastudier tillegnade Sophus Bugge på hans 60-åra födelsedag den 5 januari 1893.* 194-225. Uppsala: Almqvist & Wiksell, 1892.

Critical notes to the stanzas in *Ynglingatal* treating Fjǫlnir; Sveigðir; Vanlandi, Vísburr, and Agni; and Dómarr-Yngvi. The method involves distinguishing myth and legend from various historical levels.

1965. Noreen, Adolf. "Tiveden och tibast." In *Festskrift til H. F. Feilberg fra nordiske sprog- og folkemindeforskere på 80 års dagen den 6. august 1911.* 273-84. Svenska landsmål, 1911; Maal og minne, 1911; Danske studier, 1911. Stockholm: Norstedt, Copenhagen: Gyldendal, Oslo (Kristiania): Bymaals-laget, 1911.

Argues that the Swedish placename *Tiveden* does not contain the name of the god Týr. Noreen offers also a general discussion of the principles of compounding gods' names in placenames.

1966. Noreen, Adolf. "Urkon Auðhumla och några hennes språkliga släktingar." *Namn och bygd*, 6 (1918), 169-72.

Linguistically related forms, primarily onomastic, to the name of the protocow, Auðhumla, which Noreen interprets as "the hornless, powerful cow."

1967. Noreen, Adolf. "Yngve, Inge, Inglinge m. m." *Namn och bygd*, 8 (1920), 1-8.

Noreen derives these forms from a root originally meaning "stave, stick."

1968. Noreen, Adolf. "Ynglingatal: Text, översättning och kommentar." *Kungliga vitterhets historie och antikvitets akademiens handlingar*, 28:2 (1925), 193-254.

Edition, translation, and commentary to *Ynglingatal.*

1969. Noreen, Erik. *Till Alvíssmǫl 14.* Studier i nordisk filologi, 4:5, Skrifter utgivna av Svenska literatursällskapet i Finland, 110. Helsinki: Tidnings- & tryckeriaktiebolaget, 1913. 5 pp.

Textual note.

1970. Noreen, Erik. "Ett hednisk kultcentrum i Värmland?" *Namn och bygd*, 8 (1920), 17-31.

Theophoric placenames in Värmland, Sweden.

1971. Noreen, Erik. "Eddastudier." *Språkvetenskapliga sällskapets i Uppsala förhandlingar 1919-21; Uppsala universitets årsskrift*, 1921, pp. 1-44.

Includes a section on the age of the eddic poems, suggesting that those in *ljóðaháttr*, such as *Vafþrúðnismál* or *Skírnismál*, can date from as early as the beginning of the eighth century.

1972. Noreen, Erik. *Studier i fornvästnordisk diktning. 3de samlingen*. Uppsala universitets åsrskrift 1923, Filosofi, språkvetenskap och historiska vetenskaper, 3. Uppsala: Lundequistska bokhandeln, 1923. 61 pp.

Includes discussion of *Lokasenna* and *Þrymskviða*.

1973. Noreen, Erik. "Ordet bärsärk." *Arkiv för nordisk filologi*, 48 (1932), 242-54.

The etymology and meaning of *berserkr*: "bare-shirted."

1974. Noreen, Erik. "Ur Eddaöversättningarnas historia." *Nordisk tidskrift för vetenskap, konst och industri*, 8 (1932), 40-51.

Discussion of translations of the Poetic Edda.

1975. Noreen, Erik. "Några Eddaställen." In *Studia Germanica tillägnade Ernst Albin Kock den 6 december 1934*. 258-60. Lund: C. Blom, 1934.

Textual notes to *Skírnismál* 9, *Lokasenna* 15 and 31.

1976. Noreen, Erik. "Ur Eddaforskningens historia." *Nordisk tidskrift för vetenskap, konst och industri*, n. s., 17 (1941), 349-59.

Survey of research on the Poetic Edda.

1977. Noreen, Erik. "Grímnismál 33." *Arkiv för nordisk filologi*, 58 (1944), 235-37. Also in *Festskrift till Jöran Sahlgren 8/4 1944* (Lund: C. W. K. Gleerup, 1944), pp. 235-37.

Textual note.

1978. Normann, Einar. "Onsøy—Oden's bygd." *Syn og segn*, 50 (1944), 109-15.

Placenames and natural phenomena in Onsøy (Austfold, Norway) fitting the myth of Baldr's death.

1979. Nowotny, Karl Anton. "Die Brakteaten der Schleswiger Gruppe und die Wilde Jagd im Mythos der Völkerwanderungszeit." *Mannus*, 30 (1938), 210-22.

Interprets fifth- and sixth-century bracteates from Schleswig as representations of the wild hunt. They portray Odin, wolf and raven, and a stag representing the woman being hunted.

1980. Nutt, Alfred. "Presidential Address: The Discrimination of Racial Elements in the Folklore of the British Isles." *Folk-Lore*, 9 (1898), 30-52.

One of the "racial elements" discussed is "Teutonic," adduced almost exclusively from Scandinavian mythology.

O

1981. Ödeen, Nils. "Studier över den nordiska gudavärldens uppkomst." *Acta Philologica Scandinavica,* 4 (1929-30), 122-71.

A wide-ranging essay on the origins of Norse myth and religion. Ödeen finds the primary impulse for the creation of the Norse gods in belief in power—various powers, various gods. He offers analysis of the war between the *æsir* and *vanir* as a means of reconciling the old powers and the newer cultural influences from the south. He pays particular attention, too, to the figure of Odin, whom he sees as joining beliefs in power, animism, and the supernatural, combined with the various waves of southern influence.

1982. Ödeen, Nils. "Vanamytens religionshistoriska betydelse." In *Studier tillägnade Axel Kock, tidskriftens redaktör, 1888-1925.* 294-303. Arkiv för nordisk filologi, 40, supplement. Lund: C. W. K. Gleerup, 1929. Also issued separately, under title *Studier tillägnade Axel Kock.*

In some ways this article is ahead of its time and anticipates Dumézil's contributions. Ödeen finds that the war between the *æsir* and *vanir* reflects not a war of peoples with different cults but rather a symbolic opposition. Odin is an ancient god among the Germanic peoples, with Indo-European antecedents, and the myth of the *vanir* was necessary to redefine him after he assumed some characteristics of other gods from the south.

1983. Oelmann, Franz. "Zum Problem des gallischen Tempels." *Germania,* 17 (1933), 169-81.

Points out the similarity of Gallic temples to the nearly square Germanic temples of Uppsala and Sæból.

1984. Ørsnes, Mogens. "Der Moorfund von Ejsbøl bei Hadersleben und die Deutungsprobleme der grossen nordgermanischen Waffenopferfunde." In *Vorgeschichtliche Heiligtümer und Opferplätze in Mittel- und Nordeuropa: Bericht über ein Symposium in Reinhausen bei Göttingen vom 14.-16. Oktober 1968,* ed. Herbert Jankuhn, 172-87. Abhandlungen der Akademie der Wissenschaften in Göttingen, phil.-hist. Kl., 3. Folge, 74. Göttingen: Vandenhoeck & Ruprecht, 1970.

Methodological remarks on archaeological evidence for cult.

1985. Østergaard, K. Høgsbro. "En trehovet gud? To mærkelige stenskulpturer fra Glejberg og Bramminge." *Kuml*, 1954, pp. 55-77. Summary in English.

Relates two finds to a widespread iconographic feature: three-headed gods. Some discussion of the Skog tapestry.

1986. Oesterley, William Oscar Emil. *The Sacred Dance: A Study in Comparative Folklore*. Cambridge: University Press, New York: Macmillan, 1923. x, 234 pp.

Cult dance; some reference to Germanic materials.

1987. Östvold, Torbjörg. "The War of the Æsir and the Vanir—A Myth of the Fall in Nordic Religion." *Temenos*, 5 (1969), 169-202.

Interprets the war as a myth of the fall of mankind from grace.

1988. Ohlmarks, Åke. "Totenerweckungen in Eddaliedern." *Arkiv för nordisk filologi*, 52 (1936), 264-97.

Postulates a generic "lay of awakening," realized in various eddic poems. The weight of the analysis is on *Vǫluspá*, which Ohlmarks breaks into four parts: 1) the *ek* poem—strophes in which the seeress uses the first person pronoun; 2) a cosmogonic poem; 3) the *hon* poem—strophes in which the seeress, in the third person, recounts mythic history; 4) the lay of Ragnarǫk.

1989. Ohlmarks, Åke. *Heimdalls Horn und Odins Auge: Studien zur nordischen und vergleichenden Religionsgeschichte*, vol. 1: *Heimdall und das Horn*. Lund: C. W. K. Gleerup, Copenhagen: Levin & Munksgaard, 1937. vii, 399 pp.

Ohlmarks's dissertation was to have been the first of two volumes on Heimdallr's horn and Odin's eye. The second never appeared, and the relationship between horn and eye is not made explicit in this volume. It begins with a long methodological introduction on the *Kulturkreislehre* then popular in Europe (it was, indeed, in 1937 that Wilhelm Schmidt codified the method in his *Handbuch der Methode der kulturhistorischen Ethnologie*). Ohlmarks's view, then, is essentially comparative, and he introduces material from all over the world. In this the work may be compared with Birger Pering's Lund dissertation on the same subject, issued just four years later (1941); it remains always in the Nordic area.

The bulk of Ohlmarks's book consists of two monographs, a long one on Heimdallr and a shorter one on his horn. As was customary with Swedish dissertations, much attention is devoted to source criticism—for example, Ohlmarks spends 145 pp. discussing the sources pertaining to Heimdallr, and they are not many—and the bibliography is reasonably thorough.

Ohlmarks's conclusions have not become popular. He found Heimdallr a sun god of the second rank, belonging by nature to patriarchal cultures, by degree to ruler-cultures. His horn Ohlmarks understood as a cult item used in ritual drinking and representing the sun's ray.

Readers familiar with Swedish will recognize many of the German stylistic idiosyncrasies.

1990. Ohlmarks, Åke. "Anmärkningar och genmäle angående Heimdall." *Arkiv för nordisk filologi*, 54 (1939), 354-63.

Response to criticism of the author's monograph *Heimdalls Horn und Odins Auge* (1937) by I. Lindquist, "Guden Heimdall enligt Snorres källor" (1937), and by B. Pering in an immediately preceding review in the same number of the journal.

1991. Ohlmarks, Åke. "Arktischer Schamanismus und altnordischer seiðr." *Archiv für Religionswissenschaft*, 36 (1939), 171-80.

A survey of parallels between *seiðr* and arctic shamanism, suggesting possible association, perhaps particularly in the person of Odin.

1992. Ohlmarks, Åke. "Stellt die mythische Bifrǫst den Regenbogen oder die Milchstrasse dar? Eine textkritische-religionshistorische Untersuchung zur mythographischen Arbeitsmethode Snorri Sturlusons." *Meddelanden från Lunds astronomiska observatorium*, ser. 2, 110 (1941), 1-40.

Following remarks on Snorri's mythographic method, Ohlmarks argues that Bifrǫst originally meant the Milky Way; confronted with the three terms *Bifrǫst*, *Bilrǫst*, and *Ásbrú*, Snorri interpreted the bridge as a rainbow.

1993. Ohlmarks, Åke. "Alt-Uppsala und Arkona: Zur Rekonstruktion des Uppsalatempels und Entstehung der westslawischen Kulte." *Vetenskapssocietetens i Lund årsbok*, 1943, pp. 77-120.

Separates the reconstruction of the temple at Uppsala from that of the Wends at Arkona; each must be understood, Ohlmarks stresses, in its own cultural context.

1994. Ohlmarks, Åke. "'Toalettredskapen' och solreligionen under yngre bronsåldern." *Fornvännen*, 40 (1945), 337-58. Summary in English, p. 358.

An explanation of toilet articles—razors, tweezers, etc.—found atop cremated bones in ship graves from the younger Bronze Age in Scandinavia. The shape and ornamentation on the articles suggest horses and ships, both associated by scholars with the worship of the sun. Ohlmarks adduces rituals from various other cultures and suggests that the toilet articles enabled the deceased to make himself as much like the sun as possible and thus enjoy resurrection with the rising sun.

1995. Ohlmarks, Åke. *Gravskeppet: Studier i förhistorisk nordisk religionshistoria.* Stockholm: H. Geber, 1946. 236 pp.

On *skeppsättningar* and ship burials, put in their archaeological, literary, and religious context. The binding religious notion, according to Ohlmarks, is the cult of the sun.

1996. Ohlmarks, Åke. *Svenskarnas tro genom årtusendena,* vol. 1: *Hedendomen.* Stockholm: Norlin, 1947. 459 pp.

This was to be the first of an ambitious series of volumes covering the history of the religious beliefs of the Swedes. Treated are the Stone Age, the (Bronze Age) sun god, the Iron Age, the Migration period, foreign gods, and gods of the Svear and Götar from Gamla Uppsala to the mission of Ansgar. That is a lot of territory, but the book is hefty, and Ohlmarks had already written a very detailed study of Heimdallr (*Heimdalls Horn und Odins Auge,* I (1937)) and several other contributions to early Germanic religion. Although many of the hypotheses advanced here now seem improbable, it is interesting to read Ohlmarks's attempt to survey the vast subject, and the shamanistic parallels adduced to Odin myths are noteworthy (cf. his "Arktischer Schamanismus und altnordischer seiðr" (1939)), even if the suggestion that Odin originated as an Asiatic shaman-god is not.

1997. Ohlmarks, Åke. *Eddans gudasånger: Tolkade samt försedda med inledning och kommentarer.* Stockholm: H. Geber, 1948. 318 pp.

Swedish translation of mythological eddic poems, with introduction (pp. 7-53) and commentary (pp. 211-311).

1998. Ohlmarks, Åke. *Svenskarnas tro genom årtusendena,* vol. II: *Missionstid och katolsk tid.* Stockholm: Norlin, 1950. 611 pp.

Second of a projected series of volumes surveying the religious beliefs of the Swedes; useful for its coverage of the Christian mission and the conversion to Christianity.

1999. Ohlmarks, Åke. *Havamal: Det fornnordiska visdomskvädet i svensk tolkning och med kommentarer.* Stockholm: Eden, 1962. 92 pp.

Swedish translation of *Hávamál,* with commentary. Includes block prints by Per Engström.

2000. Ohlmarks, Åke. *Asar, vaner och vidunder: Den fornnordiska gudavärlden, saga, tro och myt.* Stockholm: A. Bonnier, [1963]. 304 pp.

Popular handbook for a Swedish audience.

2001. Ohlmarks, Åke. *Hällristningarnas gudar: En sammanställning och ett förklaringsförsök.* Stockholm: Kronos/Tiden, [1963]. 144 pp.

Presentation of the rock carvings and their possible religious significance.

2002. Ohlmarks, Åke. *Nordisk gudatro.* N.p.: Gummesons läromedel, 1970. 102 pp.

Popular handbook for a Swedish audience, especially adolescents.

2003. Ohlmarks, Åke. "Valcamonica, die südschwedischen Felsbilder und die Bernsteinstrasse." *IPEK, Jahrbuch für prähistorische und ethnographische Kunst*, 24 (1974-77), 102-23.

Interpretation of southern Swedish rock carvings in light of northern Italian parallels brought about by a possible link with the amber trade.

2004. Ohlmarks, Åke. *Vårt nordiska arv: Från 10,000 f. Kr. till medeltidens början.* Stockholm: Stureförlaget, 1979. 264 pp.

A popular survey of Germanic religion in Sweden from 10,000 B. C. until the time of the Christian mission (tenth century). Speculative and undocumented.

2005. Ohrt, Ferdinand. "Wodans eller Kristi ridt." *Danske studier*, 13 (1916), 189-93.

Review of R. Th. Christiansen, *Die finnischen und nordischen Varianten des zweiten Merseburgerspruches* (1915).

2006. Ohrt, Ferdinand. "Om galdersange." *Danske studier*, 20 (1923), 183-86.

Review of I. Lindquist, *Galdrar* (1923).

2007. Ohrt, Ferdinand. "Hammerens lyde–jærnets last (Til Skáldskaparmál kap. 33)." In *Festskrift til Finnur Jónsson 29. maj 1928.* 195-98. Copenhagen: Levin & Munksgaard, 1928.

A Finnish parallel to the myth of the imperfect creation of Thor's hammer by the dwarf Brokkr, when the dwarf is stung by a fly.

2008. Ohrt, Ferdinand. "Odin paa træet." *Acta Philologica Scandinavica*, 4 (1929-30), 273-86.

On *Hávamál* 138-42. Ohrt finds that popular rather than learned Christian conceptions have been adapted to the pagan myth. A separate section (pp. 279-86) discusses some of the runes Odin took up, in light of folk medicine, and concludes that whatever its sources, the poem has a pagan outlook.

2009. Ohrt, Ferdinand. "Runetrolddom." *Danske studier*, 29 (1932), 178-81.

Review of H. Brix, *Systematiske beregninger i de danske runeindskrifter* (1932).

2010. Ohrt, Ferdinand. "Eddica og magica." *Acta Philologica Scandinavica*, 9 (1934-35), 161-76.

Pp. 163-69 argue that the speaker of the *ljóðatal* of *Hávamál* (str. 146-63) was not originally Odin but a human; pp. 170-76 argue that a supposed heathen charm from Småland, Sweden, does not descend fom the pagan period.

2011. Ohrt, Ferdinand. "Gondols ondu." *Acta Philologica Scandinavica*, 10 (1935-36), 199-207.

The words occur in a magic spell recited by a woman in fourteenth-century Norway against a former lover. The valkyrie name Gǫndul is probably not involved; rather we have, according to Ohrt, a mixture of southern European and Nordic elements: *Gondols* may reflect an underlying **gand-úlfr* "magic wolf."

2012. Ohrt, Ferdinand. "Sunnr at Urðarbrunni." *Acta Philologica Scandinavica*, 12 (1937-38), 91-101.

Eilífr Goðrúnarson's stanza to Christ; Ohrt interprets the words *sitja sunnr á setbergs Urðarbrunni* as a reference to Christ sitting by the well of paradise, located atop a mountain. The *Urðar brunnr* is thus displaced mythically into Christian sentiment.

2013. Ohrt, Ferdinand. "Om Merseburgformlerne som galder: En efterladt afhandling." *Danske studier*, 35 (1938), 125-36.

On formal characteristics of magic charms.

2014. Olafsen, O. *Ulvik i fortid och nutid.* Norheimsund: Skaars boktrykkeri, 1925. 2 vols. Vol. 1, viii, 451 pp.; vol. 2, 341 pp.

Concludes that the god's name *Ullr* is not the first component of the place-name *Ulvik.*

2015. Ólafsson, Ólafur M. "Völuspá Konungsbókar." *Landsbókasafn Íslands, Árbók*, 22 (1965), 86-124.

A commentary to the Codex Regius text of *Vǫluspá*, which the author regards as complete.

2016. Ólafsson, Ólafur M. "Endurskoðun Völuspár." *Landsbókasafn Íslands, Árbók*, 23 (1966), 110-93.

This long article takes up the fundamental question of the text and transmission of *Vǫluspá*; the poem is found, in rather different forms, in Codex Regius and Hauksbók and was used in the *Gylfaginning* of *Snorra edda.* Through detailed comparison, the author argues that Codex Regius contains the definitive text. From it the Hauksbók version may be derived, and this derivation may be the work of a twelfth-century cleric who sought to revise the poem for a

Christian audience. Snorri used mostly this earlier version of the text but knew both.

2017. Ólafsson, Ólafur M. "Eiðstafur heiðinna manna." *Andvari*, 1970, pp. 103-10.

On pagan oaths. The author offers the intuition that the formula *inn almáttki áss* could refer to either Odin or Thor and therefore could be used by worshippers of Odin or Thor.

2018. Oldeberg, Andreas. "Fisk- och fågelfigurer på en bronskniv från Bohuslän." *Fornvännen*, 30 (1935), 343-55. Summary in German, pp. 354-55.

Discussion of the few Nordic Bronze Age fish and bird figures, including their possible association with cult. The bird may have to do with European tree cult and/or conceptions of the movable soul; the fish may be related to Near Eastern fish cult.

2019. Olrik, Axel. "Runestenes vidnesbyrd om dansk aandsliv." *Dania*, 4 (1897), 25-42, 106-22.

Materials in L. Wimmer's *De danske runemindesmærker* (1893 ff.) relating to Danish Viking Age and medieval culture. Magic and divinatory uses of runes are discussed.

2020. Olrik, Axel. "Odinsjægeren i Jylland." *Dania*, 8 (1901), 139-73.

Thorough study of the recent folk legends of the Wild Hunt in Jutland, sometimes called *Odensjægeren* "Odin's hunter." Here the name of the god has been associated with folk beliefs deriving, according to Olrik, from the sound of the wind or flocks of birds.

2021. Olrik, Axel. "Sivard den digre, en vikingesaga fra de danske i Nordengland." *Arkiv för nordisk filologi*, 19 (1902-03), 199-223.

Danish original of Olrik's "Siward Digri of Northumberland" (1908-09).

2022. Olrik, Axel. "Om Ragnarok." *Årbøger for nordisk oldkyndighed og historie*, 1902, pp. 157-291.

First part of Olrik's major study of Ragnarǫk, later translated as *Ragnarǫk: Die Vorstellungen vom Weltuntergang* (1922). The broad subjects treated here are the nature motifs, the battle of the gods, renewal, and *Vǫluspá*.

2023. Olrik, Axel. *Danmarks heltedigtning: En oldtidsstudie*, vol. 1: *Rolf krake og den ældre Skjoldungrække*. Copenhagen: G. E. C. Gad, 1903. 352 pp.

The first part of Olrik's study of older Danish heroic traditions, some of which were euhemeristic. Revised translation by Lee M. Hollander, *The Heroic Legends of Denmark* (1919).

2024. Olrik, Axel. "Nordisk og lappisk gudsdyrkelse." *Danske studier*, 2 (1905), 39-57.

A comparison of Lapp religious beliefs and practices (as based on seventeenth-century records) and those of Bronze Age and (by implication) Viking Age Scandinavia. Relevance to Scandinavian mythology regards primarily Thor, the Lapp Horagalles. The Lapp thunder god has a companion, like Þjálfi, Týr, or Loki, and not one but two hammers; this may be a Lapp innovation.

2025. Olrik, Axel. "Tordenguden og hans dreng." *Danske studier*, 2 (1905), 129-46.

The article has two parts. "Thor og Thjalfe" (pp. 129-40) uses Lapp mythology and recent Swedish folklore to argue the existence in Sweden of a figure parallel to Þjálfi. This figure may, Olrik thinks, have derived from a natural phenomenon such as the rumble that preceeds and follows thunder. "Thor og Loke" (pp. 140-46) presents an Estonian tale of the "thunder-son" as an archaic version of the role Loki gays as Thor's companion.

Olrik sees, then, Þjálfi and Loki as divergent developments in later mythology of the same figure, the thunder god's servant or companion.

2026. Olrik, Axel. "Tordenguden og hans dreng i Lappernes myteverden." *Danske studier*, 3 (1906), 65-69.

A Lapp myth as the reflection of an archaic trait from Norse mythology: instead of capturing the thunder god's weapon, a giant has captured the god himself.

2027. Olrik, Axel. "Episke love i Gote-ættens oldsagn." *Danske studier*, 4 (1907), 193-201.

In this review of G. Schütte, *Oldsagn om Godtjod* (1907), Olrik demonstrates the presence of such epic laws as *vorvægt* and *bagvægt* and the rule of three, the latter in various Germanic origin stories, including Tuisto/Mannus in Tacitus and Buri/Bórr/Odin in the eddas.

2028. Olrik, Axel. "Et finsk sidestykke til Baldersagnet." *Danske studier*, 4 (1907), 141-42.

Response to K. Krohn, "Lemminkäinens Tod < Christi > Balders Tod" (1905).

2029. Olrik, Axel. "Forårsmyten hos Finnerne." *Danske studier*, 4 (1907), 62-64.

Response to K. Krohn's writings on the relationship between Germanic religion and Finnish folklore ("Sampsa Pellervoinen < Njordr, Freyr?" (1904), and "Lemminkäinens Tod < Christi > Balders Tod" (1905).

2030. Olrik, Axel. "Svinefylkning og 'hamalt': Et par bemærkninger til Sakses sagnverden." *Danske studier*, 4 (1907), 214-20.

Brief references to Odin's role as the discoverer of the military formation *hamalt*.

2031. Olrik, Axel. "Siward Digri of Northumberland: A Viking-Saga of the Danes in England." *Saga-Book of the Viking Society*, 6 (1908-09), 212-37.

Altered version of Danish original, translated by Henry Goddard Leach (fn. 1). Olrik discusses Odinic figures in heroic legend, particularly Rostar in the traditions about Ragnar loðbrók.

2032. Olrik, Axel. "Finsk og lappisk mytologi." *Danske studier*, 5 (1908), 240-41.

Response to K. Krohn, "Lappische Beiträge zur germanischen Mythologie" (1906).

2033. Olrik, Axel. "Loke i nyere folkeoverlevering, I: De vestlige nybygder." *Danske studier*, 5 (1908), 193-207.

This, the first of two articles on Loki in recent folklore, surveys traditions about Loki in the Scandinavian colonies of the western expansion. Topics treated are Lokki in Faroese ballads and tales; Lok' in an English charm; Icelandic and Shetlandic linguistic traces; and the Norwegian fire demon and night troll Lokje.

2034. Olrik, Axel. "At sidde på höj: Oldtidens konger og oldtidens thulir." *Danske studier*, 6 (1909), 1-10.

An interpretation of the textual tradition that kings sit on mounds. Olrik sees it as the reflection of a ceremonial/magical function once filled by Germanic kings and parallel to the soothsaying of the *þulr*.

2035. Olrik, Axel. "Loke i nyere folkeoverlevering, II: De gammelnordiske lande." *Danske studier*, 6 (1909), 69-84.

This, the second of two articles on Loki in recent folklore, treats traditions about Loki in the Scandinavian homelands. Topics covered include: the Danish Lokke as a phenomenon of the air; Lokke/Lokje as a fire figure in Telemark (Norway) and Sweden; Loke as a teasing night figure in Telemark. Here, too, is the conclusion to both articles: Loki/Lokke of folk tradition did not derive from the eddic Loki, but the latter may have borrowed some characteristics from the former, and these may help to unlock some of the puzzles about Loki.

2036. Olrik, Axel. *Danmarks heltedigtning: En oldtidsstudie,* vol. 2, *Starkad den gamle og den yngre Skjoldungrække*. Copenhagen: G. E. C. Gad, 1910. 322 pp.

The second and concluding part of Olrik's study of older Danish heroic traditions, some of which were euhemeristic.

2037. Olrik, Axel. "Gefion." *Danske studier*, 7 (1910), 1-31.

Analysis of the Gefjon myth, with two major parts. The first treats the plowing myth and concludes that it was an origin myth for Sjælland; Gefjon, the plowing goddess, obtained the land from a sea-king, Gylfi, who ruled over the Sjælland-South Scandinavian flatlands, perhaps in the mountain Kullen in Skåne. The second part treats the plowing goddess and her worship. It tries to establish her as a fertility goddess with a fully developed cult. She was once perhaps married to the thunder god. The article ends with appendices on placenames, possibly related Eskimo legends, and Plough Monday in England.

Olrik relies often on modern folklore to support his arguments.

2038. Olrik, Axel. "Irminsul og gudestøtter." *Maal og minne*, 1910, pp. 1-9.

Lapp sacral columns and idols, and the Saxon Irminsûl, as keys to the Nordic high-seat posts: free-standing sacral posts, mythically holding up the world.

2039. Olrik, Axel. "En oldtidshelligdom." *Danske studier*, 8 (1911), 1-14.

On Sevel (Jutland, Denmark), a putative cult site, as placename evidence of ancient settlement patterns.

2040. Olrik, Axel. "Myterne om Loke." In *Festskrift til H. F. Feilberg fra nordiske sprog- og folkemindeforskere på 80 års dagen den 6. august 1911*. 548-93. Svenska landsmål, 1911; Maal og minne, 1911; Danske studier, 1911. Stockholm: Norstedt, Copenhagen: Gyldendal, Oslo (Kristiania): Bymaals-laget, 1911.

Distinguishes four chronological layers of Loki tradition. The oldest had Loki as culture-hero; the second involved cycles centering on Odinic and Thor-like characteristics and affinities; the third, dominant during the Viking Age, involved the evil Loki; and the fourth focused on younger folk traditions. A separate, concluding section treats the etymology and meanings of Loki's name.

See *Maal og minne*, 1912, p. 116, for a comment on this article by Ragnvald Iversen, and *Maal og minne*, 1913, pp. 46-47, for comments by F. Bull and Reidar Th. Christiansen.

2041. Olrik, Axel. "Nyere myteforskning." *Danske studier*, 8 (1911), 37-40.

Review article on mythological research during the period 1904-10, stressing the Lappish and Finnish connections.

2042. Olrik, Axel. "Efterslæt til Loke-myterne, II: Den sidste bog om Loke." *Danske studier*, 9 (1912), 90-95.

Review article on H. Celander, *Lokes mytiska ursprung* (1911).

2043. Olrik, Axel. "Efterslæt til Loke-myterne, III: Lukki og Laviatar i finske tryl-leformler." *Danske studier*, 9 (1912), 95-101.

Note following Olrik's studies on Loki, discussing the evidence from Finnish charms presented by E. N. Setälä, "Louhi und ihre Verwandten" (1912).

2044. Olrik, Axel. "Om Ragnarok, anden afdeling: Ragnaroksforestillingernes udspr-ing." *Danske studier*, 10 (1914), 1-283.

Second part of Olrik's major study of Ragnarǫk, later translated as *Ragnarǫk: Die Vorstellungen vom Weltuntergang* (1922). This portion of the study focuses on origins.

2045. Olrik, Axel. "Svinefylking endnu en gang." *Maal og minne*, 1915, pp. 113-44.

The short section "Odin og svinefylking" (pp. 142-44) attempts to explain Odin's association with the battle formation *svínfylking* by a logical association: so great a genius as was required to create the formation cannot have been mortal. As the cleverest god Odin would naturally have been chosen.

2046. Olrik, Axel. "Eddamytologien." *Nordisk tidskrift*, 1917, pp. 91-93.

According to Olrik, skaldic poetry represents a better source for the study of Germanic religion than does eddic poetry; skalds were imbued with religious tradition, whereas eddic poets had individual artistic freedom.

2047. Olrik, Axel. "Yggdrasil." *Danske studier*, 14 (1917), 49-62.

A study of Yggdrasill, emphasizing the natural background. As ash trees and large stags occur together only in Denmark and western Norway, Olrik assigns the provenance of the motif to this area. He argues further that it must be old, as the transparent etymology, "Odin's steed," relates to no retained narrative. When the motif reached Iceland, the *Vǫluspá* poet reinterpreted tree and stag as supernatural.

2048. Olrik, Axel. "Eddamythologie." *Neue Jahrbücher für das klassische Altertum, Geschichte und deutsche Literatur und für Pädagogik*, 41-42 (1918), 38-48.

The mythology of the eddas. Olrik distinguishes the relative artistic freedom of eddic poets from the fixed forms of the skalds and from less artistic popular conceptions, but he admits that Snorri's version of the mythology builds on eddic and skaldic sources. Above all, eddic mythology—the Poetic Edda and *Snorra edda*—are narrative. In characterizing this mythology, Olrik stresses the dualistic opposition between gods and giants.

2049. Olrik, Axel. "Gudefremstillinger på guldhornene og andre ældre mindesmærker." *Danske studier*, 15 (1919), 1-35. Olrik's remarks end on p. 34, followed by a postscript by G. K. (i.e., Gunnar Knudsen).

Olrik identifies the figures on the Gallehus gold horns as earlier forms of the

Norse gods: Odin with spear and ring, Thor with ax (an early form of his hammer according to Olrik), and the ithyphallic Freyr with staff in one hand and in the other a tool for harvesting grain.

2050. Olrik, Axel. *The Heroic Legends of Denmark*. Scandinavian Monographs, 4. New York: American-Scandinavian Foundation, London: Humphrey Milford, Oxford University Press, 1919. xviii, 530 pp. Translated by Lee M. Hollander. Rpt. Kraus Reprint Co., 1956.

A revised translation of Olrik's *Danmark's heltedigtning*, vol. 1, *Rolf Krake og den ældre Skjoldungrække* (1903). Particularly relevant are the reconstruction of *Bjarkamál*, including the section "Othin in the Biarkamal" (pp. 151-58), and the remarks on "Hrolf's Berserkers" (pp. 348-80) and on Skjǫldr, including the section "Scyld as the Son of Othin" (pp. 429-35).

2051. Olrik, Axel. *Ragnarök: Die Sagen vom Weltuntergang*. Berlin and Leipzig: W. de Gruyter, 1922. xvi, 484 pp. Translated by Wilhelm Ranisch.

Olrik's classic studies of Ragnarǫk are best known in this German version, which combines his "Om Ragnarok" (1902) and "Om Ragnarok, anden afdeling: Ragnaroksforestillingernes udspring" (1914). He traces possible origins and parallels but stresses Scandinavian features. Contents: Sources, motifs from nature (pp. 1-50); the slaughter of the gods (pp. 51-103); renewal (pp. 104-09); *Vǫluspá* (pp. 110-32); the bound giant in the Caucasus (pp. 133-290); the bound wolf (pp. 291-326); the Persian conceptions of Ragnarǫk (pp. 327-62); the burning of the world (pp. 363-98); the destruction of the world among primitive peoples (pp. 399-420); retrospective on the destruction of the world (pp. 421-63); appendix (pp. 464-78); index (pp. 478-84).

Olrik essentially believed in the diffusion of his materials through time and space and found Avestan Persia the source of many of the more important conceptions of Ragnarǫk.

2052. Olrik, Axel. "Odins ridt." *Danske studier*, 22 (1925), 1-18.

An incomplete paper on the second Merseburg charm, printed posthumously with an afterword (pp. 17-18) by Hans Ellekilde. Apparently originally begun as the formal faculty opposition to R. Th. Christiansen's doctoral dissertation, *Die finnischen und nordischen Varianten des zweiten Merseburgerspruches* (1914), the paper stresses the similarities between the charm and eddic mythology and opposes the then prevailing notion that the charm was of Christian origin and should be understood in a Christian context.

2053. Olrik, Axel. "Skjaldemjøden." *Edda*, 24 (1925), 236-41.

Text of a lecture, printed posthumously by Hans Ellekilde. Olrik posits a development from the nature myths of "mankind's childhood" telling of the acquisition of water from a beast guarding it at the end of the world, through the ritual use of a myth telling of the acquisition of the gods' drink (as when Indra obtains soma), to the Norse stage, where the mead has become a symbolic expression of poetry.

2054. Olrik, Axel. *Viking Civilization*. New York: The American-Scandinavian Foundation—W. W. Norton & Co., 1930. 246 pp.

A popular introduction to Norse literature. Chapters relevant to myth and religion include: "The Development of the Myth" (pp. 28-43), "Worship of the Gods" (pp. 44-59), and "Paganism and Christianity" (pp. 128-52). Outmoded but still of interest.

The not always felicitous English translation follows Hans Ellikilde's (lightly) revised 1927 edition of the 1907 Danish original. German and Swedish translations were also undertaken.

2055. Olrik, Axel, and Hans Ellekilde. *Nordens gudeverden*. Copenhagen: G. E. C. Gad, 1926-51. vii, xii, 1184 pp. 2 vols., consecutively paginated.

Handbook of Scandinavian mythology.

2056. Olrik, Jørgen, and Axel Olrik. "Asgård." *Danske studier*, 11 (1914), 1-8.

The title refers not to the stronghold of the gods but to a canal dug during the twelfth century to supply a Danish monastery with water. It is possible, according to the authors, that the canal was so named because of its high walls. If so, we have a popular retention of Norse mythology after the conversion to Christianity.

2057. Ólsen, Björn M. "Små bidrag til tolkningen af Eddasangene." *Arkiv för nordisk filologi*, 9 (1893), 223-35.

Textual notes to, inter alia, *Hávamál* str. 2 and *Lokasenna* str. 3.

2058. Ólsen, Björn M. "Hvar eru Eddukvæðin til orðin?" *Tímarit hins íslenzka bókmenntafélags*, 15 (1894), 1-133.

Criticism of Finnur Jónsson's view on the origin of eddic poetry.

2059. Ólsen, Björn M. "Um Völuspá: Kafli úr firirlestri." *Skírnir*, 86 (1912), 372-75.

On the interplay of pagan and Christian elements in *Vǫluspá*. Whether the poet was pagan or Christian, he was a product of his time (the end of the tenth century) and was moved by sentiments of impending doom: the end of the world in 1000 A. D.

2060. Ólsen, Björn M. "Til Eddakvadene, I: Til Vǫluspá." *Arkiv för nordisk filologi*, 30 (1914), 129-69.

Commentary to *Vǫluspá*, str. 2, 34, 46-47, 50-52, 56.

2061. Ólsen, Björn M. "Til Eddakvadene, II: Til Hávamál." *Arkiv för nordisk filologi*, 31 (1915), 52-95.

Commentary to *Hávamál*, str. 4, 17, 22, 24, 25, 33, 36-37, 41, 52, 53, 54, 58, 66, 69, 73, 74, 83, 90, 107, 127, 135-36, 137, 138, 139, 151, 152.

2062. Ólsen, Björn M. "Hávamál v. 155 (Bugge): Efterslæt til afhandlingen om Hávamál i Arkiv XXXI." *Arkiv för nordisk filologi*, 32 (1916), 71-83.

Extended comment on *Hávamál*, str. 155. Response by L. Fr. Läffler, "Till Hávamáls strof 155" (1915-16).

2063. Ólsen, Björn M. "Um nokkra staði í Svipdagsmálum." *Arkiv för nordisk filologi*, 33 (1917), 1-21.

Commentary to *Grógaldr* (str. 3, 6, 10, 14) and *Fjǫlsvinnsmál* (str. 1-3, 5, 11-12, 13-14, 24, 26, 28, 30, 32, 38).

2064. Ólsen, Björn M. "Til Eddakvadene, III: Til Vafþrúðnismál." *Arkiv för nordisk filologi*, 38 (1922), 195-96.

Commentary to *Vafþrúðnismál*, str. 2.

2065. Olsen, Magnus. *Det gamle norske ønavn Njarðarlǫg*. Christiania videnskabs-selskabets forhandlinger, 1905, 5. Oslo: J. Dybwad, in commission, 1905. 29 pp. Rpt. in Olsen, *Norrøne studier* (1938), pp. 63-85.

Treats the Old Norwegian placename *Njarðarlǫg*. Olsen argues that the name reflects worship of Nerthus/Njord associated with a holy lake; this worship, he suggests, was brought to Norway by the Hǫrðar (Harudes) from Denmark.

2066. Olsen, Magnus. "Til Hávamál strofe 152." *Arkiv för nordisk filologi*, 23 (1907), 189-90.

Textual note to *Hávamál*, str. 152.

2067. Olsen, Magnus. "Hærnavi: En gammel svensk og norsk gudinde." *Norske videnskaps-akademi i Oslo; Forhandlinger i videnskabs-selskabet i Christiania*, 1908, 6 (1908), 1-18.

The placename *Hærnevi* reflects, according to the author, the West Scandinavian name for Freyja, *Hǫrn*, who will have been an important East Scandinavian goddess.

2068. Olsen, Magnus. "Fra gammelnorsk myte og kultus." *Maal og minne*, 1909, pp. 17-36.

Olsen's interpretation of *Skírnismál* is one of the few older myth-ritual readings still frequently cited. The myth derives, according to Olsen, from an early stage of Norse religion, when Freyr was a sky god controlling Draupnir, Hliðskjálf, and the power of runes; these Odin subsequently acquired, as his cult spread in the North. Gerðr's name has to do with *garðr* "yard, farm," and she would represent, thus, the fertility of the earth. From the underworld she follows Freyr's servant, perhaps representative of a ray of sunshine, to meet the sky god, so that she (and the earth) will not wither. The location of their meeting is *barri*, which Olsen understands as "in the seed"; later the *Skírnismál* poet misunderstood the old dative as a placename.

From a mythological and philological perspective, this interpretation appears rather speculative.

2069. Olsen, Magnus. "Tjǫsnur og tjǫsnublót." *Arkiv för nordisk filologi*, 26 (1910), 342-46.

Tjǫsnur were the pegs used to mark the field for a duel. Proceeding etymologically, Olsen finds that *tjasna* (singular) meant "phallus" and argued for a consequent connection between duel and fertility ritual.

2070. Olsen, Magnus. "Hvad betyder oprindelig ordet skald?" In *Festskrift til H. F. Feilberg fra nordiske sprog- og folkemindeforskere på 80 års dagen den 6. august 1911*. 221-25. Svenska landsmål, 1911; Maal og minne, 1911; Danske studier, 1911. Stockholm: Norstedt, Copenhagen: Gyldendal, Oslo (Kristiania): Bymaals-laget, 1911.

Olsen argues that *skáld* derives from a Germanic root **skawa-* and means "he who pays attention," i.e., who has contact with supernatural wisdom and powers. Olsen then attempts to apply this distinction to the description of the priest of the Nerthus cult in *Germania*, ch. 40.

2071. Olsen, Magnus. "Kung Orre: Et bidrag til gammel nordisk folketro." *Maal og minne*, 1912, pp. 1-26.

In seeking to explain the Swedish exression *på Kung Orres tid* "in King Orre's time, i.e., long ago," Olsen postulates a winter festival and sacrifice during the Old Scandinavian month *Þorri* and a mythic personification of the month with the same name. Then **blót-Þorri* > **blot-torre* > **blot-orre*, whence finally King Orre. There is little compelling evidence for these assumptions.

See *Maal og minne*, 1912, p. 114, for comments on this subject by Oluf Kolsrud and B. Symons. Hugo Jungner rejected the entire hypothesis in an article entitled "Om kung Orre: Några funderingar" (1914).

2072. Olsen, Magnus. *Stednavnestudier*. Oslo: Aschehoug, 1912. 130 pp.

Includes essays on "Gevjons pløining og ønavnet Sjælland" (proposes an etymology for the placename Sjælland based on a hypothetical **sulhf-* "plow" and thereby associated with the myth of Gefjon's plowing) and "Fitjungs søner" (associates the sons of Fitjungr (*Hávamál* 78) with the placename Fitjar, Norway).

2073. Olsen, Magnus. "Spredte bemerkninger til Eddadigte." In *Festskrift til Professor Alf Torp paa hans 60 aars fødelsedag 27. september 1913.* 115-21. Kristiania (Oslo): H. Aschehoug, 1913.

Includes notes on *Skírnismál*, str. 19, and *Lokasenna*, str. 47.

2074. Olsen, Magnus. *Hedenske kultminder i norske stedsnavne.* Skrifter utg. av det norske videnskaps-akademi i Oslo, hist.-filos. kl., 1914, 2:4. Oslo: J. Dybwad in commission, 1915. x, 315 pp.

Olsen's first major study of pagan placenames in Norway. The focus is on Oppland, whose cult remnants Olsen explores in great detail, but the chart on pp. 73-78 indicates the distribution of theophoric placenames throughout Norway.

2075. Olsen, Magnus. "Om troldruner." *Edda*, 5 (1916), 225-45. Rpt. as vol. 2 of Fordomtima, Skriftserie, utg. av Oskar Lundberg, (Uppsala, 1917), and in Olsen, *Norrøne studier* (1938), pp. 1-23, there with the modern spelling "Om trollruner."

Magic runes in the elder and younger futhark. Special attention to Egill Skallagrímsson's *níðvísur.*

2076. Olsen, Magnus. "Varðlokur: Et bidrag til kundskap om gammelnorsk trolddom." *Maal og minne*, 1916, pp. 1-21.

Varðlokur is the term used for the song sung by women to accompany the seeress's performance in *Eiríks saga rauða*, ch. 4. Olsen associates the first component with *vǫrðr* "guardian," a word sometimes connected with the otherworld, and the entire term *warlock.* He concludes that *varðlokur* originally were the persons who accompanied the performance of a seeress.

Henrik Ussing, Heinz Hungerland, and the author contributed additional notes on the topic in *Maal og minne*, 1917, pp. 65-66.

2077. Olsen, Magnus. "Ullevaal." *Maal og minne*, 1917, pp. 47-50. Rpt. in Olsen, *Norrøne studier* (1938), pp. 102-05.

On the second component of the Norwegian farm name *Ullevaal* (the first component being, presumably, the name of the god Ullr). Olsen argues that *-vaal* is equivalent to Old Norse *hváll* "hill" and adduces examples of cult activities on small hills.

2078. Olsen, Magnus. "'Bú er betra—': En tekstrettelse til Hávamál 36, 37." *Maal og minne*, 1918, pp. 60-68. Rpt. in Olsen, *Norrøne studier* (1938), pp. 169-77.

Textual note.

2079. Olsen, Magnus. "Fröi og Pellon-Pekko." *Arkiv för nordisk filologi*, 34 (1918), 174-75.

Corrects a reading imputed to Olsen in W. von Unwerth, "Fiolnir" (1917).

2080. Olsen, Magnus. "Er 'han' i upersonlige uttrykk Njord?" *Maal og minne*, 1920, pp. 101-02.

Rejects the notion of K. Kopperstad, "Det pers. pron. 'Hann' som subjekt for 'upersonlege' verber" (1920), that Njord may be the underlying subject of the sentence *hann rignir* "it is raining."

2081. Olsen, Magnus. "Haneberg og Hanehaug." *Namn och bygd*, 8 (1920), 35-39.

Includes remarks on a possible cult of Freyr.

2082. Olsen, Magnus. "Til Rök-indskriften." *Arkiv för nordisk filologi*, 37 (1921), 201-32.

Reads the Rök runic inscription as virtually entirely an expansion of the formula "May Thor hallow this monument." This reflects, he concludes, an East Scandinavian version of Thor, known as much for his wisdom as for his strength.

2083. Olsen, Magnus. "Cruces eddicae I." *Arkiv för nordisk filologi*, 39 (1923), 303-20.

Philological notes on *Alvíssmál* 3 and *Rígsþula* 32.

2084. Olsen, Magnus. *Minner om guderne og deres dyrkelse i norske stedsnavn*. Oslo: P. F. Steensballes boghandel, 1923. 40 pp.

Separate printing of the author's contribution to the third edition of P. A. Munch's *Norrøne gude- og heltesagn* (1922), where it replaced an essay by Olaf Rygh. After a summary of the various elements of theophoric placenames, Olsen surveys Norway, district by district.

2085. Olsen, Magnus. "Om Balder-digtning og Balder-kultus." *Arkiv för nordisk filologi*, 40 (1924), 148-75.

Argues that traditions about Baldr derive from a pagan parody of the cult of Christ.

2086. Olsen, Magnus. "Hjadningekampen og Hallfreds arvedraapa over Olaf Tryggvason." In *Heidersskrift til Marius Hægstad fra vener og æresveinar 15de juli 1925*. 23-33. Oslo: O. Norli, 1925.

Hallfreðr's *Erfidrápa Óláfs Tryggvasonar* as a source of the traditions about the *Hjaðningavíg*.

2087. Olsen, Magnus. "Kǫrmt og Örmt." In *Germanica: Eduard Sievers zum 75. Geburtstage 25. November 1925*. 247-57. Halle a. d. S.: M. Niemeyer, 1925. Rpt. in Olsen, *Norrøne studier* (1938), pp. 178-88.

On the river names *Kǫrmt* and *Örmt* in *Grímnismál* 29. Olsen argues that they were invented by the poet, probably with the myth of Thor's journey to Geirrøðr in mind.

2088. Olsen, Magnus. *Ættegård og helligdom: Norske stedsnavn sosialt og religionshistorisk belyst*. Instituttet for sammenlignende kulturforskning, ser. A: Forelesninger, 9A. Oslo: H. Aschehoug (W. Nygaard), Leipzig: O. Harrassowitz, Paris: H. Champion, 1926. 302 pp.

Norwegian original of *Farms and Fanes of Ancient Norway* (1928).

2089. Olsen, Magnus. "'Haldit maðr á keri—': Bidrag till Edda-tolkning (Hávamál 19)." *Maal og minne*, 1926, pp. 103-109. Rpt. in Olsen, *Norrøne studier* (1938), pp. 158-65.

Interprets the sentiment of the strophe thus: one should drink neither too little (holding one's cup while others drink off theirs) nor too much.

2090. Olsen, Magnus. "Hávamál 33." In *Festskrift til Hjalmar Falk fra elever, venner og kolleger*. 202-04. Oslo: H. Aschehoug, 1927.

Brief textual note. The sentiment of the strophe is that one should not eat as early as usual before visiting, so as to avoid an appetite that eliminates one from conversation.

2091. Olsen, Magnus. *Farms and Fanes of Ancient Norway: The Place-Names of a Country Discussed in their Bearings on Social and Religious History*. Instituttet for sammenlignende kulturforskning, ser. A: Forelesninger, 9. Oslo: H. Aschehoug (W. Nygaard), Leipzig: O. Harrassowitz, Paris: H. Champion, 1928. xiv, 349 pp.

English translation (by Th. Gleditsch) of Olsen's *Ættegård og helligdom* (1926). This remains the classic study of social history and theophoric place-names in a Nordic country, although it may now be regarded as somewhat exaggerated. The first eight chapters are given over largely to social history, but to Olsen social history included also the history of religion and cult, so these receive regular treatment, especially in Chapter 8 on the parish names. Chapter 9 treats the placename elements *hof* and *hǫrgr* and analyzes religious continuity, and Olsen devotes Chapter 10, the final chapter, to "The Great Sanctuaries" (i.e., public cult) and to mythology, specifically the placename element *skjálf* as supposed representation of myths of Odin and Baldr.

2092. Olsen, Magnus. "Hávamál 33." In *Festskrift til Finnur Jónsson 29. maj 1928.* 202-204. Copenhagen: Levin & Munksgaard, 1928.

Interpretation of the verse and the custom behind it.

2093. Olsen, Magnus. "En iakttagelse vedkommende Balder-diktningen." In *Studier tillägnade Axel Kock, tidskriftens redaktör, 1888-1925.* 169-77. Arkiv för nordisk filologi, 40, supplement. Lund: C. W. K. Gleerup, 1929. Also issued separately, under title *Studier tillägnade Axel Kock.*

On *Hávamál* 160-63 (the final four stanzas of the *ljóðatal*) and more specifically on the Odin name *Hroptatýr* (*Hávamál* 160 and elsewhere). *Hávamál* 160-63 all have to do, according to Olsen, with the Baldr myth: Odin refers to the rune magic which enabled him to seduce Rindr and thus beget an avenger for Baldr. *Hroptatýr* would then, whenever the name is used, refer regularly to this mythologem. Its first component, *Hroptr*, belonged originally to a sacral poetry celebrating Odin as master of magic.

2094. Olsen, Magnus. *Stedsnavn og gudeminner i Land.* Avhandlinger utgitt av det norske videnskaps-akademi i Oslo, II. hist.-filos. kl., 1929, 3. Oslo: J. Dybwad, in commission, 1929. 95 pp. Rpt. in O. Kolsrud and R. Th. Christiansen, ed., *Boka om Land*, 2 (1952), 55-126.

Includes a section on theophoric and cult names in Land, Norway. Njord, Freyr, and Ullinn (Ullr) are represented.

2095. Olsen, Magnus. "Valhall med de mange dörer." *Acta Philologica Scandinavica*, 6 (1931-32), 157-70. Rpt. in Olsen, *Norrøne studier* (1938), pp. 109-29.

Olsen explores the possibility that Roman ampitheatres may have influenced the conception of Valhalla in Norse literature. The Colosseum offers a particularly tempting model, for crowds issued daily from its many doors and scenes of combat took place within. Despite its plausibility, this hypothesis has not gained general favor.

2096. Olsen, Magnus. "Cruces eddicae II." *Arkiv för nordisk filologi*, 47 (1931), 216-26.

Philological notes on *Hymiskviða* 37, *Lokasenna* 10 and 39, *Þrymskviða* 28.

2097. Olsen, Magnus. "Yddal (*Ýdalr) i Strandvik." *Maal og minne*, 1931, pp. 131-33. Rpt. in Olsen, *Fra norrøn filologi* (1949), pp. 85-88

Response to O. Hanssen, "Stadnamn med voksternamn," which immediately precedes it in this number of *Maal og minne.* Olsen agrees that the farm-name *Yddal* may derive from older *ýdalr* "yew-dale" and thus is identical with the name of Ullr's dwelling. Olsen finds the worldly "yew-dale" to have been the model, and not vice-versa, and since alliteration between *ýdalr* and Ullr could occur only after loss of initial *w-* in **wulþuz* (> Ullr) during the seventh century, the equation must be limited to the last centuries of paganism.

2098. Olsen, Magnus. "Fra Eddaforskningen: Grímnismál og den höiere textkritikk." *Arkiv för nordisk filologi*, 49 (1933), 263-78. Rpt. in Olsen, *Norrøne studier* (1938), pp. 130-44, with supplement, pp. 144-49.

The text of an address delivered at the Seventh meeting of Nordic philologists held in Lund in August, 1932. Olsen proceeds through the text, arguing coherence and internal consistency and denying interpolation and patchwork. The poem takes its structure from its situation and follows Odin's visions between the fires; its intent is not didactic. The supplement draws a parallel to the myth of Odin's self-sacrifice in *Hávamál.* It follows the Norwegian manuscript on which Olsen's lectures in France in 1933 were based; these were printed as "Le prêtre-magicien et le dieu-magicien" (1935).

2099. Olsen, Magnus. "Fra Hávamál til Krákumál." In *Festskrift til Halvdan Koht på sextiårsdagen 7de juli 1933.* 93-103. Oslo: H. Aschehoug, 1933. Rpt. in Olsen, *Norrøne studier* (1938), pp. 234-44.

The influence of *Hávamál* on *Krákumál.*

2100. Olsen, Magnus. "Helkunduheiðr." *Namn och bygd*, 21 (1933), 12-27.

Olsen explains this Icelandic placename as "the heath of a being descended from Hel" (**helkunda*), i.e., a troll.

2101. Olsen, Magnus. "Þundarbenda." *Maal og minne*, 1934, pp. 92-97.

The title refers to a name applied by Glúmr to his son in *Víga-Glúms saga* (ch. 23); Olsen thinks it may mean "omen from Odin."

2102. Olsen, Magnus. *Universitetets radioforedrag: Hvad våre stedsnavn lærer oss.* Oslo: J. M. Stenersen, 1934. 66 pp.

Texts of popular radio addresses, one on reflections of paganism in Norwegian placenames.

2103. Olsen, Magnus. "Le prêtre-magicien et le dieu-magicien dans la Norvège ancienne." *Revue de l'histoire des religions*, 111 (1935), 177-221.

Olsen finds the "magician-priest" on the text of the Kårstad runic inscription: the runemaster, according to Olsen, says he is one of the Boii (an ancient Germanic people); and Olsen understands the reference, as he understands runic *erilaR*, as denoting the magician in a sacral context. Olsen finds the magician-god in *Grímnismál*, in the person of Odin, who gains divine power and averts the threat of Ragnarǫk. Much of this discussion, but not the conclusion, was prefigured in Olsen's "Fra eddaforskningen" (1933).

Also treated is the role of the priest in connection with fertility deities and Olsen's contention about the origin of Valhalla, already published in "Valholl med de mange dører" (1931).

2104. Olsen, Magnus. "Commentarii scaldici, I: 1, Sonatorrek." *Arkiv för nordisk filologi*, 52 (1936), 209-55.

Textual notes to *Sonatorrek*. In discussing str. 22, Olsen analyzes Egill's attitude toward Odin and his status as an Odinic hero.

2105. Olsen, Magnus. "Gjøre bro for ens sjel." *Maal og minne*, 1936, pp. 210-12. Rpt. in Olsen, *Norrøne studer* (1938), pp. 24-27.

The title refers to the custom of building a bridge for the soul of the dead, as mentioned in many runestones. Olsen sets the practice in association with pagan conceptions of the difficult and dangerous journey to the world of the dead.

2106. Olsen, Magnus. "Runespennen fra Bratsberg i Gjerpen, 2: Runeinnskriften." *Viking*, 1 (1937), 61-73. Rpt. in Olsen, *Fra norrøn filologi* (1949), pp. 30-42.

The second part of a description of a runic find (the first part, by Bjørn Hougen (pp. 53-60), treats the circumstances of the find and the style and dating of the artifact). Olsen discusses the sacral terms *erilaR* and *gudija*.

2107. Olsen, Magnus. "Kǫgurbarn og kǫgursveinn." *Maal og minne*, 1940, pp. 9-16. Rpt. in Olsen, *Fra norrøn filologi* (1949), pp. 271-78.

Thor calls Odin a *kǫgursveinn* in *Hárbarðsljóð* 13 and is in turn called one by Útgarða-Loki in *Gylfaginning*; the term derives, according to Olsen, from the more widely attested *kǫgurbarn*. Olsen explains the term as a compound with *kǫgurr* "coarsely woven cloth"; this would suit giants and those in the lowest social orders and hence would be a term of opprobrium.

2108. Olsen, Magnus. "Reynir er bjǫrg Þórs." *Maal og minne*, 1940, pp. 145-46. Rpt. in Olsen, *Fra norrøn filologi* (1949), pp. 89-91.

Olsen claims to find the origin of the supposed proverb that the rowan is Thor's rescuer, attested in the account of Thor's visit to Geirrøðr in *Snorra edda*, in the Norwegian custom of using scraped bark, particularly from the rowan, for fodder in times of need. Thus this motif would be Norwegian and hence would antedate the settlement of Iceland.

2109. Olsen, Magnus. *Sigtuna-amuletten: Nogen tolkningsbidrag.* Avhandlinger utgitt av det norske videnskaps-akademie i Oslo, II. hist.-filos. kl., 1940, 3. Oslo: J. Dybwad, in commission, 1940. 48 pp.

Argues that the Sigtuna amulet makes reference to Thor, who will raise his hammer against the wolf mentioned later in the inscription.

2110. Olsen, Magnus. "Kultminne i stadnamn, 3: Norge." In *Religionhistorie*, ed. Nils Lid, 59-73. Stockholm: A. Bonnier, Oslo: H. Aschehoug, Copenhagen: J. H. Schultz, 1942.

Exuberant survey of references to cult in Norwegian placenames.

2111. Olsen, Magnus. "Ti lønnstaver." *Maal og minne*, 1948, pp. 122-24.

This interpretation of secret charms in *Egils saga* calls on *Skírnismál* 36 in the context of magic charms against a woman's happiness.

2112. Olsen, Magnus. *Fra norrøn filologi*. Oslo: H. Aschehoug, 1949. 308 pp.

A collection of the author's earlier essays. Those relevant to Norse mythology and religion and entered separately in this bibliography include: "Yddal (*Ýdalr) i Strandvik" (1931), pp. 85-88; "Runespennen fra Bratsberg i Gjerpen" (1937), pp. 30-42; "Kǫgurbarn og kǫgursveinn" (1940), pp. 271-78; and "Reynir er bjǫrg Þórs" (1940), pp. 89-91.

2113. Olsen, Magnus. "Nykøbing-innskriften." *Acta Philologica Scandinavica*, 22 (1952), 1-10. Summary in English, p. 10.

Olsen finds the beginning of a futhark on this inscription (*Danmarks runeindskrifter*, no. 244) and argues that protective supernatural powers were attributed to such inscriptions (p. 10).

2114. Olsen, Magnus. *Edda- og skaldedvad: Forarbeidar til kommentar,* vol. 5: *Hávamál*. Avhandlinger utgitt av det norske vitenskaps-akademie i Oslo, II. hist.-filos. kl., n.s. 3. Oslo: Universitetsforlaget, 1960. 58 pp.

Commentary on the eddic poem *Hávamál.*

2115. Olsen, Magnus. *Edda- og skaldekvad: Forarbeidar til kommentar,* vol.*1: Hárbarðsljóð*. Avhandlinger utgitt av det norske vitenskaps-akademie i Oslo, II. hist.-filos. kl., 1960, 1. Oslo: Aschehoug (in commission), 1960. 89 pp.

Commentary on the eddic poem *Hárbarðsljóð*.

2116. Olsen, Magnus. *Edda- og skaldekvad: Forarbeidar til kommentar,* vol. 2: *Lokasenna*. Avhandlinger utgitt av det norske vitenskaps-akademie i Oslo, II. hist.-filos. kl., 1960, 3. Oslo: Aschehoug (in commission), 1960. 56 pp.

Commentary on the eddic poem *Lokasenna*.

2117. Olsen, Magnus. *Edda- og skaldekvad: Forarbeidar til kommentar,* vol. 6: *Eyvindr Skáldaspillir, Glúmr Geirason, Einarr Skálaglamm*. Avhandlinger utgitt av det norske vitenskaps-akademie i Oslo, II. hist.-filos. kl., n.s. 4. Oslo: Universitetsforlaget, 1962. 53 pp.

Commentaries on the verse of three later tenth-century skalds. Of special interest is the thorough treatment of Eyvindr's *Hákonarmál.*

2118. Olsen, Magnus. *Edda- og skaldekvad: Forarbeidar til kommentar,* vol. 7: *Gudedikte.* Avhandlinger utgitt av det norske vitenskaps-akademie i Oslo, II. hist.-filos. kl., n.s. 5. Oslo: Universitetsforlaget, 1964. 57 pp.

Comments on selected passages from *Vǫluspá, Vafþrúðnismál, Grímnismál, Hymiskviða,* and *Alvíssmál*; overall interpretation of *Skírnismál.*

2119. Olsen, Olaf. "Hørg, hov og kirke: Historiske og arkæologiske vikingetidsstudier." *Årbøger for nordisk oldkyndighed og historie,* 1966, pp. 1-307. Also diss. Copenhagen. Summary in English.

This important monograph treats as its major theme the continuity of worship from paganism to Christianity in Scandinavia, primarily by gauging the extent "to which worship took place in association with sacral buildings at the end of the heathen period" (p. 277). It subjects both written and archaeological materials to rigorous scrutiny and concludes that early Christian churches were not built on pagan sacral ground. Pagan worship seldom if ever took place in enclosed buildings. The *hǫrgr,* originally a pile of stones central to nature worship, may in the course of time have been covered, and the *hof* may have had extensive secular usage. Indeed, most remains associated with pagan worship may be interpreted as dwellings or similar structures.

After introductory and methodological chapters, the work treats cult buildings in historical sources (pp. 19-54), the temple at Uppsala (pp. 116-66), other archaeological evidence (pp. 167-235), and the correlation of cult place and church (pp. 236-75). With its critical sense and extensive reference, Olsen's work is one of the important studies of Nordic paganism of recent times.

2120. Olsen, Olaf. "Die alte Gesellschaft und die neue Kirche." In *Kirche und Gesellschaft im Ostseeraum und im Norden vor der Mitte des 13. Jahrhunderts.* 43-54. Acta Visbyensia, 3; Visby-symposiet för historiska vetenskaper 1967. Visby: Museum Gotlands Fornsal, 1969.

Lecture delivered at an international symposium on church and society in Scandinavia and the Baltic before the mid-thirteenth century; offers programmatic treatment of the relationship among social structure, paganism, and early Christianity, with important implications. Olsen argues that ancient cult was neither highly structured nor primarily public, but mostly a matter of large social movements and private or family cult, with emphasis on wealthy landowners. According to this reasoning, conversion to Christianity cannot have been instituted from above, without receptive attitudes among these wealthy landowners and their dependents. Olsen devotes the latter part of his essay to the case of Denmark and suggests that the early, relatively easy conversion to Christianity was conditioned by contact with the Christian Danelaw.

2121. Olsen, Olaf. "Vorchristliche Heiligtümer in Nordeuropa." In *Vorgeschichtliche Heiligtümer und Opferplätze in Mittel- und Nordeuropa: Bericht über ein Symposium in Reinhausen bei Göttingen vom 14.-16. Oktober 1968,* ed. Herbert Jankuhn, 259-78. Abhandlungen der Akademie der Wissenschaften in

Göttingen, phil.-hist. Kl., 3. Folge, 74. Göttingen: Vandenhoeck & Ruprecht, 1970.

Negative evaluation of the evidence of pre-Christian temples and the like in Scandinavia; cf. Olsen, *Hørg, hov og kirke* (1966).

2122. Olsen, Olaf. "The 'Sanctuary' at Jelling, With Some Observations on Jelling's Significance in the Viking Age." *Mediaeval Scandinavia*, 7 (1974), 226-34.

Part of a larger discussion, with various participants, on "Jelling problems." Olsen argues against the notion that there was a *vé* "sanctuary" at Jelling.

2123. Olson, Emil. "Ortnamn och bebyggelseshistoria." *Ymer*, 48 (1928), 111-18.

Commentary on M. Olsen, *Ættegård og helligdom* (1926).

2124. Olson, Emil. "Neuere Beiträge zur altnordischen Religionsgeschichte." *Archiv für Religionswissenschaft*, 31 (1934), 213-71.

Critical research survey.

2125. Olson, Oscar L. "The Relation of the Hrólfs saga Kraka and the Bjarkarímur to Beowulf." *Scandinavian Studies*, 3 (1916), 1-104.

With remarks on the apearance of Odin in the Norse texts (pp. 17-19).

2126. Opland, Jeff. *Anglo-Saxon Oral Poetry: A Study of the Traditions.* New Haven and London: Yale University Press, 1980. xi, 289 pp.

Although focusing on Anglo-Saxon oral poetry, this work is useful for the light it throws on oral poetry and its contexts, particularly as it sifts the evidence of divine inspiration and a poetry related to Woden/Odin.

2127. Oppel, Horst. "Lebensgeschichte des altgermanischen Götterlieds." *Zeitschrift für Deutschkunde*, 54 (1940), 305-20.

On the difficulties of reconstructing ancient Germanic religious poetry. The mythological poems of the Poetic Edda, the obvious major point of departure, cannot live up to their promise for this purpose, as they are too clearly bound up with their own period and area.

2128. Opsund, Enok. *Snorre Sturlasson: Den norrøne gudeheimen, Gylfaginning og gudesegnene i Skáldskaparmál og Snorra edda.* Oslo: O. Norli, 1929. 144 pp.

Norwegian translation of *Gylfaginning* and mythological passages from *Skáldskaparmál*.

2129. Ordish, T. Fairman. "English Folk-Drama: II." *Folk-Lore*, 4 (1893), 149-75.

Gefjon and the Plough-Monday play (pp. 163-65).

2130. Orluf, Fr. "Gefionmythen hos Brage den gamle." *Danske studier*, 20 (1923), 22-30.

Essentially a discussion of Snorri's use of the Gefjon myth and Bragi's Gefjon stanza. Orluf believes that Snorri misunderstood the verse and created a myth of Gefjon plowing in Sweden.

2131. Orluf, Fr. "Hærormene fra Lindholm og Kragehul." *Danske studier*, 28 (1931), 60-74.

No numerological magic on the Lindholm runic amulet.

2132. Orluf, Fr. "Runestenene i Jelling." *Vejle amts årbog*, 1943, pp. 99-126.

Proposes reading the word *kændusk* on the larger Jelling stone, which yields the interpretation that King Harald "adjudged" the Danes Christian in a kind of legal action. If correct (which few have accepted), the supposition would have implications concerning the nature of royal power in Denmark's conversion to Christianity.

2133. Osborn, Marijane. "The Finnsburg Raven and *Guðrinc Astah*." *Folklore*, 81 (1970), 185-94.

On two Old English passages, the Finnsburg fragment and *Beowulf* 1118. Osborne associates both with a more widely Celtic-Germanic bird psychopomp. "I suggest that this mythic association of ravens, women and war, which survives in both cultures in early inscriptions and in later literature, reflects an actual ritual correspondence between the prognostic raven that hovers over battles and the priestess who chants prophecies at the funerals of fallen warriors" (p. 188).

Óskar Halldórsson, *see* Halldórsson, Óskar.

2134. Osterman, Anna Z. "En studie över landskapet i Vǫluspá." *Scripta Islandica*, 4 (1953), 15-30.

Although the article promises, and to some extent delivers, a discussion of the landscape of *Vǫluspá*, it is perhaps most noteworthy because it goes on to suggest that Brennu-Njáll, the eponymous sage of *Njáls saga*, may have composed the poem.

2135. Owen, Gale R. *Rites and Religions of the Anglo-Saxons*. Newton Abbot, Devon: David & Charles, Totowa, N. J.: Barnes & Noble, 1981. 216 pp.

A presentation of the sources for the study of Anglo-Saxon paganism and early Christianity. The opening chapter, "Gods and Legends," draws on Scandinavian materials.

P

2136. Paasche, Fredrik. *Snorre Sturlason og Sturlungerne*. Oslo: Aschehoug, 1922. x, 359 pp.

A discussion of Snorri and his family, based largely on *Sturlunga saga*.

2137. Paasche, Fredrik. *Møtet mellom hedendom og kristendom i Norden: Olaus Petri-forelesninger ved Uppsala universitet våren 1941*. Ed. Dag Strömbäck. Oslo: H. Aschehoug (W. Nygaard), 1958. 163 pp.

These eight lectures on the meeting between paganism and Christianity are preceded by introductory essays on the author and his theories and followed by a selection of notes, all this provided by the editor, Dag Strömbäck. The text proper (pp. 73-155) provides a broad survey, from the Christian mission through the high points of Icelandic literature.

2138. Page, R. I. "Dumézil Revisited." *Saga-Book of the Viking Society*, 20 (1978-79), 49-69.

Criticism of the philological details of Dumézil's theories as applied to Norse mythology.

2139. Palm, Thede. "Der Kult der Naharvalen." *Archiv für Religionswissenschaft*, 36 (1939), 398-405.

On the account in *Germania*, ch. 43, on the cult of the Naharvales, illuminated by the Kivik (Sweden) grave monument and by modern lore. Palm's conclusion is that the description given by Tacitus is likely to be genuine and that the cult act is wholly Germanic.

2140. Palm, Thede. "Stav och blotträ." *Namn och bygd*, 28 (1940), 15-19.

Palm suggests that a "holy tree" replaced the notion of a phallus cult in certain placenames in *-stav* relating to Njord/Nerthus.

2141. Palm, Thede. "Uppsalalunden och Uppsalatemplet." *Vetenskapssocietetens i Lund årsbok*, 1941, pp. 79-109.

The central burden of the argument is that the cult in Uppsala, with its grove, spring, and tree, was separate from and anterior to the temple at Uppsala. The location of the altars in the temple, with Thor the most important, is evidence of the origin of the temple in the late Viking Age.

The article includes much discussion of cult and temple in Scandinavia.

2142. Palm, Thede. *Trädkult: Studier i germansk religionshistoria*. Skrifter utgivna av vetenskaps-societeten i Lund, 33. Lund: C. W. K. Gleerup, 1948. 131 pp. Summary in English, pp. 125-29.

Monographic treatment of tree cult in Germanic religion. Topics discussed include sacral groves, the grove of the Semnones (Tacitus, *Germania*, ch. 39), the Donar-oak in Geismar, the Irminsûl, and sacrificial poles.

2143. Palme, Sven Ulrik. "Die Kirche in der Gesellschaft der Landschaftsgesetze." In *Kirche und Gesellschaft im Ostseeraum und im Norden vor der Mitte des 13. Jahrhunderts*. 55-63. Acta Visbyensia, 3; Visby-symposiet för historiska vetenskaper 1967. Visby: Museum Gotlands Fornsal, 1969.

Lecture delivered at an international symposium on church and society in Scandinavia and the Baltic before the mid-thirteenth century; treats the attitude toward paganism in early Swedish laws as a source-critical question.

2144. Palmér, Johan. "Baldersbrå." *Arkiv för nordisk filologi*, 34 (1918), 138-47.

On the plant name *Baldersbrå* (Old Norse *Baldrs brár*), which Snorri (*Gylfaginning*, ch. 22) equates with the brows of Baldr. Palmér offers a different etymology and sees the connection with Baldr as a learned conjecture, perhaps first undertaken by Snorri himself.

2145. Palmér, Johan. "Luggude härads namn." *Sydsvenska ortnamnssällskapets årsskrift*, 1925, pp. 19-24.

The term *Luggude härad* may mean "folk-god's district," in which case one is dealing with public rather than private cult.

2146. Palmér, Johan. "Sigrdrífumál 13." In *Festskrift til Finnur Jónsson 29. maj 1928*. 244-51. Copenhagen: Levin & Munksgaard, 1928.

Parallels between *Sigrdrífumál* 13-14 and *Hávamál* 139-40. *Sigrdrífumál* 13 means "Odin created *hugrúnar* after drinking the mead of poetry."

2147. Palmér, Johan. "Till Vǫluspá." In *Studier tillägnade Axel Kock, tidskriftens redaktör, 1888-1925*. 108-18. Arkiv för nordisk filologi, 40, supplement. Lund: C. W. K. Gleerup, 1929. Also issued separately, under title *Studier tillägnade Axel Kock*.

On *Vǫluspá* 16-17, the creation of human beings. Palmér attempts an astrological explanation: *lá* means "blood"; Hœnir is a sun god; Lóðurr is Mars; *iviþi* means "in space."

2148. Palmér, Johan. "Betydelseutvecklingen i isl. heiðr." *Acta Philologica Scandinavica*, 5 (1930-31), 289-304.

Semantic history of *heiðr*. The first section (pp. 289-93) treats the development from "shine" to "honor" and includes remarks on "shining" as an epithet for gods; here Ullr receives special mention. Later the association of the root with magic and magicians is discussed.

2149. Pálsson, Hermann. "Áss hinn almáttki." *Skírnir*, 130 (1956), 187-92.

Argues that *áss hinn almáttki* "the all-powerful god," called on in oaths, was Ullr. The god will have maintained his legal function, according to Hermann Pálsson, long after he ceased to be worshipped in Iceland.

2150. Pálsson, Hermann. "Átrúnaður Hrafnkels Freysgoða." *Skírnir*, 142 (1968), 68-72.

On the change of religious faith attributed to Hrafnkell Freysgoði "Freyr's priest" in the saga bearing his name. Hermann Pálsson doubts the authenticity of the saga's remarks about Hrafnkell's paganism and questions the use of any family sagas in the study of Norse paganism.

2151. Pappenheim, Max. "Zum ganga undir jarðarmen." *Zeitschrift für deutsche Philologie*, 24 (1892), 157-61.

On the brotherhood ritual of going under earth together, stressing its symbolic nature.

2152. Patch, Howard. *The Other World According to Descriptions in Medieval Literature.* Smith College Studies in Modern Languages, n. s., 1. Cambridge: Harvard University Press, 1950. ix, 386 pp. Rpt. New York: Octagon Books, 1970.

Contains a discussion of "Germanic mythology" (pp. 60-79), based largely on the primary sources. Five features distinguish the Germanic conceptions: 1) it is surrounded by a river barrier; 2) the river is fiercely dangerous; 3) the bridge is a steady feature; 4) the road thither is through a dark forest; 5) it may be located in a rocky mountain.

2153. Patzig, Hermann. "Zum Text der Liederedda." *Zeitschrift für deutsches Altertum*, 58 (1920), 65-87.

Philological notes to eddic poems.

2154. Patzig, Hermann. "Zur Etymologie von Muspilli." *Zeitschrift für vergleichende Sprachforschung*, 53 (1925), 86-88.

Derives the first component of *Muspilli*, medieval German term for the destruction of the world, from *mund* "time."

2155. Paulsen, Peter. *Axt und Kreuz bei den Nordgermanen.* Deutsches Ahnenerbe, Reihe B: Fachwissenschaftliche Untersuchungen, Arbeiten zur Ur-, Vor- und Frühgeschichte, 1. Berlin: Ahnenerbe-Stiftung-Verlag, 1939. 267 pp.

Archaeological discussion of ax and cross in Germanic (primarily viking) culture, with remarks on the religious-historical context. 158 illustrations.

2156. Pedersen, Jørg., Gudmund Schütte, Knud B. Jensen, and Gunnar Knudsen. "Er *Tørrild* et *Thor-hillæ*?" *Danske studier*, 43 (1946-47), 135-41.

Four authors debate the possibility that the Danish placename Tørrild may be compounded with the name of the god Thor.

2157. Pering, Birger. "Den fornnordiska gudavärlden: Dess uppkomst och möte med kristendomen." *Svensk teologisk kvartalsskrift*, 17 (1941), 219-27.

One hardly has any right to expect in eight pages full treatment of the origin of the world of the Norse gods and its meeting with Christianity. Remarks on Heimdallr are included.

2158. Pering, Birger. *Heimdall: Religionsgeschichtliche Untersuchungen zum Verständnis der altnordischen Götterwelt.* Lund: C. W. K. Gleerup, 1941. 298 pp.

Pering's was the second of two Lund dissertations on Heimdallr to appear within a mere four years and as such invites comparison with the other, Åke Ohlmarks's *Heimdalls Horn und Odins Auge,* vol. I: *Heimdall und das Horn* (1937). Perings's survey of the sources (chapter 1), previous scholarship (chapter 2), and his methodology (chapter 3) are all shorter and tighter than those of Ohlmarks and therefore more accessible. Where Ohlmarks made use of the then popular European *Kulturkreislehre* to assert that Heimdallr was a sun god of the second rank, Pering stayed closer to Nordic ethnography, and his procedure and conclusion seem less dated, if no more acceptable.

For Pering the key to Heimdallr is the expression *vǫrðr goða.* Snorri understood it as "guardian of the gods," but Pering finds this a late speculation. He argues instead that *vǫrðr* meant "guardian spirit" as it does in modern Scandinavian languages—but not in any other Old Norse contexts. Heimdallr, then, was not a god but the *hustomte* or brownie of the land of the gods. He has nine mothers because he inherited the protective function of earlier female figures such as the norns or the *matronae.*

Pering expends a good deal of energy and cleverness bending the texts to fit the hypothesis. A measure of his relative success is doubtless the title de Vries chose for his 1955 essay on the same god: "Heimdallr, enigmatic god."

2159. Perkins, Richard. "The Dreams of *Flóamanna saga.*" *Saga-Book of the Viking Society*, 19 (1974-77), 191-238.

Includes discussion of the dreams in which Thor appears and of the demonization of Thor and pagan gods in general (pp. 197-208).

2160. Persson, Axel W. "Åkerbruksriter och hällristningar." *Fornvännen*, 25 (1930), 1-24. Summary in German.

Interprets the rock carvings in the light of agricultural ritual, partly also in light of Near Eastern parallels. The central figures are humans with zoomorphic features such as tails (previously identified as swords) and animal heads.

2161. Persson-Mirea, Victoria. "Les religions et les divinités dans l'ornament scandinave sur les amulettes, sur les tissus et las tapis, sur les dentelles, sur les outils et les vases en bois." In *Actes du Ve congrès international d'histoire des religions à Lund, 27-29 août 1929*. 215-18. Lund: C. W. K. Gleerup, 1930.

Lecture and discussion from an international congress on the history of religion.

2162. Pestalozzi, Rudolf. "Die germanische Götterdämmerung." *Neue Jahrbücher für das klassische Altertum, Geschichte und deutsche Literatur und für Pädagogik*, 16:31 (1913), 706-20.

Discussion of Ragnarǫk in terms of *Völkerpsychologie*; emphasis on *Vǫluspá*.

2163. Peterich, Eckart. *Götter und Helden der Germanen: Kleine Mythologie*. dtv, 119. Munich: Deutscher Taschenbuch Verlag, 1963. 158 pp. 1st ed. (1937) bore title: *Kleine Mythologie: Götter und Helden der Germanen*; new. ed. with Pierre Grimal: *Götter und Helden: Die klassichen Mythen und Sagen der Griechen, Römer und Germanen* (Olten: Walter, 1917. 365 pp.).

Popular survey of Germanic mythology.

2164. Peters, R. A. "OE *ælf, -ælf, ælfen, -ælfen*." *Philological Quarterly*, 42 (1963), 250-57.

Includes discussion of the *álfar* "elves."

2165. Petersen, Henry. *Om nordboernes gudedyrkelse og gudetro i hedenold: En antikvarisk undersøgelse*. Copenhagen: C. A. Reitzel, 1876. 137 pp.

In this early treatment of Scandinavian paganism, Petersen treats cult in the first two chapters and the mythology in the third and longest chapter (pp. 33-137). The treatment is historical and traces the replacement of Thor as chief god by Odin.

2166. Petersen, Henry. "Hypothesen om religiøse offer- og votivfund fra Danmarks historiske tid." *Årbøger for nordisk oldkyndighed og historie*, 1890, pp. 209-52.

Urges caution in interpreting depot finds as votive.

2167. Petersen, Jan. "Overtro fra gravhaug." *Maal og minne*, 1914, pp. 106-09.

An explanation for the presence of heavy stones in three boat graves of the Viking Age: to keep the corpse from returning.

2168. Petersen, Theodor. *Nogle bemærkninger om de saakaldte 'hellige hvide stene'*. Kongelige norske videnskabs selskabs skrifter, 1905, 8. Trondheim: Kongilige norske videnskabs selskab, 1905.

A catalog and analysis of the "holy white stones" of archaeology, identified here as phallic props of fertility cult, white because in Germanic gleaming has numinous properties. Petersen argues that chronology and distribution suggest association with the *vanir*, particularly Njǫrðr.

2169. Petersen, Theodor. "Zwei neugefundene Kultobjekte aus der älteren Eisenzeit." In *Festschrift Eugen Mogk zum 70. Geburtstag 19. Juli 1924*. 484-99. Halle a. d. S.: M. Niemeyer, 1924.

Discusses two "holy white stones" (cf. Th. Petersen 1905), their hypothetical association with fertility cult, and possible linguistic reflexes in Old Norse.

2170. Petré, Bo. "Björnfällen i begravningsritualen—statusobjekt speglande regional skinnhandel?" *Fornvännen*, 75 (1980), 5-14. Summary in English.

Correlating bear phalanges in grave finds from the Roman Iron Age through the Viking Age with indications of regional prosperity, Petré suggests that burial on bearskin reflected the status of the deceased and is evidence of fur trade. He does not take up the obvious mythological implications, but Åke V. Ström does later in his "Björnfällen och Oden-religion" (1975).

2171. Petri, Erik. "Våluspá och bibeln." *Bokvännen*, 21 (1966), 229-30.

Associates *Vǫluspá*, str. 5, with Joshua 10:12-13 (the sun stands still), and *Vǫluspá*, str. 57, with Matthew 24:29 (end of the world).

2172. Peuckert, Will-Erich. "Germanische Eschatologien." *Archiv für Religionswissenschaft*, 32 (1935), 1-37.

Adduces the following parallels between Germanic and Iranian, Mandean, and/or Manichaean eschatological literature: 1) use of the term "wolf-age"; 2) presence of two specially powerful figures after the end of the world (*Hyndluljóð* 43-44; and cf. "the powerful one" mentioned in the final strophe of the *Hauksbók Vǫluspá*); 3) a final battle between forces of good and evil, imagined as a series of individual combats between corresponding figures; 4) association of the south with evil and "dark fire." Peuckert concludes that the Germanic conceptions must have been borrowed from Mandean/Manichaean, ultimately deriving from Iranian tradition. He proposes two routes of dissemination: one over the Balkans to southern Germany, the other through Russia to Scandinavia. Response by Fr. Börtzler, "Edda und Muspilli vom Manichäismus beeinflusst?" (1935).

2173. Peuckert, Will-Erich. *Geheimkulte.* Heidelberg: C. Pfeffer, 1951. 664 pp.

Peuckert includes in his worldwide survey of secret cult a chapter on berserks (pp. 88-100) and remarks on Vǫlsi (pp. 403-05) and Freyr in Uppsala (pp. 419-20). Like any ethnographic potpourri, the book makes fascinating reading, but the perspective on the Norse material, while not the usual one, does not represent a major source of interest.

2174. Pfannenschmid, Heino. "Der mythische Gehalt der Tellsage: Ein Beitrag zur deutschen Mythologie." *Germania,* 10 (1865), 1-40.

Anchors the mythic background for the legend of Wilhelm Tell in an Indo-European myth of Indra and Odin as solar archers.

2175. Pfister, Friedrich. "Die Religion und der Glaube der germanischen Völker und ihrer religiöser Führer: Eine Problemstellung." *Archiv für Religionswissenschaft,* 33 (1936), 1-14.

Programmatic essay on the research problems of the religion and belief of the Germanic peoples and their leader, including references to contemporary Germany.

2176. Philippson, Ernst Alfred. *Germanisches Heidentum bei den Angelsachsen.* Kölner anglistische Arbeiten, 4. Leipzig: B. Tauchnitz, 1929. 238 pp.

A thorough study, rich in detail, of paganism among the Angles, Saxons, and Jutes, before and after the migration to England. Topics treated include: nature cult; the dead; "soul-demons" (includes valkyries and norns); spirits of nature; gods in animal form; fertility ritual; worship of sun and moon; the *vanir*; the *æsir*; Ēastre; Baldr; other echoes; cult and ritual; magic; prophecy; and fate.

Thorough review and summary by E. Voigt in *Zeitschrift für deutsche Philologie,* 56 (1931), 327-40.

2177. Philippson, Ernst Alfred. "Die agrarische Religion der Germanen nach den Ergebnissen der nordischen Ortsnamenforschung." *Publications of the Modern Language Association,* 51 (1936), 313-27.

Indications of agrarian religion in Nordic placenames, primarily theophoric.

2178. Philippson, Ernst Alfred. "Neuere Forschung auf dem Gebiet der germanischen Mythologie." *Germanic Review,* 11 (1936), 4-19.

Research survey.

2179. Philippson, Ernst Alfred. "Runenforschung und germanische Religionsgeschichte." *Publications of the Modern Language Association,* 53 (1938), 321-32.

Primarily on theories of runic origins, stressing the relationship between runes, magic, and the cult of Odin.

2180. Philippson, Ernst Alfred. *Die Genealogie der Götter in germanischer Religion, Mythologie, und Theologie.* Illinois Studies in Language and Literature, 37:3. Urbana: University of Illinois Press, 1953. iv, 94 pp.

This classic "historicist" study of Norse mythology and Germanic religion departs from the genealogy of the gods in an attempt to analyze their origins and relative chronology. Following Paula Philippson, the author argues the existence of three stages of genealogy. The first is numinous, the second mythic, the third theological. The numinous contains such aspects as the *hieros gamos* or the dying god; the mythic explores ordinary forms of genealogy and thus departs from the religion itself; and the theological is a highly speculative derivative of the mythic, particularly characteristic of the late Viking Age.

2181. Philippson, Ernst Alfred. "Phänomenologie, vergleichende Mythologie, und germanische Religionsgeschichte." *Publications of the Modern Language Association*, 77 (1962), 187-93.

A criticism of the theories of Georges Dumézil concerning Indo-European origin and structure of Germanic religion.

2182. Phillpotts, Bertha S. "Surt." *Arkiv för nordisk filologi*, 21 (1905), 14-30.

Concludes that Surtr is a "volcano-giant" and therefore that *Vǫluspá* is of Icelandic origin.

2183. Phillpotts, Bertha S. "Temple-Administration and Chieftainship in Pre-Christian Norway and Iceland." *Saga-Book of the Viking Society*, 8 (1912-13), 264-84.

A still useful article surveying the literary evidence connecting temple administration and chieftainship in Norway and Iceland. Phillpotts concludes that the connection was strong and important in both areas.

2184. Phillpotts, Bertha S. "Germanic Heathenism." In *The Cambridge Mediaeval History*, vol. 2. 480-95. Cambridge: University Press, 1913.

Brief survey of Germanic religion; interesting for its attempt to draw on folklore as well as ancient and medieval written sources.

2185. Phillpotts, Bertha S. *The Elder Edda and Ancient Scandinavian Drama.* Cambridge: University Press, 1920.

Phillpotts offers the bold hypothesis that ritual dramas underlie much extant eddic poetry.

She argues first a sharp distinction between eddic poems in *ljóðaháttr* and those in *fornyrðislag*. The *ljóðaháttr* poems were Norwegian and originated in pagan times; the *fornyrðislag* poems were largely postpagan and Icelandic. In Norway *ljóðaháttr* poems made up the texts of ritual dramas, performed in temples or other holy places for sacral and magic purposes. Subjects of the ritual dramas included death of a god (e.g., Baldr) or of a god's adversary (e.g., Hrungnir), ritual marriage, and fertility drama (e.g., Skírnir/Freyr and Gerðr). These dramas were performed in an archaic religious context inclining toward totemism.

The book received admiring but noncommittal reviews when it appeared, and few have subsequently been persuaded by it.

2186. Phillpotts, Bertha S. *Edda and Saga*. The Home University Library of Modern Knowledge, [150]. New York: Holt, 1931. 255, [1] pp.

General introduction to Old Norse literature, with emphasis on the Poetic Edda, including the mythological poems.

2187. Philpot, Mrs. J. H. *The Sacred Tree: Or, the Tree in Religion and Myth*. London and New York: Macmillan, 1897. xvi, 179 pp.

Popular treatment of the subject, including mention of Yggdrasill.

2188. Piebenga, G. A. "Fridrek, de eerste buitenlandse zendeling op Ijsland: Een bronnenstudie." *Amsterdamer Beiträge zur älteren Germanistik*, 17 (1982), 129-44.

Summary of the sources concerning Friðrekr's mission in Iceland.

2189. Piebenga, G. A. "Fridrek, den første utenlandske misjonæren på Island: En undersøkelse av påliteligheten i de islandske tekstene som beretter om ham." *Arkiv för nordisk filologi*, 99 (1984), 79-94.

Text-critical analysis of the accounts concerning Friðrekr's mission in Iceland. The first part of the article is a translation of the author's "Fridrek, de eerste buitenlandse zendeling op Ijsland" (1982).

2190. Piekarcyzk, Stanisław. *O społeczeństwie i religii w Skandynawii VIII-XI w*. Warsaw: Państwowe wydawn. naukwe, 1963. 257 pp.

"On society and religion in Scandinavia during the eighth to the eleventh centuries." In Polish. See the detailed summary and review by G. Schramm in *Anzeiger für deutsches Altertum*, 67 (1966), 52-58.

2191. Piekarczyk, Stanisław. "Funkeje spoleczne religii a moranos'ć bogów skandynawskich." *Euhemer-przeglad religioznawczy*, 7 (1963), 3-24.

"Social functions of religion and the morality of the Scandinavian gods."

2192. Pineau, Léon. *Les vieux chants populaires scandinaves (Gamle nordiske folkeviser): Étude de littérature comparée,* vol. 2: *Époque barbare: La légende divine et héroïque.* Paris: É. Bouillon, 1901. 584 pp.

The first part (pp. 29-167) treats mythological remnants in the Scandinavian ballads. These have largely to do with Thor.

2193. Pipping, Hugo. *Eddastudier I.* Studier i nordisk filologi 16:2, Skrifter utgivna av Svenska literatursällskapet i Finland, 182. Helsinki: Mercator tryckeri, 1925. 52 pp.

Wide ranging textual comments to *Vǫluspá* 1 (*mǫgu Heimdallar*) and 2:5-8 (especially on the word *mjǫtviðr/mjǫtuðr*). Pipping discusses particularly the implications of understanding the name *Heimdallr* literally as "world tree."

2194. Pipping, Hugo. *Eddastudier II.* Studier i nordisk filologi, 17:3, Skrifter utgivna av Svenska literatursällskapet i Finland, 189. Helsinki: Mercator tryckeri, 1926.

A continuation of *Eddastudier I* (1925), comprising essentially a commentary to *Vǫluspá.* Strophes treated specifically in this section of the work are: 4:5-6, 5:1-4, 11:2-3, 13:7, 14, 17:7, 19, 22, 25:5-8, 32:1-4, 35:1-4, 40:1-2, 41:1-2, 42, 46-47, 50:5-7, 51:1-3, 52:1-4, and 63:1-2. Pipping's central hypothesis is that the language of *Vǫluspá* is not West Norse but a mixture of East and West Norse, and he interprets many words and expressions accordingly (these are summarized on pp. 117-18). He concludes that the poem originated in Uppsala, was reformed in Hedeby, and thence was transported to Norway, perhaps with the skalds and warriors of Hákon jarl.

A second major thrust is continued interpretation of Heimdallr, summarized on pp. 120-30. According to Pipping, Heimdallr is a god, similar to figures among Finno-Ugric and other peoples to the east of Scandinavia, who embodies the world tree and the heavens supported by the tree.

Pp. 132-38 contain an index to *Eddastudier I-II.*

2195. Pipping, Hugo. *Eddastudier III.* Studier i nordisk filologi, 18:4, Skrifter utgivna av Svenska literatursällskapet i Finland, 197. Helsinki: Mercator tryckeri, 1928. 57 pp.

A commentary to various eddic passages: *Hávamál* 2:4-6, 31, 53:1-2, 75:3, 152:3, 153:1-3, 161:1-2; *Vafþrúðnismál* 16:1-3, *Grímnismál* 49:10, *Hárbarðsljóð* 42:1-2, *Hymiskviða* 31:7, *Lokasenna* 3:4-5, *Alvíssmál* 5:6, *Hyndluljóð* 37:6, 39:1-4, 43, 49:4, *Grógaldr* 6:3, *Fjǫlsvinnsmál* 14-15. The central hypostheses are those of Pipping's *Eddastudier* II. P. [58] contains an index, to this part of the *Eddastudier* only.

2196. Pipping, Hugo. "Zur Lesung und Deutung von Hǫvamǫl 39." *Neuphilologische Mitteilungen*, 29 (1928), 83-86.

Proposed addition to the lacuna in *Hávamál* 39:4: *fikinn* "greedy, eager."

2197. Pipping, Hugo. "Zur Deutung der Inschrift auf dem Runenstein von Rök." *Acta Philologica Scandinavica*, 4 (1929-30), 247-69.

The interpretation calls forth remarks on ritual and number magic.

2198. Pipping, Hugo. "Hávamál 136." In *Studies in Honor of Hermann Collitz*. 155-58. Baltimore: Johns Hopkins University Press, 1930.

The term *baugr* means "anus"; thus the second helming of *Hávamál* 136 counsels one to aim the anus at a stranger to avoid curses.

2199. Pipping, Hugo. *Sigtuna-amuletten*. Studier i nordisk filologi, 23:4, Skrifter utgivna av Svenska literatursällskapet i Finland, 238. Helsinki: Mercator tryckeri, 1933. 14 pp.

Reads the newly discovered (1931) Sigtuna runic amulet as a magic charm, but without the reference to Thor found by M. Eriksson and D. O. Zetterholm, "En amulett från Sigtuna" (1933).

Cf. also I. Lindquist, *Religiösa runtexter, 1: Sigtuna-galdern* (1932).

2200. Pipping, Hugo. "Nya stöd för gamla åsikter." *Arkiv för nordisk filologi*, 58 (1944), 40-41. Also in *Festskrift till Jöran Sahlgren 8/4 1944* (Lund: C. W. K. Gleerup, 1944), pp. 40-41.

Textual notes to *Hávamál* 136 and the Rök runic inscription.

2201. Pipping, Rolf. *Oden i galgen*. Studier i nordisk filologi 18:2, Skrifter utgivna av Svenska literatursällskapet i Finland, 197. Helsinki: Mercator tryckeri, 1928. 13 pp.

Argues that Odin's self-sacrifice on the tree (*Hávamál* 138) reflects shamanic ritual, particularly parallel to Finnish tradition: the shaman obtains magic powers and through hanging a glimpse into the world of the dead. Further, the verb *váfir* may mean "swings" and thus may perhaps be involved in the Odin name *Váfuðr*.

2202. Pipping, Rolf. "Om Gull-veig-stroferna i Vǫluspá." In *Festskrift til Finnur Jónsson 29. maj 1928*. 225-28. Copenhagen: Levin & Munksgaard, 1928.

Proposed readings in *Vǫluspá* 23: *afráð* "improper sexual conduct"; *gildi eiga* "to be guilty."

2203. Pipping, Rolf. *Vǫluspá 5:4 och Staffansridningen*. Studier i nordisk filologi, 18:3, Skrifter utgivna av Svenska literatursällskapet i Finland, 197. Helsinki: Mercator tryckeri, 1928. 8 pp.

Following H. Pipping's reading in *Vǫluspá* 5:4: *himiniódýr* (*Eddastudier* II (1926) pp. 19ff.), the author attempts to isolate aspects of horse cult and similar folk belief in the Swedish Staffan ballads and customs.

2204. Pipping, Rolf. "Hugo Pipping: Minnesteckning." *Societas Scientiarum Fennica, årbok*, 24:4 (1946), 1-24.

Includes discussion of Birger Pering, *Heimdall* (1941), in which Hugo Pipping's use of non-Scandinavian parallels was criticized. Rolf Pipping argues the value of such sources, particularly Finno-Ugric.

2205. Pira, Sigurd. "Den helige Tores källa." *Namn och bygd*, 33 (1945), 1-10.

Considers possible association of Thor with holy springs.

2206. Pizarro, Joaquín Martínez. "On *Níð* Against Bishops." *Mediaeval Scandinavia*, 11 (1978-79), 149-53.

Níð against bishops in Gregory of Tours, *Historia Francorum* IV:39 (not previously noticed by scholars); Paul the Deacon, *Historia Langobardorum* V:38, *Kristni saga* ch. 4, and *Sverris saga* ch. 131. "The repeated confrontation of worldly and ecclesiastical powers in the context of a *níð*-episode points to a tradition of mockery of the Christian clergy among the pagan and semi-pagan Germans. The principles and models of behavior of the Christian church clashed strongly with Germanic values of honor and virility, and priests who were zealous and consistent in their Christianity must often have been exposed to charges of *ergi*" (p. 152).

2207. Pjetursson, Helgi. "Opinberun, Völuspá og stjörnulífffræði." *Iðunn*, 16 (1932), 310-19.

Unusual discussion of the astronomical background of Revelations and *Vǫluspá*. Although he constantly compares them, the author stresses his view that *Vǫluspá* did not borrow from Revelations.

2208. Ploss, Emil. "Haarfärben und -bleichen (Zu Standeszeichen und Schwurritual der Germanen)." *Germanisch-Romanisch Monatsschrift*, 40 (1959), 409-20.

In seeking the age of the motif of the bleaching of their hair when Brynhild and Guðrún quarrel, according to *Skáldskaparmál*, Ploss builds on the findings of O. Höfler, *Germanische Sakralkönigtum* (1952). He analyzes primarily the oath of the Batavian Iulius Civilis in 69 A.D. and concludes that coloring the hair took place in the context of warrior cult and indicated the status of the warrior and the characteristics of the god(s) involved.

2209. Ploss, Emil. *Siegfried–Sigurd, der Drachenkämpfer: Untersuchungen zur germanisch-deutschen Heldensage, zugleich ein Beitrag zur Entwicklungsgeschichte des alteuropäischen Erzählgutes.* Beihefte der Bonner Jahrbücher, 17. Cologne and Graz: Böhlau, 1966. 128 pp.

A study of the archaeological and iconographic background of Germanic narratives about dragon-slaying. Besides the clear relevance to traditions about Thor, the book is of interest for its attempt to refute Otto Höfler's theory (*Siegfried, Arminius und die Symbolik* (1961)) that the Siegfried materials represent a mythic and cultic recasting of the victory of Arminius over the Romans in 9 A.D.

2210. Pollak, Hans W. "Zur altwestnordischen Namensform Þórr." *Arkiv för nordisk filologi*, 27 (1911), 93-94.

Pollak thinks the form of the god Thor's name, *Þórr*, must originally derive from a plural.

2211. Polomé, Edgar C. "L'Étymologie du terme germanique **ansuz* 'dieu souverain.'" *Études germaniques*, 8 (1953), 36-44.

The etymology of Germanic **ansuz* > *áss* (plural *æsir*). Through comparison with Indo-European cognates, Polomé argues that the term originally referred only to sovereignty. Its application to sovereign gods occurred in Germanic via the semantic link of magic, which sovereign gods controlled.

2212. Polomé, Edgar C. "À propos de la déesse Nerthus." *Latomus*, 13 (1954), 167-200.

Polomé argues that at the time Tacitus described the Nerthus ritual, agriculture was essentially a female activity; only later did it become masculine, with the concomitant emergence of the gods Ing, Freyr, and Njord. Thus Polomé understands the Nerthus ritual as the celebration of the arrival of spring, a symbolic reenactment of renewal intended to promote fertility and regenerate the life force of the Terrae Mater. The approach employs Eliade's notion of the celebration of spring as a cosmic event through symbol and ritual.

2213. Polomé, Edgar C. "La religion germanique primitive: Reflet d'une structure sociale." *Le flambeau*, 37 (1954), 437-63.

Polomé dedicated this essay to Georges Dumézil, and indeed it is little more than a popular presentation of Dumézil's then current thinking.

2214. Polomé, Edgar C. "Notes sur le vocabulaire religieux du germanique, I: Runique *alu*." *La nouvelle clio*, 6 (1954), 40-55.

Etymology and analysis of the use of the term *alu* in runic inscriptions. It had a prophylactic force, and from the same verbal root the oldest word for beer derives (Norse *ǫl*), for beer was part of ritual; and cf. the mead of poetry.

2215. Polomé, Edgar C., ed. *Old Norse Literature and Mythology: A Symposium*. Austin and London: Published for the Department of Germanic Languages of the University of Texas, Austin, by the University of Texas Press, 1969. 347 pp.

In this volume honoring Lee M. Hollander, the following papers, entered separately in this bibliography, are relevant to Scandinavian mythology: A. Margaret Arent, "The Heroic Pattern: Old Germanic Helmets, *Beowulf*, and *Grettis saga*" (pp. 130-99); Winfred P. Lehmann, "On Reflections of Germanic Legal Terminology and Situations in the *Edda*" (pp. 227-43); E. O. G. Turville-Petre,

"Fertility of Beast and Soil in Old Norse Literature" (pp. 244-64); Edgar C. Polomé, "Some Comments on Vǫluspá, Stanzas 17-18" (pp. 265-90).

2216. Polomé, Edgar C. "Some Comments on Vǫluspá, Stanzas 17-18." In *Old Norse Literature and Mythology: A Symposium*, ed. Edgar C. Polomé, 265-90. Austin and London: Published for the Department of Germanic Languages of the University of Texas, Austin, by the University of Texas Press, 1969.

Polomé sets as his task the identification of the divine trio who imbue Askr and Embla with life in the seventeenth and eighteenth stanzas of *Vǫluspá*. Odin presents no problem; he gives *ǫnd*, which Polomé understands as "life giving power." Hœnir gives *óðr* "inspired mental activity"; Polomé interprets this as "the instrument of godly wisdom, the one who utters the message conveyed by outside widsdom. Therefore he remains mute in the discussion of the Þing of the vanir when this inspiration, embodied by Mimir, fails him. . . . Therefore, also, he appears in a sacerdotal function after Ragnarǫk" (p. 272). The rest of the article considers Lóðurr. Polomé rejects the association of this figure with the *logaþore* of the runic inscription on the Nordendorf brooch. The key to Polomé's interpretation of Lóðurr is a new etymology he proposes for the quality given by Lóðurr to man, *lá*, from PIE **lah*, cognate with Hittite *lek*, with the sense "mien." He also revives an etymology of Adolf Noreen, according to which *lá* means "hair." In either case the emphasis is on man's appearance, and then Lóðurr should be of the *vanir*. He may, Polomé suggests, be the male counterpart of the fertility goddess Ludhgodha identified by Jöran Sahlgren on toponymic evidence.

2217. Polomé, Edgar C. "The Indo-European Component in Germanic Religion." In *Myth and Law Among the Indo-Europeans: Studies in Indo-European Comparative Mythology*, ed. Jaan Puhvel, 55-82. Publications of the UCLA Center for the Study of Comparative Folklore and Mythology, 1. Berkeley and Los Angeles: University of California Press, 1970.

After a useful survey of the question of the Indo-European component of Germanic religion, Polomé investigates the myth of Baldr's death. He finds Dumézil's notion of the cosmic importance of the myth exaggerated and prefers de Vries's analysis equating it with Odin ritual.

2218. Polomé, Edgar C. "Approaches to Germanic Mythology." In *Myth in Indo-European Antiquity*, eds. Gerald James Larson, C. Scott Littleton, and Jaan Puhvel, 51-65. Berkeley and Los Angeles: University of California Press, 1974.

"The first part of the text is essentially an expanded version of the first pages of my contribution, 'The Indo-European Component in Germanic Religion' [1970]. . . . The remainder of the paper is a rebuttal of the critique of Georges Dumézil's work by Ernst A. Philippson in his article 'Phänomenologie, vergleichende Mythologie und germanische Religionsgeschichte' [1962]" (p. 51, fn.).

2219. Porru, Giula Mazzuoli. "Considerazioni in nota alla Germania di Tacito: Le antiche divinità germaniche." *Studi germanici*, 8 (1970), 373-85.

On the basis of the *Germania* of Tacitus, Porru proposes a stratification of

Germanic theogony. It begins with the earth mother, followed by the hermaphroditic Tuisto (cf. Nerthus). Tuisto's son is the progenitor Mannus, whose offspring fall into a tripartite division: Ingvi-Freyr, Tiwaz-Irmin, and Istraz (corresponding to the Ingwaeones, Erminones, and Istaevones). They represent, respectively, fertility, supreme power, and wisdom. Tiwaz descends from Tiwaz-Irmin and assumes a function of military power, and Wodanaz descends from Istraz, expanding the latter's wisdom into magic; at this level Donar enters the picture as a representative of benign physical force.

2220. Potkowski, Edward. "Eschatologia germanska." *Euhemer-przeglad religioznawczy*, 7 (1963), 25-39.

"Germanic eschatology."

Præstgaard Andersen, Lise, *see* Andersen, Lise Præstgaard.

2221. Powell, F. York. "Recent Research on Teutonic Mythology." *Folk-Lore*, 1 (1890), 118-26.

Review article, treating works of M. Hirschfeld, V. Rydberg, and E. H. Meyer.

2222. Psilander, Hjalmar. "Alvíssmál 1, 6." In *Nordiska studier tillägnade Adolf Noreen på hans 50-årsdag den 13 mars 1904, af studiekamrater och lärjungar.* 486-87. Uppsala: K. W. Appelberg, 1904.

Brief textual note.

2223. Puhvel, Jaan, ed. *Myth and Law Among the Indo-Europeans: Studies in Indo-European Comparative Mythology.* Berkeley and Los Angeles: University of California Press, 1970. x, 276 pp.

"Most of the works gathered into this volume were originally presented at a symposium held under the auspices of the Center [for the Study of Comparative Folklore and Mythology, UCLA] and of the Section of Indo-European Studies [Department of Classics, UCLA] on March 17-18, 1967" (p. vi). Articles relevant to Scandinavian mythology and entered separately in this bibliography include: Calvert Watkins, "Language of Gods and Language of Men: Remarks on Some Indo-European Metalinguistic Traditions" (pp. 1-18); Edgar C. Polomé, "The Indo-European Component in Germanic Religion" (pp. 55-82); C. Scott Littleton, "The 'Kingship in Heaven' Theme" (pp. 83-122); Donald J. Ward, "The Threefold Death: An Indo-European Trifunctional Sacrifice?" (pp. 123-42); idem, "The Separate Functions of the Indo-European Divine Twins" (pp. 193-202); James L. Sauvé, "The Divine Victim: Aspects of Human Sacrifice in Viking Scandinavia and Vedic India" (pp. 173-92).

The work contains a bibliography (pp. 247-68) that claims to "constitute the documentation of the new Indo-European mythology" (p. vi).

2224. Puhvel, Jaan. "Transposition of Myth to Saga in Indo-European Epic Narrative." In *Antiquitates Indogermanicae: Studien zur indogermanischen Altertumskunde und zur Sprach- und Kulturgeschichte der indogermanischen Völker: Gedenkschrift für Hermann Güntert zur 25. Wiederkehr seines Todestages am 23. April 1973*, eds. Manfred Mayrhofer, Wolfgang Meid, Bernfried Schlerath, and Rüdiger Schmitt, 175-84. Innsbrucker Beiträge zur Sprachwissenschaft, 12. Innsbruck: Institut für Sprachwissenschaft der Universität Innsbruck, 1974.

Peripheral remarks on Norse materials.

2225. Puhvel, Jaan. "*Remus et frater.*" *History of Religions*, 15 (1975), 146-67.

The author uses both Tacitus (Mannus and Tuisto) and Norse mythology (the slaying of Ymir) as evidence in his attempt to reconstruct the Indo-European origin myth, which he believes revolved around Primeval Man's slaying of his twin and fashioning of the world and society from his remains.

2226. Puhvel, Martin. "The Legend of the Church-Building Troll in Northern Europe." *Folklore*, 72 (1961), 567-83.

Primarily a study of the modern legends apparently related to the story of the building of Asgard. Puhvel finds himself most in agreement with von Sydow, less so with Sahlgren and Fossenius.

2227. Puhvel, Martin. "The Blithe-Hearted Morning Raven in *Beowulf*." *English Language Notes*, 10 (1972-73), 243-47.

On *Beowulf* 1801: Odin's ravens as a good omen.

2228. Puhvel, Martin. "The Deicidal Otherworld Weapon in Celtic and Germanic Mythic Tradition." *Folklore*, 83 (1972), 210-19.

Puhvel discusses the use of a special weapon in Celtic and Germanic myth and older literature by one sun or lightning god to kill another. Material adduced from Scandinavian mythology includes *Þrymskviða* (Þrymr as a thunder god) and Baldr's death. Puhvel inclines more to descent from an Indo-European origin than to influence of Celtic or Germanic.

R

2229. Raabe, Jens. *Nordiske gude- og heltesagn: Fortællinger fra Norges sagatid,* vol. 1. Oslo: A. W. Brøgger, 1911. 91 pp.

Popular retelling of Scandinavian myth and legend.

2230. Rabe, A. "Zur Edda: Ein Versuch." *Am Urdhs-Brunnen,* 1 (1881-83), 5:2-6, 6:4-6, 10:4-8, 11:13-15, 12:2-9.

Celtic influence on the Poetic Edda.

2231. Rabe, A. "Die Weltsage der Edda (Völuspá?): Unter Zuhülfenahme des Keltischen übersetzt." *Am Urdhs-Brunnen,* 2 (1884), 149-57.

Translation of *Vǫluspá* with discussion stressing Celtic influence.

2232. Raddatz, Klaus. "Religionsgeschichtliche Probleme des Thorsberger Moorfundes." In *Vorgeschichtliche Heiligtümer und Opferplätze in Mittel- und Nordeuropa: Bericht über ein Symposium in Reinhausen bei Göttingen vom 14.-16. Oktober 1968,* ed. Herbert Jankuhn, 188-97. Abhandlungen der Akademie der Wissenschaften in Göttingen, phil.-hist. Kl., 3. Folge, 74. Göttingen: Vandenhoeck & Ruprecht, 1970.

Traces a ritual chronology through the evidence of the Thorsbjærg moor find.

2233. Radzin, Hilda. "The Names of the Gods and Goddesses in Snorri Sturluson's Edda." *Literary Onomastics Studies,* 8 (1981), 39-45.

Following a schematic literary-historical introduction, Radzin offers very brief listing of a few names of gods in *Snorra edda.*

2234. Radzin, Hilda. "Names in the Mythological Lay *Grímnis-Mál.*" *Literary Onomastics Studies,* 10 (1983), 261-68.

"In proceeding to offer a few brief observations on the most interesting names of *Grímnis-Mál,* we shall. . . chiefly regard the myths under a physical and psychological point of view, occasionally giving some of Finn Magnusen's astronomical explanations" (p. 263).

2235. Rafnsson, Sveinbjörn. "Um Kristinsboðsþættina." *Gripla*, 2 (1977), 19-31.

Discusses the literary relationships of the various *þættir* or short narratives dealing with the Christian mission and conversion in Iceland. The author associates *Þorvalds þáttr víðfǫrla* with Hólar and Þingeyrar and assigns the composition of *Þangbrands þáttr* to the early twelfth century.

2236. Ralph, Bo. "The Composition of the Grímnismál." *Arkiv för nordisk filologi*, 87 (1972), 97-118.

Contra Fleck, "The Knowledge Criterion in the *Grímnismál*" (1971), Ralph investigates the composition of the poem itself without reference to implicit ritual. He concludes that the stanzas of *Grímnismál* are highly reminiscent of those of the *þulur*; they present mythological information, frequently on the basis of a name, and often the second half of the verse comments on the topic raised in the first half. Using this framework, Ralph interprets *Grímnismál* 42: *hverr* (line 3) means "kettle" (cf. line 6) and refers to the sun.

Thus Ralph reads *Grímnismál* as a poem stressing its mythological content, not the mythic situation. The frame would be a literary addition.

2237. Ralph, Bo. "Om tillkomsten av *Sonatorrek*." *Arkiv för nordisk filologi*, 91 (1976), 153-65.

On the background and circumstances of composition of *Sonatorrek*, with suggestive remarks on the consonance of skaldic poetry, prophecy, and *seiðr* as magic arts.

2238. Ralph, Bo. "Ett ställe i Skáldskaparmál 18." *Scripta Islandica*, 28 (1977), 27-44.

A discussion of the passage in *Skáldskaparmál* in which Thor grasps a rowan tree to avoid being drowned by the giantess flooding the river Vímur: *því er þat orðtak haft, at reynir er bjǫrg Þórs.* Ralph concludes that *orðtak* refers here to the use of the image in a kenning of Grettir, and that that kenning was Snorri's immediate source for his remark that the rowan saved Thor. Thus the rowan myth would have no basis in tradition. To strengthen this assertion, Ralph offers arguments against the common association of the hypothetical Norse rowan cult with the Lapp thunder god.

2239. Ramskou, Thorkild. "Ragnarok." *Kuml*, 1953, pp. 182-92. Summary in English.

Interprets the decoration of ninth-century bowl-shaped brooches as the death of Odin and the vengeance of Víðarr and concludes that Víðarr was a more important god than Odin.

2240. Ramskou, Thorkild. "Stavgård og bautavi." *Kuml*, 1957, pp. 86-90. Summary in English.

The south tumulus at Jelling as a sacred enclosure associated with ancestor worship.

2241. Ranke, Friedrich. "Das wilde Heer und die Kultbünde der Germanen." *Niederdeutsche Zeitschrift für Volkskunde*, 18 (1940), 1-33. Rpt. in Ranke, *Kleinere Schriften*, ed. Heinz Rupp and Eduard Studer, Bibliotheca germanica, 12 (Bern and Munich: Francke, 1971), pp 380-408.

A long, critical review of Otto Höfler's *Kultische Geheimbünde der Germanen* (1934), probably the most effective skeptical evaluation of Höfler's theory. Ranke objected that conceptions of the Wild Hunt were relatively recent and had nothing to do with the cult of Odin.

2242. Ranke, Friedrich. "Der Altersspruch der Seherin (Zu Vǫluspá Str. 2)." *Zeitschrift für deutsches Altertum*, 78 (1941), 51-61.

On *Vǫluspá* 2: the seeress stakes her authority on her great age, stretching back to mythic prehistory. Ranke detects Celtic influence.

2243. Raszmann, A. "Zu Wôdan." *Germania*, 8 (1863), 380-81.

Notes that some Hessian dogs bear the name *Wodan* and presumes a connection with the Wild Hunt.

2244. Raszmann, A. "Wodan und die Nibelunge." *Germania*, 26 (1881), 279-316.

An attempt to reconstruct an original legend of the Nibelungen and Odin's role in it as starter and finisher of the action.

2245. Rehfeldt, Bernard. "Recht, Religion und Moral bei den frühen Germanen." *Zeitschrift der Savigny-Stiftung für Rechtsgeschichte*, Germanistische Abteilung, 71 (1954), 1-22.

A discussion of law and religion in ancient Germanic times, drawing heavily on *Ynglinga saga.*

2246. Reichardt, Konstantin. "Hymiskviða 1." *Arkiv för nordisk filologi*, 45 (1929), 337-38.

Textual comment to *Hymiskviða*, str. 1-3: Ægir has enough kettles for meat, but not to brew mead for all.

2247. Reichardt, Konstantin. "Hymiskviða: Interpretation. Wortschatz. Alter." *Beiträge zur Geschichte der deutschen Sprache und Literatur*, 57 (1933), 130-56.

Linguistic evidence that *Hymiskviða* is a late poem, probably recorded after *Gylfaginning.* Snorri does not seem to know it, and the question *hverr kann um þat goðmálugra gǫrr at skilja* (*Hymiskviða*, str. 38) refers, according to Reichardt, to Snorri and further to *Gylfaginning*, the poet's source. On this particular point see further Jan de Vries, "Das Wort Godmálugr" (1954).

2248. Reichardt, Konstantin. *Runenkunde*. Jena: E. Diederichs, 1936. 126 pp.

With a section on magic.

2249. Reichardt, Konstantin. "Die Liebesbeschwörung in Fǫr Skírnis." *Journal of English and Germanic Philology*, 38 (1939), 481-95.

Argues that str. 26-36 of *Skírnismál*, detailing Skírnir's magic charms, are interpolated from a single poem; goes on to analyze that poem and proposes a revised order for the extant stanzas.

2250. Reichardt, Konstantin. "Die Thorsdrápa des Eilífr Goðrúnarson: Textinterpretation." *Publications of the Modern Language Association*, 63 (1948), 329-91.

A thorough interpretation of the *Þórsdrápa*, including commentary to each stanza and translation. Fundamental for the textual problems.

2251. Reichardt, Konstantin. "Odin am Galgen." In *Wächter und Hüter: Festschrift für Hermann J. Weigand zum 17. November 1957*, eds. Curt von Faber du Faur, Konstantin Reichardt, and Heinz Bluhm, 15-28. New Haven: Department of Germanic Languages, Yale University, 1957.

Reichardt explores German and English parallels to Odin's words when he was hanging on the tree. These parallels occur in the context of popular lore concerning medicinal and magic herbs created by Christ on the cross. Reichardt sees possible ninth-century northern British influence on the scene in *Hávamál*.

2252. Reichborn-Kjennerud, I. "Lægeraadene i den eldre Edda." *Maal og minne*, 1923, pp. 1-57.

Discussion of the medical charms in *Hávamál*, str. 137.

2253. Reichborn-Kjennerud, I. *Mimameiðs aldin*. Studier i nordisk filologi, 17:2. Helsinki: Mercator, 1926. 3 pp.

Mímameiðr a juniper tree.

2254. Reichborn-Kjennerud, I. *Mimameiðs aldin*. Studier i nordisk filologi, 17:2, Skrifter utgivna av Svenska literatursällskapet i Finland, 189. Helsinki: Mercator tryckeri, 1926. 3 pp.

On *Fjǫlsvinnsmál* 21-22 and the medicinal and superstitious properties of the juniper.

2255. Reichborn-Kjennerud, I. "Dvergnavnet Móðsognir." *Maal og minne*, 1931, pp. 116-17.

On the dwarf's name Móðsognir (*Vǫluspá* 10): Reichborn-Kjennerud understands the name as "strength-sucker," hence a reference to some sort of parasite.

2256. Reichborn-Kjennerud, I. "Tunga er hǫfuðs bani." *Maal og minne*, 1933, pp. 69.

Parallels to a line in *Hávamál*, str. 73.

2257. Reichborn-Kjennerud, I. "Den gamle dvergetro." In *Studia Germanica tillägnade Ernst Albin Kock den 6 december 1934*. 277-88. Lund: C. Blom, 1934.

Contra de Boor, "Der Zwerg in Skandinavien" (1924), Reichborn-Kjennerud attempts to restore dwarfs to genuine folk belief during the older period. He surveys the numerous references to dwarfs' appearance in the eddas and sagas and then finds the same characteristics in recent Norwegian folklore, suggesting a continuation of folk belief.

2258. Reichborn-Kjennerud, I. "Eldr við sóttom—ax við fjǫlkyngi." *Maal og minne*, 1934, pp. 149.

Parallels in Nordic folk belief to *Hávamál*, str. 137.

2259. Reichborn-Kjennerud, I. "Et kapitel av Hauksbók." *Maal og minne*, 1934, pp. 144-48.

The chapter from *Hauksbók* under discussion, which includes such bits of folk belief as the notion that foolish women put out food for the *landvættir*, states that it follows St. Augustine. Reichborn-Kjennerud finds the probable link to Augustine in a sermon of Ælfric.

2260. Reichborn-Kjennerud, I. *Vår gamle trolldomsmedisin*, vol. 5. Skrifter utg. av det norske videnskaps-akademi i Oslo, 1947, 1. Oslo: J. Dybwad, in commission, 1947. 253 pp.

The final volume of the author's monumental study of folk medicine, this contains sections on werewolves and berserks.

2261. Reichert, Hermann. "Zum Sigrdrífa—Brünhild—Problem." In *Antiquitates Indogermanicae: Studien zur indogermanischen Altertumskunde und zur Sprach- und Kulturgeschichte der indogermanischen Völker: Gedenkschrift für Hermann Güntert zur 25. Wiederkehr seines Todestages am 23. April 1973*, eds. Manfred Mayrhofer, Wolfgang Meid, Bernfried Schlerath, and Rüdiger Schmitt, 251-65. Innsbrucker Beiträge zur Sprachwissenschaft, 12. Innsbruck: Institut für Sprachwissenschaft der Universität Innsbruck, 1974.

The final pages discuss the relationship between heroic legend and myth.

2262. Reier, Herbert. "Der Eggjumstein—ein Schandstein." *Acta Philologica Scandinavica*, 21 (1950-52), 73-86.

Attempts to remove the Eggjum runestone from the realm of cult and religion.

2263. Rein, Kurt. "Die Bedeutung von Tierzucht und Affekt für die Haustierbenennung: Untersucht an der deutschen Synonymik für *capra domestica*." In *Deutsche Wortforschung in europäischen Bezügen, 1*, ed. Ludwig Erich Schmidt, 191-295. Beiträge zur deutschen Philologie, 21. Giessen: W. Schmitz, 1958.

This monograph on words for "goat" in Germanic languages includes an excursus on "the position of the goat in the myth and culture of the Germanic peoples" (pp. 220-22).

2264. Reinskou, Finn. "Er Eddaen norsk eller islandsk? Den nye klanganalyse." *Nordisk tidskrift för vetenskap, konst och industri*, 1924, pp. 220-25.

Remarks on Eduard Sievers's theories on the location of the eddic poems in Norway.

2265. Reiss, Edmund. "*Havelok the Dane* and Norse Mythology." *Modern Language Quarterly*, 27 (1966), 115-24.

Locates a hypothetical parallel to Odin within *Havelok the Dane* in the figure Grim. Reiss goes on to argue the presence of other mythological elements and suggests that the poem may be of pre-Christian origin.

2266. Reitzenstein, Richard. "Weltuntergangsvorstellungen: Eine Studie zur vergleichenden Religionsgeschichte." *Kyrkohistorisk årsskrift*, 24 (1924), 129-212.

Comparative study of eschatologies, arguing relatively late influence of Near Eastern traditions, Iranian or Manichaean, on Germanic and Norse conceptions.

2267. Renauld-Krantz. *Structures de la mythologie nordique*. Paris: Maisonneuve & Larose, 1972. 234 pp.

This is a strange book. As an attempt at an overall reading of Norse mythology it is noteworthy, and it bristles with shrewd observations. On the other hand, its basic aim, to relate the structures of Norse mythology to man and the universe, leads the author into a kind of neo-romantic pseudo-mythology of man and nature.

Renauld-Krantz accepts Dumézil's assignment of the major Norse gods into the three major functions: Odin and magic sovereignty, Thor and force, the *vanir* and fertility. These are, according to Renauld-Krantz, only a *sociological* division, and myth relates equally also to man and the cosmos.

Like Dumézil, Renauld-Krantz centers his remarks on individual gods and relies heavily on the thirteenth-century literary sources. Odin (pp. 35-110) is the grand ancestor, the creator, the sovereign of gods and men; he derives his power from magic and control of spiritual ecstasy. His realm is the sky and the wind, his element the air, and in Renauld-Krantz's corporeal metaphor Odin correlates with the brain. Thor (pp. 111-79) is a god of storms, whose element is fire. As he reigns in the realm between sky and earth, "so he reigns in the small universe that is man in that intermediate zone, between high and low, between the head and the stomach, which is the seat of the heart: the torso" (p. 178). The two gods bear comparison (pp. 181-94) for the oppositions father-son, air-fire, mind-body, and so forth. As *æsir*, inhabitants of the upper regions, they are structurally opposed to the *vanir* (pp. 195-212), inhibitants of the nether regions, whose elements are earth (Freyr) and water (Njord) and whose body part is the stomach. A conclusion (pp. 213-18) enumerates these oppositions in almost Hegelian fashion.

In this summary I have stressed the most questionable part of Renauld-Krantz's analysis, the correlation of the gods with natural realms and elements, for which the sources give but small support, and with the human body, for which the sources give no support at all. Taken as metaphors, however, these correlations can be instructive, and the book remains worthwhile for its stimulating interpretation of details as well as for its attempt at a systematic reading.

2268. Restrup, Ole. *Odin og Tor: Vikingeguder fra Eddaernes verden.* Copenhagen: G. E. C. Gad, 1953. 109 pp.

Popular handbook.

2269. Reuschel, Helga. "Der Göttertrug im Gunnarsþáttr helmings." *Zeitschrift für deutsches Altertum*, 71 (1934), 155-66.

Rejects the *Gunnars þáttr* from the canon of texts significant to the history of religion. Reuschel presents arguments that it is a product of the fourteenth century, based on international migratory materials.

2270. Reuschel, Karl. "Literaturbericht 1912-1915: Germanisches Altertum; Mythologie." *Zeitschrift für den deutschen Unterricht*, 30 (1916), 127-36.

Research survey.

2271. Reuter, Otto Sigfrid. *Das Rätsel der Edda und der arische Urglaube.* Sontra: Deutsch-Ordens-Land, 1921. 174 pp.

Speculation on the religious values of the Aryans, as supposedly exemplified in eddic poetry.

2272. Reuter, Otto Sigfrid. "Astronomie und Mythologie: Zur Methodik (Vortrag, gehalten in der Sitzung der Gesellschaft für deutsche Vorgeschichte zu Berlin, am 1. Dezember 1925)." *Mannus*, 18 (1926), 33-78.

Text of a lecture. Reuter argues for the importance of applying astronomy to mythological problems and offers several "solutions" from Old Norse cosmology. These include analysis of *Vǫluspá*, str. 3-5, and several passages from *Grímnismál.*

2273. Reuter, Otto Sigfrid. *Germanische Himmelskunde: Untersuchungen zur Geschichte des Geistes.* Munich: J. F. Lehmann, 1934. xvi, 766 pp.

On the astronomical achievements and knowledge of the Germanic peoples, with various asides on myth and religion. Reuter seeks evidence everywhere of ancient and untrammeled Germanic thought.

2274. Reuterskiöld, Edgar. *De nordiska lapparnas religion.* Populära etnologiska skrifter, 8. Stockholm: Cederquists grafiska aktiebolag, 1912. 149 pp. Summary in French, pp. 145-49.

Treats borrowings of Nordic myth and cult into Lapp religion.

2275. Richert, Mårten Birger. *Försök till belysning af mörkare och oförstådda ställen i den poetiska Eddan.* Uppsala universitets årsskrift. Uppsala: E. Edquist, 1877. iii, 57 pp.

Textual notes to eddic poetry, including these mythological passages: *Hávamál*, str. 2, 13, 32, 33, 41, 107; *Hárbarðsljóð*, str. 13; *Hymiskviða*, str. 2; *Alvíssmál*, str. 5.

2276. Rieger, Gerd Enno. "Þkr. 20 *við scolom aka tvau.*" *Skandinavistik*, 5 (1975), 7-10.

Rieger draws attention to the neuter plural pronoun *tvau* "two" in *Þrymskviða* 20: *við scolom aka tvau* "we two shall go" and analyzes its context. It is suitable, he argues, because Loki accepts his feminine role (as Thor/Freyja's servant) but Thor does not (whence the neuter, which is used in the plural for groups of male and female together).

2277. Rieger, Max. "Ingävonen Istävonen Herminonen." *Zeitschrift für deutsches Altertum*, 11 (1856-59), 177-205.

Germanic tribal division, with many remarks on myth and cult.

2278. Rieger, Max. "Über den nordischen Fylgjenglauben." *Zeitschrift für deutsches Altertum*, 42 (1898), 277-90.

Survey of the literary evidence concerning belief in *fylgjur*, with some evaluation.

2279. Riegler, Richard. "Schwedisch *tordyvel* 'Mistkäfer.'" *Neuphilologische Mitteilungen*, 26 (1925), 179-81.

Swedish *tordyvel* "dung beetle" as a pagan-Christian formation (Thor-devil). See the following item.

2280. Riegler, Richard. "Nochmals schwedisch *tordyvel* 'Mistkäfer.'" *Neuphilologische Mitteilungen*, 27 (1926), 13-14.

Retraction of the above item.

2281. Ringbom, Lars-Ivar. *Graltempel und Paradies: Beziehungen zwischen Iran und Europa im Mittelalter.* Kungliga vitterhets, historie, och antikvitetsakademiens handlingar, 73. Stockholm: Wahlström & Widstrand, in commission, 1951. 546 pp.

Chapter 15, "Das Paradies in den Mythen der heidnischen Völker" (pp. 312-29), explores the hypothesis that traditions of the invasion of the *æsir* from Asia may have been true and that conceptions of Asgard therefore derive from the East.

2282. Ringgren, Helmer, and Åke V. Ström. *Religions of Mankind: Today and Yesterday.* Ed. J. C. G. Greig. Edinburgh and London: Oliver & Boyd, 1967. xlii, 426 pp. Translated by Niels L. Jensen.

Pp. 80-101 survey Germanic religion.

2283. Robinson, J. "Ethnologisches in der Edda." *Das Ausland*, 66 (1893), 609-11.

Naive observation of ethnographic parallels to various eddic motifs. Relevant to the mythology are remarks on the sun and moon, blood, divine judgment, and snakes.

2284. Rochholz, E. L. "Ohne Schatten, ohne Seele: Der Mythus vom Körperschatten und vom Schattengeist." *Germania*, 5 (1860), 69-94, 175-207.

On shadows, souls, and attendant spirits in ancient Germanic culture. Hel, the valkyries, and *fylgjur* enter into the discussion.

2285. Rochholz, E. L. "Gold, Milch und Blut: Mythologisch." *Germania*, 7 (1862), 385-428.

Wide-ranging early article on the symbolic role of liquids, milk, blood, and mead. In connection with the latter Rochholz draws on Norse mythology.

2286. Rödiger, Max. "Der grosse Waldesgott der Germanen." *Zeitschrift für deutsche Philologie*, 27 (1895), 1-14.

Against the postulation of F. Kauffmann, in his *Deutsche Mythologie* (1890) and elsewhere, of an archetypal Germanic god of the forest, expressed in Víðarr, Heimdallr, Hœnir, Váli, Ullr, deus Requalivahanus, and Ziu/Týr.

2287. Rohan, Michael Scott, and Allan J. Scott. *The Hammer and the Cross.* Oxford: Alder Publishing, 1980. 64 pp.

Popular account (suitable for older children) of the conversion to Christianity in Scandinavia.

2288. Rokkjær, C. C. "Arkæologisk datering af poetiske tekster." *Arkiv för nordisk filologi*, 74 (1959), 277-78.

Response to B. Nerman, "Det heliga tretalet och Vǫluspá" (1959).

2289. Rolfsen, Perry. "Den siste hedning på Agder." *Viking*, 44 (1981), 112-28. Summary in English.

Archaeological description of the last three pagan graves in Aust-Agder, Norway, from late in the Viking Age. "Even though the three burials are pagan, we cannot from this infer that the man [who was buried] and his family were unfamiliar with the Christian faith. We should, rather, interpret the pagan burial practice as an attempt at upholding religious and cultural traditions. And thus these three graves demonstrate the deep roots of the Norse religion among certain families" (p. 127).

2290. Romdahl, Axel L. "Bildstenar och yxor." *Fornvännen*, 41 (1946), 1-10. Summary in English

On the "geometric" decorated stones from Gotland. Romdahl believes that they portray axes and would have had a prophylactic purpose in burial ritual.

2291. Rooth, Anna Birgitta. *Loki in Scandinavian Mythology*. Skrifter utgivna av kungliga humanistiska vetenskapssamfundet i Lund, 61. Lund: C. W. K. Gleerup, 1961.

Using classical folklore methodology of the "Finnish school," Rooth attempts to strip away hypothetical accretions to the Loki figure; she concludes that the original Loki was a spider, a meaning the term *locke* bears in some Swedish dialects. Philologists have not accepted the book with enthusiasm.

2292. Rooth, Anna Birgitta. *Den onde Loki och den symboliska tolkningen av myterna*. Lund: Studentliteratur, 1969.

Summary of the author's *Loki in Scandinavian Mythology* (1961).

2293. Rooth, Anna Birgitta. *Det gudomliga ruset: Ett kulturhistoriskt axplock från myt och kult*. Lund: Studentliteratur, 1969.

The text of a radio address surveying substances used to induce religious intoxication, including the mead of poetry.

2294. Rooth, Anna Birgitta. *Loke, Locke och nätet*. Lund: Studentliteratur, 1969.

A radio address, later printed in a daily newspaper, on Loki, the folk figure Locke, and the net. Superseded by the author's *Loki in Scandinavian Mythology* (1961).

2295. Rooth, Erik. "Furan på fjällhyllan." *Svenska landsmål*, 89 (1967), 1-23. Summary in German.

On the word *þorp* in *Hávamál* 50. Rooth suggests that in this context it may mean "mountain ledge."

2296. Ropeid, Andreas. "Vilhelm Kiil og Tors-kulten." *Norveg*, 10 (1963), 123-28.

Criticism of Kiil, "Fra andvegissúla til omnkall" (1960).

2297. Rosell, Erland. *Värmländsk medeltid i ortnamnsperspektiv*. Karlstad: Press förlag, 1981. 219 pp.

Chapter 4 (pp. 171-87) of this discussion of placename evidence concerning the Middle Ages in Värmland (Sweden) treats, in a cautious and rather general way, pagan cult and culture.

2298. Rosenberg, Carl. *Nordboernes aandsliv fra oldtiden til vore dage,* vol. 1: *Hedenold.* Copenhagen: Samfundet til den danske literaturs fremme, 1878. 501 pp.

Besides a chapter on mythological poetry (pp. 149-217), this treatment of the culture of ancient Scandinavia includes as the final chapter discussion of belief, cult, and ethics.

2299. Rosenfeld, Hellmut. "Nordische Schilddichtung und mittelalterliche Wappendichtung: Ihre Beziehung zum griechischen Schildgedicht und ihre literarische Auswirkung." *Zeitschrift für deutsche Philologie*, 61 (1936), 232-69.

Important for the study of skaldic poetry (a principal source of Norse mythology), this article brings skaldic shield poems into association with European shield poems.

Section 3, "Die religiöse Wurzel des griechischen und nordischen Schildgedichts" (pp. 244-48), attempts to anchor the tradition in cult.

2300. Rosenfeld, Hellmut. "Die vandalischen Alkes 'Elchreiter', der ostgermanischer Hirschkult und die Dioskuren." *Germanisch-Romanisch Monatsschrift*, 28 (1940), 245-58.

Interpretation of the word *alcis* (Tacitus, *Germania*, ch. 43) in the context of East Germanic stag cult and, more generally, of Mediterranean veneration of divine twins.

2301. Rosenfeld, Hellmut. "Die Inschrift des Helms von Negau." *Zeitschrift für deutsches Altertum*, 86 (1955-56), 241-65.

Dismisses the inscription on the helmet from Negau from the realm of cult. In the last pages, Rosenfeld discusses the origin of the runic alphabet in light of the names of deities embodied in the rune-names: no Odin, no Thor, no goddesses, but *Ingwaz* and *alkiz* point to the Vandals.

2302. Rosenfeld, Hellmut. "Name und Kult der Istrionen (Istwäonen), zugleich Beitrag zu Wodankult und Germanenfrage." *Zeitschrift für deutsches Altertum*, 90 (1960-61), 161-81.

Separates the Istriones (Istaevones) from the cult of Odin and reads the names simply as "men in the cult place." Living in the area between the Weser and the Rhine, this people took over pre-Indo-European cult (the matrones).

2303. Rosenfeld, Hellmut. "Germanischer Zwillingsgottkult und indogermanischer Himmelsgottglaube: Elbe, Hirsche und Pferd in der urarischen Mythologie." In *Märchen, Mythos, Dichtung: Festschrift zum 90. Geburtstage Friedrich von der Leyens am 19. August 1963*, eds. Hugo Kuhn and Kurt Schier, 269-86. Munich: C. H. Beck, 1963.

Traces the hypothetical evolution of the Indo-European twin gods from the twin animals and their equipment that pull the sun's chariot.

2304. Rosenfeld, Hellmut. "Die Namen der Heldendichtung, insbesondere Nibelung, Hagen, Wate, Hetel, Horand, Gudrun." *Beiträge zur Namenforschung*, Neue Folge, 1 (1966), 231-65.

Four of the six names of the title give this article its relevance to Scandinavian mythology. They are Hagen, Wate, Hetel, and Horund, all part of the Hilde-Hetel heroic legend and all explained etymologically by F. R. Schröder as derivations of the myth-ritual he believed to be behind the legend (F. R. Schröder, "Die Sage von Hetel und Hilde," 1958). Rosenfeld argues against "mythological" etymological interpretations of names: these ignore the corpus of names with similar components and seek an interpretation based only on a narrow textual context.

2305. Rosenfeld, Hellmut. "Phol ende Wuodan vuorun zi holza: Baldermythe oder Fohlenzauber?" *Beiträge zur Geschichte der deutschen Sprache und Literatur* (Tübingen), 95 (1973), 1-12.

The second Merseburg charm contains no Baldr myths, only "foal-magic."

2306. Rosenfelder, Karl. "Die Christianisierung Nordgermaniens." *Reden und Aufsätze zum nordischen Gedanken*, 18 (1934), 60-73.

A nationalistic German view of the conversion to Christianity.

2307. Rosén, Helge. "Freykult och djurkult." *Fornvännen*, 8 (1913), 213-44.

Freyr cult and animal cult. Animals considered are the boar, the horse, the ox, and the dog.

2308. Rosén, Helge. *Om dödsrike och dödsbruk i fornnordisk religion.* Lund: Distrib. by Gleerupska universitets-bokhandeln, 1918. xii, 252 pp. Diss. Lund.

The world of the dead and customs associated with death in ancient Scandinavian religion. The author treats the origin of the various dwellings of the dead, the island of the dead, the Baldr myth, the rowan tree, Hel-shoes (*Gísla saga*), and other customs associated with death in Norse literature and in recent folk belief. The perspective is essentially comparative.

2309. Rosén, Helge. "Om Lapparnas dödsrikesföreställningar." *Fataburen*, 1919, pp. 16-27.

Includes consideration of Norse-Lapp equivalences, of which Odin-Ruto is the most significant.

2310. Rosén, Helge. *Studier i skandinavisk religionshistoria och folktro.* Lund: C. Blom, 1919. 79 pp.

Contains three studies, of which the first ("The power of water") relates largely to recent folklore. The second, "Freyr's ship, Skiðblaðnir," suggests that the conception may derive from an area where a fertility god was believed to live on an island. The third, on Heimdallr, sees a combination of factors behind conceptions of the god: ancient beliefs, skaldic speculations, and perhaps Celtic loans.

2311. Rosenstand, Nina. *Mytebegrebet.* Gads filosofi-serie. Copenhagen: G. E. C. Gad, 1981. 108 pp.

In this general exposition of the concept of myth, Rosenstand concentrates on Yggdrasill as an example of a mythic model (pp. 65-74) interpretable in various ways.

2312. Ross, Alan S. C. "Jomali." *Acta Philologica Scandinavica*, 12 (1937-38), 170-73.

On the relationship between Finnish *jumala* "god" and Norse *Jómali*, according to *Heimskringla* and *Bósa saga* the god of the Bjarmar.

2313. Ross, Anne. "Severed Heads in Wells: An Aspect of the Well Cult." *Scottish Studies*, 6 (1962), 31-48.

In the course of presenting Celtic materials relating to the preservation of severed heads, their association with wells and powers of prophecy, Ross suggests that these aspects of Mímir in Norse mythology derive from Celtic conceptions (p. 41).

2314. Ross, Margaret Clunies. "Hildr's Ring: A Problem in the Ragnarsdrápa, Strophes 8-12." *Mediaeval Scandinavia*, 6 (1973), 75-92.

The passage in question involves the offering of a ring by the abducted Hildr to her father Hǫgni, a scene in the legend of the Hjaðningavíg. By analyzing various texts, the author argues that the ring here and elsewhere has the secondary meaning "anus" and served in insults of *ergi* "passive homosexuality."

Among the passges discussed is *Hárbarðsljóð* 42-47, where Clunies Ross finds much sexual innuendo, and *Vatnsdœla saga*, ch. 33, where she sees passage under turf (*jarðarmen*) as encompassing anal insult.

2315. Ross, Margaret Clunies. "Style and Authorial Presence in Skaldic Mythological Poetry." *Saga-Book of the Viking Society*, 20 (1978-81), 276-304.

Starting from the intuition that mythological skaldic poetry involved a "double focus" (the poetic description of an object such as a shield in the presence of the ruler who had given it to the skald and hence was implicitly praised by the content as well as by the situation of the performance of the poem), Clunies Ross analyzes the political aspects of mythological skaldic poetry and such stylistic aspects—irony and the grotesque—as may be understood in light of the politics and the "double focus." Poems treated are *Ragnarsdrápa*, *Haustlǫng*, *Húsdrápa*, and *Þórsdrápa*.

2316. Ross, Margaret Clunies. "The Myth of Gefjon and Gylfi and its Function in Snorra Edda and Heimskringla." *Arkiv för nordisk filologi*, 93 (1978), 149-65.

The myth originally turned on sexual involvement between king and traveling woman, as part of a deceptive land bargain; Bragi reduced the sexual component and used the story in a professional skaldic mnemonic; and Snorri found the tale so compelling that he used it twice, in *Snorra edda* and in *Ynglinga saga*. "I suggest that the reason why the story of Gefjon's plowing suited Snorri's grand plan for *Snorra edda* and *Heimskringla* so well that he used it twice over was that the deceptive land purchase motif which was central to it drew a clear parallel between early Scandinavian history and the history of Britain as told by Geoffrey of Monmouth" (pp. 162-63).

2317. Ross, Margaret Clunies. "An Interpretation of the Myth of Þórr's Encounter with Geirrøðr and his Daughters." In *Speculum Norroenum: Norse Studies in Memory of Gabriel Turville-Petre*, eds. Ursula Dronke, Guðrún P. Helgadóttir, Gerd Wolfgang Weber, and Hans Bekker-Nielsen, 370-91. N.p.: Odense University Press, 1981.

Aims to "analyze the structural pattern of the Old Norse myth of Þórr's visit to the giant Geirrøðr and thereby attempt an interpretation of it and, in the process, to examine some of the important cruces in Eilífr Goðrúnarson's *Þórsdrápa*" (p. 370).

The myth is ontogenic. Thor overcomes the flowing river, understood by Clunies Ross as menstrual blood of Jǫrð, and the two giantesses who seek to elevate him from below: in these cases, the young god rejects the sexual advances of chthonic female beings of his primary bonding (p. 385). He turns to females with whom he can associate by affinity—the rowan, understood by Clunies Ross as symbolic of Sif, and the giantess Gríðr, who confers on him the staff symbolic of her sexual power. In the third episode Thor kills Geirrøðr, whom Clunies Ross interprets as the divine smith (frequently the young god's father) of the great weapon; thus the glowing iron bolt which Thor hurls back at Geirrøðr is Mjǫllnir. The myth's "central concern is how the young god Þórr frees himself from the potential threat to his career as an active, virile, ordering deity posed by the dual forces of excessive attachment to the female objects of his primary bonding and the destructive rivalry with his father, whose weapon he must acquire for himself" (p. 390). This provocative essay adduces many useful comparative data.

2318. Ross, Margaret Clunies. "Snorri Sturluson's Use of the Norse Origin-Legend of the Sons of Fornjótr in his *Edda*." *Arkiv för nordisk filologi*, 98 (1983), 47-66.

On Snorri's anthropomorphic representation of natural phenomena as giants, his "projection of early Scandinavian man's understanding of the nature of the macrocosm"(p. 65). Although the author leaves open the possibility that the sons of Fornjótr may represent genuine older tradition, she strives generally to place Snorri's reasoning in a learned medieval context.

2319. Rostvik, Allan. *Har och harg*. Skrifter utgivna av kungliga Gustav Adolfs akademien, 44. Uppsala: Almqvist & Wiksell, 1967. 175, [15] pp. Summary in German, pp. 156-59.

The placename and dialect evidence bearing on the term *hǫrgr*. Originally it must have meant "pile of stones." The cultic association, although old, must be secondary, perhaps via a semantic link "cultic stone heap, stone altar."

2320. Rostvik, Allan. "Ortnamnet *Harv*." *Namn och bygd*, 57 (1969), 75-82. Summary in English.

The placename element *harv* is equivalent to *harg*; thus, *harg/hǫrgr* names are also known in Fenno-Swedish speech areas.

2321. Routh, Harold Victor. *God, Man, and Epic Poetry: A Study in Comparative Literature*. Cambridge: University Press, 1927. xii, 283 pp.

Includes a discussion of "religious sentiments in early northern poetry" (pp. 25-67).

2322. Rudolf, Adalbert. *Edda: Runen aus germanischem Urwalde: Beiträge zur deutschen Götterlehre*. Hamburg: G. A. Rudolph, 1898. 154 pp.

Treatise on eddic mythology, with focus on cosmic history (*Vǫluspá*) and Baldr's death.

2323. Rüdiger, Hans Helmut. *Liederedda und germanische Seele*. Berlin: Dr. Emil Ebering, 1939. 243 pp.

This study of the "germanic soul" considers the world of eddic poetry under three rubrics: man and nature, man and life, man and mystery. Although it has little to say directly about myth, its discussion of the eddic poems is informative.

2324. Rühfel, Josef. *Die drei Nornen: Ein Beitrag zur germanischen Mythologie mit besonderen Berücksichtigung süddeutscher Überlieferungen*. Dresden: Aurora, 1920. 148 pp.

Southern German folk traditions of three females as alleged evidence of the survival of "more original" conceptions of the norns than those of Scandinavian mythology.

2325. Rühs, Friedrich. *Die Edda: Nebst einer Einleitung über nordische Poesie und Mythologie und einem Anhang über die historische Literatur der Isländer*. Berlin: Realschulbuchhandlung, 1812. vi, 288 pp.

Translation of *Gylfaginning* and portions of *Skáldskaparmál* from *Snorra edda*, preceded by a lengthy introduction (pp. 1-160) and followed by an index and an appendix on Icelandic historical literature. Rühs treats the mythology on pp. 120-60, stressing its connection with poetry and Christianity.

2326. Ruggerini, Maria Elena. *Le invettive di Loki*. Testi e studi di filologia, 2. Rome: Istituto di glottologia, Università di Roma, 1979. 121 pp.

The text of *Lokasenna*, with an Italian translation and extensive commentary. Ruggerini argues that the poet imitated such poems as *Hávamál*, *Skírnismál*, *Vǫlundarkviða*, *Hárbarðsljóð*, and *Alvíssmál* and had some classical training. She dates the poem to the twelfth century and thinks the prose sections are not original.

2327. Rupp, Theophil. "Fiölsvinnsmâl." *Germania*, 10 (1865), 433-46.

Reads the poem as a marriage between sun and moon.

2328. Rupp, Theophil. "Baldur." *Germania*, 11 (1866), 424-35.

Contrasts the German and Nordic traditions and stresses the ethical nature of the latter versus the nature mythology of the former.

2329. Rupp, Theophil. "Hrafnagaldr Odhins." *Germania*, 11 (1866), 311-20.

Commentary to the poem.

2330. Rupp, Theophil. "Nachtrag zu Baldur." *Germania*, 12 (1867), 100-01.

Brief addendum to the author's "Baldur" (1866), taking up the question of the mistletoe.

2331. Rupp, Theophil. *Eddische Studien*. Vienna: C. Gerolds Sohn, 1869. 62 pp.

Includes chapters on Baldr and Freyja.

2332. Ryan, J. S. "Othin in England: Evidence from the Poetry for a Cult of Woden in Anglo-Saxon England." *Folklore*, 74 (1963), 460-80.

Reflections of Odin in English royal genealogies, spells, references to beasts of battle, and the wild hunt.

2333. Rydberg, Viktor. "Astrologien och Merlin: (Om källorna till stjärneskildringen i Galfrids Historia Regum Britanniæ)." *Nordisk tidskrift för vetenskap, konst och industri*, 4 (1881), 377-409. Rpt. in Rydberg, *Skrifter* (Stockholm: A. Bonnier), vol. 12 (1898), pp. 435-84.

Detailed criticism and ultimate dismissal of the theories of Sophus Bugge concerning Western influence on *Vǫluspá*.

2334. Rydberg, Viktor. "Sibyllerna och Völuspå." *Nordisk tidskrift för vetenskap, konst och industri*, 4 (1881), 1-29.

Criticism of A. Chr. Bang, *Völuspaa og de sibyllinske orakler* (1879).

2335. Rydberg, Viktor. "Sibyllinerna og Völuspa." *Nordisk tidskrift för vetenskap, konst och industri*, 4 (1881), 317-434. Rpt. in Rydberg, *Skrifter* (Stockholm: A. Bonnier), vol. 12, pp. 317-434.

Detailed criticism and ultimate dismissal of A. Chr. Bang, *Völuspaa og de Sibyllinske orakler* (1879).

2336. Rydberg, Viktor. *Undersökningar i germanisk mythologi*. Stockholm: A. Bonnier, 1886-89. 755, vi; 628, xxxvii pp. 2 vols.

Swedish original of Rydberg's *Teutonic Mythology* (1889).

2337. Rydberg, Viktor. *Fädernas gudasaga berättad för ungdomen*. Stockholm: A. Bonnier, 1887. 248 pp. Rpt. in Rydberg, *Skrifter* (Stockholm: A. Bonnier), vol. 12, pp. 3-309, with sep. title page labeled 2nd. ed.

Popular treatment of the mythology, ostensibly for juvenile readers. The last section is a name index with extensive comments.

A German translation was also issued: *Die Göttersage der Väter: Für die Jugend erzählt* (Stockholm: A. Bonnier, n. d., 232 pp.).

2338. Rydberg, Viktor. *Teutonic Mythology: Gods and Goddesses of the Northland*. London: S. Sonnenschein, 1889. xii, 706 pp. Translated by Rasmus B. Anderson.

As the title of the Swedish original of this work indicates (*Undersökningar i germansk mytologi*, 1886-89), Rydberg offers "investigations" rather than, strictly speaking, a handbook. The organization of the lengthy work thus seems rather loose. Despite its philological emphasis and broad sweep, the work now commands little more than historical interest—and this largely because of Rydberg's status as a poet.

S

2339. Sachs, Emmy. "Zu aisl. 'gaglviðr'." *Wörter und Sachen*, 6 (1914-15), 141-43.

On the etymology of *gaglviðr (Vǫluspá*, str. 42); no obvious mythological import.

2340. Sahlgren, Jöran. "Mansnamnet Locke och ortnamnen Låckerud och Låcktorp." *Namn och bygd*, 2 (1914), 252-54.

Concludes that the personal name Locke had nothing to do with the god Loki, contra Olrik, "Loke i nyere folkeoverlevering," (1908 and 1909).

2341. Sahlgren, Jöran. "Förbjudna namn." *Namn och bygd*, 6 (1918), 1-40.

This paper deals with linguistic tabus in Scandinavian. Section 4, "Nerthus, Freyr och Freyja" (pp. 22-27), finds that each of these names was a tabu form for a fertility deity and gently criticizes but in effect follows Axel Kock, "Die Göttin Nerthus und der Gott Niorþr" (1896), 299ff. Section 5, "Luggude, Ludgo och Luggavi," discusses fertility figures allegedly attested in placename evidence.

2342. Sahlgren, Jöran. "De skånska häradena och deras namn: En översikt." *Namn och bygd*, 8 (1920), 54-62.

Includes discussion of reflection in placenames of worship of Odin and of a goddess Ludguda, whom Sahlgren identifies with Freyja.

2343. Sahlgren, Jöran. "Är mytosofien en vetenskap?" *Vetenskaps-societeten i Lund, årsbok*, 1923, pp. 27-36.

Mythosophy, Sahlgren's term for overly zealous identification of theophoric elements in placenames, is to the history of religion as astrology is to astronomy; it is no science. Sahlgren was to sound this theme throughout his career, but here he is at his most sarcastic. The butt of the sarcasm is primarily Magnus Olsen, but Adolf Noreen and Hugo Jungner are also condemned. Most of the examples cited here turn up elsewhere in Sahlgren's writings, but here they are adorned with particular contempt.

2344. Sahlgren, Jöran. "Nordiska ortnamn i språklig och saklig belysning, 6: Oäkta *vi*-namn." *Namn och bygd*, 11 (1923), 110-34.

In that it represents the first important reaction to the then prevailing tendency to interpret placenames as theophoric on scanty evidence, this article on false names in -*vi*- (cf. Norse *vé* "holy place") is important.

2345. Sahlgren, Jöran. "Mera om de oäkta *vi*-namn." *Namn och bygd*, 12 (1924), 37-40.

Primarily on Hugo Jungner, "Om Friggproblemet" (1924) and *Gudinnan Frigg och Als härad* (1922).

2346. Sahlgren, Jöran. "Häradsnamnet Luggude." *Sydsvenska ortnamnssällskapets årsskrift*, 1925, pp. 25-27.

*Ludhgudha a fertility goddess.

2347. Sahlgren, Jöran. "Vrindevi: Ett genmäle." *Sydsvenska ortnamnssällskapets årsskrift*, 1925, pp. 47-48.

Contra A. Nordén, "Den heliga murgrönans offerställe" (1925): *Vrindevi* is not a *vi*-name and does not contain the name Rindr.

2348. Sahlgren, Jöran. *Eddica et scaldica: Fornvästnordiska studier 1-2.* Nordisk filologi, undersökningar och handlingar, 1. Lund: C. W. K. Gleerup, 1927-28. viii, 318 pp. 2 vols. with continuous pagination.

Contains five separate studies, of which three are studies of texts relevant to Norse mythology. These are *Eiríksmál* (pp. 1-37), *Hákonarmál* (pp. 39-109), and *Skírnismál* (pp. 209-303). The results, besides various proposals for new readings and reconstituted texts, include the following.

Eiríksmál imitated *Hávamál* (first part), *Vafþrúðnismál*, and *Þrymskviða*, and borrowed from *Helgakviða Hundingsbana I*.

Hákonarmál is actually two poems, which probably produced the model for *Hyndluljóð*.

Skírnismál does not, as Magnus Olsen suggested, reflect ancient fertility myth. Rather it reflects folktale patterns, particularly those of Irish saga. This essay is particularly suggestive in its analysis of placenames and gods' names.

2349. Sahlgren, Jöran. "Nordiska ordstudier, 4: Fvn. *kǫgurr, kǫgursveinn*." *Arkiv för nordisk filologi*, 40 (1927-28), 258-71.

Relevant to *Hárbarðsljóð* 13, in which Thor calls the disguised Odin a *kǫgursveinn*, and to *Gylfaginning*, in which Utgarða-Loki uses the term at least equally disparagingly of Thor. Sahlgren's explanation of the word as "small boy" draws on Nordic placenames.

2350. Sahlgren, Jöran. "Sagan om Frö och Gärd." *Namn och bygd*, 16 (1928), 1-19.

Sahlgren dismisses Magnus Olsen's interpretation of *Skírnismál* as a derivative of fertility cult ("Fra gammelnorsk myte og kultus" (1909)) and argues instead that a folktale (with Celtic analogs) lies at the heart of the poem; like a folktale prince, Freyr obtains a bride from the realm of the sea-king.

2351. Sahlgren, Jöran. "Järular och heruler." *Saga och sed*, 1932-34, pp. 83-90.

In this paper (arguing no connection between the southest Swedish dialect term *järul* and the Heruli) Sahlgren speculates in passing whether Thor's *megingjǫrð*, usually understood as a belt of strength, may not simply have been a goatskin belt or sash enabling the god to assume the form of a goat (p. 89).

2352. Sahlgren, Jöran. *Vad våra ortnamn berätta*. Verdandis småskrifter, 351. Stockholm: A. Bonnier, 1932. 73 pp.

With a section on ancient and medieval religion.

2353. Sahlgren, Jöran. "Gunnar Gröpa en jättekäring." *Namn och bygd*, 30 (1942), 159-70.

Includes discussion of recent folklore survivals of the valkyries (p. 167f.).

2354. Sahlgren, Jöran. "Reaktion och korrektion: En språkpsykologisk och språkhistorisk studie." *Namn och bygd*, 35 (1947), 97-126.

Pernicious homonymy illustrated in part with *Odin-*, *Thor-*, and *hǫrgr* names.

2355. Sahlgren, Jöran. "Hednisk gudalära och nordiska ortnamn: Kritiska inlägg." *Namn och bygd*, 38 (1950), 1-37.

Sahlgren takes up a series of earlier explanations of placenames as theophoric and offers in each case a nonreligious explanation. Treated are possible horse and sun cults (cf. Elias Wessén, "Hästskede och lekslätt" (1921)), including criticism of the "kilometer method" (two deities are related if they appear in placenames situated near one another; Sahlgren condemns the method unless the names are also contemporary), and the possible reflection of a cult of the Dioscurii (*alces*) in Nordic placenames in *Älg-*.

Midway through the paper, almost in passing, Sahlgren offers a not very flattering judgement of Magnus Olsen's great works on theophoric placenames. Although Sahlgren was in the forefront of the reaction against overly zealous identification of theophoric elements in placenames, it is safe to say that by 1950 his position was no more than moderate and was shared by most placename scholars.

2356. Sahlgren, Jöran. "Skövde: Förberedande meddelande." *Ortnamnssällskapets i Uppsala årsskrift*, 1951, pp. 47-50.

Against the interpretation of the placename *Skövde* as *Skadevi* "Skaði's holy place." Sahlgren offers instead an explanation based on natural formations.

2357. Sahlgren, Jöran. "Aktuella frågor inom modern ortnamnsforskning." *Ortnamnssällskapets i Uppsala årsskrift*, 1952, pp. 11-26.

Includes on pp. 22-26 a reprint of Sahlgren's remarks against Magnus Olsen's interpretation of *Hærnevi* placenames (1908), reprinted from "Hednisk gudalära och nordiska ortnamn" (1950).

2358. Sahlgren, Jöran. "Västergötlands häradsnamn." *Ortnamnssällskapets i Uppsala årsskrift*, 1953, pp. 1-10.

Text of an address delivered in 1934, including Sahlgren's doubts that the placename *Frövi* has anything to do with Freyja or Freyr.

2359. Sahlgren, Jöran. "Gudhem." In *Scandinavica et Finno-Ugrica: Studier tillägnade Björn Collinder den 22 Juli 1954.* 1-7. Stockholm: Almqvist & Wiksell, 1954. Summary in French, p. 7.

Sahlgren questions whether *Goðheimr* "gods' home," attested in Old Norse literature, is somehow parallel to the continental Scandinavian placename *Gudhem.* He concludes that it is not. *Gudhem* is regularly associated with the Church and is therefore a loan translation of *locus dei.*

2360. Sahlgren, Jöran. "*Alavi*, fsv. Aluerui." *Namn och bygd*, 46 (1958), 159-62.

Another "false *vi*-name" (cf. Sahlgren, "Nordiska ortnamn i språklig och saklig belysning, 6: Oäkta *vi*-namn" (1923), and "Mera om de oäkta *vi*-namn" (1924)).

2361. Sahlgren, Jöran. "Gamla svenska ånamn." *Namn och bygd*, 47 (1959), 1-54.

This discussion of ancient Swedish river names includes a section on *Þunð* (*Grímnismál* 21).

2362. Sahlgren, Jöran. "Odens kulle på Axvalls hed." In *Septentrionalia et Orientalia: Studia Bernhardo Karlgren A.D. III non. oct. anno mcmlix dedicata.* 368-76. Kungliga vitterhets historie och antikvitets akademiens handlingar, 91. Stockholm: Kungliga vitterhets historie och antikvitets akademien, 1959.

On antiquarian descriptions of early excavation of a grave-site called "Odin's hill"; the name probably represents late, popular usage, the name *Oden* here simply indicating that the hill is large.

2363. Sahlgren, Jöran. "Væta ǫgur, Arsvätan och Ballblötan: Till Hárbarðsljóð 13." *Namn och bygd*, 49 (1961), 1-8.

Support for the interpretation of *ǫgur* (*Hárbarðsljóð* 13), offered by Magnus Olsen and Ferdinand Holthausen, as *membrum virile*: Nordic placenames referring to the wetting of parts of the body.

2364. Sahlgren, Jöran. "Lunden Barre i Skírnismál." *Namn och bygd*, 50 (1962), 193-203. Summary in English, p. 233.

Additional remarks contra Magnus Olsen's interpretation of *Barri* (*Skírnismál* 39, 41; see Olsen, "Fra gammelnorsk myth og kultus," (1909)). Sahlgren draws on etymological, onomastic, and ethnographic evidence.

2365. Sahlgren, Jöran. "Nordisk hedendom: Kritiska anmärkningar." *Namn och bygd*, 51 (1963), 162-68.

A review article on Folke Ström's *Nordisk hedendom: Tro och sed i förkristen tid* (1961), criticizing some of Ström's etymologies and his unwillingness to accept the views Sahlgren had put forth, particularly on *Skírnismál.*

2366. Salberger, Evert. "Vi*n*zflot: En skriftnotis till Alvíssmál 22." *Arkiv för nordisk filologi*, 70 (1955), 188-95.

Palaeographic note on *Alvíssmál*, str. 2.

2367. Salberger, Evert. "Rístu nú, Skírnir! Ett textställe i Skírnismál 1." *Arkiv för nordisk filologi*, 72 (1957), 173-92.

Textual note on *Skírnismál*, str. 1.

2368. Salberger, Evert. "Vel glýioð eller velglýioð: En text-detalj i Vǫluspá 35." *Scripta Islandica*, 22 (1971), 46-52.

Philological note on *Vǫluspá*, str. 35.

2369. Salberger, Evert. "Heill þú farir! Ett textproblem i Vafþrúðnismál 4." *Scripta Islandica*, 25 (1974), 23-30.

Proposes an emendation to *Vafþrúðnismál*, str. 4.

2370. Salberger, Evert. "Eldens namn hos vanerna: En heiti-studie i Alvíssmál 26." *Gardar*, 10 (1979), 52-63. Summary in German.

Reads the *vanir*'s term for fire (*Alvíssmál*, str. 26), as *vágr* "wave."

2371. Salin, Bernhard. "Heimskringlas tradition om asarnes invandring: Ett arkeologiskt-religionshistoriskt utkast." In *Studier tillägnade Oscar Montelius 19.9.03 af lärjungar*, eds. Bernhard Salin, Oscar Almgren, and Sune Ambrosiani, 133-41. Stockholm: Norstedt, 1903.

Associates the description in *Heimskringla* (*Ynglinga saga*) of the entry of the *æsir* into Scandinavia under the direction of Odin with archaeological evidence of an invasion of Scandinavia by peoples from north of the Black Sea during the third and fourth centuries A.D.

2372. Salin, Bernhard. "Några ord om en Fröbild." In *Opuscula Archæologica Oscari Montelio Septuagenario Dicata d. IX. m. Set. a. MCMXIII.* 405-[12]. Stockholm: I. Hæggström, 1913.

Discussion of an image of Freyr discovered in 1904 near Nyköping, Sweden, dating from around the year 1000.

2373. Salus, Peter H. "More 'Eastern Echoes' in the *Edda*? An Addendum." *Modern Language Notes*, 79 (1964), 426-28.

An "addendum" to R. A. Fowkes, "Eastern Echoes in the *Wessobrunner Gebet*?" (*Germanic Review*, 37 [1962], 83-90). Fowkes "offered Rig-Vedic and Armenian 'echoes' of a motif in the *Wessobrunner* verses. As those Old High German lines have been frequently noted as similar to the Old Norse *Vǫluspá*, we might consider the Vedic and Armenian as analogs of the Eddic poem. . . . Curiously enough, another echo of oriental cosmogony in the *Edda* is visible in the *Vafþrúðnismál*" (p. 426). Salus finds this echo in str. 20-26, in the dialog on creation of the various parts of the cosmos.

2374. Salus, Peter H., and Paul Beekman Taylor. "*Eikinskialdi, Fjalarr,* and *Eggþér*." *Neophilologus*, 53 (1969), 76-81.

On names in *Vǫluspá*. The authors read *Eikinskialdi* (str. 16) as "with an oaken shield" and *Fjalarr* as "he who hides or deceives" or "all-wise." They believe that only the dwarf in *Vǫluspá* 16 actually bears the name; the figures in *Vǫluspá* 42, *Hávamál* 14, and *Hárbarðsljóð* 26 bear the name through extension. The authors compare *Eggþér* (*Vǫluspá* 42) to Ecgtheow in *Beowulf* and understand him as a shepherd tending the wolf-cubs mentioned in str. 40. His name "is a descriptive agnomen deriving from the giants' hatred of the gods and his function of arousing the giants to battle" (p. 80).

2375. Samplonius, Kees. "Zu Nordals Datierung der 'Vǫluspá.'" *Amsterdamer Beiträge zur älteren Germanistik*, 19 (1983), 139-45.

Dismissal of one of the primary bases of Sigurður Nordal's dating of *Vǫluspá* to ca. 1000 A.D.: fear of the end of the world with the coming of the millennium. Samplonius argues that the anxiety expressed by the poet has to do with a fear of hell and that the eschatological material in the poem turns up in other contexts both well before and after the year 1000. He offers no alternative dating.

2376. Sander, F. *Eddastudier: Brages samtal om skaldskapets uppkomst m.m.* Stockholm: P. A. Norstedt, 1882. 155 pp.

A series of loosely related and, to the modern reader, not very useful essays about eddic and mythological subjects: Bragi and the origin of poetry; Freyja and the *Brísingamen*; Sleipnir; the stages of mythic action (the most interesting of the essays); *Baldrs draumar*; and heroic and runic topics.

2377. Sander, F. *Harbardssången jämte grundtexten till Völuspá: Mythologiska undersökningar.* Stockholm: P. A. Norstedt, 1891. 72 pp.

Argues against identifying Hárbarðr with Loki (an implausible hypothesis in any case) and against reconstruction of earlier versions of the text.

2378. Sander, F. *La mythologie du nord, éclairée par des inscriptions latines en Germanie, en Gaul et dans la Bretagne anncienne des premiers siècles de notre ère.* Stockholm: P. A. Norstedt, 1892. 188 pp.

Continental inscriptions and Norse mythology. Like much of Sander's work, this book was rejected as worthless by contemporary scholars; see, e.g., F. Kauffmann in *Anzeiger für deutsches Altertum*, 20 (1894), 79-80.

2379. Sander, F. *Rigveda und Edda: Eine vergleichende Untersuchung der alten arischen und der germanischen oder nordischen Mythen.* Stockholm: P. A. Norstedt, 1893. 71 pp.

Dated comparison between Vedic and Norse mythology.

2380. Sandnes, Jørn. "Gno. *hǫrgr* i gardsnavn." *Maal og minne*, 1964, pp. 113-20.

A survey of farm names in western Norway (Vestlandet and Trøndelag) including the appellative *hǫrgr* "mountain" or "pagan cult site." Sandnes concludes that all are based on the first meaning and therefore have nothing to do with pagan religion.

2381. Santillana, Giorgio de, and Hertha von Dechend. *Hamlet's Mill: An Essay on Myth and the Frame of Time.* Ipswich: Gambit, 1969. xxiii, 505 pp.

This ambitious and curious book, which attempts to locate the origin of myth in astronomical cosmological speculation, departs from Scandinavian materials (the Hamlet story in the *Gesta Danorum* of Saxo Grammaticus) and uses them throughout. A chapter on "The Twilight of the Gods" (pp. 149-64) offers a reading of Norse mythic history, as based on *Vǫluspá*. As with any undertaking of this scale, the details are suspect, and errors in interpreting Norse myth derive from a lack of familiarity with the original language and the full range of secondary literature.

2382. Sass, Günther. "Sagazeugnisse zur Gewaltmissionierung des alten Nordens." *Reden und Aufsätze*, 18 (1934), 17-53.

Stresses, in an anti-Christian, pro-German(ic) spirit, the conversion of Scandinavia as an act of force and aggression.

2383. Saubert, B. *Germanische Welt- und Gottanschauung in Märchen, Sagen, Festgebräuchen und Liedern*. Hannover: Helwing, 1895. 285 pp.

Alleged association between Märchen and Germanic mythology.

2384. Saussaye, P. D. Chantepie de la. *Geschiedenis van den godsdienst der Germanen vóór hun overgang tot het Christendom*. Haarlem: De erven F. Bohn, 1900. vii, 302 pp.

The (somewhat less full) Dutch original of the author's *Religion of the Teutons* (1902).

2385. Saussaye, P. D. Chantepie de la. *The Religion of the Teutons*. Handbooks on the History of Religion, 3. Boston and London: Ginn, 1902. vii, 504 pp. Translated by Bert J. Vos.

What separates this handbook from others of the period is the emphasis on the Germanic cultural background on the one hand and on cult and survivals on the other.

2386. Sauvé, James L. "The Divine Victim: Aspects of Human Sacrifice in Viking Scandinavia and Vedic India." In *Myth and Law Among the Indo-Europeans: Studies in Indo-European Comparative Mythology*, ed. Jaan Puhvel, 173-91. Publications of the UCLA Center for the Study of Comparative Folklore and Mythology, 1. Berkeley and Los Angeles: University of California Press, 1970.

A comparison of Odin's self-sacrifice (*Hávamál* 138-42) with Indic traditions. "The ultimate divine act of self-sacrifice was perceived as the eschatological mystery wherein the last possible cosmic potentiality was actualized in the person of the sacrificer" (pp. 190-91).

2387. Sawyer, Peter H. *Kings and Vikings: Scandinavia and Europe AD 700-1100*. London and New York: Methuen, 1982. x, 182 pp. 16 pp. of plates.

Includes a clear-eyed chapter on "Pagans and Christians" (pp. 131-43).

2388. Scardigli, Piergiuseppe. "La conversione dei goti al cristianesimo." In *La conversione al cristianesimo nell'Europa dell'alto medioevo: 14-19 aprile 1966*. 47-86. Settimane di studio del centro italiano di studi sull'alto medioevo. Spoleto: Presso la sede del centro, 1967.

A contribution to an international symposium on the conversion of the European peoples to Christianity; treats the Goths.

2389. Scargill, M. H. "Evidence of Totemism in Edda and Saga." *American-Scandinavian Review*, 40 (1952), 146-49.

"To sum up: Scandinavian Mythology, as revealed in written records, must be a development of earlier beliefs, and there are traces of these beliefs in verse and prose. These earlier beliefs are of such a nature that one is led to assign them to the Totemic Age, the period of transition between Primitive Man and the Age of Heroes and Gods" (p. 149).

2390. Schach, Paul. "Antipagan Sentiment in the Sagas of Icelanders." *Gripla*, 1 (1975), 168-81.

Schach surveys the sagas of Icelanders (family sagas) to determine the attitude of their authors toward paganism and Christianity. He concludes that there is no basis for the old romantic notion that the sagas are sympathetic to paganism.

2391. Schach, Paul. "The Theme of the Reluctant Christian in the Icelandic Sagas." *Journal of English and Germanic Philology*, 81 (1982), 186-203.

Surveying the theme of the reluctant Christian in the family sagas, Schach concludes that these texts are essentially anti-pagan.

2392. Schach, Paul. "Some Thoughts on *Völuspá*." In *Edda: A Collection of Essays*, eds. Robert J. Glendenning and Haraldur Bessason, 86-116. The University of Manitoba Icelandic Studies, 4. N. p.: University of Manitoba Press, 1983.

An edition with English translation of *Vǫluspá*, embodying the author's interpretation and commenting from time to time on recent scholarship on the poem. Schach stresses the Icelandic nature of *Vǫluspá*, its pagan theme and accommodation to Christianity.

2393. Schaefer, Albert. *Die Kunde der Vala: Götterdämmerung: Aus der Edda*. Berlin: Kranich, 1935. 31 pp.

Commentary to *Vǫluspá*. A supplement contains *Þrymskviða*.

2394. Schäfer, Hermann. *Götter und Helden: Über religiöse Elemente in der germanischen Heldendichtung*. Tübinger germanistische Arbeiten, 25. Stuttgart and Berlin: W. Kohlhammer, 1937. vi, 126 pp.

Concludes that religious elements in the heroic poetry of the Migration period were very few and of little importance, for the elevated social class that peopled and used the verse was wholly impious, and the verse served primarily esthetic purposes.

2395. Schahl, A. "Freyr-Frô-Phol." *Archiv für Religionswissenschaft*, 35 (1938), 174-78.

Supposed idols of Freyr in medieval German church art.

2396. Scher, Steven P. "Rígsþula as Poetry." *Modern Language Notes*, 78 (1963), 397-407.

"Although *Rígsþula* is a significant source for the cultural history of Nordic civilization, it is primarily an exceptionally original piece of poetry" (p. 397). "This controversial poem is unparalleled for its curiously semi-mythological, semi-philosophical, semi-historical and semi-didactic content framed by an artistic sequence of descriptive names. Its author emerges from the concise stanzas written in free *fornyrðislag*. . . as a learned and original thinker as well as a master of Old Norse poetic expression" (p. 407).

2397. Scheving, Hallgrímur. "Kritisk undersögelse om et par stropher i den saa kaldte Voluspa, især om det sted, der omtaler menneskets skabelse." *Det skandinaviske litteraturselskabs skrifter*, 6 (1810), 175-220.

An interesting early essay on aspects of the mythology of *Vǫluspá*. Scheving comments extensively on str. 17-18 and compares them with *Snorra edda* and *Ynglinga saga*. He finds that Hœnir and Loki (whom he takes Loðurr to be) were ancient gods with a close relationship to Odin, who had a strong interest in the creation of mankind.

2398. Schier, Kurt. "Die Erdschöpfung aus dem Urmeer und die Kosmogonie der Vǫluspá." In *Märchen, Mythos, Dichtung: Festschrift zum 90. Geburtstage Friedrich von der Leyens am 19. August 1963*, eds. Hugo Kuhn and Kurt Schier, 303-34. Munich: C. H. Beck, 1963.

Vǫluspá suggests a creation myth not found in Snorri: the rising of the earth from the sea. Schier reviews the typological parallels to this myth, which in *Vǫluspá* seems to have a very archaic form.

2399. Schier, Kurt. "Freys und Fróðis Bestattung." In *Festschrift für Otto Höfler zum 65. Geburtstag*, eds. Helmut Birkhan and Otto Gschwantler, 389-409. Vienna: Notring, 1968.

Schier argues the essential unity between the descriptions of the burial of Freyr (*Ynglinga saga*, ch. 10, and *Flateyjarbók*) and King Frode in the fifth book of the *Gesta Danorum* of Saxo Grammaticus. A scheme of the essential elements shows them all to be present in the description given by Herodotus (book 4) of a royal funeral among the Scythians. Schier explores possible explanations for this correspondence without arguing preference for any single one. He concludes, however, that the account of Herodotus strengthens the bond between Freyr and Fróði and makes it clear that Fróði, too, was a god. It also certifies, Schier argues, that Freyr belongs to the type of the dying god.

2400. Schier, Kurt. "Balder." In *Reallexikon der germanischen Altertumskunde,* 2nd. ed., vol. 2, ed. Heinrich Beck et al., 2-7. Berlin and New York: W. de Gruyter, 1976.

Besides being a useful encyclopedia summary with many references, this article finds a way to revive the parallel between Baldr and the Near Eastern "dying gods." De Vries's "Der Mythos von Balders Tod" (1955) had apparently undermined this parallel by demonstrating that the point of the Baldr story is that

Baldr stays in the world of the dead and does not return, but Schier argues that in fact many of the Near Eastern figures (Tammuz, Attis, Osiris) undergo the same fate.

2401. Schier, Kurt. "Die Húsdrápa von Úlfr Uggason und die bildliche Überlieferung altnordischer Mythen." In *Minjar og menntir: Afmælisrit helgað Kristjáni Eldjárn 6. desember 1976*, eds. Bjarni Vilhjálmsson, Jónas Kristjánsson, Þór Magnússon, and Guðni Kolbeinsson, 425-43. Reykjavik: Bókaútgáfa Menningarsjóðs, 1976.

The most interesting part of this article is the suggestion that Úlfr may have been working in the tradition of the jarls of Hlaðir when he composed his *Húsdrápa*. If so, even more of our picture of late paganism in Scandinavia centers on the Trondheim area than was previously thought.

2402. Schier, Kurt. "Zur Problematik der Beziehung zwischen Bilddetail und Bildganzem." In *Medieval Iconography and Narrative: A Symposium*, eds. Flemming G. Andersson, Esther Nyholm, Marianne Powell, and Flemming Talbo Stubbkjær, 167-82. Odense: Odense University Press, 1980.

A contribution to the methodology of interpreting iconographic material. A major example is the Smiss (Gotland) stone, on which some scholars see an androgynous proto-being, others representatives of Luxuria or classical prototypes.

2403. Schier, Kurt. "Edda." In *Enzyklopädie des Märchens: Handwörterbuch zur historischen und vergleichenden Erzählung*, vol. 3, ed. Kurt Ranke, 979-1003. Berlin and New York: W. de Gruyter, 1981.

Schier offers a lengthy encyclopedia article covering both *Snorra edda* and the Poetic Edda. Topics discussed include origins and age, contents, and the role of folktales in the eddas. The article is particularly valuable for its extensive references and bibliography.

2404. Schier, Kurt. "Zur Mythologie der *Snorra Edda*: Einige Quellenprobleme." In *Speculum Norroenum: Norse Studies in Memory of Gabriel Turville-Petre*, eds. Ursula Dronke, Guðrún P. Helgadóttir, Gerd Wolfgang Weber, and Hans Bekker-Nielsen, 405-20. N.p.: Odense University Press, 1981.

Snorri's emphasis on cosmology and eschatology and in general his systematizing are, according to Schier, the result of his sources. In *Gylfaginning* Snorri relies primarily on *Vǫluspá*, which de Boor sought to associate with the language of the skalds of the Hlaðir jarls (Trondheim area) of the late tenth century (see de Boor, "Die religiöse Sprache der Vǫluspá" (1930)). In *Skáldskaparmál* skalds cited who provide mythological information center again on the circle of the Hlaðir jarls. The mythology of these circles will have been influenced by tension between paganism and Christianity, and particularly by the Christian notion of the the impending end of the world in A. D. 1000. Snorri's mythology thus reflects the mythological speculation prevalent among the Hlaðir jarls during the later tenth century.

2405. Schierenberg, G. August B. *Secretiora Germaniae oder Deutschlands heilige Berge: Fragmentarische Beiträge zur (sogenannten) nordischen Göttersage und zur deutschen Heldensage.* Detmold: F. Böger, 1872. xxiii, 152, 72 pp.

Eddic myth, esp. *Vǫluspá*, applied to the *Germania* of Tacitus.

2406. Schierenberg, G. August B. *Deutschlands Olympia (Secretiora Germaniae) oder vom Gottesgericht über Roms Sieggötter! Vermuthungen und Untersuchungen über die deutsche Götter- und Heldensage, die wahre Heimath der Eddalieder, ihren Ursprung und ihre Bedeutung.* Frankfurt a. M.: Jaeger, [1875]. xcviii, 167, 136 pp.

Patriotic treatment of eddic myth.

2407. Schierenberg, G. August B. *Die Götterdämmerung und die Goldtafeln des Idafelds oder die Teutoburger Schlacht in den Liedern der Edda: Eine Streitschrift über die Heimat und Bedeutung der Eddalieder (Zur Widerlegung der neuerlich darüber veröffenlichten Ansichten des Prof. Bugge und Dr. Bang dienend).* Detmold: (C. Schenk), 1881. xxxii, 156 pp.

The German and Germanic origins of Ragnarǫk.

2408. Schierenberg, G. August B. *Der Ariadnefaden für das Labyrinth der Edda oder die Edda eine Tochter des Teutoburger Waldes.* Frankfurt a. M.: Reitz & Köhler, 1889. xviii, 96 pp.

The alleged German connection of Norse mythology.

2409. Schierenberg, G. August B. *Die Götter der Germanen oder Vom Eddarausch der Skandinavier und ihrem Katzenjammer, eine Stimme vom Teutoburger Walde.* Detmold: Schenk, 1894. lii, 224 pp.

The contents actually come close to living up to the title: derives Norse mythology from the battle between Arminius and Wittekind. Includes translations of *Vǫluspá*, *Grímnismál*, and other texts.

2410. Schirmeisen, Karl. "Buchstabenschrift, Lautwandel, Göttersage und Zeitrechnung." *Mannus*, 3 (1911), 255-78.

Schirmeisen postulates an original futhark of sixteen runes, each of them a symbol of a Norse god or goddess. These he understands as related to the solstice or equinox, and he arranges them according to the zodiac.

2411. Schirokauer, H. "Ahd. gelimit—mhd. gelime(t)." *Zeitschrift für deutsche Philologie*, 71 (1951-52), 183-86.

On the word *gelimida* in the last verse of the second Merseburg charm.

2412. Schjødt, Jens Peter. "Om Loke endnu engang." *Arkiv för nordisk filologi*, 96 (1981), 49-86.

Schjødt proposes a new examination of Loki, aiming not at reconstruction of an original Loki but rather at an interpretation of the Loki of the sources. He isolates and comments at some length on eighteen motifs, which he reads as a kind of chronology. Long ago Loki swore blood-brotherhood with Odin (for Odin needed access to Loki's chthonic powers), and as mythic history proceeded Loki's relationship with the gods grew worse, until he arranged Baldr's death, slew Fímafengr and slandered the gods, was bound by the gods, and led the forces of evil at Ragnarǫk. Schjødt finds the key to this history in Loki's role as mediator; he changes sexes and form, and is now with the gods, now with the giants. Such mediation, Schjødt argues, breaks down natural oppositions and thus leads to destruction.

2413. Schjødt, Jens Peter. "Völuspá—cyklisk tidsopfattelse i gammelnordisk religion." *Danske studier*, 76 (1981), 91-95.

On the last strophe of *Vǫluspá* (str. 66): the arrival of the dragon and sinking of the sybil. In the light of Eliade's *Myth of the Eternal Return*, Schjødt reads the strophe as an indication of cyclic time in Old Scandinavian religion.

2414. Schlauch, Margaret. *Romance in Iceland.* Princeton: Princeton University Press, New York: American-Scandinavian Foundation, 1934. viii, 201 pp.

Schlauch's study of the translated and native Icelandic romances remains fundamental to study of the Icelandic late Middle Ages. Chapter 2, "The Old Gods and Heroes" (pp. 18-41), surveys the appearance of pagan gods in the romances and in *fornaldarsögur* and Saxo's *Gesta Danorum.*

2415. Schlender, Ida Hedwig. *Germanische Mythologie: Religion und Leben der Germanen.* Berlin: H. Stubenrauch, 1937. 280 pp. 6th rev. ed. by Richard von Kienle.

Popular handbook.

2416. Schlottig, Karl Helmut. "Sind die Inschriften der *ehu*-Brakteaten undeutbar?" In *Beiträge zur Runenkunde und nordischen Sprachwissenschaft: Gustav Neckel zum 60. Geburtstag.* 74-77. Leipzig: O. Harrassowitz, 1938.

Are runic *ehu*- bracteates uninterpretable? Not according to the author, who thinks *e* might stand for Odin.

2417. Schmidt, August F. *Danmarks helligkilder: Oversigt og literaturfortegnelse.* Danmarks folkeminder, 33. Copenhagen: Det schønbergske forlag, 1926. 159 pp.

Sacred springs in Denmark.

2418. Schmidt, August F. "Helligkilder i Svendborg amt." *Årbog for Svendbo amts historiske samfund*, 1926, pp. 3-38.

Sacred springs in Jutland.

2419. Schmidt, August F. "Lejrskov." *Danske studier*, 23 (1926), 77-81.

Danish placename with hypothetical cult activity.

2420. Schmidt, August F. "Fra Kongeåegnen." *Sønderjysk månedsskrift*, 4 (1927), 81-86 and 97-103.

Theophoric placenames and placenames reflecting cult in an area of southern Jutland.

2421. Schmidt, Kurt. "Tiernamen als Zeugen altniederdeutschen Glaubens bei Wilhelm Busch." *Zeitschrift für deutsche Philologie*, 66 (1941), 64-67.

Mythological reminiscences in Wilhelm Busch's collection of Low German folk traditions, *Geschichten ut ôler welt.* Freyr is paramount.

2422. Schmidt, Ludwig. *Geschichte der deutschen Stämme bis zum Ausgang der Völkerwanderung,* vol. 1, *Die Ostgermanen.* Munich: C. H. Beck, 1934. viii, 218 pp.

Classic treatment of the ancient Germanic peoples, with remarks on religion.

2423. Schmidt, Ludwig. *Geschichte der deutschen Stämme bis zum Ausgang der Völkerwanderung,* vol. 2:1, *Die Westgermanen.* Munich: C. H. Beck, 1938. viii, 218 pp.

Classic treatment of the ancient Germanic peoples, with remarks on religion.

2424. Schmidt, Ludwig. *Geschichte der deutschen Stämme bis zum Ausgang der Völkerwanderung,* vol. 2:2, *Die Westgermanen.* Munich: C. H. Beck, 1940. viii, 218 pp. 2nd ed., with Hans Zeuss.

Classic treatment of the ancient Germanic peoples, with remarks on religion.

2425. Schmidt, Philip. "Reexamination of Chaucer's Old Man of The Pardoner's Tale." *Southern Folklore Quarterly*, 30 (1966), 249-55.

Against R. A. Barakat, "Odin: Old Man of *The Pardoner's Tale*" (1964).

2426. Schmieder, Arno. *Wider die Lüge der germanischen Götterlehre,* vol. 2: *Die Asensage und ihr geschichtlicher Hintergrund.* Leipzig: Hammer, 1937-38. 392 pp.

The second part of Schmieder's rehabilitation of his Germanic ancestors' religion centers on making *Gylfaginning* a historical source. Includes a lengthy commentary to *Gylfaginning.*

2427. Schmieder, Arno. *Wider die Lüge der germanischen Götterlehre,* vol. 1: *Die Götterlieder der älteren Edda.* Leipzig: Hammer, 1937. 319 pp.

Because Germans in 1937 considered themselves such a lofty race, writers like Schmieder took it upon themselves to demonstrate that the polytheism of the eddas could not reflect the reality of their Germanic ancestors.

2428. Schmied-Kowarzik, Walther. *Frühe Sinnbilder des Kosmos: Gotteserlebnis und Welterkenntnis in der Mythologie: Eine religionsphilosophische Studie.* Ed. Wolfdietrich Schmied-Kowarzik. Ratingen: Henn, 1974. 203 pp.

Philosophically oriented study of images of the cosmos, with discussion of Scandinavian mythology.

2429. Schneider, Hermann. *Germanische Religion vor dreitausend Jahren.* Leipzig: J. J. Weber, 1934. 30 pp. With fourteen plates, unpaginated.

Brief account of the symbols and figures on Scandinavian rock carvings, primarily from Bohuslän, Sweden. Emphasis of interpretation is on seasonal myths.

2430. Schneider, Hermann. "Muspilli." *Zeitschrift für deutsches Altertum,* 73 (1936), 1-32.

The only thing pagan about the entire poem *Muspilli* is the word *muspilli.*

2431. Schneider, Hermann. *Über die ältesten Götterlieder der Nordgermanen.* Sitzungsberichte der bayerischen Akademie der Wissenschaften, phil.-hist. Abt., 7. Munich: C. H. Beck, 1936. 54 pp.

Schneider attempts to use skaldic poetry with religious content to draw conclusions about the preceding eddic religious poetry. He reasons that this older eddic poetry will have shown greater reverence to the gods than do the extant eddic poems.

2432. Schneider, Hermann. *Die Götter der Germanen.* Tübingen: J. C. B. Mohr (Paul Siebeck), 1938. vii, 273 pp.

This is Schneider's personal statement on the gods of the Germanic peoples. His view is essentially historical: the *vanir* are age-old, non-Germanic fertility gods, and the *æsir* are a more unified, Germanic group, with some Indo-European antecedents. His portrayals of the individual gods consider cult and especially myth and also touch on social factors and Germanic worldview. Schneider is honest about the limits of our knowledge of Germanic religion.

2433. Schneider, Hermann. "Loki." *Archiv für Religionswissenschaft*, 35 (1938), 237-51.

After surveying what skaldic and eddic poems have to say about Loki, Schneider concludes that he is not a force of nature, nor a poetic invention, nor a trickster, nor any sort of god. He is a demon of folk belief: a destroyer, who aroused feelings of disgust.

2434. Schneider, Hermann, ed. *Germanische Altertumskunde.* Munich: C. H. Beck, 1939. xii, 504 pp.

This handbook of Germanic culture, undertaken by the German Academy, intended to present as thorough a picture of its subject as was possible, given limitations of length. As such, it sums up German scholarship in Germanic antiquities up to World War II. At least two of the essays are directly relevant to Scandinavian mythology and are entered separately in this bibliography: Hermann Schneider, "Glauben" (pp. 222-305), and Helmut de Boor, "Dichtung" (pp. 306-430). Of more peripheral interest are Helmut de Boor, "Staat und Gesellschaft" (pp. 123-70), which mentions ritual contacts, Hans Kuhn, "Sitte und Sittlichkeit" (pp. 171-221), on morality and ethics, and Wilhelm von Jenny, "Kunst" (pp. 460-82), a short survey of art with occasional reference to myth and religion.

2435. Schneider, Hermann. "Glauben." In *Germanische Altertumskunde*, ed. Hermann Schneider, 222-305. Munich: C. H. Beck, 1939.

A historical survey of pagan religious belief among the Germanic peoples, written for a comprehensive handbook of early Germanic culture. The treatment is similar but less comprehensive than in Schneider's *Die Götter der Germanen* (1938). Of particular importance for the study of mythology are Schneider's ongoing remarks about religious belief in the various literary documents.

2436. Schneider, Hermann. "Beiträge zur Geschichte der nordischen Götterdichtung." *Beiträge zur Geschichte der deutschen Sprache und Literatur*, 69 (1947), 301-50.

Defense of the author's postulation of a layer of mythological poems, now lost, in Norway during the Viking Age. The bulk of the article, pp. 312-50, comprises a discussion of the verse, extant and lost, relating to Baldr. Schneider postulates a lost cycle of Baldr verse and attempts to reconstruct its content.

2437. Schneider, Hermann. *Eine Uredda: Untersuchungen und Texte zur Frühgeschichte der eddischen Götterdichtung.* Halle: M. Niemeyer, 1948. 119 pp.

The title of this monograph is interesting but in a sense misleading. The indefinite article admits that by the late 1940s scholars had abandoned the notion of recreating *the* proto-Edda; Schneider's proto-text purports to be the final stage before the extant poems, from the close of the pagan period.

The first section considers *Vǫluspá* and *Hyndluljóð*. From these Schneider extracts three poems: the *Vǫluspá* proper (str. 27ff., an eschatological poem), a cosmological poem (*Vǫluspá* 1-26), and a later, imitative reworking of very primitive eschatological material (*Vǫluspá en skamma*, str. 29-44 in *Hyndluljóð*).

The second section considers the editorial principles at work in linking the various parts of Odin's wisdom poems, *Hávamál*, *Vafþrúðnismál*, and *Grímnismál*. The emphasis is on *Hávamál*, which Schneider regards as originally having treated Odin's accession to the godhead of divine wisdom. This section ends by advancing the notion that individual strophes originally bore and nurtured religious belief.

The third section contains Schröder's reconstructed texts. There is no index or bibliography.

Although the work cannot be said to have succeeded in reconstructing pagan poetry from which extant mythological and gnomic poems grew, its commentary remains of value.

2438. Schneider, Hermann. "Die Geschichte vom Riesen Hrungnir." In *Edda, Skalden, Saga: Festschrift zum 70. Geburtstag von Felix Genzmer*. 200-10. Heidelberg: C. Winter, 1952.

Schneider concerns himself primarily with the textual history of the Hrungnir story. He distinguishes four layers: an ancient epic; the *Haustlǫng* of Þjóðólfr of Hvín (or Hvin); a detailed prose tale; Snorri's version in *Skáldskaparmál*.

2439. Schneider, Karl. *Die germanischen Runennamen: Versuch einer Gesamtdarstellung: Ein Beitrag zur idg./germ. Kultur- und Religionsgeschichte*. Meisenheim am Glan: A. Hain, 1956. xii, 635 pp.

The author's central hypothesis is that the runic writing system belonged primarily to cult and only secondarily came to be used as a mode of ordinary written communication. The monograph seeks to reconstruct the names of the runes and to associate them with Germanic religion. Schneider divides the names into areas of society, cult (burial, sun, and fire), and cosmology-mythology (ice, marriage of sky father and earth mother, tree, and serpent). An excursus on Germanic religion in comparative and historical context (pp. 300-58) prepares the ground for a chapter on the gods reflected in the names of the runes and their putative use (Týr, Ing, Odin, and Thor, and the divine brothers) and on fate (Urðr, *wyrd*). Additional sections treat the origins of the various futharks and offer new readings of certain inscriptions, based on the interpretations presented earlier in the book.

There is much here on Norse mythology, and a thorough knowledge of the textual traditions, but the book should be used with the understanding that it has not proved successful with runologists or historians of religion.

2440. Schneider, Karl. "Zu den Inschriften und Bildern des Franks casket und einer ae. Version des Mythos von Balders Tod." In *Festschrift für Walther Fischer*. 4-20. Heidelberg: C. Winter, 1959.

According to the author, the right side of the Franks (Auzon) casket presents textual and scenic representation of the death of Baldr. The specifically Old

English version presented is far closer to Saxo's than to Snorri's and may be summarized thus.

Baldr (Old English Erdæg) and Hǫðr (Old English *Heaðu) compete for the hand of Nanna, the daughter of the sun. Baldr wins her favor and the two are engaged to marry. Hǫðr's longing for Nanna is so great that he determines to kill Baldr. With the help of the primeval god Hegil ("Hail"), he fashions a spear from a branch of the world tree. In heaven, Hegil blesses Hǫðr and the spear with a leafy branch. Hǫðr meets three nymphs preparing a potion of strength for Baldr and tricks them into giving it to him. He slays Baldr, who is put in a grave mound. Nanna sits grieving on a horse before the mound. The three nymphs, who were unable to prevent the tragedy, reproach themselves bitterly.

Needless to say, extraction of such a version from the short inscription and few scenes on the casket requires a good deal of imagination.

2441. Schnetz, Joseph. "Germanische Völkernamen, 1: Ingvaeones." *Zeitschrift für Ortnamenforschung*, 11 (1935), 201-09.

The etymology of **Ingwaz*: "he with a large voice."

2442. Schnittger, Bror. "Storken som livsbringare i våra fäders tro." *Fornvännen*, 11 (1916), 104-18.

Departing initially from recent folk beliefs about the stork as bringer of human life, Schnittger offers an etymological argument that the name of the god Hœnir originally meant "stork" (derived, however, not from an Indo-European base form but from Latin *ciconia*). In belief formulated, according to the author, as early as the Bronze Age, Hœnir the stork or bird god brought liquid, the essence of life (cf. *Vǫluspá* 18: *óð gaf Hœnir*). Schnittger goes on to discuss later evidence linking religious beliefs with water.

2443. Schnittger, Bror. "En hällristning vid Berga-Tuna i Södermanland: Jämte några allmänna synpunkter på hällristningsproblemen." *Fornvännen*, 17 (1922), 77-112. Summary in German, pp. 267-69.

After describing one recently discovered rock carving, Schnittger discusses generally the purpose of the rock carvings. He finds that the bulk of them involved sympathetic magic used in hunting. Although he denies that they could have been used for a cult of the dead, he does accept the likelihood of various kinds of fertility cults.

2444. Schnittger, Bror. "Hällristningarnas kronologi och betydelse: Ett genmäle till docent Ekholm." *Fornvännen*, 17 (1922), 222-39. German summary, p. 284.

Response to G. Ekholm, "Hällristningsproblemet" (1922), defending the findings of the author's "En hällristning vid Berga-Tuna" (1922).

2445. Scholes, Robert, and Robert Kellogg. *The Nature of Narrative*. London, Oxford, New York: Oxford University Press, 1966. 326 pp.

Chapter 2, "The Oral Heritage of Written Narrative," contains remarks on Norse traditions, including the Poetic Edda. These are helpful in understanding the possible transmission of pagan myth.

2446. Schomerus, Rudolf. *Die Religion der Nordgermanen im Spiegel christlicher Darstellung*. Borna: Noske, 1936. Diss. Göttingen.

A thorough attempt to analyze the effects of the Christian "mirror" through which Scandinavian paganism is reflected, especially in the works of Snorri, Saxo, and the sagas. In general Schomerus inclines toward skepticism and believes that much of what is retained is late or gives a false picture of paganism.

2447. Schoning, O. *Dødsriger i nordisk hedentro*. Studier fra sprog- og oldtidsforskning, 57 [vol. 13:1]. Copenhagen: Kleins forlag (C. Klein), 1903. 54 pp.

Important early study of the realms of the dead in Old Norse belief. Schoning distinguishes *hel* as a realm of shades from the land of the giants, which he regards as a place under Loki's direction where corpses are devoured. Valhalla is a later development.

2448. Schott, Georg. *Weissagung und Erfüllung im deutschen Volksmärchen*. Munich: H. A. Wiechmann, 1925. 204 pp.

Alleged association between Märchen and Germanic mythology.

2449. Schottman, H[ans]. "Christentum der Bekehrungszeit: Die altnordische Literatur." In *Reallexikon der germanischen Altertumskunde,* 2nd ed., vol. 4, ed. Heinrich Beck et al., 563-77. Berlin and New York: W. de Gruyter, 1981.

An encyclopedia article on the Norse literature of the conversion period. Extensive references and bibliography.

2450. Schrader, Otto. *Reallexikon der indogermanischen Altertumskunde: Grundzüge einer Kultur- und Völkergeschichte Alteuropas*. Strassburg: K. J. Trübner, 1901. xl, 1048 pp. 2nd. ed. (without subtitle) published 1917 (vol. 1, Strassburg: K. J. Trübner) and 1929 (vol. 2, ed. A. Nehring, Berlin and Leipzig: W. de Gruyter).

An encyclopedia of Indo-European culture, still useful to put Germanic and Scandinavian in its Indo-European context. Of the numerous articles relevant to Norse mythology, the most important are "Gott," "Opfer," and "Religion."

2451. Schramm, Percy Ernst. "Nordeuropa im Licht der Staatssymbolik." In *Kirche und Gesellschaft im Ostseeraum und im Norden vor der Mitte des 13. Jahrhunderts*. 99-112. Acta Visbyensia, 3; Visby-symposiet för historiska vetenskaper 1967. Visby: Museum Gotlands Fornsal, 1969.

Lecture delivered at an international symposium on church and society in early Scandinavia and the Baltic. The author, an authority on royal symbols and insignia, discusses the situation in Scandinavia and devotes several pages to the continuation of pagan symbols in Christian royal paraphernalia.

2452. Schreuer, Hans. "Das Recht der Toten: Eine germanische Untersuchung." *Zeitschrift für vergleichende Rechtswissenschaft*, 33 (1915), 333-423. [Part 1, "Die Rechtspersönlichkeit des Toten."]

First part of a study of the roles of the dead in Germanic law, with many comments on mythology and literary texts. This part deals with the dead person as a legal being.

2453. Schreuer, Hans. "Das Recht der Toten: Eine germanische Untersuchung." *Zeitschrift für vergleichende Rechtswissenschaft*, 34 (1916), 1-208. [Part 2, "Das Personenrecht des Toten."]

Continuation of the author's study of the roles of the dead in Germanic law, with many comments on mythology and literary texts. This part deals with the legal rights surrounding a dead person.

2454. Schröder, Edward. "Balder in Deutschland." *Namn och bygd*, 10 (1922), 13-19.

Personal and placename evidence for the worship of Baldr in Germany.

2455. Schröder, Leopold. *Germanische Elben und Götter beim Estenvolke*. Sitzungsberichte der Akademie der Wissenschaften in Wien, phil.-hist. Kl., 153:1. Vienna: A. Hölder, 1906. 92 pp.

A study of possible Germanic loans in Estonian tradition (and to some extent also in Finnish). The suggestions Schröder makes in the area of the "higher mythology" include Thor's journey to Geirrøðr and his retrieval of his hammer, some Loki myths, and others.

2456. Schrodt, Richard. "Der altnordische Beiname 'Sýr.'" *Arkiv för nordisk filologi*, 94 (1979), 114-19.

The nickname *Sýr* (often associated with Freyja), according to Schrodt's linguistic and etymological reasoning, originally meant "protectress." It soon became confused with the near homonym *sýr* "sow."

2457. Schröder, Edward. "Belisars Ross." *Zeitschrift für deutsches Altertum*, 35 (1891), 237-44. Addendum in *Anzeiger für deutsches Altertum*, 16 (1891), 184.

Etymological interpretation of Baldr as "the gleaming or bright."

2458. Schröder, Edward. "Walburg, die Sibylle." *Archiv für Religionswissenschaft*, 19 (1916-19), 196-200.

Reads the name Wal(u)burg as *walus* "staff" and, in connection with *gandr* "magic staff," associates the name with the accoutrements of a seeress.

2459. Schröder, Edward. "Irminsûl." *Zeitschrift für deutsches Altertum*, 72 (1935), 292.

Separates the hypothetical god Irmin from the word *irminsûl.*

2460. Schröder, Franz Rolf. "Hœnir, eine mythologische Untersuchung." *Beiträge zur Geschichte der deutschen Sprache und Literatur*, 43 (1918), 219-52.

After a long and fascinating review of scholarship on Hœnir, stretching back nearly a century, Schröder launches his own interpretation. It is at base etymological; Hœnir was **Hauhinijaz*, an adjectival form of **hauhinaz*, itself a parallel form to **hauhaz* "soul of the dead." Schröder understands it as a collective and reads the adjective as "belonging to the band of souls," whence "leader of the band of souls," i.e., Odin. Thus, Hœnir is an Odin name, according to Schröder, and Hœnir was Odin.

2461. Schröder, Franz Rolf. *Germanentum und Hellenismus: Untersuchungen zur germanischen Religionsgeschichte.* Germanische Bibliothek, II. Abteilung, 17. Heidelberg: C. Winter, 1924. viii, 160 pp.

The subject of this important book is the supposed influence of Near Eastern religious conceptions on Germanic religion. The first chapter treats such cosmic conceptions as the many doors of Valhalla (*Grímnismál* 23), conceptions of the dead and the growth of Valhalla, and identification of Bifrǫst as the Milky Way (not, as Snorri has it, the rainbow). The second chapter treats the reflection of vegetation cult in gods, myth, and legend: Sigrún and Helgi (*Helgakviða Hundingsbana II*) reveal ancient fertility ritual; the name Nerthus/Njord is cognate with Sanskrit *nrtu* "dance" and has to do with ritual dance; Freyr and Freyja derive from Semitic conceptions of fertility, perhaps transmitted by the Goths. The third chapter presents the Germanic conceptions of Baldr, distinguished from Hellenistic traditions, which make up the subject of the fourth chapter. To the Germanic conceptions belong native rites of the dying god, but the mistletoe was a novelistic addition. Besides a putative poetic lay of Baldr's death, there was a poetic lay of Hermóðr. It originated ca. 575 and influenced *Skírnismál*, which Schröder assigns to ca. 600. Loki belongs to the Hellenistic version of the story. In the cult of Isis he is parallel to Seth, and Sigyn—whom Schröder regards as equivalent to Frigg—is parallel to Isis.

Much of Schröder's argument now seems exaggerated, particularly in the analysis of Baldr, but the book is methodologically valuable for its attempt to elucidate the laconic and sparse Germanic texts by means of material from other cultures which possibly were in contact with Germanic peoples.

2462. Schröder, Franz Rolf. "Ase und Gott." *Beiträge zur Geschichte der deutschen Sprache und Literatur*, 51 (1927), 29-30.

Etymological notes on the words *áss* and *guð*.

2463. Schröder, Franz Rolf. "Die altgermanische Religion." In *Die Religionen der Erde*, ed. Carl Clemen, 243-60. Munich: F. Bruckmann, 1927.

Handbook article; translated as Schröder, "Teutonic Religion" (1931).

2464. Schröder, Franz Rolf. "Njords nackte Füsse." *Beiträge zur Geschichte der deutschen Sprache und Literatur*, 51 (1927), 31-32.

Associates Skaði's choice of Njord as husband by his feet with footprints on rock carvings and with later marriage ritual.

2465. Schröder, Franz Rolf. "Thor im Vimurfluss." *Beiträge zur Geschichte der deutschen Sprache und Literatur*, 51 (1927), 35-40.

Greek, Egyptian, and recent parallels (Holberg!) to Snorri's account of Thor's problem with the swelling river Vimur.

2466. Schröder, Franz Rolf. "Thor und der Wetzstein." *Beiträge zur Geschichte der deutschen Sprache und Literatur*, 51 (1927), 33-35.

Relates the whetstone in Thor's head to nails or flints in Lapp idols, used for striking a spark for fire.

2467. Schröder, Franz Rolf. "Zu 'Germanentum und hellenismus'." *Beiträge zur Geschichte der deutschen Sprache und Literatur*, 50 (1927), 430-31.

Addendum to Schröder's book (1924), addressed primarily to E. Brate, "Völuspá" (1914).

2468. Schröder, Franz Rolf. "Rituelle Barfüssigkeit." *Germanisch-Romanisch Monatsschrift*, 16 (1928), 167-68.

Addendum to the author's "Njords nackte Füsse" (1927).

2469. Schröder, Franz Rolf. *Altgermanische Kulturprobleme*. Berlin: W. de Gruyter, 1929. 151 pp.

Twenty-one short essays make up this continuation of Schröder's attempt to demonstrate the dependence of much of Germanic religion on Hellenistic and Near Eastern ritual and religious conceptions (see Schröder, *Germanentum und Hellenismus*, 1924). Of particular interest are the early remarks on the question of Germanic borrowing. Other topics of general interest include mystery cults, the planetary week, and creation stories.

2470. Schröder, Franz Rolf. "Neuere Forschungen zur germanischen Altertumskunde und Religionsgeschichte." *Germanisch-Romanisch Monatsschrift*, 17 (1929), 177-92, 241-55, 401-20.

Research survey.

2471. Schröder, Franz Rolf. "Germanische Schöpfungsmythen I-II: Eine vergleichende religionsgeschichtliche Studie." *Germanisch-Romanisch Monatsschrift*, 19 (1931), 1-26 (I), 81-99(II).

Schröder's point of departure in this important study of creation myths in Germanic tradition is Snorri's account of the creation of the cosmos. This Schröder regards as a whole series of somewhat contradictory myths loosely joined, which he separates for analysis. His method is comparative; by ample use of Iranian, Indic, Babylonian, Semitic, and other traditions, primarily Near Eastern, and also of recent ritual, Schröder places the Norse creation materials in broader religious contexts and seeks to identify the origins of the various Norse conceptions. The nine subheads of the study are: 1). *Snorra edda*; 2). Polarity; 3). Ymir; 4). Nerthus-Njǫrðr; 5). Gayomard; 6).Adam; 7). Auðumla; 8). Borr's sons; 9). Askr and Embla.

2472. Schröder, Franz Rolf. "Teutonic Religion." In *Religions of the World: Their Nature and their History*, ed. Carl Clemen, 227-42. New York and Chicago: Harcourt, Brace & Co., 1931. Translated by A. K. Dallas. Rpt. Freeport, N. Y.: Books for Libraries Press, 1969.

Handbook article; translation of Schröder, "Die altgermanische Religion" (1927).

2473. Schröder, Franz Rolf. "Germanentum und Alteuropa." *Germanisch-Romanisch Monatsschrift*, 22 (1932), 157-212.

Part III (pp. 181-212) treats problems relating to the history of religion. Schröder attempts to observe the building up of later Nordic religion on "old European" (pre-Indo-European) grounds. The emphasis is on myth and ritual of fertility, where Schröder sees a "masculinization" of deities as part of the growth of Germanic culture.

2474. Schröder, Franz Rolf. *Quellenbuch zur germanischen Religionsgeschichte für Übungen und Vorlesungen*. Teubners philologische Bibliothek, 14. Berlin and Leipzig: W. de Gruyter, 1933. 182 pp.

Reader in Germanic religion.

2475. Schröder, Franz Rolf. *Germanische Heldendichtung: Ein Vortrag nebst einer Studie zur Heroisierung des Mythos*. Philosophie und Geschichte, 55. Tübingen: J. C. B. Mohr (Paul Siebeck), 1935. 48 pp.

The supplement is on the heroicization of a mythic archetype in the union of Sigmundr and his sister Signý in the Vǫlsung traditions.

2476. Schröder, Franz Rolf. "Der Ursprung der Hamletsage." *Germanisch-Romanisch Monatsschrift*, 26 (1938), 81-108.

Assigns the origin of the Hamlet legend to myth and the sacral: conceptions of the dying god, with Baldr the major Germanic parallel.

2477. Schröder, Franz Rolf. "Germanische Urmythen." *Archiv für Religionswissenschaft*, 35 (1938), 201-36.

Two parts. In part 1, "Thor und Thjalfi" (pp. 201-22), Schröder equates Þjálfi with Thielver of the Gotlandic origin story *Guta saga*, whom he then proceeds to identify as a phallically-oriented fire demon who enjoys a cosmogonic marriage with the earth goddess. His relation to Thor, argues Schröder, parallels that of Vishnu to Indra; he is a prototype or representation of the god's power of procreation, possibly of pre-Indo-European origin.

In part 2, "Wodan und Wölsi" (pp. 223-36), Schröder argues a similar relationship between Vǫlsi and Odin.

2478. Schröder, Franz Rolf. "Ursprung und Ende der germanischen Heldendichtung." *Germanisch-Romanisch Monatsschrift*, 27 (1939), 325-67.

Important for the theory of a mythic and ritual background to Germanic heroic poetry.

2479. Schröder, Franz Rolf. *Untersuchungen zur germanischen und vergleichenden Religionsgeschichte,* vol. I: *Ingunar-Freyr*. Tübingen: J. C. B. Mohr (Paul Siebeck), 1941. vi, 74 pp.

Schröder investigates Norse myth and ritual associated with a holy tree (usually a yew), which he holds always to have been associated with a female deity. Various figures mated with her: chronologically they were Ullr, Thor, Odin, and finally Ingunar-Freyr. The latter is, however, also the oldest of these, for Ingun (and Ívaldi; cf. *Ívalda synir* in *Grímnismál*, str. 43) was a name of this goddess; the form *Ingunar*, then, would be genitive singular. The relationship of fertility goddess to younger god as consort reappears in the pairs Skaði and Njord, Nerthus and Týr (elicited from placenames), and, in literature, Þorgerð hǫlgabrúð and Hǫlgi.

2480. Schröder, Franz Rolf. *Untersuchungen zur germanischen und vergleichenden Religionsgeschichte,* vol. 2: *Skadi und die Götter Skandinaviens*. Tübingen: J. C. B. Mohr (Paul Siebeck), 1941. iv, 167 pp.

Schröder finds that Skaði is the name given in Scandinavia to a primal goddess, a mistress of animals, and a great mother figure. Most commonly she assumed the form of a goat, and this, argues Schröder, is the etymological meaning of her name. Like Artemis, Skaði was goddess of the forest and of hunting. Over time, she was associated with various gods: Ullr, Thor, Odin, Freyr—and finally Njord; this "marriage" was relatively late and so, accordingly, was the opposition of mountain and sea implicit in Snorri's narrative of Skaði and Njord. In general Skaði's association with gods reflects a general move from the feminine to the masculine principle in the history of Germanic religion.

The last chapter (pp. 162-67) argues the etymology of Scandinavia: "island of Skaði."

2481. Schröder, Franz Rolf. "Erce und Fjorgyn." In *Erbe der Vergangenheit: Festgabe für Karl Helm zum 80. Geburtstage*, ed. Ludwig Wolff, 25-36. Tübingen: M. Niemeyer, 1951.

An Old English charm is addressed to Erce, "mother of earth"; Fjǫrgyn is said to be the mother of Thor (*Vǫluspá* str. 26, *Hárbarðsljóð* str. 56) and may therefore be identical with earth. Schröder sees Proto-Indo-European **perkālu-* "furrow" behind both forms and suggests that they may derive from an ancient goddess of the furrow.

2482. Schröder, Franz Rolf. "Das Symposion der Lokasenna." *Arkiv för nordisk filologi*, 67 (1952), 1-29.

Points out the similarity of *Lokasenna* to the classical genre of the symposion, particularly as represented by Lucian. Although Schröder admits that there may be no actual relationship, he inclines to the notion that *Lokasenna* is indeed a Norse symposion.

2483. Schröder, Franz Rolf. "Balder und der zweite Merseburger Spruch." *Germanisch-Romanisch Monatsschrift*, 34 (1953), 161-83.

In the second Merseburg charm, Schröder analyzes Sinhtgunt as "the nightly wanderer," i.e., the moon, and takes Phol for a fertility figure parallel to Freyr and identical with Baldr, who is mentioned two lines later. Baldr is a fertility god, whose name Schröder derives from the Proto-Indo-European root **bhel-* "to swell," here referring to strength. The center of the Baldr myth is the god's death, which Schröder regards as the reflection of an ancient ritual in which the participants attacked the god and tore him to pieces so that his blood fell to the earth and promoted fertility. Schröder adduces numerous parallels from Mannhardt; in many cases the deity is burned. Schröder finds a further source in the *runot* of the *Kalevala*, which according to him "are of inestimable value, for they present an older and more original form of the Baldr legend than does the version of *Snorra edda*" (p. 177). He regards Lemminkäinen as a "gleaming god of Spring," who also is cut into pieces. The charm which Lemminkäinen's mother uses to put him back together reminds Schröder of the second Merseburg charm, and he concludes that it retains the same story, the reuniting of the pieces of the god's body and his resurrection in cult. The charm mingles two traditions: a horse charm without reference to Baldr (lines 1-2) and the Baldr tradition.

2484. Schröder, Franz Rolf. "Eine indogermanische Liedform: Das Aufreihlied." *Germanisch-Romanisch Monatsschrift*, 35 (1954), 179-85.

Continuing a theme of his 1939 "Ursprung und Ende der germanischen Heldendichtung," Schröder here adduces additional Indic and Greek parallels to Vetrliði Sumarliðason's and Þorbjǫrn dísarskáld's late tenth-century praise poems to Thor. He attempts thereby to strengthen his postulation of an Indo-European poetic form, the "string-poem" (*Aufreihlied*), in which basic reference to deeds of active gods such as Indra, Thor, and Herakles are strung together, rather like beads.

2485. Schröder, Franz Rolf. "Das Hymirlied: Zur Frage verblasster Mythen in den Götterliedern der Edda." *Arkiv för nordisk filologi*, 70 (1955), 1-40.

The particular interest of this article is summed up in the subtitle. Schröder assigns the extant *Hymiskviða* to the twelfth or early thirteenth century in Iceland, but he believes he can uncover a much older mythic core. This he does through a specific eight-point comparison with the Indic traditions of Indra and Tvastar, which turns primarily on the identity of soma and the poetic mead. The last pages of the article take up *Lokasenna* as the continuation of *Hymiskviða* and pose the question of an ancient mythic core for this—in Schröder's view—equally late poem.

2486. Schröder, Franz Rolf. "Mythos und Heldensage." *Germanisch-Romanisch Monatsschrift*, 36 (1955), 1-22. Rpt. in Karl Hauck, ed., *Zur germanisch-deutschen Heldensage* (Darmstadt: Wissenschaftliche Buchgesellschaft, 1965), pp 285-315.

Schröder's aim is to derive the hero of Germanic heroic legend, in particular Sigfrid (Siegfried), from the mythic archetype of the divine son. Offspring of sky father and earth mother, the divine son rules the middle area between them (the air) and mediates their opposition. He brings order to the chaos of earth by slaying a monster. He is a demi-god, the first king and first priest. Stressing one or the other of these functions produces the strong hero or the wise hero.

Whatever his possible historical antecedents, the Sigfrid of heroic legends follows this archetypal pattern, according to Schröder.

2487. Schröder, Franz Rolf. "Die Welt der Mutter und die Welt des Vaters." *Germanisch-Romanisch Monatsschrift*, 38 (1957), 182-201.

Masculine and feminine principles in Indo-European myth, religion, and culture, with some attention to Germanic tradition.

2488. Schröder, Franz Rolf. "Indra, Thor, und Herakles." *Zeitschrift für deutsche Philologie*, 76 (1957), 1-41.

The major purpose of this article is to demonstrate that the Greek hero Herakles belongs to the Indo-European archetype reconstructable from comparison of Indra and Thor. That archetype is the "god's son," the one son of the divine proto-couple, sky father and earth mother. The son-god parts his parents, establishes the world pillar (cf. Irminsûl), and rules over the sky, the realm between earth and heaven. He may also retain aspects of the polarity of his parents' union. Thor's relation to this archetype is one aspect of the article.

2489. Schröder, Franz Rolf. "Die Sage von Hetel und Hilde." *Deutsche Vierteljahrsschrift für Literaturwissenschaft und Geistesgeschichte*, 32 (1958), 38-70.

Derives the legend of Hetel and Hilde from fertility ritual.

2490. Schröder, Franz Rolf. "Grímnismál." *Beiträge zur Geschichte der deutschen Sprache und Literatur* (Tübingen), 80 (1958), 341-78.

Although not all can accept Schröder's attempts at reconstruction, this essay is among the most useful modern treatments of the eddic poem *Grímnismál.* After a consideration of the frame, adding details to the accepted view that it combines folktale and myth, Schröder argues that the verse itself derives from an ancient Odin monolog which had nothing to do with the frame. This monolog comprised a cosmic vision and was used in pagan cult. There someone seeking inspiration or a vision fasted, sat in fires, and meditated. Schröder adduces Nordic and Indic evidence to support this hypothesis.

In remarks on the names Odin cites for himself, Schröder finds parallels in Near Eastern materials, particularly in the total of fifty names (which he reaches by paring away four names from the manuscript versions of the poem).

2491. Schröder, Franz Rolf. "Die Göttin des Urmeeres und ihr männlicher Partner." *Beiträge zur Geschichte der deutschen Sprache und Literatur* (Tübingen), 82 (1960), 221-64.

On the goddess of the proto-sea and her male partner: discussion centers on traditions of Nerthus and Njǫrðr but ranges widely.

2492. Schröder, Franz Rolf. "Nerthus und die Nuithones." *Die Sprache*, 6 (1960), 135-47.

The Nuithones are the seventh of the peoples who according to Tacitus, *Germania*, ch. 39, participated in the cult of Nerthus. Schröder proposes reading the name as *Nurthones* "worshippers of Nerthus." His arguments include interesting remarks on the relationship between names of gods and names of Germanic tribes.

2493. Schröder, Franz Rolf. "Sigfrids Tod." *Germanisch-Romanisch Monatsschrift*, 41 (1960), 111-22.

The death of Sigfrid/Sigurðr and the attached boar hunt as a heroicization of the myth of the death of the god of vegetation. Hagen/Hǫgni was, according to Schröder, once the boar.

2494. Schröder, Franz Rolf. "Sinfjötli." In *Hommages à Georges Dumézil.* 193-200. Collection Latomus, 45. Brussels: Latomus, Revue d'études latines, 1960.

Explores the question whether the episode of Sigmundr and Sinfjǫtli in the grave mound (*Vǫlsunga saga*, ch. 8) derives from myth. Using archaeological and literary parallels from the Middle East (primarily Sumeria), Schröder associates the episode with the myth (and cult) of the dying vegetation god; he also derives from myth Sinfjǫtli's association with wolves and werewolfism.

2495. Schröder, Franz Rolf. "Balder-Probleme." *Beiträge zur Geschichte der deutschen Sprache und Literatur* (Tübingen), 84 (1962), 319-57.

Extended response to J. de Vries, "Der Mythos von Balders Tod" (1955). Schröder stresses the importance of agricultural rites and seasonal myth as a background to the Baldr story and cites many Near Eastern parallels. He postulates two lost poems, "Baldr's death" and "Hermóðr's ride," and puts the latter into the context of such similar eddic verse as *Skírnismál* and *Svipdagsmál.* His conclusion is that Baldr belongs among the *vanir* and that elements of his story are as old as the introduction of agriculture in northern Europe and therefore Germanic.

2496. Schröder, Franz Rolf. "Der Riese Vǫrnir." *Beiträge zur Geschichte der deutschen Sprache und Literatur* (Tübingen), 84 (1962), 1-4.

Derives the name of the giant Vǫrnir (attested only in a *þula* of *Snorra edda*) from the same root as the Indic god Varuna and sees in the giant the possibility of a god fallen from Indo-European times. This god may have been the *heros eponymos* of the Varni.

2497. Schröder, Franz Rolf. "Die eddischen 'Balders Träume.'" *Germanisch-Romanisch Monatsschrift*, 45 (1964), 329-37.

A short essay on some of the problems of interpretation in the eddic poem *Baldrs draumar*, which Schröder assigns to the late twelfth century. He finds the beginning of the poem not original to it, comments on parallels in eddic poetry and ballads, and reads the final riddle (str. 12) as a reference to waves and hence to Baldr's ship funeral.

2498. Schröder, Franz Rolf. "Thors Hammerholung." *Beiträge zur Geschichte der deutschen Sprache und Literatur* (Tübingen), 87 (1965), 1-42.

On the ancient background of the myth behind *Þrymskviða.* Besides some ancient formulas and analogs, Schröder deals with two important sources. Comparison of Greek and Hittite texts permits reconstruction of a myth of the theft of the thunder weapon, which probably reached Scandinavia via an eastern route about three millennia ago. It was combined with a second myth, reconstructable from Indic and Islamic sources, of the theft and retrieval of soma or the water of life.

2499. Schröder, Franz Rolf. "Svipdagsmál." *Germanisch-Romanisch Monatsschrift*, 47 (1966), 113-19.

Separates an underlying myth of a god of light from the extant text and its features of Märchen.

2500. Schröder, Franz Rolf. "Heimdall." *Beiträge zur Geschichte der deutschen Sprache und Literatur* (Tübingen), 89 (1967), 1-41.

A lengthy study of Heimdallr, placing him in the context of Indo-European and Near Eastern gods.

2501. Schröder, Franz Rolf. "Odins Verbannung." *Germanisch-Romanisch Monatsschrift*, 48 (1967), 1-12.

Odin's exile occurred, according to Saxo, after he had sired Bous on Rinda. Schröder separates the apparent holy marriage from Celtic tradition, against H. Wagner, "Eine irisch-altnordische hieros gamos-Episode" (1955). He presents Odin as the wind god, who, parallel to the Sumerian Enlil, is exiled on ethical grounds.

2502. Schröder, Franz Rolf. "Helgi und Heimdall?" *Germanisch-Romanisch Monatsschrift*, NF 19 (1969), 454-56.

Here Schröder adds briefly to his remarks on Heimdallr (1967). He presents evidence from various traditions for natural calamities and the birth of the fire or weather god and suggests further that the birth of Helgi in *Helgakviða Hundingsbana II* derives from the birth of Heimdallr.

2503. Schröder, Franz Rolf. "Merowech." *Beiträge zur Geschichte der deutschen Sprache und Literatur* (Tübingen), 96 (1974), 241-45.

On the Merovingian origin legend.

2504. Schröder, Joh. Henr. "Anmärkningar om Eddamythernes fordna allmänlighet i Norden: Med anledning af en här meddelad gammal swensk folkvisa om Thor och hans hammar." *Iduna*, 8 (1820), 113-27.

Romantic argument that the Nordic myths were once widespread through Scandinavia, based on the ballad of Thor and his hammer.

2505. Schröer, K. J. "Mythisches vom dem durch den Gunzenlê gefeierten Konrad." *Germania*, 16 (1871), 286-93.

Possible Odinic background to a medieval German chronicle.

2506. Schrönghamer-Heimdal, Franz. *Vom Ende der Zeiten: Das Wissen vom Weltende nach Edda, Wissenschaft und Weissagung*, 2nd ed. Augsburg: Haas & Grabherr, 1918. x, 99 pp. 1st ed. 1918.

Presses the eddic conception of Ragnarǫk into service for speculative philosophy. The eddic materials (mostly *Vǫluspá*) are treated specifically in the first chapter (pp. 1-26).

2507. Schück, Henrik. "Smärre bidrag till nordisk litteraturhistoria." *Arkiv för nordisk filologi*, 12 (1896), 217-40.

Part 3 (pp. 233-40) deals with the introductory stanzas of *Ynglingatal* and attempts to refute A. Noreen, "Mytiska beståndsdelar i Ynglinga tal" (1892). Noreen had sought *Ynglingatal*'s "missing" verses about Freyr in the stanzas about Dómarr, but Schück locates the "missing" verses, which he believes were about the Ingvaeonic hero Ingunar-Freyr, in Snorri's prose in *Ynglinga saga*.

2508. Schück, Henrik. *Studier i nordisk litteratur- och religionshistoria.* 2 vols. Stockholm: H. Geber, 1904. Vol. 1: 214 pp.; vol. 2: 319 pp.

Attempts to describe ancient literary and religious history, primarily in Sweden. Vol. 1 treats primarily the mead of poetry, vol. 2 Baldr.

2509. Schück, Henrik. *Nordisk folktro och fornnordisk religion.* Studentföreningen Verdandis småskrifter, 134. Stockholm: A. Bonnier, 1905. 25 pp.

Brief treatment, for Swedish university students, of Scandinavian folk belief and ancient Scandinavian religion.

2510. Schück, Henrik. "Ingunar Freyr." *Fornvännen*, 35 (1940), 289-96. Summary in German, p. 296.

Interprets Ingunar Freyr as "the spouse of or one who makes Ingunn (the earth mother) pregnant."

2511. Schück, Henrik. "Odin, Vili och Vé." *Fornvännen*, 36 (1941), 22-29. Summary in English.

Argues identification of the triad Odin, Vili, and Vé with that of Odin, Thor, and Freyr in Adam of Bremen's description of the pagan temple at Uppsala and further with that of Fjǫlnir, Sveigðir, and Vanlundi in *Ynglingatal.*

2512. Schütte, Gudmund. "Die Schöpfungssage in Deutschland und im Norden." *Indogermanische Forschungen*, 17 (1904-05), 444-57.

Schütte's aim is to establish the textual relationship of the creation stories in the Old High German *Muspilli* and *Wessobrunner Gebet*, the Middle High German *Anegenge*, an Old Frisian tale of Adam, and the eddic traditions. He advances the curious idea that *Alvíssmál* is a catalog of glosses to the creation story in which the common Germanic terms were recognized and identified as the language of the Goths (Germans), not of the gods (*goð*), as most would read the poem. For a convincing refutation see Karl Helm, "Die germanische Weltschöpfungssage und die Alvíssmál" (1907).

2513. Schütte, Gudmund. *Oldsagn om Godtjod: Bidrag til etnisk kildeforsknings metode med særligt henblik på folke-stamsagn.* Copenhagen: H. Hægerup, 1907. xi, 204 pp. Diss. Copenhagen.

Attempts a taxonomy and assesses the source-value of Germanic origin legends and creation myths.

2514. Schütte, Gudmund. "Gotthonic Names." *Scandinavian Studies*, 1 (1911-14), 69-98.

With remarks on the "mythical conceptions" of the origins of names of Germanic peoples (pp. 71-72 and passim).

2515. Schütte, Gudmund. "The Cult of Nerthus." *Saga-Book of the Viking Society*, 8 (1912-13), 29-43.

Associates the cult with Jutland and the Ingvaeones.

2516. Schütte, Gudmund. "Lidt om soldyrkelse." In *Troldesagn og dunkel tale: Fra den gamle skattegravers omraader.* 147-58. Danmarks folkeminder, 17. Copenhagen: Det Schønbergske forlag, 1917.

Solar worship allegedly reflected in the legendary placename *Sólfjǫll* (*Helgakviða Hundingsbana I*, 8).

2517. Schütte, Gudmund. *Offerpladser i overlevering og stedminder.* Studier fra sprog- og oldtidsforskning, 112. Copenhagen: V. Pio, P. Branner, 1918. 80 pp.

Traditional and toponymic evidence of places where sacrifice supposedly took place. Treated are wagon finds, possible animal sacrifice, and theophoric placenames.

2518. Schütte, Gudmund. *Hjemligt hedenskab i almenfattelig opstilling: Medomfattende folkeviser samt Saxes og Evald Tang Kristensens sagnstof.* N. p.: Gyldendal, 1919. 244 pp.

Danish original of the author's *Dänisches Heidentum* (1923).

2519. Schütte, Gudmund. "En gammel kulturvej fra Lilleasien til Skandinavien." *Danske studier*, 19 (1922), 40-54.

Promises a reorganization of the arguments concerning Near Eastern influence on Scandinavia, as advanced by G. Neckel (*Die Überlieferungen vom Gotte Balder*, 1920) and others. The discussion falls into two parts: material culture (pp. 42-43), and religious culture (pp. 43-54). Under the latter rubric, Schütte advances twelve points of contact, most of them mythological.

2520. Schütte, Gudmund. *Dänisches Heidentum.* Kultur und Sprache, 2. Heidelberg: C. Winter, 1923. 154 pp.

German version of the author's *Hjemligt hedenskab* (1919), an attempt to write a history of Danish—as opposed to Germanic or Nordic—paganism. Given the sparseness of actual Danish sources, Schütte had recourse to several flights of fancy.

2521. Schütte, Gudmund. "Danish Paganism." *Folk-Lore*, 35 (1924), 360-71.

Briefly sketches, in English, the author's *Hjemligt hedenskab* (1919) and *Dänisches Heidentum* (1923).

2522. Schütte, Gudmund. "Sagnet om soen og den sunkne gaard." *Danske studier*, 22 (1925), 117-32.

Argues the pagan background of some Danish local legends.

2523. Schütte, Gudmund. "Hedenske levn i tilknytning til helligkilder." *Danske studier*, 23 (1926), 157-66.

On holy springs in Denmark. Schütte finds that those of eastern Denmark tended more to be sacred to male deities, those of western Denmark to a single goddess who can be traced back to Nerthus.

2524. Schütte, Gudmund, and Gunnar Knudsen. "Himmerlands tyr." *Danske studier*, 23 (1926), 183-88.

Debate on possible traces of Cimbrian mythology in the bull of Himmerland.

2525. Schütte, Gudmund. "Haruderne eller Hardsysselboerne." *Hardsyssels årbog*, 1928, pp. 155-67.

Ulborg, Denmark, as an Ullr placename.

2526. Schütte, Gudmund. "Eponyme Götter und Heroen." *Zeitschrift für deutsches Altertum*, 69 (1932), 129-36.

Survey of eponymous gods, goddesses, and, to a lesser extent, heroes, with focus on Nordic—especially Danish—circumstances. Schütte calls for greater consideration of the eponymous function of mythological figures.

2527. Schütte, Gudmund. *Gotthiod und Utgard: Altgermanische Sagengeographie in neuer Auffassung.* 2 vols. Copenhagen: Aschehoug dansk forlag, Jena: Frommannsche Buchhandlung, 1935-36. Vol. 1: 336 pp; vol. 2: 372 pp.

Cosmology in ancient Germanic culture: division into outer zone, mid-zone, inner zone, and zero zone. Extensive discussion of texts.

2528. Schütte, Gudmund. "Popular Distinction of Languages and Onomastic Restrictions." *Acta Philologica Scandinavica*, 14 (1940), 173-80.

Includes remarks on patterns of personal naming following the conversion to Christianity (pp. 176-77).

2529. Schütte, Gudmund. "The Lumber-Room of Ancient Geography: Distorted, Imaginary or Badly Localized Place-Names." *Acta Philologica Scandinavica*, 17 (1943-45), 168-70.

The "lumber-room" contains, inter alia, Herthadal, the valley not of the goddess Hertha but of garden peas. Schütte assigns Hertha herself to the lumber-room: "A goddess Hertha never existed; the true form of her name is Nerthus" (p. 168); perhaps this equation, too, belongs in some lumber-room.

2530. Schütte, Gudmund. "Et sallingsk Eddasagn." *Skivebogen*, 1944, pp. 57-63.

Alleged parallel in recent Jutlandic folk belief to the midgard serpent.

2531. Schütte, Gudmund. "Where is Gefjon's Lake Situated?" *Acta Philologica Scandinavica*, 18 (1944), 306-08.

It is identical with lake Vänern (Sweden), according to the author.

2532. Schütte, Gudmund. "Til kritik av danske stednavneforsknings metode." *Årbøger for nordisk oldkyndighed og historie*, 1945, pp. 122-35. Summary in French, appendix, pp. xiv-xvii.

Criticism of S. K. Amtoft, "Stednavnene som bebyggelses- og religionshistorisk kildestof" (1941).

2533. Schütte, Gudmund. "Gottonsk kosmologi." *Danske studier*, 43 (1946-47), 41-48.

Survey of reconstructed Germanic cosmology: the upper zone, the middle zone, the under zone, the outer zone; with attempts to align these zones with actual European geography.

2534. Schütte, Gudmund. "Nerthus nytydet." *Danske studier*, 43 (1946-47), 125-26.

In a not particularly convincing note, the author associates *Nerthus* with words for "north."

2535. Schütte, Gudmund. "Urmytiske geografispekulationer." *Årbøger for nordisk oldkyndighed og historie*, 1948, pp. 285-93. Summary in English.

Criticism of S. K. Amtoft, *Nordiske gudeskikkelser i bebyggelseshistorisk belysning* (1948).

2536. Schütte, Gudmund. "Sæhrímnir spøger i Hardsyssel." In *Festskrift til museumsforstander H. P. Hansen, Herning på 70-årsdagen den 2. oktober 1949*, eds. Peter Skautrup and Axel Steensberg, 303-05. Copenhagen: Rosenkilde og Bagger, 1949.

An alleged modern folklore parallel from Jutland to the motif of Sæhrímnir.

2537. Schütte, Gudmund. "Forsømte gottonske navneproblemer." *Arkiv för nordisk filologi*, 66 (1951), 16-37.

Pp. 20-21 contain a brief presentation of central cult placenames with simplex forms.

2538. Schullerus, A. "Zur Kritik des altnordischen Valhollglaubens." *Beiträge zur Geschichte der deutschen Sprache und Literatur*, 12 (1887), 221-82.

A development of the conceptions, origin, and development of Valhalla. Schullerus concludes that the conceptions originated during the first half of the ninth century and developed in Scandinavia in connection with myths of Odin under the influence of Christianity. An excursus (pp. 271-82) treats *Grímnismál* and argues that the text exhibits a poetic mythologizing.

2539. Schultz, Wolfgang. "Zeitrechnung und Zeitordnung bei den Germanen." *Mannus*, 16 (1924), 119-26.

Among Schultz's remarks on chronology and the ordering of time are some dealing with myth and religion: there was no Germanic sun worship, and the myths of the gods are fundamental to the ordering of time.

2540. Schultz, Wolfgang. "Vorgeschichte und Mythenforschung." *Mannus*, 4, Ergänzungsband (1925), 76-89.

Text of a lecture on prehistory and mythological research, with remarks on the relationship between Germanic/Scandinavian myth and ancient Germanic decorative art. Schultz concludes that each discipline informs the other.

2541. Schultz, Wolfgang. "Balder, das Oseberggrab und südrussisch-sakische Parallelen." *Mannus*, 5, Ergänzungsband (1927), 129-36.

Text of a lecture. Schultz links details of Baldr's funeral and the Oseberg find with Ibn Fadlan's account of the Rus funeral and concludes that a southern Russian conduit brought conceptions ultimately of Iranian origin to the Germanic peoples.

2542. Schultz, Wolfgang. "Thors Bergung." In *Festgabe für den 70jährigen Gustaf Kossinna von Freunden und Schülern*. 316-23. Mannus, 6, Ergänzungsband. Leipzig: C. Kabitzsch, 1928.

On Thor's self-rescue from the swollen river he crosses on his visit to Geirrøðr. Schultz presents several possible parallels from other Indo-European traditions (Estonian, Irish, Greek, Iranian) and speculates on the possible original form and home of the myth.

2543. Schultz, Wolfgang. "Die Felsritzung von Hvitlycke und das Edda-Lied von Thrym." *Mannus*, 21 (1929), 52-71.

Taking *Þrymskviða* for a cultic text, Schultz reads it against the Hvitlycke and other rock carvings and finds that it concerns a mythic drama focusing on fertility. The article includes a translation of the entire poem, using different type faces to clarify its structure.

2544. Schultz, Wolfgang. "Die altgermanische Zwillingsgötter (Auszug)." *Mannus*, 8, Ergänzungsband (1931), 74-76.

Summary of a lecture. Schultz connects the representations of paired figures (gods?) on Bronze Age rock carvings with later narrative traditions of the Alciis and stresses the age and importance of the traditions.

2545. Schultz, Wolfgang. "Die Felsbilder Skandinaviens und Nordafrikas." *Mitteilungen der anthropologischen Gesellschaft in Wien*, 61 (1931), 239-68.

Essentially a review of O. Almgren, *Hällristningar och kultbruk* (1926-27), treating the Egyptian parallels adduced by Almgren to Nordic rock carvings. Schultz argues against direct influence and for parallel development.

2546. Schultz, Wolfgang. "Steuer, Faltboot und Rammspitze im Schiffsbaue der jüngeren Bronzezeit nach den Ritzungen auf Schabmessern und Felsen und nach bisher unerklärten Stellen der Skalden und der jüngeren Edda über Skidbladnir, Hallinskidi und Gullintanni." *Mannus*, 24 (1932), 40-56.

Working from the rock carvings, Schultz comes to the remarkable conclusion that references to pocketing Skíðblaðnir may derive from actual folding boats. *Hallinskíði*, then, he identifies as "ship" and finds that it only later became (mis-)identified with Heimdallr.

2547. Schulz, Walther. "Deutungsversuch einer Felsenzeichnung." *Mannus*, 6 (1914), 324-25.

Interpretation of the rock carving from Tuvene, Bohuslän, Sweden. Accompanied by a small companion, Thor kills a giant, thus freeing a goddess with whom he couples.

2548. Schulz, Walther. "Archäologisches zur Wodan- und Wanenverehrung." *Wiener prähistorische Zeitschrift*, 19 (1932), 161-72.

Archaeological comparison of the worship of Wodan/Odin and the *vanir*; emphasis on the cult of the dead.

2549. Schulz, Walther. "Die Langobarden als Wodanverehrer." *Mannus*, 24 (1932), 215-31.

The evidence for worship of Wodan/Odin among the Langobards. Pp. 229-30 offer a useful chronological table.

2550. Schwartz, Friedrich Leberecht Wilhelm. *Der Ursprung der Mythologie dargelegt an griechischer und deutscher Sage*. Berlin: W. Hertz, 1860. xxiv, 299 pp.

Remnants of pagan mythology in Germany.

2551. Schwartz, Friedrich Leberecht Wilhelm. *Der heutige Volksglaube und das alte Heidenthum mit Bezug auf Norddeutschland, besonders die Mark Brandenburg und Mecklenburg: Eine Skizze,* 2nd ed. Berlin: W. Hertz, 1862. xiv, 142 pp.

Pagan remnants in north Germany.

2552. Schwartz, Friedrich Leberecht Wilhelm. *Prähistorisch-anthropologische Studien: Mythologisches und Kulturhistorisches.* Berlin: W. Hertz, 1884. viii, 520 pp.

Nature-mythological studies, some relating to Norse mythology.

2553. Schwartz, Stephen. *Poetry and Law in Germanic Myth.* University of California Publications, Folklore Studies, 27. Berkeley and Los Angeles: University of California Press, 1973. 61 pp.

The subject of this brief monograph is the notion advanced by Grimm of interrelationships between Germanic law and Germanic poetry; Schwartz finds this interrelationship in myth. He follows an evolutionist path, deriving the judicial god Forseti from the Frisian figure Foseti, surveying the assumption of judicial function by Odin, god of poetry, at the expense of Týr: addition of Foseti to the Norse pantheon and the disqualification of Týr as a god of legal contract through the loss of his hand.

2554. Schwartz, W. *Indogermanischer Volksglaube: Ein Beitrag zur Religionsgeschichte der Urzeit.* Berlin: O. Seehagen, 1885. xxiv, 280 pp.

A reconstruction of the so-called "lower mythology," using Greek, Roman, and Scandinavian sources. Schwartz is a nature-mythologist for whom the sun and sky play a major role. Of the "higher" Scandinavian mythological figures, Odin, Baldr, and Yggdrasill receive particular attention.

2555. Schwarz, Hans. "Varin und das ältere Futhark." *Beiträge zur Geschichte der deutschen Sprache und Literatur* (Halle), 78 (1956), 323-56.

Hypothetical oracular use of runes and rune names.

2556. Schwietering, Julius. "Der erste Merseburger Spruch." *Zeitschrift für deutsches Altertum*, 55 (1914-17), 148-56. Rpt. in Schwietering, *Philologische Schriften*, ed. Friedrich Ohly and Max Wehrli (Munich: W. Fink, 1969), pp. 118-26.

Argues the Christian origin of the first Merseburg charm.

2557. Schwietering, Julius. "Wodans Speer." *Zeitschrift für deutsches Altertum*, 60 (1923), 290-92. Rpt. in Schwietering, *Philologische Schriften*, ed. Friedrich Ohly and Max Wehrli (Munich: W. Fink, 1969), pp. 234-36.

Suggests that the spear-equipped Wodan/Odin replaced the sword-equipped Tiuz/Týr as chief god, first along the lower Rhine, partly as the result of the refinement of techniques using spears in battle.

2558. Scovazzi, Marco. *Il diritto islandese nella Landnámabók.* Milan: Giuffrè, 1961. iii, 238 pp.

In this attempt to delineate the state of Icelandic law in *Landnámabók*, Scovazzi concludes that the law Norwegian settlers established in Iceland was that of the ancient, peaceful "vanir society."

2559. Scovazzi, Marco. "Paganesimo e cristianesimo nelle saghe nordiche." In *La conversione al cristianesimo nell'Europa dell'alto medioevo: 14-19 aprile 1966.* 759-84. Settimane di studio del centro italiano di studi sull'alto medioevo. Spoleto: Presso la sede del centro, 1967.

A contribution to an international symposium on the conversion of the European peoples to Christianity. Scovazzi scrutinizes Icelandic literature, i.e., family sagas, *Landnámabók*, *Íslendingabók*, from a historical perspective, with special emphasis on the conversion. Throughout he stresses the unity of Icelandic society, the need for varying elements to find accommodation.

2560. Scovazzi, Marco. "Dalla Scandinavia all'Islandia." In *I normanni e la loro espansione in Europa nell'alto medioevo: 19-24 aprile 1968.* 131-54. Settimane di studio del centro italiano di studi sull'alto medioevo, 16. Spoleto: Presso la sede del centro, 1968. Discussion on pp. 165-68.

Scovazzi's survey of the evolution of Icelandic culture out of mainland Scandinavian culture, undertaken for a conference on the Normans in Europe, stresses religious elements: Harald Fairhair's religious tyranny as a cause for emigration from Norway; the Icelanders' attempt to return to an older, more tolerant form of paganism; and the importance of peace, the nature of property ownership, and law.

2561. Scovazzi, Marco. "Tracce di concezioni germaniche nel culto delle *Matronae* e delle *Matres.*" *Studi germanici*, 8 (1970), 169-78.

Traces of Germanic conceptions in the cult of the Matronae and Matres considered here include Vár and the *dísir.*

2562. Scovazzi, Marco. "Tuisto e Mannus nel II capitolo della *Germania* di Tacito." *Istituto Lombardo: Accademia di scienze e lettere, rendiconti, classe di letteri*, 104 (1970), 323-36.

A discussion of Tuisto, Mannus, and the creation story according to ch. 2 of the *Germania* of Tacitus.

2563. Seaton, M. E. "A Remark on Snorri's Edda." *Arkiv för nordisk filologi*, 29 (1913), 343.

A parallel to Árvakr and Alsviðr in Shirley's *Triumph of Peace*, a seventeenth-century masque.

2564. See, Klaus von. "Der Alter der Rígsþula." *Acta Philologica Scandinavica*, 24 (1957), 1-12. Rpt. in von See, *Edda, Saga, Skaldendichtung* (1981), pp. 84-95, with addendum pp. 514-16.

Argues a late date of origin for *Rígsþula.*

2565. See, Klaus von. "Das Walkürenlied." *Beiträge zur Geschichte der deutschen Sprache und Literatur* (Tübingen), 81 (1959), 1-15. Rpt. in von See, *Edda, Saga, Skaldendichtung* (1981), pp. 329-43.

On *Darraðarljóð*; von See denies that the valkyries weave fate or make any sort of magic. He reads *vefr darraðar* as a simple kenning for battle and assigns the valkyries the role they take in other early praise poetry, such as *Hákonarmál.*

2566. See, Klaus von. "Rígsþula Str. 47 und 48." *Beiträge zur Geschichte der deutschen Sprache und Literatur* (Tübingen), 82 (1960), 318-20. Rpt. in von See, *Edda, Saga, Skaldendichtung* (1981), pp. 96-98, with addendum, pp. 514-16.

Textual note, supporting a thirteenth-century Norwegian origin of *Rígsþula.*

2567. See, Klaus von. "Berserker." *Zeitschrift für deutsche Wortforschung,* 17 (1961), 129-35. Rpt. in von See, *Edda, Saga, Skaldendichtung* (1981), pp. 311-17.

Argues that berserks were a literary invention—perhaps of Þorbjǫrn hornklofi in *Haraldskvæði*—which blossomed during the twelfth century.

2568. See, Klaus von. "Zwei eddische Preislieder: Eiríksmál und Hákonarmál." In *Festgabe für Ulrich Pretzel, zum 65. Geburtstag dargebracht von Freunden und Schülern*, eds. Walter Simon, Wolfgang Bachofer, and Wolfgang Dittmann, 107-17. Berlin: E. Schmidt, 1963. Rpt. in von See, *Edda, Saga, Skaldendichtung* (1981), pp. 318-28, with addendum pp. 522-25.

Von See concludes that *Eiríksmál* is later than and influenced by *Hákonarmál.*

2569. See, Klaus von. *Altnordische Rechtswörter: Philologische Studien zur Rechtsauffassung und Rechtsgesinnung der Germanen.* Hermaea, 16. Tübingen: M. Niemeyer, 1964. vii, 263 pp.

The overall aim of this study of Germanic legal terminology is to remove older Germanic law from the sphere of myth and ritual and transfer it to the realm of details of everyday life. Part 3 "Recht und Religion" raises the question of the hypothetical sacral context of Germanic law in connection with an examination of the Norse terms *goði* "chieftain-priest" and *heilagr* "holy."

2570. See, Klaus von. "Skop und Skald: Zur Auffassung des Dichters bei den Germanen." *Germanisch-Romanisch Monatsschrift*, 45 (1964), 1-14. Rpt. in von See, *Edda, Saga, Skaldendichtung* (1981), pp. 347-60.

In making the Germanic poet a scolder, von See argues against a Germanic priestly or ecstatic poetry inspired by the gods.

2571. See, Klaus von. "Der Spottvers des Hjalti Skeggjason." *Zeitschrift für deutsches Altertum*, 97 (1968), 155-58. Rpt. in von See, *Edda, Saga, Skaldendichtung* (1981), pp. 380-83.

Hjalti's famous verse, declaimed at the Icelandic *alþingi* before the conversion to Christianity, may be read literally or figuratively: "I do not wish to bay at the gods, [for] Freyja seems a bitch to me," or "I do not wish to blaspheme the gods, [but] Freyja seems a whore to me."

2572. See, Klaus von. "Sonatorrek und Hávamál." *Zeitschrift für deutsches Altertum*, 99 (1970), 26-33.

Opposes Nordal's interpretation (1924) that *Sonatorrek* represents the spiritual crisis of Egill's belief in Odin. Because of verbal similarities to *Hávamál* von See argues that the theme of the poem is nothing more than the hopelessness of an old man bereft of his sons.

2573. See, Klaus von. *Germanische Heldensage: Stoffe, Probleme, Methoden: Eine Einführung*. Frankfurt a. M.: Athenäum, 1971. 178 pp.

Von See's introduction to Germanic heroic legend contains a lengthy chapter on heroic legends and myth (pp. 31-60; of the eight chapters, only the one on the historical background of heroic legend is longer). Its survey reveals the presence of mythic elements throughout Germanic heroic traditions. In general, von See inclines toward the view that these elements derive from a gradually increasing tendency, particularly relevant in Scandinavia, to apply myth to heroic legend, and not from any ancient equation between heroic poetry, myth, and cult.

2574. See, Klaus von. *Die Gestalt der Hávamál: Eine Studie zur eddischen Spruchdichtung*. Frankfurt a. M.: Athenäum, 1972. 70 pp.

Before the appearance of this monograph, the most recent work on the origin and structure of the eddic poem *Hávamál* was Ivar Lindquist's *Die Urgestalt der Hávamál* (1956), which attempted a reconstruction of the original form of the poem. Von See's is an entirely different approach. He regards the poem as we have it in the manuscript not as an opportunity to reconstruct but rather as the unified work of a medieval redactor attempting to impose order on a variety of stanzas. Von See argues that the redactor imitated the literary model of such Odin poems as *Vafþrúðnismál* and *Grímnismál*. *Hávamál* would be, then, a poem spoken by Odin, proceeding through an increasing realization of the god and his power. Thus Odin begins with the gnomic stanzas and then tells various narratives about himself and the power they conferred upon him. To cement his work, the redactor composed some transitional stanzas.

This hypothesis is important for drawing attention to the extant *Hávamál* and not to unknowable earlier stages of the text. It bears, however, on the mythological background of the text, for according to von See the redactor worked not out of any living mythic conception but rather with purely literary ones, in the mind.

For detailed considerations of the hypothesis, see H. de Boor's review in *Beiträge zur Geschichte der deutschen Sprache und Literatur* (Tübingen), 95 (1973), 366-76, and S. Beyschlag, "Zur Gestalt der Hávamál" (1974). Cf. also von See, "Disticha Catonis und Hávamál" (1972), and "Probleme der altnordischen Spruchdichtung" (1975).

2575. See, Klaus von. "Disticha Catonis und Hávamál." *Beiträge zur Geschichte der deutschen Sprache und Literatur* (Tübingen), 94 (1972), 1-18. Rpt. in von See, *Edda, Saga, Skaldendichtung* (1981), pp. 27-44, with addendum p. 513.

In this companion piece to his monograph on *Hávamál* (*Die Gestalt der Hávamál* (1972)), von See attempts to set the eighty gnomic stanzas of the poem in their learned European context by suggesting possible direct or indirect influence from the *Disticha Catonis*, the widely known medieval gnomic poem, rendered into Norse as the *Hugsvinnsmál*. Besides direct influence in certain passages of *Hávamál*, von See sees possible further influence in the choice of sentiments treated and perhaps too in the structure of their thirteenth-century realization. These the thirteenth-century redactor will have put into the mouth of Odin.

2576. See, Klaus von. "Probleme der altnordischen Spruchdichtung." *Zeitschrift für deutsches Altertum*, 104 (1975), 91-118. Rpt. in von See, *Edda, Saga, Skaldendichtung* (1981), pp. 45-72.

Here von See responds to the critical reception of his 1972 works on *Hávamál* (*Die Gestalt der Hávamál* and "Disticha Catonis und Hávamál"); he addresses his remarks particularly to the reviews of de Boor (1973) and Beyschlag (1974). On pp. 108-18 von See investigates the age of the Odin name Hár/Hávi (gen. *Háva* as in *Hávamál* "words of the high one"), as opposed to Hárr "hoary." He concludes that in *Hávamál* use of this form of the name is due to the redactor, who will have got it from the *Gylfaginning* of *Snorra edda*. Further, von See believes the redactor composed stanza 1 also on the model of *Gylfaginning*. Thus the composition of *Snorra edda* in the third decade of the thirteenth century provides a terminus post quem for *Hávamál* in its present form.

2577. See, Klaus von. "Was ist Heldendichtung?" In *Europäische Heldendichtung*, ed. Klaus von See, 1-38. Wege der Forschung, 500. Darmstadt: Wissenschaftliche Buchgesellschaft, 1978. Rpt. in von See, *Edda, Saga, Skaldendichtung* (1981), pp. 154-93.

In this introductory essay to a collection of thirty-three essays on Indo-European, Greek, Roman, Germanic, French, Spanish, Serbo-Croatian, Russian, and Celtic heroic poetry, von See offers a research history of definitions of "heroic poetry" keyed to possible or hypothetical origins in Indo-European or Germanic culture or in myth. As in his other writings (e.g., *Germanische Heldensage* (1971)), he minimizes the role of myth, stressing instead the hero as an exaltation of the individual.

2578. See, Klaus von. *Edda, Saga, Skaldendichtung: Aufsätze zur skandinavischen Literatur des Mittelalters*. Skandinavistische Arbeiten, 6. Heidelberg: C. Winter-Universitätsverlag, 1981. 539 pp.

Contains these essays, separately entered above: "Das Alter der Rígsþula" (1957); "Das Walkürenlied" (1959); "Rígsþula Str. 47 und 48" (1960); "Berserker" (1961); "Zwei eddische Preislieder" (1963); "Skop und Skald" (1964); "Der Spottvers des Hjalti Skeggjason" (1968); "Disticha Catonis und Hávamál" (1972); "Probleme der altnordischen Spruchdichtung" (1975); "Was ist Heldendichtung?" (1978).

2579. Segerstedt, Torgny. "Den heliga eken." *Ymer*, 26 (1906), 341-46.

Worship of oak trees in Europe.

2580. Segerstedt, Torgny. "Nordiska vapengudar." In *Skrifter tillägnade Pehr Gustaf Eklund*. 663-95. Lund: C. W. K. Gleerup, 1911.

Prehistoric cults of sword and spear, later associated with Týr and Odin; remarks on these gods as "weapon-gods."

2581. Seip, Didrik Arup. "Musen som Lokes arvtager." *Maal og minne*, 1915, pp. 230.

Comment on R. Iversen's article with the same title (1912).

2582. Seip, Didrik Arup. "'Ættegård og helligdom'." *Nordisk tidskrift för vetenskap, konst och industri*, 2 (1926), 593-605.

Critical discussion of Magnus Olsen's book with the same name (1926).

2583. Seip, Didrik Arup. "Har nordmenn skrevet opp Edda-diktningen?" *Maal og minne*, 1951, pp. 3-33.

Argues that the eddic poems were originally recorded in Norway. English review by Anne Holtsmark in *Humaniora Norvegica* 2 (1950-52), 214-16 [1958].

2584. Seip, Didrik Arup. "On the Original of the Codex Regius of the Elder Edda." In *Studies in Honor of Albert Morey Sturtevant*. 103-06. Lawrence: University of Kansas Press, 1952.

Brief rehearsal of some of the arguments supporting the author's view that Codex Regius of the Poetic Edda is a copy of a Norwegian original.

2585. Seip, Didrik Arup. "Om et norsk skriftlig grunnlag for Edda-diktningen eller deler av den." *Maal og minne*, 1957, pp. 81-207.

Continues the discussion begun in Seip, "Har nordmenn skrevet opp Edda-diktningen" (1951), concerning possible Norwegian provenance of the written forms of some of the eddic poems.

2586. Seipp, Horst. *Entwicklungszüge der germanischen Religionswissenschaft (von Jacob Grimm zu Georges Dumézil)*. Bonn: E. Reuter, 1968. Diss. Bonn.

A thorough survey of research in Germanic religion, from Jacob Grimm to Dumézil's theories as of 1959, with an extensive bibliography covering works up to that date. The dissertation is divided into five parts. 1: The early nineteenth century; 2: The science of religion and cultural history; 3: History of religion and phenomenology (*Wesensdeutung*); 4: Belief in fate and the conversion to Christianity; 5: Sociology and the science of religion. The exposition is based on ample use of quotations.

2587. Setälä, E. N. "Aus dem Gebiete der Lehnbeziehungen." In *Festgabe für Vilhelm Thomsen,* part 1. 161-289. Finnisch-Ugrische Forschungen, 12. Leipzig: O. Harrassowitz, 1912.

Includes discussion of mythological words and expressions (pp. 170-264) in which the author derives much Finnish and Finno-Ugric mythological tradition from Norse mythology. Loki and the Baldr myth receive particular treatment.

2588. Sharpe, Eric J. "Salvation, Germanic and Christian." In *Man and his Salvation: Studies in Memory of S. G. F. Brandon*, eds. Eric J. Sharpe and John R. Hinnells, 243-62. Manchester: Manchester University Press, Totowa, N. J.: Rowman & Littlefield, 1973.

Asks "whether the Germanic mind of the early Middle Ages was soteriologically a *tabula rasa*, upon which the Christian scheme of salvation could easily be written; or whether certain presuppositions were present which caused the Christian message to be received and understood in a distinctive way, and which brought about the emergence of an equally distinctive Germanic Christian view of salvation." Sharpe attempts to demonstrate the latter view through a presentation of such elements of Scandinavian religion and myth as sacrifice, conceptions of Thor and Odin, dualism, and reception of Christ.

2589. Siebs, Theodor. "Beiträge zur deutschen Mythologie." *Zeitschrift für deutsche Philologie*, 24 (1892), 145-57, 433-61.

Part I, "Der Todesgott ahd. Henno Wôtan Mercurius" (pp. 145-57), reconstructs a German god of the dead, Henno, still reflected in folklore, who was more powerful and more important in early Germanic times than Odin. Part II, "Things und die Alaisiagen" (pp. 433-57), treats the Borovicium altars and argues that *Things* was the name of the chief god, equated with Mars, and later replaced by Tius/Týr. Part III, "Zur Hludanae-Inschrift" (pp. 457-61), reads Hludana as a sea goddess allegedly parallel to Nerthus.

2590. Siebs, Theodor. "Der Gott Fos(e)te und sein Land." *Beiträge zur Geschichte der deutschen Sprache und Literatur*, 35 (1909), 535-53.

On the Frisian god Fosete, including consideration of his relationship with the eddic Forseti (this relationship is, according to Siebs, slight). Siebs concludes that Foseti was not a god of law or judgment, only a major god whose cult required human sacrifice.

2591. Siecke, Ernst. *Die Liebesgeschichte des Himmels: Untersuchungen zur indogermanischen Sagenkunde.* Strassburg: K. J. Trübner, 1892. vii, 131 pp.

Indo-European solar and lunar mythology, with some Nordic materials.

2592. Siecke, Ernst. *Die Urreligion der Indogermanen: Vortrag, gehalten im Verein für Volkskunde.* Berlin: Mayer & Müller, 1897. 38 pp.

Text of a lecture reducing Indo-European deities, including many from the Germanic world, to primitive reflections of the sun and moon.

2593. Siecke, Ernst. *Mythologische Briefe: I, Grundsätze der Sagenforschung; II, Uhland's Behandlung der Thor-sagen.* Berlin: F. Dümmler, 1901. 258 pp.

The second part (the last dozen of some forty "letters") is a criticism of Uhland's interpretation of Thor, pointing out that the extant myths do little to connect Thor with thunder.

2594. Sierke, Sigurd. *Kannten die vorchristlichen Germanen Runenzauber?.* Schriften der Albertus-Universität, geisteswissenschaftliche Reihe, 24. Königsberg and Berlin: Ost-Europa, 1939. 127 pp.

Did the pre-Christian Germanic peoples know runic magic? The author answers affirmatively, seeing such magic in many cases associated with its medium; thus, for example, magic aimed at fertility or physical love tends to be the aim of runes carved on bone. Not a work of great importance.

2595. Sievers, Eduard. "Die angebliche Göttin *Ricen.*" *Beiträge zur Geschichte der deutschen Sprache und Literatur*, 16 (1892), 366-68.

Discusses a hypothetical Germanic/Old English goddess, Ricen (proposed on the basis of a gloss).

2596. Sievers, Eduard. "Sonargǫltr." *Beiträge zur Geschichte der deutschen Sprache und Literatur*, 16 (1892), 540-44.

On a term applied to cult. Sievers thinks the first component is not, as some observers held, *són* "atonement."

2597. Sievers, Eduard. "Grammatische Miscellen, 8: Altnord. *Váli* und *Beyla.*" *Beiträge zur Geschichte der deutschen Sprache und Literatur*, 18 (1894), 582-84.

Etymologies of two mythological figures. Sievers derives *Váli* from **wanila*, perhaps "extremely beautiful" or related to *vanir*, and Beyla from **Baunilo* "Bean."

2598. Sievers, Eduard. "Zur Lokasenna." *Beiträge zur Geschichte der deutschen Sprache und Literatur*, 18 (1894), 208.

Textual note to *Lokasenna*, str. 3.

2599. Sievers, Eduard. "Zur Chronologie der Eddalieder." In *Festschrift Eugen Mogk zum 70. Geburtstag 19. Juli 1924.* 15-29. Halle a. d. S.: M. Niemeyer, 1924.

Concludes that most eddic verse is Icelandic from the period 950-1100; a small amount is Norwegian from before 950, and the Icelandic material up to around 1100 must be treated cautiously.

2600. Sievers, Eduard. "Zur Snorra Edda." *Beiträge zur Geschichte der deutschen Sprache und Literatur*, 50 (1926), 89.

Supports E. Mogk, "Zur Bewertung des Cod. Upsaliensis der Snorra-Edda" (1924-25): Codex Upsaliensis the best manuscript of *Snorra edda.*

2601. Sievers, Eduard. "Zur Snorra Edda." *Beiträge zur Geschichte der deutschen Sprache und Literatur*, 50 (1927), 89.

Addendum to E. Mogk, "Zur Bewertung des Cod. Upsaliensis der Snorra-Edda" (1924).

2602. Sijmons, B., and Hugo Gering. *Die Lieder der Edda,* vol. 1: *Text,* part. 1: *Götterlieder.* Germanistische Handbibliothek, 7. Halle a. d. S.: Waisenhaus, 1888. xvi, 222 pp. Rpt. Hildesheim: G. Olms, 1971.

Edition of the mythological poems of the Poetic Edda.

2603. Simon, Karl. "Die Runenbewegung und das arianische Christentum." *Zeitschrift für deutsche Philologie*, 53 (1928), 41-48.

Brief note on the cultural influences proceeding from the South to Germany and Scandinavia: runic writing, the cult of Odin, and Arian Christianity.

2604. Simonsen, P. "The Rock Art of Arctic Norway." *Bolletino del centro comuno di studi preistorici*, 11 (1974), 129-50.

Possible influence from the South on the motifs of Scandinavian rock carvings, which the author associates with fertility.

2605. Simpson, Jacqueline. "Mímir: Two Myths or One?" *Saga-Book of the Viking Society*, 16 (1962-65), 41-53.

Following a survey of the apparently contradictory literary references to Mímir, Simpson points out the many Celtic parallels adduced by Anne Ross ("Severed Heads in Wells" (1962)), in which severed heads dwell in wells as guardians of healing waters. Simpson argues against the possibility of direct

Celtic influence by citing parallel folktales from England and Norway (Buskebrura "The Bushy Bride" in Asbjørnsen and Moe's *Samlede eventyr*). In these, three heads rise from a well to test a heroine. These tales appear to suggest that "the association of head and well was once widespread" (p. 49). Further parallels may indicate that the association between Mímir and the world tree is not unusual. Simpson concludes that Mímir is "essentially the head, an otherworld deity" (p. 50); he is neither of the *æsir* nor *vanir*, neither of the living nor the dead. He is the source and guardian of wisdom, perhaps of the mead of poetry—a complex figure clarified by parallels.

2606. Simpson, Jacqueline. "A Note on the Folktale Motif of the Heads in the Well." *Saga-Book of the Viking Society*, 16 (1962-65), 248-50.

In this postscript to her study of "Mímir: Two Myths or One" (1962-65), Simpson summarizes the findings of Warren Roberts concerning the tale type of "The Kind and the Unkind Girls." A small number of these tales have the heads in the well, and the centers of distribution are England and Scandinavia. Roberts postulated diffusion from England to Scandinavia. These findings lead Simpson to further speculation on the possible reflection of the myth of Mímir.

2607. Simpson, Jacqueline. "Otherworld Adventures in an Icelandic Saga." *Folklore*, 77 (1966), 1-20.

Two of the adventures of the hero in *Þorsteins þáttr bæjarmagns* have clear affinities with myths of Thor. The first has to do with Thor's hammer, the second with the god's journey to Geirrøðr. Simpson adduces analogs and parallels to the latter and explains a saga motif not found in the myth as the result of Celtic influence.

2608. Simpson, Jacqueline. "Some Scandinavian Sacrifices." *Folklore*, 78 (1967), 190-202.

Text of a paper read at the Folklore Symposium held at Folkestone on June 18, 1967 in connection with the Folkstone International Folklore Festival. Simpson reviews the evidence of animal sacrifices in which the body or head of the slaughtered animal is suspended on a tree or pole, and the related customs of the *níðstǫng* and horse heads; and she compares them with practices, possibly related, of recent English folklore.

2609. Simpson, Jacqueline. "The King's Whetstone." *Antiquity*, 53 (1979), 96-100.

Suggests that the whetstone may have been a terrestrial representation of the sky god's thunderbolt.

2610. Simpson, John. "Comparative Structural Analysis of Three Ethical Questions in Beowulf, The Nibelungenlied, and The Chanson de Roland." *Journal of Indo-European Studies*, 3 (1975), 239-54.

The Germanic reflection of Dumézil's second (warrior) function in three poems of Germanic peoples.

2611. Simrock, Karl. *Vaticinii Valae Eddici Carminis Antiquissimi Vindiciae*. Bonn: A. Marcus, 1853. 11 pp.

Remarks on Ragnarǫk in *Vǫluspá*.

2612. Simrock, Karl. *Handbuch der deutschen Mythologie mit Einschluss der nordischen,* 6th ed. Bonn: A. Marcus, 1869. 643 pp. 1st ed. 1853.

Handbook.

2613. Simrock, Karl. *Die Edda*. Ed. Gustav Neckel. Berlin: Deutsche Buch-Gemeinschaft, 1926. 434 pp.

As the editor of this new edition of Simrock's translation of the Poetic Edda, Neckel provided an introduction summing up his position on several of the major issues.

2614. Singer, Samuel. "Die Grundlagen der *Thrymskvidha.*" *Neophilologus*, 17 (1931), 47-48.

Arabic and Indo-European parallels to *Þrymskviða*.

2615. Singer, Samuel. *Sprichwörter des Mittelalters,* vol. 1: *Von den Anfängen bis ins 12. Jahrhundert*. Bern: H. Lang, 1944. viii, 198 pp.

Includes treatment of *Hávamál*, *Sigrdrífumál*, *Hamðismál*, and *Vólundarkviða*, with citation of many parallels to the gnomic material in these poems.

2616. Skard, Eiliv. "Kong Adils." *Maal og minne*, 1933, pp. 162.

Proposes an emendation to *Historia Norvegiae* suggesting a cult act: riding a horse about the hall of the *dísir*.

2617. Skautrup, Peter. "Nogle højnavne i Hardsyssel." *Hardsyssels årbog*, 1927, pp. 120-35.

The terms *jǫtunn* and *jǫtul* "giant" in names of mounds in Denmark.

2618. Skautrup, Peter. "Nogle højnavne i Hardsyssel." *Hardsyssels årbog*, 1929, pp. 156-58.

Placenames in *Ul-* do not contain the name of the god Ullr.

2619. Skautrup, Peter. "Runologiske oplevelser, 1: Vinterlevstenene." *Sprog og kultur*, 1 (1932), 3-16.

Interpretation of a new runic find. The inscriptions involve magic and may have had to do with burial. But cf. Skautrup, "Vinterlevstenene" (1935).

2620. Skautrup, Peter. "Vinterlevstenene." *Sprog og kultur*, 3 (1935), 99-100.

The Vinterlev stones are recent. Cf. Skautrup, "Runologiske oplevelser, 1" (1932).

2621. Skovgaard-Petersen, Inge. "Saxo, Historian of the Patria." *Mediaeval Scandinavia*, 2 (1969), 54-77.

Saxo the nationalistic historian in his medieval context.

2622. Skovgaard-Petersen, Inge. *The Way to Byzantium: A Study in the First Three Books of Saxo's History of Denmark*. Ed. Karsten Friis-Jensen. Copenhagen: Museum Tusculanum Press, 1981.

Informative analysis of Saxo's mythography in books 1-3 of *Gesta Danorum*. Saxo uses Norse sources in a personal way and "mingles them with Christian and classical conceptions" (p. 130). To take the example of the Baldr story: Skovgaard-Petersen finds it possible that Saxo knew no more of Norse mythology than we do and adapted the Baldr story to fit his purposes.

Skovgaard-Petersen distinguishes Saxo's euhemerism from that of Snorri and explains the location of the *æsir* in Byzantium as Saxo's adaptation of the contradiction between Greek wisdom and Greek paganism—both later replaced by Christianity.

2623. Skrede, Sverro Mo. "*Myrar*." *Heimen*, 12 (1961-63), 481-505.

The Norwegian farm name *Myrar* may reflect prehistoric cult activity.

2624. Slawik, Alexander. "Kultische Geheimbünde der Japaner und Germanen." *Wiener Beiträge zur Kulturgeschichte und Linguistik*, 4 (1936), 675-764.

As the title suggests, Slawik identifies parallels between Japanese *Männerbünde* and Germanic (after O. Höfler, *Kultische Geheimbünde der Germanen* (1934)).

2625. Smári, Jakob Jóh. "'Áss hinn almáttki.'" *Skírnir*, 110 (1936), 161-63.

The expression refers to a nameless creator, not to Odin or Thor.

2626. Smith, Emil. "Gude- og dæmonsprog." *Maal og minne*, 1918, pp. 9-18.

Setting *Alvíssmál* alongside Norwegian folklore and Greek literature showing similar phenomena, Smith evaluates possible explanations for the conception of different languages for supernatural beings. He concludes that the best explanation has to do with the power of the spoken word.

2627. Smolian, J. "Vehicula Religiosa: Wagen in Mythos, Ritus, Kultus und Mysterium." *Numen*, 10 (1963), 202-27.

General treatment of the cult wagon, with much use of Germanic sources. Useful for the general context of such mythic motifs as Thor's chariot or Freyja's being pulled by cats and of such cultic moments as Nerthus in her wagon.

2628. Sørensen, John Kousgård. "*Odinkar* og andre navne på -kar." *Namn og bygd*, 62 (1974), 108-16.

The author refutes the notion that the typically Danish personal name *Odinkar* is compounded with Odin. The second component meant originally "curved, bent," secondarily "obstinate, reluctant," and was always semantically related to the first component. Thus Old Danish *o thænkar* will have been a compound adjective whose first component was a noun *o thæn* "rage, madness" (derived from the same root as *Óðinn*), and the name meant "one inclined to rage or madness."

2629. Sørensen, Preben Meulengracht. *Saga og samfund: En indføring i oldislandsk litteratur*. Berlingske lexikon bibliotek, 116. Copenhagen: Berlingske forlag, 1977. 191 pp.

This "Introduction to Old Icelandic Literature" is unusual (within Norse literary criticism) in its attempt to relate society and literature. Its discussions of worldview relate to myth, and the last chapter contains an overtly mythic reading (pp. 159-64) of the episode of Vanlandi and Vísburr from *Heimskringla* (*Ynglinga saga*, ch. 13-14).

2630. Sørensen, Preben Meulengracht. "Starkaðr, Loki og Egill Skallagrímsson." In *Sjötíu ritgerðir helgaðar Jakobi Benediktssyni 20. júli 1977*, vol. 2, eds. Einar G. Pétursson and Jónas Kristjánsson, 759-68. Stofnun Árna Magnússonar á Íslandi, rit 12. Reykjavik: Stofnun Árna Magnússonar, 1977.

A discussion of parallels and contrasts among three well-known "trickster" figures in Norse tradition: Loki, Starkaðr, and Egill Skallagrímsson—the latter two noted Odin heroes.

2631. Sørensen, Preben Meulengracht. *Norrønt nid: Forestillingen om den umandige mand i de islandske sagaer*. Odense: Odense University Press, 1980. 134 pp.

Danish original of *The Unmanly Man* (1983).

2632. Sørensen, Preben Meulengracht. *The Unmanly Man: Concepts of Sexual Defamation in Early Northern Society*. The Viking Collection, 1. Odense: Odense University Press, 1983. 115 pp. Translated by Joan Turville-Petre.

Translation of the author's *Norrønt nid* (1980); treatment of *níð* in its thirteenth-century literary and social context.

2633. Sokolicek, Ferdinand. "Der Hinkende im brauchtümlichen Spiel." In *Festschrift für Otto Höfler zum 65. Geburtstag,* eds. Helmut Birkhan and Otto Gschwantler, 423-32. Vienna: Notring, 1968.

Although it makes only passing reference to Germanic materials, this wide-ranging essay relating limping to the figure of the smith and ultimately to shamanism and initiation is clearly relevant to Wayland the smith and perhaps more distantly to the maiming of Odin and Týr.

2634. Solger, Friedrich. "Sturmgott und Sternengott." In *Festgabe für den 70jährigen Gustaf Kossinna von Freunden und Schülern.* 310-15. Mannus, 6, Ergänzungsband. Leipzig: C. Kabitzsch, 1928.

Reads Germanic myth as the irreconcilable opposition between a storm god (Donar/Thor) and star gods (typified by Nerthus). This opposition, Solger claims, was later rationalized by the myths of the *æsir* and *vanir.*

2635. Sommerfelt, Alf. "Har syden og vesten vært uten betydning for nordisk hedenskap?" *Maal og minne,* 1962, pp. 90-96.

Sommerfelt attempts to supplement a weakness he perceives in F. Ström's *Nordisk hedendom* (1961)—the lack of influences from the south and west. By this, Sommerfelt meant primarily from Ireland, and the article constitutes in effect a brief catalog of evidence for Irish influence.

2636. Spehr, Harald. "Literaturbericht." *Archiv für Kulturgeschichte,* 22 (1932), 92-116, 262-72, 342-51.

Research survey.

2637. Spehr, Harald. "Literaturbericht." *Archiv für Kulturgeschichte,* 26 (1935), 227-63.

Research survey.

2638. Sperber, Hans. "Embla." *Beiträge zur Geschichte der deutschen Sprache und Literatur,* 36 (1910), 219-22.

The etymology of Embla: < **ambilo n,* parallel to Greek *ámpelos* "vine." This would indicate a soft wood, into which a hard wood like ash (Askr) was bored to make fire.

2639. Sperber, Hans. "Exegetische Miscellen." *Beiträge zur Geschichte der deutschen Sprache und Literatur,* 37 (1911), 148-56.

Textual notes to, inter alia, *Hávamál,* str. 84, and to the runic text of Cotton Caligula A 15 (reference to Thor).

2640. Springer, Otto. "Germanic Bibliography 1940-1945: Books and Articles in the Field of Germanic Philology Published in Europe, Especially in Germany and in the Scandinavian Countries, During the War." *Journal of English and Germanic Philology*, 45 (1946), 251-326.

Contains a section on "Religion and Heroic Legend" (pp. 292-95), including mythology.

2641. Ståhl, Harry. "Tisdag, Tyr och Tisaren." *Ortnamnssällskapets i Uppsala årsskrift*, 1949, pp. 18-22.

Against the interpretation of the placename *Tisaren* (Närke, Sweden) as containing the name of the god Týr.

2642. Stauff, Philipp. *Märchendeutungen: Sinn und Deutung der deutschen Volksmärchen*. Berlin: Priber & Lammer, 1914. iii, 244 pp.

Alleged association between Märchen and Germanic mythology.

2643. Steblin-Kamenskij, M. I. *Kul'tura Islandii*. Leningrad: Izdatelystvo Nauka, 1967. 181, [1] pp.

Popular treatment of Icelandic culture, with a section on mythology.

2644. Steblin-Kamenskij, M. I. *The Saga Mind*. Odense: Odense University Press, 1973. 171 pp. Translated by Kenneth H. Ober.

This study is of interest primarily for its advancement of the theory of "syncretic truth:" the notion that medieval man had a different and wider notion of what was "true" than does modern man. The last chapter, in which the author describes a meeting with a revenant in a hotel in Reykjavik, is quite witty. The book led to a debate with Peter Hallberg on the subject of "syncretic truth."

2645. Steblin-Kamenskij, M. I. "Some Considerations on Approaches to Medieval Literature." *Mediaeval Scandinavia*, 8 (1975), 187-91.

A response to Hallberg (1974); part of the debate on "syncretic truth."

2646. Steblin-Kamenskij, M. I. "Further Considerations on Approaches to Medieval Literature." *Mediaeval Scandinavia*, 9 (1976), 167-72.

Response to Hallberg (1976); final entry in the debate on "syncretic truth."

2647. Steblin-Kamenskij, M. I. *Mif.* Iz istorii mirovi kul'tury. Leningrad: Nauka, 1976. 102, [2] pp.

Russian original of the author's *Myth* (1982).

2648. Steblin-Kamenskij, M. I. "On the History of Laughter." *Mediaeval Scandinavia*, 11 (1978-79), 154-62.

Uses Norse texts, including *níð* poetry, *Hárbarðsljóð*, and *Lokasenna*, as evidence that ". . . the history of laughter consists, roughly speaking, in a gradual differentiation of directed laughter from non-directed laughter . . . or, to put it in yet another way, the function of literature has increasingly become to ridicule something and not merely to provoke mirth" (p. 154).

2649. Steblin-Kamenskij, M. I. *Drevneskandinaviskaya literatura.* Moscow: Vysshaya Shkola, 1979. 190 pp.

Intended as an introduction to Old Icelandic literature, this volume contains a stimulating chapter on eddic poetry. The author discusses some of the themes of his *Myth*, e.g., mythic time, heroic poetry, and the individual.

2650. Steblin-Kamenskij, M. I. *Myth.* Ann Arbor: Karoma, 1982. 150 pp. Translated by Mary P. Coote with the assistance of Frederic Amory.

A translation of the author's *Mif* (1976). The study proper (pp. 21-102) is divided into four chapters. The first seeks to define myth as an outgrowth of human consciousness; the second treats space and time and the third "personality" in Norse mythology; and the fourth contrasts modern notions of personality and conscious authorship with more archaic conceptions. Overall, the study traces the emergence of this consciousness from earlier stages by reviewing the relationship and attitude of an author to his subject.

The English translation includes an unappreciative "Critical Introduction" (pp. 1-21) by Sir Edmund Leach and an "Epilogue and Biobibliography" by Anatoly S. Liberman.

2651. Steblin-Kamenskij, M. I. "Valkyries and Heroes." *Arkiv för nordisk filologi*, 97 (1982), 81-93.

Deals with the heroes and heroines of Norse heroic poetry: the second half of the Poetic Edda. The author finds a distinction between heroes, who merely perform, and heroines, who feel. These heroines have both a profane aspect (as human women) and a sacral aspect (as valkyries; and cf. Tacitus, *Germania*, ch. 8); the latter may be an expression of the heroines' ability to feel and show emotion.

2652. Steenstrup, Johannes. "Hammer og kors." In *Studier tillägnade Axel Kock, tidskriftens redaktör, 1888-1925.* 44-61. Arkiv för nordisk filologi, 40, supplement. Lund: C. W. K. Gleerup, 1929. Also issued separately, under title *Studier tillägnade Axel Kock.*

Hammer and cross on Swedish runestones. Steenstrup concludes that Christianity was widespread in central Sweden by the eleventh century.

Stefán Einarsson, *see* Einarsson, Stefán.

Stefán Karlsson, *see* Karlsson, Stefán.

2653. Steffen, Richard. "Blåkulla—dödsgudinnan." In *Festskrift til H. F. Feilberg fra nordiske sprog- og folkemindeforskere på 80 års dagen den 6. august 1911.* 536-40. Svenska landsmål, 1911; Maal og minne, 1911; Danske studier, 1911. Stockholm: Norstedt, Copenhagen: Gyldendal, Oslo (Kristiania): Bymaalslaget, 1911.

Blåkulla is the traditional site of the witches' sabbath in Nordic folk belief. Steffen attempts to explain the apparent placename as "goddess of death." Folk belief seems to associate the putative goddess with Freyja, but Steffen argues association with Frigg, as a wind goddess (she is wife of Odin, the "wind-god").

2654. Steffensen, Jón. "Lækningagyðjan Eir." *Skírnir*, 134 (1960), 34-46.

Seeks to answer the question why Eir, according to Snorri the goddess of healing, is not mentioned as such in other sources. Steffensen argues that Eir was indeed a pagan goddess of healing who perhaps reached Scandinavia from the Celts via England. The conversion to Christianity will have vitiated her position, however; medicine became a male rather than female activity, and Christian formulas replaced pagan in medicinal magic charms.

2655. Steffensen, Jón. "Aspects of Life in Iceland in the Heathen Period." *Saga-Book of the Viking Society*, 17 (1966-69), 177-205. Revised translation of "Nokkrir þættir úr menningu hins íslenzka þjóðfélags í heiðni," *Árbók hins íslenzka fornleifafélags*, 1967, pp. 25-44.

Steffensen examines nicknames, cures and charms, and the meaning and practice of baptism, in each case considering practices both before and after the conversion to Christianity in Iceland. Direct reference to mythology is minimal.

Steingrímur Matthíasson, *see* Mattíasson, Steingrímur.

2656. Steinhauser, Walter. "Die Wodansweihe von Nordensdorf bei Augsburg (Runenspange A)." *Zeitschrift für deutsches Altertum*, 97 (1968), 1-29.

Reads the portion of the inscription usually transcribed *logaþore wodan* as *log akore Wo dan* "May Wodan approve the agreement." The agreement would be the sacral bonds of the Odin cult, in the way it has been explained by O. Höfler.

2657. Steinsland, Gro. "Treet i Vǫluspá." *Arkiv för nordisk filologi*, 94 (1979), 120-50.

A well-nuanced study of the role of the world tree in the mythology of *Vǫluspá*. The tree provides structural and thematic unity, appearing at key moments: it is seed in str. 2, symbol of completed creation in str. 19, gathering point of the gods in str. 27, ancillary to Baldr's death in str. 31, symbol of gathering chaos in str. 46-47 and of a new regime in str. 63. "The tree is the image that expresses the process the poet wished to describe: history" (p. 148).

2658. Steinsland, Gro. "Antropogonimyten i Vǫluspá: En tekst- og tradisjonskritisk analyse." *Arkiv för nordisk filologi*, 98 (1983), 80-107.

Steinsland reads *Vǫluspá* 17-18, on the creation of man, in connection with what precedes it in the poem: the creation and activity of dwarfs. According to this reading, dwarfs create the forms (*manlícon*, *Vǫluspá* 10) of the proto-humans, and the gods animate these forms. Close comparison with other texts does not, according to Steinsland, undermine this reading. Snorri misunderstood portions of the underlying text and systematized; *Hávamál* 49 appears to Steinsland to be a genuine mythologem deriving from the same underlying tradition as *Vǫluspá*'s anthropogonic myth; *Rígsþula* has a kind of creation with similar circumstances.

2659. Steinsland, Gro, and Kari Vogt. "'Aukinn ertu Uolse og vpp vm tekinn': En religionshistorisk analyse av *Vǫlsaþáttr* i *Flateyjarbók*." *Arkiv för nordisk filologi*, 96 (1981), 87-106.

A full reading of the cultic and mythic implications of *Vǫlsa þáttr*. The authors read the pesky term *Mǫrnir* as "giantesses" and refer it to the *brúðkonur* of an earlier strophe and ultimately to Skaði. We have here, in their opinion, a *hieros gamos*, undertaken in the private cult of a *vǫlva* "seeress." King Olaf has in the written version replaced Odin, whose sphere of activity from time to time intersected that of *vǫlur* but who had an uneasy relationship with them.

2660. Stenberger, Mårten. "Gudingsåkrarna." *Gotländskt arkiv*, 15 (1943), 18-24.

Swedish votive hoards from the Viking Age, with emphasis on Gotland. Mostly weapons, they may represent offerings to a god of war.

2661. Stenberger, Mårten. *Det forntida Sverige*. Stockholm: Almqvist & Wiksell, 1964. 870 pp.

Comprehensive treatment of ancient Sweden, up to the conversion to Christianity, stressing the archaeological record. Several chapters relate to cult and religion, e.g., those dealing with rock carvings (pp. 228-49), burials (pp. 72-80, 121-30, 177-90, 208-12, 253-63, 523-28, 602-21, 696-716), and votive finds (pp. 423-49, 739-46, 793-99).

2662. Stenberger, Mårten. "Christliche Einflüsse im archäologischen Material der Wikingerzeit in Schweden." In *Kirche und Gesellschaft im Ostseeraum und im Norden vor der Mitte des 13. Jahrhunderts*. 9-20. Acta Visbyensia, 3; Visbysymposiet för historiska vetenskaper 1967. Visby: Museum Gotlands Fornsal, 1969.

A paper delivered at an international conference on church and society in viking Scandinavia and the Baltic; treats Christian influences on archaeological artifacts of the Viking Age in Sweden. The focus is on grave materials.

2663. Stenton, Frank M. "The Historical Bearing of Place-Name Studies: Anglo-Saxon Heathenism." *Transactions of the Royal Historical Society*, 4th ser., 23 (1941), 1-24. Rpt. in Doris Mary Stenton, ed., *Preparatory to Anglo-Saxon England: Being the Collected Papers of Frank Merry Stenton*, (Oxford: Clarendon Press, 1970), pp. 281-97.

A major study of theophoric placenames in England.

2664. Stephens, George. "Týr hæb us, ye Týr ye Odin." *Årbøger for nordisk oldkyndighed og historie*, 1875, pp. 109-16.

Alleged Northumbrian survival of a pagan formula invoking Týr and Odin, associated with a festival.

2665. Stephens, George. "Prof. S. Bugge's studier over nordisk mythologi: Oversat efter 'Memoires des antiquaires du nord 1882-84' og gjennenset af forf." *Årbøger for nordisk oldkyndighed og historie*, 18 (1883), 215-363. Index in supplement, xvii-xxv.

Translation (by the author) of eight public lectures delivered in English at the University of Copenhagen in 1881.

2666. Stephens, George. "Prof. S. Bugges studier over nordisk mythologi: Supplement." *Årbøger for nordisk oldkyndighed og historie*, 1884, pp. 1-47.

Anglo-Norse and Danish rock carvings.

2667. Stephens, John. "The Mead of Poetry: Myth and Metaphor." *Neophilologus*, 56 (1972), 259-68.

"I suggest that there existed a quantity of poetic lore centering on mead as an intrinsically potent force, and continually drawn on by poets until eventually the feelings and emotions accruing to it were projected into myths" (p. 261). Stephens investigates this move, concentrating particularly on Snorri's version of the myth of the mead of poetry.

2668. Stertzing, G. F. "Kleine Beiträge zur deutschen Mythologie." *Zeitschrift für deutsches Altertum*, 3 (1843), 358-68.

German charms and supersititions.

2669. Stichtenoth, Dietrich. "Abalus und die Nerthusinsel." *Zeitschrift für deutsches Altertum*, 86 (1955-56), 161-92.

Associates the account of Tacitus concerning the island of Nerthus with many other accounts of holy islands, including Atlantis (see the interesting chart on p. 188) and suggests that all may have to do with the amber trade and cult centers near the mouth of the Oder river.

2670. Stjernquist, Berta. "Germanische Quellenopfer." In *Vorgeschichtliche Heiligtümer und Opferplätze in Mittel- und Nordeuropa: Bericht über ein Symposium in Reinhausen bei Göttingen vom 14.-16. Oktober 1968*, ed. Herbert Jankuhn, 78-99. Abhandlungen der Akademie der Wissenschaften in Göttingen, phil.-hist. Kl., 3. Folge, 74. Göttingen: Vandenhoeck & Ruprecht, 1970.

Discussion of the methodology of interpreting archaeological evidence of cult; analysis of specific recent finds from Skåne, Sweden. For discussion see T. Capelle, "Ringopfer" (1970).

2671. Storm, Gustav. "Om Thorgerd Hölgebrud." *Arkiv för nordisk filologi*, 2 (1885), 124-35.

On Þorgerðr Hǫlgabrúðr as a goddess of Hákon jarl's family.

2672. Storm, Gustav. "Vore forfædres tro paa sjælevandring og deres opkaldelsessystem." *Arkiv för nordisk filologi*, 9 (1893), 199-222.

The movable soul.

2673. Storm, Gustav. "Musen som Lokes arvtager?" *Maal og minne*, 1914, pp. 45. (Signed G. S.)

Addendum to R. Iversen's article with the same title.

2674. Streuvels, Stijn (pseudonym for Frank Lateur). *Ijslandische godensagen*. Amsterdam: L. J. Veen, 1938. 173 pp.

Popular survey.

2675. Strid, Jan Paul. "Veiðar námo—ett omdiskuterat ställe i Hymiskviða." *Scripta Islandica*, 33 (1982), 3-9.

Textual note to *Hymiskviða* 1. The phrase *veiðar námo* means "they [the gods] were hunting" (not "eating").

2676. Ström, Åke V. "The King-God and his Connection with Sacrifice in Old Norse Religion." In *Atti dell'viii congresso internazionale di storia delle religioni (Roma 17-23 Aprile 1955)*. 371-73. Florence: G. C. Sansoni—Editore, 1956.

Summary of an address at the eighth international conference on the history of religions: the king as priest, receiver, and object of sacrifice.

2677. Ström, Åke V. "Die Hauptriten des wikingerzeitlichen nordischen Opfers." In *Festschrift Walter Baetke dargebracht zu seinem 80. Geburtstage am 28. März 1964*, ed. Kurt Rudolf et al., 330-42. Weimar: H. Böhlau, 1964.

Despite the apparent lack of genuine pagan religion in the medieval Norse written sources, Ström believes that knowledge of cult may be recovered from them, primarily through examination of fixed verbal expressions. He divides his analysis between blood-rituals (coloring red and drinking blood) and banquets (gathering together to drink beer, slaughter, coloring red, eating, drinking). Pp. 339-41 offer a Dumézilian analysis of the cups employed in ritual drinking.

2678. Ström, Åke V. "Indogermanisches in der Völuspá." *Numen*, 14 (1967), 167-208.

After an introduction on the state of research, Ström treats general Indo-European motifs in *Vǫluspá*, motifs specifically shared between *Vǫluspá* and the Iranian Bundahišn (there are twenty-one of these, which Ström ascribes to common inheritance), and the "powerful one" (*inn ríki*) of str. 65H (perhaps an Indo-European/Germanic god Eiríkr, misinterpreted by a scribe). A thought-provoking article.

2679. Ström, Åke V. "Scandinavian Belief in Fate: A Comparison between Pre-Christian and Post-Christian Times." In *Fatalistic Beliefs in Religion, Folklore, and Literature: Papers Read at the Symposium on Fatalistic Beliefs Held at Åbo on the 7th-9th of September, 1964*, ed. Helmer Ringgren, 63-88. Scripti Instituti Donneriani Aboensis, 2. Stockholm: Almqvist & Wiksell, 1967.

Presentation of pre-Christian and twentieth-century belief in fate in Scandinavia, followed by a comparison of these disparate topics. The discussion of the pre-Christian situation comprises a brief research history, analysis of some important literary passages, and some philological remarks on terminology for fate. The comparison has this conclusion: "Comparative religion finds an amazing multitude of remnants from pre-Christian religion, still alive in the Northern countries. . . . But the modern belief in fate is decidedly not a 'survival' of ancient religion but the spontaneous creation of a secularized culture."

2680. Ström, Åke V. "Tradition und Tendenz: Zur Frage des christlichen-vorchristlichen Synkretismus in der nordgermanischen Literatur." In *Syncretism: Based on Papers Read at the Symposium on Cultural Contact, Meeting of Religions, Syncretism Held at Åbo on the 8th-10th of September, 1966*, ed. Sven S. Hartman, 240-62. Scripti Instituti Donneriani Aboensis, 3. Stockholm: Almqvist & Wiksell, 1969.

Ström's study of syncretism has a heavily bibliographic orientation and is useful for the history of the scholarship in the area. He treats forms of syncretism, eschatology, and sagas; and his own contribution is to point out that what appears to be borrowed from the Near East may in fact be Indo-European inheritance.

2681. Ström, Åke V. "Formes de mystique dans le nord préchrétien." In *Mysticism: Based on Papers Read at the Symposium on Mysticism Held at Åbo on the 7th-9th September, 1968*, eds. Sven S. Hartman and Carl-Martin Edsman, 220-48. Scripti Instituti Donneriani Aboensis, 5. Stockholm: Almqvist & Wiksell, 1970.

After an introduction on the literature on mysticism, Ström treats various forms of mysticism: dreams and visions, prophecy, and so forth, citing primarily saga evidence. He concludes with a discussion of *Vǫluspá* as an example of prophetic ecstasy.

2682. Ström, Åke V. "Gottesstaat und Götterstaat unter den vorchristlichen Germanen." In *The Myth of the State: Based on Papers Read at the Symposium on the Myth of the State Held at Åbo on the 6th-8th September, 1971.* 143-59. Scripti Instituti Donneriani Aboensis, 6. Stockholm: Almqvist & Wiksell, 1972.

Concludes that the Germanic peoples possessed, at the time the texts came to be recorded, two myths of the state. The first was the myth of a state of law on earth, under divine control, and with a strict differentiation between ruler and object; the second was that of a heavenly state of gods, where a similar division of power obtained between Odin and the other gods. Sacral kingship bound the two conceptions of the state.

2683. Ström, Åke V. "Björnfällar och Oden-religion." *Fornvännen*, 75 (1980), 266-70.

Departing from the findings of Bo Petré, "Björnfällen i begravningsritualen" (1975), Ström associates burial ritual involving bear phalanges with Odin and berserks.

2684. Ström, Folke. *On the Sacral Origin of the Germanic Death Penalties.* Lund: H. Ohlsson, 1942. 229 pp. Translated by Donald Burton.

Reconsideration of the evidence for the sacral origin of capital punishment in Germanic law. Ström argues against such an origin and indeed can find little of the sacred in the Germanic death penalities; his discussion of the individual elements calls on various aspects of folk belief and apotropaic techniques.

2685. Ström, Folke. *Den döendes makt och Oden i trädet.* Göteborgs högskolas årsskrift, 53:1. Gothenburg: Elander, 1947. 91 pp. Summary in English.

An excellent monograph on the power of the dying person and its relation to myths of Odin. The first chapter treats the representation of this power in Norse texts, the second and third its phenomenological background, and the fourth Odin on the tree (*Hávamál* str. 138-39). This chapter is the major contribution, as it traces Odin's quest to obtain the wisdom and secret lore belonging to the dead; voluntarily he hangs himself on the tree and suffers a near-death in pursuit of knowledge.

An excursus treats *seiðr.*

2686. Ström, Folke. *Den egna kraftens män: En studie i forntida irreligiositet.* Göteborgs högskolas årsskrift, 54:2. Gothenburg: Elander, 1948. 78 pp. Summary in English.

This little monograph deals with men who put themselves outside society, who trusted in their own powers and not those of the gods. It includes a survey of the relevant saga incidents and of the etymology and semantics of the terms used to describe this state.

2687. Ström, Folke. *Loki: Ein mythologisches Problem.* Göteborgs universitets årsskrift, 62:8. Gothenburg: Elander, 1950. 147 pp.

Loki as a hypostasis of Odin in a cult drama (the death of Baldr) in which Odin sacrifices to himself the sacral king.

2688. Ström, Folke. *Diser, norner, valkyrjor: Fruktbarhetskult och sakralt kungadöme i Norden.* Kungliga vitterhets, historie, och antikvitetsakademiens handlingar, filologisk-filosofiska serien, 1. Stockholm: Almqvist & Wiksell, in distribution, 1954. 102 pp. Summary in German, pp. 99-102.

A study of the female figures in Norse mythology, focusing on their roles in cult and myth. The first two chapters survey the cult of the *dísir* in West and East Scandinavia: *Vǫlsa þáttr* assigns a high degree of fertility to the *dísablót,* whereas *Ynglingatal* also brings into play the question of sovereignty of the Uppsala kings. Chapter 3 notes the similarities between Freyja and Odin, especially through their use of *seiðr.* Chapter 4 draws the valkyries into the discussion and chapter 5 the norns. Chapter 6 concludes that association of the *dísir* with conceptions of the soul is secondary.

More generally, Ström's concern is to demonstrate the continuity of conceptions in myth (primarily West Norse) and cult (primarily centered in Uppsala). He finds that sacral kingship provides a logical locus for this continuity.

2689. Ström, Folke. "'Fimbulvintern' ur religionshistorisk synpunkt." *Fornvännen,* 51 (1956), 3-5.

Part of a series of short essays by T. Bergeron et al., "'Fimbulvintern'" (1956). Ström quickly reviews the sources and points out parallels from outside Scandinavia.

2690. Ström, Folke. "Guden Hœnir och odensvalan." *Arv,* 12 (1956), 41-68. Summary in English.

Nominates specifically the black stork (*Ciconia negra*) as the background to Hœnir and identifies a connection with Odin.

2691. Ström, Folke. "Kung Domalde i Svitjod och 'kungalyckan.'" *Saga och sed,* 1967, pp. 52-66.

On the sacrifice of King Dómaldi by his subjects (*Ynglinga saga,* ch. 15, and *Ynglingatal* 5). Ström argues against Walter Baetke, *Yngvi und die Ynglingar* (1964), and Lars Lönnroth, "Kroppen som själens spegel—ett motiv i de isländska sagorna" (*Lychnos,* 1963-64), who sought to derive the concept of "luck" from notions of God's grace in contemporary Latin texts. According to Ström, the Dómaldi episode is anchored in genuine pagan conceptions: when the king's "luck" failed, he could no longer continue as king.

2692. Ström, Folke. *Nordisk hedendom: Tro och sed i förkristen tid,* 2nd ed. Gothenburg: Gumpert, 1967. 208 pp. 1st ed. 1961.

A handbook of pre-Christian religion in the North, intended for a Swedish audience. Part I (pp. 9-67) covers prehistoric times, part II (pp. 69-249) the Viking Age. Topics discussed include social forms, cult, creation, the gods, fate, conceptions of the soul, death, magic, eschatology, and the waning of paganism. Emphasis on the literary sources.

2693. Ström, Folke. "Nid och ergi." *Saga och sed,* 1972, pp. 27-47.

A discussion of *níð* and *ergi,* relevant to Loki and Odin.

2694. Ström, Folke. *Níð, Ergi and Old Norse Moral Attitudes.* The Dorothea Coke Memorial Lecture Delivered 10 May 1973 at University College London. London: Published for the College by the Viking Society for Northern Research, 1974. 20 pp.

Text of a lecture, focusing particularly on ancient attitudes toward *níð/ergi* and homosexuality in general.

2695. Ström, Folke. "Poetry as an Instrument of Propaganda: Jarl Hákon and his Poets." In *Speculum Norroenum: Norse Studies in Memory of Gabriel Turville-Petre,* eds. Ursula Dronke, Guðrún P. Helgadóttir, Gerd Wolfgang Weber, and Hans Bekker-Nielsen, 440-58. N. p.: Odense University Press, 1981.

Ström's discussion of the skaldic panegyrics to Hákon jarl (tenth century, Norway) stresses the use of mythological imagery for political purposes.

2696. Ström, Folke. "Hieros gamos-motivet i Hallfreðr Óttarssons Hákonardrápa och den nordnorska jarlavärdigheten." *Arkiv för nordisk filologi,* 98 (1983), 67-79.

Hallfreðr Óttarsson's *Hákonardrápa* is understood to celebrate Hákon jarl's victory at Hjǫrungavágr and contains an apparent example of a *hieros gamos* between Odin and the earth—here presumably Norway. Drawing on the tale of Hǫlgabrúðr's aid to Hákon at the battle, Ström sees a double context: a myth of Odin and Jǫrð and a specific conception among the Hlaðir jarls that the current jarl entered into an erotic relationship with a local fertility goddess.

2697. Ström, Krister. "Thorshammerringe und andere Gegenstände des heidnischen Kults." In *Systematische Analysen der Gräberfunde,* ed. Greta Arwidsson, 127-40. Birka: Untersuchungen und Studien, 2:1. Stockholm: Kungliga vitterhets historie och antikvitets akademien / Almqvist & Wiksell, 1984.

A chapter in the major archaeological report of the excavations at Birka (Björkö, Sweden). Ström concludes that his results hardly support the older view of Thor's hammers as deliberate symbolic opposites of the Christian cross, except perhaps during the later missionary period.

2698. Strömbäck, Dag. "Fvn. *Gaglviðr* och några därmed besläktade ord." *Språkvetenskapliga sällskapets i Uppsala förhandlingar*, 1927, pp. 23-33.

On the term *gaglviðr* (*Vǫluspá* 42): "the high tree." Discussion of other related terms.

2699. Strömbäck, Dag. "Att helga land: Studier i Landnáma och det äldsta rituella besittningstagandet." In *Festskrift tillägnad Axel Hägerström den 6 september 1928 av filosofiska och juridiska föreningarna i Uppsala*. 198-220. Uppsala and Stockholm: Almqvist & Wiksell, 1928. Rpt. in Strömbäck, *Folklore och filologi*, pp. 135-65.

A study of the rituals employed when settlers claimed land during the Icelandic *landnám*. These included procession over or around the territory with fire, shooting a flaming arrow over the territory, or erecting a pole or something similar (e.g., a Thor's hammer) and reciting a magic formula. According to Strömbäck, the aim of such rituals was to claim the territory from its original inhabitants, the *landvættir*, whom Strömbäck regards as nature beings.

2700. Strömbäck, Dag. "Lytir—en fornsvensk gud?" In *Festskrift til Finnur Jónsson 29. maj 1928*. 283-93. Copenhagen: Levin & Munksgaard, 1928.

Lýtir as a Swedish name for Freyr. It means "defiler" and was formulated in a spirit of anti-paganism.

2701. Strömbäck, Dag. "Banaþúfa och heillaþúfa: Några text- och traditionsanmärkningar." In *Studier tillägnade Axel Kock, tidskriftens redaktör, 1888-1925*. 69-83. Arkiv för nordisk filologi, 40, supplement. Lund: C. W. K. Gleerup, 1929. Also issued separately, under title *Studier tillägnade Axel Kock*.

Analysis of two terms having to do with mounds: *banaþúfa* and *heillaþúfa*. Following the entry in Finnur Jónsson's revision of Sveinbjörn Egilsson's *Lexicon Poeticum*, Strömbäck agrees that *banaþúfa* originally meant "the hillock on which the mortally wounded was placed to ease his death throes." He notes a parallel Swedish dialect term in which the notion of fate seems to play a role.

2702. Strömbäck, Dag. *Sejd: Textstudier i nordisk religionshistoria*. Nordiska texter och undersökningar, 5. Stockholm: H. Geber, Copenhagen: Levin & Munksgaard, 1935. xxiv, 209 pp.

The major study of *seiðr*, a form of magic with evil connotations, associated in the mythology especially with Odin but said to have been taught to the *æsir* by Freyja. As the subtitle indicates, Strömbäck's approach is text-critical. He analyzes virtually all the passages in classical Old Norse literature in which *seiðr* appears, arranging this analysis according to genre: eddic poems, skaldic poems, kings' sagas, family sagas, *fornaldarsögur*, legal materials. As most of the attestations occur in the family sagas and *fornaldarsögur*, these receive greatest attention (pp. 49-77 and 79-106 respectively). Following the textual analysis are discussions of terminology (pp. 108-41), "white" and "black" *seiðr* (pp. 142-59), and shape-changing (pp. 160-90). A concluding chapter draws shamanism into the discussion.

2703. Strömbäck, Dag. "Till Codex Wormianus av Snorre-Eddan: Textkritiska och lexikaliska bidrag till dess Wb-redaktionen." *Arkiv för nordisk filologi*, 51 (1935), 90-120.

A text-critical and lexical study of one of the manuscripts of *Snorra edda*, focusing on a section ("Wb") so different from the rest of the manuscript that it is frequently treated independently. Most of the words treated occur in *Skáldskaparmál*.

2704. Strömbäck, Dag. "Philologisch-kritische Methode und altnordische Religionsgeschichte: Einige Bemerkungen anlässlich einer Heimdal-Monographie." *Acta Philologica Scandinavica*, 12 (1938), 1-24.

The Heimdallr monograph in question is that of Åke Ohlmarks, *Heimdalls Horn und Odins Auge* (1937). Strömbäck analyzes a number of instances in which Ohlmarks has committed philological or source-critical errors and concludes: "The work seems to me quickly written, more an experiment than the result of careful analysis and deeper penetration into the material" (p. 24).

2705. Strömbäck, Dag. "Hade de germanska dödsstraffen sakralt ursprung?" *Saga och sed*, 1942, pp. 51-69.

Remarks occasioned by Folke Ström, *On the Sacral Origin of the Germanic Death Penalties* (1942). Strömbäck focuses his discussion on Ström's interpretation of *Germania*, ch. 12, especially the role of the anger of the gods and the importance of hanging. Adducing some of his evidence from Norse mythology and religion, Strömbäck concludes that Ström's attempt to eliminate the sacral from the Germanic death penalties may have been hasty.

2706. Strömbäck, Dag. "Om draumkvädet och dess källor." *Arv*, 2 (1946), 35-70. Rpt. in Strömbäck, *Folklore och filologi* (1970), pp. 1-33.

Strömbäck's analysis of the Norwegian dream-ballad and its sources includes discussion of the Gjallarbrú, which seems to have survived from Norse mythology here and in other Christian visions and later traditions.

2707. Strömbäck, Dag. "Cult Remnants in Icelandic Dramatic Dances." *Arv*, 4 (1948), 132-45.

The dances in question are postmedieval, but Strömbäck traces them to ancient mumming, perhaps associated with fertility ritual.

See also Stefán Einarsson, "Horse Dance in the Sturlunga saga" (1960).

2708. Strömbäck, Dag. *Tidrande och disarna: Ett filologiskt-folkloristiskt utkast*. Lund: C. Blom, 1949. 59 pp. Rpt. in Strömbäck, *Folklore och filologi* (1970), pp. 166-91.

An important study of the *dísir*. The first part (pp. 166-81 in *Folklore och filologi*—the more readily available version of the work, as the original was apparently printed in only 100 copies) treats *Þiðranda þáttr dísabana*, attempting to place the text in the context of medieval vision literature. The second part (pp. 181-91) treats the *dísir* more generally, using philological-folkloristic methodology.

2709. Strömbäck, Dag. "Att binda helskor: Anteckningar till Gisle Surssons saga." *Kungliga humanistiska vetenskaps-samfundet i Uppsala, årsbok,* 1952, pp. 139-48. Rpt. in Strömbäck, *Folklore och filologi* (1970), pp. 192-200.

On *Gísla saga*, particularly the funeral of Vésteinn and the Hel-shoes put on him by Þorgrímr. Strömbäck argues that the scene preserves a genuine bit of folk belief from the tenth century; the Hel-shoes should aid the deceased on his journey to the world of the dead.

2710. Strömbäck, Dag. "Till Ynglingatal 10 och nordisk ödestro." In *Septentrionalia et Orientalia: Studia Bernhardo Karlgren A.D. III non. oct. anno mcmlix dedicata.* 386-92. Kungliga vitterhets historie och antikvitets akademiens handlingar, 91. Stockholm: Kungliga vitterhets historie och antikvitets akademien, 1959. Rpt. in Strömbäck, *Folklore och filologi* (1970), pp. 201-08

Textual note to *Ynglingatal* 10; on the expression *at skǫpum* "according to fate" and its relation to Old Scandinavian conceptions of fate.

2711. Strömbäck, Dag. *Folklore och filologi: Valda uppsatser utgivna av kungl. gustav adolfs akademien 13.8.1970.* Skrifter utgivna av kungliga Gustav Adolfs akademien, 48. Uppsala: Kungl. Gustav Adolfs Akademien, 1970. 306 pp.

Collection of Strömbäck's essays, of which the following are pertinent to the mythology and entered in this bibliography: "Att helga land: Studier i Landnáma och det äldsta rituella besittningstagandet" (1928); "Banaþúfa och heillaþúfa: Några text- och traditionsanmärkningar" (1929); "Om draumkvädet och dess källor" (1946); *Tidrande och disarna: Ett filologiskt-folkloristiskt utkast* (1949); "Att binda helskor: Anteckningar till Gisle Surssons saga" (1952); "Till Ynglingatal 10 och nordisk ödestro" (1959).

2712. Strömbäck, Dag. "The Concept of the Soul in Nordic Tradition." *Arv,* 31 (1975), 5-22.

Primarily on the *fylgja* and parallels in recent Nordic folk belief. These indicate a conception of the soul as a separate and mobile element of man.

2713. Strömbäck, Dag. *The Conversion of Iceland: A Survey.* Viking Society Text Series, 6. London: Viking Society for Northern Research, 1975. xii, 109 pp. Translated by Peter Foote.

Translation (expanded) of a series of popular lecures on the conversion. Critical approach to the sources, including the verse of the skald Hallfreðr vandræðaskáld.

2714. Strömbäck, Dag. "Resan till den andra världen: Kring medeltidsvisionerna och Draumkvädet." *Saga och sed*, 1976, pp. 15-29.

Strömbäck applies the survey of medieval vision literature undertaken here to Norse mythology, especially *Vǫluspá* (p. 25f.).

2715. Stroh, Friedrich. *Handbuch der germanischen Philologie*. Berlin: W. de Gruyter, 1952. xx, 820 pp.

Handbook of Germanic philology, including a section on religion.

2716. Strutynski, Udo. "History and Structure in Germanic Mythology: Some Thoughts on Einar Haugen's Critique of Dumézil." In *Myth in Indo-European Antiquity*, eds. Gerald James Larson, C. Scott Littleton, and Jaan Puhvel, 29-50. Berkeley and Los Angeles: University of California Press, 1974.

Contra Haugen, "The Mythical Structure of the Ancient Scandinavians" (1967). Strutynski argues for the superiority of Dumézil's "empirical" approach over Haugen's "theoretical" approach; the latter relies a priori on patterns of binary opposition derived from Prague school phonology and, according to Strutynski, thus precludes an empirical approach to the data.

2717. Strutynski, Udo. "Germanic Divinities in Weekday Names." *Journal of Indo-European Studies*, 3 (1975), 368-84.

Correlates the names of the weeks from Tuesday through Friday with Dumézil's tripartite functional scheme: Týr (Tuesday) and Odin (Wednesday) represent the dual aspects of sovereignty, Thor (Thursday) represents the warrior, and Frigg (Friday) represents fertility. Application of these gods' names was not haphazard but reflected an inherited Indo-European structure here applied to time reckoning.

2718. Strutynski, Udo. "Philippson contra Dumézil: An Answer to the Attack." *Journal of Indo-European Studies*, 5 (1977), 209-19.

A summary of some of Philippson's criticisms of Dumézil, issued from the "historicist" viewpoint, and a rebuttal.

2719. Stubbs, H. W. "Troy, Asgard, and Armageddon." *Folklore*, 70 (1959), 440-59.

Stubbs finds many parallels between Greek and Norse tradition. He organizes them according to the following categories (p. 450): The Stolen Bride: Helen/Thetis/Freyja; The Misleader: Eris?/Aphrodite/Gullveig; The Enemy Castle: Troy/(Jǫtunheimr/Vanaheimr; The Enemy Chief: Priam/Paris/Apollo/Freyr?; The Spy: Odysseus/Prometheus/Loki. Two additional categories, The Hero (Achilles) and The Bridegroom (Menelaus or others), are not found in Norse tradition. Stubbs understands the war between the *æsir* and *vanir* as "symbolizing a ritual, or actual, struggle between the castes" (p. 451).

2720. Stübe, R. "Kvasir und der magische Gebrauch des Speichels." In *Festschrift Eugen Mogk zum 70. Geburtstag 19. Juli 1924*. 500-09. Halle a. d. S.: M. Niemeyer, 1924.

Surveys the anthropological context of the creation of Kvasir through the mixture of spittle of the *æsir* and *vanir*.

2721. Stumpfl, Robert. *Kultspiele der Germanen als Ursprung des mittelalterlichen Dramas*. Berlin: Junker und Dünnhaupt, 1936. xiv, 448 pp.

As the title indicates, Stumpfl attempts to derive medieval drama from ancient Germanic cult dramas: the German Shrovetide play from *Männerbünde*, Easter plays from cult drama of the dying god.

2722. Sturtevant, Albert Morey. "The Old Norse Hávamál in Modern Norwegian Folk Song." *Journal of English and Germanic Philology*, 9 (1910), 340-55.

The folk song in question is "Aka paa isen haale," published in 1903. It treats the fickleness of women and is, according to Sturtevant, in part an almost literal translation of *Hávamál* 90, in part a paraphrase and extension of other stanzas (79, 81-95) dealing with Odin's amorous adventure with Billingr's daughter. Sturtevant thus derives the song from this passage of *Hávamál* and argues the validity of the song as evidence for the arrangement of stanzas in an earlier version of *Hávamál*.

2723. Sturtevant, Albert Morey. "A Note on the *Hárbarðsljóð*." *Scandinavian Studies*, 1 (1911-14), 157-64.

Interpretation of *Hárbarðsljóð* 18. Two themes are present and adumbrated: Odin's wit and his seduction of giantesses.

2724. Sturtevant, Albert Morey. "A Study of the Old Norse Word *mein*." *Scandinavian Studies*, 1 (1911-14), 221-50.

The word means "evil" or "injury" in *Lokasenna* 3; "bodily injury" or "destruction" in *Hávamál* 151; "evil fate" or "doom" in *Sigrdrífumál* 20; "evil deed" or "shameful act" in *Lokasenna* 32 and 56. The article concludes with some general remarks on *Lokasenna*.

2725. Sturtevant, Albert Morey. "The Relation of Loddfáfnir to Odin in the Hávamál." *Journal of English and Germanic Philology*, 10 (1911), 42-55.

Extended analysis of *Hávamál* 163 and the surrounding circumstances. Sturtevant concludes that Loddfáfnir is a mythic character, a poetic realization of Odin's audience. *Hávamál* 163 (in which Odin announces the existence of a charm he will reveal to none) is a valid mythic reflection of the unanswerable riddle of Odin's final words whispered in Baldr's ear on the funeral pyre.

2726. Sturtevant, Albert Morey. "A Note on the Sigrdrífumál." *Scandinavian Studies*, 2 (1914-15), 79-91.

On the *límrúnar* (*Sigrdrífumál* 11) and other magic "runes" of the poem, with reference to *Hávamál*, *Skírnismál*, and *Hárbarðsljóð*.

2727. Sturtevant, Albert Morey. "A Study of the Old Norse Word *regin*." *Journal of English and Germanic Philology*, 15 (1916), 251-66.

Sturtevant's essay traces the "fading in meaning" that *regin* "gods" underwent in Old Norse; it derives from the root **rag* "power" (usually supernatural) but when used as first component in compounds seems to be only an intensifier in most cases. Two compounds are of special interest for the mythology, and these are discussed: *reginkunnr* (*Hávamál* 80) and *regindómr* (*Vǫluspá* 66). Sturtevant grants each a mythological meaning.

2728. Sturtevant, Albert Morey. "Semological Notes on Old Norse *heim-* in Compounds." *Scandinavian Studies*, 3 (1916), 253-64.

Includes discussion of *Hávamál* 155 and of *Vǫluspá* 56 (*heimstǫð*).

2729. Sturtevant, Albert Morey. "Old Norse Notes." *Scandinavian Studies*, 8 (1924-25), 199-209.

One of these notes (pp. 203-04) treats the word *-fambi* "fool" (*Hávamál* 103).

2730. Sturtevant, Albert Morey. "Old Norse Semasiological and Etymological Notes." *Scandinavian Studies*, 8 (1924-25), 37-47.

Most of the words treated are found primarily or exclusively in eddic mythological contexts: *afi* "man" (*Skírnismál* 1, *Grógaldr* 5); *api/glapi* "fool" (*Hymiskviða* 21, *Hávamál* 17); *-fákr* "horse" (*Hymiskviða* 27).

2731. Sturtevant, Albert Morey. "Notes on the Poetic Edda." *Scandinavian Studies*, 9 (1926-27), 31-36.

One of these notes (p. 32) treats the expression *tveir'u einherjar* (*Hávamál* 73).

2732. Sturtevant, Albert Morey. "Some Etymologies of Certain Old Norse Words Dealing With the Supernatural." *Scandinavian Studies*, 9 (1926-27), 151-59.

The words treated are *dólgr* "enemy, fiend, monster"; *flyka* "phantom"; *reimt* "haunted"; *skars/skass* "monster, giantess"; *skí* "sorcery, jugglery"; and *skrípi* "phantom."

2733. Sturtevant, Albert Morey. "Some Old Norse Etymologies." *Journal of English and Germanic Philology*, 25 (1926), 216-26.

The etymology and meaning of 1) Líf-þrasir: "one who is heroic, mighty, sturdy in life (i.e., in surviving death; one hard to kill" (p. 224) and 2) Mǫgþrasir (*Vafþrúðnismál* 49): *þorp Mǫgþrasis* is "'the hill of man', i.e., that hill where the race of man is to be saved from the destruction of Ragnarökkr" (p. 225).

2734. Sturtevant, Albert Morey. "Some Etymologies of Old Norse Poetic Words." *Scandinavian Studies*, 16 (1940-41), 220-25.

Includes the etymology of Gná, one of Frigg's maids (< **ga-naha* "sufficiency") and Kerti, a mythological horse (< *kart-uz* "horse-cart").

2735. Sturtevant, Albert Morey. "Semantic and Etymological Notes on Old Norse." *Scandinavian Studies*, 20 (1948), 129-43.

Includes discussion of mythological terms: *Vitnir* "wolf" (< **vitan* "see, visit, guard, watch over"); *-þrasir* (Lífþrasir "one stubbornly, persistently maintaining life, one hard to kill"); *Mǫsma* (*Rígsþula* 38, < **mas-* "stripe"); *Úlfs hnitbróðir* (*Hymiskviða* 24, wolf and midgard serpent from the same brood).

2736. Sturtevant, Albert Morey. "Etymologies of Old Norse Proper Names Used as Poetic Designations." *Modern Language Notes*, 64 (1949), 486-90.

The etymologies of Þuðr and Uðr (Odin names), Viþofnir (*Fjǫlsvinnsmál* 18), Loddfáfnir (*Hávamál* 111), and Drǫttr (*Rígsþula* 12).

2737. Sturtevant, Albert Morey. "Etymological Comments on Certain Words and Names in the Elder Edda." *Publications of the Modern Language Association*, 66 (1951), 278-91.

Mythological expressions treated include *dags vera*, *Kerlaug*, *Naglfar*, *Sviðrir*, *hara*, *Fjalarr*, *Surtr*, and *Lagastafr*.

2738. Sturtevant, Albert Morey. "Etymological Comments Upon Certain Old Norse Proper Names in the Eddas." *Publications of the Modern Language Association*, 67 (1952), 1145-62.

Mythological names treated include *Þjalfi, Vǫn, Kvasir, Læráðr, Loptr, Bestla, Hengi-Kjǫptr, Rígr, Bilskirnir,* and *Víðarr.*

2739. Sturtevant, Albert Morey. "Regarding the Name Ása-Þórr." *Scandinavian Studies*, 15 (1953), 15-16.

Brief note on Thor's designation as *Ása-Þórr*, which Sturtevant understands as a kind of honorific: best of the clan of the *æsir*.

2740. Sturtevant, Albert Morey. "Comments on Mythological Name-Giving in Old Norse." *Germanic Review*, 29 (1954), 68-71.

Etymological comments on the names Huginn and Muninn, Góin and Móinn, and Ókólnir.

2741. Stutz, Elfriede. "Ein Widerschein von Hávamál 138 bei Elisabeth Langgässer." In *Antiquitates Indogermanicae: Studien zur indogermanischen Altertumskunde und zur Sprach- und Kulturgeschichte der indogermanischen Völker: Gedenkschrift für Hermann Güntert zur 25. Wiederkehr seines Todestages am 23. April 1973*, eds. Manfred Mayrhofer, Wolfgang Meid, Bernfried Schlerath, and Rüdiger Schmitt, 467-73. Innsbrucker Beiträge zur Sprachwissenschaft, 12. Innsbruck: Institut für Sprachwissenschaft der Universität Innsbruck, 1974.

Although the use of Norse mythology by a twentieth-century poet sheds only dim light at best on the mythology itself, the author's review (p. 471) of some of the pagan-Christian implications of *Hávamál* 138 may be of interest.

2742. Süsskand, Peter. *Germanisches Leben im Spiegel der altnordischen Dichtung.* Berlin: Junker & Dünnhaupt, 1936. 123 pp.

Application of Old Norse-Icelandic literature to study of Germanic culture; largely derivative. Topics specifically treated include paganism and ethics; the skald and Valhalla; the fall of the Nibelungs and Ragnarǫk; the world ash and the conversion of Iceland.

Sveinbjörn Rafnsson, *see* Rafnsson, Sveinbjörn.

2743. Sveinsson, Einar Ól. *Verzeichnis isländischer Märchenvarianten mit einer einleitenden Untersuchung.* FF Communications, 83. Helsinki: Suomalainen tiedeakatemia, 1929. xcii, 176 pp.

Pp. xiv-xvi contain a survey of works dealing with the relationship between folktale and Norse mythology.

2744. Sveinsson, Einar Ól. "Lítil athugasemd." *Skírnir*, 122 (1948), 146-51.

Opposes the immediately preceding note by Stefán Einarsson, "Eddu-smælki." Einar Ól. Sveinsson argues that the word *hórdómr* in the description of Ragnarǫk in *Vǫluspá* 44 reflects not Norwegian but Icelandic churchly use, and he considers more generally the circumstances of religious language and sentiment around the time of the conversion in Iceland.

2745. Sveinsson, Einar Ól. "Vísa í Hávamálum og írsk saga." *Skírnir*, 126 (1952), 168-77.

On *Hávamál* 129 and specifically the expression *verða at gjalti.* Einar Ól. Sveinsson adduces a possible Irish source, namely traditions about the Irish warrior Suibne geilt.

2746. Sveinsson, Einar Ól. *Íslenzkar bókmenntir í fornöld*, vol. 1 [all that appeared]. N.p.: Allmenna bókafélagið, 1962. vii, 532 pp.

Literary history of Old Icelandic poetry, focusing on the Poetic Edda. Three chapters treat the mythological poetry, and the division is chronological: older poetry; the conflict of faith, younger poetry.

2747. Sveinsson, Einar Ól. "The *Edda* and Homer." In *IV International Congress for Folk-Narrative Research in Athens (1.9-6.9 1964): Lectures and Reports*, ed. Georgios A. Megas, 531-52. Laographía, 22. Athens: Laographía, 1965.

With remarks on the formula *jǫrð fanns æva né uphiminn* in accounts of creation and destruction in Germanic literature (pp. 539-41).

van Sweringen Baur, Grace, *see* Baur, Grace van Sweringen.

2748. Sydow, C. W. von. "Studier i Finnsägnen och besläktade byggmästarsägner." *Fataburen*, 1907, pp. 65-78, 199-218.

Pathfinding study of the Masterbuilder legend in Norway, Denmark, and Sweden.

2749. Sydow, C. W. von. "Studier i Finnsägnen och besläktade byggmästarsägner: Finnsägnens förhistoria." *Fataburen*, 1908, pp. 19-27.

Continuation of von Sydow's study of the Masterbuilder legend. The oldest Nordic form of the tale may be found in *Alvíssmál*; the building of Ásgarðr represents a literary branch and the Finn legend a popular branch of the legend.

2750. Sydow, C. W. von. "Tors färd till Utgård." *Danske studier*, 1910, pp. 65-105; 145-82.

This still important article on Thor's journey to Útgarða-Loki is in three parts, which correspond to the logical division of the story: the slaughtering of the goats (pp. 65-105); the Skrýmir episode (pp. 145-67); and the actual visit to Útgarðr (pp. 167-82). These, von Sydow believes, all derive from Celtic—for the latter two, definitely Irish—tradition. The entire episode may date from the tenth century and would owe its current form to Scandinavian reformation of the originally Celtic materials.

2751. Sydow, C. W. von. "Jätten Hymes bägare." *Folkminnen och folktankar*, 1 (1914), 113-50.

A study of the episode in *Hymiskviða* in which Thor breaks Hymir's cup by throwing it against the giant's head. Von Sydow derives the episode from an originally European folktale, sharing some characteristics with the tale of the giant without a head. Pp. 145-50 contain methodological remarks setting forth von Sydow's views on the value of folklore in the study of myth.

2752. Sydow, C. W. von. "Jättarna i mytologi och folktro." *Folkminnen och folktankar*, 6 (1919), 52-96.

A study of giants in Scandinavian mythology and in later folk tradition.

2753. Sydow, C. W. von. "Iriskt inflytande på nordisk guda- och hjältesaga." *Vetenskaps-societeten i Lund, årsbok*, 1920, pp. 19-29.

Irish mythic material will have been preserved, according to the author, in Christian narrative for a few hundred years and then have influenced Norse. Concrete examples cited include *Rígsþula*, Mímir's well and head, the construction of the stronghold at Ásgarðr, and motifs within the story of Thor's journey to Geirrøðr. Von Sydow finds the Finn cycle a likely source for much of this.

2754. Sydow, C. W. von. "Scyld Scefing." *Namn och bygd*, 12 (1924), 63-95.

This article on Scyld Scefing (*Beowulf* 1-19) includes remarks opposing the existence of a hypothetical Norse god Skjǫldr.

2755. Sydow, C. W. von. "Germansk tradition: Föredrag vid det 8:de nordiska filologmötet i Köpenhamn 14 aug. 1935." *Saga och sed*, 1935, pp. 49-59.

Theoretical considerations concerning Germanic tradition, primarily religion.

2756. Symons, Barend. "Untersuchungen über die sogenannte Völsunga saga." *Beiträge zur Geschichte der deutschen Sprache und Literatur*, 3 (1876), 199-303.

The fourth part of this monograph on *Vǫlsunga saga* treats the prehistory of the legends involved (pp. 287-303) and has much to say about Odin.

2757. Symons, Barend. "Bijdrage tot de dagteekening der Eddaliederen." *Verslagen en mededeelingen der koninklijke akademie van wetenschappen*, Afd. letterkunde, 3. r., 4 (1887), 220-42. Also issued separately (Amsterdam: J. Müller).

On dating the eddic poems; Symons stresses more the method than the conclusions.

2758. Symons, Barend. *De ontwikkelingsgang der germaansche mythologie*. Redevoering uitgesproken bij de overdracht van het rektoraat der rijks-universiteit te Groningen, den 20sten september 1892. Groningen: J. B. Wolters, 1892. 28 pp.

Text of an address on Norse mythology and the scholars who have studied it.

2759. Szcepański, G. von. *Der romantische Schwindel in der deutschen Mythologie und auf der Opernbühne, I: Das humoristische altisländische Gedicht von Harbard oder Charon, Fährmann weiland in der griechischen Unterwelt.* Eberfeld: Bädeker, 1885. 39 pp.

Classical origins of Norse mythology.

2760. Szcepański, G. von. *Der romantische Schwindel in der deutschen Mythologie und auf der Opernbühne, II: Wer ist Loki?* Eberfeld: Bädeker, 1885. 27 pp.

Roman parallels to Loki myths.

2761. Szcepański, G. von. *Der romantische Schwindel in der deutschen Mythologie und auf der Opernbühne, III: Odin, Baldur und Hödr.* Eberfeld: Bädeker, 1885. 46 pp.

Classical parallels to the myth of Baldr's death.

2762. Szcepański, G. von. "Der germanische Kriegsgott Tyr." *Am Urds-Brunnen*, 6 (1888-89), 8-10, 18-22, 41-44, 52-58, 68-72.

Criticism of R. Goette, "Die Schwertrune und der Schwertgott" (1887-88); Szcepański sees Roman sources.

2763. Szcepański, G. von. "Die Frage- und Ausrufungszeichen des Herrn R. Goette." *Am Urds-Brunnen*, 6 (1888-89), 117-19.

Response to R. Goette, "Erwiderung auf die Abhandlung des Herrn. Sz 'Der germanische Kriegsgott'" (1888-89).

2764. Szcepański, G. von. "Die Quellen der Edda." *Am Urds-Brunnen*, 6 (1888-89), 161-64.

Roman sources in the Poetic Edda.

T

2765. Talbot, Annelise. "The Withdrawal of the Fertility God." *Folklore*, 93 (1982), 31-46.

On the substance of *Skírnismál*. Talbot cites parallels from Finnish, Irish, and Hittite tradition, in which a fertility god withdraws from the world because of strong emotion. She concludes: "they are all seasonal myths inspired by man's fear of starvation, and a 'sacred wedding' between the powers who protected his fields and made his corn grow was the means by which he hoped to ensure a good harvest" (p. 44).

2766. Talley, Jeannine E. "Runes, Mandrakes and Gallows." In *Myth in Indo-European Antiquity*, eds. Gerald James Larson, C. Scott Littleton, and Jaan Puhvel, 157-68. Berkeley and Los Angeles: University of California Press, 1974.

The three nouns of the title come together in the context of Odin's self-sacrifice to gain the runes (*Hávamál*) seen against later folk traditions associating mandrake and gallows. As these imply fertility, Talley assigns a component of fertility to the Odin myth/ritual.

2767. Tapp, Henry L. "Hinn almáttki áss—Thor or Odin?" *Journal of English and Germanic Philology*, 55 (1956), 85-99.

Thor, according to the author.

2768. Taylor, Paul Beekman. "The Structure of *Völundarkviða*." *Neophilologus*, 47 (1963), 228-36.

Reads the poem as a myth of regeneration. Vǫlundr loses his potency with the loss of his swan-maiden wife and theft of her ring. Níðuðr represents the powers of winter and death, from which Vǫlundr frees himself by seducing Bǫð vildr and regaining the ring. "The structure of the myth is a series of archetypal patterns. The archetype of ritual death and regeneration describes the whole structure, but there are a number of subordinate archetypes" (p. 234).

2769. Taylor, Paul Beekman. "Heorot, Earth and Asgard: Christian Poetry and Pagan Myth." *Tennessee Studies in Literature*, 11 (1966), 119-30.

Mostly on the Christian and pagan elements of *Beowulf*.

2770. Taylor, Paul Beekman, and W. H. Auden. *The Elder Edda: A Selection*. London: Faber, New York: Random House, 1969. 173 pp. Rpt. New York: Vintage, 1970.

Partial translation of the Poetic Edda, with an introduction by Peter H. Salus and Paul B. Taylor and notes to the individual poems by Salus.

Teilgård Laugesen, Anker, *see* Laugesen, Anker Teilgård.

2771. Terry, Patricia. *Poems of the Vikings: The Elder Edda*. Indianapolis: Bobbs-Merrill, 1969. xxvi, 269 pp.

Translation of the Poetic Edda, with an introduction by Charles W. Dunn.

2772. Tessier, Georges. "La conversion de Clovis et la christianisation des Francs." In *La conversione al cristianesimo nell'Europa dell'alto medioevo: 14-19 aprile 1966*. 149-89. Settimane di studio del centro italiano di studi sull'alto medioevo. Spoleto: Presso la sede del centro, 1967.

A contribution to an international symposium on the conversion of the European peoples to Christianity; treats Clovis and the Franks.

2773. Teudt, Wilhelm. *Germanische Heiligtümer: Beiträge zur Aufdeckung der Vorgeschichte, ausgehend von den Externsteine, den Lippequellen und der Teutoburg,* 4th ed. Jena: E. Diederichs, 1936. 378 pp.

Enumeration and discussion of actual (according to the author) cult places and cult objects in north Germany.

2774. Therman, Erik. *Eddan och dess ödestragik*. Helsinki: Söderström, 1938. 224 pp.

A study of fate in eddic poetry. The focus is on the mythological verse, and the figure of Odin receives lengthy treatment. There are separate studies of *Vǫluspá*, *Baldrs draumar*, *Vafþrúðnismál*, *Hárbarðsljóð*, *Grímnismál*, and *Hávamál*.

2775. Thompson, Lawrence S., ed. *Norse Mythology: The Elder Edda in Prose Translation*. Hamden, Conn.: Archon Books, 1974. 124 pp.

The prose translations are from the *Corpus Poeticum Boreale* of Vigfússon and Powell (1883) and hence are rather outdated. The editor has provided a short preface and headnotes to the individual poems.

2776. Thümmel, A. "Der germanische Tempel." *Beiträge zur Geschichte der deutschen Sprache und Literatur*, 35 (1909), 1-123. Also issued separately as diss. Leipzig (Halle a. d. S.: Karras).

A long, rather outmoded study of the "temple" in Germanic culture.

2777. Thyregod, O. "Lovstridigt hedenskab i Norden: Uddrag af gamle love." *Dania*, 3 (1895-96), 337-55.

Paganism and Christianity in early Scandinavian laws.

2778. Tiefenbach, Heinrich. "Geli mida (Zum Verständnis der letzten Zeile des zweiten Merseburger Spruchs." *Frühmittelalterliche Studien*, 4 (1970), 395-97.

The word is to be understood as a collective noun, from the verb *ge-li men* "conglutinare."

2779. Tihany, Leslie C. "A Note on Grimm's *Deutsche Mythologie*, I, 296, N. 1." *Journal of English and Germanic Philology*, 36 (1937), 551-53.

Correction to a footnote in Grimm's *Deutsche Mythologie* (*Teutonic Mythology*, 1875) on the origin of a Hungarian phrase.

2780. Tille, Alexander. *Yule and Christmas: Their Place in the Germanic Year*. London: D. Nutt, 1899. 218 pp.

Annual festivals among the Germanic peoples, often in the context of their religious beliefs. Stresses the Christian aspects of Yule.

2781. Timerding, Heinrich. *Die christliche Frühzeit Deutschlands in den Berichten über die Bekehrer,* Erste Gruppe: *Die irisch-fränkische Mission*. Frühgermanentum, 3. Jena: E. Diederichs, 1929. 277 pp.

Early Christianity in Germany, as revealed in accounts of the missionaries.

2782. Timmer, B. J. "Wyrd in Anglo-Saxon Prose and Poetry." *Neophilologus*, 26 (1941), 24-33, 213-28.

Study of Old English *wyrd.* Timmer concludes that the term originally meant men's fate, perhaps even a goddess of fate, but under Christianity it came to refer to events rather than to fate.

2783. Tögel, Hermann. *Germanenglaube,* 2nd ed. *His* Der Werdegang der christlichen Religion, 5. Leipzig: J. Klinkhart, 1935. 236 pp.

The belief of the Germanic poeples in a form supposedly applicable to contemporary Germans.

2784. Toorn, M. C. van den. *Ethics and Moral in Icelandic Saga Literature*. Assen: Van Gorcum, 1955. 153 pp.

With discussion of the ethics of *Hávamál.*

2785. Toporov, V. N. "K balto-skandinaviskim mifologicheskim svyazyam." In *Donum Balticum to Professor Christian S. Stang on the Occasion of his Seventieth Birthday, 15 March 1970*, ed. Velta Ruke-Dravina, 534-43. Stockholm: Almqvist & Wiksell, 1970. English summary, p. 543.

Equates Baltic Teljavelj with Þjálfi and argues contact by borrowing.

2786. Trathnigg, Gilbert. "Glaube und Kult der Semnonen." *Archiv für Religionswissenschaft*, 34 (1937), 226-49.

Methodological objections to A. Closs, "Die Religion des Semnonenstammes" (1936).

2787. Trier, Jost. "Irminsul." *Westfälische Forschungen*, 4 (1941), 99-133.

Departing from the monk Rudolf's description, Trier studies the Irminsûl in detail. Trier holds that it is a kind of architectural metaphor for the universe, based on the construction of actual buildings. He takes the Lapp traditions as Germanic loans and argues Indo-European origin.

2788. Trier, Jost. "Zaun und Mannring." *Beiträge zur Geschichte der deutschen Sprache und Literatur*, 66 (1942), 232-64.

This important article may stand for Trier's contributions concerning the importance of enclosures for early Indo-European and Germanic culture. For Trier, enclosure sets off an area from the ordinary and confers on it a sense of the holy. Matters specifically relevant to Norse mythology receive occasional mention, e.g., Garmr (p. 246) and the *þulr* (p. 252).

2789. Trillmich, Werner. "Die Krise des nordgermanischen Heidentums." *Die Welt als Geschichte*, 12 (1952), 27-43.

The crisis of north Germanic heathendom was its confrontation with Christianity and the ultimate resolution of that encounter in the conversion. Trillmich treats that crisis, focusing on West Scandinavian circumstances and the period just before 1000 A.D.

2790. Trolle, Henrik af. *Om ordalierna hos de germanska folken: Ett bidrag till processrättens historia*. Stockholm: Nordiska bokhandeln, 1916. iv, 157 pp.

On prophecy and conceptions of the judgment of the gods among the Germanic peoples.

2791. Trotzig, Gustaf. "Gegensätze zwischen Heidentum und Christentum im archäologischen Material des 11. Jahrhunderts auf Gotland." In *Kirche und Gesellschaft im Ostseeraum und im Norden vor der Mitte des 13. Jahrhunderts*. 21-30. Acta Visbyensia, 3; Visby-symposiet för historiska vetenskaper 1967. Visby: Museum Gotlands Fornsal, 1969.

Paper delivered at an international symposium on church and society in early

Scandinavia and the Baltic; treats the opposition between paganism and Christianity in eleventh-century graves on Gotland. The author suggests that the custom of putting food in the grave was a pagan reaction to the spread of Christianity.

2792. Tunberg, Sven. "Svearne: En historisk fantasi." *Nordisk tidskrift för vetenskap, konst och industri*, n. s., 21 (1945), 81-103.

On the ancient kingdom of the Svear, with remarks on sacral kingship and on von Friesen's proposed etymology of the word *konungr* "king."

2793. Tuppa, Gerlinde. "Bemerkungen zu den Tierträumen der Edda." In *Festschrift für Otto Höfler zum 65. Geburtstag*, eds. Helmut Birkhan and Otto Gschwantler, 433-43. Vienna: Notring, 1968.

The animal dreams of the Poetic Edda (all of them in the "heroic" second section) derive not from Byzantine or classical influence but more probably from general symbols of the human mind (Freud and Jung are both cited). The animals themselves are to be associated with theriomorphic warriors (berserks, *úlfheðnar*) rather than with *fylgjur*.

2794. Turville-Petre, Gabriel. "Liggja fylgjur þinar til Íslands." *Saga-Book of the Viking Society*, 12 (1937-45), 119-26. Rpt. in Turville-Petre, *Nine Norse Studies* (1972), pp. 52-58.

Turville-Petre discusses the origin and usage of the terms *fylgja* and *hamingja*, both used of fetches in Old Norse literary tradition. He isolates a primarily concrete sense for *fylgja* and a primarily abstract one for *hamingja* (i.e., "fate"), although each may be either abstract or concrete.

2795. Turville-Petre, Gabriel. *The Heroic Age of Scandinavia*. Hutchinson's University Library: History. London: Hutchinson University Library, 1951. 196 pp.

With incidental remarks on paganism (pp. 102-05, 176-77, and passim).

2796. Turville-Petre, Gabriel. "Professor Georges Dumézil." *Saga-Book of the Viking Society*, 14 (1953-57), 131-34.

Review article, basically approving of Dumézil's approach and work.

2797. Turville-Petre, Gabriel. *Origins of Icelandic Literature*. Oxford: Clarendon Press, 1953. vii, 260 pp.

As the origins of Icelandic literature seem to stretch back in certain cases to paganism, Turville-Petre devotes early chapters of this work to "Pagan Iceland" (pp. 1-47), "The Conversion of Iceland" (pp. 48-69), and "The First Century of Christianity" (pp. 70-87). The bulk of the book treats Iceland's early Christian literature.

2798. Turville-Petre, Gabriel. "Dreams in Icelandic Tradition." *Folklore*, 69 (1958), 93-111. Comment by the author on pp. 26-70. Rpt. with a postscript in Turville-Petre, *Nine Norse Studies* (1972), pp. 30-51.

In this, the first of three articles dealing with dreams and dream symbolism in Icelandic tradition, Turville-Petre remarks briefly on fetches.

2799. Turville-Petre, Gabriel. "Professor Dumézil and the Literature of Iceland." In *Hommages à Georges Dumézil*. 209-14. Collection Latomus, 45. Brussels: Latomus, Revue d'études latines, 1960.

"So long as Icelandic literature was studied solely by those who studied nothing else, the road was blocked" (p. 210). Dumézil's theories opened the road, and they suggest further that "Snorri had undergone a strict training in Norse mythology" (p. 213).

2800. Turville-Petre, Gabriel. "Thurstable." In *English and Medieval Studies Presented to J. R. R. Tolkien*, eds. Norman Davis and C. L. Wrenn, 241-49. London: Allen & Unwin, 1962. Rpt. in Turville-Petre, *Nine Norse Studies* (1972), pp. 20-29.

In Essex hundred is the place Thurstable, which Turville-Petre follows others in identifying as *Þures stapel* or "Thunor's pillar." Thunor is the Old English form of Thor, and in Icelandic tradition that god is particularly associated with the "high seat pillars" (*ǫndvegisúlur*) which many settlers are said to have transported from Norway to Iceland and which have strong sacral significance. A further analog is in Tacitus, *Germania*, ch. 34, where we read of "pillars of Hercules" (*Herculis columnas*) among the ancient Germans. These may be identified with the *Irminsûl* of the Saxons, for which Turville-Petre adduces evidence that it was a vast column holding up the universe. Whether Tacitus referred to an otherwise unknown god Irmin or to Thor is unclear. "Irmin and Þórr resembled Hercules in that all three were gods of supporting pillars. While the *Irminsûl* supported the world of the Saxons, Þórr, with his *ǫndvegisúlur*, upheld the house of the Icelandic farmer, and with his stapel he assured the security of the Essex hundred" (p. 247).

2801. Turville-Petre, Gabriel. *Myth and Religion of the North: The Religion of Ancient Scandinavia*. New York: Holt, Rinehart and Winston, 1964. ix, 340 pp.

Turville-Petre's handbook of Scandinavian mythology and pagan religion is the best in English. As a philologist, Turville-Petre stressed the literary sources, which he knew extremely thoroughly, but he never ignored the question of cult. Scholars whose lead he most often follows include de Vries, Dumézil, and to a lesser extent Magnus Olsen. After an excellent introduction to the sources, the book is organized by the individual gods, surveying in separate chapters Odin, Thor, Baldr, Loki, Heimdallr, the *vanir*, and some of the lesser-known deities. A list of the subheads of the Odin chapters shows the scope of coverage and something of the organizational principles Turville-Petre used: God of Poetry, Lord of the Gallows, God of War, Father of Gods and Men, Óðinn and his Animals, Óð inn's Names, Óðinn's Eye, the Cult of Óðinn, Woden-Wodan. As relegation of the continental manifestations of Odin to the final subchapter suggests, Turville-Petre concerned himself primarily with the Scandinavian aspects of Germanic religion. These he treated at least as thoroughly as did Jan de Vries in the standard *Altgermanische Religionsgeschichte*, which, however, also covers non-Scandinavian materials.

Besides the chapters on the gods, there follow several chapters devoted to aspects of religion and belief. These are: The Divine Kings; The Divine Heroes; Guardian Spirits; Temples and Objects of Worship; Sacrifice; Godless Men; Death; and The Beginning of the World and its End.

Although the notes and references are not as exhaustive as those of de Vries, they are useful, and a descriptive bibliography closes the volume. Where Turville-Petre's work shows its superiority over other handbooks is in the author's thorough knowledge of the sources and the vast secondary literature about them.

2802. Turville-Petre, Gabriel. "Dream Symbols in Old Icelandic Literature." In *Festschrift Walter Baetke dargebracht zu seinem 80. Geburtstage am 28. März 1964*, ed. Kurt Rudolf et al., 343-54. Weimar: H. Böhlau, 1966.

Contains remarks on *Þiðranda þáttr, dísir*, and *fylgjur*.

2803. Turville-Petre, Gabriel. "Fertility of Beast and Soil in Old Norse Literature." In *Old Norse Literature and Mythology: A Symposium*, ed. Edgar C. Polomé, 244-64. Austin and London: Published for the Department of Germanic Languages of the University of Texas, Austin, by the University of Texas Press, 1969.

Turville-Petre surveys apparent fertility ritual and fertility deities in Scandinavia from the Bronze Age chariot and disk from Trundholm, through the Nerthus of Tacitus and theophoric placenames to the *vanir* of the Norse literary sources. Much of the material mentioned is already discussed in Turville-Petre's *Myth and Religion of the North* (1964), and the article is valuable for its summarizing rather than for new analysis.

2804. Turville-Petre, Gabriel. *Nine Norse Studies*. Viking Society Text Series, 5. London: Viking Society; University College London, 1972. 180 pp.

The following papers relate to mythology and are separately entered in this bibliography: "The Cult of Óðinn in Iceland" (1972), "Thurstable" (1962), "Dreams in Icelandic Tradition" (1958), "Liggja fylgjur þínar til Íslands" (1937-45).

2805. Turville-Petre, Gabriel. "The Cult of Óðinn in Iceland." In *Nine Norse Studies*. 1-19. Viking Society Text Series, 5. London: Viking Society; University College London, 1972. Originally published as "Um Óðinsdýrkun á Íslandi," *Studia Islandica*, 17 (1958), 5-25.

Landnámabók mentions the Law of Úlfljótr, which tells of practices in heathen temples in early Iceland. One practice was the swearing of an oath to Freyr, Njord, and the "all-powerful god" (*hinn almáttki áss*). Turville-Petre's aim is first to determine whether, as the eddas might imply and so many scholars have suggested, this god is Odin. He argues that Odin was essentially a god of lawlessness, popular among courtly circles in southeast Norway and Denmark under such ruthless kings as Harald Fairhair and Erik Bloodaxe. In Iceland, however, Odin can hardly have been popularly worshipped, for the settlers had left Norway to avoid Harald's lawlessness. Turville-Petre surveys also some of Dumézil's findings and concludes: "The highest gods did not, among all these [Indo-European] peoples, correspond with the Indian Mitra-Varuna, but men chose their chief god according to their social system, their way of life, and their needs. The Swedes depended on fertility of the soil and, therefore, their chief god was the fertility god, Freyr. Inhabitants of western Norway, and hence the Icelanders as well, chose the trusty Þórr, who must have been *hinn almáttki áss* in their eyes" (p. 18).

Turville-Petre leaves unexplained the preponderance of Odin in Icelandic literary sources.

2806. Turville-Petre, Gabriel, and A. S. C. Ross. "Agrell's 'Magico-Numerical' Theory of the Runes." *Folk-Lore*, 47 (1936), 203-13.

"Summarizing, we may say that the underlying idea of Agrell's theory—that the distorted order of the runic alphabet is primarily magical, and that certain runic inscriptions are of purely magical significance—is very plausible. The details of the late antique connection, however, as worked out by him, still remain rather unconvincing" (p. 213).

2807. Turville-Petre, Joan. "Hengest and Horsa." *Saga-Book of the Viking Society*, 14 (1953-57), 273-90.

Medieval Kentish origin legends tell of Hengest and Horsa, brothers whose names mean "horse." Turville-Petre associates them with the cults of twin deities and of the horse, then proceeds to the reception and adaptation of these figures by medieval historians.

2808. Turville-Petre, Joan. "On Ynglingatal." *Mediaeval Scandinavia*, 11 (1978-79), 48-67.

Treats the origin of *Ynglingatal*, medieval analogs in the form of other genealogical records, and the poem's internal structure. The author concludes that in genealogies, "Symbolic figures are required, to express the concept that every dynasty originated in a world of non-human powers. Divine appellatives are appropriate, and these form the top layer of a properly-constructed genealogy. Some intermediary figures are needed to make a connexion between the divine world and the world of heroic legend. The conventions established are largely the result of problems to be solved with such material as was available. They persisted into literate tradition, to be used and adapted by scholars whose view of origins was based on book-learning. It is instructive to compare the ancestor-list of *Ynglingatal* with the interpretations devised by Icelandic scholars of the twelfth and thirteenth centuries" (p. 66).

2809. Tveitane, Mattias. "Sjá í gaupnir sér." *Maal og minne*, 1972, pp. 1-6.

The title is an expression, found in the *Legendary Saga of St. Olaf*, and sometimes understood as part of a magic oracular process. Tveitane locates a possible source in the Norse translation of *Gregory's Dialogues*.

2810. Tveitane, Mattias. "Omkring det mytologiske navnet *Ægir* 'vannmannen.'" *Acta Philologica Scandinavica*, 31 (1976), 81-95. Summary in English, p. 95.

Tveitane argues that attestations of the mythological name *Ægir* indicate two different words: *Ægir* "water-man" and *ægir* (neut. collective) "mass of water, sea." The latter word would replace the commonly postulated *ægir* as first component of placenames and compounds.

2811. Tveitane, Mattias. "On a New Account of Germanic Religion." *Arv*, 35 (1979), 141-50.

Criticism of Åke V. Ström, "Germanische Religion" (1975). ". . . I do not believe that Åke V. Ström's book can give satisfactory service as an up-to-date and reliable handbook. Its deficiencies are particularly clear in the treatment of linguistic problems and source-criticism" (p. 150).

U

2812. Uhland, Ludwig. *Der Mythus von Thôr nach nordischen Quellen*. Stuttgart and Augsburg: J. G. Cotta, 1836. 223 pp. Also in Uhland, *Schriften zur Geschichte der Dichtung und Sage*, 6 (Stuttgart), pp. 3-128.

Early study of Thor, noteworthy for its thorough treatment of the various myths and motifs. The approach is more descriptive than interpretive.

2813. Uhlenbeck, C. C. "Zur deutschen Etymologie." *Beiträge zur Geschichte der deutschen Sprache und Literatur*, 35 (1909), 161-80.

Pp. 166-67 discuss the etymology of *Baldr*.

2814. Uhlenbeck, C. C. "G. Schütte: Dänisches Heidentum." *Acta Philologica Scandinavica*, 1 (1926-27), 293-300.

Extended critical discussion of the German version of Schütte's presentation of Danish paganism (1923).

2815. Ulvestad, Bjarne. "How Old Are the Mythological Eddic Poems?" *Scandinavian Studies*, 26 (1954), 49-69.

A useful research survey of attempts to date the mythological eddic poems.

2816. Unruh, G. "Der Fenriswulf und der Mondhund." *Am Urdhs-Brunnen*, 1,10 (1882), 1-4.

Zoomorphic features of Fenrir and Mánagarmr.

2817. Unruh, G. "Die Thiermasken der drei Nornen." *Am Urdhs-Brunnen*, 1,6 (1882), 1-3.

Zoomorphic features of the norns.

2818. Unruh, G. "Die Thiermasken des Freyr und der Freyja." *Am Urdhs-Brunnen*, 1,7 (1882), 1-4.

Zoomorphic features of Freyr and Freyja.

2819. Unruh, G. "Die Thiermasken des Heimdall." *Am Urdhs-Brunnen*, 1,9 (1882), 1-5.

Zoomorphic features of Heimdallr.

2820. Unruh, G. "Die Thiermasken des Thor." *Am Urdhs-Brunnen*, 1,11 (1882), 1-5.

Zoomorphic features of Thor.

2821. Unruh, G. "Die Thiermasken des Tyr und der Hel." *Am Urdhs-Brunnen*, 1,8 (1882), 1-4.

Zoomorphic features of Týr and Hel.

2822. Unwerth, Wolf von. *Untersuchungen über Totenkult und Óðinnverehrung bei Nordgermanen und Lappen, mit Excursen zur altnordischen Literaturgeschichte.* Germanistische Abhandlungen, 37. Breslau: M. & H. Marcus, 1911. xii, 178 pp.

Building on comparisons between accounts of cult activity in Icelandic sagas and what is known of Lapp religion, von Unwerth tries to build a clearer picture of both Scandinavian and Lapp paganism. His basic premise is that Lapp paganism (known from only relatively recent sources) borrowed much from and often closely reflects Scandinavian paganism. Topics treated include the abode of the dead in a mountain, the dead as instigators of disease, and the hypothetical equivalence of Lapp Rota and Odin in light of these equivalences.

2823. Unwerth, Wolf von. "Oðinn und Rota." *Beiträge zur Geschichte der deutschen Sprache und Literatur*, 39 (1914), 213-21.

Identifies Odin with the Lapp god Rota.

2824. Unwerth, Wolf von. "Zur Deutung der längeren Nordendorfer Runeninschrift." *Zeitschrift des Vereins für Volkskunde*, 26 (1916), 81-85.

Concludes that the inscription's *logaþore* is identical with Loki and should be understood as "fire-*þore*" (fire demon?).

2825. Unwerth, Wolf von. "Fiolnir." *Arkiv för nordisk filologi*, 33 (1917), 320-35.

Fjǫlnir is attested as an Odin name and as a legendary king in *Ynglingatal.* Basing his interpretation on an etymology from **felduni nir* "field being," von Unwerth equates Fjǫlnir with the Finnish *pellon Pekko* and with Byggvir and sees in him a field god and representative of barley who sacrifices himself to the production of mead.

2826. Usener, Hermann. *Götternamen*. Bonn: F. Cohen, 1896. x, 391 pp.

Theoretical study of ancient mythology, a subject which in the Germany of the 1890s routinely included Norse mythology. The theory involves a development from locally bound to conceptual gods.

V

2827. Vågslid, Eivind. "Ásló—Ósló." *Norsk måltidende*, 3 (1938), 348-52.

Argues that the first component of the placename *Oslo* was *áss* "god."

2828. Vågslid, Eivind. "Litt um Vòluspå." *Frem daa, frendar*, 7 (1965), 99-133.

Translation of *Vǫluspá*. In the introduction Vågslid assigns the provenance of the poem to Norway ca. 1000 A. D.

2829. Vaughan-Sterling, Judith A. "The Anglo-Saxon *Metrical Charms*: Poetry as Ritual." *Journal of English and Germanic Philology*, 82 (1983), 186-200.

"In this paper I have attempted to show that Anglo-Saxon ritual magic and established poetry are not so distantly related as scholars have supposed" (pp. 199-200).

2830. Vernaleken, Theodor. *Mythen und Bräuche des Volkes in Österreich: Als Beitrag zur deutschen Mythologie, Volksdichtung und Sittenkunde.* Vienna: W. Braumüller, 1859. viii, 386 pp.

Pagan remnants in Austria; includes discussion of Wodan/Odin myths and myths of Wodan/Odin and death.

2831. Vesper, Ekkehart. "Das Menschenbild der Älteren Hávamál." *Beiträge zur Geschichte der deutschen Sprache und Literatur* (Halle), 79, Supplement (1957), 13-31.

The ethics of the gnomic section of *Hávamál.*

2832. Vestlund, Alfred. "Åskgudens hammare förlorad: Ett bidrag till nordisk ritforskning." *Edda*, 11 (1919), 95-119.

Vestlund attempts to reconstruct a ritual enacting the recovery of Thor's hammer from a giant and connected ultimately with fertility. He finds it not only in *Þrymskviða*, but also in the myths of Thor's encounters with Geirrøðr and Hymir.

2833. Vetter, Ferdinand. "Zum Muspilli: Kritisches und Dogmatisches." *Germania*, 16 (1871), 121-55.

Brings up Ragnarǫk in the closing pages but declines to speculate on knowledge of Ragnarǫk in Germany.

2834. Vetter, Ferdinand. "Freyr und Baldr, und die deutschen Sagen vom verschwindenden und wiederkehrenden Gott." *Germania*, 19 (1874), 196-211.

German legend traditions derived from the dying and returning god, including the Schwanenritter, Siegfried, Ortnit/Wolfdietrich, and Baltram/Sintram. See p. 209 for a table of the parallels, under the rubrics departure, return, opponent (a natural force), and symbol of the returning spring.

2835. Vogt, Walther Heinrich. "'Wenn du nach Runen forschest—': Ein Nachtrag zu Meissners *Ganga til fréttar*, ein Beitrag zu Olsens Deutung des Eggjumsteins." *Zeitschrift des Vereins für Volkskunde*, 35-36 (1925-26), 7-13.

The evidence of *Hávamál* 80 and 142 on cult speech, applied to the Eggjum runic inscription.

2836. Vogt, Walther Heinrich. "Hroptr rǫgna." *Zeitschrift für deutsches Altertum*, 62 (1925), 41-48.

The expression is in *Hávamál* 42 and refers to Odin. Vogt reads *Hroptr* as "conjurer, magician" (*rǫgna* "of the gods").

2837. Vogt, Walther Heinrich. "Der frühgermanische Kultredner: Þulr, þula und eddische Wissensdichtung." *Acta Philologica Scandinavica*, 2 (1927), 250-63.

On the Norse *þulr* (reciter of ancient knowledge) and his Germanic context. According to Vogt, the position had both secular and sacred aspects: cult-narrator, prophet, teacher, initiator of youths.

2838. Vogt, Walther Heinrich. *Stilgeschichte der eddischen Wissensdichtung*, vol. 1. Breslau: F. Hirt, 1927.

An attempt at a history of the style of the wisdom poetry of the Poetic Edda. The *þulr* as a position with secular and sacred aspects: cult-narrator, prophet, teacher, initiator of youths.

2839. Vogt, Walther Heinrich. "Zum Problem der Merseburger Zaubersprüche." *Zeitschrift für deutsches Altertum*, 65 (1928), 97-130.

Exploration of the language, form, and meaning of the Merseburg charms, stressing the possibility that they retain native Germanic mythological material.

2840. Vogt, Walther Heinrich. "Þórs Fischzug: Eine Betrachtung über ein Bild auf Bragis Schild." In *Studier tillägnade Axel Kock, tidskriftens redaktör, 1888-1925*. 200-16. Arkiv för nordisk filologi, 40, supplement. Lund: C. W. K. Gleerup, 1929. Also issued separately, under title *Studier tillägnade Axel Kock*.

Textual analysis of the portion of Bragi's *Ragnarsdrápa* dealing with Thor's encounter with the midgard serpent (str. 14-19).

2841. Vogt, Walther Heinrich. "Bragis Schild: Maler und Skalde." *Acta Philologica Scandinavica*, 5 (1930-31), 1-28.

Includes interpretation of the Gefjon stanza (*Ragnarsdrápa* 3).

2842. Vogt, Walther Heinrich. "Die altgermanische Kultrede." In *Actes du Ve congrès international d'histoire des religions à Lund, 27-29 août 1929*. 236-38. Lund: C. W. K. Gleerup, 1930.

Lecture and discussion from an international congress on the history of religion. Vogt sets forth some of the material developed at length in his *Die þula zwischen Kultrede und eddischer Wissensdichtung* (1942).

2843. Vogt, Walther Heinrich. "Von Bragi zu Egil: Ein Versuch zur Geschichte des skaldischen Preisliedes." In *Deutsche Islandforschung 1930,* vol. 1: *Kultur*, ed. Walther Heinrich Vogt, 170-209. Veröffentlichungen der Schleswig-Holsteinischen Universitätsgesellschaft, 28:1. Breslau: F. Hirt, 1930.

Vogt begins his history of the skaldic encomium with a brief discussion (pp. 171-75) of encomiastic cult verse, i.e., the praise of Thor voiced by Vetrliði Sumarliðason and Þorbjǫrn dísarskáld.

2844. Vogt, Walther Heinrich. *Altnorwegens Urfehdebann und der Geleitschwur: Tryggðamál und Griðamál, Form- und Stoffgeschichte, Die Wortlaute, Übersetzungen*. Forschungen zum deutschen Recht, 2:1. Weimar: H. Böhlau, 1936. ix, 213 pp.

With occasional suggestions of pagan verbal formulas underlying Christian formulas.

2845. Vogt, Walther Heinrich. "Zwei Flüche der Griðamál." *Arkiv för nordisk filologi*, 52 (1936), 325-39.

Formulaic reminiscence of *galdr* and a tripartite formula (earth:heaven:sea) in *Griðamál.*

2846. Vogt, Walther Heinrich. "Binnenreime in der Edda." *Acta Philologica Scandinavica*, 12 (1937-38), 228-62.

On assonance and internal rhyme (formal elements primarily of skaldic poetry) in the Poetic Edda. Remarks on the style of Bragi's *Ragnarsdrápa* and of *Vǫluspá*.

2847. Vogt, Walther Heinrich. "Fluch, Eid, Götter—altnordisches Recht." *Zeitschrift der Savigny-Stiftung für Rechtsgeschichte,*, Germanistische Abteilung, 57 (1937), 1-57.

The religious nature of oaths and role of the gods in oaths, with discussion of the word *heilagr* and conceptions of the holy.

2848. Vogt, Walther Heinrich. "Religiöse Bindungen im Spätgermanentum." *Archiv für Religionswissenschaft*, 35 (1938), 1-34.

Religious attitudes in late Germanic paganism, especially Scandinavian sources. The methodology follows Rudolf Otto and centers on conceptions of the holy.

2849. Vogt, Walther Heinrich. *Die Þula zwischen Kultrede und eddischer Wissensdichtung.* Nachrichten der Akademie der Wissenschaften in Göttingen, phil.-hist. Kl., 1942:1. Göttingen: Vandenhoeck & Ruprecht, 1942.

A classic and valuable study of the institution of the *þula* or versified list in its social and ritual context.

2850. Vonbun, Franz Josef. *Beiträge zur deutschen Mythologie: Gesammelt in Churrhätien.* Chur: L. Hitz, 1862. 137 pp.

Legends in Switzerland containing pagan remnants.

2851. Vordemfelde, Hans. *Die germanische Religion in den deutschen Volksrechten,* vol. 1: *Der religiöse Glaube.* Religionsgeschichtliche Versuche und Vorarbeiten, 18:1. Giessen: A. Töpelmann, 1923. 165 pp.

Systematic treatment of possible remains of Germanic religion in German legal texts. Categories treated are fetishes, nature worship, worship of plants, worship of animals, worship of humans, belief in the dead, and (pp. 160-65) the pagan gods.

2852. Vries, Jan de. "Der altnordische Rasengang." *Acta Philologica Scandinavica*, 3 (1928-29), 106-35. Rpt. in de Vries, *Kleine Schriften* (1965), pp. 89-112.

Saga literature contains several scenes in which men lift and go under a piece of turf; often they mix their blood together and swear oaths. Adducing far-ranging ethnographic parallels, de Vries explains the pre-Christian meaning of this ritual as a means of creating a blood-brother relationship: "An outsider cannot enter the family, for it is not a social but a natural unit. One can only be born into it. To effect that, one must first transfer oneself to the world of the dead; there the outsider must be bound to the family through the ritual of mixing blood, and then only through magic participation in the closed circle of the family is he in a position to be reborn as a member of it" (*Kleine Schriften*, pp. 109-10).

2853. Vries, Jan de. "Over de dateering der Þrymskviða." *Tijdschrift voor nederlandse taal- en letterkunde*, 47 (1928), 251-372.

In this short but oft-cited monograph de Vries analyzes the following points in arguing that *Þrymskviða* is a very late poem: metrics, language, relation to other eddic poems, content, relation to Thor poems, interchange between old and new esthetics. He concludes that *Þrymskviða* was composed in the thirteenth century, during the period when ballads were replacing eddic poetry.

2854. Vries, Jan de. "Ginnungagap." *Acta Philologica Scandinavica*, 5 (1930), 41-66. Rpt. in de Vries, *Kleine Schriften* (1965), pp. 113-32.

With this article de Vries seems to have solved the problem of Ginnungagap. He rejects Mogk's postulation of a personification, *Ginnungi ("Ginnungagap" (1882)); it fails because development to Ymir cannot be proved. Further, de Vries finds association with *gína* "to gape" unacceptable and connects the first component of Ginnungagap with such words as *ginnheilar, ginnregin*, the *ginArunAr* "magic runes" of the Björketorp and Stentoften stones, and related terms, and defines Ginnungagap as "the proto-space filled with magic powers" (p. 65). It is more than nothingness, however, for it is charged with potency. Thus Ginnungagap and Ymir are not identical, but Ymir gives form to the potential of Ginnungagap, "for he incorporates the double function of creation, conception, and birth" (p. 66).

2855. Vries, Jan de. "Studien over germaansche mythologie, I: Fjǫrgyn en Fjǫrgynn." *Tijdschrift voor nederlandsche taal- en letterkunde*, 50 (1931), 1-25.

The form *Fjǫrgynn* is late; association with the Baltic Perkunas is unlikely. The root originally meant "life, vital power."

2856. Vries, Jan de. "Über Sigvats álfablót-Strophen." *Acta Philologica Scandinavica*, 7 (1932-33), 169-80.

Str. 4-8 of Sighvatr Þorðarson's *Austrfararvísur* mention an *álfablót* in western Sweden which the skald witnessed. Departing from the conclusions of Olrik and Ellekilde, *Nordens gudeverden*—which he finds hasty—, de Vries proceeds through the five stanzas and then offers his own conclusions: the stanzas tell humorously of a private ritual, undertaken in every household, to honor the dead. This leads de Vries to further considerations: the name *"lvir*, borne by peasants in some of the households, may perhaps reflect a priestly function relating to the *dísablót*, a public sacrifice to fertility goddesses taking place in Sweden in February, in Norway around Yule. *Hervarar saga ok Heiðreks konungs* is not a trustworthy source.

2857. Vries, Jan de. "Die Bedeutung der Volkskunde für mythologische und religionsgeschichtliche Untersuchungen." *Germanisch-Romanisch Monatsschrift*, 20 (1932), 27-39.

Methodological statement, urging caution in the use of recent folklore to interpret ancient Germanic myth and religion.

2858. Vries, Jan de. "Endnu en gang om Sighvats alfeblotstrofer." *Acta Philologica Scandinavica*, 8 (1933-34), 292-94.

Response to H. Ellekilde, "Om Sighvat skjalds alfeblotstrofer og Alfhildsagnet i Hervarar saga" (1933-34), itself a response to de Vries, "Über Sigvats Álfablót-Strophen" (1932-33).

2859. Vries, Jan de. *The Problem of Loki*. FF Communications, 110. Helsinki: Suomalainen tiedeakatemia, 1933. 306 pp.

An important monograph devoted to all the traditions about Loki, in recent folklore as well as in medieval sources. De Vries concludes that Loki was a double figure: culture-hero and trickster. From this "original conception" the later traditions may be derived. The volume is thorough and draws upon ethnographic material from all over the world.

2860. Vries, Jan de. *De skaldenkenningen met mythologischen inhoud*. Nederlandsche bijdragen op het gebied van germaansche philologie en linguistiek, 4. Haarlem: H. D. Tjeenk Willink & Zoon, 1934. 85 pp.

In this classic study of skaldic kennings following the conversion of Iceland, de Vries contended that poets eschewed kennings based on mythological allusions for the first century and a half or so of Christianity. Only with the "renaissance" of the twelfth century in Iceland were mythological kennings taken up again.

2861. Vries, Jan de. "Odin am Baume." In *Studia Germanica tillägnade Ernst Albin Kock den 6. december 1934*. 392-96. Lund: C. Blom, 1934.

De Vries explores here the classical (largely Greek) background of Odin's self-sacrifice on the world tree (*Hávamál* 138-41). The parallels, which include hanging on a tree and marking with a spear, suggest an association with chthonic forces. De Vries concludes that Odin's self-sacrifice is an age-old conception and need not be derived from Germanic paganism. It should be considered together with the classical parallels, either as a common inheritance or as a loan (de Vries seems inclined toward the latter interpretation).

2862. Vries, Jan de. "Om Eddaens visdomsdigtning." *Arkiv för nordisk filologi*, 50 (1934), 1-59.

The aim of de Vries in this long article is to examine similarities of structure and content in eddic wisdom poetry and to offer suggestions regarding the origins of various poems. He surveys *Grímnismál*, *Alvíssmál*, *Vafþrúðnismál*, *Reginsmál*, *Fáfnismál*, *Sigrdrífumál*, *Hávamál*, *Svipsdagsmál*, *Sǫgubrot*, and the Heiðrekr riddles of *Hervarar saga*, offering specific remarks on each text. By way of conclusion he divides this material into two groups (this division also indicates his treatment of *Hávamál* and *Grímnismál*). The first group contains poems which present wisdom in narrative context, often in the form of a catalog with internal numbering. The poems of this group are *Hávamál* 1-80, its *Loddfáfnismál* and its *ljóðatal*; also *Sigrdrífumál*, *Grógaldr*, and *Grímnismál* (the dwellings of the gods and the descriptions of cosmic wisdom).

The other group contains poems which set the wisdom in a narrative frame and tend toward elaborate internal structures of the content rather than toward catalogs with their own numbering systems. To this group belong: *Vafþrúðnismál*, *Alvíssmál*, *Svipsdagsmál*, *Fáfnismál*, the *Heiðreksgátur*, and *Sǫgubrot*. Inclusion of the Heiðrekr riddles here suggests the similarity between riddles and mythic wisdom.

The article is important for its attempt to delineate the ways in which mythic material is preserved in the extant mythology.

2863. Vries, Jan de. "Studien over germaansche mythologie, VI: Over enkele godennamen." *Tijdschrift voor nederlandsche taal- en letterkunde*, 53 (1934), 192-210. This and the following entry comprise a single consecutively paginated article.

The gods' names discussed are the parallel pairs Óðr/Óðinn and Ullr/Ullinn and also Thor, whose name is explained as meaning the force of thunder.

2864. Vries, Jan de. "Studien over germaansche mythologie, VII: De skaldenkenningen met de namen der godinnen Freyja en Frigg." *Tijdschrift voor nederlandsche taal- en letterkunde*, 53 (1934), 210-17. This and the preceding entry comprise a single consecutively paginated article.

Skaldic kennings with the names of the goddesses Freyja and Frigg. Cf. de Vries, *De skaldenkenningen met mythologischen inhoud* (1934), which focused largely on Odin and devoted little detail to these goddesses.

2865. Vries, Jan de. "Über die Datierung der Eddalieder." *Germanisch-Romanisch Monatsschrift*, 22 (1934), 253-63.

On the problems of dating the mythological eddic poems. Following his discussion of a lull in mythological kennings during the first century and a half of Christianity (*De skaldenkenningen met mythologischen inhoud,* 1934), de Vries argues that it is unlikely that mythological eddic poems could originate during this period. He thus sees two layers: pre-1000, when the bulk of eddic mythological poems originated, and post-1150, when poets could take an antiquarian interest in mythological material.

2866. Vries, Jan de. "Studien over germaansche mythologie, IX: De oudnoorsche god Heimdallr." *Tijdschrift voor nederlandsche taal- en letterkunde*, 54 (1935), 53-81.

General treatment of Heimdallr, stressing etymology and the god's role in Norse mythology.

2867. Vries, Jan de. "Die Völuspá." *Germanisch-Romanisch Monatsschrift*, 24 (1936), 1-14.

General treatment of *Vǫluspá* as the expression of a single poet. The poet did not adapt an already existing source.

2868. Vries, Jan de. *Edda: Vertaald en van inleidingen voorzien.* Amsterdam: U. M. Elsevier, 1938. 284 pp.

Dutch translation of the Poetic Edda, with general introduction, headnotes to the poems, and commentary.

2869. Vries, Jan de. "Rood, wit, zwart." *Volkskunde*, 2 (1942), 1-10.

"The color triad red-white-black, which occurs so widely in folk traditions and in folk magic, is a recollection of the symbolic functions of the colors in the religious conceptions of our Indo-European ancestors of the distant past" (p. 62). De Vries presents these functions in terms of Dumézil's theory of the tripartite division of Indo-European myth and social structure and cites examples from Norse mythology.

2870. Vries, Jan de. "HagustaldaR." *Arkiv för nordisk filologi*, 58 (1944), 93-104. Also in *Festskrift till Jöran Sahlgren 8/4 1944* (Lund: C. W. K. Gleerup, 1944), pp. 93-104.

The term refers, according to de Vries, to the guardian of a royal, sacred enclosure.

2871. Vries, Jan de. "Die Götterwohnungen in den Grímnismál." *Acta Philologica Scandinavica*, 1952, pp. 172-80.

The eddic poem *Grímnismál* contains references to the dwellings of Thor, Freyr, and Ullr in stanzas 4-5. Str. 6 begins a second catalog, calling Válaskjálf (identified by Snorri as Odin's hall) the third and continuing to name gods' dwellings and giving each a number in the ordering, but all have a different form than 6 (str. 6-16). De Vries resolves this obvious paradox by assigning to the original, pagan Odin poem only the dwellings of 4-6, i.e., those of Thor, Freyr, Ullr, and Odin. Odin calls on a Dumézilian triad, then, in his torment between the fires: Odin and Ullr (first function), Thor (second function), Freyr (third function). However, de Vries regards str. 6 as the clumsy adaptation of a later redactor, who had a numbered catalog of gods' dwellings and wanted to add it to the poem. Thus, the original of 6:1 *Bœr er sá inn þriði* is the redactor's, while the rest of the stanza may be genuine.

2872. Vries, Jan de. *Edda*, vol. 1: *Godenliederen*. Klassieke galerij, 67. Antwerp: De Nederlandsche boekhandel, 1952. xvii, 142 pp.

Dutch translation of the mythological poems of the Poetic Edda, with introduction, headnotes to the poems, and brief commentary.

2873. Vries, Jan de. "La valeur religieuse du mot germanique *irmin*." *Cahiers du sud*, 36 (1952), 18-37.

In a primarily linguistic argument, treating etymology and semantics, de Vries argues the existence of a Germanic god *Ermanaz, realized in Old Saxon as Irmin and perhaps parallel to the Indic Aryaman. **ermana-* denotes the people and summarizes the bonds that maintain it; *Ermanaz may have been a "third-sovereign" beside Odin and Tīwaz/Týr (see Dumézil, *Le troisième souverain: essai sur le dieu indo-iranien Aryaman et sur la formation de l'histoire mythique de l'Irlande*, Collection Les dieux et les hommes, 3, Paris: G. -P. Maisonneuve).

2874. Vries, Jan de. "Das germanische Sakralkönigtum: Betrachtungen zu Otto Höfler, *Germanisches Sakralkönigtum*, I. Band: Der Runenstein von Rök und die germanische Individualweihe (Tübingen 1952)." *Germanisch-Romanisch Monatsschrift*, 34 (1953), 183-89.

Largely favorable remarks on Höfler's book on sacral kingship.

2875. Vries, Jan de. "Das Motiv des Vater-Sohn-Kampfes im Hildebrandslied." *Germanisch-Romanisch Monatsschrift*, 34 (1953), 257-74. Rpt., with substantial postscript, in Karl Hauck, ed., *Zur germanisch-deutschen Heldensage: Sechzehn Aufsätze zum neuen Forschungsstand*, Wege der Forschung, 14 (Darmstadt: Wissenschaftliche Buchgesellschaft, 1965), pp. 248-84.

The purpose of this penetrating essay is to probe the formation of the heroic legend of the confrontation in which Hildebrand kills his son Hadubrand in the Old High German poem *Hildebrandslied*. De Vries argues that the historical event behind the story was quickly reformulated according to Indo-European mythic archetypes: a god sires a son, semi-divine, on an earthly woman; the son becomes rebellious and the father must slay him. This leads both to initiation ritual and, in a Germanic context, to parallel heroic legend (Sigmundr and Sinfjǫtli) and myth (Odin and Baldr—de Vries understands Hǫðr as a hypostasis of Odin).

2876. Vries, Jan de. "Baum und Schwert in der Sage von Sigmundr." *Zeitschrift für deutsches Altertum*, 85 (1954-55), 95-106.

Mythic and cultic interpretation of the sword in the tree in the legend of the Vǫlsungs.

2877. Vries, Jan de. *Betrachtungen zum Märchen: Besonders in seinem Verhältnis zu Heldensage und Mythos*. FF Communications, 150. Helsinki: Suomalainen tiedeakatemia, 1954. 184 pp.

Passing references to Odin; pp. 133-35 argue a sacral origin of Germanic heroic legend.

2878. Vries, Jan de. "Das Wort Godmálugr in der Hymiskvida." *Germanisch-Romanisch Monatsschrift*, 35 (1954), 336-37.

Contra Reichardt, "Hymiskviða" (1933), 151f., who understood the word as "theologian, mythograph," a reference to Snorri and therefore evidence that the composition of *Hymiskviða* postdated *Snorra edda*. De Vries reads instead "poeta theologus," a common medieval term here applied to the twelfth-century poet of *Hymiskviða* by a thirteenth-century interpolater.

2879. Vries, Jan de. "La toponomie et l'histoire des religions." *Revue de l'histoire des religions*, 145 (1954), 207-30.

Critical survey of the problems and methods of placename research as it applies to the history of Germanic religion, especially Scandinavian. The author questions many of the assumptions of such scholars as M. Olsen, E. Elgqvist, and the "historicist" school generally, and he urges caution in using nature names to support hypotheses about the practice of cult.

2880. Vries, Jan de. "Über das Verhältnis von Óðr und Óðinn." *Zeitschrift für deutsche Philologie*, 73 (1954), 337-53.

Much of this article is directed against Hollander, "The Old Norse God Óðr" (1950), and Philippson, *Die Genealogie der Götter* (1953), both of whom sought to separate Óðr wholly from Odin. De Vries argues their association, largely on etymological grounds, and then surveys stories in Saxo and *Ynglinga saga*. In these Odin travels because of some action of his wife; another figure takes his place; he returns and regains his power and glory. Snorri's brief remarks on Óðr and Freyja (*Gylfaginning*, ch. 10) are compatible with this scheme, and de Vries concludes that we have here a parallel occurrence of the same myth, with independent characters.

2881. Vries, Jan de. "Über das Wort 'Jarl' und seine Verwandten." *La nouvelle clio*, 4 (1954), 461-69.

On the word *jarl* and related forms, particularly *erilaR* on runic inscriptions and the tribal name *Heruli*. The age-old distinction between *jarl* and *karl* is reflected in the mythological notion that the jarls belong to Odin, the karls to Thor.

2882. Vries, Jan de. "Der Mythos von Balders Tod." *Arkiv för nordisk filologi*, 70 (1955), 41-60.

This paper represents a fundamental contribution to modern understanding of the myth of Baldr's death.

Against the previously reigning understanding of Baldr as a vegetation god of the Near Eastern type, who undergoes death and resurrection, de Vries stresses the simple fact that the gods were unable to reverse Baldr's death and retrieve him from the world of the dead. On one plane, then, the myth is about death, for it represents death's first appearance. With Baldr's stately funeral Odin initiates the custom of funerary burning (cf. *Ynglinga saga*, ch. 8). The attempt to overcome or reverse death fails before an unfillable condition, and death thereafter becomes irrevocably part of man's fate. Other mythologies show ample parallels.

In removing Baldr from the fertility of the dying god, de Vries cleared the way for further interpretation based on initiation ritual. He sees Hǫðr as a hypostasis of Odin, blind in both eyes while Odin is blind in one. He kills the initiand, Baldr, who may then be reborn (as Váli?) in the cult of Odin. Mistletoe is the perfect weapon; it "kills" and then, as the plant of life, awakens the initiand to his new existence.

So long as the myth deals only with death, Loki is unnecessary. But motivation for the tragedy makes room for him, and on him the gods may heap their revenge.

Although the details of the initiation sequence may remain not wholly clear, and although the typological parallel with Near Eastern dying gods may be greater than de Vries thought (cf. Kurt Schier, "Baldr" (1976)), further study of Baldr cannot ignore this interpretation.

2883. Vries, Jan de. "Die Starkadsage." *Germanisch-Romanisch Monatsschrift*, 36 (1955), 281-97. Rpt.in de Vries, *Kleine Schriften* (1965), pp. 20-36.

Surveying the tradition of Starkaðr, de Vries concludes that he was from the start a half-mythic figure who symbolized the sacred bonds of warrior and king. But like Odin he was to be feared, for these bonds were never quite secure: "in the frequent dynastic feuds it was often difficult to determine to whom one's allegiance belonged" (p. 35). Those outside of these bonds will also have feared and distrusted them. Certain legends of Starkaðr, the Odin retainer, portray this distrust in worshippers of Thor and throw light in a dramatic way on religious history.

2884. Vries, Jan de. "Heimdallr, dieu énigmatique." *Études germaniques*, 10 (1955), 257-68.

In surveying a few problems associated with Heimdallr, de Vries offers a new interpretation based largely on the etymology of the second component of the god's name. He derives it from the root **dal-* "flowering" (cf. Greek *thallō, thalléo)* with the suffix -**þu-*. "The word *-dallr* corresponds to a god representing spontaneous energy, manifesting himself at the beginning of the world and keeping watch with uninterrupted attention over the well-being of creation" (p. 266). The first component of the god's name, *heimr* "world," would be a late addition stressing his sphere of action; cf. Mardǫll, a goddess who would exercise the same power over the sea (*marr* "sea" + *dǫll*, feminine of *dallr*).

The suffix -**þu-* also formed other gods' names. Ullr and Óðr are first function figures, Njord third function. De Vries suggests that *Dallr was a second function god and argues consequent association with Thor.

2885. Vries, Jan de. "Kenningen und Christentum." *Zeitschrift für deutsches Altertum*, 87 (1956-57), 125-31.

A short note on the effects of Christianity on the kenning system and on Christian kennings, responding to Hans Kuhn, "Das nordgermanische Heidentum in den ersten christlichen Jahrhunderten" (1942). De Vries defends his conclusion that "pagan" kennings were avoided by skalds in the first century and a half after the conversion.

2886. Vries, Jan de. "Das Königtum bei den Germanen." *Saeculum*, 7 (1956), 289-309.

A linguistic study of words for "king" in the Germanic languages, this essay is relevant to Norse mythology for its views on the sacral nature of Germanic kingship.

2887. Vries, Jan de. "Die Helgilieder." *Arkiv för nordisk filologi*, 72 (1957), 123-54.

On the textual history of the Helgi lays, focusing on the extant texts but deriving them ultimately from a cult legend. Pp. 129-34 discuss valkyries.

2888. Vries, Jan de. "L'état actuel des recherches sur la religion germanique." *Diogène*, 18 (1957), 91-106.

Research summary.

2889. Vries, Jan de. "Ein Problem in der Bekehrungsgeschichte Islands." *Zeitschrift für deutsches Altertum*, 89 (1958-59), 75-82.

On the episode in the conversion of Iceland in which the pagan lawspeaker Þorgeirr retires under his cloak and decides that Iceland should be Christian. De Vries argues that Þorgeirr made contact with the *vættir* or spirits of the land and thus that a religious act had taken place.

2890. Vries, Jan de. "Die Sage von Wolfdietrich." *Germanisch-Romanisch Monatsschrift*, 39 (1958), 1-18. Rpt. in de Vries, *Kleine Schriften* (1965), pp. 37-55.

In the course of this study of the German legendary figure Wolfdietrich, de Vries draws attention to Odin cult and sees the first component of Wolfdietrich's name as an indication that he led a band of warriors whose initiation retained elements of the Odin cult (*Kleine Schriften*, p. 51).

2891. Vries, Jan de. "Die 'Tierverehrung' in Gallien." *Saga och sed*, 1958, pp. 48-62.

Primarily on ancient Celtic animal worship, but with brief reference to Germanic materials.

2892. Vries, Jan de. "Loki . . . und kein Ende." In *Festschrift für Franz Rolf Schröder: Zu seinem 65. Geburtstage September 1958*, ed. Wolfdietrich Rasch, 1-10. Heidelberg: C. Winter, 1959.

Departs from the analyses of Dumézil (1948), which he favors, and Ström (1956), which he rejects. Here de Vries regards Loki as a demon of the prototime, of chaos and destruction, whose intellectual gifts are for a time harnessed by the gods.

2893. Vries, Jan de. "Die Interpretatio Romana der gallischen Götter." In *Indogermanica: Festschrift für Wolfgang Lange zum 65. Geburtstage am 18. September 1960 von Fachgenossen und Freunden dargebracht*. 204-13. Heidelberg: C. Winter, 1960.

The *interpretatio romana* of the Gallic gods, based largely on Caesar's reporting and interpreted in light of Dumézil's scheme of Indo-European myth. Much reference to Germanic parallels.

2894. Vries, Jan de. *Kelten und Germanen*. Bibliotheca Germanica, 9. Bern and Munich: Francke, 1960. 139 pp.

A re-examination of the relationship between Celtic and Germanic peoples, stressing not historical contact but Indo-European inheritance. Cult and religion, which play a major role in the discussion, are ultimately interpreted according to Dumézil's theories.

2895. Vries, Jan de. "Sur certains glissements fonctionnels de divinités dans la religion germanique." In *Hommages à Georges Dumézil*. 83-95. Collection Latomus, 45. Brussels: Latomus, Revue d'études latines, 1960. Rpt. in de Vries, *Kleine Schriften* (1965), pp. 151-61.

Using Dumézil's framework, de Vries argues that second function figures among some Germanic peoples (e.g., the Saxons) lost their role as head of a group of warrior demons. Gods of the first function then assumed this role.

2896. Vries, Jan de. *Forschungsgeschichte der Mythologie*. Orbis Academicus, 1:7. Freiburg: K. Alber, 1961.

In this wide-ranging book, de Vries attempted a history of virtually all western mythography. There are, therefore, remarks on both Snorri Sturluson and Saxo Grammaticus. These are of particular interest in that they place the two great medieval Scandinavian mythographers in their international context. Discussion of later important students of Scandinavian mythology are also sound and of great interest.

2897. Vries, Jan de. "Theodorich der Grosse." *Germanisch-Romanisch Monatsschrift*, 42 (1961), 319-30.

Here de Vries supports the interpretation of Otto Höfler, *Kultische Geheimbünde der Germanen* (1934) and *Germanisches Sakralköigtum* (1952), that legends of Theodoric grew out of the context of an ecstatic warrior cult. Theodoric was regarded as a hypostasis of Odin.

2898. Vries, Jan de. "Celtic and Germanic Religion." *Saga-Book of the Viking Society*, 16 (1962-65), 109-23.

The purpose of this address, one of the O'Donnell lectures, delivered at Oxford in May 1962, was to sketch a picture of Celtic religion using Caesar's remarks on Gallic and Germanic religion (*Gallic War*, book 6) as a starting point. De Vries uses Germanic materials to reconstruct the scanty Celtic ones, e.g., Odin and Lug, Týr and Nuadu, in a Dumézilian framework. His only comment addressed directly to Germanic conditions is the suggestion that Germanic priesthood may once have been more complex, more like the Druids.

2899. Vries, Jan de. *Altnordisches etymologisches Wörterbuch,* 2nd rev. ed. Leiden: E. Brill, 1962. 1st ed. 1957-60; rpt. 1977.

Standard etymological dictionary of Old Norse-Icelandic; includes entries on the names of the gods.

2900. Vries, Jan de. "Vǫluspá Str. 21 und 22." *Arkiv för nordisk filologi,* 77 (1962), 42-47.

Textual note; argues that Gullveig was the creation of the *Vǫluspá* poet.

2901. Vries, Jan de. "Wodan und die Wilde Jagd." *Die Nachbarn,* 3 (1962), 31-59.

Casts doubt on the specifically Germanic nature of legends of the Wild Hunt and therefore their association with cult of Odin.

2902. Vries, Jan de. *The Study of Religion: A Historical Approach.* New York: Harcourt, Brace & World, 1967. xxiii, 231 pp.

Translation of the author's *Godsdienstgeschiedenis in vogelvlucht* (Utrecht: Het Spectrum, 1961), a historical survey of the study of myth and religion. De Vries offers brief, often acerbic remarks on the methodology of many writers, including some who discuss Norse mythology: Snorri Sturluson, Sophus Bugge, Georges Dumézil, Jacob Grimm, Kaarle Krohn, and Viktor Rydberg.

2903. Vries, Jan de. *Altgermanische Religionsgeschichte,* vol. 1: *Einleitung—Vorgeschichtliche Perioden—religiöse Grundlage des Lebens—Seelen- und Geisterglaube—Macht und Kraft—Das Heilige und die Kultformen,* vol. 2: *Die Götter—Vorstellungen über den Kosmos—Der Untergang des Heidentums,* 3rd ed. Grundriss der germanischen Philologie 12:1-2. Berlin: W. de Gruyter, 1970. 1st ed. 1935-37; 2nd ed. 1956-57.

Since Grimm, Germanic philologists have considered myth and religion a part of their subject. Thus the original *Grundriss der germanischen Philologie* contained coverage of Germanic mythology by Eugen Mogk (1st ed. 1891; 2nd ed. 1900). De Vries contributed a two-volume study of the history of Germanic religion, *Altgermanische Religionsgeschichte* (1935-37), to the revived, larger *Grundriss* and almost immediately undertook an extensive revision as he became familiar with the works of Georges Dumézil. This 2nd edition was in proof by 1945 but was seized by the occupation authorities (vol. 1, p. v) and did not appear until eleven years later. In 1970, a photomechanical reprint of the 2nd (1956-57) edition was issued as the 3rd edition. It is the standard handbook of Germanic religion and Scandinavian mythology. During the fifteen years or so when the fate of the work was unclear, de Vries continued to read and to publish specialized investigations, and the list of references to this work (vol. 1, pp. ix-xlix), with some one thousand entries, contributes a thorough if incomplete bibliography of the subject through the early 1950s.

The author of important monographs on Odin (1931), Loki (1933), mythological kennings (1934), ten "Studien over germaansche mythologie" in his native Dutch, and numerous other articles and books in Dutch, German, English, and French, de Vries was eminently well equipped to write a history of Germanic religion. (An all but indefatigable writer, he also contributed a two-volume history of Norse literature, etymological dictionaries of Old Norse and Dutch, books on heroic poetry, mythological scholarship, and many other subjects.)

In the 1956-57 revision of the *Altgermanische Religionsgeschichte* de Vries abandoned the division into south and north Germanic of the first edition and following Dumézil attempted treatment of Germanic religion as a whole. For this he drew the criticism of those with a more "historicist" view. As the work is organized now, vol. 1 considers matters more purely devoted to religion, such as the religious foundation of life, conception of souls and spirits, power, the holy and cult, while vol. 2 focuses on subjects usually associated with mythology, such as the gods and the cosmos. The study is overtly historical, however, in that it opens with prehistory and closes with the end of paganism.

In the more mythological second volume, de Vries surveys the gods systematically, with chapters on *Tīwaz/Týr, Woden/Odin, Donar/Thor, Ullr and Ullin, the *vanir*, the *æsir-vanir* war, Baldr, Heimdallr, twin gods, Loki, and other gods and goddesses. The section on cosmology covers creation, world picture and worldview, and destruction. As the chapter titles indicate, the focus is Germanic, but the Scandinavian materials receive very full treatment.

De Vries attempts explanation of myth and cult. For myth his views are essentially those of Dumézil; for cult he combines literary reference with other data. The maps of theophoric placenames are particularly good. Although it has a mass of detail, this handbook is easy to use, as it has a series of indices to the entire work.

2904. Vries, Jan de. "La religion des germains." In *Histoire des religions,* vol. 1: *Les religions antiques—la formation des religions universelles et les religions de salut en Inde et en extrême-orient.* 747-79. Encyclopédie de la Pléiade, 29. Paris: Gallimard, 1970.

Brief survey of Germanic religion, for a collective volume of essays on the world's religions. The treatment offered by de Vries follows the structural principles of Dumézil and thus focuses mostly on the mythology.

W

2905. Wackernagel, Wilhelm. "Die Anthropogonie der Germanen." *Zeitschrift für deutsches Altertum*, 6 (1848), 15-20.

Origin legends of Germanic peoples, including the eddic triad Odin, Vili, Vé.

2906. Wadstein, Elis. "Alfer ock älvor: En språkligt-mytologisk undersökning." In *Uppsalastudier tillegnade Sophus Bugge på hans 60-åra födelsedag den 5 januari 1893*. 152-79. Uppsala: Almqvist & Wiksell, 1892.

A survey of the terminology of the elves in Germanic languages. Wadstein's position is that the original term for elves meant "god" or "higher powers," but that homonymy and other factors caused the elves to be relocated to the wilds of the earth.

2907. Wadstein, Elis. "Bidrag till tolkning ock belysning av skalde- ock Edda-dikter, I: Till tolkningen av Ynglingatal." *Arkiv för nordisk filologi*, 11 (1895), 64-82.

On the interpretation and dating of *Ynglingatal*.

2908. Wadstein, Elis. "Bidrag till tolkning ock belysning av skalde- ock Edda-dikter, II: Om Ynglingatals avfattningstid ock förhållande till Háløygiatal." *Arkiv för nordisk filologi*, 11 (1895), 83-92.

On the interpretation and dating of *Ynglingatal*. Wadstein sees the kings of the early stanzas as reflections of gods, but he dates the poem to after the year 1000 A.D.

2909. Wadstein, Elis. "Bidrag till tolkning ock belysning av skalde- ock Edda-dikter, V: Till Vǫluspǫ́." *Arkiv för nordisk filologi*, 15 (1899), 158-61.

Textual note.

2910. Wadstein, Elis. "Bidrag till tolkning ock belysning av skalde- ock Edda-dikter, VI: Till Hymeskuiþa." *Arkiv för nordisk filologi*, 15 (1899), 161-65.

Textual note.

2911. Wadstein, Elis. "Bidrag till tolkning ock belysning av skalde- ock Edda-dikter, VII: Till Alvíssmǫl." *Arkiv för nordisk filologi*, 15 (1899), 165-67.

Textual note.

2912. Wadstein, Elis. "Beowulf: Etymologie und Sinn des Namens." In *Germanica: Eduard Sievers zum 75. Geburtstage 25. November 1925*. 323-26. Halle a. d. S.: M. Niemeyer, 1925.

Beowulf as a wind demon.

2913. Wadstein, Elis. "Svinnegarn, ett gammalt kultcentrum i Svealand, urhem för sveanamnet." *Rig*, 20 (1937), 28-54.

Svinnegarn, Sweden, as an ancient center of Svealand; water and stone cults have left traces.

2914. Wagner, Felix. "Völuspa ou prédictions de la prophétesse: Analyse et interprétation." *Revue belge de philologie et d'histoire*, 13 (1934), 45-56.

Commentary to *Vǫluspá*.

2915. Wagner, Felix. *Les poèmes mythologiques de l'Edda*. Bibliothèque de la faculté de philosophie et lettres de l'université de Liège, 71. Liège and Paris: E. Droz, 1936. xi, 272 pp.

French translation of the Poetic Edda, with introduction and notes.

2916. Wagner, Felix. "Que signifie le mot 'Edda'?" *Revue belge de philologie et d'histoire*, 18 (1939), 962-64.

The title *Edda* must, according to Wagner, mean "great-grandmother" and allude to ancient stories.

2917. Wagner, Heinrich. "Eine irisch-altnordische hieròs gámos-Episode." *Beiträge zur Geschichte der deutschen Sprache und Literatur*, 77 (1955), 348-57.

Reconstructs a portion of the Baldr story: after the death of Baldr (who is "a function of Odin"), Odin sires Bous (Váli) on the earth goddess Rinda (Rindr), with the aid of runic magic, and this son grows quickly (he avenges Baldr when only one night old), thus replacing the fertility god Baldr. Wagner presents the Irish myth of the Dagda, the river goddess Boann, and her son Aengus as a parallel, but he leaves open the exact nature of the relationship.

2918. Wagner, Heinrich. "Irisches in der Edda." *Ériu*, 20 (1966), 178-82.

On the languages of gods and of men in *Alvíssmál*.

2919. Wagner, Norbert. "Dioskuren, Jungmannschaften und Doppelkönigtum." *Zeitschrift für deutsche Philologie*, 79 (1960), 225-40.

The religious and cult background of hypothetical double kingship in Germanic culture, as derived from Indo-European.

2920. Wagner, Norbert. "Irmin in der Sachsen-Origo: Zur Arbeitsweise des Widukind von Corvey." *Germanisch-Romanisch Monatsschrift*, 59 (1978), 385-97.

Insignia and early religious beliefs of the Saxons.

2921. Wagner, Norbert. "Zu zwei Triaden in Tacitus' 'Germania.'" *Zeitschrift für deutsches Altertum*, 108 (1979), 209-18.

Concludes that Tacitus had more information at his disposal than he used in *Germania*, for his aim there was organizational and stylistic. A major organizing principle was the triad, which in his descriptions of Germanic religion realizes itself as father god (*regnator omnium deus*), mother god (Nerthus), youthful deities (the Alciis).

2922. Wagner, Norbert. "Zur Neunzahl von Lejre und Uppsala." *Zeitschrift für deutsches Altertum*, 109 (1980), 202-08.

Bishop Thietmar of Merseburg (d. 1018) mentioned in his chronicle a pagan cult site at Lejre. There the Danes sacrifice every ninth year ninety-nine men and ninty-nine dogs and roosters (the latter in the place of hawks or falcons); the number ninety-nine has been corrected from ninety. This account has reminded many observers of Adam of Bremen's description of the sacrifice at Uppsala where every ninth year men and animals are killed and hung in a tree; there the total of those sacrificed is said to be seventy-two after the nine days of the cult.

Wagner's aim is to refute the claim of R. Schmidt that these numbers derive from Christian numerology; nine symbolizes the death of Christ and the cross; eight the resurrection (whence the seventy-two hanged victims in Uppsala) and so forth. Wagner's method is to attempt to anchor in Nordic ritual the beasts slaughtered at Uppsala. Adam's eyewitness mentioned horse and hound, and Thietmar mentioned roosters as a substitute for hawks or falcons. With horse, hound, and hawk Wagner has three animals of the hunt, perhaps sacred to Odin. To these he adds bull, ram, goat, and boar, all substantiated in Germanic cult. With men the total is eight, and one of each per day yields the seventy-two corpses Adam's eyewitness saw. Wagner thinks that Thietmar originally wrote of nine victims. Mere exaggeration raised the number to ninety or ninety-nine.

2923. Wahlgren, Erik. "*Góð kona.*" *Scandinavian Studies*, 16 (1940-41), 185-93.

The expression "good woman" or its equivalent is found in four passages in *Hávamál*, all associated with Odin (str. 101, 102, 108, 130). Wahlgren argues that the adjective is used ironically in all four cases.

2924. Wais, Kurt. "Ullikummi Hrungnir Armilus und Verwandte." In *Edda, Skalden, Saga: Festschrift zum 70. Geburtstag von Felix Genzmer*, ed. Hermann Schneider, 211-61. Heidelberg: C. Winter, 1952.

On the relationship of the Hrungnir myth to story material in Hittite and other ancient traditions.

2925. [Wallman, J. H.]. "Odin och Budha." *Iduna*, 10 (1824), 179-242.

Comparison of Odin and Buddha, focusing primarily on the areas of the sun, wisdom, victory in battle, godhead, and creative powers. The author thinks a historical connection is likely.

2926. Wallner, Anton. "Eiris sazun idisi." *Zeitschrift für deutsches Altertum*, 50 (1908), 214-18.

Battle fetters in the first Merseburg charm.

2927. Walter, Emil. *Okouzlení krale Gylfa: Edda za staré íslandštiny*. Prague: Arkún, 1929. 157 pp.

Czech translation of *Gylfaginning* and *Vǫluspá*.

2928. Walter, Ernst. "Quellenkritisches und Wortgeschichtliches zum Opferfest von Hlaðir in Snorris Heimskringla (Hák. góð. c. 17)." In *Festschrift Walter Baetke dargebracht zu seinem 80. Geburtstage am 28. März 1964*, ed. Kurt Rudolf et al., 359-67. Weimar: H. Böhlau, 1966.

In ch. 17 of *Hákonar saga góða* in *Heimskringla*, King Hákon the good—a Christian—attends a pagan feast at Hlaðir. When he makes the sign of the cross over the drinking horn, Jarl Sigurðr protects him by explaining to the pagans that Hákon has made the sign of Thor's hammer. According to Ernst Walter's analysis, this anecdote is of scant value in the study of Scandinavian paganism: Snorri cannot have found it in anything like this form (particularly the dialog) in his sources, and his religious terminology is not that of tenth-century paganism but of thirteenth-century Christianity.

2929. Wanscher, Vilhelm. *Kivik guldhorn og edda*. Copenhagen: P. Haase & søn, 1935. 43 pp.

The supposed derivation from Egyptian religion of figures on the Gallehus horns, stone-carvings at Kivik, and Norse mythology. The "evidence" consists of fantastic etymologies.

2930. Ward, Donald. *The Divine Twins: An Indo-European Myth in Germanic Tradition*. University of California Studies in Folklore, 19. Berkeley and Los Angeles: University of California Press, 1968. x, 137 pp.

Seeks to demonstrate the continuation of an Indo-European myth of the *dioscurii* or divine twins in Germanic myth, historical writing, heroic literature, iconography, and later folk traditions. Within the corpus of Norse mythology *Skírnismál* is singled out as the repository of an ancient dioscurian myth, with Njord, Freyr, and Freyja making up a dioscurian triad. *Ynglingatal* is also treated.

2931. Ward, Donald. "The Threefold Death: An Indo-European Trifunctional Sacrifice?" In *Myth and Law Among the Indo-Europeans: Studies in Indo-European Comparative Mythology*, ed. Jaan Puhvel, 123-42. Publications of the UCLA Center for the Study of Comparative Folklore and Mythology, 1. Berkeley and Los Angeles: University of California Press, 1970.

Ward's argument is that human sacrifice, legal execution, and reflected literary usage within Germanic tradition indicate a correlation of means of death and Dumézilian function: hanging is associated with the first function, death by weapon with the second function, and drowning (or burial alive) with the third function. Ward admits that the evidence is meager, and he does not adequately address the question of Odin sacrifice with weapons, e.g., Víkarr and Baldr.

The article discusses a wide range of material.

2932. Warnatsch, Otto. "Phol und der 2. Merseburger Zauberspruch." *Zeitschrift für deutsche Philologie*, 64 (1939), 148-55.

Reads the first line as follows: *Pholende Wodan vuor unzi holza* "The Devil Wodan was up to the forest."

2933. Waschnitius, Viktor. *Perht, Holda und verwandte Gestalten: Ein Beitrag zur deutschen Religionsgeschichte*. Sitzungsberichte der kaiserlichen Akademie der Wissenschaften in Wien, phil.-hist Kl., 174:2. Vienna: A. Hölder, in commission, 1913. 184 pp.

Analysis of two figures from "lower mythology" in Germany, touching on the Wild Hunt.

2934. Watkins, Calvert. "Language of Gods and Language of Men: Remarks on Some Indo-European Metalinguistic Traditions." In *Myth and Law Among the Indo-Europeans: Studies in Indo-European Comparative Mythology*, ed. Jaan Puhvel, 1-17. Publications of the UCLA Center for the Study of Comparative Folklore and Mythology, 1. Berkeley and Los Angeles: University of California Press, 1970.

The purpose of this essay is to analyze the semantic and lexical operation of the figure "language of gods and language of men" and to add Irish analogs to the known Norse (*Alvíssmál*) and Indic occurrences. The "language of men" uses unmarked members of the lexicon, whereas the "language of gods" uses marked members. In the case of a language rich in poetic synonyms (e.g., Norse), "it is a simple matter to multiply (or subdivide) the divine or semi-divine groups" (p. 11), as in *Alvíssmál*.

2935. Weber, Edmund. *Kleine Runenkunde*. Berlin: Nordland, 1941. 120 pp.

Popular introduction to runology, with a section on Odin as god of runes.

2936. Weber, Gerd Wolfgang. "Die Lausavísa des Þorvaldr inn veili." *Zeitschrift für deutsches Altertum*, 97 (1968), 158-60.

Þorvaldr's verse, directed against the missionary Þangbrandr, does not make appeal to Germanic death penalties (so Ólafur Lárusson, "Vísa Þorvalds veila" (1928)), but merely threatens to drive Þangbrandr away from Iceland.

2937. Weber, Gerd Wolfgang. *Wyrd: Studien zum Schicksalsbegriff der altenglischen und altnordischen Literatur*. Frankfurter Beiträge zur Germanistik, 8. Bad Homburg v. d. H., Berlin, and Zurich: Gehlen, 1969. 175 pp.

A study of the concept of fate embodied in Old English *wyrd* and Old Norse *urðr*. Starting from the paradox that most of the attestations occur in Old English, the Germanic literature most steeped in medieval Christendom, Weber argues that Old English *wyrd* reflects *fortuna fatalis* and similar medieval Christian conceptions. The basis for a common Germanic concept of fate is thus shaken.

Pp. 149-54 are devoted to attestations of Old Norse *urðr*.

2938. Weber, Gerd Wolfgang. "Die Christus-Strophe des Eilífr Goðrúnarson." *Zeitschrift für deutsches Altertum*, 99 (1970), 87-90.

Weber identifies in Eilífr's strophe to Christ an unclear word, *setberg*, as a reference to a topos "king on a mound." Thus he interprets the strophe: Rome's king (Christ) sits on a mound (rules) at the well of Urðr (the old þing place).

2939. Weber, Gerd Wolfgang. "Das Odinsbild des Altunasteins." *Beiträge zur Geschichte der deutschen Sprache und Literatur* (Tübingen), 94 (1971), 323-34.

The iconographic representation of Odin on the Altuna runestone. Weber associates the upper image on the left narrow side with Hliðskjálf.

2940. Weber, Gerd Wolfgang. "'Sol per terrae marginem dicitur circuire' auch in Vǫluspá 5, 1-4?" *Germanisch-Romanisch Monatsschrift*, 29 (1971), 129-35.

A possible classical analog in *Vǫluspá*.

2941. Weber, Gerd Wolfgang. "Odins Wagen: Reflexe altnordischen Totenglaubens in literarischen und bildlichen Zeugnissen der Wikingerzeit." *Frühmittelalterliche Studien*, 7 (1973), 88-99.

On the expression *reið Rungnis* in *Sigrdrífumál* 15. Weber reads *Rungnis* as *Rǫgnis*, gen. sing. of Rǫgnir, an Odin name. Weber therefore translates the phrase "Odin's cart" and relates it to the carts and sledges of the Oseberg and Gokstad grave ship finds, to descriptions of royal funerals with references to carts (in *Helreið Brynhildar* and the *Sǫgubrot*), and to iconography on Gotland picture stones. The wagon will have been part of the ritual of bringing the dead to Odin.

2942. Weber, Gerd Wolfgang. "Irreligiosität und Heldenzeitalter: Zum Mythencharakter der altisländischen Literatur." In *Speculum Norroenum: Norse Studies in Memory of Gabriel Turville-Petre*, eds. Ursula Dronke, Guðrún P. Helgadóttir, Gerd Wolfgang Weber, and Hans Bekker-Nielsen, 474-505. N.p.: Odense University Press, 1981.

The expression "mythic" is used here in the modern sense employed by Northrop Frye. The study analyzes the apparent ideology of the Icelandic family sagas in their thirteenth-century context.

2943. Weber, Leopold. *Die Götter der Edda*. Munich: Musarion, 1919. 195 pp.

Presentation of Norse mythology as "living" material for a German audience, including portions from *Snorra edda* rendered into alliterative verse.

2944. Weinhold, Karl. "Niordhr, Nordhr, Niorun, Norn, Neorxu." *Zeitschrift für deutsches Altertum*, 6 (1848), 460-61.

Associates etymologically the words in the title and concludes therefore that norns were originally giant water goddesses.

2945. Weinhold, Karl. "Zu Völuspâ." *Zeitschrift für deutsches Altertum*, 6 (1848), 311-18.

The argument that the extant *Vǫluspá* was assembled from older poems is followed by specific textual notes.

2946. Weinhold, Karl. "Die Sagen von Loki." *Zeitschrift für deutsches Altertum*, 7 (1849), 1-94.

Survey of the myths and recent legends of Loki, aiming at an inner history. Weinhold seeks Loki's essence in fire, water, and air, but admits contradictions and permits Loki to be both provider and destroyer.

2947. Weinhold, Karl. "Die Riesen des germanischen Mythus." *Sitzungsberichte der kaiserlichen Akademie der Wissenschaften*, phil.-hist. Kl., 26 (1858), 225-306.

In arguing that the giants originally were the oldest family of gods, Weinhold divides the giants into natural spheres of activity: water, air, fire, and earth.

2948. Weinhold, Karl. "Die deutschen Zwölfsgötter." *Zeitschrift für deutsche Philologie*, 1 (1869), 129-32.

Remarks on the lists of twelve gods in *Snorra edda* and their possible application to German mythology. Weinholds thinks that the notion of twelve gods is ancient.

2949. Weinhold, Karl. "Tius things." *Zeitschrift für deutsche Philologie*, 21 (1889), 1-16.

Reading of the inscriptions on the Borovicium altars.

2950. Weinhold, Karl. "Über den Mythus vom Wanenkrieg." *Sitzungsberichte der königlich preussischen Akademie der Wissenschaften zu Berlin, phil.-hist. Kl.*, 1890, pp. 611-25.

Weinhold sees the war between the *æsir* and *vanir* as the reflection of the meeting between two cults: the sun cult of the *vanir* and the chthonic cult of Odin.

2951. Weinhold, Karl. *Die mystische Neunzahl bei den Deutschen*. Abhandlungen der königlichen Akademie der Wissenschaften zu Berlin, phil.-hist. Kl, 1897, 2. Berlin: Verlag der königlichen Adademie der Wissenschaften, 1897. 61 pp.

Weinhold discusses a very broad range of cases in ancient and modern culture where the number nine is of importance. Direct analysis of myth is rare, but the mythology is commonly mentioned.

2952. Weiser-Aall, Lily. *Altgermanische Jünglingsweihen und Männerbünde: Ein Beitrag zur deutschen und nordischen Altertums- und Volkskunde*. Bausteine zur Volkskunde und Religionswissenschaft, 1. Bühl in Baden: Konkordia, 1927. 94 pp.

Classic delineation in Germanic culture of closed male societies with initiation of youth in a sacral context. A great deal of the evidence derives from Scandinavian sources, especially those having to do with Norse mythology.

2953. Weiser-Aall, Lily. "Zur Geschichte der altgermanischen Todesstrafe und Friedlosigkeit." *Archiv für Religionswissenschaft*, 30 (1933), 209-27.

Study of capital punishment and outlawry, tied to the author's theories about ancient *Männerbünde*: the legal process and its judgments were in certain cases carried out within the *Bund* and bore its symbolic tokens.

2954. Weiser-Aall, Lily. "Hugrinn—vindr trollkvenna." *Maal og minne*, 1936, pp. 76-78.

The ethnographic backgound of the kenning *vindr trollkvenna* "wind of the troll women."

2955. Weisweiler, Josef. "Beiträge zur Bedeutungsentwicklung germanischer Wörter für sittliche Begriffe: Erster Teil." *Indogermanische Forschungen*, 41 (1923), 13-77.

Discussion of *ergi* and *níð*.

2956. Weisweiler, Josef. "*Seele* und *See*: Ein etymologischer Versuch." *Indogermanische Forschungen*, 57 (1939), 25-55.

Argues, on the basis of etymology, that in the ancient Germanic conceptual world lakes and similar bodies of water were regarded as the abode of unborn and deceased souls.

2957. Weninger, Ludwig. "Feralis exercitus." *Archiv für Religionswissenschaft*, 9 (1906), 201-47.

Part A, "Das schwarze Heer der Harier" (pp. 201-23), treats the remarks of Tacitus on the Harii and draws them ultimately into contact with Odin and Germanic beliefs in the soul and the realm of the dead.

2958. Wennström, Torsten. "Om runor och magi." In *Studier tillägnade Josua Mjöberg den 11 September 1926*. 260-94. Lund: C. W. K. Gleerup, 1926.

Runes, magic, death, and burial mounds.

2959. Werenskiold, W. "Ymesfjell." *Maal og minne*, 1934, pp. 152-53.

Against the "popular explanation" of the placename *Ymesfjell* as a reference to the giant Ymir.

2960. Werlich, Egon. *Der westgermanische Skop: Der Aufbau seiner Dichtung und sein Vortrag*. Münster: Issuer not indicated, 1964. xxix, 379 pp. Diss. Münster.

Derives the West Germanic **skop* (Old English *scop*) from a chanting, dancing poet with priestly function. The **skop* is parallel to the *woðbora*, who achieves religious ecstasy through ritual drinking of mead; the first component of the term is cognate with the name of Odin (*Óðinn*, Old English *Woden*).

For criticism see Ida Masters Hollowell, "*Scop* and *woðbora* in OE Poetry" (1978).

2961. Werlich, Egon. "Der westgermanische Skop: Der ursprung des Sängerstandes in semasiologischer und etymologischer Sicht." *Zeitschrift für deutsche Philologie*, 86 (1967), 352-75.

Traces a development from Germanic priest to court poet and concludes that the West Germanic scop is a "secularized Germanic priest." Much discussion of poetry, singing, dance, and cult.

2962. Werner, Joachim. *Die beiden Zierscheiben des Thorsberger Moorfundes: Ein Beitrag zur frühgermanischen Kunst- und Religionsgeschichte.* Commission des deutschen archäologischen Instituts zu Frankfurt a. M., Römisch-germanische Forschungen. Berlin: W. de Gruyter, 1941. v, 77 pp.

Detailed analysis of two artifacts from the Thorsbjærg (Denmark) moor. One shows a warrior and a goose, which leads Werner to discussion of the relationship between the war god Týr and the goose and the possible magico-religious use of the object.

2963. Wesche, Heinrich. *Das Heidentum in der althochdeutschen Sprache,* vol. 1: *Die Kultstätte.* Göttingen: Dieterich, 1932. 45 pp. Diss. Göttingen.

The first of three studies on the vocabulary of German paganism; treats cult places.

2964. Wesche, Heinrich. "Beiträge zu einer Geschichte des deutschen Heidentums." *Beiträge zur Geschichte der deutschen Sprache und Literatur,* 61 (1937), 1-116.

The vocabulary of priest and worship in German paganism. The priestly caste is treated on pp. 2-25; worship on pp. 26-114.

2965. Wesche, Heinrich. *Der althochdeutsche Wortschatz im Gebiete des Zaubers und der Weissagung.* Untersuchungen zur Geschichte der deutschen Sprache, 1. Halle a. d. S.: M. Niemeyer, 1940. vi, 110 pp.

Magic and prophecy in German paganism as reflected in vocabulary. The index also covers Wesche's studies of cult places (1932) and priests and worship (1937).

2966. Wessén, Elias. "Om kuiða i namn på fornnordiska dikter: Ett bidrag till Eddadiktningens historia." *Edda,* 4 (1915), 127-41.

On the poetic terms *-mál* and *-kviða.* The remarks on *-mál* relate to Norse mythology. According to Wessén, the term was originally applied to didactic poems spoken by Odin (e.g., *Hávamál*) only later to didactic poetry in a narrative frame (*Vafþrúðnismál, Grímnismál*), and finally to narrative poetry in general (e.g., *Skírnismál*) and/or in the meter *málaháttr* (e.g., *Eiríksmál*).

2967. Wessén, Elias. "Forntida gudsdyrkan i Östergötland." *Meddelanden från Östergötlands fornminnes- och museiförening,* 1921, pp. 85-147.

First of a two-part study based on theophoric placenames in Östergötland, Sweden. Starting from the placenames Ullevi and Mjärdevi, Wessén discusses public worship of the linked gods Ullr and Njord and includes remarks on their personae in the mythology. Pp. 127-46 include geographic and alphabetic lists of theophoric placenames in Östergötland.

2968. Wessén, Elias. "Hästskede och Lekslätt." *Namn och bygd*, 9 (1921), 103-31.

On placenames in *-skeið*, which Wessén associates with worship of the fertility gods Ullr and Freyr.

2969. Wessén, Elias. "Forntida gudsdyrkan i Östergötland, II." *Meddelanden från Östergötlands fornminnes- och museiförening*, 1922, pp. 1-48.

Second of a two-part study based on theophoric placenames in Östergötland, Sweden. Names discussed here are Skedevi (connection with horses) and Götevi and Götala (connection with Odin).

2970. Wessén, Elias. "Till de nordiska äringsgudarnas historia." *Namn och bygd*, 10 (1922), 97-118.

A review article on H. Jungner, *Gudinnan Frigg och Als härad* (1922).

2971. Wessén, Elias. *Minnen av forntida gudsdyrkan i mellan-Sveriges ortnamn: Föredrag vid Svenska filolog- och historikermötet i Helsingfors 17-19 aug. 1922.* Studier i nordisk filologi, 14:1, Skrifter utgivna av Svenska literatursällskapet i Finland, 170. Helsinki: Mercator tryckeri, 1923. 26 pp.

The placename evidence for cult activity in central Sweden, stressing close proximity of cult places for related gods and goddesses and the differences between central and western Swedish traditions. Of the many gods and placename components mentioned, Ullr and *-åker* "field" receive special attention. Three maps are included.

2972. Wessén, Elias. "Gestumblinde." In *Festskrift tillägnad Hugo Pipping på hans sextioårsdag den 5 november 1924.* 537-48. Skrifter utg. av Svenska litteratursällskapet i Finland, 175. Helsinki: Mercators tryckeri, 1924.

On the character and name of Gestumblindi, i.e., Odin, in *Hervarar saga.* The name was, according to Wessén, originally applied to a character who urged Heiðrekr to kill his brother Angantýr; later it was put to use in the frame story of the riddle encounter in the saga. Wessén derives the name from a hypothethical form meaning "the blind guest," i.e., Odin.

2973. Wessén, Elias. *Studier till Sveriges hedna mytologi och fornhistoria.* Uppsala universitets årsskrift 1924, filosofi, språkvetenskap och historiska vetenskaper, 6. Uppsala: Almqvist & Wiksell, 1924. 198 pp.

Study of early Swedish religion and settlement, based primarily on placenames. Major subjects treated are Yngvi-Freyr and Odin in Götaland; the relationship between Götaland and Gotland; Njord; and Adam of Bremen's description of the pagan temple at Uppsala.

2974. Wessén, Elias. "Ynglingatal." *Upplands forminnesförenings tidskrift*, 10 (1925-26), 64-70.

Comments on portions of *Ynglingatal* relating directly to Uppland: Fróði, Eysteinn, Óláfr trételgja.

2975. Wessén, Elias. *Nordiska namnstudier*. Uppsala universitets årsskrift 1927, filosofi, språkvetenskap och historiska vetenskaper, 3. Uppsala: Lundequistska bokhandeln, 1927. 118 pp.

Includes a section on Old Scandinavian farmers' names compounded with the names of gods: *Þór-*, *Frey-*, *Óðin-*.

2976. Wessén, Elias. "Om den äldsta kristna terminologien i de germanska fornspråken." *Arkiv för nordisk filologi*, 44 (1928), 75-108.

The oldest Christian vocabulary in the ancient Germanic languages. Wessén offers a careful measurement especially of the role of Gothic as the initial receiver and transmitter of this vocabulary at the missionary stage.

2977. Wessén, Elias. "Schwedische Ortsnamen und altnordische Mythologie." *Acta Philologica Scandinavica*, 4 (1929-30), 97-115.

A survey of Swedish placename evidence for cult activity, interpreted in light of Norse mythology. Figure 6 (p. 107) offers a useful table: on the vertical axis all the gods represented, on the horizontal axis the placenames' second components (*-vi*, *-harg*, *-lund(a)*, *-åker*, *-tuna*). The most widely represented god is Ullr, followed by Thor, Frö (Freyr), and Skædh (Skaði). The most widely attested second component is *-lund(a)*. In the last pages Wessén argues that the male Njord is descended from a goddess and that Freyr replaced Ullr.

2978. Wessén, Elias. "Introduction." In *Codex Regius to the Younger Edda: MS no. 2367 4to in the Old Royal Collection in the Royal Library of Copenhagen*. 1-30. Corpus Codicorum Islandorum Medii Ævi, 14. Copenhagen: Munksgaard, 1940.

The introduction to a facsimile of the major manuscript of *Snorra edda*. The work will have been written "backwards": first *Háttatal*; then *Skáldskaparmál* in further explanation of the poetic language in *Háttatal* and elsewhere; then *Gylfaginning*, to explain further the kenning system; finally the Prologue, to make the work acceptable in a Christian context. This view of the origin of *Snorra edda* is generally accepted.

2979. Wessén, Elias. "Den isländska eddadiktningen: Dess uppteckning och redigering." *Saga och sed*, 1946, pp. 1-31.

Approaches the problem of the recording of eddic poetry, based on the relationships between the two major manuscripts, the fairly complete Codex Regius (GkS 2365 4to) and the fragmentary "A" (AM 748 4to). Both agree almost word for word in parallel passages, thereby indicating a common original, but the order of the poems included is altogether different, and "A" contains a poem

(*Baldrs draumar*) not found in Codex Regius. Wessén's solution to this problem is to postulate a series of recordings of poems from oral tradition onto separate leaves. Codex Regius and "A" both used these leaves, but the scribe of Codex Regius systematically ordered his material and mistakenly omitted *Baldrs draumar*.

The collection of eddic poetry was inspired by *Snorra edda* (and Snorri himself was probably responsible for the redaction of *Hávamál*) and carried out by learned men who composed some (but not all) of the prose now to be found within the poems.

2980. Wessén, Elias. "Nytt om Rök-stenen." *Fornvännen*, 48 (1953), 161-77. Summary in German.

Commentary on O. Höfler, *Der Runenstein von Rök und die germanische Individualweihe* (1952).

2981. Wessén, Elias. "Det fattiga hemmet och det ensamma trädet: Till tolkningen av ett par strofer i Hávamál." *Svio-Estonica*, 14 (1958), 19-24.

Str. 36-37 and 50 of *Hávamál*.

2982. Wessén, Elias. *Runstenen vid Röks kyrka*. Kungliga vitterhets, historie, och antikvitetsakademiens handlingar, filol.-filos. serien, 5. Stockholm: Almqvist & Wiksell, 1958. 111 pp. Summary in German

Points out the similarities of the Rök stone to the picture stones and sees the entire complex as a kind of pagan literature.

2983. Wessén, Elias. *Hávamál: Några stilfrågor*. Filologiskt arkiv, 8. Stockholm: Almqvist & Wiksell, 1959. 31 pp.

Snorri the redactor of *Hávamál*? (pp. 8-9).

2984. Wessén, Elias. "Ordspråk och lärodikt: Några stilformer i Havamal." In *Septentrionalia et Orientalia: Studia Bernhardo Karlgren A.D. III non. oct. anno mcmlix dedicata*. 455-73. Kungliga vitterhets historie och antikvitets akademiens handlingar, 91. Stockholm: Kungliga vitterhets historie och antikvitets akademien, 1959.

On proverbs and stylistic features of the gnomic section of *Hávamál*, specifically on the relationship between proverb and commentary (verses in the first person). Wessén finds that this section of the poem (str. 1-80) must be "one or a couple of generations older than *Hákonarmál*," which he dates to 960 A. D.

2985. Wessén, Elias. "Havamal." *Modersmålslärarnas förening, årsskrift*, 1960-61, pp. 3-14.

Str. 1-80 of *Hávamál* the work of a single poet from before the middle of the tenth century.

2986. Wessén, Elias. "Teodorik–myt eller hjältesaga." *Arkiv för nordisk filologi*, 79 (1964), 1-20.

Part of the debate with Höfler on the Rök stone.

2987. Wessén, Elias. "Svar till Professor Höfler." *Arkiv för nordisk filologi*, 81 (1966), 255-57.

More in the debate with Höfler on the Rök stone.

2988. Wessén, Elias. "Rök, ett fornminne och ett ortnamn." *Fornvännen*, 70 (1975), 5-15. Summary in English.

Useful for two purposes: 1) warns against interpreting the placename *Rök* as involving a cult-site; 2) contains a reasonably exhaustive bibliography on the Rök runic inscription.

2989. Wessén, Elias. "Rökstenen ännu en gång: Tillika ett svar till Professor Höfler." *Arkiv för nordisk filologi*, 91 (1976), 42-50.

Perhaps the final entry in the debate with Höfler on the Rök stone.

2990. Westman, K. G. "Bidrag till problemet om Nerthus-Frökulten i Sverige." *Saga och sed*, 1943, pp. 199-204.

Recent folklore recordings from Sweden which, according to the author, reflect traces of fertility cult similar to that of Nerthus as described by Tacitus in *Germania*.

2991. Whistler, Charles W. "Odinic Traces in Somerset." *Saga-Book of the Viking Society*, 2 (1897-1900), 42-50.

An amateur's discussion of a hypothetical *vé* (holy place) in Somerset, England.

2992. Whistler, Charles W. "Survival of an Odinic Riddle." *Saga-Book of the Viking Society*, 2 (1897-1900), 151-52.

Report of a folklore parallel to one of the riddles of Gestumblindi in *Heiðreks saga*.

2993. Whistler, Charles W. "Tradition and Folklore of the Quantocks." *Saga-Book of the Viking Society*, 5 (1906-07), 142-50.

Alleged survivals of Norse mythology in Wessex are discussed on pp. 145-46.

2994. Whitaker, Ian. "Some Anthropological Perspectives on *Gretla*: A Response to Motz." *Arkiv för nordisk filologi*, 92 (1977), 145-54.

A dismissal of L. Motz, "Withdrawal and Return" (1973).

2995. Whitelock, Dorothy. "The Conversion of the Eastern Danelaw." *Saga-Book of the Viking Society*, 12 (1937-45), 159-76.

Attempts "to bring together any evidence relating to the ecclesiastical history of this area" (p. 159) from 869 to ca. 970.

2996. Wiberg, Albert. "'At festa skip': En studie i fornnordisk begravningsritual." *Fornvännen*, 32 (1937), 99-108. Summary in German, p. 108.

On the ship funerals in *Gísla saga*. Wiberg disputes the notion that the ritual was meant to discourage the deceased from becoming a revenant, for he would plague his enemies, not his family who carry out the ritual. Rather, argues Wiberg, the Hel-shoes are intended for use in the grave, and the expression *at festa skip* means to ballast the ship correctly.

2997. Widéen, Harald. "Till diskussionen om Uppsala hednatempel." *Fornvännen*, 46 (1951), 127-31.

Urges caution in applying Adam of Bremen for reconstructing the pagan temple at Uppsala and challenges the archaeological surmise that evidence under the existing church must relate to the pagan temple and not to an earlier church.

2998. Wieden, Helge bei der. "Bragi." *Zeitschrift für deutsche Philologie*, 80 (1961), 83-86.

Concludes that the human poet Bragi preceded the god with the same name.

2999. Wieden, Helge bei der. "Einige Bemerkungen zum religionsgeschichtlichen Ort der Lokasenna." *Zeitschrift für deutsche Philologie*, 83 (1964), 266-75.

Surveys four positions on the importance of *Lokasenna* for the history of religion: 1) the poem is the work of a pagan; 2) the poem is the work of a Christian; 3) the poem derives from syncretism; 4) the poem reflects antique literary models. Of these, bei der Wieden inclines toward the third.

3000. Wieseler, Karl. *Untersuchungen zur Geschichte und Religion der alten Germanen in Asien und Europa*. Leipzig: J. C. Hinrich, 1881. vi, 178 pp.

Naive and exaggerated identifications of Germanic peoples and their religion in Europe and Asia.

3001. Wieselgren, Peter. *Völo-spa hoc est Carmen Veledae Islandice et Latine: Commentariolis Strictim Illustratum*. Gothenburg: Berling, 1829. 84 pp.

Edition of and commentary to *Vǫluspá*.

3002. Wikander, Stig. "Från Bråvalla till Kurukshetra." *Arkiv för nordisk filologi*, 75 (1960), 183-93.

Wikander attempts to locate Indo-European eschatological themes in Saxo's account of Harald wartooth's last battle at Brávellir. For a rebuttal see Wistrand (1970).

3003. Wikander, Stig. "Germanische und indo-iranische Eschatologie." *Kairos*, 2 (1960), 83-88.

Parallel features in the eschatological systems of Norse and Indo-Iranian sources.

3004. Wikman, K. Rob. V. "Fröreligionen och Priapos-hypotesen." *Budkavlen*, 2 (1923), 12-18.

Criticism of H. Jungner, *Gudinnan Frigg och Als härad* (1922).

3005. Wikman, K. Rob. V. "Världsträdet och livskällan: Några randanteckningar till fornnordisk kosmologi." *Budkavlen*, 6 (1927), 1-11.

Building largely on H. Pipping's *Eddastudier* (1925 and 1926), Wikman focuses on Heimdallr as a personification of the world tree and analyzes his relationship to the well.

3006. Wilber, Terence. "The Interpretation of Vǫluspá 22,4: *vitti hon ganda*." *Scandinavian Studies*, 31 (1959), 129-36.

Wilber reads the line "she consecrated the staves."

3007. Wilke, Georg. "Der Weltenbaum und die beiden kosmischen Vögel in der vorgeschichtlichen Kunst." *Mannus*, 14 (1922), 73-99.

Although there is no particular focus on Germanic or Scandinavian materials in this broad article on the world tree and the two cosmic birds in prehistoric art, they do crop up occasionally, and the whole provides interesting background to the Scandinavian mythological conceptions of the world tree. Wilke argues finally that this group of motifs deserves an astral interpretation.

3008. Wilke, Georg. "Ein altgermanisches Haaropfer." *Mannus*, 16 (1924), 64-73.

Archaeological evidence for a Germanic hair ritual.

3009. Wilken, E. "Der Fenriswolf: Eine mythologische Untersuchung." *Zeitschrift für deutsche Philologie*, 28 (1896), 156-98, 297-348.

Lengthy study of the Fenrir myth, with essentially nature-mythological premises. Wilken finds that the wolf was bound by night, in heaven, and he therefore argues that the mythic kernel reflects a constellation called *ulfs keptr* somewhere in or near the Milky Way and that the battle of Fenrir against Odin and Víðarr is for the sun.

3010. Wilken, E. "Zur Ordnung der Völuspá." *Zeitschrift für deutsche Philologie*, 30 (1898), 448-86.

Analysis of the arrangement of stanzas and events of *Vǫluspá*, aiming ultimately at reconstruction of a proto-text.

3011. Wilken, E. "Zur Erklärung der Vǫluspá." *Zeitschrift für deutsche Philologie*, 33 (1901), 289-330.

Extensive notes to Wilken's earlier article, "Zur Ordnung der Vǫluspá" (1898), focused on a hypothetical proto-form of the poem.

3012. Wilken, E. *Die prosaische Edda im Auszuge nebst Vǫlsungasaga und Nornagests-þáttr*. 2nd ed. Vol. 1: *Text*; vol. 2: *Glossar*. Bibliothek der ältesten deutschen Literatur-Denkmäler, 11-12. Paderborn: F. Schöningh, 1912-13. xv, 264; vii, 284 pp.

An edition of the narrative portions of *Snorra edda* and two other relevant texts. The glossary, vol. 2, is useful for its grammatical information.

3013. Wilkinson, James John Garth. *The Book of Edda Called Völuspá: A Study in its Scriptural and Spiritual Correspondences*. London: J. Speirs, 1897. xvi, 195 pp.

Swedenborgian reading of *Vǫluspá*.

3014. Will, Gerd. *Die Darstellung der Gemütsbewegungen in den Liedern der Edda*. Nordische Brücke, Deutsche Studien zur nordischen Sprach-, Literatur- und Kulturgeschichte, 2. Hamburg: Friedrichsen, de Gruyter, 1934. 84 pp.

Literary analysis of the representation of emotions in eddic poetry, arguing metrical distribution: more representation of emotion in *fornyrðislag* than in *ljóðaháttr*.

3015. Winther, Chr. "Tydning af nogle helleristningsfigurer." *Danske studier*, 36 (1939), 81-96.

Interpretation of Bronze Age rock carvings, in part through comparison with Mexican artifacts. Illustrated.

3016. Winther, Chr. "Tydning af nogle helleristningsfigurer II-III." *Danske studier*, 37 (1940), 127-49.

Continuation of a study of certain figures on the Bronze Age rock carvings. Part II (pp. 127-36) considers the possible presence of the signs of the Zodiac; part III (pp. 136-49) of pictorial "signatures."

3017. Winther, Chr. "Tydning af nogle helleristningsfigurer IV." *Danske studier*, 40 (1943), 1-19.

Continuation of a study of certain figures on the Bronze Age rock carvings. Here Winther argues that certain groups of figures follow a definite order. On pp. 18-19, he discusses the possibility that the rock carvings may have a less strongly expressed religious impulse than scholars usually grant.

3018. Wipf, Karl A. "Die Zaubersprüche im Althochdeutschen." *Numen*, 22 (1975), 42-69.

General treatment of the Old High German magic spells, from the point of view of primitive magic. According to the author, it is impossible ultimately to distinguish pagan and Christian in the charms.

3019. Wipf, Karl A. "Wotan: Der Aufstieg Wotans im germanischen Götterpantheon." *Triebschener Blätter: Zeitschrift der schweizerischen Richard-Wagner-Gesellschaft*, 42 (1978), 1-32.

Although it is specifically aimed at Wagner's Wotan, this essay attempts a historical development of the religious and literary background of the figure.

3020. Wirth, Werner. *Der Schicksalsglaube in den Isländersagas.* Veröffentlichungen des orientalischen Seminars der Universität Tübingen, 11. Stuttgart: W. Kohlhammer, 1940. viii, 160 pp. Also issued as: Neue Folge Veröffentlichungen des Arischen Seminars, 1.

Belief in fate and "luck" in the Icelandic family sagas.

3021. Wislicenus, Hugo. *Die Symbolik von Sonne und Tag in der germanischen Mythologie: Mit Beziehung auf die allgemeine Mythologie: Untersuchungen.* Zurich: Schabelitz'sche Buchhandlung (C. Schmidt), 1867. iv, 92 pp. 2nd ed. 1892.

Solar mythology.

3022. Wissowa, Georg. "Interpretatio Romana: Römische Götter im Barbarenlande." *Archiv für Religionswissenschaft*, 19 (1916-19), 1-49.

The last ten pages or so treat directly the Germanic circumstances, and the entire article is useful for the context of the *interpretatio romana* of Germanic myth and religion.

3023. Wistrand, Magnus. "Slaget vid Bråvalla—en reflex av den indoeuropeiska mytskatten?" *Arkiv för nordisk filologi*, 85 (1970), 208-22.

Contra Wikander, "Från Bråvalla till Kurukshetra" (1960). Wistrand argues that Wikander based his analysis on Saxo, but *Sǫgubrot af fornkonungum*, a better source, fails in key places to corroborate the supposed Indo-European parallels.

3024. Wolf, Alfred. "Die germanische Sippe *bil*: Eine Entsprechung zu *Mana*: Mit einem Anhang über den Bilwis." *Språkvetenskapliga sällskapets i Uppsala förhandlingar*, 1928-30, pp. 17-156.

An attempt to locate a concept of *mana* in Germanic; the root *bil* means "supernatural power."

3025. Wolf, Alois. "Zitat und Polemik in den 'Hákonarmál' Eyvinds." In *Germanistische Studien*, eds. Johannes Erben and Eugen Thurnher, 10-32. Innsbrucker Beiträge zur Kulturwissenschaft, 15. Innsbruck: Institut für Vergleichende Sprachwissenschaft der Universität Innsbruck, 1969.

In part a response to K. von See, "Zwei eddische Preislieder" (1963), attempting to restore the usual chronology: Eyvindr used *Eiríksmál* as a source for *Hákonarmál.*

3026. Wolf, Alois. "Sehweisen und Darstellungsfragen in der Gylfaginning: Thors Fischfang." *Skandinavistik*, 7 (1977), 1-27.

Wolf investigates aspects of Snorri's literary technique in *Gylfaginning*, dividing his essay into four parts. 1) The distribution of roles in the *sjónhverfing* and *ginning*: Gylfi/Gangleri takes the role of Odin the questioner as in *Vafþrúð nismál*, and Hár and the others are also Odin figures; thus we have the ironic situation of Odin putting questions to Odin. 2) On the theme of truth in *Gylfaginning*: Snorri uses verbal formulas of "truth/faith" and "wisdom" ironically and gradually approaches and merges the two; beneath it all, Snorri is the great man of wisdom. 3) The Thor episodes: these are examples of Snorri's ironizing, particularly the fishing expedition for the midgard serpent. Here Snorri reduces the eschatological element and instead stresses the human aspects of the story, linking the old traditional elements into a comic/grotesque narrative. 4) On *Hymiskviða*: Wolf sees the poem as a late, conscious literary reworking of the same material Snorri used, but to different effect. Where Snorri humanized, the *Hymiskviða* poet heightened the mythic aspects of the incident. The two versions reveal a picture of the presence of the old myths in thirteenth-century Iceland.

3027. Wolf, J. W. *Beiträge zur deutschen Mythologie,* vol. 1: Götter und Göttinnen. Göttingen: Dieterichs, Leipzig: F. C. W. Vogel, 1852. 267 pp.

Collection of materials from many sources relating to German mythology. The approach is reminiscent of that of J. Grimm, and some of the chapters are keyed to Grimm's *Deutsche Mythologie.*

3028. Wolf, J. W. *Beiträge zur deutschen Mythologie,* vol. 2. Göttingen: Dieterichs, 1857. xi, 468 pp.

Continuation of the author's collection of materials relating to German mythology. This volume relates mostly to the so-called lower mythology.

3029. Wolff, Ludwig. "Eddisch-skaldische Blütenlese." In *Edda, Skalden, Saga: Festschrift zum 70. Geburtstag von Felix Genzmer,* ed. Hermann Schneider, 92-107. Heidelberg: C. Winter, 1952.

On the substance of the kenning: it makes direct reference to the mythic and heroic background insofar as the subject of the kenning seeks to link his feelings, his prowess and bravery, with the mythic-heroic past. Thus Snorri holds that words meaning "giant" are inadmissible base-words for man-kennings in encomia, but the elves, who were the objects of cult, are acceptable. Specific examples are discussed from *Atlakviða, Hákonarmál,* and *Sonatorrek.*

3030. Wolff, Ludwig. "Die Merseburger Zaubersprüche." In *Die Wissenschaft von deutscher Sprache und Dichtung: Methoden, Probleme, Aufgaben [Festschrift für Friedrich Maurer zum 65. Geburtstag am 5. Januar 1963],* ed. Siegfried Gutenbrunner et al., 305-19. Stuttgart: E. Klett, 1963.

The Merseburg charms as examples of Germanic charm tradition. The second charm reflects conceptions of Baldr in Germany.

3031. Wolfram, Herwig. "Methodische Fragen zur Kritik am 'sakralen' Königtum germanischer Stämme." In *Festschrift für Otto Höfler zum 65. Geburtstag,* eds. Helmut Birkhan and Otto Gschwantler, 473-90. Vienna: Notring, 1968.

The author calls for a thorough philological study of the documents on which postulation of a Germanic sacral kingship might be based—particularly a close comparison with Latin documents in which similar notions seem to be suppressed.

3032. Wolf-Rottkay, W. H. "Baldr and the Mistletoe: A Note." *Scandinavian Studies,* 39 (1967), 340-44.

Comments on Aage Kabell, *Baldr und die Mistel* (1965); specifically directed against Kabell's proposed emendation of *vǫllum* to *vǫlu* in *Vǫluspá* 31.

3033. Wood, Frederic T. "A Note on *Vǫluspá* 24." *Scandinavian Studies,* 15 (1938), 84-86.

Interprets the word *vígspár* (*Vǫluspá* 24) as "exposed to warfare."

3034. Wood, Frederic T. *Eddic Lays.* [Charlottesville? Va.]: [No issuer], 1940. v, 227 pp. Place of publication and issuer not indicated.

An edition of eddic poems, including many mythological texts, with introduction and glossary.

3035. Wood, Frederic T. "Order in the *Codex Regius* of the *Poetic Edda.*" In *Humanistic Studies in Honor of John Calvin Metcalf.* 107-19. University of Virginia Studies, 1. Charlottesville, Va. [New York]: [Columbia University Press], 1941.

On the organization of the poems in Codex Regius of the Poetic Edda. Regarding the mythological poems, Wood asserts that the manuscript represents the interests of the upper classes, in that it places poems of Odin and Freyr first, and only puts Thor in other contexts. He "is seen first with a god (Óðinn, Týr) as opponent or comrade, then alone, and finally with a demonic being as opponent in one poem and comrade in the other" (p. 114).

3036. Wood, Frederic T. "Grímnismál 33." *Scandinavian Studies*, 17 (1942), 110-13.

Textual note.

3037. Wood, Frederic T. "The Vǫluspá and its Name." *Scandinavian Studies*, 20 (1949), 209-16.

The semantic component of *-spá.*

3038. Wood, Frederic T. "The Transmission of the Vǫluspá." *Germanic Review*, 34 (1959), 247-61.

Concludes that the recorded texts of *Vǫluspá* represent two versions, "final late recastings of traditional material drawn from ancient oral sources" (p. 247). The versions differ "more in point of view than in actual content" (p. 260).

3039. Wood, Frederic T. "The Age of the 'Vǫluspá.'" *Germanic Review*, 36 (1961), 94-107.

Concludes that "a Goth, imbued with Hellenistic ideas and living, as it were, in the midst of them, composed this work [*Vǫluspá*] perhaps as long ago as the fourth or fifth century, if not earlier, in these southern regions" (p. 106).

3040. Wormald, C. Patrick. "Viking Studies: Whence and Whither?" In *The Vikings*, ed. R. T. Farrell, 128-53. London and Chichester: Phillimore, 1982.

In proposing an "alternative model" for studies of the Viking Age, Wormald discuses conceptions of sacral kingship and social organization (pp. 144-46).

3041. Wrenn, C. L. "Magic in an Anglo-Saxon Cemetery." In *English and Medieval Studies Presented to J. R. R. Tolkien on the Occasion of his Seventieth Birthday*, eds. Norman Davis and C. L. Wrenn, 306-20. London: Allen & Unwin, 1962.

Possible runic and archaeological evidence for burial magic in a cremation urn from Caistor-by-Norwich.

3042. Wrenn, C. L. "Some Earliest Anglo-Saxon Cult Symbols." In *Franciplegius: Medieval and Linguistic Studies in Honor of Francis Peabody Magoun, Jr.*, eds. Jess B. Bessinger, Jr. and Robert P. Creed, 40-55. New York: New York University Press, 1965.

Possible runic and archaeological evidence for Anglo-Saxon cult; passing reference to Odin and Yggdrasill.

Y

3043. Young, Jean I. "Does Rígsþula Betray Irish Influence?" *Arkiv för nordisk filologi*, 49 (1933), 97-107.

Young thinks it does: sleeping with his vassal's wife was the Irish king's right, and Heimdallr was popular throughout the British Isles.

Z

3044. Zachrisson, R. E. "Topographical Names Containing Primitive Germanic **geb.*" *Namn och bygd*, 14 (1926), 51-64.

Includes remarks on Gylfi and Gefjon in *Gylfaginning*.

3045. Zaks, N. A. "Snorri Sturluson i sotsial'naya deystvitel'nost" rannesrednevekovoy skaldinavij." *Skandinaviskij sbornik*, 25 (1980), 7-18. Summary in Swedish.

An interpretation of aspects of *Snorra edda* in the light of changing social institutions.

3046. Zatočil, Leopold. "Hárbardsljóð 50,3-4." *Zeitschrift für deutsches Altertum*, 71 (1934), 168.

Textual note.

3047. Zehme, Arnold. *Germanische Götter- und Heldensage: Unter Anknüpfung an die Lektüre für höhere Lehranstalten, namentlich für den deutschen Unterricht, sowie zur Selbstbelehrung nach den Quellen dargestellt.* Prague: F. Tempsky, 1901. xi, 258 pp. Several other editions.

Handbook of Germanic myth and legend, intended primarily for student use.

3048. Zeiss, Hans. *Das Heilsbild in der germanischen Kunst des frühen Mittelalters.* Sitzungsberichte der bayerischen Akademie der Wissenschaften, Phil.-hist. Abt., 1941, 2:8. Munich: Verlag der bayerischen Akademie der Wissenschaften, 1941. 71 pp.

A survey from prehistoric to early medieval times of the artwork intended to confer health and/or sacral power.

3049. Zetterholm, Delmar Olof. *Studier i en Snorre-text: Tors färd till Utgård i Codices Upsaliensis DG 11 4to och Regius Hafn. 2367 4to.* Nordiska texter och undersökningar, 17. Stockholm: H. Geber, Copenhagen: E. Munksgaard, 1949. 100 pp.

Subjects to close stylistic scrutiny the episode in *Gylfaginning* of Thor's journey to Útgarða-Loki, comparing the versions in Codex Regius and Codex

Upsaliensis. To the old question of which is closer to the original Zetterholm has a new answer: each is at one remove from the original, having followed a different stylistic ideal.

3050. Zeune, A. "Aelteste altdeutsche heidnische Gedichte." *Germania*, 5 (1843), 12-19.

Presentation of and commentary to the Merseburg charms.

3051. Zeune, A. "Idisi und Diedesi." *Germania*, 6 (1844), 141-43.

Commentary to the first Merseburg charm.

3052. Zimmer, H. "Parjanya Fiörgyn, Vâta Wôdan: Ein Beitrag zur vergleichenden Mythologie." *Zeitschrift für deutsches Altertum*, 19 (1876), 164-81.

Early comparative study. The Vedic Parjanya is equivalent to the male Fjǫrgynn, who was replaced by Thor, while the female Fjǫrgyn remained; Vâta is equivalent to Odin, who grew in importance as Dyaus/Týr, the father of Parjanya/Fjǫrgynn, faded.

3053. Zingerle, J. V. "Zu Donar." *Zeitschrift für deutsche Mythologie und Sittenkunde*, 4 (1859), 149.

Alleged survival of Donar/Thor worship in the Tirol.

3054. Zingerle, J. V. "Wuotan, Ziu." *Germania*, 5 (1860), 68.

Brief note pointing out use of the names of the pagan gods to refer to Satan.

3055. Zotto, Carla del. *La Hymiskviða e la pesca di Þórr nella tradizione nordica*. Testi e studi di filologia, 1. Rome: Istituto di glottologia, Università di Roma, 1979. ix, 149 pp.

An edition of *Hymiskviða* with Italian translation and extensive commentary; includes also relevant skaldic texts with Italian translation. The author dates the poem to the reign of Óláfr kyrri (1066-93).

3056. Zupitza, Julius. "Zur ältern Edda." *Zeitschrift für deutsche Philologie*, 4 (1873), 445-51.

Pp. 450-51 contain a textual note to *Hávamál*, strophe 17.

3057. Zutz, Lothar F. "Totenfurcht und Aberglaube bei den Germanen der Völkerwanderungszeit." *Volk und Rasse*, 7 (1932), 185-93.

Conceptions of death and the dead during the Migration period.

Þ

3058. Þórðarson, Matthías. "Um eina tegund innskota í goðakvæðunum fornu." *Árbók hins íslenzka fornleifafélags*, 1918, pp. 14-23.

On redundant lines and similar textual matters in *Vǫluspá*, str. 21; *Hávamál*, str. 1, 74, 105, 109, 111, 112, 142, 155, 156, and 162; *Grímnismál*, str. 45; *Skírnismál*, str. 10, 27, 28, 32, 34, and 42; and *Lokasenna*, str. 23 and 62.

3059. Þorðarson, Matthías. "Ynglingar." *Skírnir*, 95 (1921), 35-64.

An attempt to anchor the Ynglingar in history.

Index

C

E

F

N

O

X

Y